Latin American Political Yearbook 2000

Volume Three

Latin American Political Yearbook 2000

Robert G. Breene, Jr.
editor
United States

Alphonse Emanuiloff-Max
associate editor
Montevideo

José Carlos Graça Wagner
associate editor
São Paulo

Mario Rosenthal
associate editor
El Salvador

James R. Whelan
associate editor
Mexico

Routledge
Taylor & Francis Group
LONDON AND NEW YORK

First published 2002 by Transaction Publishers

Published 2017 by Routledge
2 Park Square, Milton Park, Abingdon, Oxon OX14 4RN
711 Third Avenue, New York, NY 10017, USA

First issued in paperback 2018

Routledge is an imprint of the Taylor & Francis Group, an informa business

Copyright © 2002 by Latin American News Syndicate®

All rights reserved. No part of this book may be reprinted or reproduced or utilised in any form or by any electronic, mechanical, or other means, now known or hereafter invented, including photocopying and recording, or in any information storage or retrieval system, without permission in writing from the publishers.

Notice:
Product or corporate names may be trademarks or registered trademarks, and are used only for identification and explanation without intent to infringe.

ISSN: 1097-4997

ISBN 13: 978-1-138-51153-8 (pbk)
ISBN 13: 978-0-7658-0044-2 (hbk)

Contents

1. Elections and Status of Political Forces (SPF) in Latin America ... 1
   A Realistic Definition of the Political Left ... 1
   Elections and SPF in Central America ... 2
   Political Situation in the MERCOSUR Nations ... 16
   The Andean Nations Go to the Polls ... 34
   Caribbean Nations ... 70
   Notes ... 85

2. Politico-Economic Backgrounds in Latin America ... 89
   Liberals and Neoliberals ... 89
   Argentina ... 92
   Bolivia ... 109
   Brazil ... 110
   Ecuador ... 115
   El Salvador ... 115
   Guatemala ... 121
   Haiti ... 121
   Mexico ... 122
   Panama ... 125
   Venezuela ... 136
   Notes ... 140

3. Three Hemispheric Heads of State: Pinochet, Ortega and Clinton ... 145
   Augusto Pinochet Ugarte ... 145
   Daniel Ortega Saavedra ... 164
   William Jefferson Clinton ... 173
   Notes ... 186

4. The Hemispheric Left ... 191
   Introduction ... 191

Fidel Ruz Castro	193
The HL: Umbrella Organizations and Activities	216
Brazil	220
Cuba	226
Mexico	245
Nicaragua	277
Peru	287
Notes	297

5. The Hemispheric Left (HL) in Colombia — 303
   Introduction — 303
   A. The Diplomacy of the Subversion — 304
   B. Minor Terrorist Coups in Subversive Diplomacy — 322
   C. The Self Defense Patrols — 356
   D. The Pastrana Peace Process — 364
   E. Death of a Terrorist Cleric — 385
   Notes — 386

6. The Hemispheric Left Support — 393
   Introduction — 393
   Colombia — 395
   Mexico — 415
   Notes — 422

7. Latin American International Organizations — 427
   General — 427
   Central American Bank of Economic Integration (BCIE) — 427
   Inter-American Development Bank (BID) — 429
   Andean Community of Nations (CAN) — 435
   Central American-Dominican Free Trade — 437
   Latin American Infancy Summit (CIAL) — 438
   Summit of the Americas (CLA) — 439
   Summit of the Peoples of America (CPA) — 446
   Conference of Foreign Ministers (CMCA) — 448
   Presidents of Iberian-American Democratic Parliaments (CPPIA) — 449
   Entrepreneurial Forum of the Americas (FEA) — 451
   Coexistence and Citizen Security (FCSC) — 454

Grupo de Río and UE	454
Common Market of the Southern Cone (MERCOSUR)	458
The "Non-Aligned" Nations (MNNA)	459
The Organization of American States (OAS)	462
Commerce Ministers Meetings (RMC)	472
Latin American Economic System (SELA)	473
Central American Economic Integration System (SICA or SIECA)	479
Notes	482
Contributors	487
Name Index	491
Subject Index	501

1

Elections and Status of Political Forces (SPF) in Latin America

As was of course the case in previous yearbooks, coherency of description of the kaleidoscope of elections in LA (Latin America) is aided by a system of subdivisions. Once again, that which is used here is CA (Central America), MERCOSUR, the Andean Nations, and four of the Caribbean nations to include Mexico. It remains appropriate to preface the discussion with a definition of the Left.

A Realistic Definition of the Political Left

In what follow the "Left" will be taken to mean the "political Left." The lexicon which has evolved began with "Left" and "Right," progressed through "Center" to "right center" and "left center," the ultimate stage in this dubious progression perhaps reached with "center center." Since there is no real definition of these terms, they can and have been used to confuse and disguise. Here only "Left" will be used, "Right" entering only briefly as a counterpoint.

In the French National Assembly, the States General of 1789, the "privileged classes,"[1] the clergy and the nobility were seated on the right of this august body. The Right (physically) were therefore "conservatives," those wishing to maintain the *status quo*, those opposed to maintaining it, the Left. Some 143 years later the Reichstag was seated in Berlin, the representatives of the National Socialist German Workers Party (the Nazi Party) seated on the right. These people certainly had no desire to maintain the status quo, but it was of quite specific benefit to the, by definition, Left MLs (Marxist-Leninists) to classify them as "rightists." As it was so to classify the Fascists[2] of the socialist Mussolini, whose prewar "Mussoliniani" included the famous Italian communist, Gramsci.[3] Thus was perpetrated the great twentieth-century fraud which established the Nazis and Fascists on the Right, the MLs on the Left[4]

In actuality, ML, Fascism, and Nazism are all appropriately lumped together into the Left. In LA (Latin America) the influence of these three Left ideologies have been strong in certain nations, relevant examples of this having been encountered in YRBK97*(*Latin American Political Yearbook 1997*, Transaction Publishers, 1998. ISBN: 1-56000-350-2, YRBK98 *mutatis mutandi**).

The Left can therefore be taken as the collectivist doctrine having little use for individual liberties and administered at the whim of bureaucrats. The military caudillos who arose in the 1970s in reaction to the lawlessness of the Left generally constituted special "reactionary" cases which need hardly be assigned positions in the political spectrum.

Elections and the SPF in Central America

COSTA RICA

THE COSTA RICAN GENERAL ELECTIONS OF 1 FEBRUARY 1998 (WKLY 5.5, 5 FEBRUARY 1998)

The Costa Rican (CR) general elections were held on 1 February 1998 in that Central American (CA) nation. The last such elections were held on 6 February 1994. In those elections José María Figueres Olsen of the National Liberation Party (PLN-Social Democrat) won the presidency with 49.7 percent of the vote, his closest rival Miguel Angel Rodríguez Echeverría of the Social Christian Unity Party (PUSC) with 47.5 percent. In the unicameral national legislature the PLN won 28 of the 57 seats, the PUSC 25 and the Democratic Force Party (PFD) 2.

Parties in the Presidential Elections

In the last three elections (1986, 1990, 1994) about 18 percent of the registered voters have not cast ballots, the high being 35 percent in 1958.

The 1998 presidential ticket included the presidential and two vice presidential candidates, 13 parties fielding such tickets. As will be seen, this was basically a two-party race, but six of the other parties

---

* Also hereinafter 1YRBK98 will mean chapter 1, YRBK98.

will be remarked here. With all voting places canvassed (numbers in parentheses are vote totals) the six parties are: PUSC (650,399), PLN (616,600), PFD (41,922), National Integration Party (PIN) (20,266), Costa Rican Renovation Party (PRC) (19,103), Democrat Party (PD) (13,599), Libertarian Movement Party (PML) (5849). A brief description of each of the six also-ran parties follows, these taken from the platitudinous self descriptions of the parties which frequently tell the careful reader more than the party intended.

PLN

This party was formed about 1944 by a generally misunderstood José (Pepe) Figueres [1906-1990] who came to power four years later largely due to the Caribbean Legion. He has been discussed briefly in 1YRBK97. The PLN won the presidency in 1953, 1962, 1970, 1977, 1982, 1986 and, under Figueres' son, in 1994.

"Five principles which govern the new form of political action [are] Honesty (decency)...We will arrive in the Government to serve the Country without arrogating to ourselves privileges of any kind...Truth...The truth is the primary source of our discourse and our behavior...Justice...A society which is not just is damaging, dehumanizing and egotistical. Justice for all is our political expression in order [to describe] endowing all the people with access to the material, intellectual and spiritual goods which the society produces...Liberty...is the basis of a society with participative democracy...Fairness (equity)...Our *social democrat*[5] conception of development considers all sectors of Costa Rican society in an equitable, just and fraternal manner..."

The party is proposing twelve "Political Propositions" which may be summarized as follows: "1. We will propose new mechanisms to regulate political, economic and social relations in Costa Rican society and its institutions..." No specifics are given. "2. We will impel a great tax reform according to which each citizen pays taxes according to his income and economic capacity..."[6] "3. We will promote a participative democracy...4. We will promote the increase of production and savings and improve the methods of distribution of wealth, the only way to reduce poverty, recover fraternity and generate employment..." In short, anti-neoliberalism. From this point the platform promises to "reform" education (No.5), develop Culture, Sport and Recreation

(No.6), "regulate and promote national development" (No.6), adjust the state to the "new necessities" (No.7), "guarantee the environment and biodiversity" (No.8), "watch over citizen security" (No.9), "reinforce health and social security systems" (No.10), "guarantee future generations and [a] better country" (no.11) and "rescue gender equity" (No.12).

PFD

"The country is in bad shape, navigating without a course, in the hands of a pact between two worn out parties, the PLN and the PUSC incapable of raising national production...CR needs a change...FD, as a young political party...wishes a prosperous, just and democratic CR [and] invites all CRs to rise up against the bad administration, corruption and incapacity of the exhausted parties..." The method which the PFD is suggesting to accomplish this is an antineoliberal, statist one similar to that of the PLN above.

The stated solutions are divided into five categories, (I) "we will confront the high cost of living," (II) "we will raise national production and generate employment, (III) "we will battle corruption," (IV) "we will give a renovating impetus to democracy" and (V) "we will strengthen State solidarity in order to foment sustainable development." Only anecdotal illustration is possible.

In category I.2[7] "the weight of indirect, especially sales, taxes will be reduced," in I.3, government regulation of basic services will be defended, in I.4 "speculation" in rents will be fought, as in I.5 will privatization of "social services" such as "health, education and social security." In category II FD will "promise to foment a productive economy which will generate development, insure creation of employment and generate a just distribution of wealth." Trans national enterprises beware (II.6) while agriculture is to be subsidized (II.3), the "strategic function of the State and public enterprise in the development of national production" will be defended and stimulated (II.8) while "sustainable development" and "environmental preservation" will be sponsored (II.12).

The PFD position is most succinctly set forth in category V with "FD is not in accord with the implantation of that neoliberal model in CR since as has recently been stated by the Order of Jesuits...," the Jesuit statement against neoliberalism (free market) being essentially the position of Fidel Castro.

PIN

Wálter Muñoz Céspedes, the physician PIN candidate for president, wishes to stimulate "a new and different project [which] will bring back the hope of constructing the Costa Rica of the XXI Century with solidarity, well being and social stability." In his "Call" he bemoans "the lack of short and medium term policies [which] has stopped the initiation of solutions of the great problems of health, education, economy, environment and housing among others." In his "Vision" he tells of his 10 years of "analyzing national problems in the permanent Forum, Perspectives of CR for the XXI Century," as president and founder of the International Federation of XXI Society he has "dedicated [himself] to the analysis of the world situation" and concluded that CR "needs to confront globalization as an employer and not an employee." As a physician he expresses considerable concern with health-related matters although matters of economic concern are not extensively discussed.

PRN

According to Sherman Thomas, PRN president, this party was formed during a night meeting at the Institute of Intellectual Development in Hatillo, a San José suburb, on 8 May 1995. Its founding date was taken as 3 June 1995. "PRN is a political party committed to God, Country and Family in order to carry out the transformations which the elevation of the quality of life of all CR citizens demands...The CR society which the PRN visualizes is inspired by and based on the highest Christian values...The family is the pillar and nucleus on which is constructed a society of peaceful coexistence...In the family is where the spiritual principles are developed and to the State corresponds its safeguarding as the nucleus of society...We reiterate the conviction in entrepreneurial freedom with social responsibility. Private enterprise must be a part for social development with freedom."

PD

"On Sunday, 28 April 1996, a group of distinguished intellectuals challenged me [PD President Alvaro González Espinosa] in order that a new political party be created...[as a consequence] of the pessimism of the CRs with respect to the conduct of the traditional parties." Which Mr. González did. "On presenting the registration of the movement framed in an authentic INDIGENOUS philosophy, outside obsolete economic doctrines and socio-political tendencies, divorced from honor, labor and decency, we suffered a serious reverse..." The electoral commission would not register the party which, however, won through eventually to registration.

Among the principles enunciated is "The spiritual and social affirmation that all the ELDERS and CHILDREN [capitalization as furnished by Mr. González] have rights. The first to a dignified life [apparently to be furnished by the State], with enjoyment of necessary alimentation within the geriatric conceptions and clothing, shelter, medications, diversions and geriatric attention..." This goes on to the creation of a "CITY FOR THE AGED," then to "THE GOLDEN CITY OF THE CHILD." Another long paragraph creates a "NATIONAL TAX OF THE CAMPESINO" which will "free the campesino from the very serious injustices" and will provide that worthy with "a bank of unlimited resources."

PML

"We Libertarians think," said PML presidential candidate Federico Malavassi Calvo, "that CR is cornered in an economic and moral crisis. The traditional politicians raise the cost of living, drive us into debt and charge us with taxes, and cause unemployment, poverty, privileges and corruption which inundate us. Those politicians reward the vagabond, the inept and the criminal and castigate the capable and honest worker...The basic principle of the Libertarian Movement is that every man is the master of himself...and he can do what he wishes with his body, his mind and his honestly acquired belongings...we must assume the responsibility of respecting the same rights of others. Or be it, we must assume liberty with responsibility. From this principle are derived the basic rights of each person, the violation of which is immoral

"We Libertarians denounce the inflation the Central Bank causes by issuing money without backing, devaluing the value of our salaries, pensions and savings. We seek to break the monopoly of the State in the emission of money. Dolarization of the economy is the first step in doing this. Without inflation, we will have salaries, pensions and savings which have value, stable prices, confidence to make investments which create employment and a more secure and prosperous future.

"For the Libertarian, a State immersed in everything neglects that which it should be enhancing: the security of its citizens. Therefore, we wish to withdraw the State from that which we think it should not be doing (like being an impresario) and put the police where they should be: watching the streets."

There is of course more, but the idea should percolate. This is apparently the only free-enterprise, free-man party which does not look to the State for the solution of society's problems.

The PUSC Wins the Presidency

The four political parties, which formed the Unity Coalition [*Coalición Unidad*] in 1978, were the Calderón Republican Party (PRC), the Democratic Renovation Party (PRD), the Popular Union Party (PUP) and the Christian Democrat Party (PDC). Under the CU banner that year Rodrigo Carazo Odio won the CR presidency. On 17 December 1983, the National Assemblies of the PRC, the PRD, the PUP and the PDC created the PUSC. Rafael Angel Calderón Fournier was elected president in 1994 as the PUSC candidate.

In the elections of 1 February 1998 the PUSC ticket won the presidency with the totals which have been given above. The presidential candidate was Miguel Angel Rodríguez Echeverría, the first vice presidential candidate Astrid Fischel Volio, the second vice presidential candidate Elizabeth Odio Benito.

On 15 September 1997 Mr. Rodríguez, the "social Christian" candidate, presented his Program of Government, entitled "Solutions for the Future," which will allegedly constitute "a guide for his action" as president.

The "social Christian Program of Government will revolve around twelve promises considered priorities in order to assure solutions and the well being of families. These would appear to cover the waterfront beginning with "1. More and better jobs through economic reactivation," through "6. Excellency in education for all which guarantees quality, coverage and access" to "12. Our agreement with the moral doctrine," health, women, security and ecology of course being included.

Considerable attention is devoted to "3. Government of all through the Triangle of Solidarity" and hence perhaps should be mentioned. After presenting a litany of national woes—security, education, health, deficit, inflation, unemployment—the Triangle is introduced as "a new form of making social politics." [The vertices of] a triangle made up of [1] "the municipalities, [2] public institutions and [3] organized communities will mutually support each other in order to impel local development projects."

Presidential Percentages

Using the vote total of 1,387,287 LANS has obtained the following percentages: PUSC 48.3 percent, PLN 44.4 percent, PFD 3.0 percent, PIN 1.5 percent and PD < 1.0 percent. In the 1994 elections the PLN candidate won with slightly (1.4 percent) more of the vote, the PUSC candidate lost with 3.3 percent more of the vote. The PFD candidate remained in third place in 1998 but this time with 1.4 percent more of the vote.

The CR Congress

The following numbers will probably be officially confirmed. The PUSC won 27 seats in the unicameral national legislature, two more than in the last legislature, the PLN won 23, five less than in the last legislature. The PFD won 3 seats, the PML won 2 seats, the PIN 1 and the Alajuela [Province] Labor Action Party (PALA) 1. Generally speaking, the minority party leaders are occupying these seats. The results by province are:

SAN JOSE: 8 PUSC, 8 PLN, 2 PFD, 2 PML, 1 PIN.
CARTAGO: 3 PUSC, 3 PLN.
ALAJUELA: 4 PUSC, 4 PLN, 1 PALA, 1 PFD.
HEREDIA: 3 PUSC, 2 PLN.
PUNTARENAS: 4 PUSC, 2 PLN.
LIMON: 2 PUSC, 2 PLN.
GUANACASTE: 3 PUSC, 2 PLN.

EL SALVADOR

LATIN-AMERICAN ELECTIONS, 1997-1998
(WKLY 5.9, 5 MARCH 1998)

March 1997

Salvadoran Municipal and Legislative elections were held in March 1997 and have been discussed in Wkly 3.13 (1YRBK98). The presidential elections are to be held in 1999. The results were essentially a dead heat in the unicameral legislature, the National Republican Alliance (ARENA) winning 28 seats, the ex terrorist Farabundo Martí National Liberation Front (FMLN) 29.

IN EL SALVADOR ARENA SELECTS ITS PRESIDENTIAL CANDIDATE (WKLY 5.16, 23 APRIL 1998)

With the Chapultepec Accords of 16 January 1992, the Farabundo Martí National Liberation Front (FMLN) entered the political arena with a power which neither its military nor its political impotence would have gained for it. With the off-year elections of 1997 this ex terrorist but still Marxist Leninist (ML)[8] party won almost the same number of seats in the national legislature as did the National Republican Alliance. As has been suggested in Wkly 3.13 (YRBK98), the apparent reason for what amounted to an ARENA loss was that 11 deputies simply moved to the National Reconciliation Party (PCN), the latter thus effectively acquiring 11 deputies whom ARENA lost. LANS has received reports to the effect that these defections were the result of the conception that ARENA is no longer the free-market, anti-ML party which it once was or once was conceived as being. What is happening now may strengthen this viewpoint in some quarters.

Ruben Zamora was the Democratic Convergence (CD) candidate in the general elections of 1994, the FMLN *per se* having fielded no candidate. However, as has been discussed in these reports (pp.4-5,YRBK97), CD was little more than a front for the FMLN from its formation in 1987, so that Zamora may be considered the *de facto* FMLN presidential candidate in 1992. The intricate maneuvering which preceded and has followed ARENA's nomination of a presidential candidate renders all this of considerable interest.

The ARENA National Executive Committee (COENA), under the party president, Alfredo Cristiani, invited some 800 delegates to the Assembly which, on 29 March 1998, nominated the party's candidate for president in the elections of 7 March 1999. Francisco (Paco) Flores Pérez (38), described as a "philosopher and economist," was president of the Legislative Assembly until February 1998 when he resigned to declare himself a candidate for the ARENA presidential nomination. Mr. Cristiani duly declared that there was a *motón* (pile, load, etc.) of qualified candidates to vie for the nomination. No one emerged from the motón, and the ARENA movers and shakers— Mr. Cristiani, Pres. Calderón, head of ARENA legislative bloc Juan

Duch, etc.—began lining up behind what was apparently the foreordained nominee. On 29 March this was confirmed, and Mr. Flores, in trousers and open-necked white shirt, gave his acceptance speech before an enormous banner portraying him in suit and tie with right forefinger raised in symbolic gesture.

If elected president he will assure citizen security, "fight corruption" and do various other things which have not yet really been decided, what amounts to a poll being projected to clarify this. As to the "free market," once allegedly an ARENA priority, "I believe," said Mr. Flores, "that day by day, privatization has had effects which one must moderate..." The entire process is interesting, but perhaps most interesting is the individual who has emerged as most likely vice presidential running mate for Flores, Ruben Zamora.

Before the Assembly, it was bruited about that Zamora was to be the ARENA vice presidential candidate. Was this the Central American Yeltsin, transmogrified from an ML into a free-enterprise democrat? In reply to *El Diario de Hoy*'s "Who will occupy the vice presidency," Mr. Flores answered, "Then ... Ehhh, there is an opening in the party; today they told me that president (of COENA) Cristiani, is contemplating the possibility of Ruben Zamora..." He went on to disclaim any knowledge of this affair.

Will another 11 ARENA deputies move to the PLN banc?

GUATEMALA

The most recent Guatemalan general elections were held in 1995, the next to be held in November 2000. In the last elections the National Advance Guard Party (PAN) won 43 of the 80 seats in the unicameral legislature, the Guatemalan Republican Front (FRG) picking up 21 seats while three other parties won less than 10 seats. In the runoff election of 7 January 1996 PAN presidential candidate Alvaro Arzú Irigoyen won with 51.22 percent, his FRG opponent, Alfonso Portillo losing with 48.78 percent.

HONDURAS

LATIN AMERICAN ELECTIONS, 1997-1998
(WKLY 5.9, 5 MARCH 1998)

November, 1997

This CA nation has two major parties, the Honduran Liberal Party (PLH) and the Honduran National Party (PNH), their combined vote in presidential elections routinely being over 90 percent. Nevertheless, theirs is not technically a two-party system since a certain number of minority parties are rewarded for being small and weak. The general elections were held on 30 November, the presidency won by PLH candidate, Carlos Roberto Flores Facussé with 52.8 percent, his PNH opponents, Nora Gúnera de Melgar, polling 42.6 percent. The 128-chair unicameral National Congress will probably be made up as follows: The PLH will have 70 seats, the PNH 54, the Innovation and Unity Party (PINU) 3 and the Democratic Unification (UD) 1. Among the mayoral races, the PNH won in the capital city (population 624,542), the PLH in San Pedro Sula (326,943) and the UD in La Paz (11,238).

NICARAGUA

ATLANTIC COAST ELECTIONS IN NICARAGUA, 1 MARCH 1998
(WKLY 5.9, 5 MARCH 1998)

The second Nicaraguan elections since the Esquipulas II Accords allegedly transmogrified that nation into a democracy were held in October 1996. Liberal Alliance (AL) candidate Arnaldo Alemán won the presidency with 904,880 votes, trailed by Sandinista National Liberation Front (FSLN) candidate Daniel Ortega with 669,443 (Wkly 2.15). Of the 20 other parties fielding presidential candidates only two captured more than 10,000 votes, the Christian Road Party (CC) polling 76,621 and the Conservative Party 40,096 (Wkly 2.15). In the unicameral national legislature AL won a slender advantage over the FSLN in number of deputies (Wkly 2.12), but hardly enough to ward off the low-level chaos which Ortega and his FSLN have maintained since that time.

The Atlantic Coast of Nicaragua is Indian country, Miskito, Sumo and Rama (3YRBK97,n.114). The area lies generally within Zelaya Department which was named after General José Santos Zelaya who overthrew the Sacasa Government in 1893, his position regularized by the Constitution of 1894. The 61,479 km^2 of the coastal region is delimited by its division into two political units, the Autonomous North Atlantic Region (RAAN) with capital at Puerto Cabezas of about 40,000 km^2 and the Autonomous South Atlantic Region with capital at Bluefields of about 20,000 km^2.

On 1 March 1998 elections were held at 683 voting places (JRVs) in order to elect 33 regional counselors to the RAAN Regional Council and 30 regional counselors to the RAAS Regional Council. The

Organization of American States (OAS) observers declared their "general satisfaction" with the conduct of the election which may or may not mean anything. In the 1996 elections there was a surfeit of "observers" from an array of organizations—the OAS, the Carter Center, etc.—who trampled each other getting out of Managua after the election had taken place. Whether true or false, LANS has since received various reports to the effect that this haste in departure left much to be "observed" in the National Assembly races.

The AL has been mentioned in connection with Alemán. In this alliance is the Constitutional Liberal Party (PLC) which he has headed since he emerged from the Sandinista prison and under whose banner the Liberals ran in Zelaya. The other parties in the races were the FSLN, the Yátama Party, the Multi-Ethnic Indigenous Party (PIM) and the Coastal Alliance. The results were as follows:

RAAN: PLC 17, FSLN 11, Yátama 5.
RAAS: PLC 10, FSLN 8, Yátama 4, PIM 6, Coastal Alliance 2.

Alemán claimed victory which is technically true: PLC won a slim one-vote majority in RAAN, more votes than any other party but no majority in RAAS. Corn Island is 50 sm (statute miles) northwest by west of Bluefields. PIM won its votes and what was a substantial victory there. Although Ortega's FSLN made a showing, it can hardly be claimed a victory and could have been expected to evoke the cries of foul with which he has greeted every previous loss. Perhaps such were not forthcoming because the erstwhile caudillo had other things on his mind, things such as adopted daughters and sexual assault which are treated in Chapter 3.

PANAMA

THE PANAMANIAN PRIMARIES
(SPCL 5.15, 9 MAY 1998)

In the Panamanian elections of 8 May 1994 (pp.8-9,YRBK97) Ernesto (Toro) Pérez Balladares of the Democratic Revolutionary Party (PRD) won the presidency with 33.3 percent of the vote, trailed by Mireya Moscosa of the Democratic Alliance (AD) with 29.1 percent, Ruben Blades of the Papa Egoro Movement (MPE) with 17.1

percent and Ruben Carles of Cambio 94 with 16.1 percent. The election ritual is now in its primary phase in that nation, and, judging by the attacks on Pres. Pérez Balladares, he, though not yet the official nominee of his party, is the "man to beat."

Ms. Moscosa was chosen by the Arnulfista Party (PA) in its 29 March 1998 primary as its presidential candidate. During the credentials ceremony at the National Elections Committee (CNE) she declared, *inter alia*, "they are taking this country into a civil dictatorship through the PRD" (*El Siglo* (Panama) 3 Apr 98). The Christian Democrat Organization (ODC) of America, with Panamanian CD power Ricardo Arias Calderón conspicuously present, exhorted Pres. Pérez that he "abide by the Constitution which prohibits immediate reelection..." (*El Siglo* 6 Apr 98). Peoples Nationalist Party (PNP) vice president Roberto Díaz Herrera avowed that they should "add ourselves to the Pro Democratic Front and fight the project of" reelection (*El Siglo* 7 Apr). To which PNP Pres. Jorge Flores added his voice the following week as did Civilist Renovation Party (PRC) Pres. Sandra Escorcia who strongly asserted the necessity of "defeating the reelectionist pretensions of Pres. Pérez..." And, it may be said, so on.

Important in all this is the "Yankee Go Home" theme which figures prominently in the routinely linked sentiment against the Multilateral Anti Drug Center (CMA) (Wkly 5.3).

Arising naturally from this rhetoric is the question: Can Pres. Pérez run for reelection? The answer is both "No" and "Probably." This week he cannot run for president; in three months he probably can.

The Panamanian Constitution and the Panamanian Presidency

The Political Constitution of the Republic of Panama came into being on 11 October 1972, it being thereafter amended by two Reform Acts (5/10/78 and 25/10/78) and a Constitutional Act (24/4/83). Title VI (The Executive Branch of Government) contains the relevant article as follows:

> ARTICLE 173. The citizen who has been elected President or Vice-President of the Republic may not be reelected for the same office in the two Presidential terms immediately following.

Therefore, Pres. Pérez could not now be reelected president. However, Art. 308 provides the method whereby the Constitution may be amended so that he may be reelected. There are actually two ways in which such amendment could be effected, only the one in use being detailed here.

This is a three-step process. First, the enabling amendment must be passed in a session of the National Assembly. This was done in the last session of the present Assembly which ended with December 1997. Second, the enabling amendment must be passed a second time in a different session of the National Assembly. The Pérez Balladares forces expect this to happen during the week of 10-17 May 1998, at the latest during May. If this occurs, the amendment must be submitted to a referendum of the electorate no less than 90 days after the second legislative approval.

Ernesto (Toro) Pérez Balladares

A few points on the incumbent's background are perhaps worthy of remark. As the LANS Editor learned in Panama immediately before the 1994 elections, Toro's father was a physician, Pérez Balladares, who reputedly fled Nicaragua to escape the Somoza dictatorship, only to have his son take up the cudgels for the Torrijos dictatorship. According to Panamanian sources at that time, in 1994 Pérez B. ran under the banner of the Torrijos-Noriega[9] dictatorship, that banner emblazoned with an "11" commemorating the coup of 11 October 1968 which initiated it.

In 1994 various Panamanians considered Pérez B. to be the candidate of US Pres. William Clinton—"the gringos are at it again"— this apparently based on the assertion that Toro and Clinton were friends and fellow students at Georgetown University. Mr. Clinton had also invited Toro to his 1993 inauguration although this was probably not a particularly selective action. The establishment of the CMA would appear to be an extrapolation of the good relations between Messers Clinton and Pérez B., although the ultimate effects to be expected on the elections would be risky to judge.

More or less in the same vein, it is interesting to recall that, in 1994, "Toro" Pérez Balladares invited the well-known US "political scientists," Jesse Jackson and Oliver Stone to be "election observers."

The Opposition

The runner-up in the 1994 presidential race was Mireya Moscosa de Gruber. Ms. Moscosa is the widow of thrice-Pres. Arnulfo Arias, whose forename appears in the Arnulfista Party designation, and wife of Arias' secretary, Gruber. After a "spirited" primary battle with Alberto Vallarino—she declared that he "was buying votes," he that she was "hurling threats"—she won her party's nomination on 29 March 1998. Ms. Moscosa's entourage when she appeared to collect her election credentials included:

Guillermo Ford, ex Panamanian vice president and president of the Liberal Republican National Movement (MOLIRENA) which had been a member of Carles' Democratic Opposition Alliance (ADO) in 1994; Rubén Arosemena Valdes, president of the PDC; a representative of Joaquín José Vallarino, president of the National Renovation Movement (MORENA) which had also been in Carles' ADO in 1994.

Whether an alliance supporting Moscosa will emerge from all this remains to be seen. Nor is it assured that other parties such as the Civilista Renovation Movement (MRC), Sandra Escorcia president, and the Authentic Liberal Party (PLA) will finally form a part of such a coalition. But various of these political groupings did gather on 26 April 1998 in a "No to Reelection!" Conference under the general direction of the coordinator of the Pro Democracy Front (FPD), Joaquín J. Vallarino.

Present at this "Stop Pérez" rally were the presidents or representatives of seven political parties, these the PA, the PRC, the PNP, MORENA, the PLA, MOLIRENA and the ODC. As was to be expected, all conferees agreed that Pres. Pérez B. must be stopped from seeking a second term. Coordinator Vallarino suggested that the very concept of reelection be "impugned" because President Pérez Balladares "swore to uphold a Constitution which forbids reelection, and he is now reforming it so as to present himself as a candidate." The notion is an interesting one, but it remains to be seen if it carries legal support. It was also suggested that the FPD propagandize against reelection

At the same time the anti-neoliberal (anti free market) theme entered into this anti-Pérez dialog, the routine accusation that "neoliberal laws increased unemployment" being frequently encountered among them. Which should hardly be taken as indicating that Pérez's PRD is the "party of free enterprise," however. The Panamanian president has gone along with certain privatization as required by the international lending agencies, but he appears to be motivated by a desire for the money being dispensed by them.

Pérez Allies

There are a number of individuals who seek to run under the PRD banner who might therefore be classified as "allies." For example, Carlos Alberto Duque, life president of the PRD, Sra. Dora de Pérez B. and Baby Arango. Perhaps most interesting, however, is a PRD candidate for first vice president, Rubén Blades. Perhaps this salsa singer head of Papa Egoro (Mother Earth) and darling of the "Hollywood left" would complement the man who wanted Jackson and Stone as election observers.

The Political Situation in the MERCOSUR Nations

ARGENTINA

October 1997

Elections were held in October 1997 for deputies to the lower house of the national bicameral legislature, deputies and senators to the bicameral provincial legislatures, constitutional convention delegates and City of Buenos Aires deputies. These elections were discussed in Wkly 4.18 (1YRBK98). President Menem's Justicialista Party (PJ) received almost exactly the same vote as did his principal opposition, ALIANZA, which amounted to a substantial setback for the PJ.

BOLIVIA

LATIN AMERICAN ELECTIONS, 1997-1998
(WKLY 5.9, 5 MARCH 1998)

June 1997

Bolivian general elections were held in June 1997 and have been discussed in Wkly 3.21 (1YRBK98). Patriotic Accord (AP) candidate Hugo Banzer Suarez won the presidency, and the PA coalition with the Revolutionary Left Movement (MIR) won control of the legislature.

BRAZIL

LATIN AMERICAN ELECTIONS, 1997-1998
(WKLY 5.9, 5 MARCH 1998)

October 1998 Brazil

Ex President Fernando Collor de Mello was removed from office for embezzlement on a vast scale (Spcl 1.10). Nothing daunted, he declared his intention of running again in 1998. In January the Brazilian courts apparently put an end "to his pretensions." Luiz Inácio (Lula) da Silva, Fidel Castro confidant and co-founder of the Foro São Paulo (Wkly 1.6), ran second to Cardoso in the 1994 elections with 27.04 percent of the vote. His "retirement" from political activity was short lived and, as 1998 opened, he was running second in the polls. (An analysis of the Cardoso candidacy campaign will be distributed later this spring.) Itamar Franco, vice president under Collor de Mello and then president, announced that he would run under the PMDB label, but this does not appear to have created much of a stir.

THE BRAZILIAN GENERAL ELECTIONS OF 4 OCTOBER 1998
(WKLY 6.14, 8 OCTOBER 1998)

In the Brazilian general elections of 4 October 1998 some 14,415 candidates were vying for 1,627 opportunities to serve the Brazilian people or themselves, depending on your point of view. All 1,600 of these positions can hardly be considered here. Instead, an overview of the national elections will be attempted. Most importantly, of course, is the run for the presidency followed perhaps by that for the National Congress. As with the thousands of local positions, LANS does not yet have the final results of the elections for the House of Deputies; an approximate report will be given here. The raw data for the National Senate races has been treated by LANS and will be briefly discussed. First, however, a word on the Constitution and the most prominent political parties is in order.

Elections and the Brazilian Constitution

The Brazilian Constitution of 1993, as amended on 28 January 1997 to allow President Cardoso's run for a second term, has been briefly reviewed in Spcl 6.8. Here a few articles necessary as background to the elections of 4 October 1998 will be abstracted.

Organization of Authorities. By Art.18 the Federative Republic of Brazil comprises the Union, the States, the Federal District and the Municipalities. The Federal Territories also comprise the Union.

Nationality. By Art. 12 only native-born Brazilians may hold the offices of President, Vice President, President of the House of Representatives, President of the Federal Senate, Justice of the Federal

Supreme Court, pursue a Diplomatic Career or be an Officer in the Armed Forces.

State Executive. By Art. 28 the State Governors and Vice Governors are elected for a term of four years, the election held 90 days before the end of their predecessors' term. They take office on 1 January of the following year.

State Legislative Assembly (SLA). By Art. 27 the number of representatives in the SLA is three times the number the State has in the Federal House of Representatives (FHR). When the number of State Representatives (SR) reaches 36, it is increased by as many as there are Federal Representatives (FR) in excess of 12. The term of office is four years.

Municipalities (Munis). By Art. 29 Mayors, Vice Mayors and City Councilmen (CC) are elected for four years, the election 90 days before the expiration of their predecessors' terms. Munis elect CCs as follows: Munis < 1 million (m) population elect between 9 and 21 CCs, Munis with one to five m elect between 33 and 41 CCs, Munis with more than 5 m elect 42 to 55 CCs.

Federal District (DF). By Art. 32 the DF may not be divided into Munis. Governor, Vice Governor and DF Representatives elected as with state offices.

Territories. By Art. 33 These may be divided into Munis. The Governor is appointed. Territorial House is elected.

National Congress (NC). By Art. 44 the National Congress is composed of a House of Representatives and a Federal Senate. A legislature has a four-year duration.

National House (NH). By Art. 45 NH members are elected by a proportional representation system in each State, Territory and the DF. Each State elects from 8 to 70 Representatives, the number adjusted for population the year before the election. Each Territory elects four Representatives.

Federal Senate (FS). By Art. 46 each State and the DF elects three Senators for eight-year terms. One third and two thirds are renewed alternately each four years

President and Vice President. By Art. 77, if no presidential candidate receives an absolute majority, a second round is held between the two candidates receiving the most votes within 20 days of result announcement.

Reelection. By Art. 82 presidential reelection was forbidden. This restriction was amended out of existence as remarked.

Political Parties

About 40 political parties were created in the Brazil of the latter 1980s, relatively few of which are of sufficient interest to warrant inclusion. Here only the eight parties with the largest representation in the 1994 NC plus the PCdoB, PPS and the PSD will be described briefly. A few other parties will be listed with their Party Numbers. In discussing these parties no attempt will be made to describe them with the Political Correctness (PC) inherent in the familiar descriptions—center right, center left, etc. Such descriptions are routinely created with an inherent left bias which spreads confusion rather than clarification. Example: Cardoso's PSDB is described as having "a center-left social agenda." In contradistinction to such a description, Cardoso has effectively supported the "low-intensity warfare" of the Hemispheric Left (HL) through "Agrarian Reform" as carried out by the Marxist Leninists (ML) of the MST (Landless Peasant Movement) (cf. 106ff, YRBK97 and later reports). This is appropriate for this socialist sociologist, who may be first remarked establishing the Marx Seminary at the University of São Paulo in 1958 to study the work of Heinrich Karl Marx, and whose first book was *Capitalism and Slavery in Meridional Brazil*.

PMDB (Brazilian Democratic Party Movement). This largest of the Brazilian parties was registered with the TSE (Supreme Electoral Tribunal) in 1966. The PMDB had 13 Senate and 107 House seats in the NC elected in 1994. Party No. 15.

PFL (Liberal Front Party). The PFL was founded in 1985 by members of the Democratic Social Party who opposed the candidacy of Paulo Maluf. The PFL had 11 Senate and 89 House seats in the 1994 NC. Party No. 25.

PSDB (Brazilian Social Democracy Party). This is the party of the now two-term president, Cardoso. It had 10 Senate and 62 House seats in the 1994 NC. Party No. 45.

PDT (Democratic Workers Party). The PDT was formed in 1980 by Leonel Brizola who first came to general notice as the brother-in-law of Jango Goulart, "the fondest hope of the Kremlin."[10] The Castroite Brizola orchestrated the Navy rebellion the reaction to which led to Jango's ouster (p.58, YRBK97). The PDT had 4 Senate and 34 House seats in the 1994 NC. Party No. 12.

PP (Progressive Party). The PP resulted from a merger of the

Renovating Workers Party and the Social Workers Party. It held 4 Senate and 37 House seats in the 1994 NC. Party No. 11.

PPB (Brazilian Progressive Party). The PPB was put together in 1995 by the merger of the PPR (Reformed Progressive Party), the PP (Progressive Party) and the PRP (Progressive Republican Party). Its Red-Black symbol is apparently not intended to indicate any affinity for the Sandinistas. Party No. 11.

PT (Workers Party). This is the party formed under the tutelage of Frei Betto by the Castro intimate, Lula da Silva. Castro and Lula, in the Havana of 1989, formed what is now the principal instrument of the HL, the São Paulo Forum (FSP) (Chapter 3, YRBK97). Da Silva describes his PT as made up of "Trotskyites, Castroites, activists of the Brazilian Communist Party (PCB) ... Liberation Theologists... FMLN ... M-19."[11] The PT won 4 Senate and 49 House seats in 1994, apparently 52 of the latter when coalitions are included. Party No. 13.

PTB (Brazilian Labor Party). The PTB was founded in 1945 and presently has strength only in a few western states. It captured 3 Senate and 28 House seats in the 1994 elections. Party No. 14.

PPR (Progressive Renewal Party). The PPR was formed in 1993 from the merger of Maluf's Democratic Social Party and the Christian Democrat Party. This party took 2 Senate and 52 House seats in the 1994 elections.

PL (Liberal Party). The PL advocates neoliberalism and a flat tax. It won 13 House seats in the 1994 elections. Party No. 22.

PSB (Brazilian Socialist Party). The PSB was founded in 1946 and has been a Lula supporter. It took 14 House seats in the 1994 election, part in coalition. Party No. 40.

PCdoB (Communist Party of Brazil). The PCdoB was founded in 1922 at the urging of an agent of the South American Propaganda Bureau (SAPB) of the Third International.[12] Party No. 65.

PPS (Peoples Socialist Party). Doubtless aware that there is little of consequence in a name, the PCB (Brazilian Communist Party), organized at about the same time as the PCdoB with the authorization of the SAPB, changed its name to PPS in 1992. Party No. 23.

PSD (Social Democrat Party). One of the parties in Cardoso's winning coalition. The Social Democrat parties are those of Venezuela's Pérez and Peru's Garcia. These parties are linked through

the Socialist International, the lineal descendant of Heinrich K. Marx's First International. Party No. 41.
PMN (National Mobilization Party). Party No. 33.
PRONA (National Order Reconstruction Party). Party No. 56.
PSC (Social Christian Party). Party No. 20.
PSD (Social Democrat Party). Party No.40.
PSN (National Solidarity Party). Party No. 31.
PSTU (Unified Socialist Workers Party). Party No. 16.
PTN (National Workers Party). Party No. 19.
PV(Green Party). Party No. 43.

President

By 7 October 1998 94.68 percent of the polling places had been canvassed which was reported as corresponding to 75.63 percent of the vote. There is therefore apparently no question as to the relative placement of the presidential candidates beginning with the first-round victor. There is also no question as to the relative placement of the second through fourth place finishers in this race. Therefore, although the following candidates may have slightly different percentages in the final results, this relative standing will remain as indicated (name, party, vote percentage):

(1) Fernando Henrique Cardoso. 52.83 percent PSDB
(2) Luíz Ignácio (Lula) da Silva. 31.93 percent PT
(3) Ciro Gomes. 11.05 percent PPS
(4) José Maria Eymael ~3 percent PSDC

Also rans with lesser percentages, no particular order: José M. de Almeida (PSTU), Sergio Bueno (PSC), Enéas Carneiro (PRONA), Ivan Frota (PMN), Vasco de Azevedo Neto (PSN), Thereza Ruiz (PTN), Alfredo Sirkis (PV), João de Deus de Jesus (PCdoB).

Cardoso's running mate and new vice president is Marco Maciel of the PFL. The new president was elected on a coalition ticket including the PFL, the PPB, the PSD and the PSDB.

The National Senate

The 26 Brazilian states and the DF each send three senators to the Senate for a total of 81. There were 54 senators elected in 1994 so that there were 27 senators elected in 1998, one from each voting region. LANS has used the raw data from these, which is not complete, and selected the candidate with the highest number of votes as of the report. It is possible that there will be a few shifts here but probably not many. In this manner then the Senators apparently elected in 1998 by party are as follows.

PMDB 12; PFL 5; PT 4; PSDB 4; PPB 2.

In 1994 three Senators were elected, one each from three parties, the details on which LANS does not now have. Otherwise, the parties which assuredly will have more than 1 Senator are as follows.

PMDB 25; PFL 16; PSDB 14; PT 8; PDT 4; PP 4; PTB 3; PPB 2; PPR 2.

The PPB may already have a senator and could hence increase its banc to 3.

Obviously the first-round victory of President Cardoso did not carry many of his PSDB members in on his coattails, although his party remained more or less even with that of Lula. Other analysis can of course be carried out, and it is possible that the results for the House of Deputies will not vary excessively from these for the Senate.

National House of Deputies

The information which follows is early and fragmentary.

It appeared that about 45 percent of the Deputies will be replaced with new faces. The PFL, which was being reported as having 111 Deputies before the elections, was expected to remain the largest banc in the House with perhaps 115. The PMDB with 88 was expected to exceed 100 while the PSDB fell at least to 80. The PT had something like 50 Deputies—much of this depends on how such a party is tallied in and out of coalitions—and was expected to increase to over 60. The PPB was predicted to fall from 77 "to under" 70 and the PTB with 23 could have even less than this number.

BRAZILIAN CONGRESSIONAL ELECTIONS
(WKLY 6.16, 22 OCTOBER 1998)

On 4 October 1998 some 14,415 candidates vied for the 1,627 opportunities to serve themselves or the Brazilian people, depending on your viewpoint, in elections which have been generally treated in Wkly 6.14. The complete results in the congressional elections were not available at that time; these results are reproduced here thanks to the kindness of the Head of the Congressional Section of the Brazilian Embassy in Washington, DC, Councillor Nilo Barroso.

As has been discussed in Wkly 6.14, the number of senators in the bicameral national legislature is fixed. The number of deputies in the lower house of the legislature, however, varies with the populations of the 26 states and Federal District. In the 1998 elections there was no such variation, the number of deputies remaining the same, namely, 513. Therefore, the makeup of the two houses of the legislature by political party is now as follows:

Senate

PMDB (Brazilian Democratic Party Movement) 27; PFL (Liberal Front Party) 20; PSDB (Brazilian Social Democrat Party) 16; PT (Workers Party) 7; PPB (Brazilian Progressive Party) 4; PSB (Brazilian Socialist Party) 3; PDT (Democratic Workers Party) 2; PPS (Peoples Socialist Party) 1; PTB (Brazilian Labor Party) 1.

House of Representatives

PFL 106; PSDB 99; PMDB 82; PPB 60; PT 58; PTB 31; PDT 25; PSB 19; PL (Liberal Party) 12; PCdoB (Communist Party of Brazil) 7; PPS 3; Others 11.

CHILE

LATIN AMERICAN ELECTIONS, 1997-1998
(WKLY 5.9, 5 MARCH 1998)

November 1997

In these off-year elections a plethora of political parties ran candidates for both houses of the bicameral legislature (Wkly 4.23). Senate seats were captured by the Christian Democrat Party (PDC), Independent List B (IL-B), the Independent Democratic Union (UDI), the National Renovation (RN) and the Chilean Socialist Party (PSC). With the lineup of appointed members this will continue the majority enjoyed in that chamber by the *concertación* (government bloc). In the race for Chamber of Deputy seats there were 16 sets of candidates, even more than in the Senate. Seats were captured by the PDC, the RN, the UDI, the Party for Democracy (PPD), the PSC, the IL-B, the Social Democrat Radical Party (PRSD), the Party of the South (PDS) and the Progressive Center-Center Union (UCCP) and Independents.

[By 10 March 1998 all the senators-for-life (*senadores vitalicios*) will have taken office. These will be detailed in chapter 3, this volume, which will be largely devoted to one of them, General Pinochet Ugarte.]

PARAGUAY

LATIN AMERICAN ELECTIONS, 1997-1998
(WKLY 5.9, 5 MARCH 1998)

May 1998

The situation here revolves around General Lino Santos Oviedo (Ret) who last year obtained the Colorado Party presidential nomination and whom that party's governmental junta declared it would support (AFP 9 January 1998). President Wasmosy recently stated that "he wishes general election on 10 May" (EFE 17 February 1998) which may be true or may be some part of a personal vendetta. Unfortunately, this situation appears to have been complicated considerably (Wkly 4.14).

THE PARAGUAYAN ELECTIONS OF 10 MAY 1998
(WKLY 5.17, 7 MAY 1998)

EDITOR'S INTRODUCTION

As with the murder of ousted Brazilian President Collor de Mello's "treasurer," P. C. Farias (pp.63-66,YRBK97), the last punditical[13] pontification may not yet have been made on Paraguay's *l'affaire Oviedo* (pp.72-73,YRBK97).

As has been pointed out, the conflict between Pres. Wasmosy and General Oviedo was early and ostentatiously joined by the US. Recently, the US has been huffing and puffing again [*Washington Post*, 10 Apr 98] although perhaps not with the certainty it displayed earlier. Meanwhile, Oviedo remains in duress vile for a coup attempt which, he maintained in a book, "never happened." And it has apparently not been proven that it did. Doctor Emanuiloff-Max, LANS associate editor in Montevideo, discussed the situation and the rather demagogic Gen. Oviedo late last year (Wkly 4.14,YRBK98). Herein LANS' correspondent in Río de la Plata further discusses the background of next Sunday's Paraguayan elections.

* * *

PARAGUAY IS TORN BETWEEN VAGUE LOYALTIES
LANS CORRESPONDENT
RÍO DE LA PLATA
ARGENTINA

The Paraguayan presidential elections of Sunday, 10 May 1998, will be a contest between Raúl Cubas Grau and Domingo Laíno. Outside this panorama, a prisoner in a military post, General Lino Oviedo, will be the third actor in a conflict which—from all indications—will extend its crucial effects far beyond that date.

It is significant, both qualitatively and quantitatively, that the questions which arise on the destiny of Paraguay are always linked to the fate which will finally overtake General Oviedo, located as he is at the core of the political panorama.

Analyzing the complex situation in which Paraguay exists today, a Uruguayan diplomatic source recalled the array of similarities which the political scene in that country offered to the Argentine situation in 1945. These are, a worn-out process of military governments, generalized corruption, international isolation and the emergence of a "messianic" figure within the Army strongly supported in some quarters and markedly rejected in others.

"Yesterday there was (Juán Domingo) Perón and today there is Oviedo," said the diplomat, "both personalities of strong populist style with strong support among the masses." "As was partially true then, Perón won the 1945 elections running against the US ambassador (Spruille Braden), and something very similar is happening today with the Paraguayan general," this through his confrontations—at the international level with the US and with the chancelleries of the neighboring countries.

The instability of that country awakens enormous concern in the MERCOSUR nations. Argentina, Brazil and Uruguay make up a sub-regional bloc with Paraguay which, from its creation (1991), has demonstrated a very important commercial dynamic which soon will include new "partners" (Bolivia and Chile) and which is governed by a "democratic clause."

This means that the four countries agree to maintain the democratic and republican form of government as a matter of principle and with the conviction that institutional stability is the key in today's world for investor tranquility.

Therefore, the other three partners expressed themselves actively and immediately when, in May 1996, an incident occurred between General Oviedo and the constitutional president, Juan Carlos Wasmosy. This incident resulted in the political problems of today.

At that time it was Brazil which made the decisive decision, releasing reports of the decision to cut all commercial connection with Paraguay, to close its doors to the exports of that country and—most importantly—to suspend payment for electrical energy generated by the binational dam of Itaipú. This amounts to more than 25 percent of the Paraguayan budget.

But what really happened at that time? According to the official version, General Oviedo knew that he would be passed over and retired, and he confined himself to barracks, promoting an uprising against the country.

"There was nothing like that," if sources close to the general are given credence. These sources recall that later Oviedo was turned over to the courts and found not guilty. "There was neither anyone who could show an order confining the troops to barracks nor a member of the military who could say that he had received such an order," they maintain. They likewise maintain the "messiness" of the president's resolution. This resolution ordered the general's retirement without there appearing therein any date or hour when this should take place.

The episode was confused: In his capacity as commander in chief, Oviedo had his home in a barracks so that, after his dispute with the president, he could well have retired to his residence to nurse his grievance.

During the episode Wasmosy waffled on more than one occasion. When the crisis was in full bloom he offered Oviedo the job of Minister of Defense which the general accepted. A little later the president withdrew the offer.

At the same time there arose strong international pressure under the aegis of the three MERCOSUR ambassadors and the US ambassador. Weeks later it would be learned that Wasmosy traveled secretly to Brazil days before the dispute in order to inform his colleague, Fernando Henrique Cardoso, that in some barracks there was "saber rattling."

The Brazilian president gave his support to the constitutional president, and this appeared to be fundamental to overcoming the crisis which was unleashed a little later. Also it permitted the consolidation of a dream of "intra MERCOSUR" intervention, according to the report by the Uruguayan diplomat who mentioned the satisfaction of Itamaraty (Brazilian Minister of Foreign Relations) and his associates at Uruguay's prominence in the affair. Brazilian diplomats were heard to comment on the demonstrable capacity to face the crisis in the neighboring country, as well as to denigrate the (US) Department of State. "They cannot find a solution to the problem in Haiti which is mere miles from Miami," was the scathing comment.

Coup d'Etat or merely an argument? This is an aspect of the situation which is most difficult to clarify. If it is clear that the pressure from the neighboring countries aborted the first, it is also certain that a civil court found Oviedo innocent. This assured, moreover, that he never wanted a *coup d'etat* and that, to the contrary, it was Wasmosy who did come around to carrying one out because "the Parliament did not allow him to govern."

The episode evolved into a strong confrontation between Oviedo and Wasmosy which carried over into the civil domain. In 1997 the general put himself into the political campaign by launching his candidacy for nomination to the presidency of the republic through the Colorado Party. This is Wasmosy's party, and the party which has held power since 1954.

Oviedo won the "officialist"[14] nomination in a campaign marked by a strong populist tone in which he promised "better conditions of life," "a more just country for all Paraguayans" and "putting an end to corruption" with heavy and direct accusations against Wasmosy.

The credibility of Oviedo as a candidate is based on elements of considerable significance in Paraguay: He speaks Guaraní, the native tongue which is spoken by the lower classes and campesinos. In the second place, his life in the army permitted him to have very direct contact with the youths called to military service. These youths enter the service from the depths of the villages in order not only to receive instruction in the manual of arms but also to learn to read and to be trained for a position.

The paternalism of the general did not arise then overnight but during a process of years which bore fruit as soon as he decided to enter the political arena.

The effects of the victorious internal election were magical for Oviedo: He immediately initiated a tour through the neighboring countries; the neighboring countries opened their doors to him.[15] He gained international recognition, and the diplomatic respect of the neighboring countries was added to that of the German ambassador who has long demonstrated signs of support. His collaborators say that the German support was very important in order that "the General" remain isolated. They recall that he took courses in the military academies of that country, and amicable relations are assumed as an undeniable fact.

The selfsame Cardoso received Oviedo in Brazil, and, moreover, consented to displace Ambassador Marcio Dias who was odious to the general. Dias proved to be a frontline actor in the drama wherein Oviedo had the confrontation with Wasmosy.

According to the military, the ambassador has personal interests in the support of the president because he is connected to the construction firm, "Andrade Gutiérrez," ready to construct a bridge over the Paraná River.

The export of soy is one of the keys of Paraguayan commerce, and that production is sold either to Brazil or to countries overseas. In both cases it is transported by trucks which cross Brazilian territory, trucks for which the "Friendship Bridge" proves absolutely insufficient during harvest season.

Hence the necessity of constructing a second bridge, between Ciudad del Este (Paraguay) and Foz do Iguazú (Brazil), a plan to which Oviedo is radically opposed since "Wasmosy wants to build the bridge with one of his own companies," according to an accusation which he has repeated time and again.

The initiative reached the Paraguayan Parliament, and the opposition of the six Colorado senators, who responded directly to Oviedo, resulted in the wreck of the government proposal for the bridge.

With matters thus, in December 1997 a special military tribunal condemned Oviedo to 10 years in prison for insubordination immediately after the events of the previous year. The general's partisans speak of "flagrant unconstitutionality," "abuse of power" and the illegality of being tried twice for the same offense. The government maintains nothing more than that existing laws are being applied.

In this context Wasmosy made an attempt to postpone the date of the elections, but it was found that the apparatus which he had put in motion the previous year was hostile to such an attempt. As much from the Embassy of the US as from the MERCOSUR countries very clear signs were being sent to the effect that such a postponement would not be acceptable.

With Oviedo a prisoner the Colorado Party conjured up the candidacy of the engineer Cubas Grau. At first, and in the opinion of the Oviedistas "it would have to be something very like the Argentine elections of March 1973 in which Héctor Cámpora ran but Perón won."

Thus then, and before the triumph of Cubas Grau, "he will pardon Oviedo and call free elections without any sort of disqualification."

Nevertheless, things do not look straightforward, not for the Colorado Party and even less for the general's partisans. This is simply because his *dauphin*[16] initiated a process of rapprochement with the sectors which were defeated in the internal elections of 1997. These are the same ones who were, at that time, denounced as "corrupt" and "continuists."

The question which everyone is asking is what Cubas Grau will do if he wins the elections. Will he free Oviedo and call again on the citizenry to vote? Or, on the contrary, will he be supported by the old rivals and seek to consolidate his own power?

Meanwhile, the other candidate for the Presidency of the Republic, the Social Democrat Domingo Laíno, travels about Paraguay denouncing the rapprochement of Cubas Grau with the other Colorados as a bastard maneuver to keep himself in power.

Nevertheless, the internal divisions, which the Colorados have presented until now, open up an excellent opportunity for Laíno to attain the presidency. His running mate is the Socialist Juan Carlos Filizzoli, and the opportunity which they have to win the elections appears almost unbeatable. In that case it remains to be seen whence his capacity for action will be directed and by what method he will utilize the Colorado Party and the Army, decisive factors in the harnessing of power for half a century of Paraguayan history.

[Translated from the Spanish by the Editor, LANS]

THE PARAGUAYAN ELECTIONS
(WKLY 5.18, 14 MAY 1998)

Perhaps the most interesting aspect of the Paraguayan general elections which took place on 10 May 1998 was the Oviedo Episode which has been discussed in Spcl 5.15. By election day General Oviedo, the National Republican Association (ANR) or Colorado Party presidential candidate, had been tucked away in duress vile for some time. He had also been replaced at the head of the Colorado ticket by Raul Cubas whose running mate was Dr. Luis María Argaña. The principal opposing ticket, that of the Alliance, was headed by Dr. Domingo Laíno, his running mate Dr. Carlos Filizzoli.

By 14 May 1998 69 percent of the vote had been counted, and the Cubas ticket had captured 54 percent, the Laíno ticket 42 percent. There would appear to be little doubt that Cubas will be the next Paraguayan president.

THE PARAGUAYAN GENERAL ELECTIONS
(WKLY 5.19, 21 MAY 1998)

The double land to the southeast of Bolivia includes the arcadian Parana Plateau –a modest 1000 to 2000 feet in altitude—to the east of the Paraguay River, the dry and forbidding Chaco to the west. On 4 May 1954 the war hero, General Alfredo Stroessner, gave President Federico Chávez his marching orders and brought the land out of the chaos in which it had become embedded.[17] The old caudillo had held his post for 34 years when he was displaced by Gen. Andrés Rodríguez on 3 February 1989, the blessings of democracy allegedly showering down on the land with Rodríguez's election that December and the constitution of 18 June 1992. Under whatever modified form, however, Stroessner had bequeathed power to the Colorado Party or National Republican Association (ANR) which, on 9 May 1993, won the general elections (p.14,YRBK97). Juan Carlos Wasmosy occupied the presidential palace. Wasmosy could not run again in the elections of 10 May 1998, and this was at least partly responsible for the most interesting aspect of the campaign: the Wasmosy-Oviedo battle. The LANS correspondent in Río de la Plata has covered this affair above.

Since Wasmosy had Oviedo, the ANR candidate, languishing in duress vile, the party selected Lic.[18] Raul Cubas. As has been reported (Wkly 5.18), Cubas appears to have won the presidency with an ample majority, and his opponent, Alliance candidate Dr. Domingo Laíno, has conceded as much. The ANR has also apparently won control of the bicameral legislature, but none of these results will be official until they are declared so later this month by the Supreme Electoral Tribunal (TSJE). Specifics will be given at that time. Here the framework of these general elections will be discussed.

Paraguay has 17 departments, each with a governor. In what follows the population of a department will follow its name in parentheses. The departments elect a number of representatives to the lower house, the Chamber of Deputies, of the national legislature which is proportional to department population. The upper house, the Senate, is elected from national slates of the various parties.

Deputy Distribution

The lower house of the bicameral national legislature has 80 deputies. None of these deputies are elected "at large" as is done in certain other Latin American (LA) countries. Thus, since there are 3,646,650 people in the country, the number of deputies from a given department is *related* to the quotient of the national and departmental population. But there is no simple formula which yields the relation, the notion that there is hence one deputy for every 45,600 people in a given department being complicated by the fact that departments are not populated with even multiples of 45,600 people. Therefore, at this time, the only departments of which LANS is sure of representation are Central—the "federal district" for which the winners in the *18* races are already known—and the two smallest, Boquerón and Alto Paraguay, both with one. LANS has, however, carefully calculated the *probable* number of deputies from each department. While these numbers are generally correct there may be some errors which will be corrected. With this caveat:

The Chaco

There are now three departments in the Chaco, President Hayes (64,417), Boquerón (29,060) and Alto Paraguay (12,156). The total population is thus 105,333. The surface area of the Chaco is 95,300 square miles (mi^2) giving a population density of 1.105 people/$mi.^2$ (All such numbers to slide-rule accuracy.) For comparison, Central

Department (866,856) has a population density of 913 people/mi.² During the *stroñato* the Chaco had five departments, the northern portion of what is now Boquerón being Nueva Asunción, the northwest portion of what is now Alto Paraguay being Chaco. It is asserted that these political divisions existed only for political reasons, that is, as sources of appointments for political cronies.

As Paraguayan Councilor Ricardo Caballero was kind enough to tell LANS, Rutherford B. Hayes, nineteenth president of the US, arbitrated a territorial dispute between Paraguay and Argentina in 1878, awarding the disputed territory to the former. Therefore, the department in the southeast portion of the Chaco was named after him as was its capital, Villa Hayes. Other tributes to Hayes exist in the country.

The following shorthand will be used in departmental description:

Pres. Hayes [Pop: 64,417; A: 28,100; D: 2; ALIANZA: PLRA, PEN]. Pres. Hayes is the department. "Pop" is the population of the department; "A" is surface area of the department in mi.²; "D" is the number of deputies to be elected. Generally speaking, there are two groups running, ANR and ALIANZA. In this case one of the two ALIANZA candidates belongs to the Authentic Radical Liberal Party (PLRA), the other to the National Encounter Party (PEN).[19] The other two Chaco departments are:

Boquerón [Pop: 29,060; A: 35,400; D: 1; ALIANZA: PEN]

Alto Paraguay [Pop: 12,156; A: 31,800; D: 1, ALIANZA: PLRA]

Parana Plateau

The Parana River flows south out of Brazil to form the eastern border between the two nations, then describes a long, sweeping curve to the west, forming Paraguay's southern border before joining the Paraguay River at the southeastern tip on the country. A rough idea of the departments in this eastern section of the country may be given as follows:

Neembucú Department fills this southeastern corner, to its east and northeast abutting on Misiones, to its north on Paraquari. Itapúa borders Misiones to its east, Paraquarí to its north and Caazapá to its northeast. Alta Parana is defined by the Parana River, the international boundary, the department lying north of Itapua and east of Caazapá. Bordering Neembucú to the south and Paraquari to the east is Central wherein lies the capital of Asunción. To the east of

Central is Guairá, to its north Cordillera, Caaquazú north of the former. Above these departments lie the four which complete these political divisions, from west to east, San Pedro and Canindeyú making up the first tier, Concepción and Amambay the second. The data on these departments follows:

Neembecú [Pop: 69,770; A: 4,690; D: 2; ALIANZA: PLRA, PRF[20]]
Missiones [Pop: 89,018; A: 3,690; D: 2; PEN, PLRA]
Caazapá [Pop: 129,352; A: 3,660; D: 3; ALIANZA: PEN, PLRA]
Itapuá [Pop: 377,536; A: 6,370; D: 8; ALIANZA: PLRA, PEN]
Paraguarí [Pop: 208,527; A: 3,360; D: 4; ALIANZA: PLRA, PEN]
Alto Parana [Pop: 406,584; A: 5,750; D: 9; ALIANZA: PEN, PLRA]
Central [Pop: 866,856; A: 953; D: 18; ALIANZA: PLRA, PEN]
In Central Department, in addition to ALIANZA and the ANR, the PRF fielded a 17-candidate slate, the Christian Democrat Party (PDC), the Blanco Party and the Morena parties 18-candidate slates.
Guairá [Pop: 161,991; A: 1,480; D: 4; ALIANZA: PEN, PLRA]
Cordillera [Pop: 198,701; A: 1,910; D: 4;[21] ALIANZA: PLRA[22]]
Caaguazú [Pop: 386,412; A: 5,690; D: 8; ALIANZA: PEN, PRLA]
San Pedro [Pop: 280,336; A: 7,720; D: 6; ALIANZA: PEN, PLRA]
Canindeyú [Pop: 103,785; A: 5,660; D: 2; ALIANZA: no data; PRF is running a two-candidate slate]
Concepción [Pop: 162,289; A: 6,960; D: 4; there appears to have been 1 ALIANZA (PLRA) and 1 PRF candidate]
Amambay [Pop: 99,860; A: 4,990; D: 2; ALIANZA: PLRA, PEN]

URUGUAY

The Uruguayan presidential elections in November 1994 were won by Colorado Party candidate Julio María Sanguinetti with 31.36 percent of the vote in a race which was virtually a three-way tie. In that race Progressive Encounter candidate Mariana Arana had about 3.5 percent fewer votes than Sanguinetti, National Party candidate Alberto Volonte about 2.5 percent less than Arana. This will, however, be the last near tie in a presidential election, the citizenry having approved amendment of the Constitution in a referendum which was itself almost a tie. One of the amendments established a runoff election between the two top presidential candidates if none of these obtains more than 50 percent of the vote in the first.

Since the general elections take place every five years in October,

Uruguay will choose its president and the members of both houses of the bicameral legislature in October 1999.

The Andean Nations Go to the Polls

COLOMBIA

LATIN AMERICAN ELECTIONS, 1997-1998
(WKLY 5.9, 5 MARCH 1998)

October 1997

In accordance with Art.262 of the Colombian Constitution the elections of 1997-1998 have been and will be held as follows: The departmental and municipal elections were held on 26 October 1997, the congressional elections to be held on 8 March 1998, the presidential elections on 31 May 1998. The Marxist Leninist (ML) terrorists of the Colombian Revolutionary Armed Force (FARC) and the National Liberation Army (ELN) murdered and kidnapped substantial numbers of citizens in an unsuccessful attempt to prevent these elections. The departmental and municipal elections were considered in Spcl 4.13 (1YRBK98). While the Liberals at the national level were being buffeted by various scandals, their party was doing as well as ever at the local level. Of the gubernatorial contests Liberal candidates won 75 percent, Conservative 23 percent and the single "other" (Independent) 3 percent, a remarkably small change. [The variation from a total of 100 percent is of course a function of rounding off. The races were tied in two departments, and LANS has simply given one to each.] When it is recalled that the Liberals won 72 percent of the governorships in 1993, the Conservatives 25 percent, these results are remarkably close to the earlier ones.

March-May 1998

The first phase of the three-phase Colombian election process has been discussed immediately above under 1997. The second phase, the elections for the national legislature, will be held on 8 March 1998, earlier talk of postponement apparently having been dispensed with appropriately. Although not as remarkably a two-party system as that of Honduras above, Colombia nevertheless provides the presidency and the majority in the two houses of the legislature to either the PLC or the PCC, more frequently to the former. The nation emerged from the 1994 elections with, in the Senate, the PLC with 56 seats, the PCC with 20 (Wkly 2.11). In the House of Representatives, the PLC captured 88 of the 165 seats, the PCC 40. No attempt at prediction is being made here. However, continued PLC dominance in the recent local elections would perhaps indicate that the congressional situation will not change much.

The last or presidential phase occurs on 31 May. Several of the candidates have been discussed (Wkly 4.20), the changes since that discussion being that Horacio Serpa Uribe is now the official PLC candidate and Andrés Pastrana Arango the acknowledged PCC candidate. The position of Serpa may be complicated by the continuing presence of Alfonso Valdivieso Sarmiento, the dissident PLC candidate. Perhaps General Harold Bedoya (Ret) is not yet to be eliminated either.

THE COLOMBIAN ELECTIONS OF 1997-1998. II.
THE CONGRESSIONAL ELECTIONS
(WKLY 5.11, 19 MARCH 1998)

The three-phase Colombian elections began with the local and departmental elections of 27 October 1997 which have been discussed in Wkly 4.20 (1YRBK98). The second phase of these elections consists of the election of the senators and representatives or deputies who make up the national bicameral legislature, this phase having taken place on 8 March 1998. The third phase is, of course, the presidential election which will take place in May 1998. Although the official Liberal Party (PLC) candidate appears to be the front runner now, if his advantage is insufficient, there will be a runoff election in June.

Senate Elections

According to Art. 132 of the Colombian Constitution of 1991 the Senators and Representatives (Deputies) in the bicameral national legislature, who were elected on 8 March, will begin their four-year terms of office on 20 July 1998.

According to Art. 171 the Senate will consist of 100 members elected in a national district (*circunscripción*), that is, the entire nation. According to the same article two additional senators will be elected by a national district consisting of the indigenous communities for a total Senate strength of 102 members.

According to Art. 172 a senatorial candidate must be over 30 years of age at the time of the election and must be Colombian by birth and exercising citizenship. An individual may not be elected if related through the third degree of consanguinity (blood relationship) to functionaries exercising civil or political control. [Parents are first; grandparents, grand children and brothers examples of second; and nephews are examples of third.] The same exclusion operates for the first three degrees of affinity (relation by marriage) and for parents or children by adoption.

Senate

In the senatorial elections of 1994 the Colombian Liberal Party (PLC) won 56 seats, the Colombian Conservative Party (PCC) 40, the ex terrorist Democratic Alliance 19 April Movement (ADM-19) 1 and various independent groups 23 (Wkly 2.11; 1YRBK97). In the elections of 8 March 1998 a divided PLC won 54 seats and an also divided PCC 29, a slight loss for the former and a serious one for the latter. But the losses by the (apparently) ex terrorist tickets were worse. After the Senate races *per se* are considered, the Tercería political alliance, more concerned with the presidential race than the congressional, will be discussed briefly. For the nonce, this group can be considered as an alliance of presidential candidates Valdivieso, Mockus and Sanín.

It will be recalled (Wkly 5.7) that incumbent President Ernesto Samper's man, Horacio Serpa Uribe, handily emerged from the PLC convention with that party's presidential nomination. As did Andrés Pastrana Arango from the PCC convention. However, dissident PLC presidential candidates continue their political activities, in alliance and otherwise, as do independent candidates.

In the ongoing campaigns there has been considerable railing against *continuismo*, that is, the same tired and allegedly corrupt statesmen (politicians) occupying the same government positions. This has been suggested as the reason for the 1998 vote being almost twice that of 1994 in Bogotá, increasing from 600,000 (1994) to 1,100,000 (1998). But of course such a theory comes a cropper when one finds that 80 percent of the senators will return to their curule chairs next summer, these ladies and gentlemen to include Amylkar Acosta, the Senate president. Perhaps another barren exercise is provided by attempted prediction of the coming presidential race through polling of the senators elect as to their choice of presidential candidate, then adding up the senatorial constituencies to find the winner.

El Tiempo (Bogotá) polled 82 of the 100 newly-elected senators and found 38 favoring Serpa, 17 favoring Pastrana, 1 favoring whoever the Tercería candidate may be and 25 undecided. For example, Martha Catalina Daniels Guzman, first on the list of Serpistas, secured her seat with 48,187 votes. So one would add this total to that of the second Serpista, Edgar José Perea Arias (69,935), to that of the fourth, the aforementioned Amylcar David Acosta Medina (58,708) and so on to arrive at the Serpista vote. Which is *a priori* nonsensical but furnishes an absorbing activity for certain political pundits.

The leading vote getter in the Senate races was the young, but apparently over 30, lady, Ingrid Betancourt Pulecio, who received 155,316 votes. Because it appears most frequently in the press as Betancourt, this spelling is apparently correct. Nevertheless, this former deputy's name has likewise been rendered in the press as Betancur, a former president mentioned in these reports, and Betancurt. The poll placed her in the "undecided" or "Tercería" column which appears appropriate enough since her party is the Liberal Oxygen (Oxígeno) Movement (MOL). Javeriana University political scientist Rodrigo Lozada [*El Pais* (Cali) 10 March 1998] commented that her triumph "reflects only that there is a sizable part of the electorate which appreciates her style." Assuredly she is a physically active and highly enthusiastic young lady. Along with Ms. Betancourt 17 other members of the Chamber of Deputies will move to the Senate next summer, 13 men and 4 women.

Several terrorist or ex terrorist parties lost their representation in the Senate. Among these were ADM-19, M-19, the Socialist Renovation Current (CRS),[23] the Patriotic Union (UP)[24] and the Independent Revolutionary Workers Party (MOIR).[25]

Tercería or Opción Vida

Presidential candidates Alfonso Valdivieso Sarmiento, Noemí Sanín de Rubio and Antanas Mockus have been discussed, *inter alia*, in Wkly 4.12 (1YRBK98). Earlier this year the trio formed a political alliance from which a single candidate was to have emerged in order to oppose the "official" candidate, Serpa. On 12 March, however, Valdivieso announced that he was resigning from Tercería, giving four reasons for this action of which only one appears to have been considered of any consequence. The former attorney general felt that the alliance should be seeking a "grand national accord" which included retired General Harold Bedoya and PCC presidential nominee Pastrana. On 13 March he visited Ms. Sanín at 0700 and Mr. Mockus about 1300 in order personally to inform them of his decision. At which point the torch of coalition was picked up by Sanín-Mockus

It is interesting to remark that former Attorney General Valdivieso's action was considerably strengthened by the letter of support which Pastrana had received from 45 former PLC ministers supporting the PCC candidate. The latest in the great coalition campaign occurred on 14 March.

In the company of presidential candidate Carlos Lleras de la Fuente, Sanín and Mockus announced the formation of a new coalition named Life Option (*Opción Vida*) in which they were joined by Lleras de la Fuente. The group plans on uniting behind the results of a survey which it will sponsor. The survey will begin on 16 March and its results will be released on 1 April. The release will be a symbolic act which is scheduled to take place on the Bridge of Boyacá, hallowed by its location as the place of consummation of Colombian independence. In the meantime a Valdivieso-Pastrana alliance was mentioned on that same 14 March.

All of this is of course related more to the upcoming presidential elections than to the congressional elections which are the concern of this report. Nevertheless, their obtrusion on these congressional elections is relevant.

The House of Representatives (Chamber of Deputies)

By Art. 176 of the Colombian Constitution of 1991, the House of Representatives will be elected in territorial and special districts. It will have two representatives for each territorial district and one more for each 250,000 inhabitants or major fraction of 125,000 over the units of 250,000. For the election of representatives each department and the Bogotá District Capital will constitute a territorial district. By Art. 177 a candidate for Representative must be over 25 years of age and an active citizen of Colombia. Consanguinity and Affinity requirements are the same as for election to the Senate.

For example, Atlantico Department in northern Colombia sends seven deputies to the lower house of the national legislature, which means that five of these are assigned the department as a function of its population which therefore must be between one million and one million 250,000. In practice, the top seven vote getters in this department will go to the Chamber of Deputies, but, for complete accuracy, there is a further complication.

This further complication arises from the existence of the "quotient" (*cuociente*) and the "residue" (*residuo*). A "quotient" in a given department is obtained by dividing the number of votes cast—to include blank ballots—in the department by the number of deputies to be elected. If one million votes are cast in a department fielding 10 deputies, the "quotient" is 100,000. A candidate receiving more than 100,000 votes is thus elected "by quotient" (*por cuociente*); candidates elected with lesser number of votes are thus "by residue." In the recent elections only four candidates were elected "by quotient," ex terrorist chief Antonio José Navarro Wolff and journalist María Isabel Rueda Serboussek in Santafé de Bogotá, José María Imbett Bermúdez in Bolivar Department and Joaquín José Vives Pérez in Magdalena, albeit, the residue deputies in the two departments—and elsewhere—will go as surely to the lower house.

The numbers of deputies elected per department were as follows: 18: Santa Fé de Bogotá; 17: Antioquia; 13: Valle del Cauca; 7: Atlantico, Cundinamarca, Santander; 6: Bolívar, Boyaca, Tolima; 5: Caldas, Córdoba, Magdalena, Nariño, Norte de Santander; 4: Cauca, Cesar, Huila, Risaralda; 3: Meta, Sucre; 2: Amazonas, Arauca, Caquetá, Casanare, Choco, Guainia, Guaviare, La Guajira, Putumayo, Quindio, San Andres, Vaupes, Vichada.

An Example: Atlantico

In what follows LANS will present gross election results as they appeared in *El Tiempo* (Bogotá) on 11 March 1998. LANS feels it has found errors in the *El Tiempo* presentation, however, which for reasons of space will only be discussed for Atlantico Department. This statement is in no sense an indictment of that newspaper; this statement is based on the assumption that the data available from the Colombian Electoral Organization (CEO) (*Organización Electoral, Registraduría Nacional del Estado Civil*) is correct.

In Atlantico Department seven candidates won seats in the lower house. Their names are not important for this discussion, but their party election numbers are. Each candidate has a party election number, that is, the number which indicates the candidates party in that department. For example, No. 114 means the candidate belongs to a particular coalition in Antioquia, the Liberal Party in Atlantico, the Conservative Party in Cauca and so on. In the order in which these numbers are to be treated for Atlantico the seven winning candidates had the following numbers, not in the order of victory: 106, 114, 115, 116; 122; 108; 104.

According to CEO, the first four numbers in Atlantico (106-116) correspond to the Liberal Party, No.122 corresponds to the Independent Conservative Movement, No.108 to the Democratic Alternative Movement (MAD) and No.104 to the Peoples Participation Movement (MPP). *El Tiempo* gives names and not numbers, but, by number, it gives: Liberals: 106, 114, 115; Independent Conservative: 122; Citizens Movement: 116; Others: 108, 104. Since the MAD and the MPP can be lumped as "Others," the only disagreement is in the placement of No.116. It would appear that the PLC obtained four deputies from Atlantico and not three as reported by *El Tiempo*. Even so the following numbers of representatives by department are probably roughly correct.

AMAZONAS: PLC 1, Peoples Convergence (PC): 1. ANTIOQUIA: PLC 8, PCC 4, Progressive Force (FP) 4, Coalition (Co) 1. ATLANTICO: PLC 4, Independent Conservative (IC) 1, Other 2. ARAUCA: PLC 1, Co 1. BOLÍVAR: PLC3, PCC 1, National Conservative (NC) 1, Other 1. BOYACÁ: PLC 2, PCC 4. CALDAS: PCC 2, NC 1. CAQUETÁ: PLC 1, Co 1. CASANARE: PLC 2. CAUCA: PLC 3, PCC 1. CESAR: PLC 3, Others 1. CUNDINAMARCA: PLC 5, New Colombia 1, New Democratic Force (NFD) 1. BOGOTÁ: PLC 6, NC 1, National Christian Party (PNC) 1, National Salvation Movement (MSN) 1, NFD 1, Other 5, Co 2. CHOCÓ: PLC 2. GUAJIRA: PLC 1, Co 1. GUAINÍA: PLC 1, Indigenous Social Alliance (ASI) 1. GUAVIARE: PLC 1, PCC 1. HUILA: PLC 1, PCC 2, Peoples Civil Convergence Movement (MCPC) 1. MAGDALENA: PLC 5. META: PLC 1, PCC 2. NARIÑO: PLC 1, PCC 1, IC 1, Others 2. NORTE DE SANTANDER: PLC 3, PCC 1, Others 1. PUTUMAYO: PLC 1, PCC 1. QUINDÍO: PLC 1, NFD 1, Co. 1. RISARALDA: PLC 3, PCC 1. SAN ANDRÉS: PLC 2. SANTANDER: PLC 4, Co 3. SUCRE: PLC 4, Co 3. TOLIMA: PLC 3, PCC 2, Co 1. VALLE: PLC 8, PCC 3, Co 1, Other 1. VAUPÉS: ASI 1, Civico 1. VICHADA: PLC 2.

THE COLOMBIAN PRESIDENTIAL ELECTIONS

MIGUEL POSADA S.[26]
BOGOTÁ, COLOMBIA
(WKLY 5.19, 21 MAY 98)

EDITOR'S INTRODUCTION

The three-phase Colombian general elections began with the local and departmental elections of 27 October 1997 (Wkly 4.20, 1YRBK98). They continued on 8 March 1998 with the elections for the bicameral legislature in which the Colombian Liberal Party (PLC) maintained its majority over the Colombian Conservative Party (PCC) in both the Senate and the Chamber of Deputies (Wkly 5.11 above). The third phase of these elections is the presidential election, the first round of which will be held on 31 May 1998. The candidates have been discussed from time to time (cf. Wkly 4.12,1YRBK98). The 15 original protagonists have apparently been reduced to the following four sets of president-vice president candidates: Horacio Serpa and María Emma Mejía; Andrés Pastrana and Gustavo Bell; Noemí Sanín and Antanas Mockus; Harold Bedoya and Jorge García Hurtado. If there is a second round as is expected, it will be held in June. LANS wishes to thank the Inter-American Economic Press Agency (AIPE) for permission to reproduce this article.

* * *

The next elections in Colombia will determine whether the country will continue along the road of economic opening, privatization and entry into the global economy or whether it will return to the old mercantilistic, statist and protectionist system which ruled in Latin America for decades. The official candidate of the Liberal Party which now holds the presidency is Horacio Serpa who represents the old and unsuccessful system. His opponents, Andrés Pastrana, Noemí Sanín and General Harold Bedoya (Ret), represent the opposite to a greater or lesser degree.

In the past the presidential elections were a test of strength between the two traditional parties, the Liberal and the Conservative, which shared, with small differences, the same economic theory. The National Front,[27] an accord which obligated the Liberal and Conservative Parties to share power, erased the ideological differences. Nevertheless, Liberal Pres. Gaviria, who governed between 1990 and 1994, accepted the movement, initiated by Chile, toward economic opening and privatization, what has come to be known as "Neoliberalism." His successor, Ernesto Samper, weakened from the beginning by having received narcotrafficking money in his campaign, could not, in spite of his inclinations toward the old mercantilism and statism, reverse the achievements of Gaviria. Nevertheless, those of his functionaries, who were closest to him in economic matters, behaved quite differently.

Two of these functionaries were Carlos Wolff, the director of the Social Security Institute and Cecilia López, the Minister of Agriculture and later director of National Planning. As with Serpa, these two have made very clear their radical inclination toward interventionism and great "social" programs administered by enormous bureaucracies. Wolff and Lopez have been, for example, bitter enemies of a privatized pension system wherein there is individual capitalization managed by private administrators who invest the reserves in the capital markets through the stock exchanges. They have sought to preserve the Social Security Institute which operates under a distribution system and whose reserves the government manages at its whim.[28]

The Serpa campaign will have the support of a few very powerful economic groups. These economic groups, whose proprietors or presidents have been called "the ruckus raisers" (*los cacaos*), have generously financed the Samper campaign. When the latter was attacked by the unions for hot money in his campaign, they supported him, misappropriating in passing the voice of the entrepreneurial sector. Serpa succeeded in being at the time, incredible as it seems, the favorite candidate of Samper, of the "cacaos" who have obtained special privileges under his government, of the corrupt politicians who are benefited by the budget of the state system, of the state unions and of the guerrilla who today is the associate of the narcotrafficker.

Everything indicates that the elections will be determined in the second round because no candidate will obtain an absolute majority in the first. In the second round the two candidates who received the highest percentages in the first round of voting will face each other. The opponents will probably be Horacio Serpa and Andrés Pastrana. This will not be a confrontation between two parties but between two economic systems. One of these will be the old system which kept Latin America at a standstill for decades and the other, the new system which recognizes that in private enterprise, regulated by market forces under conditions of equality for all and inserted in the global economy, exists the unique hope of achieving the prosperity of our people.

[Translated from the Spanish by the LANS Editor]

THE COLOMBIAN PRESIDENTIAL ELECTIONS OF 31 MAY 1998
(WKLY 5.21, 4 JUNE 1998)

In Wkly 5.19 Doctor Miguel Posada correctly predicted that "the elections will be determined in the second round because no candidate will obtain an absolute majority in the first." Which is precisely what happened.

With 10,502,140 votes counted (97.78 percent), the four principal candidates for president ranked as follows: Horacio Serpa Uribe of the Liberal Party received 34.60 percent. Andrés Pastrana Arango, originally under the Conservative banner but running as the candidate of the Grand Alliance for Change, received 34.32 percent. Noemí Sanín Posada of Option for Life received 26.89 percent. Gen. Harold Bedoya Pizarro (Ret) of the Colombian Force received 1.83 percent. Serpa and Pastrana will face off in a second round on 21 June 1998.

Serpa won in 20 departments, Pastrana in 12 and Sanín in two (Meta and Bogotá). Ms. Sanín carried the cities of Bogotá, Cali and Medellín. Perhaps the most discussed aspect of this contest was the failure of the polls which, at times, had predicted a strong advantage in favor of Pastrana.

The question now is where Sanín's near two million votes will go in latter June, and the candidate herself has not helped much in the answer, having allegedly freed her followers with no suggestions as to whom they should give their votes on the twenty-first. The two front runners were quick to tell the lady how magnificent a statesman she had demonstrated herself to be.

Said Serpa, *inter alia*, in a statement, "Far from the cold electoral results, I want to recognize that here you had another grand triumph: that of Noemí Sanín and her message. Doctor Sanín: the success which you achieved in recent weeks ... No one ever fails in seeking their ideals ..."

And Pastrana added, in his statement, "...Today, Noemí Sanín has demonstrated that soon, very soon, a woman will arrive in the presidency of the republic ... I recognize the achievements of Noemí in this campaign and share, with all the members of the Grand Alliance, her desire for change..."

Apparently there is yet no indication that either statement will produce the desired result.

COLOMBIAN PRESIDENTIAL ELECTIONS, SECOND ROUND
(WKLY 5.24, 25 JUNE 1998)

The first round of the 1998 Colombian presidential elections have been discussed in Wkly 5.19. Since neither of the two leading candidates received more than 40 percent of the vote, a second round between these two was scheduled for 21 June. This runoff duly took place.

With 98.62 percent of the votes tabulated, the Colombian Conservative Party (PCC) candidate, Andrés Pastrana, won the election with 50.39 percent of the vote (6,086,507), trailed by his Colombian Liberty Party (PLC) opponent, Horacio Serpa, with 46.53 percent of the vote (5,620,719).

Marcos Calarca was the spokesman on that day for the Marxist Leninist (ML) terrorists of the Colombian Revolutionary Armed Forces (FARC). He is reported as stating that the terrorists for whom he speaks hope that the Pastrana Government is capable of initiating a "process of national reconciliation." In the past, this ML-speak has meant providing a victory for the terrorists, as in Central America (Wkly 3.8ff, YRBK98).

ECUADOR

LATIN AMERICAN ELECTIONS, 1997-1998
(WKLY 5.9, 5 MARCH 1998)

November 1997

As a consequence of the removal from office of the bizarre Ecuadoran president, Abdala Bucaram Ortiz (Wkly 3.7, Wkly 3.19), a plebiscite was held in May (Wkly 3.20) to determine if a National Assembly was to be elected for the purpose of amending the Constitution (Question 3). To which 59 percent of the voters answered "Yes" so that an election was held on 30 November for this purpose. In this election the Social Christian Party captured 19 seats, the

Peoples Democracy (DP) 10, the Ecuadoran Roldos Party (PRE) 8 and Pachakutik 7. Eleven other parties and coalitions captured lesser numbers of seats as given in Wkly 4.23.

THE ECUADORAN ELECTIONS OF 31 MAY 1998
(WKLY 5.21, 4 JUNE 1998)

One of the amusing episodes of 1997 was the ejection of the truly bizarre Abdala Bucaram Ortiz from the presidential palace in Quito (Wkly 3.7 and 3.19, YRBK98). With the subsequent approval of a plebiscite (Wkly 3.20), an election was held on 30 November (Wkly 4.23) for a Constituent Assembly from which emerged a new Ecuadoran Constitution. The first general elections under this constitution took place on 31 May 1998 and will be preliminarily described herein.

In these elections the citizens voted for a new president to succeed the interim president who replaced the ousted Bucaram. They also voted for the 121 deputies to the unicameral national legislature, the 56 provincial councilors and the 631 municipal councilors. There having been elections in 18 provinces in which 11 registered political parties took part, it is clear that a large number of statesmen were seeking office.

The Presidential Election

There were six sets of presidential and vice presidential candidates. In no particular order these were: (1) The Peoples Democracy Party (DP) ran Jamil Mahuad for president and Gustavo Naboa for vice president. (2) New Country (NP) ran Freddy Ehlers for president and Jorge Gallardo for vice president. (3) Democratic Left (ID) ran Rodrigo Borja for president and Carlos Baquerizo for vice president. (4) The Ecuadoran Roldos Party (PRE) ran Alvaro Noboa for president and Alfredo Castillo for vice president. (5) The Independent Movement (MIRA) ran Rosalía Arteaga for president and Guido Carranza for vice president. (6) The Democratic Peoples Movement (MPD) ran María Eugenia Lima for president and Ricardo Rodríguez for vice president.

If no candidate for the presidency gains 40 percent of the vote, there is a second round between the top two candidates, this year on 12 July 1998. Therefore, quite early it was known that such a runoff would take place between Mahuad and Noboa, the projections for the candidates then being: Mahuad 36.66 percent, Noboa 29.75

percent, Borja 14.66 percent, Ehlers 12.97, Arteaga 3.97 percent and Lima 1.97 percent. And now the horse trading begins.

The LANS correspondent in Ecuador, Mr. Julien Valvois, is widely and intimately acquainted with Ecuadoran political affairs. Before the elections the Editor asked him for a candid description of the presidential candidates which he furnished with his usual gusto.

THE ECUADORAN PRESIDENTIAL ELECTIONS

JULIEN VALVOIS
LANS CORRESPONDENT
QUITO, ECUADOR

In February of 1997, the usually mild-tempered Ecuadorans organized mass demonstrations against the abuses of power and the corruption of President Abdala Bucaram and his «Gang of 40,000 Thieves.» Bucaram left for Panama, and an interim president was elected to serve until August 1998. Now, only a short time later, there is a likelihood that Bucaram´s friend and supporter, the multi-millionaire lawyer and businessman, Alvaro Noboa Ponton, may win this presidential election. Many Ecuadorans await the poll results with concern, some in near panic.

How is it possible that, after the disastrous Bucaram regime, the majority might elect one of his close allies? It is widely believed that, if Noboa is elected, the «Bucaram Gang» will return from Panama in full force and out for vengeance. More optimistic souls hope that, if elected, Noboa will end his alliance with the Bucarams. His father, Luis Noboa, accumulated a massive fortune in banana export and other enterprises. But the scions of great wealth often have agendas very different from their forebears. Noboa has been spending millions to give rice, medicines and so on to the impoverished masses on the coast, a "charity" which is widely considered a vote-buying scheme. It remains to be seen whether the Roldosista candidate conforms to the dire predictions of his opposition.

The other candidate, who appears most likely to win the presidential race, is the popular ex-mayor of Quito, Jamil Mahuad, of the Peoples Democracy Party (DPP). Mahuad's political experience has been as Minister of Labor and principal of a high school in a nearby suburb. The high school almost closed its doors because of financial problems and had to be rescued by the parents of the students. But he has what, in Ecuador, is called «Carismo,» that is, "personal appeal," an attribute which overrides whatever his administrative blunders may have been. Most of those who will vote for Jamil say they have chosen the lesser of the various evils which are being offered. Jamil has recently been the target of unfavorable publicity connected with a sale to his brother of property belonging to the ex drug Czar of Ecuador, Jorge Reyes, the transaction falling under a cloud of questionable circumstances.

Jamil and Noboa are the two candidates chosen to win in most polls. During Jamil's term as Mayor of Quito, a trolley system was installed which has caused many serious traffic problems in the city. It has been strongly criticized by well informed people who maintain that a foreign company should have been given the contract to build a subway in Quito. Jamil has been reported as receiving a substantial commission for the Trolley Contract with a Spanish company.

Another major candidate is ex-President Rodrigo Borja. Many will vote for him simply because he had a quiet, conservative term, which did little damage to the country, and was not accused of any major corruption. He and Ehlers are a toss up for third place in the race, although, in this Land of a Thousand Wonders, Rodrigo could be a Dark Horse Candidate and win.

T.V. Commentator Freddy Ehlers is a relative newcomer on the political scene. Even so, he is a source of worry for many who remember his association with communism as a student, his populist promises to the masses, his connections with the ever-socialistic Indian group, and his paucity of experience in administration. It is unlikely that he will receive enough votes to make it to the second round of voting.

In Ecuador, if a candidate does not receive at least 40 percent of the total vote, a run-off is held between the two receiving the most votes. This applies only for the office of president. It is after the first round that the horse-trading begins for the votes of the defeated candidates. Many have maintained that Bucaram made more money losing two presidential elections and selling his votes to the remaining candidates than if he had won

Another candidate is Bucaram's vice president, Rosalía Arteaga, who stayed on as Vice President when her cohort was packed off to

Panama. She was the self-proclaimed "President For One Day." Her party is the National Alliance.

[End Valvois Report]

Voting Method

The Supreme Electoral Commission (TSE) decided that, in the 31 May elections, the voter will vote for the national deputies by List (*plancha*) and for the provincial deputies, the provincial councilors and the municipal councilors by Candidate (*listas abiertas*). In List voting the voter indicates the list of his choice on the ballot, in Candidate voting he indicates the candidates—the 14 deputies he desires in Pichincha Province for example—from one or more lists.

The National Legislature Elections

There are 121 deputies in the unicameral national legislature, 20 of these elected in the country at large, the remaining 101 deputies elected by province as follows:

From GUAYAS Province: 18.
From PICHINCHA Province: 14.
From MANABI Province: 8.
From AZUAY, EL ORO, LOS RÍOS Provinces: 5.
From CHIMBORAZO, ESMERALDAS, LOJA, TUNGURAHUA Provinces: 4
From BOLIVAR, CAÑAR, CARCHI, COTOPAXI, IMBABURA, MORONA SANTIAGO, NAPO, SUCUMBIOS Provinces: 3.
From GALÁPAGOS, PASTAZA, ZAMORA CHINCHIPE: 2.

There were, according to the LANS count, 14 party and alliance lists of national deputy candidates, all 20-candidate lists. For example, List 1 corresponded to the alliance of the Conservative Party and the National Union and, incidentally, was headed by former Pres. Durán Ballén. List 4 corresponded to the Peoples Concentration of Forces Party, first on this list being Averroes Bucaram, fifth Jorge Bucaram. This gave 280 Ecuadoran statesmen the opportunity to run for national political office. The same sort of arrangements of course prevailed in the providence races, Azuay a fertile field for statesmen.

The voter votes for his candidates either *plancha* in the case of national deputies or *lista abierta* in the case of the other categories of candidates. The winners in the *plancha* races are the 20 top vote getters. If the votes received by a given slate yield sufficient only to elect one candidate, that party sends the number one man on its list to the legislature. The early returns indicate that the winners by party will be as follows:

The SOCIAL CHRISTIAN PARTY (PSC, List 6) won 6 deputies, these beginning with Jaime Nebot and concluding with Raúl Riva.

PEOPLES DEMOCRACY (DP, List 5) won 4, these beginning with Juan José Pons and concluding with José Cordero.

The DEMOCRATIC LEFT (ID, List 12) won 4, these beginning with Paco Moncayo and concluding with Marcelo Farfan.

The ECUADORAN ROLDOSISTA PARTY (PRE, List 10) won 4, these beginning with Adolfo Bucaram and concluding with Vicente Estrada.

The ECUADORAN CONSERVATIVE PARTY (PCE, List 1) won 1 who had to have been Durán Bellén since he headed the list.

The NEW COUNTRY—SOCIALIST—PACHAKUTIK Alliance[29] (List 21-18-17) won 1, this León Roldós.

Although the new constitution created a congress with 121 deputies instead of the 82 provided by the old (August 1979), thus giving 39 more statesmen the opportunity to serve, it is still possible to see considerable similarity between the possible makeup of the old and the new congresses. First, the PSC had the largest number of deputies (27) although not a majority as appears to be indicated in 1998. PRE and DP followed with 19 and 12, respectively, as they appear to be doing here, although ID had no more than it does now (4).

The legislative results will be reported by party when they appear which was originally scheduled for 5 June, although the TSE has until 20 June to furnish the results.

THE ECUADORAN GENERAL ELECTIONS OF 1998. II
(SPCL 6.1, 2 JULY 1998)

The party abbreviations which will be encountered in this report are: the CFP (Concentration of Popular Forces), the DP (Peoples Democracy), the FRA (Alfarista Radical Front), the ID (Democratic Left), the MPD (Peoples Democratic Movement), the NP (New Country), the PCE (Ecuadoran Conservative Party), the PRE (Ecuadoran Roldos Party), the PSC (Social Christian Party), the PSE (Ecuadoran Socialist Party)

Ecuador held general elections on 31 May 1998 which have been preliminarily discussed in Wkly 5.21 above. In the presidential election none of the six candidates in the field captured 40 percent of the vote. Therefore, there will be a run-off election on 12 July 1998 between the two leading candidates in that first round, Jamil Mahuad of the Peoples Democracy Party (DP), and Alvaro Noboa of the Ecuadoran Roldos Party (PRE).

Deputies Elected Nationwide

Under Ecuador's brand new Constitution there are 20 deputies elected to the national legislature in the country at large, 101 elected by province. In Wkly 5.21 the preliminary results are reported before the complete vote count was canvassed. In these early returns the PSC had 6 seats (now 5), the ID had 4 (now 3), the Broad Front 1 (now 2) and the MPD none (now 1). DP and PRE maintained their counts.

By party affiliation, the results of these elections were as follows:

5 PSC members won seats, among these Jaime Nebot, who had lost the presidential run-off election against Abdala Bucaram in 1996, and Heinz Moeller, who had held an important position in the congress during the Bucaram ouster of 1997 (Wkly 3.7ff, YRBK98).

4 DP members captured seats. As an aside, it might be remarked that the four winners—Pons, Rivera, González and Cordero—occupied the first four positions on List 5, the DP list. Of the 14 lists LANS has on hand, the PSC winners occupied the top five positions on List 6, the ID victors the top three positions on List 12, the Frente Amplio winners the top two positions on List 21-18-17, the single PCE winner the top spot on List 1, the MPD victor the top spot on List 15.

4 PRE members captured seats, their leader being Adolfo Bucaram of the clan which produced the bizarre ex president. According to the Supreme Election Tribunal announcement, the third and fourth winners here were Alberto Andrade and Jorge Marún. Andrade does not appear on the List 10, the PRE list and apparently substituted for Vicente Estrada. Raú Marum appears in the third place on List 10. Presumably, the victor was Jorge Marún and not Raú Marum.

3 ID members captured seats, these corresponding to the first three names on List 12. Leading this list was Paco Moncayo who was chairman of the joint chiefs of staff during the Abdala Bucaram ouster.

2 Broad Front members, Léon Roldós, a former president of Ecuador, and Nina Pacari, occupied the first two slots on List 21-18-17 and were assigned the chairs. The Broad Front consisted of the Pachakutik, PN and PSE.

1 PCE candidate won a seat, this being the former Ecuadoran president, Sixto Durán Ballén who headed List 1.

1 MPD candidate, Jaime Hurtado, another former Ecuadoran president, occupied the first slot on List 15 and captured a seat. In the second spot on this list was Stalin Vargas.

Deputies Elected by Province

The 101 provincial delegates provided by the new Constitution are as follows:

Guayas 18; Pichincha 14; Manabi 8; Azuay, El Oro and Los Ríos 5 each; Chimborazo, Esmeraldas, Loja and Tungurahua 4 each; Bolivar, Cañar, Carchi, Cotopaxi, Imbabura, Morona Santiago, Napo and Sucumbios 3 each; Galápagos, Pastaza and Zamora Chinchipe 2 each.

These numbers check out. However, as will be seen below, the number of deputies by party, which was allegedly released by the TSE and has been here taken from *La Hora* (29 Jun 98), do not add as they should. Because the results, however, cannot be changed by enough to affect the party blocs, this is not particularly important at this time.

The Congress which is to be installed on 1 August 1998 will include 105 male and 16 female deputies. These will serve until August 2002. The total number of deputies by party, to include both national and provincial deputies, according to the TSE, is as follows.

> The DP has 32 deputies.
> The PSC has 26.
> The ID has 16.
> Pachakutik has 6.
> The FRA has 3.
> The PCE has 2.
> The MPD has 2.
> The DP-ID-PSC alliance has 2.
> The DP-FRA alliance has 1.
> The DP-Pachakutik alliance has 1.

The PSE-Pachakutik alliance has 1.
The NP-PSE-Pachakutik alliance has 1.
The FRA-PSE alliance has 1.
The PSC-CFP alliance has 1.

There are, of course, various familiar names in this group of deputies, some of whom have been mentioned earlier. Elsa Bucaram is the sister of the ousted president, Abdala, now residing in Panama. With all save six of the 6,154 voting place in Guayas County, she won a seat in 16th place with 186,811 votes. This former mayor of Guayaquil is a PRE deputy. Winning a deputy post under the banner of the DP-FRA alliance from Imbabura Province was Luis Mejía, the former president of the Constituent Assembly which had just drawn up the new Ecuadoran Constitution.

It is of some interest to compare the congressional blocs elected in 1996 with those chosen in 1998, although the results are only qualitative. In doing so the bloc size from 1996 is increased by 50 percent because of the constitutional increase in deputies. (For example, PSC actually won 26 seats in '96, a number increased here to 26(150 percent)=39.) PSC won 39 in '96, 26 in '98; PRE won 28 in '96, 32 in '98; DP won 18 in '96, 32 in'98.

PERU

PERUVIAN MAYORAL ELECTIONS
(SPCL 6.13, 2 NOVEMBER 1998)

ONPE (National Electoral Proceedings Office) has just released the official results of the 11 October 1998 municipal elections in the 24 departments of Peru and the Constitutional Province of Callao. These results will only be given here for the departmental capitals. The results are official with percentages of the vote tallies as indicated. These results are reproduced using the following notation:

MOYABAMBA (San Martín); 99.57 percent; MIVV (Independent Neighbors Movement) 7,498 (28.04 percent) means: With 99.57 percent of the vote counted, the MIVV candidate won the mayoral election in Moyabamba, capital of San Martín Department with 7,498 votes or 28.04 percent of the total. Using the notation the mayoral results in the departmental capitals, the results are as follows:

CHACHAPOYAS (Amazonas); 100 percent; MI6J (6 June Independent Movement); 5,576 (34.66 percent). HUARAZ (Ancash);

100 percent; SH (We Save Huaraz); 14,425 (28.30 percent). ABANCAY (Apurímac); 89.45 percent; MIVV 6,447 (26.35 percent) & NI (New Left) 6,675 (27.29 percent): undecided. AREQUIPA (Arequipa); 98.99 percent; ATF (Arequipa Tradition and Future) 261,022 (67.26 percent). HUAMANGA (Ayacucho); 98.90 percent; MIVV 17,163 (26.44 percent) & MIC (Cealamaqui Independent Movement) 13,659 (21.05 percent). CAJAMARCA (Cajamarca); 98.75 percent; FIRJP (Peru Together Independent Regional Front) 31,871 (35.47 percent) & MIVV 28,229 (31.42 percent). CALLAO (Callao); 97.72 percent; Cimpum Callao 213,399 (67.24 percent). CUSCO (Cusco); 86.75 percent; MIVV 26,938 (23.39 percent) & MISP (We Are Peru Independent Movement) 22,510 (19.55 percent) & FA (Broad Front) 25,078 (21.78 percent). HUANCAVELICA (Huancavelica); 100 percent; MDAP (Peru Decentralized Now Movement) 15,583 (42.33 percent). HUÁNUCO (Huánuco); 95.80 percent; MISP 23,612 (32.94 percent). ICA (Ica); 100 percent; FIP (Independent Peoples Front) 51,399 (38.44 percent). HUANCAYO (Junín); 91.09 percent; FVI (Independent Local Front) 85,251 (53.95 percent). TRUJILLO (La Libertad); 96.57 percent; APRA (Peruvian Aprista Party) 154,532 (55.31 percent). CHICLAYO (Lambayeque); 96.90 percent; AC (Forward Chiclayo) 111,322 (40.31 percent). LIMA (Lima); 97.99 percent; SP (We Are Peru) 1,804,598 (58.80 percent). MAYNAS (Loreto); 96.13 percent; FL (Lorteana Force) 63,141 (47.07 percent). TAMBOPATA (Madre de Dios); 100 percent; MIVV 5,451 (31.19 percent). MARISCAL NIETO (Moquegua); 99.59 percent; MIVV 10,399 (34.07 percent) & MISP 10,198 (33.41 percent). PASCO (Pasco); 100 percent; MIVV 16,132 (33.76 percent). PIURA (Piura); 98.08 percent; RD (Reconstruction and Development) 99,797 (52.27 percent). PUNO (Puno); 98.10 percent; FIJOF (Independent Front for Fixed Works) 34,660 (39.14 percent). MOYABAMBA (San Martín); 99.57 percent; MISS 7,498 (28.04 percent). TACNA (Tacna); 99.18 percent; MITU (Independent Tacna United Movement) 29,945 (31.22 percent). TUMBES (Tumbes); 100 percent; ADT (Tumbusina Democratic Alliance) 16,678 (36.46 percent). CORONEL PORTILLO (Ucayalí); 100 percent; MIP 2000 (2000 Pucalipa Independent Movement) 26,997 (31.98 percent)

Alberto Andrade Carmona, Mayor of Lima and head of MISP was reelected with 58.8 percent, former Prime Minister Juan Carlos Hurtado Miller, the MIVV candidate receiving 32.5 percent of the vote. MISP has 24 seats on the Municipal Council, MIVV 13, while Peoples Action and APRA have one each.

In the Constitutional Province of Callao, Mayor Alexander Kuori was reelected in the Callao mayoral race with 68 percent of the vote.

VENEZUELA

THE VENEZUELAN ELECTIONS OF 1998
(WKLY 5.14, 9 APRIL 1998)

On 6 December 1998 what is being described as "the most complex elections" of the 40 years since the "restoration of democracy," that is, the overthrow of the caudillo Marcos Pérez Jiménez, will take place. The president, 46 senators, 326 national assembly deputies, 330 mayors, 370 regional assembly deputies, 2404 city councilors and 3082 parish boards will be elected.

As has been frequently mentioned in these reports, the comely Irene Sáez (37), Miss Universe 1981 and now mayor of Chacao, has been leading the presidential polls for almost two years by substantial margins. Indeed, the polling firm Datos reported a figure of 39 percent for her in a poll taken between 13 November and 11 December 1997. But the same poll had what was once a familiar name in second place, Hugo Chávez Frías, with 14 percent. The "dissident" Social Democrat, Claudio Fermín, the Democratic Action (AD) candidate in 1993 (p.24,YRBK97), was in third place with 13 percent, Henrique Salas Römer, the ex governor of the State of Carabobo,[30] in fourth place with 8 percent. Eduardo Fernández, who lost the presidential elections to Carlos Andrés Pérez in 1988 (p.74,YRBK97) and the present mayor of Caracas, Antonio Lodezma, both trailed this field with 3 percent.

But the most interesting hopeful to appear in the poll would prove to be Chávez, for, according to a CVI poll disseminated by the Caracas press in latter March, this ex lieutenant colonel was polling 34.2 percent against Ms. Sáez's 29 percent by that time. Although this impressive improvement may not yet presage a Chávez victory, it renders him worthy of special consideration. This latterday Velasco Alvarado,[31] as International Economic Press Agency (AIPE) director Carlos Ball has described him, is of the left. This renders his rise to fame in a 1992 *coup d'etat* attempt against the leftist Venezuelan President Carlos

Andres Pérez of more interest than it might otherwise have and demands a brief review of the great embezzler himself.

Carlos Andrés Pérez

Any discussion of Pérez in turn demands previous mention of Rómulo Betancourt, for it was as "private secretary" to the latter that the former emerged from his political egg.

The Venezuelan, Betancourt (b.1908), was communist party chief in Costa Rica from 1930 to 1935 (*La Hora* (San José) 25 September 1934). When he left Costa Rica for bigger and better things in Venezuela he bequeathed the CP to his brother-in-law, Manuel Mora Valverde who, unable to move on to b&bt, faithfully fulfilled his CP boss duties, for many years under Castro, until his recent death (p.3, YRBK97). There are those who feel that Betancourt shed his ML (Marxist Leninist) skin with his migration back to his native Venezuela, these perhaps typified by Alexander (*THE VENEZUELAN DEMOCRATIC REVOLUTION: A Profile of the Regime of RB*, Rutgers University Press, 1964. LCC: 64-19176). Although such appears to be the PC view, there has been divergence from it, Senator Olin Johnston (D, SC)—who was in a position to know—calling him the "communist leader of LA (Latin America)," the LANS Editor's old friend, now deceased, placing him in the "Caribbean Comintern."

On his return to Venezuela Betancourt formed the Venezuelan Revolutionary Party (ORVE) which evolved into AD, the vehicle for Pérez's political power in his native Venezuela (pp.74ff,YRBK97). His "secret meeting"[32] with Castro, Ortega et al in Caracas after his second election as president indicated that he remained well attached to the left. Which is relevant to the fact that a "leftist" revolution was attempted against him some 2½ years later.

Although worthy of note, this is probably as simple as Pérez surrendering to neoliberalism—and its privatizations—in order to reap the monetary benefits offered by the international lending agencies. Pérez's socialist successor, Caldera, would enter the presidency with unkind words for neoliberalism, only to surrender and join its proponents for this cash. And perhaps Castro, like the Romans and Persians with the Himyarite-Axum struggles, was simply stoking the fires to his own ends.

All of which may be "over analysis" based more on hindsight than reality, for reports at the time indicated that Chávez had been agitating for a *coup* for at least five years, that is, since two years before Pérez returned to the presidential palace.

Hugo Chávez Frías

In 1987 Chávez was an instructor at the Venezuelan Military Academy. It was reportedly at this time that he began his creation of a clandestine officers group, CoMaCaTe, which stood for colonels, majors, captains, lieutenants. Someone apparently reported his pamphleteering activities to this end. Out of this effort seems to have arisen his Bolivar Revolutionary Movement 200 (MBR 200), although caution should probably be used in applying this name to the first *coup* attempt. It was in use by the second such (November 1992) at which point Chávez was in duress vile.

In any event, Chavéz's objectives are demonstrably leftist, but primarily power seeking. To this point he has been able to create what may be a sizable constituency. The details of the *coup* attempt need hardly be given *in extenso*: Pérez was apparently to have been murdered after his aircraft touched down at the Francisco de Miranda Air Force Base, but, through late arrival, he was forced to land 30 miles away at the International Airport. He got to the Miraflores Palace, then away by a secret tunnel—of which the golpistas were unaware—and under a coat as Chávez's men broke in. So much for the failed *coup*.

Chávez ended in jail, but not for long; Caldera would pardon him, thus allowing him to make a legal run for the presidency in 1998. The golpistas' manifesto had complained of this and that, but perhaps most notably of "unpunished corruption"—and Pérez would be out of the presidency the following year for precisely this reason (pp.73ff, YRBK97)— and "privatization of state companies," i.e., moves toward the free market. The "ex" golpista would parrot the same themes.

The Chávez 1998 Presidential Run

On the sixth anniversary of his attempted *coup*, 4 February 1998, Chávez (43) told his followers and the world, "I am a soldier of humanity, of the people." But he told the interviewer for *VenEconomy Monthly* (March 1998), Yana Marull, considerably more, revealing a simplistic view of economic reality but one which allows him to hew to the Castroite "anti-neoliberal" line. He is advocating a government economy. It was just such an economy that plunged Venezuela into that slough of economic despond which has not allowed it to emerge, as Vladimir Chelminski (pp.76ff,YRBK97) put it, from "socialist prehistory." This, or the example provided by Castro's economic catastrophe, are not allowed to enter his thought or his discourse. For such ideas would drive away those leftists who are, and have been, so important to him.

In 1992 Movement Toward Socialism (MAS), one of the organizations in Castro's Foro São Paulo (p.99,YRBK97), deputy and ex terrorist, Teodoro Petkoff, was unearthed by James Brooke (*New York Times* 9 February 1992) for a few hundred words of Chávez eulogy. On 17 February 1998 Venezuelan Communist Party (PCV) director Pedro Ortega Díaz declared that "The program of Chávez coincides with that which the PCV is creating, it represents the aspirations of the working class..." (AFP)

Pepe Figueres (p.3,YRBK97) was wont to remark that "I am not a communist, I am just good friends with them," albeit, some of his personal friends have told the LANS editor a different story. This is apparently the position Chávez appears to be essaying in the same wire dispatch. Whether friends or *compañeros*, however, enough of them probably signed his petition so that he was able to present the Venezuelan Supreme Election Council (CSE) on 16 January 1998 with the 100,000 signatures necessary to legalize his V Republic Movement party and establish himself as a serious contender.

Because the former lieutenant colonel, as leader in the polls, is a serious contender, the synopsis of the superb interview by Yana Marulla is reproduced below. It was translated into English by Russell Maddicks. This is reproduced with the gracious permission of the *VenEconomy* publisher, Mr. Robert Bottome.

HUGO CHÁVEZ HAS HIS EYE ON MIRAFLORES AGAIN
YANA MARULL
VENECONOMY
CARACAS, VENEZUELA

On Feb. 14, 1992 Lieutenant Colonel Hugo Chávez was on the point of taking the Presidential Palace of Miraflores by force. Now, six years after the failed coup attempt by a group of young officers, Chávez has his eye set on Miraflores again, but this time he'll be taking the electoral route, and it looks like he's moving up: He's second[33] in the polls, behind former Miss Universe and mayor of Chacao Irene Sáez, and his support continues to grow.

What stands out most in the years since the coup is 43-year-old Chavez's change of style. Originally from the Llanos of Barinas,[34] Chávez has transformed himself from an aggressive army officer in the military fatigues and red beret of the parachute regiment into the charismatic leader of the "anti-politics" movement, complete with civilian suit and tie. Gone are the veiled threats and extremist stance, smoothed over and expanded to present a more moderate and less simplistic position. In fact, give him a few minutes and he's capable of quoting from Mao, the Bible, Archimedes ("give me where to stand and I will move the world"), Simón Bolívar ("Damned be the soldier who takes up arms against his own peoples"), Montesquieu, Jesus Christ, the Pope, and Dante.

It certainly makes for a change from six years ago when he only spoke of Bolívar's revolt against corruption. Now he details his future government's policies: "We are not going to kick out international companies" if elected president, he says, while at the same time keeping a "revisionist" line up his sleeve on the contracts already signed by the State with foreign multinationals. In Chavez' economic system, basic industries should belong to the State. In the economic system he envisions a possible economic integration with Mercosur, although the time has not yet come for hemispheric integration.

Will he apply exchange controls? Will he put up with the current monetary and exchange system? The answer is that it all depends on circumstances. External debt is another point he would renegotiate. (He doesn't want to say not pay).

A SOLDIER OF THE PEOPLE

"I am a soldier committed to a nation," but not "a dictator or a king," says the former coup-maker, who now has the official support of the left-wing party Patria Para Todos (PPT) for the elections, and who has promised a much more active role for the armed forces in the future "for the development of the country."

If he wins the elections, he pledges to form a Constituent Assembly which would imply the dissolution of Congress—elected the same day as the president. The first step would be to hold a referendum, which would give his plan a seal of democratic approval. How the Assembly would be elected, who would take part in it, and how it would work are all things that have yet to be decided.

WOLF IN SHEEP'S WARDROBE

"There is a dramatic change in the way he projects his image:

Chávez, the wolf, has put on a variety of sheep's clothing so that now he's seen as a nice, pleasant, friendly, guy, and a skilled debater," says Alfredo Keller, president of Consultores 21. But he adds, "Chávez won't admit his weaknesses now. He won't admit he is a subversive, responsible for the deaths caused by his coup attempt, and the economic fallout it left behind. Just as he won't talk about who's backing him."

For Chávez, the last six years have gone well: his popularity has improved and he has discovered the skill of appealing to the more extreme segments of the political left and right as well as those who usually abstain. Consultores 21 gives him 17 percent in the polls, with a tendency to rise, and predicts that figure could reach 30 percent in May or June. One electoral scenario would see a three-way split, with Sáez taking a third of the vote, Chávez another third, and the last third being fought over, perhaps by COPEI[35] and AD.

Chávez' mark is evident all over the country: His "sphinx" logo appears on walls and "Welcome to Bolivarian Territory" greets visitors at the entrances to the poor areas surrounding Caracas. In the 23 de Enero slum they well remember his epic deeds. The chanting of his name after the coup attempt rang through the hills. Many consider him a hero for taking on then-president Carlos Andrés Pérez, who in 1989 used harsh measures to put down the popular insurrection known as the "Caracazo" and pushed through a program of economic reforms, similar to those now in force, but which in those days had a very different impact.

"It was like a light being turned off. We knew that there was going to be a coup here, people were armed, rebel soldiers stayed the night, and we went out together to fight the government," explains a resident of the 23 de Enero. For a family member of a victim of Feb. 4, who recently made a public appeal on a radio program, "he's no savior. Don't forget the dead he left behind."

Rafael Caldera has twice given Chávez a nod of approval, once as President, when he issued amnesty to the coup-maker, and before, in 1992, when he compared the coup attempt to a repetition in "military garb" of the 1989 "Caracazo."

He has become a hero to some and a danger to others. To win the elections, he has to appeal to more voters than he can count on at the moment, and not just those on the fringes of the political spectrum. With that in mind, he has softened his tone. Now he has to make sure that he can attract that section of the electorate that supports him but usually abstains from voting. He says that to be elected he will call on the abstainers and beat the rest of the field with an incontestable margin of 2 or 3 million votes. He also says that the military will back his campaign, but only by guaranteeing fair elections.

THE VENEZUELAN GUBERNATORIAL AND CONGRESSIONAL
ELECTIONS OF 8 NOVEMBER 1998
(WKLY 6.19, 12 NOVEMBER 1998)

Venezuelan Geography

Beginning with the easternmost of the northern tier of Venezuelan states, the State of Zulia encloses Lake Maracaibo. To its east the State of Falcon occupies the southern-curving coastline to be adjoined to its east by Yaracuy, Carabobo and the narrow strip of coast which is the Federal District and the State of Vargas. Following the coast on to the east the State of Anzoátegui is next encountered, this state extending south to the Orinoco River as does the State of Monagas to its east, albeit, separated from the sea by the State of Sucre save for a short window on the Gulf of Pavia. Yet farther to the east of Monagas and enclosing the mouth of the Orinoco is the Territory of Delta Amacuro.

Fronting on Lake Maracaibo to its west and the State of Zulia to its north is the small State of Trujillo, it in turn bordered by the States of Lara to its northeast and Portuguesa to its east. To its east are the States of Cojedes, then Guarico, this pair bordered on their north by Aranda and Miranda. Which leaves only the broad expanses of the States of Apure and Bolivar to the east, these bordered by the Territory of Amazonas to their south, this part of the Amazon Basin thrusting between Colombia to the west and Brazil to the east.

Election Generalities

On 8 November 1998 gubernatorial elections were held for the 23 Venezuelan states and the Federal District and for the representatives of these states in the upper house (senators) and lower house (deputies) of the national legislature. The gubernatorial elections are straightforward, the legislative elections deserving of specific consideration.

Art. 148 of the Venezuelan Constitution deals with the election of senators, there being two of these elected by direct vote from each state and the Federal District. Art. 151 deals with the election of deputies, there being at least two of these elected by direct vote from each state, the actual number so elected being a function of the latest population figures for the various states. There was originally to be at least one deputy elected by direct vote from each territory, but there are no longer any territories. Additional deputies are to be elected by "proportional representation of minorities," "minorities" here referring to political parties of small to miniscule membership.

An example of the "minority" nature of these minority parties may be obtained from the data on the senatorial elections. There were, of course, 48 senators to be elected on 8 November. Over 48 parties entered candidates in the country, these of course splitting up the 4,999,172 votes which a 95.97 percent vote count showed to have been cast. The maximum number of votes gained by any party was the 1,226,032 (24.52 percent) won by AD. The tenth-ranked party (IRENE) picked up 62,497 (1.25 percent), the twentieth (RENACE) 12,088 (0.24 percent), the fortieth (EL) 920 (0.02 percent) while the forty-eighth, apparently a family affair, (FIN) received 138 (<.01 percent). LANS queries of Venezuelan Embassy political experts revealed that votes received in previous elections determined whether a given party was placed on the ballot.

Political Parties

It is clearly neither possible nor desirable to deal with "all" the political parties of Venezuela if, indeed, anyone has a notion of such an entity. A few are, however, a necessity for relatively rational discussion of elections in that nation. Any such discussion must perforce begin with Rómulo Betancourt had he done nothing more than play godfather to Carlos Andrés Pérez. But he did considerably more. The first 10 parties on the senators' list will be given briefly below in order of their appearance, the votes drawn by each following their description.

AD

As has been discussed in Wkly 5.14 immediately above, Betancourt, back in Venezuela from his Costa Rican adventures, put together ORVE (Venezuelan Revolutionary Party), to some extent from ARDI (Left Revolutionary Group). On 13 September 1941 AD (Democratic Action Party) evolved as Mr. Betancourt's official vehicle for political activity, Pérez becoming his secretary therein by 1945.[36] (1,226,032)

MVR (Fifth Republic Movement)

Lt. Col. Chávez, the apparent Castroite, attempted the overthrow of the Pérez regime in 1992 with an MBR200 (Bolívar Revolutionary Movement) consisting of 200 members of a military lodge (1992). For reasons best known to Caldera, the latter pardoned the former in 1994, the pardonee launching his presidential campaign in 1997. Chávez, as the front runner in the presidential elections merits further coverage which he will receive. (983,239)

COPEI (Independent Political Electoral Organization Committee— Christian Socialist)

This is of course the party formed in 1946 by the incumbent president of Venezuela, Rafael Caldera. With whatever accuracy, it traces its beginnings back to the 1934 meeting in Rome of the World Catholic Youth, held for the purpose of creating an international network of Christian Democrat Movement Parties. Caldera was one of the COPEI founders in 1946. Dissidents from this "Christian Socialist" party joined MAS (Movement Toward Socialism) and PCV (Venezuelan Communist Party) to elect that Caldera who may have given the *coup de grace* to the Venezuelan economy. (614,323)

PRVZL (Project Venezuela)

In September 1997 Salas Römer established this vehicle for a run at the presidency. There will be more on Dr. Salas; his son, Salas Feo, will be encountered as a successful gubernatorial candidate. This party is allegedly "social christian." (498,166)

MAS (Movement Toward Socialism)

Founded by the ML, Teodoro Petkoff, and certain of his PCV (Venezuelan Communist Party) associates, this party is appropriately represented by its clenched-fist logo. It represents itself as "communism of a new time" and justifies its claim with militancy in Castro's FSP (São Paulo Forum). (457,293)

PPT (Country for Everyone)

This is an offshoot of Causa R (below) which was put together in 1996 by alleged "dissidents" of that organization although the name has undergone certain evolution. It claims to be "humanist," "participative" and "democratic," which would have described the apparently defunct USSR. It supports Chávez. (167,351)

Causa R (Radical Cause)

This aptly named group allegedly arose out of certain ML terrorist groups, the last mentioned being the FMPR (Manuel Ponte Rodríguez Front), to which were added "dissidents" of the PCV, then of MAS (1979). That it arose from these ML groups is not in question, but, as always, the matter of dissidence is. (147,577)

APERTURA

Perhaps the last gasp of that old socialist, Carlos Andrés Pérez, who was put down but not finished by his immense peculations which have been described in these reports. (122,779)

CONVERGENCIA

This is the largely marxist coalition which Caldera put together to eke out a presidential victory in 1994. (118,189)

IRENE (Integration, Representation and New Hope)

This party name began with the first name of Irene Sáez, adding words to fit, e.g., NE = Nueva Esperanza. This comely ex Miss Universe is now mayor of Chacao and was front runner in the presidential sweepstakes until the Chávez campaign was well underway. (62,497)

Senate

The results in the senate races by state and party affiliation were as follows:

Amazonas: AD 1; COPEI 1. Anzoategui: AD 1; MVR 1. Apure: AD 2. Aragua: MAS 1; MVR 1. Barinas: AD 1; Coalition (MVR, PPT, etc.) 1. Bolívar: AD-Convergencia 1; MVR 1. Carabobo: PRVZL 1; MVR 1. Cojedes: AD 1; COPEI 1. Federal District: MVR 2. Delta Amacuro: AB-COPEI 1; MAS 1. Falcon: AD 1; COPEI 1. Guarico: AD 1; MVR 1. Lara: AD 1; MAS 1. Merida: AD 1; MVR 1. Miranda: PPT 1; PRVZL 1. Monagas: AD 1; Coalition (MVR-PPT-MAS) 1. Nueva Esparta: AD 1; COPEI 1. Portuguesa: AD 1; Coalition (MAS-MVR-PPT). Sucre: AD 1; MAS 1. Tachira: COPEI 1; APERTURA 1. Trujillo: AD 1; Coalition (PCV, Polo Patriotica) 1. Vargas: AD 1; Coalition (MVR, MAS, PPT, etc.) 1. Yaracuy: CONVERGENCIA 2. Zulia: AD 1; COPEI 1.

In the Senate AD will perhaps have 18 "constitutional" (elected) senators and one senator-for-life, ex Pres. Jaime Lusinchi. MVR now has 13 and will perhaps have fewer, COPEI 8, MAS 4, PRVZL 2 and CONVERGENCIA 2.

Chamber of Deputies

As an example, the results by direct vote and proportional representation will be given for a small-population state (Amazonas) and the larger-population political division (Federal District). In Amazonas AD won 1 seat by direct vote (DR) and 1 seat by proportional representation (PR) while COPEI gained 1 seat by DR. In the Federal District AD won 2 seats by DR; MAS won 1 seat by DR and 1 seat by PR; MVR won 1 seat by DR and 5 seats by PR; PPT won 1 seat by PR and PRVZL won 4 seats by DR.

Although there will apparently be some adjustments, the principal parties now appear to have about the following numbers of deputies: AD 59; MVR 58; MAS 30; COPEI 27; PRVZL 25; Causa R 6; PPT 4 and CONVERGENCIA 2.

Gubernatorial Races

There is considerably less attention to party labels in these races for the governor's chairs than in the national races. While there appear to have been six winning governors on AD tickets, three on COPEI and a scattering of wins by other parties, "Independent" appears more appropriate here.

Perhaps most independent was Orlando Fernández Medina who won the governorship in the State of Lara running under the OFM banner, that is, his own initials. The 70-year-old Rafael "Fucho" Tovar clearly labeled himself an Independent and won the gubernatorial race in the State of Nueva Esparta. The Black militant of Polo Patriotico, Alfredo Laya, won the governor's race in the State of Vargas. Among the other triumphant wavers-and-smilers was Enrique F. Salas Feo in the State of Carabobo whose father, Dr. Salas, is seeking the presidency with much less chance of success than young Salas enjoyed. And, apparently appropriately and under the banner of his son's MVR, Hugo de los Reyes Chávez was elected governor of the State of Barinas.

THE VENEZUELAN PRESIDENTIAL ELECTIONS
(WKLY 6.22, 3 DECEMBER 1998)

Whether or not Nostradamus could and/or did accurately forecast "the future" appears to be a subject for debate, learned or otherwise. Whether any of the substantial number of contemporary tea-leaf readers can forecast the future of the HL (Hemispheric Left) terrorist boss, Fidel Castro, remains an interesting speculation. It can be said, however, that those prognosticators who have confidently predicted, during the last decade and more, the political demise of Castro have so far been belied by events. It can also be said, if seldom admitted, that, quite to the contrary, Castro's political position has substantially improved.

Such improvement should be brought home to the most casual observer of the political scene if Cmdte. Chávez wins the Venezuelan presidential elections of 6 December 1998. The polling data indicates that he will do just this.

Presidential Elections Preliminaries

Those who have perused LANS Wkly 6.19 (above) will encounter little difficulty in accepting the assertion that Venezuela has "more political parties than any nation in the world" (AFP 11 February 1995)—"Every man his own political party." When the Venezuelan CSE (Supreme Electoral Commission) performed minor surgery on this vast body of political parties in early 1995 by canceling the certification of 22 national and 88 regional parties, there still remained more than 1000 parties on the rolls, all of which had allegedly received at least 1 percent of the national vote in the then most recent election.

In Wkly 6.19 the attempt had to be made to provide a reasonably comprehensive account without simply trivializing it with this party plethora. In the presidential elections, however, such a conundrum does not really arise. As will be seen, there were some 11 candidates, one of whom—Hugo Rafael Chávez Frías—will be discussed in detail. As a matter of historical interest, a candidate with little apparent chance of winning the presidential sweepstakes, will be discussed first.

Irene Lailin Sáez Conde

The quite comely, blonde Ms. Sáez attained international prominence in 1981 when she was selected as Miss Universe. Since she threw her hat into the presidential ring in 1996, certain segments of the press have looked down their prominent proboscises with thinly-veiled scorn at this quite comely, blond lady running for president of Venezuela. The viability of this view may remain to be demonstrated, but it certainly can now be said that she could never destroy the economy of that nation as have the scoundrels (e.g., Carlos Andrés Pérez (CAP)), socialists (e.g., Rafael Caldera) and MLs (Marxist Leninists) (e.g., Teodoro Petkoff, the Caldera right arm) previously occupying the Miraflores Palace.

The political career of Ms. Sáez, a licenciado in political science, may be said to have begun when she was elected mayor of Chacao in 1992. Chacao is a suburb (municipality) of Caracas, and the same proboscises have described this suburb as occupied by the "rich," a derogatory term in the lexicon of these people save when looking for a loan or a donation. She was reelected for a second three-year term in December 1995 as an Independent with the support of AD and COPEI. AD was of course the creation of Rómulo Betancourt and long the bailiwick of CAP. COPEI was formed by Pres. Caldera and associates in 1946. (For more information on these and other of the parties to be encountered, cf. Wkly 6.19.)

However reflective of reality the polls may have been, Ms. Sáez's performance in them is worthy of attention during the last two and one-half years. She began in June 1996 in first place with a modest 10 percent, climbed into the forty-percent range which she maintained until the end of 1997 when, in tandem with the rising numbers of Chávez, her numbers fell until, by mid October 1998 they were being reported by a CIRM Market Research poll as 15 percent.

The fall did not stop there nor was this the extent of her misfortunes.

At one point she was effectively the candidate of both AD and COPEI. But not long ago COPEI removed her endorsement and bestowed it elsewhere. Then, less than a week before the election was to take place, CSE Vice Pres. García announced that the CSE had decided "unanimously" that AD could change its affiliation from Luis Alfaro Ucero to the man in second place, Enrique Salas Römer. Venezuelan politicians were "deeply concerned" over a possible victory by Chávez.

It would appear that Ms. Sáez is out of the running which may have annoyed her enough to induce her comments to *El Universal* of 2 December 1998. She declared that the Venezuelans "will react against the pacts," going on to maintain that "The people are very sad... to see these last minute, under the table pacts," which of course could be true to whatever extent. If it is, this would apparently work in favor of Chávez. She then claimed that "One pole against another pole is not being dealt with ...but the consensus of the people ..." The original "pole" is of course that in Chávez's party name, Patriotic Pole (Polo Patriótico), the "other pole" the alliance that is being formed against him. In essence she is saying that the latter pole will not work.

In the meantime, Ms. Sáez is continuing her campaign under the banner of the party which she formed in 1992 for her mayoral campaign, IRENE (Integración Representación Nueva Esperanza—New Hope Integration Representation). The party was originally registered only in the single state relevant to her mayoral campaign; in 1997 she extended it to a national party.

Hugo Rafael Chávez Frías

LANS will assuredly not predict the winner of the 6 December 1998 presidential election in Venezuela. However, various rather astute political figures in that nation have made such a prediction or have indicated their belief in such an outcome with their bustling activities in support of Chávez -blocking coalitions. Among the former is Carlos Andrés Pérez.

Septuagenarian ex Pres. Pérez may be criticized for various of his activities during a long life, but it can hardly be denied that he has vast experience as a practical politician. Which renders his remarks of latter November 1998 worthy of remark. He told EFE that "Chávez

...will be the winner" of the 6 December elections, that "The Venezuelan people expressed an unequivocal will (for this) ...in the parliamentary ...elections of 8 November ..." and, finally, that the efforts to form a front to oppose his election will fail. Whether Pérez proves right or wrong, the bases of his remarks appear sound.

Hugo Chávez (b. 1955) is a marxist, proof of this surfacing virtually with his every appearance and utterance. But he is also a military man, and LANS sources in Venezuela have compared the government which he can be expected to form with that of another military marxist, Peru's Gen. Velasco Alvarado.[31]

He graduated from the VMA (Venezuelan Military Academy) in 1976. By 1987 he was an instructor at the VMA, an ideal position for his subversive propensities to surface. As they apparently did, for at that time he had formed a clandestine officers group, CoMaCaTe (Colonels, Majors, Captains and Lieutenants) which was suspected of circulating subversive pamphlets. But nothing came of it, and his career continued. By 4 February 1992, Chávez had advanced in rank to LTC (lieutenant colonel) and formed a new subversive organization, MBR (Bolivarian Revolutionary Movement). Choosing 4 Feb for his attempted golpe (coup d'etat), allegedly because it is Gen Sucre's birthday, MBR personnel amounting to about a battalion—about 133 officers and 925 enlisted men were later captured—under Chávez set out to take over the government.

The plotters failed to murder Pres. Pérez as they had planned, he escaping through a tunnel under a raincoat, a reality which some feel saved the day for the Venezuelan Government. Such is of course to some extent conjectural. In any event Chávez was jailed, and *The New York Times* (NYT) was allegedly able to locate any number of people who greatly admired the golpista boss, among them the man who would be Pres. Caldera's "economic expert," Teodoro Petcoff, the marxist founder of MAS (Movement Toward Socialism).

"The Venezuelan people applaud the putschists (golpistas)," Petkoff told Brooke (NYT, 9 Feb 92) who would claim there to have been "silent cheers from a large part of the population." Through it all the golpistas and their promoters in the press parroted the HL (Hemispheric Left) line of Fidel Castro against "neoliberalism," as if this gaggle of MLs (Marxist Leninists) would take any position other than this anti-free market one. But perhaps most interesting in this situation was the continuing pro-

Chávez position which the president-to-be, Rafael Caldera, would assume.

Chávez was jailed for his rebellion but not for long. Rafael Caldera replaced the ousted Pérez as president in December of 1993 and subsequently pardoned the golpista and returned his military rank with which Chávez retired. Venezuelan sources have told LANS that Caldera did this because he supported the Chávez efforts to overthrow Pérez. Which is in keeping with the facts and with the views of Caldera's cohorts such as Petkoff.

"I am not a communist," Chávez recently told *El Universal* (24 Nov 98) in repetition of a favorite theme. In the sense that his name is not on the roll of a communist party—such as those which are in his coalition—this is probably true. But that he appears to be a ML and dutiful member of Castro's HL the evidence all seems to indicate as does the makeup of the coalition[37] which he brought with him to the presidential ballot. First the question of the parties in his coalition.

The Chávez alliance of course includes the candidate's own MVR which is essentially an outgrowth of his MBR200 (Bolívar Revolutionary Movement) based on the 200 members of a military lodge with which his coup of 1992 was attempted. Some of the other groups in his coalition are: MAS was founded by Petkoff and certain of his PCV associates. PCV is also in the coalition. PPT is an offshoot of Causa R which in turn arose out of certain ML terrorist groups and "dissidents" from PCV and MAS. The three remaining are IPC (Independents for the Community), MSI (Independent Solidarity Movement) and AA (Agricultural Action).

That Chávez is leading what is effectively a ML coalition into the elections would seem to be undeniable. That he is leading it under the banner of Castro's HL may be inferred from various statements by the candidate, but he perhaps made his most convincing statement during the love feast between the candidate and the caudillo when the latter welcomed the former in the Aula Magna (Great Lecture Room) of the University of Havana on Chávez's arrival there in December 1994. The LANS files contain the video of the Venezuelan's talk and the Cuban dictator's reply. The performance can best be described as classic and endless ML rhetoric. Our colleague, Ariel Remos, has aptly distilled it with the Chávez remarks (*Diario las Américas* 24 Sep 98),

"I do not deserve this honor, I aspire to deserve it some day... Some day we hope to come to Cuba ... extending our arms in a LA (Latin American) revolutionary project, imbued as we are... with (the idea of) an Hispanic American continent integrated as a single nation ..." And the "soviet-type" LA union again arises, this to be either under Castro or his successor.[38]

Henrique Salas Römer

No endorsement of polls in general or these presidential polls in particular is intended here. However, it would appear that the only other candidate with any chance of victory is Salas. He appears in the second spot on the ballot, just below the ill fated Luís Alfaro Ucero, with three political parties given as in support. Two of these have been encountered above, AD and COPEI. The third party, PRVZL (Project Venezuela), is allegedly "social Christian" and has been encountered in Wkly 6.19. This party was created by Salas for his presidential run.

This account will be completed with what appears to be the latest poll rating the presidential hopefuls. The poll was taken by the polling firm, Consultores 21 on Friday, 27 November 1998 and published in *El Nacional* (Caracas) on 29 November 1998. The results are:

Chávez	57 percent
Salas	26 percent
Alfaro	6 percent
Sáez	3 percent

Caribbean Nations

DOMINICAN REPUBLIC

THE DOMINICAN MIDTERM ELECTIONS
(WKLY 5.19, 21 MAY 1998)

Francisco Peña Gomez was the leftist who appeared prominently on the platform at the January 1995 Sandinista rally in Managua, his importance to the Hemispheric Left (HL) attested at the IV São Paulo Forum when, as LANS Associate Editor Graça Wagner pointed out, "18 Dominican parties were coalesced. From this arose the candidacy of Peña."

The leftist was allegedly beaten by Balaguer in the Dominican elections of 1994. In reporting the elections of 16 May 1998, Tibisay Soto (AFP 17 May) curiously describes this as "the scandalous election of 1994." It was so described by the Peña forces, but a careful reading of the situation at the time does not prove as much. The election may have been stolen by the Balaguer forces, but this was hardly demonstrated. In any event, the US Government forced Balaguer to cut his last presidential term by one half, and new elections were held in 1996 (pp.25ff,YRBK97). Which Peña lost.

Not long before the recent midterm elections Peña died of cancer and was given a hero's sendoff, Tomás Borge and other such individuals prominent at his funeral. In the flood of eulogistic printers' ink, Peña's leftwing past could not be detected. And it may well have been this flood which brought what the press called Peña's defeat—from the tomb—of Pres. Fernández. Results are incomplete, but Peña's Dominican Revolutionary Party (PRD) apparently took 24 of the 30 Senate seats and 83 of the 145 House of Deputy seats, proving, if anything, the power of the press.

MEXICO

THE 1998 MEXICAN LOCAL ELECTIONS
(WKLY 5.24, 25 JUNE 1998)

The United Mexican States held general elections on 21 August 1994, Institutional Revolutionary Party (PRI) candidate Ernesto Zedillo Ponce de León winning the presidency with 48.77 percent of the vote and trailed by National Action Party (PAN) candidate Diego Fernández de Cevallos with 25.94 percent, Democratic Revolutionary Party (PRD) candidate Cuauhtémoc Cárdenas Solórzano with 16.60 percent and Workers Party (PT) candidate Cecilia de Soto with 2.74 percent. The next general elections will be held in 2000.

Perhaps the second most important position in Mexican political affairs is that of governor of the Federal District (DF), the territory including and surrounding the nation's capital. Prior to 1997 this position was an appointive one, the president of Mexico making the appointment. By the date (7 July 1997) of the midterm elections (Wkly 4.2, YRBK98), however, reforms had rendered this an elective position. PRD candidate Cuauhtémoc Cárdenas won this gubernatorial election with 48 percent, PRI trailing with 26 percent, PAN with 16 percent and various others with lesser percentages.

Local Elections

"Local" elections will be taken as referring to the contests for state governors, state legislatures and town councilors. The governors are chosen in local elections every six years. The local legislature is made up of deputies who are chosen by popular election every three years. There is a new feature in the 1998 local elections in that primary elections will be held within the PRI ranks in order to select the PRI candidate for governor. There is apparently no other political party which has adopted this method of candidate selection.

During 1998 local elections have been held or will be held in 14 Mexican states. In this report these will be generally described for those held before 25 June, the remainder to be described in a December 1998 report. The location of these 14 states, given in the order in which they are holding their elections, is as follows:

(The Mexican State of) Yucatan is the northernmost and central one of the three states of the Yucatan Peninsula, its capital (Merida) about 625 sm (statute miles) East by Northeast (ENE) from Mexico City (MC). Baja California borders the US to the North (N), its capital (Mexicali) about 1400 sm Northwest (NW) of MC. Chihuahua borders US to N, its capital (Chihuahua) 780 sm NW by N (NWN) MC. Durango is S of Chihuahua, its capital (Durango) 490 sm NW MC. Zacatecas is SE of Durango, its capital (Zacatecas) 340 sm NW MC. Aguascalientes is a small state on and within southern border of Zacatecas, its capital (Aguascalientes) 285 sm NW MC. Oaxaca on Pacific with Guerrero to its W and Chiapas to its E, its capital (Oaxaca) 225 sm SE MC. Veracruz has Gulf of Mexico to NE, it capital (Jalapa Enríquez) 150 sm E MC. Chiapas has Pacific SW, Guatemala E, capital (Tuxtla Gutiérrez) 405 sm SEE MC. Tamaulipas (Tamps) has Gulf of Mexico E, its northern border abutting on Texas, its capital (Victoria) 300 sm N MC. Sinaloa is on the Pacific, Sonora to N, its capital (Culiacán) 690 sm NW MC. Michoacán has Pacific to SW, the DF to E, its capital 135 sm W MC. Tlaxcala a small state immediately E DF, its capital (Tlaxcala) 60 sm E MC. Puebla extends from NE to SE MC, its capital (Puebla) 75 sm ESE.

The following code will be used to designate the elections taking place in 1998 in these 14 states. YUCATÁN 0; 25; 106; 24/5 means that, in Yucatán (1) no governor will be elected; (2) 25 deputies will be elected; (3) 106 town councils will be elected; (4) the elections will take place on 24 May. With this code the Mexican local elections of 1998 may be given as:

YUCATÁN 0; 25; 106; 24/5. BAJA CALIFORNIA 0; 25; 5; 28/6. CHIHUAHUA 1; 33; 67; 5/7. DURANGO 1; 25; 39; 5/7. ZACATECAS 1; 30; 56; 5/7. AGUASCALIENTES 1; 27; 11; 2/8. OAXACA 1; 42; 570; 2/8 & 4/10. VERACRUZ 1; 45; 0; 2/8. CHIAPAS 0; 40; 111; 4/10. TAMAULIPAS 1; 32; 43; 25/10. SINALOA 1; 40; 18; 8/11. MICHOACÁN 0; 30; 113; 8/11. TLAXCALA 1; 32; 60; 8/11. PUEBLA 1; 39; 217; 8/11.

The totals for the year are thus 10 governors, 465 deputies and 1,416 town councils. There will also be 10 PRI primary elections for the gubernatorial races.

Elections in Yucatán

There was no gubernatorial election. Insofar as election of deputies to the state legislature is concerned, the "tricolor" of PRI has apparently maintained control of the legislature. In the reports of 25 May PRI was maintaining this control with 13 deputies, PAN in second place with 10, its deputy total having reportedly fallen from 12 in the last election. For the first time PRD was reported as having been able to elect two deputies. Neither PT nor the Green Ecology Party (PVEM) was able to capture any deputy seats. The presumably more accurate reports of 26 May, when the vote count was over 90 percent, gave PRI 15, PAN 9 and PRD 1.

As an example of the voting by municipality where all five parties received some votes, in the municipality of Ticul PRI received 6776 votes, PAN 4720, PRD 723, PVEM 2 and PT 1, the PT candidate presumably voting for himself, the PVEM candidate joined by his spouse. Election day was not without its lively moments.

In the Oxzkutzcab municipality 1000 perredistas (PRD), led by their mayoral candidate, Filiberto Lugo Rubio, erupted into the seat of the Municipal Election Council, throwing all the standees to the floor. Encouraged by the success of this operation, Cárdenas' democrats moved on to the Municipal Palace, shouting imprecations against PRI candidate Juan Magaña Arana, throwing rocks and generally comporting themselves in a democratic fashion. Reports of virulent complaints against alleged misbehavior of the PRI personnel by the PAN personnel were fairly widespread and included the charge that the governor had been buying votes with promises, generally considered fair play in democratic elections.

All in all, some 64 percent of the voters turned out in the elections of 24 May in Yucatán. With 95 percent of the voting tables tabulated PRI had obtained 307,000, PAN 204,666 and PRD, PT and PVEM together 56,851.

PRI Gubernatorial Primaries

As has been pointed out in the election compilation above, Tamaulipas will hold its local elections on 25 October, Sinaloa and Puebla holding theirs on 8 November. On 24 May for the first time PRI had primary elections for its gubernatorial candidates in these three states.

In Tamaulipas, the ex State Finance Secretary, Tomás Yarrington Ruvalcaba, was declared the winner of the primary with 51.19 percent of the vote (141,359) over the ex Chiapas Peace Commissioner, Marco Antonio Bernal Gutiérrez. Mr. Bernal apparently assured all that "these results were being manipulated." In Sinaloa Senator Juan S. Millán won the nomination, although considerably more press attention was given to PAN complaints that to the primary itself.

Senator Melquiades Morales Flores won the PRI nomination for Puebla governor with 53 percent of the vote, trailed by José Luis Flores with 29 percent and Germán Sierra with 18.9 percent.

It would appear to be generally agreed, or at least maintained, by the notables in PRI that these first primary elections were a rousing success.

THE 1998 MEXICAN LOCAL ELECTIONS
(WKLY 6.4, 30 JULY 1998)

"Local" elections are taken to mean those elections involving state governors, state legislators and town councilors. The 14 Mexican states within which such elections are being held in 1998 are listed in Wkly 5.24 above. The results of the Yucatán State elections are also listed there. Here the June and July 1998 election results will be discussed. In doing so LANS expresses its appreciation to Señor Manuel Carrillo Poblano, Director of the Federal Electoral Institute (Mexico), for the material furnished by his organization.

In Wkly 4.2 (YRBK98) the details of "direct election" (MR) and "proportional representation" (RP) are discussed with regard to the national legislature. Qualitatively speaking, MR means the election of a candidate in a given voting district by his having received a plurality of the votes cast in said district. Only a certain percentage of the legislative seats may be won by a given party through MR. Parties with fewer than this maximum number of seats may be assigned seats through RP depending on their vote over a number of districts.

Baja California (28 June)

Excelsior (Mexico 29 Jun 98) described this election with "abstencionism triumphs," apt since abstencionism amounted to some 55 percent of the "vote." There was no gubernatorial election, and the National Action Party (PAN) lost some ground relative to the Institutional Revolutionary Party (PRI), although it maintained a plurality in the state Chamber of Deputies.

PAN won the mayoral elections in 16 municipalities all told, these including Tijuana, Mexicali and Playas de Rosarita, the last of which had been given to PRI in the early returns. PRI, on the other hand, won the mayor's office in Tecate and Ensenado, the latter having been assigned to PAN in early returns.

In the Baja California Chamber of Deputies PAN won 11 seats by MR and 1 by RP for a total of 12 and a plurality in the legislature. PRI won 5 MR seats and 5 or 6 RP seats depending on how the final tally assigns the latter. The Democratic Revolution Party won no seats by MR and 3 or 2 seats, depending on the RP assignment for PRI and the fact that the Chamber must contain 25 deputies. The Workers Party (PT) and the local Socialist Revolution Party picked up a few votes but not enough to obtain any sort of representation.

Chihuahua (5 July)

The election results in the State of Chihuahua will not be official before 20 August 1998. This will, however, affect only the Chihuahua Congress.

There was a gubernatorial election in the State of Chihuahua which was won by the PRI candidate, Patricío Martínez.

In municipal races, PRI candidates captured the Municipal President posts in 67 municipalities, PAN those in 18 and PRD those in 2.

The makeup of the state legislature remains in doubt, PRI candidates winning deputy races in Districts XI, XVI and XIX, PRI winning those in Districts XVII and XVIII.

Durango (5 July)

The Durango State Electoral Council (CEE) has released the following numbers on the gubernatorial race. PRI candidate Angel Guerrero Mier won 38.9 percent of the vote and PAN candidate Rosario Castro Lozano 26.9 percent. The effective alliance of the Workers Party (PT) and the Mexican Green Ecology Party (PVEM) is described as the PT "supported by" the PVEM. However this left coalition is classified, its candidate, Alejandro González Yañez, was in third place with 20.8 percent of the vote, the PRD candidate, Máximo Gámiz Parral, trailing with 8.2 percent.

The state Chamber of Deputies contains 25 members, the PRI winning a clear majority therein. PRI won 14 seats, all MR. PAN won 1 seat by MR and 4 by RP for a total of 5. PRD won 2 seats, both by RP, and PT won 4 seats, all by RP.

Of the 39 municipal presidencies, PRT won 31, PAN 4, PT 3 and PRD 1.

Citizen participation was 56.66 percent.

Zacatecas (5 July)

Ricardo Monreal Avila, the gubernatorial candidate of PRD, won his race with 213,804 votes, his PRI opponent polling only 181,725.

The Zacatecas Congress contains 30 deputies. PRI won 12 seats (11 MR plus 1 RP), PRD 10 (6MR and 4 RP), PAN 6 (1 MR and 5 RP) and PT 2 (both RP). Obviously PRI does not have a majority in the congress.

There were 56 municipal president positions for which elections were held. Of these PRI won 34, PRD 10, PAN 10 and PT 2.

August Local Elections

Local elections will be held in August 1998 in the States of Aguascalientes, Oaxaca and Veracruz.

FINAL RESULTS FOR THE BAJA CALIFORNIA LEGISLATIVE ELECTION
(WKLY 6.5, 6 AUGUST 1998)

In Wkly 6.4 the local legislative elections in the Mexican States of Baja California, Chihuahua and Durango were reported. At the time the election results were not complete enough to allow a determination as to whether the Institutional Revolutionary Party (PRI) had won 5 or 6 seats by "proportional representation" (RP).[39] Since the National Action Party (PAN) figures were complete, this would have meant that the Democratic Revolution Party had won 2 or 3, the number of members of the legislature being 25. The other method of assigning seats is by "direct election" (MR). Therefore:

Party	MR	RP	Total
PAN	11	0	11
PRI	5	6	11
PRD	0	3	3
Total	16	9	25

LOCAL ELECTIONS IN AGUASCALIENTES, OAXACA AND VERACRUZ (WKLY 6.5, 6 AUGUST 1998)

On 2 August 1998 local elections were held in the Mexican States of Aguascalientes, Oaxaca and Veracruz. At the time of these elections the following political structure was in place in these three states.

AGUASCALIENTES: Otto Granados Roldán of the Institutional Revolutionary Party (PRI) was governor of the state. In the state Congress PRI (Tricolor) held 9 seats by MR and 2 by RP for a total of 11; the National Action Party (PAN) held 9 seats by MR and 4 by RP for a total of 13; the Democratic Revolution Party (PRD), the Workers Party (PT) and the Cardenist Party (PC) each held 1 seat by RP. There are 18 congressional voting districts and 27 seats in the legislature. Of the 11 municipal presidencies, 7 were held by PRI and 4 by PAN.

OAXACA: Diódoro Carrasco A. of the PRD was governor of the state. PRI held all 25 MR seats in the state legislature and hence no RP seats; PAN (Blanquiazul) held 5 seats by RP; PRD (Perredistas) held 10 RP seats; other parties holding 2. There are 25 voting districts and 42 seats in the legislature. Of the municipal presidencies, 537 were held by PRI, 4 by PAN, 26 by PRD and 13 by other parties.

VERACRUZ: Patricio Chirinos Calero of PRI was governor. PRI

held 28 seats in the state legislature, 23 by MR and 5 by RP; PAN held 6 seats, 1 by MR and 5 by RP; PRD held 4 seats, all by RP; other parties held 1 seat by RP. This added to 39 seats, but there will be 16 RP seats in the 3 August elections for a total of 40. Of the 207 municipal presidencies, 150 were held by PRI, 26 by PRD, 19 by PAN and 12 by other parties.

At press time the official assignment of RP seats in the state legislature were not available, although this will not seriously effect the various parties positions in the legislatures. With this in mind, however, the results, subject to the usual wave of protests, correspond to an over 90 percent vote count and should remain valid.

AGUASCALIENTES: Felipe González González of PAN won the gubernatorial race with 53 percent. He was trailed by Héctor Hugo Olivares Ventura of PRI with 36 percent, Alfonso Bernal Sahagún of the PRD with 7 percent and Marta Zambrano of the Workers Party (PT) with 2 percent. PAN candidates won the municipal races in 6 of the 11 municipalities to include the state capital, PRI in 4 and PT in 1 (San José de Gracia).

In the 18 voting districts PAN won 12 MR legislative seats, PRI 6, a clear 3-seat loss for PRI with the corresponding gain for PAN.

OAXACA: José Murat of PRI won the gubernatorial race with about 49 percent of the vote. He was trailed by PRI candidate Héctor Sánchez with 37 percent and PAN candidate Pablo Arnaud with 11 percent. LANS does not yet have the results in the 17 municipalities.

PRI maintained its control of the legislature with victories in 23 of the 25 districts, PRD picking up 2.

VERACRUZ: Miguel Alemán Velasco of PRI won the gubernatorial race with 48 percent. Luis Pazos of PAN trailed with 26 percent, Arturo Herviz of PRD with 18 percent and the candidate of the PT-PVE (Green Ecology Party), Ignacio Morales Lechuga, brought up the rear with 6 percent.

PRI candidates won 21 of the MR seats in the legislature, the PAN candidates 2 and the PRD candidates 1, thus assuring continued PRI dominance in that branch of state government.

MEXICAN LOCAL ELECTIONS OF 4 OCTOBER 1998
(WKLY 6.16, 22 OCTOBER 1998)

During 1998 local elections have been or will be held in 14 of the United Mexican States. In these contests some of the state governors, the deputies to the state legislatures and the town councils are selected. In Wkly 5.24 the local elections in the 14 states have been generally described. On 4 October 1998 these local elections took place in the States of Chiapas and Oxaca.

In Wkly 4.2 the two methods of electing deputies nationally have been detailed, the first, election by plurality (MR), the second, election by proportional representation (RP). Here it need only be repeated that, in a local election, a party may only receive 60 percent of the deputies available in the legislature by direct vote. If a given party received a full 60 percent of the available deputies by MR, it may not receive any deputies by RP. If it receives less than 60 percent of available deputy seats by MR, it may receive additional seats by RP.

State of Chiapas

As the local elections of 4 October 1998 approached, the offices in the State of Chiapas were divided as follows.

The governor of the state was Lic. Roberto Albores Guillén of the PRI (Institutional Revolutionary Party).

In the state congress PRI held 21 MR deputy seats and 5 RP seats for a total of 26 seats in the 40-seat legislature. PAN (National Action Party) held 2 MR seats and 3 RP seats for a total of 5, and PRD (Democratic Revolutionary Party) held 1 MR seat and 5 RP seats for a total of 6. In order to complete the 40-seat Congress other political parties held a total of 3 RP seats. In this state there are a total of 110 town councils. PRI controlled 84 of these, PRD 18, PAN 5 and the 3 remaining were the bailiwicks of other political parties.

In the elections of 4 October 24 MR deputies and 16 RP were to have been elected, the 24 from the same number of electoral districts by direct vote. There were to have been 111 municipal presidencies or mayoralties contested. However, in 3 of the 24 districts and 8 of the 111 municipalities the elections were suspended because it was felt that the security of the electorate could not be guaranteed.[40] In these 8 municipalities both climatic conditions and the unrest created by the EZLN (Zapatista National Liberation Army) terrorists[41] were given as reasons for the suspension; it appears that both reasons were justified.[42]

The continuing furor over the HR (Human Rights) situation in

Chiapas predictably created an army of "observers," both domestic and foreign, which invaded the state in a campaign lasting from about 2 to 6 October. Some 798 Mexican citizens were registered to observe the elections, these from a plethora of organizations allegedly devoted to HR. By 2 October some 34 foreign observers had descended on the state from Europe and North America, these representing the US, Canada, Spain, the United Kingdom, France and Austria, one additional country's representatives having not then yet made their appearance.

On 9-10 October 1998 the District and Municipal Electoral Councils turned over the proofs of victory to the CEE (State Electoral Commission) and to the mayoral and local deputy victors in the elections of 4 October. There were 102 mayoral-race winners declared and 21 local deputies, all the latter of course MR.

The mayoral races won by PRI decreased from 84 to 82 while PRD lost two to arrive at 15, PAN maintaining the same count with 5.

PRI was declared the winner in 18 deputy races, PAN the winner in 2 and PRD in 1.

There will be further review for those cases where certain parties claim election irregularities to exist. In District XVIII (Tapachula) PRD candidate Noel Vásquez Rodas won by 57 votes, and what amounts to a recount has apparently been demanded by PRI candidate Lydia del Carmen Abarca Pinzón. In District I (Tuxtla Gutiérrez) there are also "further investigations" while the districts in which the elections were suspended have of course to make the electoral decisions. But all these alleged peccadillos are minor compared to the challenge of Mr. López.

PRD Pres. Andrés Manuel López Obrador stated on 5 October that his party will "demand" the annulment of the Chiapas elections, these having allegedly shown that PRI was up to "its old practices." According to López, PRI was buying votes with handouts of construction materials and "cartons of beer." Whether or not PRI—and, possibly, PRD—was passing out beer, a hardly novel operation, the charge is a routine one.

To add to these festivities 300 militants of PAN, PRD and PT (Workers Party),[43] in what was doubtless a "peaceful" demonstration, took over the offices of the CEE after the recent elections and burned the ballots in what was doubtless a "peaceful" fire.

At a press conference Antonio Medrano and Ted Lewis from AI

(Amnesty International) and Global Exchange, HR organizations, grumbled about the presence of the military, calling it "the militarization of many zones" and claiming that "under these conditions" democracy will not exist. This demonstrates little if anything but the pro Zapatista bias of these ONGs, the "conditions" being nothing but a minimal government reaction to the existence of armed EZLN terrorists in the area. Various examples of AI proclivity for ML subversive groups such as the EZLN have been given in these reports,[44] It is painfully obvious, however, that where there are criminals there will be police or chaos.

State of Oaxaca

In Oaxaca 154 municipalities had mayoral elections while such officialdom was selected in the almost 600 other municipalities by the centuries-old system of "uses and customs." PRI won 113 of the 154 mayoral contests, thus maintaining its leadership over the 1,175,000 dwelling therein. In second place was PAN which triumphed in 12 municipalities with 478,000 citizens while PRD gained 29 municipalities with 383,000 inhabitants. Thus, PRI was triumphant in about 74 percent of the races.

Presently PRI has the majority in the State Congress and in both house of the Federal Legislature.

ELECTIONS IN THE MEXICAN STATE OF TAMAULIPAS ON 25 OCTOBER 1998
(WKLY 6.16, 22 OCTOBER 1998)

Local elections will be held in the State of Tamaulipas on 25 October 1998. The results will, of course, be reported when they are available. Here the background to these elections will be reviewed as will the pre-election makeup of the local Congress.

In the 1992 elections PRI candidate Manuel Cavazos won the gubernatorial contest against the PAN-PRD coalition by a mere four votes with only three of the 43 municipalities supporting the coalition. It would not appear possible with the data on hand to assign the numbers on this, but it remains a quite remarkable performance.

PAN and PRD are going their own way in the present contest, the former fielding Gustavo Cárdenas Gutiérrez, the latter Joaquín Hernández Correa while Tomás Yarrington carries the PRI banner.

In addition to the governor's race the citizens of Tamaulipas will choose mayors in 43 municipalities and MR local deputies in the 19 district of the state.

The present governor is Lic. Manuel Cavazos of PRI. The present Congress is constituted by 19 MR deputies, one from each district, and 13 RP deputies for a total of 32 distributed as follows.

PRI has 14 MR deputies and 6 RP for a total of 20. PAN has 4 MR and 3 RP for a total of 7, PRD 1 MR and 2 RP for a total of 3, PARM (Authentic Party of the Mexican Revolution)[45] 1 RP, PFCRN (Cárdenas National Reconstruction Front Party) 1 RP.

LOCAL ELECTIONS IN THE STATE OF TAMAULIPAS, MEXICO
(SPCL 6.13, 2 NOVEMBER 1998)

In a brief summary (Wkly 6.16), the makeup of the government of the Mexican State of Tamaulipas prior to the 25 October 1998 elections has been given. The governor was a PRI (Institutional Revolutionary Party) stalwart, the legislature had 20 PRI deputies, 4 PAN (National Action Party) deputies, 3 PRD (Democratic Revolution Party) deputies and one each from the PARM (Authentic Party of the Mexican Revolution) and PFCRN (Cárdenas National Reconstruction Front Party). As was listed in Wkly 5.24, a governor, 32 deputies and 43 mayors were to have been elected on 25 October.

These elections were duly held, and, amidst the cries of "fraud," "bribery," "theft" and the like which routinely followed, PRI gubernatorial candidate Tomás Yerrington Ruvalcaba was declared the winner with 60.1 percent of the vote. With 90.15 percent of the voting places tallied this had dropped to 53.54 percent, but it was still over twice the vote received by the second-place finisher. Yarrington (41) is an economist who has been a federal deputy, a treasury secretary under ex Governor Manuel Cavazos Lerma and president of the Matamoros municipality. Apparently he made something of a fetish of offering his hand in friendship to his political opponents, on this occasion doing as much for Enrique Cárdenas del Avellano, the winner in the Victoria mayoral race.

Such caring and sharing extended to his own party faithful who included Paloma Guillén, candidate for deputy from Tampico and sister of Rafael Sebastián Guillén, notorious as the ML (Marxist Leninist) terrorist chief of the EZLN (Zapatista National Liberation Army) who has frequently been discussed in these reports [3YRBK97]. Ms. Guillén appeared prominently at his acceptance speech.

In the governor's race Yarrington was trailed by PAN candidate Gustavo Cárdenas with 25.6 percent of the vote and PRD candidate Joaquín Hernández Correa with 12.7 percent. The field also included the following candidates with less than 1 percent of the vote: PARM candidate Ranulfo Pérez Ruiz, PC (Cardenista Party) candidate José Luis González Meza, PT (Labor Party) candidate Elizabeth Calderón Contreras and PVEM (Mexican Green Ecology Party) candidate Nelly López Vera.

MR deputies were elected by majority vote in the 19 voting districts, PRI capturing 17 of these 19 seats and thus assuring itself of local legislative control. PRD gained the remaining MR seats. The RP (proportional representation) seats were allocated with 3 going to PRI, 6 to PAN and 4 to PRD. Therefore the state legislature will contain 20 PRI deputies, 6 PAN deputies and 6 PRD deputies.

In the local mayoral or municipal president races there were 43 positions contested. PRI gained the advantage in 40, prominent among them being Matamoros, Altamira, Reynosa, Nuevo Laredo, Ciudad Victoria and Mante. PRD won 2 such races, these in Río Bravo and Madera. An independent candidate captured the forty-third race.

Although major changes are anticipated by no one, there are sufficient protests in the works so that there could be minor ones.

THE LOCAL RACES OF 8 NOVEMBER 1998 IN MEXICO
(SPCL 6.13, 2 NOVEMBER 1998)

As has been enumerated in Wkly 5.24, the last local Mexican elections are to be held in the States of Michoacan, Puebla, Sinaloa and Tlaxcala on 8 November 1998. Here the makeup of the various political positions which are to be refilled in these elections will be summarized.

State of Michoacán

Morelia, the capital of this department, is 125 sm (statute miles) slightly north of west of Mexico City.

The elections of 1995 were those in which MR considerations began to play an important role, PRI obtaining first place followed by PAN and then PRD. In the election of federal deputies in 1997, however, PRD overtook both PRI and PAN. Throughout this process the percentage of citizens voting fell steadily, from 77.17 percent in 1994 to 53.21 percent in 1997. All of which had no effect on the office holders who had gained their seats in 1974.

As the election approaches the governor is Lic. Víctor Tínoco Rubí of PRI. There will be no gubernatorial election this year in Michoacán.

The 18 electoral districts in the state will send 18 MR deputies to the local Congress, these supplemented by 12 RP deputies for a total of 30. In the present Congress PRI has 17 MR deputies and 1 RP deputy for a total of 18; PAN has 2 RP deputies for a total of 2; PRD has 1 MR deputy and 8 RP deputies for a total of 9; other parties have 1 RP deputy for a total of 1. In the upcoming elections there will again be 18 MR and 12 RP deputies chosen.

There are 113 municipal presidents (mayors) in the state, PRI holding 63, PRD 43, Pan 5 and other parties 2. In the upcoming elections there will be 163 mayoral contests.

State of Puebla

Puebla, the capital of the state, is 60 sm southeast of Mexico City.

In the 1992 gubernatorial election in Puebla Lic. Manuel Bartlett Díaz of PRI won. He will be replaced this year. As was the case in Michoacán, the percentage of voters decreased steadily from the 74.04 percent of 1994 to the 54.34 percent of 1997.

The present local Congress consists of 22 MR deputies from the 22 voting districts and 7 RP deputies for a total of 29. PRI holds all the MR seats and hence none of the RP for a total of 22; PAN has 4 RP seats; PRD has 1 RP seats; and other parties hold 2 RP seats. In the upcoming elections there will be 26 MR deputies and 13 RP deputies elected for a total of 39.

There are presently 217 municipal presidencies, 203 held by PRI, 4 by PAN, 4 by PRD and 6 by other parties. The number of municipal presidents selected in the upcoming elections will remain the same.

State of Sinaloa

Cullacán, the capital of the state, is 640 sm northwest of Mexico City.

PRI candidate Lic. Renato Vega Alvarado won the 1992 gubernatorial election in this state. He will be replaced in the upcoming elections.

The present state legislature contains 23 MR deputies apparently chosen by 23 of the 24 voting districts of the state and 16

RP deputies. PRI holds 23 MR seats and 1 RP seat for a total of 24. (Nota bene: Since (1) PRI allegedly could not hold all the MR seats plus 1 RP seat and (2) since 24 MR seats and 16 RP seats are to be chosen on 8 November, it is to be presumed that 1 RP deputy vanished from the Congress for some reason. However, LANS has no specific information on this.) PAN holds no MR and 13 RP seats; PRD holds no MR and 2 RP; no other parties hold any seats.

In the upcoming elections 24 MR deputies and 16 RP deputies will be chosen for a total of 40.

The state's 18 municipal presidencies are presently divided between PRI and PAN, the former holding 17 of them, the latter 1.

State of Tlaxcala

Tlaxcala, the capital of the state, is 55 sm slightly south of east of Mexico City.

In 1992 PRI candidate Lic. José Antonio Alvarez Lima won the gubernatorial context. He will be replaced in the upcoming elections. The federal elections of 1994 drew 80.87 percent of the electorate as opposed to 50.19 percent in the elections of the 1997.

The present local Congress consists of 9 MR deputies and 6 RP for a total of 15 Since PRI holds 9 MR seats and 2 RP for a total of 11, it is presumed, for reasons already given, that the number of MR seats was originally 11. While the missing 2 MR seats might have been won by one or two minority parties, it appears more likely that PAN and/or PRI holders of these seats have dropped out since the last election. In any event, PAN now holds 2 RP seats while PRD holds 2 RP seats. In the upcoming elections 19 MR deputies and 13 RP deputies will be chosen.

There are presently 39 PRI militants, 3 PAN and 2 PRD occupying the 44 Municipal presidents positions. There will be 60 such positions filled in the upcoming elections.

Notes

1. This is of course a phrase coined by those with a democratic bias.
2. The name was taken from the Fasces, a bundle of elm or birch rods bound around an axe with a penetrating head by a red strap, the emblem of official authority (strength). They were carried on the left shoulder with the left hand of the lictors who escorted the highest Roman magistrates. They were probably of Etruscan origin.

3. Antonio Gramsci is described by Carl Boggs (*The Impasse of European Communism*, Westview Press, 1982. ISBN: 091587845) as the originator of the "gradual building toward proletarian-socialist hegemony within the infrastructure of bourgeois society."
4. Harvard's Baird Professor of History, Richard Pipes ("Communism, Fascism and National Socialism," chapter 5 of *Russia under the Bolshevik Regime*, Knopf, 1993. ISBN: 0394502426), has detailed the equivalence of these totalitarian regimes while *Jerusalem Post* editor Louis Rapaport (*Stalin's War Against the Jews: The Doctor's Plot and the Soviet Solution*, Free Press, 1990. ISBN: 0029258219) has shown that the MLs aped the anti-Semitism of the Nazis.
5. The Social Democrat parties are those internationally linked in the Socialist International (SI), the direct descendant of Heinrich Karl Marx's First International
6. This is of course taken out of Marx's Manifesto [(Heinrich) Karl Marx, *Communist Manifesto*, Gateway, 1954, Samuel Moore Trans., Intro by Stefan T. Possony. LCC: 54-8138] in Chapter II ["Proletarians and Communists"] provisions are made for "2. A heavy progressive or graduated income tax."
7. This means category I, paragraph 2.
8. While there may well be some non-MLs who support this now "political party," its boss, Shafik Handal, is and long has been boss of the Salvadoran Communist Party (PCES) and continues a close collaborator of the HL, so the description is precise.
9. It will be recalled that Omar Torrijos' rule ended rather abruptly in July 1981 when his aircraft hit a mountain at Cino Marta, Colesito. Omar's brother, Hugo, says it was caused by a bomb planted by the Manuel Noriega who would succeed Torrijos. But Noriega was head of the National Intel Department, and, as such, he carried out the "investigation" and wrote the reports: "Accident."
10. So described in 1955 by Eudocio Ravines, the defector who authored *The Yenan Way* (Scribners, 1951).
11. Appendix of Pierre Broue (*Quand le Peuple Révoque le Président*, L'Harmattan, 1993. ISBN: 2738417477). The FMLN were Salvadoran terrorists, M-19 Colombian.
12. J. W. F. Dulles describes this in extensive detail on pp.163ff of *Anarchists and Communist in Brazil; 1900-1935* (University of Texas, 1973. ISBN: 0-292-70302-2).
13. From the hindi word *pandit*. The application of the word to any number of contemporary "journalists" is appropriate to that collection of beliefs—ahimsa, karma, dharma, samsura, moksha—which typifies hinduism.
14. The "officialist" party is the party holding the presidency, here the Colorado.
15. This is further discussed in Wkly 4.14 (1YRBK98).
16. It will of course be recalled that, from 1364, the eldest sons of the kings of France and hence heirs to the throne, were suzerains of Auvergne with the title Dauphin (dolphin) of Auvergne. Apparently "Dauphin" was originally a proper name. It will be recalled that Aristide's "Dauphin" won the 1996 Haitian presidential elections with an alleged 85 percent of the vote (p.26,YRBK97).
17. P. H. Lewis (*Socialism, Liberalism and Dictatorship in Paraguay*, Praeger and Hoover, 1982. ISBN: 0030615631). P. H. Lewis (*Paraguay Under Stroessner*, Univ. of North Carolina Press, 1980. ISBN:0807814377).
18. The title, *licenciado*, basically means the titled individual holds a bachelor's degree, as *maestro* means he holds a master's degree. Usually, but sometimes it is taken to mean a law degree.
19. PEN is further complicated by being an alliance formed for the 1993 elections.
20. This is the Febrerista Revolutionary Party, a social democrat party affiliated with the

Socialist International (SI).
21. LANS has inferred this number from the population figures. However, both ANR and ALIANZA are running 5-candidate slates so the number may be incorrect.
22. One of the ALIANZA candidates (Edgar Ramírez) may not have been PLRA, but the other four were.
23. This now apparently ex terrorist group broke off from the terrorist National Liberation Army (ELN) in 1993 and made peace with the government (pp.114ff, 3YRBK97).
24. The Patriotic Union (UP) was formed by the terrorist Colombian Revolutionary Armed Forces (FARC) and attained legal status in 1986.
25. This is an allegedly Maoist group.
26 Doctor Posada is director of the Center for Socio-Politcal Analysis in Santafé de Bogotá.
27. In 1957 General Gustavo Rojas Pinilla resigned, Bogotá street mobs convincing him to do as much. In Spain Liberal leader Lleras Camargo and Conservative ex-President Laureano Gómez met and agreed upon a plan which was termed "The National Front" and under which Liberal and Conservative presidents alternated in office. The plan was approved by a plebiscite and was in effect from 1958 to 1974.
28. Government-run "social security" systems are little more than immense Ponzi Schemes where we define such a scheme as the payment of "dividends" to old stockholders with the "capital" invested by new stockholders. The SS systems are even more devious, however, the politicians appropriating the funds paid in by the working population and using them to buy votes from the same population. Recent calculations have shown that, had the SS "trust" been privatized in the US, it would now furnish income from one million dollars to the average retiree instead of providing a pittance to the old "investors" with ever increasing amounts collected from the new "investors." Editor.
29. This appears to have been generally reported simply as PACHAKUTIK which appears to have been just as generally incorrect. The winner should then be León Roldos of the clan which produced the Roldosistas.
30. Carabobo is along the coast to the west of Caracas and the Federal District.
31. Simon Strong (*SHINING PATH: Terror and Revolution in Peru*, Times Books, 1992. ISBN: 0-8129-2180-1) has rather aptly described this leftist caudillo as having "swung the country's political axis toward Moscow."
32. As Pedro J. Chamorro, son of the murdered *La Prensa* (Managua) publisher, described it on 6 February 1989.
33. This was of course written before he passed Ms. Sáez (Editor, LANS).
34. Barinas is the capital of Barina State, on the eastern slope of the Merida Range of the Andes (Editor, LANS).
35. Independent Elections Commission—Christian Socialist (Editor, LANS).
36. As Professor Stokes (p.284, *LATIN AMERICAN POLITICS*, Crowell, 1959) points out, AD is the Venezuelan *Aprismo* party. According to the guru of *Aprismo*, Harry Kantor (*The Ideology and Program of the Peruvian Aprista Movement*, University of California Press, 1953), "...Aprismo or Marxism-Aprismo is a combination of Marxian socialism and the reality of America." Other examples of this have been encountered in these reports.
37. EFE reported (22 Nov 98) that Chávez's coalition included 13 parties. Only the seven which appeared on the ballot will be mentioned here, the other "lucky gambler" parties not worth the space.
38. The projected American Union of Soviet Socialist Republics was first mention by these reports on p.99 of *Latin American Political Yearbook 1997* (Transaction 1998,

ISBN: 1-56000-350-2).
39. It will be recalled that one state congressman is selected by "direct election" (MR) in each electoral district, the number of those selected by "proportional representation" (RP) then selected by voting results over collections of districts subject to the number won by a given party through MR. For example, PRI (Tricolor) had 25 MR deputies in the State of Oaxaca (all those so elected), and hence was assigned no RP deputies.
40. The 8 municipalities were Mapastepec, Pijijiapan, Huixtla, Acasiyagua, Escuintla, Villa Como Titlán, Motozintla and Siltepex.
41. These ML (Marxist Leninist) terrorists have been discussed on pp.100ff and pp.124ff of YRBK97 (*Latin American Political Yearbook 1997*, Transaction Publishers, 1998, ISBN: 1-56000-350-2) and YRBK98 (Transaction, 1999. ISBN: 1-56000-386-3).
42. The Mexican Attorney General reported last January that 14 PAC (Civil Defense Patrol) groups were present in 30 percent of the territory of Chiapas State. This report is probably reasonably reliable. However, the report by the ONG (Non Governmental Organization) AC (Civic Alliance), one more HR organization, is probably not as reliable but included here for possible value only. AC stated that six of these PACs were located in the municipalities of Tila, Palenque, Salto de Agua, Sabanilla, Tumbalá, Venustiano Carranza, San Andrés, Chenalhó, Chilón, Ocosingo, Italá, Oxchuc, Altamirano, Las Margaritas and Huixtán. AC also claimed six of these to be most important, these being Paz y Justicia, Alianza Bartolomé de los Llanos, Máscara Roja, Chinchulines, Movimiento Indigena Revolucionario Antizapatista and Tomás Munzer
43. This group, its emblem a gold PT surmounted by a star on a red field, split off in 1994 from the CNTE (Education Workers). It is generally an "also ran" party, although it of course has a certain number of RP deputies.
44. A few of AI's contributions to the flood of disinformation generated by the HLS (Hemispheric Left Support) are discussed, *inter alia*, in Wkly 3.4 of YRBK98. In other reports the testimony of the cleric who came in from the Liberation Theology cold, Luis Pellecer, has been discussed. Pellecer defected from his ML brethren when he was required to abandon propaganda and enter the real world of ML terrorist murder and mayhem. For his testimony cf. *Marxism and Christianity in Revolutionary Central America* (Senate Subcommittee on Security and Terrorism, 1983, Y4.J89/2:S.Hrg 98-755).
45. PARM arose in 1954, put together by Gen. Jacinto B. Treviño and an old group of "military revolutionaries." It has generally supported PRI save remarkably in 1988 when it supported Cárdenas Solorzano.

2

Politico-Economic Backgrounds in Latin America

"We're like Robin Hood. We take from the Rich and give to the Poor," said Pierrot. "What Poor?" asked Pierrette. "Us Poor," replied Pierrot. This can be taken as a definition of "corruption." "From each according to his ability, to each according to his need," said Heinrich Karl Marx in what can be taken as a definition of "collectivism." And the "needs" of the PP (professional politician) — Castro and his villas, Humberto Ortega and his horse-breeding estate, etc.—are much greater than those of us in the common herd. Specific study of Latin American economies appears to demonstrate that corruption and collectivism, not necessarily in order of importance, have been responsible for most, if not all, of the economic woes of the region. This is the same as saying that the political and economic woes of a given nation cannot usually be separated. Which is worthy of repetition in introduction of these politico-economic updates. As is the following general commentary by Doctor Carlos Sabino.

Liberals and Neoliberals[1]

CARLOS SABINO[2]
VENEZUELAN CENTRAL UNIVERSITY
CARACAS, VENEZUELA
(SPCL 5.14(1), 19 JUNE 1998)

EDITOR'S INTRODUCTION

Fidel Castro's Hemispheric Left (HL) first took up the cudgels against those free-market ideas which were utilized by General

Pinochet to create the hemisphere's first "economic miracle." And he was among the first to use the term "neoliberalism" as a pejorative, a practice in which a substantial portion of the press effectively emulated him. Much, if not all of this anti-neoliberal rhetoric has been fed to the public without any accompanying explanations, only inferences that, for example, this is some sort of vast conspiracy to mistreat "the poor." This clever use of a carefully crafted cant word—neoliberalism—has allowed the HL to make tremendous strides toward its objective which is the derailment of those further Latin American (LA) "economic miracles" toward which the region appeared to be heading but a few short years ago. And this derailment is at least partially due to the surprisingly widespread ignorance of what is described by "neoliberalism." Prof. Sabino describes the term quite comprehensively in the following article.

* * *

About a decade ago various LA countries began to carry out reforms in their economies. As these reforms were being introduced the clamor against neoliberalism began to be heard. The word quickly became popular and surfaced in the debate, not as a precise ideological definition but more as a denunciation. It became a sort of insult with which to disqualify those who, for example, want to pay the foreign debt, privatize government enterprises, lower inflation or reduce government employment. Neoliberals were those who turned their backs on the poor and sacrificed everything to the market, "cold and impersonal."

This caricature, which is still taken seriously by so many, has been nothing but a means for maintaining the state gigantism responsible for the backwardness of our societies. It represents the reaction of a Left which has in fact demonstrated itself to be conservative and opposed to change, and which soon began to defend the regimes which, until then, it had opposed. In this way "neoliberal" came to mean anyone who was opposed to the privileges now established or to state interventionism, and the word continued circulating without substantial analysis or specific content. From this point of view it could be said that, in actuality, neoliberals do not exist; these are merely words which have been conjured up in order to disqualify political enemies in laying out boundaries in a debate which, disgracefully, lacks almost all depth.

But, as frequently occurs, these deliberate attempts to confuse neither arose in a vacuum nor are completely artificial. Neoliberalism could mean, if we restrict ourselves to the term itself, a new version or form of liberalism,[3] a renovation of the classical ideas of liberty which have been fought for from time immemorial. The problem is that no one knows exactly what changes would be implied in the rich liberal tradition by neoliberalism.

Liberalism is a school of thought which considers that the human being possesses inalienable rights to life, liberty and property. "Inalienable" means, in this context, that such rights are antecedent and of superior form to all collective entities which seek to violate them, be these the nation, the ethnic group, the country or the State. And it is of no importance whether this state be democratic or otherwise: the liberals do not believe that conduct can be imposed, even by an ample majority, which restricts the liberty of the individual, always and when the exercise of such individual rights does not violate the liberty of the rest.

But liberalism, as a real historical movement, is something more than the affirmation of this fundamental principle: it is the conviction that human societies can be effectively constituted on the principle of liberty, that a social organization is possible and desirable which respects these rights and converts them into the cornerstone of civilized society. For these reasons the liberals have traditionally opposed as much the conservatives—who defended hereditary privileges and a closed society—as the collectivists who, be they socialists, fascists or communists, always postulate the superiority of the social aggregate to the individual.

Therefore, I prefer that they call me a liberal and not a neoliberal. In the first place, because to no one is it very clear what is meant by the prefix "neo"; the prefix could signify as much the inevitable and enriching updating which occurs with time, as technocratic and hardly liberal variations of the classical ideas. And in the second place, but no less important, because I prefer to choose for myself the ideological school to which I belong and not leave to my adversaries the privilege of assigning to me the label which pleases them most.

[Translated from the Spanish by the LANS Editor]

Argentina

THE CONFUSED ARGENTINE POLITICAL PANORAMA

LANS SPECIAL CORRESPONDENT
LA PLATA, ARGENTINA
(WKLY 6.2, 23 JULY 1998)

The so-called "re-election" of Argentine President Carlos Menem is opening up his country's political scene, provoking fear amongst his political adversaries and the ill wishes of the principal swashbucklers in his Justicialista (Peronista) Party. In particular do the latter include those closest to the governor of Buenos Aires Province, Eduardo Duhalde.

The polls reveal that Menem's popularity today is in free fall, and it is more than probable that insistence on his reelection will bring shipwreck to his party in the elections of next year. The fact is that the rejection of his reelection is being converted into a powerful cohesive force for the opposition Alliance. Moreover, the ambitions of the president oblige him and his circle of collaborators to carry out a series of maneuvers which, while of doubtful efficacy, are capable of endangering the institutional stability of the state and generating a military crisis and a social protest of substantial proportions.

Even if the principal Argentine political players, either within his party or within the opposition, discard the possibility of Menem achieving his objective, the subject will remain the principal matter for political debate in the country. Menem has occupied the presidency of the Argentine Republic since 1989 (pp.9ff, YRBK97). He was reelected in 1995 after a political pact was signed with the ex president of Argentina (1983-1989), Raul Alfonsín. The latter, of course, was at that time the principal figure in the primary party of the opposition, the Radical Civic Union (UCR) or Radicals, a party philosophically close to the European Social Democrats.

Juan Domingo Perón (pp.46ff, YRBK97), the historical leader of the Justicialismo Party, was president of Argentina from 1945 to 1955. He won the elections of 1945, promoted a constitutional reform in order to be reelected, and only a *coup d'état* separated him from power in September 1955. He was president again, from October 1973 to his death in July 1974. In 1973, after 18 years of exile, he promoted a Perón-Perón presidential formula with his wife Isabel to assure that the succession would remain "in the family."

Like Perón, Menem displays a "genetic" attachment to the presidential throne. In that sense the latter has revealed himself as an authentic successor to the general, and the search for justification of a third term of government—of very doubtful constitutionality—is seared deep into that legacy. But, more than this, from that almost "historical" resolve of which Menem is the object, his voracity for remaining in the first magistracy is neutralized by other factors, more elemental but certainly more powerful. He must be aware of the number of irregularities which mark the almost ten years of his government. Once his powerful influence has ended, the accusations against him will accumulate. His term of office has been plagued by irregularities, concrete cases of "cronyism," connections with sectors of frankly mafiosa activities and other episodes which placed Argentina in a caricature category.

Reelection Efforts

In May of next year Argentina will have national elections. Menem aspires to present himself as the candidate of the Justicialista Party, and for that purpose he has trotted out a battery of legal, political and even diplomatic contrivances. If the strategy does not bear fruit, he intends to substitute as his *dauphin* Ramon "Palito" (Little Stick) Ortega, former rock singer and ex governor of Tucumán Province.

These plans have profoundly disturbed his fellow Peronist, Eduard Duhalde, the governor of Buenos Aires Province which is the richest and most powerful in the country. For Menem's political maneuvers seriously threaten Duhalde's plan to convert himself into the next president of the country. Although the governor's reaction is important, it is also important to take into account that never has a Buenos Aires Province governor arrived in the Argentine presidential palace.

At the end of more than a century and a half of independence this political datum is generally interpreted as follows. The governor of Buenos Aires has always held a key post. However, while locating he who holds it at the pinnacle of power, it also converts him into the preferred target of Tyrians and Trojans who dedicate themselves to swallowing up his career.

Nevertheless, what appeared a remote possibility a few months ago is today a concrete fact: The president has set in motion all the elements at his command in order to maintain himself in his job. He has entrusted some of his unconditional supporters to elaborate a demand before the courts. The idea is to present the image of a citizen "proscribed" who, through the political intrigues of his internal and external rivals, remains on the margin of the citizens' decision.

The native province of Menem and the family of his ex wife, Zulema, is La Rioja. On another level, Senator Jorge Yoma of that province is heading an offensive to set in motion a constitutional mechanism. Yoma takes the position that Art. 40 of the Constitution enables a plebiscite. If this is promoted and receives the necessary support, Menem would have a "green light" to try and recapture his office for a new term. This alternative is viewed with enthusiasm by some top Peronists who do not consider themselves "unconditionals" of the president. They consider that, if the plebiscite fails to approve a new term of office as appears to be indicated by the polls, they would remain in a very weak position to confront the Alliance in the national elections.

In the last week of June Pres. Menem was on a visit to Russia and was especially concerned that his meetings with the mayor of Moscow would have ample repercussions in Argentina. Suggestively, the muscovite hierarchy has been the principal supporter of Boris Yeltsin.

Negative Image

Menem is an optimist by nature. The polls against him, he does not appear to take into account the present state of public opinion in Argentina where his image is frankly negative, and his reelection plans suffer levels of rejection which will be very difficult ti reverse. According to Argentina's principal pollsters, the government today would lose whatever proposal it submitted to the citizenry for decision. According to Mora and Araujo, the nation's principal polling firm, 60 percent to 70 percent of the citizens would say "no" to reelection because of the predominant view that "the government is worn out." The data gathered by the Graciela Römer poll agrees with this assessment: 76 percent of the Argentine citizens are opposed to reforming the Constitution to facilitate Menem's return to the Presidential Palace, and 66 percent directly reject Menem as a candidate.

These indicators have not escaped the scrutiny of the president. Some days ago it was known that the mandatory had commented to his closest followers that at present "the Alliance has twice the strength of Peronism among those intending to vote." If the elections took place today the Alliance, made up of the UCR and the National Solidarity Front [FREPASO], would win by a 35 percent margin, this still without any candidate selected for president.

Both forces in the Alliance are resolved to go to internal elections in November, and the winning sector will nominate the candidate. If the Radicals win these primaries, the candidate will be Fernando de la Rúa, and if FREPASO wins, it will be Graciela Fernández Meijide. The first is a lawyer with a long career in radicalism who is considered a "moderate." He is presently in charge of the autonomous government of the City of Buenos Aires (six million inhabitants); he is a man who, during the government of Alfonsín, maintained an adverse position with regard to rapprochement with certain sectors of the left.

Fernández Meijide has developed an image which has been very well received by the Argentine citizenry. She is intelligent and has a captivating oratory which she frequently uses to contrast the most neglected sectors of society and the lack of jobs at the departments which denounced the officialism (now Peronist) environment. In spite of being the mother of a "disappeared," she does not make use of that situation politically. With this moderation she favorably contrasts herself with the rabid declarations of Hebe de Bonafini, president of the Mothers of the Plaza of May who demands the most severe punishments, to include life imprisonment, for the military hierarchy of the 1976-1983 period (pp.159ff, YRBK97).

Contemporary Forces

Whether it be with Menem, Duhalde or some third contender, it is clear that Peronism will use the electoral campaign in much the same way. There will be at least two objectives in the campaign, these to demonstrate that, first, the Alliance is nothing more than a transitory force having no internal cohesion and, second, that the parties which make up the Alliance cannot govern effectively. These ideas are not strange to the Alliance members themselves. They have emphasized it to ex Pres. Alfonsín and Senator Carlos Alvarez in their search for accords with some Peronist sectors. Their objectives are the concretizing of their proposal for "national agreement."

There may be accord between Radicals and FREPASOs with relation to the internal elections and the form in which the presidential ticket will be defined. Nevertheless, there will be profound differences in regard to the distribution of the other jobs which are assuredly important in the Argentine political picture. So far FREPASO has acted energetically in the matter of candidacies, the party striving mightily to assure that the candidates for the governments of Buenos Aires Province and the City of Buenos Aires emerge from its ranks.

The UCR has observed this "maneuver" with a certain concern and aspires to establish an equilibrium in this affair. At the same time it hopes that, in the internal elections, the maximum number of citizens are mobilized in the interior of the country and a minimum number in Buenos Aires as a way of assuring the triumph of De la Rúa.

As with most center-left movements in Latin America, FREPASO is characterized by strong urban support, and it is here that the candidacy of Fernández Meijide obtains its most important support.

The Imprisonment of Videla

This was the agitated Argentine political scene in mid June 1998. In the midst of it there arose an episode which was not in the scenario of anyone and which produced the most varied interpretations: Judge Roberto Merquevich called "de facto" ex Pres. Jorge Videla to testify. The judge then ordered preventive imprisonment for having been found responsible for the "theft of minors," children of the left guerrillas born in captivity during the 1970s. The Attorney General who acted in the case, Rita Molina, opposed the Marquevich decision on the basis that the principle of *coza juzgada* (thing judged) operates here. She said also that, according to the laws dictated by the governments of Alfonsín and Menem, in any event it would be necessary that Military Justice judge the case.

The same opinion was expressed by Luís Moreno Ocampo who was the Attorney General in the trials conducted against the Military Juntas after the assumption of the presidency by Alfonsín (1983). Moreno Ocampo judged that the Videla Case "is a thing judged from the 'rights' point of view and, from the 'legal' point of view, was invalidated." Moreno also maintained that "the case cannot be reopened, the proofs which arise now do not serve."

The suggestion is that Marquevich initiated the proceeding when Menem was on the point of beginning a visit to France where the question of "human rights" in Argentina is the object of concern to some activist sectors. The death of some French nuns, it was thought, could be brandished during the visit to Paris and affect the participation of some investor groups. It is a fact known to observers that Marquevich is, as with other federal judges, threatened with a trial in the Chamber of Deputies which has a Peronist majority. Various irregularities have been imputed to the magistrate, in particular, his affinity with Alfredo Yabrán, a powerful impresario coming from the mafia, who committed suicide some weeks ago.

Military sources maintain that the imprisonment of Videla was decided a little before the Menem trip to France as a way to assure him a stay there without surprises. They further allege that the decision was induced by various members of the government, in particular, the Minister of the Interior, Carlos Corach, and the Minister of Security, Miguel Angel Toma. In this regard they emphasize the declaration of Corach to television: "This (Videla's imprisonment) demonstrated that, in Argentina, Justice acts, and there is protection for no one who does not obey the law."

Those same sources indicate that Menem was opposed to such an extreme method which endangered the decisions made by his own government such as the pardon of the military chiefs. Therefore the presidential discomfort produced his rapid return to Buenos Aires. According to reports, in a Council of Ministers meeting, Menem berated his collaborators for the "excess" committed, the effects of which are difficult to control.

In effect, Videla was processed so quickly that various active generals and colonels assembled in the seat of the General Staff to analyze the concern which the imprisonment of Videla had provoked in the barracks. They asked the high command for "detailed information" on the facts.

Collaborators of the president commented that, after the imprisonment of Videla and under pressure from some activist groups, some 400 naval officers could be involved in a similar situation. This would mean a "general judgment," and the same sort of thing could happen with police and gendarmery functionaries.

For the moment, Judge Marquevich is showing himself inflexible before the allegations of these same attorneys general. He has confirmed preventive imprisonment for Videla who remains a prisoner in Caseros Prison. He denied a request that the veteran general (73) be placed in house arrest because of illness. Nevertheless, Videla's attorneys declared that they will appeal the sentence; the San Martín Federal Chamber will deal with the appeal. According to the leaks which LANS has received, house arrest will "surely" be approved before the trial is continued or the solicitation for immediate recovery of liberty is honored.

In principle, the judges of the second request would declare themselves for closing the file on the case, and thus the step previous to house arrest would come into operation as a prudent decision prior to the ultimate decision.

There is also concern over the mobilization of some extremist groups such as the Socialist Workers Party (PST) which unleashed acts of pressure and street violence rendering Videla's police protection insufficient during his transfer to court. These activist sectors, of Trotskyite and anarchist tendency, keep up a radical protest of the 1976-1983 period. They are connected to the most radical sectors of the Mothers of the Plaza of May and among their slogans they demand, "neither justice, nor pardon; put them against the wall and shoot them (*parédon*)."

[Translated from the Spanish by the Editor, LANS]

ARGENTINE REPERCUSSIONS FROM THE PERU-ECUADOR BORDER SKIRMISH
(WKLY 6.12, 24 SEPTEMBER 1998)

The mills of Argentinian Justice, which began to function in March 1996 on arms smuggling, appear to grind exceeding slow, but they may prove to grind exceeding fine. Yesterday (22 September 1998) Customs Agent María Teresa Cueto was jailed for arms smuggling, the first such in this long drawn out investigation. Other arrests "will follow."

On the night of 26-27 January 1995 Peru reported an attack on a frontier position by an Ecuadoran helicopter. The resulting border skirmish has been described in Wkly 1.10 (pp.66ff, YRBK97) as have the location of the disputed territory and the historical background of the dispute. Most importantly here, the Argentine shipments of arms to Ecuador have been preliminarily described in that report. The "bare bones" details of these shipments will first be repeated here.

In responding to a discrimination complaint by Fine Airlines, Inc., a US firm, against the Government of Peru, the latter nation provided the US Department of Transportation (DOT) with an account of arms smuggling based on documents provided by the Argentine Government. These documents described the shipment by FM (*Fabricaciones Militar*) of 6324 packages of "secret military material," these weighing 167,100.5 pounds and made up of 8,000 FAL[4] rifles; 18 155mm (millimeter) field pieces; 10,000 9.0mm pistols;[5] 350 mortars; 50 heavy MGs;[6] 58,000,000 rounds of ammunition; 45,000 artillery rounds; 9,000 grenades; and 20 tons of explosive. Fine was listed as the carrier, FM as the consignor, and Restor Metals as the consignee. Fine admitted to operating several flights between Argentina and Ecuador in February 1995 but claimed that the aircraft were chartered by a Texas firm, AES (Airline Equipment Specialists), which has since "disappeared."

These were the bare bones of a smuggling operation in which AAN (Andean News Agency 10 April 1995) described a 100-ton missile cargo on a Bulgarian aircraft stopped at Cabo Verde, a similar shipment stopped in the Azores three weeks earlier. In that summer of 1996 LANS had insufficient credible evidence to suggest that there was wider involvement than Argentina and Ecuador. As the arms smuggling episode developed a life of its own in Argentina, however, considerable evidence has since developed. It would now appear that an arms smuggling operation, which the press has begun to call "triangular," was involved in the smuggling of Argentine arms, not only to Ecuador but also to Croatia.

Innocents in High Places?

On 24 January 1995 Argentine President Carlos Menem, his Minister of Defense (Oscar Camelión), his Minister of Economy (Domingo Cavallo) and his Foreign Minister (Guido Di Tella) signed Decree 103/95 which authorized the shipment of arms to Venezuela. Whether or not these four men were aware that these arms were going to Ecuador, not Venezuela, Peruvian intelligence assuredly was. Which has, in diplomatic terms, been described as "embarrassing" because Argentina, together with Brazil, Chile and the US, is one of the four countries "guaranteeing" the peace which stopped the more serious hostilities through the 1942 agreement (Wkly 1.10).

In early 1995 Arturo Ossorio Arana was Argentinian ambassador to Peru. On 6 September 1998 he told Radio América that he had sent a coded message on 13 February 1965 to his chancellery in which he passed on the warning given to him by Peruvian intelligence. Peruvian intel had warned Ossorio of the contraband airlift to Ecuador "so that those persons in control of the aircraft (can) verify this report and take appropriate measures." Arms were shipped to Ecuador under Decree 103/95 on 17, 18 and 22 February 1995 from Ezeiza International Airport. For whatever it was worth, Peru had apparently not placed the blame on the decree signers of the Menem Government for the shipments of arms to Ecuador. Nor did Ossorio. While classifying the shipments as "a crime" and refusing to make any direct accusations, the ambassador suggested that the guilty be sought among "the management of FM and among those who control air traffic" (AP 7 September 1998).

Which would, of course, almost have to be the case to some extent, but the innocence of Foreign Minister Di Tella appears to be subject to some doubt. On 7 September 1998, Di Tella submitted documents to the court of Federal Judge Jorge Urso who has been investigating this case since the spring of 1996, the Mills of Justice apparently grinding rather slowly. These documents are reported to prove that Di Tella had been alerted by the Osorio cable to the arms smuggling to Ecuador. At this point, the account becomes perhaps deliberately confused.

In March 1995 the Argentinean Attorney General requested the chancellery to produce all the documents relating to the smuggling case. Either (1) the Ossorio cable was not produced or (2) if it was produced, the ministry has no record of it having been produced. But Di Tella proclaims his innocence, pointing out that he had personally participated in the then recent peace negotiations between Peru and Ecuador. Another interesting inconsistency in the "innocence at the highest levels" has recently arisen.

Panama has no armed forces, only a police force. Which of course means, incidentally, that the isthmian nation can offer no resistance against any aggressor, determined or dilatory, should it ever actually attain complete control of that Panama Canal that the US and Major Goethals built. At any rate, it has recently been reported (*La Nacion*

12 September 1998) that Judge Urso ordered a raid on Artillery Transport Group 4 in Córdoba. It was allegedly there that the OTO Melara "105mm" *obuses*[7] (anti-tank weapons) were to have been found which ended up in Croatia, although a decree had been signed dispatching them to Panama.

Can it really be true that neither the Argentine president, nor the Argentine defense minister nor any other signer of the relevant decree was aware that the Panamanian police had no real requirement for such an anti-tank weapon?

While none of those individuals who signed the decrees has been proven "guilty" in the matter of illegal arms shipments to Croatia and Ecuador between 1991 and 1995, all heads save those of Menem and Di Tella have already rolled, and there are of course cries for these.

A Complex Smuggling Operation

Much of the "triangular" smuggling of arms from Argentina to Ecuador and Croatia was destined for, and arrived in, Croatia. However, the Ecuadoran is within the LANS purview and will be first considered here.

Whoever may eventually be convicted of complicity in this Ecuadoran smuggling operation, he/she will hardly be able to plead ignorance of any wrongdoing if only because of the extensive complexity of the operation. As has already been described, a US firm which has since disappeared, AES, had chartered another US firm, Fine Airlines, to transport the munitions from Argentina to Ecuador. The consignor was FM. But it would soon come to light that matters were not even as simple as this.

For there was another dummy organization in Ecuador which was involved and still other front enterprises, in Uruguay and elsewhere, which were important to it. On the Ecuadoran end the arrangements for and reception of the arms were handled by an organization called PRODEFENSA. As has been stated, the Argentine end was handled by FM. During the crucial 1991 - 1995 period PRODEFENSA was run by Roberto Sassan van Elsloo, FM by Luis Sarlenga. Sarlenga was the first of those to testify before Judge Urso, and he was to be followed by a parade of others who will not all be listed here.

There were two intermediary enterprises—front groups—between FM and PRODEFENSA. When this arms smuggling began with the Croatian operation in 1991, the first of these was called Debrol

S.A.[8]—International Trade and was located at 33 Orientales, 1334 Montevideo, Uruguay. In 1995 this intermediary was called Hayton Trade although its address had not changed. When the destination of the 1995 arms shipment was changed from Croatia to Ecuador, Hayton was joined by the Caribbean Group of Companies, Inc.

Arms to Croatia

Although not of primary interest here, the arms-smuggling operation to Croatia is a necessary preliminary to the Ecuador operation.

In 1991 two decrees[9] were executed for the sale of Argentine arms to the Panamanian police, 1697/91 signed on 27 August 1991 and 2283/91 signed on 31 October 1991. The Croatian operation would have continuity during the coming four years under various ministers. During this 1991-1995 period Luis Salinga was the FM administrator. As the period began Colonel Diego Palleros (Ret), now a fugitive from Argentine Justice in Singapore, was the proprietor of the intermediary enterprise, Debrol S.A.

In seven maritime shipments during this time period Argentina had provided contraband arms to Croatia. These shipments were, of course, allegedly destined for an army-less Panama as per the decrees. They were all apparently consigned by FM. However, as a result of a raid on the Directorate of Army Arsenals in the Buenos Aires District of Palermo by the indefatigable Judge Urso on 28 August 1998, evidence was uncovered which indicated that six 155mm howitzers, Nos. 0001, 0003, 0004, 0005, 0007 and 0016, had seemingly vanished, there being no legitimate record of their disposition.

The field piece under discussion here is the 155mm Howitzer L33X1415, CITEFA (CITAR) Models 77 and 81. These weapons consist of the French 155mm gun Mk F3 top carriage with a bottom carriage designed by CITEFA (Scientific and Technical Research Institute of the (Argentine) Armed Forces). This weapon has a barrel length of 5.115m, a split-trail carriage, a weight of 8,000kg and a normal range of 22,000m. Jane's Information Group, Ltd.[10] (*Jane's Armor and Artillery*) states that, *inter alia*, "A small number of these 155mm weapons has been observed in service in Croatia. (Par) Total production...believe...around 120 systems...(apparently) Argentina has a total of 109 of these systems in service" (p.673, *ibid*).

The howitzers in question belonged to GA 141 (Artillery Group 141) which, following orders received, turned the field pieces over to FM in 1994. GA 141 had been stationed in Córdoba. After turning over this artillery to FM, it was transferred to Salta and rechristened GA 15. Other examples appear to have been dug out—the OTO Melara's of Note 5 for example—but the *modus operandi* was apparently the same and need hardly be repeated here.

It was evidently toward the end of this four-year period that a buyer suddenly appeared, prepared to pay top dollar for munitions, the buyer Ecuador. The decree, 103/95, was signed on 24 January 1995, and, according to the PRODEFENSA head, Sassan, negotiation with the intermediary enterprises, Hayton-Caribbean, began on 30 January 1995, six days after decree signing. In his need for arms, Sassan had contacted the Frenchman, Jean Bernard Lasnaud, who headed Caribbean. Bernard proposed the "Argentine solution," and the operation proceeded from there.

Thus, FM, between 1991 and 1995, had provided arms to Croatia by sea, allegedly of course destined for Panama. And then in an unplanned finale, FM consigned three flights of arms to Ecuador. But whence came all this materiel? Although all the information does not yet appear to have been assembled, it seems to have been demonstrated that some or all of it came from Argentine Army supplies as has been illustrated above.

Can the "Argentine Economic Miracle" Survive?

This question was the title of Wkly 2.4 (pp.45ff, YRBK97). Since it was written, the Hemispheric Left has made impressive gains in its all-out war on "neoliberalism" which will assuredly affect any answer. Other factors affecting such an answer are (1) the strength of Carlos Menem's dedication to neoliberalism and (2) his, apparently ultimate, withdrawal from the presidential race.

THE LONG ROAD BETWEEN ARGENTINA AND VENEZUELA

LANS MERCOSUR CORRESPONDENT
LA PLATA, ARGENTINA
(WKLY 6.13, 1 OCTOBER 1998)

EDITOR'S INTRODUCTION

The Peru-Ecuador border dispute and its aftermath have been discussed in Wkly 1.10, (pp.66ff, YRBK 97) and Wkly 6.12. With the latter report the three-year investigation of Argentine contraband arms shipments had begun to loom threateningly over the Argentine Government and its president, Carlos Menem. Although this investigation has not yet been concluded, it now appears to have progressed to a stage sufficiently indicative to warrant further review and treatment. This the LANS correspondent in MERCOSUR has furnished in this report.

* * *

Argentine President Carlos Menem was far from imagining that Decree 103, which he signed in January 1995, would bring so many complications to his government and would leave behind so much evidence of a vast net of triangulation in the arms traffic to Ecuador and Croatia. The international conduct of his nation would be open to serious questioning, and the trial and dismissal of his Minister of Defense, Oscar Camilión would be in store. Until now, the judicial investigations, the testimony of certain witnesses and the quite specific denunciations in the press also lay the blame on the chief of the Argentine Army, Martín Balza, on the international trafficker Monzer Al Kassar and on Menem's brother-in-law, Emir Yoma. All of this is happening within the framework of a thickening plot which involves Argentina, Uruguay, Venezuela, Ecuador, Croatia and the United States.

As is often the case, the press was in charge of exploding the denunciations, in this case through the influential daily, *Clarín*, which put into evidence what can be qualified as the greatest case of corruption in which the Menem Government has been involved.

The decree in the case authorized the sale of Argentine arms to Venezuela, but these were transported in flights which made their way to Guayaquil (Ecuador), where they were unloaded in flagrant violation of international accords. The participation of Uruguayan corporations, in the guise of phantom enterprises, was so structured as to provide tax avoidance and banking secrecy. This permitted the operations to be carried on and was the determining factor for the Argentine judges, Marcelo Aguinsky and Jorge Urso , who, first investigated the case as criminal and, second, in order to determine the illegal acts committed by public functionaries. Moreover, two Uruguayan judges have intervened in the case.

Parallel to these activities and suggestively, almost a dozen deaths of functionaries, witnesses and other implicated persons under strange circumstances add a level of tragedy and intimidation to the situation.

The figure of Argentine Lt. Col. Diego Palleros appears to be central to this entire affair. This individual is presently to be found in South Africa, whence Argentine justice has solicited his extradition, but it was denied after a fine of US$500,000 was paid.

Declaration in Uruguay

The last official appearance of Palleros was reported some months ago in Montevideo (Uruguay). Criminal Judge Rubén Eguiluz called him before his tribunal in April 1995. The witness did not hesitate to assure the court that the authorized 10 percent commission in the negotiations amounted to seventy million dollars, although the figure was large. He rejected the idea that he had done any smuggling because, he said, it was an absolutely legal operation. "The arms were sold to Venezuela," he maintained, and, if they were diverted to Guayaquil, "it is the responsibility of the aerial enterprise."

Some days before being interrogated by the Uruguayan court, Judge José Ferreira had ordered the lifting of bank account secrecy from the Palleros enterprises. When Judge Eguiliuz was prepared to inquire into this subject, Palleros alleged exhaustion and solicited the suspension of the questioning. The judge acceded to the request and moved the inquiry to the following day. The officer disappeared, and he was not encountered again until he appeared in South Africa.

Over and above the specific responsibilities of the Argentine functionaries, the sale of arms to Ecuador and Croatia seriously eroded the credibility of the government of that country in the international arena. Decree 103 was directly signed by Menem and his then Defense Minister Oscar Camilión. In secondary degree, Finance Minister Domingo Cavallo and Foreign Minister Guido Di Tella also assumed responsibility. At that time Buenos Aires had assumed the role of mediator in the conflict which Ecuador was carrying on with Peru for the El Condor Range. It was therefore then a violation, plain and simple, of an elemental neutrality agreement.

The frontier problem between Ecuador and Peru exploded in February 1995 but had been dragging on for decades. In 1942 both nations were persuaded to postpone their differences through the Rio de Janeiro Protocol. On that occasion Argentina, Brazil, Chile and the US convinced these belligerent neighbors of the advantages of maintaining good relations. In order to assure this situation, the four mediators offered themselves as permanent guarantors, an offer which was also violated by the Argentine decision to sell arms.

The deterioration of Argentina's international image was accented by the discovery of a similar operation, carried out in almost exactly the same way. In this case the arms were sent to Croatia although their alleged destination was Panama. The Buenos Aires government involved itself in this way in the Balkan conflict at a time when the embargo decreed by the UN was in force. Above all, Argentina was, at that time, a member of the Security Council, having even sent about a thousand soldiers to the region as part of the peace keeping operation.

Concrete Denunciations

The denunciations of *Clarín* were very specific and succeeded in frustrating the last of the shipments of arms to Ecuador, these shipments carried out with DC-8 aircraft. There are Ecuadoran Army documents in which this triangular operation is designated as "Operation Gaviota." These Ecuadoran documents contain denunciations by the Ecuadoran Armed Forces that they had themselves been swindled because they considered that 62 percent of the 8,000 FAL rifles and 10 million rounds of ammunition were "unserviceable."[11]

Through the efforts of Al Kassar Ecuador bought 46 medium range Python missiles and acquired Gecko SA8[12] missiles and the Tor-mi system which is supposed to be effective against the MiG and Sukoy aircraft with which the Peruvian Air Force is equipped. The SA8s and Tor-mi were obtained from the Russian enterprise Rosvoorouzhenie State Corporation.

It is estimated that clandestine sales by Argentina exceeded US$80 million and that, for this sum 358 containers were shipped, this recently acknowledged by the commander in chief of the Argentine Army, Martín Balza. Until the accumulation of evidence made it impossible to deny this arms smuggling, President Menem asserted that the charges were a "clumsy and absurd lie, ill intentioned journalistic information."

Nevertheless, and after the action of Argentine justice, ex Minister Camilión is presently to be found undergoing trial as is the manager of Military Manufacturing, Luis Sarlengo. Sarlengo is a personal friend of the president, recruited especially from his native province of La Rioja in order to take charge armament industrial complex.

Uruguayan Corporations

Influence pedaling, the payment of commissions and the falsification of documents were all combined in this operation. In order to complete its description, the role of the enterprises, "Hayton Trade," "Debrol" and "Daforel" remain to be discussed. These three companies were all registered in Uruguay, all with the same address.

Hayton Trade acted as the manager of consignments and it has been demonstrated that this enterprise concealed the true destination of the cargoes which made possible the traffic in 75 tons of munitions and 8,000 FAL rifles to Ecuador. Debrol, for its part was put into the enterprise at the time the commissions were distributed. It is revealing that the two enterprises were acquired in Montevideo by Palleros with the objective of concealing the contraband operations. In order to give shape to the maneuver the lieutenant colonel put two Brazilian and two Venezuelan citizens at the front of the corporations.

Once Decree 103 was signed, Palleros entered into an arrangement with Sarlenga in order to acquire arms. He immediately traveled to the US where he contracted with a Miami firm in order to arrange the shipments. Hayton Trade made the arrangements with Ezeiza Airport authorities in Buenos Aires for the takeoff of the DC-8 aircraft with flight plans for the route Buenos Aires-Guayaquil-Caracas-Buenos Aires.

Commodore Nicolás Benza, Ezeiza manager, authorized the flights without a realistic verification from the Commercial Air Directorate. The departures were controlled by retired Naval Captain Horacio Estrada who was recently found dead of a head shot. If possible it was hoped to have the case closed as a suicide, but there is considerable evidence to conclude that it was not a case of self elimination.

The Thread Is Broken

The landing in Guayaquil, impossible to authorize if all had been acting properly, and the certainty that the flight from Ecuador to Venezuela was made with the cargo hold empty, gave rise to the notion that the commander of the Argentine Air Force, Juan Paulik, put Minister Camilión on notice as to the facts. That was in February 1995, and since then two departures had been effected. A few days later, then in March, *Clarin* denounced the contraband arms operation. At this point Hayton Trade had credited a sum equivalent to 10 percent of the total for the operation which was deposited in a bank of the Uruguayan capital.

Some days later Colonel Sarenga had deposited $400,000 to the account of the Daforel enterprise in the New York Branch of Manfra, Tordella and Brockers Banking (MTB). It is known that the deposit was destined to pay a commission to an Argentine intermediary, apparently related to Carlos Menem, whose name Camilión has refused to provide to the members of an Argentine investigating committee.

Argentine Federal Judge Jorge Urso initiated a judicial inquiry into the arms-trafficking scandal and decided to try Colonel Sarlenga and the other managers of Military Fabrications, Colonels Edberto González de la Vega and Roberto Franke, although he failed in his attempt to interrogate one military officer, Commodore Benza, Ezeiza Airport manager.

Throughout 1995 the Menem Government exerted pressure to slow down an inquiry on the responsibility of Camilión who had been accused in September by Paulik in front of Judge Urso. The Air Force chief denied responsibility revealing that he had alerted the minister on the diversion of the cargoes. The government succeeded in delaying a request for elimination of immunity until after the municipal elections in Buenos Aires. Nevertheless, in July 1996 Judge Urso brought the request before Congress, and Minister Camilión opted to resign in order to avoid a parliamentary debate. He solicited further that the government guarantee that he would not go to prison.

Petition to the United States

Urso sent a petition to the US Justice Department in which he solicited raising the bank account secrecy in order to follow the management of funds of some enterprises. Suggestively, the management of the Daforel enterprise went ahead to turn over the judgment of $400,000 deposited "by error" in its account in the MTB of New York.

When Palleros was interrogated by Uruguayan Justice, he admitted all his enterprises were working with MTB Banking in New York and asserted that President Menem, ex Ministers Camilión and Cavallo and the authorities of Military Farbications were familiar with his management.

He further exhibited a copy of a presidential decree in which he was authorized to sell arms to Venezuela. Palleros assured the court that "from the president on down, all were familiar with the activities" carried on by Hayton Trade and Debrol. "The president, the minister of Defense and the manager of Military Fabrications knew the situation perfectly," he asserted on that occasion.

Other investigations carried out by Uruguayan justice revealed that at some time arms containers were deposited in the free zone of Fray Bentos (some 280 km northwest of Montevideo, on the Argentine frontier) and, also, that arrangements were made, apparently through Palleros, with the state petroleum enterprise in order to solidify the acquisition of six million liters of aviation fuel.

Meanwhile the declaration of the Argentine Army commander, Martín Balza, before Urso's Court was awaited with interest. The judge called the hearing at the suggestion of Attorney General Carlos Stornelli. Until that moment Balza denied any responsibility "because I never signed or ordered anything illegal" nor "did anyone who reviewed the situation for us make it clear that someone in the Army had done so." In the face of the totality of evidence, opposition Deputy Horacio Viqueira maintained that "this is a subject which has many thorny problems to be investigated, but, if it is a question of the intermediaries and the operators, the performance of the public functions cannot be put aside, nor can the political guarantee which permitted that this sale could be carried out."

If things are well known, "Palleros was detained abroad, Estrada dead under suspicious circumstances, persons who evidently have responsibilities, but are only a part of the operation, almost necessary participants," the deputy maintained that "they did not have the capacity for assuring that Customs will control neither the ships nor the aircraft which depart with cargoes of arms destined for Ecuador and Croatia. And it is not a question of an isolated situation."

[Translated from the Spanish by the LANS Editor]

Bolivia

Hugo Banzer Suarez was, of course, elected president of that functioning enigma, Bolivia, which has a navy with no outlet to the sea and a unionized, politically active coca-leaf industry operating in the face of its illegality. As a part of the Hemispheric Left (HL) attack on those who have prevented the Marxist Leninist (ML) terrorists from taking over various Latin American (LA) nations, Bánzer was again under siege. That he had done nothing more than answer his fellow citizens' call for protection against Castro's terrorists has been discussed (pp.195ff, YRBK98). Meanwhile, the cadavers of that terrorist "legend in his own mind," Guevara, and the KGB agent assigned to watch him, Haydee Tamara Bunke Bider, were returned from Bolivia to that Holy City of hemispheric terrorism, Havana.

Brazil

THE MST,[13] DEMOCRACY, JURIDICAL SECURITY AND THE ELECTIONS OF 1998. II

JOSÉ CARLOS GRAÇA WAGNER[14]
ASSOCIATE EDITOR, LANS
SÃO PAULO, BRAZIL
(SPCL 5.18, 5 JUNE 1998)

EDITOR'S INTRODUCTION

The Landless Peasant Movement (MST), the São Paulo Forum (FSP) and the Inter-American Dialog (DI) are discussed by Doctor Graça Wagner in Part I of this article which appears in Chapter 4 of this Yearbook. In this Part II the effects of these allied organizations on the Brazilian elections of 1998 are discussed.

* * *

The Presidential Elections and the MST

The points discussed should not be viewed as strange. It is the nature of the left or internationalism to combat capitalist globalization while favoring socialist globalization. But the Brazilian Constitution does not permit the subordination of parties to foreign entities of deliberative character. The certainty is that the performance of the MST is revolutionary and will assume unforeseen proportions on feeling the lack of governmental authority. Such a posture could check the authority of the federal government, the powers of whose head are linked to the MST. And the MST hates Cardoso, feeling betrayed by him in spite of all his efforts to gain its sympathy. He has given the MST advantages which increase its capacity to mobilize as, for example, is being justified through manipulation of drought and famine only "discovered" through the MST six months after turning serious. Moreover, the MST awaits, in order to act, supporting declarations from some bishops and some judicial authorities, even giving the impression of pre-arrangement in order to justify the illegality of its acts. These have been characterized by the hijacking of vehicles and their operators.

The defiance of the institutions is patent as is evidence of the weakness of a government which cannot support the judicial order as was demonstrated recently in the attempts to process the MST directors judicially. These people emotionally place the social aspect above the law as did Hitler in coming to power. The suggestion by Min. Raul Jungmann that the MST transform itself into a political party is nothing but the Princeton solution to accommodate the guerrillas. Jungmann forgets that the Princeton solution did not work in Colombia where the guerrillas linked to the FSP occupy 40 percent of the territory. As he forgets other salient aspects of the situation. More useful for the understanding of the MST is Stédile's [*Aquestão Agrária no Brasil*, Universidad Federal Rio Grande do Sul, 1994].

The Fragilities of the Cardoso Candidacy

Fernando Henrique Cardoso was elected president of Brazil in 1994 because of his Real Plan (pp.59ff, YRBK97), still in force, which must be sustained by two anchors, those of out-of-phase exchange rates and increasing worldwide interest rates. Without these, the reform of the state could have been realized in spite of the increase in taxes and in spite of the precarious equilibrium observable in the "deficits" of public and foreign accounts.

Cardoso also owed his election in 1994 to the fear of Luís Inacio (Lula) da Silva. His political performance, both in the international and executive arenas, was characterized by his abandonment of socialist politics, quite apart from the alleged cause. There was a weak turnout of numerically important blocs of the population, these blocs only voting for him because of the impossibility of their voting for

Lula; these blocs included population sectors connected with the guarantee of public order and judicial security, the Catholic Church, agriculture and even the evangelicals.

There is increasing discontent with Cardoso among businessmen, as illustrated by those involved in supermarkets who, along with their 600,000 employees, feel threatened by the actions of the Workers Central (CUT) and the MST.[15] Now, with the offensive of the MST and similar movements, with this developing discontent among businessmen and certain other sectors, there is an increasing number who will vote for Cardoso only if there is no alternative for them. Capital flight from Brazil is beginning in another symptom of the malady as research has shown. It is no trifling matter that radical adversaries of Lula now assert support for him in order to withdraw from a tottering politician who seeks to make it believed he knows hardly any of the MST leaders. The latter continue a radical orientation, one scarcely appropriate to a social movement, while not admitting any sort of dissidence in their imposed revolutionary unity.

Research Reveals a Technical Dead Heat

The latest research, published in *Correio Braziliense*, showed a loss of six percentage points by Cardoso and a gain of three by Lula. The research of the Brazilian Institute of Public Opinion and Statistics (IBOPE) showed the same trend. In the following days, a new drop of four points for Cardoso and a gain of two for Lula resulted in a technical dead heat (27 to 30), the poll accuracy being given as ±3 percent. In cities and capitals of more than 50,000 inhabitants the technical dead heat is now a reality (27 to 26), and, in the capitals, is a scarcely different 30 against 28. It is a matter of elementary prudence to realize that the chances of reelection of the president are being exhausted by, for example, the flow of contradictions over the years and the explicit obligations which derive from these contradictions. Cardoso has experienced the difficulty of exercising authority in the face of the realities created by his own political activities which demand energetic action in order that he not be left behind by events. The president appears to be taking refuge in his international prestige which, in fact, could be useful to the country. But the international leaders are not the ones who vote; it is the voters who are concerned with what he said in an interview in Portugal who would be able to understand to what he was referring by "drought, famine and unemployment."

Short Period for Candidate Choice

The period of time remaining for the choice of the candidates for the October elections ends on 30 June. On the other hand, the MST, supported by CUT, through the Workers Party (PT)[16] and other entities, is displaying irresponsible aggressiveness in the face of the ambiguity of the head of the Federal Government and the state governments with regard to the question of juridical security. But juridical security is now broken by these followers of the MST and this, as is well known from studies of history, results in reactions whose beginning is known but whose outcome is not.

World War II, for example, arose from the manipulation, through Nazism, of social problems (*the name of the Nazi Party was National Socialist German Workers Party*). The Nazis took power through the intimidation of their opponents, through the default of the governments and social sectors of Germany and of foreign nations. They massacred their adversaries and sought to initiate the "thousand year" Reich through the occupation of Poland. In our country also, time is running out, this without there being a well defined period, for an eventual reaction or definitive default by the opponents of the MST.

But that one or the other of these shatter the juridical order will only be avoided if the society elects someone who can respond to the threats through juridical stability, through the adequate use of authority founded on law and without the present ambiguities while displaying in other areas the qualities of the current president. There is hope for the people who stand firm in the conduct of public affairs in order that there are no deviations from the lawful course in the political and institutional life.

It is not a matter of dealing with a personal question, nor of promoting someone who, at the moment, is capable of assuring internal peace and the continuity of reforms. There is a requirement by large sectors of the country. These sectors now find themselves unable to maintain political stability through the present PFL-PSDB alliance, albeit it does now have its *raison d'être*. For this alliance cannot now superimpose itself on the national interests inherent in the schemes which have been set in motion by the candidates at all levels.

The candidates in question are those of the Liberal Front Party (PFL) and the Brazilian Social Democrat Party (PSDB) who will launch their campaigns based on the ever greater fragility of the Cardoso candidacy. The basic data projects just such increasing fragility in the face of an entirely different election from that of 1994.

Antonio Carlos Magalhães Is the Solution

The PFL is the party of that political stability which is essential for administrative, economic and social stability, all of which are essential to an increasing economy and social development. Free enterprise, as much in the economy as in questions of social interest such as health, education, transportation, housing and job training, are essentials in a self respecting society. Man is made for work as the bird is made for flight. The bird is not fulfilled which is not flying. The man is not complete who is not working. And he who is not fulfilled through work frustrates his own life. Therefore, a society is not civilized which does not prioritize the work of its members, although there be immense difficulty in concretizing this objective. Never will there be a "social paradise" on earth. Governmental action cannot subordinate human labor to other objectives though such a demand enforces innovations and the mobilization of the societal resources under coordination of the governments and subordination to the totality of laws which are inherent in human nature.

Therefore, good sense, experience and the will to exercise fully the authority of the job are necessary. These characteristics are essential and must not be modified by ideological considerations which condition the means to the ends, which generate ambiguities and with these prevent the society from demarcating well the paths in order to confront the obstacles to creating progress. The PFL has the leadership, the cohesive party structure and the capacity to create the alliances necessary to the exercise of power. These conform to the example which Bahia offers to Brazil.[17] The PFL has no reason for not assuming the responsibilities of the presidency now, particularly when it is clear that the PSDB is not esteemed within the PFL, the former organization desiring the latter only as an instrument for arriving at, and remaining in, power.

Therefore, Antonio Carlos Magalhães is the solution, he being able to avoid, through appropriate use of authority, the confrontation which is approaching between the MST and those who would tend to react to the adventurism of the movement. The present analysis does not rely on any approval by anyone, much less by any of those who appear here with solutions to the problems which have arisen. It is a contribution to the evaluation of the situation in conformity with a probable evolution of the electoral picture. This is true because now it is possible to perceive the probable exhaustion of the candidacy and of the governing potential of the present candidate, Cardoso. Even elected, his new term appears as that of an amorphous government which will seek to survive through concessions and ambiguities which the country cannot support during four more years.

Amendment 16 dispenses with the ineligibility of past presidents to run for the office again, a development which also works to the advantage of Magalhães. Thus, he will be in the advantageous position of being able to return to the presidential palace in 2002 should he triumph in the elections of 1998.

[Translated from the Portuguese by the LANS Editor]

Ecuador

As has been remarked in Chapter 1, this volume, Jamil Mahuad won the presidential runoff election in what was a rather close contest. As 1998 drew to a close it was clear that the campaign of the Hemispheric Left (HL) to prevent any moves toward the free market would hardly be slowed by any so-called "honeymoon" for the new administration. Then too, the methods used by the Mahuad Administration to implement such moves would hardly prove to be well thought out and would serve to exacerbate that chronic state of crisis which is afflicting much of LA. All of this, however, would escalate to levels demanding attention in the New Year and will be treated in *Yearbook 2000*.

El Salvador

THE EL SALVADOR-HONDURAS BORDER PROTOCOL
(SPCL 5.3, 17 JANUARY 1998)

Because hostilities between El Salvador and Honduras fortuitously began (14 July 1969) immediately after three hotly-contested, world-cup qualifier, soccer games, the conflict was misnamed the "Soccer

War." It lasted only 100 hours before the Organization of American States (OAS) cobbled up a cease fire, but its ultimate resolution took a good many years. Perhaps the then 130-year-old border dispute between the two nations was in part responsible for the conflict, but certainly more immediate was the reaction of the Salvadoran Government to the Honduran decision of June 1969 to expel the 300,000 (roughly 12 percent of the Honduran population) Salvadorans previously allowed to live and work there. El Salvador closed its borders, filed a complaint with the Inter-American Commission on Human Rights and launched its attack.

From this conflict arose the so-called *bolsones territoriales* (territorial pockets) or disputed territory along the border, the biggest and most important *bolsón* that above El Salvador's Morazán Department, although there were others above Chalatenango and La Unión Departments. These bolsones—and the "refugee camps"—provided those terrorist sanctuaries, enforced by the US, which prevented the Salvadoran Armed Forces (FAES) from eliminating the terrorists, and, as such, proved of greater importance than the war itself.[18] Indeed the Morazán bolsón was the headquarters of the Farabundi terrorist "General Staff." But by now the terrorist unpleasantness has ended, to the benefit of the terrorist, and the disputed territories have disappeared.

And on 11 September 1992, after the Chapultepec Accords had established "peace," the International Court of Justice (CIJ) rendered a decision on the disputed border with which the interested parties are alleged to be satisfied. In furtherance of this decision the presidents of the two nations signed the Frontier Protocol with the other Central American (CA) presidents acting as "witnesses of honor" (Wkly 5.8). The Protocol which they signed follows:

CHAPTER I. GENERAL DISPOSITIONS

Art. 1. Each party is obliged to respect the rights and liberties of the nationals of the two states who continue living or had rights in the territories of one or the other state delimited by the decision[19] of the CIJ and especially to the right to life, personal security, liberty, nationality, property, possession and tenancy of land, ease of circulation of persons and goods, family integrity and other acquired rights.

(Authorities, etc. not to interfere with exercise of such rights...)

Art. 2. Toward the end of promoting, stimulating and facilitating the frontier integration, both states agree, within the framework of internal legislation, to guarantee that the proprietors and inhabitants of the zone may transit freely the territories which are the object of the decision, and they may market and move their goods in said zones.

Art. 3. Both states agree to respect the right of choice of the persons with reference to nationality in the territories delimited by the CIJ decision of 11 September 1992 with full respect for recognized international human rights.

Art. 4. Both parties agree to guarantee the permanency and stability of the inhabitants in the zones delimited by the CIJ decision.

Art. 5. With reference to respect for human rights, both parties reaffirm that they will adjust their conduct to the principles consecrated in Chapter VI, Title VII of the General Treaty of Peace of 30 October 1980 and in the rest of the international and regional conventions on this subject to which both states are parties.

CHAPTER II. ACQUIRED RIGHTS

Art. 6. Both parties recognize that the notion of "Acquired Rights," to which the CIJ decision refers, comprehends situations which then existed and had judicial effectiveness on the date of the CIJ decision.

(The judicial organizations of both states recognize the validity of the rights. The parties agree that the conveyance of sovereignty of one of the states in relation with the other does not imply in any way ignorance of acquired rights...The recognition of Acquired Rights implies that each juridical figure operating in one of the countries...is recognized in the other...The accord in matters of property does not eliminate the expectations of the possessors with relation to their rights...)

CHAPTER III. NATIONALITY

Art. 7. To the persons born in the territory of each state delimited by the decision of the CIJ of 11 September 1992 is recognized the right of choosing Salvadoran or Honduran nationality by birth.

(To persons who had remained in said territories and who were registered in the census...in the delimited zones...is acknowledged the right of opting for Salvadoran or Honduran nacionality...)

Art. 8. Minors of 18 years of age will determine their nationality within two (2) years after they attain said age, period in which they can opt for Salvadoran or Honduran nationality. If such minors do not make use of the option, they will keep the nationality of their parents.

Art. 9. Minors of unknown parents while they cannot exercise the right of choice and who are found in territory of whichever state, will have the nationality by birth of the state wherein they reside.

Art. 10. The nationals of one or the other state, in order to exercise the option right which corresponds to them, will present, personally or through their legal or empowered representative, a solicitation to the corresponding government political departments, accompanied solely by certificate of birth and of the proof of being included in the census...

(Certification of birth certificate will be expedited freely by the authorities and authenticated only by the Minister of Foreign Relations. Same ministers will attest to the census. In case of difference of name between birth certificate and census, municipal authority will assure that they deal with the same person. The solicitation will be resolved within 60 days...After 60 days without resolution it will be understood that this has been conceded. The state having awarded, it will record immediately on the registers...the resolution recognizing nationality. Since the present convention regulates an exceptional situation. The present convention dealing with an exceptional situation....it will be understood that the petitioners, simply by presentation of documents referred to herein, comply with all the required legal formalities.)

Art. 11. Nationals of both states who as a consequence of the decision have remained in the territory of one state or the other may keep their residence without prejudice to their nationality right, it being recognized that the proof which satisfies the municipal authority corresponds to the data in the census.

CHAPTER IV. PROPERTY, POSSESSION, TENANCY AND OTHER RIGHTS

Art. 12. The parties recognize, in the terms and to the extent established under their acquisition, the property rights such as possession, tenancy and other rights to the land in the territories delimited by the CIJ when they had been acquired by native or legal persons private right before 11 September 1992.

(Likewise they recognize, conforming to the legislation under which obtained, the other rights acquired before that date, be they real or personal. These previous recognitions will be granted without taking into account the nationality of the holders of the rights. Beginning with the present convention, the exercise and the transference of the recognized rights of this article are registered by the internal laws of each state.)

Art. 13. Each state recognizes with the same force and value as the internal legislation of the state which inscribed them before 11 September 1992, the titles and instruments in which:

a) Are constituted, recognized, transferred, modified or cancelled the dominion or possession.

b) Are constituted (etc.) rights of usufruct, inheritance, habitation or lease of real property.

c) Rental contracts on real property when they must be evaluated against third parties, and

d) Those in which are constituted, modified, extinguished or cancelled some mortgage right.

(Titles or instruments referred to in the present article will have to be inscribed in the instruments of the state which presently exercises jurisdiction...If in the three years those interested have not registered the titles or instruments referred to above, they will not be able to dispose legally of same until they are registered. During the three year period inscription will be free. Registrars of the respective states will inscribe titles and instruments within a thirty-day period.)

Art. 14. The parties recognize...the rights of precedence resulting from the presentation of titles or instruments to the property registers of each country when the presentation was effected before 11 September 1992 even when the register has not been verified.

(The state to which the jurisdiction corresponds, after the CIJ decision, will recognize the order of presentation of the register...)

Art. 15. The irregular possession or the mere tenancy of the land which nationals of one of the parties is found exercising since before the date of the CIJ decision, in the premises of individual property, and which after the decision is found in the territory of the other state, will be normalized by the selection of both states...the state or origin taking all means necessary to achieve transfer of dominion in favor of the possessors or tenants and the other state concerting in the legalization.

(The normalization of irregular possession or mere tenancy requires as a previous condition the accord of the proprietors of the real property......achieving the above understanding the award of the instruments of dominion will proceed...)

Art. 16. Relating to regular possession, this is recognized by the time transpired, as much by the possessor directly or by adding the time which it had been possessed by he who had legally acquired it, by act while alive or by cause of death.

(For such effect, there will be had as proofs the respective titles from competent state of origin authorities and the rest of the probative means...For the sole object of recognizing the status which existed on the date of the CIJ decision, housing and property. Both parties agree to award the facilities for regularizing possession and property and their corresponding inscription.)

CHAPTER V. SPECIAL DISPOSITIONS

Art. 17. Both parties accord that the situations not expressly foreseen by this convention which arise in the territories delimited by the decision of the CIJ of 11 September 1992, with relation to judicial relations, will be resolved by the competent tribunals of the state which has territorial jurisdiction, applying, if appropriate, the norms of private international law.

Art. 18. Contracts, judicial acts and acts derived from an acquired right which were produced during the interval between 11 September 1992 and the date of entering into force of the private convention, will be taken as valid in conformity with the judicial order of the country in which the contracts are generated, always not contrary to the constitutional norms of the other country wherein the property is located.

Art. 19. The transference of property and possession rights by act between living persons and the transmission by reason of death will be able to be exercised in favor of nationals of one or the other state who were born or found resident with base in the population census, living quarters and property and those who reside legally in the zones delimited by the decision of the CIJ.

CHAPTER VI. OBLIGATION OF FAITHFUL COMPLETION

Art. 20. Both states compact to the faithful completion of the present convention. In case of differences or disagreements between them over their interpretation or execution, they will attempt to find the best solutions by means of direct negotiation, taking into account the relations of peace and brotherhood among countries.

CHAPTER VII. RATIFICATION AND VALIDITY

Art. 21. The present convention will be approved and ratified by both parties in accordance with constitutional procedures and will enter into validity on the date of the exchange of the respective instruments of ratification which will take place in the city of the republic of...

Art. 22. A certified copy of the present convention will be deposited with the Secretary General of the United Nations in accordance with the effects of Art. 102 of the charter of that organization, and another in the General Secretariat of the Organization of American States.

Guatemala

The so-called Esquipulas II Accords allegedly brought "peace" with the Marxist Leninist (ML) terrorists of the Guatemalan National Revolutionary Union (URNG), although such a claim raises serious questions (pp.146ff, YRBK97). In any event, LANS has reported on the apparent unconstitutionality of these accords (pp.268ff, YRBK98), pointing out that such a peace, arrived at by unconstitutional and illegal means, hardly represents a desirable result. During 1998 this constitutionality challenge was making its painfully ponderous way through the Guatemalan courts. With the year 1999, however, it appears that something more meaningful may happen in this challenge, something which will be covered in *Yearbook 2000*.

Haiti

In one of its first Yankee Imperialist (YI) adventures the Clinton Administration choppered the defrocked Salesian Marxist and Castroite, Jean-Bertrand Aristide, to the Haitian presidential throne in 1994. In 1996 Aristide's "dauphin," René Gárcia Preval, replaced him, winning an alleged 85 percent of the vote. If Gárcia Preval succeeds in surviving the endemic Haitian chaos, which US forces have apparently been unable to control, he will purportedly be replaced by a newly-"elected" president next year. US State Secretary Albright's visits to out of the way outposts of YI seldom appear to have any beneficial effects on the lawlessness common there, her Haitian visit of April 1998 apparently conforming to such a description.

Mexico

OPERATION CASABLANCA
(SPCL 6.2, 11 JULY 1998)

On 31 March 1998 US anti-drug czar Barry McCaffrey, Mexican Foreign Minister Rosario[20] Green and their underlings concluded a "High Level Group Against Drugs" meeting. The topics covered ran the gamut to include "money laundering," and, according to Ms. Green, everything went swimmingly. But did it? Some have questioned the sincerity of the anti-drug position—perhaps "posture" is the *mot juste* — of both the US and Mexico. The continuing bizarre refusal of the US to admit Castro's long and extensive involvement in narcotrafficking would appear to render US "anti-drug" claims fraudulent (pp.165ff, YRBK). Much the same can be said of Ms. Green's recent Cancun lament for Castroite Cuba's return to the Organization of American States (OAS) (AFP 19 June 1998), a lament paraphrased by one iconclastic wag with "Curse the drug but support your hemispheric drug dealer." These self-contradictory positions cast a confusing light on the High Level Group meeting. And the confusion would compound with Operation Casablanca.

One view describes Casablanca as having more to do with a Clinton Administration drive toward a hemispheric imperium than with a serious effort to deal with "money laundering" in Mexico. The opposing view can be taken from the letter of 16 May 1998 to Mexican President Zedillo, a letter written by US Senate Majority Leader Trent Lott (R, MI). In what has been interpreted by the opposition as water-bearing for Mr. Clinton, Mr. Lott claimed it to be a "profound deception" that the operation was "a violation of your [Mexican] sovereignty...which should be welcomed by the interested governments..." The important point would appear to be whether or not Mr. Zedillo and his Institutional Revolutionary Party (PRI) associates actually knew what was going on in the operation. The howls of outrage which first arose from National Action Party (PAN) congressmen indicate, if they hardly prove, that the PAN people did not.

Operation Casablanca

Legend has it that a "maiden with a bag of gold" could traverse all of Genghis Khan's vast empire with impunity. Assuming the availability of a maiden, the lady could come closer to doing this in Las Vegas, Nevada, than in most other US cities. But if a woman, maiden or otherwise, sought lawful employment in a House of Ill Repute (Cat House) there, she would be quite unable to find it. For this, she would have to proceed northwest on Route 95, leaving Clark County and entering the vastness of Nye County. As do many each evening, for here such Houses are matters of indifference to law enforcement. Perhaps best known for such establishments is a crossroads village called Mesquite.[21]

In Mesquite is to be found the Casablanca Casino, well possessed of all the additional inducements which Mesquite has to offer. The "sting" operation which netted the 22 "mid level" Mexican bankers on the weekend of 17-18 May 1998 took place in part at this Casino: hence the name. For the record, a "sting" operation is one in which evidence against alleged criminals is gathered by law enforcement agents, themselves posing as criminals, usually in collaboration with the accused. A broad-brush coverage of what is alleged to have happened is essential. However, the details, furnished by various US officials, have varied enough so that everything should be taken as approximate.

The US Customs Service of the Treasury Department apparently began the operation in November 1995 after the Drug Enforcement Agency (DEA) allegedly found that the "cartels"—Cali and Juárez most frequently remarked—were laundering money through branches of various Mexican banks on the border of that nation with the US. This operation was later enlarged to include investigation of the financial infrastructure of the Juárez Cartel. The agents' *modus operandi* was reported as follows:

According to Treasury Under Secretary Raymond Kelly, the agents "infiltrated" the financial operations of the cartels, the details of this perhaps most interesting but understandably least discussed. These operatives collected the profits from drug sales in US cities and deposited them in bank accounts controlled by Customs. These funds were subsequently transferred electronically to Mexican banks where the executives, later to be arrested, worked. Bank drafts were then turned over to US undercover agents who in turn parceled out the money. That the arrested bankers were aware of the laundering operation would appear to be attested by the one-percent commission they pocketed.

The three-year investigation involved six countries: US, Mexico, Italy, Canada, Colombia and Aruba. Aruba is, of course, an island dependency of the Netherlands only a few miles off the north coast of Colombia. On 18 May 1998 arrests were made in Chicago, New York, El Paso, Los Angeles and Aruba, two Colombians picked up in the last named locality. Various amounts of money, drugs and so on seized during the operation have been given as have the Mexican banks affected and the number of people—largely bankers—picked up and to be picked up. The latter figure began at "about 200" and varies somewhat thereafter. All of these statistics are interesting boilerplate but hardly necessary to repeat. The following is:

Reports indicate that US Treasury Secretary Robert Rubin did not let his Mexican counterpart, José Angel Gurría, know of the arrests and, inferentially, of the operation until the former were underway.

It appears obvious that Mexican reaction could have been predicted.

Mexican Reaction

The US undercover operation appears to have been generally reported in Mexico as having been carried out "behind the back of the Mexican Government" ["*a espaldas del gobierno de México*"—cf. *La Jornada* (Mexico 19 May 1998)]. The crucial aspect of the entire affair is contained in these six words. Did the US carry out this operation "behind the Mexican back"? Or was the Mexican Government—which would probably mean PRI and not the man in the street or in PAN—aware of it but unprepared for the reaction which public awareness would evoke? What appears a logical hypothesis, but which is *not* being claimed here as factual, is the following.

The PRI hierarchy—Zedillo, Green, Gurría, etc.—may well have been aware of the operation, if not the intimate details. Therefore, contemporary statesmen (politicians) routinely ordering their behavior by "opinion" polls, there was no immediate reaction by the Mexican Government to the US announcements on Operation Casablanca. Then came Thursday, 21 May, and the thundering attack by PAN President Felipe Calderón Hinojosa, demanding the resignation of Mexican Attorney General (AG) Jorge Madrazo Cuéllar, his "inaction, carelessness and complete ineffectiveness ...leaving the country open to ridicule."

Demanding an accounting of this violation of Mexican sovereignty, Calderón had a great deal more to say to include the accusation that the Mexican authorities and the AG "not only did not protest this affair but actually applauded and put themselves under the orders of the DEA" (*La Jornada* 22 May 1998).

Mr. Calderón had considerably more to say, among which was a remark about Raúl Salinas de Gortari, brother of Zedillo's predecessor, and the justification of "the hundreds of millions of dollars which he has in Switzerland, France and the US."

With this, the PRI hierarchy figuratively wheeled its warhorse and spurred it in the opposite direction, leading the charge *against* Operation Casablanca. From this point the affair is routine and hardly need be detailed.

On 26 May 1998 Ms. Green sounded the view halloo, the fox here being the sovereignty-violating US customs agents. "The affair," Ms. Green told the press, "has moved from being a matter of money laundering to an affair of violation of Mexican sovereignty." Apparently the investigation continues, an intriguing footnote popping up in mid July. The Swiss then announced that the $100 million which Raúl Salinas had in their banks was not the fruits of narcotrafficking after all, as had been announced last December. Not to worry.

Panama

MULTILATERAL ANTI-DRUG CENTER (CMA) IN PANAMA
(WKLY 5.3, 22 JANUARY 1998)

Negotiations have been in progress between the US and Panama for several years on the question of establishing a multilateral center for the region in the latter nation, this to continue fully in force after Panama gains complete control over the Panama Canal. The idea that Panama should obtain such control of the Canal has been Politically Correct (PC) thinking for a number of years. That the isthmian nation can visualize certain problems should all US forces depart has been evidenced by President "Toro" Pérez Balladares in his careful high-wire act, one facet of which has been the CMA.

The Carter-Torrijos Treaty

Anastasio (Tacho) Somoza Debayle, the Nicaraguan caudillo and member of the West Point Class of 1946, was a staunch anti-ML. Which meant that he had little use for the Carter-Torrijos Treaty that would turn over the Panama Canal to the Panamanian caudillo and Noriega godfather, Omar Torrijos, with unpredictable benefits to the International Left and the HL. So Somoza called a classmate[22] of his in the US Congress to tell him this was madness or words to that effect. As LANS learned from various sources close to Somoza, this was not the only influential North American whom the Nicaraguan contacted. President James Earle Carter soon learned of this Somoza opposition to this centerpiece of his LA policy, an opposition to some extent responsible for the Carter vendetta against Somoza which led to the subsequent Sandinista unpleasantness.

But Carter-Torrijos became PC, and of recent years preparations for the turnover of the Panama Canal to the Panamanians by the XXI Century have apparently proceeded more or less on schedule. Of late these preparations have been interspersed with US efforts, and apparent Panamanian acquiescence, to establish a multilateral monitoring station in Panama.

Why the Monitoring Station?

Public announcements by the Governments of the US and Panama have generally referred to an anti-narcotrafficking mission for this monitoring station. "Everybody" is allegedly against narcotrafficking, although there are a substantial number of political figures who have been accused of accepting funds from narcotraffickers, some of whom have been jailed, and there have been various reports of reduced interdiction of narcotrafficking out of LA and into the US under the present US Government. All of which might provide a basis for the questions which have been raised about the mission of this station.

One report alleges that some two years ago "[Panamanian President] Pérez Balladares proposed the establishment of the CMA, as part of the discussions on the future of US military bases in Panama...which is still being criticized by LA politicians because they consider this to be an effort by the US to create a multinational force which would be able to intervene militarily in the region on the pretext of combating narcotraffic" [*El Siglo* (Panama) 11 July

1997]. Some of these "LA politicians" could well be found in neighboring Colombia, their concern perhaps excessive but something more than paranoia.

In Wkly 5.2 what might be taken as recent US interference in Colombian affairs has been remarked, other examples having appeared in earlier reports. In this case, the US State Department, spurred on by the *New York Times* (NYT), has attacked the Colombian Army for "Human Rights" Violations (HRV), the attack based on unverified charges sent to Human Rights Watch (HRW) by "perfectly unreliable Non Governmental Organizations (NGOs)" [*SEMANA* (Bogotá) No.815 1997], one NGO being a front group for the Colombian Communist Party (PCC).

There are other obvious possibilities for the projected existence of this Monitoring Center, one of which would have the wholehearted support of the HL, another its opposition. It is clearly speculative, but the Panamanian president might well wish to have such a buffer established against the incursions into Panamanian territory from Colombia by the ML narcoterrorists. If recent US State Department statements against the anti-ML Self Defense Patrols (CAP)—paramilitary in the vernacular of the HL—are to be taken at face value, the US Government might be interested in activities against these groups. The ML narcoterrorists of the Colombian Revolutionary Armed Forces (FARC) and the National Liberation Army (ELN) have been mentioned often enough in these reports so that they should require no further discussion.

There is another possible, if unacknowledged, reason for such a center which may be inferred from the "jubilation" which was expressed by various canal users, "particularly in Asia" at a continuing US military presence in the Canal Zone. These nations have stated, and it would appear a rational sentiment, that such a presence could be expected to guarantee stability in the operation of the inter-ocean waterway. While the Panamanians may feel it an insult against their national honor to suggest that they have insufficient military force to protect the canal, it would appear to be a realistic assessment. Not only could a major power take it over with little or no military effort, a relatively minor adventurer could do the same. While the 2000 or so US personnel there could hardly stop such an effort, it is to be supposed that the US would react immediately under these circumstances. Were there no US presence, the US might simply talk.

Whether or not such a scenario is to be anticipated, there are certain powers who consider it a possibility.

CAPs or Paramilitary on the Colombian Border

La Prensa [Panama 12 July 1997] ran a story entitled "Colombian Paramilitary Murder a Panamanian," the two authors having simply written down a tale told to them by an NGO member. The tale reads like that told in Acteal by the Zapas of the CAP members slicing open the abdomens of pregnant women and tearing out the fetuses as trophies, that is (Wkly 5.1), it reads as a typical ML disinformation account. Jacinto González of Panamanian Alternative Legal Assistance (ALAP) told the tale, he having allegedly just returned from a trip to Darién on the Colombian border with a member of Regional Association for Forced Migration (ARMIF). Both these organizations are NGOs.

Apparently having heard of the alleged "murder" of one Cipriano García by "paramilitaries," the pair left for the border area on 9 July, returning two days later with their tale. There are several discrepancies in Jacinto's story which the reporters apparently did not see.

First, Cipriano, allegedly murdered on the sixth, was buried on the eighth: From the story "the removal of the cadaver was done Wednesday, 8 July, by the representative of El Real..." Since there would be no embalming it was probably high time. But this precludes Jacinto from having viewed the cadaver and demands that whatever he told the reporters about it was simply word of mouth which he had received from "other" FARC terrorist collaborators, presuming that is what these people were.

And González's tale has to have simply repeated this very ML horror story. Because García was, according to González, murdered with four machete strokes, two crossed on the head, the rest mutilating his legs. Such behavior, according to the NGO man, is routine, one reason of course being the innate cruelty of anti-MLs, the other being the more practical one that the unknowns, who pay $2000 for every dead terrorist or terrorist collaborator, want proof for their money. This raises three questions:

A piece of leg may indeed indicate that someone is dead, but how does it prove it was a collaborator or a terrorist? And if this one man had been murdered for the $2000, why not murder ten for, say, $20,000? Finally, who pays this princely sum? This was glossed over quickly with "it wasn't said who paid them to commit these crimes."

The story may not be as obviously contrived as the "babies on bayonets" tale, but it is reminiscent, and its source is akin to those for such tales.

The Evolution of the CMA

The CMA was apparently first proposed by Panamanian Caudillo Manuel Noriega in 1989, albeit, he used his "unconditional ally," interim President Francisco A. Rodríguez, to voice the proposal at the UN. Various events intervened, among them what US President Bush inexplicably called the "invasion" of Panama,[23] and the project was shelved for several years. On 6 September 1995 Panamanian President Pérez Balladares and US President Clinton brought the matter up again, announcing the beginning of exploratory talks on the subject. Because of opposition within his own Revolutionary Democratic Party (PRD),[24] however, the Panamanian president again shelved the idea only to bring it back to the table at what was apparently a US suggestion of July 1997. Talks between the US and Panama were initiated in August with John Negroponte as the US negotiator. What happened next probably shows only that the HL is opposed to the CMA Treaty.

In an anti-CMA polemic which appeared in *El Siglo* (Panama 22 December 1997), Julio Blas attempted to paint Mr. Negroponte as a condoner of "Human Rights Violations" (HRV). Blas feels it important to point out that British-born Negroponte entered the US State Department in 1960, by 1980 attaining the post of Ambassador to Honduras. In this position he was allegedly, and probably, a target as an HRV condoner. The HRV campaign of the HL has occasionally been the subject of these reports, the HRV allegations emerging from Colombia treated in a recent one (Wkly 5.2). The general subject has been treated in YRBK98 with some minor attention to HRV claims such as those against Negroponte coming out of Honduras (Wkly 3.10). Perhaps because of the HRV campaign against him, perhaps in the routine progress of affairs, Negroponte was out as CMA negotiator in September 1997, to be replaced by Ambassador Thomas E. McNamara who first visited Panama on 11 September in his new capacity. The "protests" against this new "assault on Panamanian sovereignty" were well underway by this time, one "activist" cleric, Conrado Sanjur, announcing strikes, marches and various other means of "protest" in opposition while a local HR group chimed in with charges.[25]

The US replaced President Guillermo Endara (1989-1994) on the Panamanian presidential throne with Operation Just Cause. Last fall found the ex president in the forefront of those opposing CMA which he described as a "diabolical" Christmas gift from the Panamanian government for the Panamanian people. Even so, it appeared at year's end as if the CMA was coming into existence, an apparently transitory specter for Mr. Endara.

Recent Chronology

In December 1997 Panama and the US arrive at a CMA "accord in principle."

12 January 1998: The first round of multilateral talks between Colombia, Brazil and Mexico and Panama and the US concludes. Panamanian Foreign Minister Ricardo Arias says formal talks could begin in two weeks. McNamara appears somewhat "annoyed."

19 January: US Congressman Bob Barr leads congressional delegation to Panama for talks "at the highest levels." Barr tells the press that "Our principal concern is that the security of the Canal is maintained beyond 2000."

19 January: Panamanian Foreign Minister Arias says the negotiating team will travel to DC "this week" to plan initiation of multilateral negotiations.

21 January: Barr ends three days of conferences on CMA which he describes as "very informative and positive."

22 January: US Ambassador to Panama William Hughes says the DC meeting of 21 January was "positive and productive."

27 January: A Pentagon report of this date describes the "lightning journey" of Arias to DC on 21 January with two options for the Clinton Government: (1) renegotiate "substantive themes" or (2) terminate the negotiations. The Pérez Balladares Government has decided the CMA accord is "politically unacceptable to Panama." It now appears possible that there will be no post 2000 US military presence.

29 January: Arias says Ecuador, Peru and Venezuela are interested in CMA participation.

30 January: Clinton advisor McClarty meets with Pérez Balladares in Switzerland to treat unrevealed bilateral themes.

3 February: A Panamanian presidential commission reports that the negotiating staff had effected "refinements (*precisiones*) and clarifications" in the CMA document.

The CMA Structure

Until the recent breakdown in negotiations it appeared that the Center would have the following US personnel and facilities.

Numbers of US personnel ranging from 1500 to 2500 had been mentioned. Four separate facilities had been named at one time or another, although not all at the same time so that these could have undergone various changes by this time. Most frequently mentioned was (1) Howard Air Force Base at the Pacific end of the Canal, an installation with an extent of 5,280 acres. Less frequently cited was (2) Fort Sherman in Colon at the Atlantic end of the Canal. (3) Gaeta Island in the Atlantic. (4) "Some of the wharves" at the now privatized Rodman Pacific Naval Station.

The originally projected treaty was to have been in force for a twelve-year period, then to be renewable in five-year intervals thereafter. Whether this now has any validity is unknown. Finally, in the matter of the nations involved in multilaterality.

The first group to have joined Panama and the US was to have been Brazil, Colombia and Mexico, to be followed by a second including Argentina, Bolivia and Paraguay. A third group of nations including Ecuador, Peru and Venezuela was approaching membership in the CMA at about the time Arias arrived in Washington with his ultimatum.

REQUIEM FOR THE PANAMA CANAL
(WKLY 6.20, 19 NOVEMBER 1998)

Introduction

The curious one-term, 39th president of the US, James Earle Carter, was apparently the creation of the wealthy Harriman widow. In keeping with the fact that, for obvious political reasons, the wealthy routinely create men/women of the Left, so Mr. Carter may be described. In Special Reports 5.19 and 6.3 (Chapter 4) Mr. Carter's fascination for the Panamanian dictator has been discussed. This fascination probably arose from Carter's intention of bequeathing the Panama Canal Treaty as his legacy to an admiring world. As has been shown,

Carter's vendetta against Anastasio Somoza Debayle—as dictators go, less offensive than Torrijos—probably arose from Tacho's seemingly justified opposition to turning the canal over to Torrijos. The result of this was assuredly the delivery of Nicaragua to the truly virulent ML dictatorship of Ortega et al. And now we find that said delivery is PC (Political Correctness), even Torrijos coming in for a scarcely merited share.

PC is the immensely successful creation of the Left, it boding well to take over the rules of what was once civilized existence which were exemplified by such as the Ten Commandments, now of course PIC. The Left has created PC as a hardly subtle method of instilling Orwellian thought control, and it has been remarkably successful in its application of the fact of it, if not the label, to situations it wishes to promote. One of these is of course the so-called Carter-Torrijos Treaty which will turn over the Panama Canal to the miniscule, defenceless Republic of Panama by the turn of the century. Indeed, it is remarkable how successful the campaign for canal PC has been as evidenced by the support Carter-Torrijos receives from those individuals and organizations who are supposedly of the Anti-Left.

Panama and the (Alleged) Left Worldview

The Left professes to believe in "self determination" for all the world's geographical units save those, as with Tibet, under the heel of one of its satrapies, here the Peoples Republic of China (PRP). Restricting the discussion to the Western Hemisphere, Castro's HL continues to belie the "self-determination" claim with its repeatedly stated intention of creating "supra national countries" a "sort of re-edition of a soviet-type union in Latin America" (pp.98ff, YRBK97 and later). As do the claims from similar entities around the world—Libya,[26] Irak, Iran, USSR/CIS, PRP, etc.—although of course now democratic by PC definition, entities to which we must look for "protection and support" of what has long been thought to be an important waterway. When Genghis Khan's "maiden with a bag of gold" can stroll unmolested through all the world's highways and byways, then it will be appropriate to turn over the canal that the US built, and into which the US has since poured untold billions. But such analysis, however relevant, is hardly PC.

Certain pundits, apparently not consciously of the Left, even maintain that the Panama Canal is not as important as it once was. When one considers the thousands of extra miles a ship must travel around Cape Horn if the canal is denied it for passage from Atlantic to Pacific, such a statement is only comprehensible if we suppose no ship ever need make the passage. With which one can only revert to philosophical discussions of angels and pinheads.

The Constitutionality of the Carter-Torrijos Treaty

The Left gives considerable lip service to "democracy" when it suits its purposes to do so, this Panama Canal treaty frequently classified as "democracy" of some sort and hence a priori desirable. But, all other aspects ignored for the moment, if this treaty has been unconstitutionally obtained, it is unconstitutional and hence outside the law. However desirable therefore such a treaty may be, obtaining it through violation of the law—the only protection of liberty and individual rights—can in no way be so characterized. First, the question of property rights.

The obfuscation, whether by accident or by design, of the facts relating to property rights in the Panama Canal Zone (CZ) began during the presidency of Richard M. Nixon whose residence in the White House was terminated by improper conduct. In 1974 the two nations signed the "Statement of Principles" wherein three of the eight "principles" alleged the CZ to be Panamanian territory. The evidence indicates this to be incorrect. The US Supreme Court ruled in 1907 in Wilson v. Shaw that the CZ was "unincorporated US Territory." In 1972 the US Fifth Circuit Court of Appeals handed down the same ruling in US v. Roach. It would therefore appear that the basis for the treaty that followed was illegal.

And the treaty followed in 1977 under Mr. Carter. However, the treaty which the US Senate ratified contained the DeConcini Amendment which re-established US unilateral defense rights. LANS has stated that ex President Bush's classification of his own Operation Just Cause as an "invasion" was inexplicable (p.8, YRBK97). Since the only legal instrument between the US and Panama contained this amendment, this appears to be obvious. However, the telephone call between Carter and Torrijos during the night of 7 April 1978 yielded an agreement between the two men that eliminated De

Concini. This cobbled up instrument was passed by a US Senate which was not informed of the omission of DeConcini by the bill's floor manager, Sen. Paul S. Sarbanes (D, MD). Capt. Evans[27] told LANS that a 1982 survey showed that eight senators would have voted against ratification had they been aware of DeConcini's absence. Thus, this treaty was not legitimately ratified since the number voting for it was fraudulently obtained.

Not only was the US Constitution apparently violated, so also was that of Panama. Art. 163 of the Panamanian Constitution was violated by the failure of then Pres. Demetrio B. Lakas to sign the treaties, Caudillo Torrijos signing with no constitutional authority. Art. 274 was violated by the failure to have the six major changes, which the US had added to the treaty, approved by plebscite. All of which would become standard operating procedure as LANS has demonstrated with the Esquipulas Accords (allegedly) of Oscar Arias (cf., pp.268ff, YRBK98 *et seq*).

The Panama Canal Treaty would thus appear to be unconstitutional. That the canal itself is falling apart is a fact which might make no difference were it of the minor importance to which treaty supporters appear to consign to it. But, according to those who are highly qualified by their careers to evaluate the importance of the canal, such is assuredly not the case.

The Degeneration of the Canal and Its Facilities Since the Turnover Began

The US Corps of Engineers carried out the "1996 Operations and Maintenance Study." This report, which was quickly classified as "politically sensitive," told a depressing tale of "crumbling concrete and eroding infrastructure" (Evans, ibid.) coupled with a lack of "commitment to see that proper maintenance is done." Evans attributes this to the maintenance delays caused by tiny Panama's drive for more traffic and more tolls. It reflects what is appearing more like Panamanian inability to operate the canal. Were this really that "best of all possible worlds" which the Left tirelessly paints for us, this would be no serious problem: The US could simply siphon in the dollars, and the Panamanians could play canal operator.

Unfortunately, Republic of Panama Law No.5[28] (16 January 1997) promises to render such "dreams of peace" elemental irrelevancies.

Enter the Chicoms

Admiral Thomas H. Moorer (b.1912) is a seaman with experience relating to the Panama Canal and matters nautical which few if any of the Canal Treaty supporters can boast. During his career he served as Commander-in-Chief of the Pacific Fleet and of the Atlantic Fleet, as Chief of Naval Operations and as Chairman of the Joint Chiefs of Staff. His testimony before the Senate Foreign Relations Committee[29] is therefore valuable as that of an expert witness. The following extracts from this testimony bear on the ChiCom intrusion into Panama Canal affairs.

> A company called Panama Ports Company, S.A., affiliated with Hutchison Whampoa, Ltd. through its owner, Mr. Li Ka-Shing, currently maintains control of four of the Panama Canal's major ports... Panama Ports Company is 10 percent owned by China Resources Enterprise, the commercial arm of China's "Ministry of Trade and Economic Cooperation."

The Admiral then quotes from an article in the *South China Morning Post* (16 July 1997) wherein US Senator Fred Thompson identifies China Resources as "an agent of espionage—economic, military and political—for China." In this same article it is stated that China Resources "has solid relations with the Lippo Group"—which arose in the investigation of alleged Chicom contributions to the US DNC (Democrat National Committee)—"in 1992, it acquired 50 percent of the Hong Kong Chinese Bank, which is also 50 percent owned by Lippo, and sold its stake to its listed arm, China Resources Enterprise, last month."

The Admiral proceeds with

> Hutchison-Whampoa controls countless ports around the world... this company is controlled by the Communist Chinese. And they have virtually accomplished, without a single shot being fired, a stronghold[30] on the Panama Canal ...through something called "Law No.5," which provides ... 1. Responsibility for hiring new pilots for the Canal. (Pilots have complete control of all ships passing through the canal); 2. Assumes control over... Atlantic/Pacific Anchorages, including a monopoly on the Pacific side when Rodman Naval Base is vacated next year. (... Law No.5, effective 1 March 1997 ...(gives) Hutchison the right to demand possession of Rodman); 3. Authority to control the ships utilizing the entrance to the canal on the pacific side, and ...to deny ships access to the ports and entrances of the canal if they are deemed to be interfering with Hutchison's Business ... 4. The right to unilaterally transfer its rights to a third party—any company or nation of their choosing; ... 6. Included in the deal with Hutchison is US Naval Station Rodman; a portion of US Air Station Albrook; Diablo; Balboa ...; Cristobal ...; the Island of Telfers ...adjacent to Galeta Island, a critical communications center.

Toward the end of his testimony Admiral Moorer sums up with

> We are not talking about an ill-funded Nicaraguan effort against the Communists in the late 80's; we *are* talking about the control of a strategic part of the world in our hemisphere, shortly to be controlled by the largest country on Earth, Communist China, financially flush and people-strong....

Venezuela

VENZUELA'S RETURN TO BASICS
CARLOS BALL
EDITOR, AIPE
(WKLY 6.7, 20 AUGUST 1998)

EDITOR'S INTRODUCTION

Rafael Caldera Rodríguez was elected Venezuelan president as the candidate of a far-left coalition including Movement Toward Socialism (MAS) (p.24, YRBK97). His socialist policies have exacerbated the already unfortunate Venezuelan economic situation (pp.76ff, YRBK97) as was assuredly to have been expected, this contributing to the rise of Chávez (Wkly 5.14) in next December's presidential sweepstakes. There are various important facets of this situation and its background which are either not known or deliberately left unreported. In order to shed much needed light on the subject, LANS has turned to Carlos Ball. Mr. Ball is a Venezuelan journalist who, as editor, has nurtured the burgeoning success of the Inter-American Economic Press Agency (AIPE). LANS is pleased to reproduce two of his recent articles on the Venezuelan economic situation.

* * *

The politic of the Venezuelan governments of the last three decades has been to beat the petroleum *piñata* with a stick and share the best candies and toys that cascade forth among the friends who present themselves at the Miraflores Palace to tell the president how grand he is. Certainly, this leaves some scraps which fall from the table and into the hands of the people, to whom the politicians never tire of repeating what great good fortune it is for them to live in such a rich country where there is no need to work much so long as we continue electing the same clique.

Rafael Caldera—fascist in the 1930s and founder of Christian Socialism in Venezuela during the 1940s—together with his economic genius, Teodoro Petkoff[3][1]—communist guerrilla in the 1960s and founder of Movement Toward Socialism (MAS) in the 1970s—calculated badly: the cash ran out five months before the December 1998 elections. The Venzuelan Government confronted a deficit of 7 percent in the Gross Domestic Product (PIB), and the life preserver is the new minister of the treasury, Maritza Izaguirre. For years, Izaguirre was a functionary of the multilateral organisms in Washington, DC, and, therefore, possessed of the necessary experience to drive future generations of Venezuelans into maximum indebtedness trying to keep the lid on the empty budget until December. It will not be the first time that a new Venezuelan Government has been installed and found that there is not a cent in the treasury. Thus, there will soon begin to arrive in Caracas the birds of ill omen from the International Monetary Fund (IMF). As a result, we will surely have street demonstrations and Jakarta-like plundering before Christmas.

At the beginning of the year, as much the Venezuelan minister of petroleum as the president of the state petroleum monopoly were crying out like Tarzan, speaking of sovereignty and a brilliant future. Saudi Arabia, in order to clear the smoke, opened the petroleum stream and quickly Mexico and Venezuela responded—with their tails between their legs—to pact the reduced oil production with the Arabs. The reality is that the government has milked and politicized Venezuelan Petroleum to the point that, like the Central Bank, it functions as petty cash for the state, with dispensable funds for neither investment nor expansion and, much less, with anything with which to confront a fall in prices to $8.40 per barrel.

The result of this tragic comedy of errors is that the entrance of capital into Venezuela has now retroceded to 1952 levels, and 80 percent of the population is below the poverty level. It is miraculous that the Venezuelan people have peacefully borne up under this plundering by the political class. Perhaps the safety valve is the proximity of the elections, which it now appears Comandant Hugo Chávez will win by a large margin. Chávez is the principal critic of the Venezuelan partidocracy system.

Lamentably, Chávez appears to be a military man of 1970s type. Alejandro Sucre recently wrote a piece pointing out the similarities of the program of Chávez to that of Carlos Andrés Pérez[32] in 1974: nationalism, interventionism, nationalization of "basic and strategic" industry and redistribution of the wealth. The problem is that such political theories have only succeeded in redistributing poverty in all those nations where they have been applied.

But Chávez also offers the inhabitants of the Caracas and country districts the security of being able to reach their humble homes without being assaulted or having to pay tolls to bands of criminals. While the rich can hire bodyguards, the poor must depend on the government for their personal security. When the Venezuelan government has abysmally neglected its primary obligation to guarantee the life and property of its citizens, the ideological disagreements which can be had with Chávez matter little if it is guaranteed that our wives and children can go into the streets without being assaulted and hurt. For me this is the explanation of Chávez.

[Translated from the Spanish by the LANS Editor]

AFTER CALDERA, THE DELUGE[33]

CARLOS BALL
EDITOR, AIPE
(WKLY 6.7, 20 AUGUST 1998)

For many years it appeared that the Venezuelan failure was a result of the economic ignorance of the politicians, a viewpoint which would be clarified little by little as it became clear that central direction of a modern economy is an impossibility. Soon, however, one is forced to see the obvious advantage of fomenting a system of individual initiatives in such a way that those who work harder in order to please the consumers obtain success and personal fortune.

But the Venezuelan reality is much more complicated and gloomy: Forty years of socialism has propitiated the emergence of an elite whose *raison d'être* is clinging to its privileges. For such an elite, the solution to any crisis is to increase taxes and, conscious of its own ineptitude, function under the slogan, "après moi, le déluge."

The Venezuelan tragedy is that there has not arisen in our era a single political leader who said, "wait a moment; the function of government is not to fix the problems of every Venezuelan but to establish a legal framework which guarantees the life and property of the citizens, permitting each one to make the best use of his abilities and inclinations in order to attain his personal happiness, always and when the process does not violate the rights of the rest."

For decades the Venezuelans have been free to vote in order to elect their councilors, deputies, senators and presidents. But all those politicians, together with a million and a half bureaucrats employed by the government once in power have devoted themselves to imposing the most varied collection of laws and regulations which, whether well or evil intentioned, have put a straitjacket on the citizenry.

Among the worst political crimes against the Venezuelan we should remark:

1. The politization of the Central Bank has destroyed the value of the money, whereby it is impossible to save, there is no long term financing of homes and, with interest rates at more than 50 percent, it is impossible for those who are not rich to buy an automobile. Solution: To change the people's bolivars for dollars and close the Central Bank.

2. Public education is worse every day. The teachers are totally demoralized and frequently on strike because they cannot feed their families with their miserable salaries. Solution: Sell or give the schools to the employees and the teachers, converting them into impresarios who compete for students. Thus, if there are bad teachers and bad administrators, they will have to dedicate themselves to something for which they are better equipped. If they are good teachers, they will be successful and will open other schools, benefiting principally the youth and the future of the nation. The state would deal with basic education for the poor, distributing coupons with which the parents can send their children to the school of their choice. The "free" university has always been a subsidy for those who are not poor.

3. Lack of liberty and equality of opportunity. More than half of the Venezuelan workers labor in the underground economy because they do not have the money or the politico-union connections to gain access to the formal economy. The regulatory enthusiasm of politicians and public functionaries has condemned the mass of the population to working on the margin of the law owing to the cost of

legality. Solution: A campaign of annulling counter productive laws and regulations based on the cost of compliance in relation to the average income of the people. If compliance costs more in time or money than a day's salary, the law should surely be eliminated.

4. Privatization of the subsoil, in such a way that the citizens and not the state are the proprietors of the mineral riches, at the same time that the Petroleum Monopoly (PDVSA) is eliminated, distributing the shares of PDVSA among all the Venezuelans. Thus would be realized the old official deception that the petroleum belongs to everybody.

5. Elimination of import tariffs and export subsidies. It is absurd to manufacture internally anything that can be imported more cheaply, and, without the state monopolies, the Venezuelans would be able to enjoy to the maximum our comparative advantages. In Venezuela there have been two classes of citizens: those for whom it is possible to travel abroad and buy what they want and those who only have access to the goods and services that the bureaucracy permits them.

These are only five key ideas for projecting Venezuela into the new millenium. The tragedy is that the candidates in the December presidential election do not believe in the capacity of the citizenry to do what is best for them in the absence of the nursemaid state which has ruined and corrupted them. With grand arrogance they believe it much better that they decide what we must do, generally with foreseen good of some multilateral bureaucracy like the IMF.

It is ironic that, at the same time, they think that we Venezuelans are quite capable of bringing them to the presidential palace, naming one of them dictator for the next five years.

[Translated from the Spanish by the Editor, LANS]

Notes

1. LANS gratefully acknowledges the permission to publish this article granted by the Inter-American Economic Press Agency.
2. Doctor Sabino is Professor of Sociology at the Venezuelan Central University.
3. Prof. Sabino is not referring to the sort of political philosophy which is inferred in the US in the latter part of Century XX by the term "Liberalism" and typified by government gigantism; he is referring to the "classical" liberalism of free men, free markets and the property right.
4. There are two versions of the FN-FAL (Fabrique Nationale Fusil Automatique Léger) or simply FAL which Argentina has manufactured, both at Fabrica Militar de Armas Portatiles "Domingo Matheu." The first is the 7.62mm rifle with which the

Army is largely equipped. The second is the 5.56mm.
5. This 9mm pistol is manufactured at "Domingo Matheu" with license from FN Herstal SA in two military and one "detective" models.
6. This is apparently the 7.62mm FAP (Heavy Automatic Rifle) Model 2, which is a heavy-barreled version of the FAL with a bipod.
7. The word *obúse* can mean "mortar," "howitzer," "shell," in short, it is not precise. However the Italian munitions firm, OTO-Melara SpA of La Specia, is producing recoilless rifles, anti tank weapons, the MAF [Manportable Missile System]. This consists of a missile in its container launcher and a firing post. The two-stage missile is laser-beam guided and has a range in excess of 3 km. Missile diameter is 130mm.
8. Sociedad Anónima, that is, incorporated.
9. The most recent information (cf. *La Nación* 16 September 1998) states that there were three decrees, but LANS has not acquired the third.
10. LANS is deeply grateful for information supplied by Jane's Information Group, in particular, by their Public Relations Officer, Mr. Joe Dougherty.
11. Details of the munitions shipments to Ecuador have been provided in Wklys 1.10 and 6.12.
12. This all weather, low altitude surface-to-air missile system was put into service by the USSR in 1974. It is self propelled, having a tube length of 3.15m, a missile diameter of 0.21m and a wing span of 0.64m. It is self propelled by a solid-fuel rocket. There are two models, the SA-8A having a range of 12,000m, the SA-8B a range of 15,000m.
13. An introduction to the facts relative to the dual international entities analyzed herein, the São Paulo Forum and the Inter-American Dialog, were obtained by Doctor Graça Wagner in August 1993 by chance from a client who had an office in Miami. The client had been informed, by his Cuban manager without any proof, that there had been a politico-strategic pact consummated between Fidel and Lula during the previous week in Havana. Because the indications were at that time that Lula would be elected Brazilian president in 1994, Doctor Graça Wagner immediately began an investigation with the files of *Granma*, the official organ of the Cuban Communist Party, at the North-South Center of the University of Florida. He has continued this investigation throughout the continent to the present time.
14. Doctor Graça Wagner, now Coordinator of International Affairs for the Tancredo do Neves Institute of São Paulo, has devoted himself to public affairs since his days as a student. During this time he has participated in various political, social and professional movements, holding numerous important positions within these organizations and receiving hosts of awards and recognitions for his efforts. For a number of years the FSP and the DI have been important subjects of his broad-ranging research.
15. The MST has been extensively discussed in Part I (Spcl 5.17) and earlier (pp.106ff, YRBK97).
16. This is the Workers Party which Lula formed under the tutelage of Frei Betto and which Lula himself described in Pierre Broue [*Quand le Peuple Révoque le Président*, L'Harmattan, 1993. ISBN: 2-738-41747-7] by classifying its militants as "Trotskyites, Castroites, activists of the Brazilian Communist Party (PCB) ... liberation theologists ... Sandinistas..." and more.
17. Magalhães has long been the power in the National Democratic Union (UDN) party in the State of Bahia.
18. Destacamento Militar IV (reinforced regiment) was headquartered at San Francisco Gotera, just south of the bolsón, in and about which the LANS Editor spent time in

the middle 1980s. An amusing example of the almost complete misinformation on this "war" which existed in the US was given by a national newsmagazine about the time he returned from one such visit. To his surprise he found the bustling departmental capital described as "a ghost town."

19. The word used is *sentencia* (sentence), but this appears a proper "interpretation."
20. This is apparently the proper spelling, although the individual in question is assuredly a woman.
21. In Nevada's other famous city, Reno, a similar situation exists. Here the lady would have to proceed east on Interstate 80, ducking south out of Washoe County into Storey County to find Mustang Ranch. In addition to being some 500 miles farther from the Mexican border, Operation Mustang would hardly have had the same ring to it.
22. This individual was later allegedly caught in some sort of embezzlement, neither the details of which nor the individual's name need be mentioned here.
23. *OPERATION JUST CAUSE: The Storming of Panama.* Thomas Donnelly, Margaret Roth, Caleb Baker. Macmillan. 1991 ISBN: 0-669-24975-0.
24. In actuality, this was Caudillo Noriega's party which, in one of those puzzling pieces of US "diplomacy," the US effectively put in Noriega's place by replacing Endara on the presidential throne, then walking away and leaving the Torrijos-Noriega Constitution in force.
25. One of the Panamanian HR activists and the LibTheo (Liberation Theology) clerics who worked for the Tupac Amaru Revolutionary Movement terrorists during the Japanese Embassy Operation in Lima have been touched upon in Wkly 3.6.
26. In brief the Socialist People's Libyan Arab Jamahiriya whose dictator, Khadafy, financed Ortega's recent run for the Nicaraguan presidency.
27. G. Russell Evans, *Death Knell of the Panama Canal*, National Security Center, 997. ISBN: 0-9658348-0-8.
28. A copy of the 32-page document is, thanks to Capt. Evans, in the LANS files. On p.1 "THE LEGISLATIVE ASSEMBLY DECREES" begins the purveyal of the Ports of Balboa (Pacific) and Cristobal (Atlantic) to what appear to be agents of the PRP.
29. *Hearings. Panama. Testimony of Adm.Thomas H. Moorer.* Senate Committee on Foreign Relations. 16 June 1998. Y4.F76/2: s.hrg. 105ff.
30. This may have originally been "stranglehold," albeit, the verb "accomplished" is not as appropriate as it might be in either reading.
31. The son of Bulgarian immigrants, his mother a physician, Teodoro Petkoff joined the Venezuelan Communist Party (PCV) after entering Liceo Andrés Bello in Caracas in 1949. He entered medical training at the Venezuelan Central University (UCV) and joined the staff of the communist paper, *Tribuna Popular*, abandoning the medical training after two years for a degree in "political economics" (1960). By 1961 he had risen to the Central Committee (CC) of the PCV joining Douglas Bravo in 1962 to establish one of the first Venezuelan Marxist Leninist (ML) terrorist groups. In and out of duress vile, he escaped for good in 1967 and is alleged to have turned "peaceful" in 1971 to join other MLs in forming Movement Toward Socialism (MAS). Petkoff is Caldera's "Minister of Planning," largely responsible for the latter's "economic" policies.
32. Pérez has been the *eminence gris* of the Hemispheric Left (cf. pp.73ff, YRBK97), his fine Italian hand in or near every terrorist operation for many years, and an embezzler on a truly grand scale (*ibid* and p.24, *ibid*) whose malversations have probably only been surpassed by Brazil's Collor.

33. Louis XV was the great-grandson and successor of the Sun King, Louis XIV. He is supposed to have said, realizing what a chaotic state of affairs his long, do-nothing reign had created, "After me, the deluge," but this has been hard for some to believe. Le Marquis D'Argenson (*Memoires*, 1857 *et seq*) wrote that, at the council table Louis "opened his mouth, said little and thought not at all" and that "under the appearance of personal monarchy it was really anarchy that reigned." That Louis ever said anything as perceptive as "Après moi..." is highly unlikely but nonetheless appropriate to the present discussion.

3

Three Hemispheric Heads of State: Pinochet, Ortega and Clinton

Three men, each of whom has been or is a hemispheric chief of state, captured enough international attention during 1998 to warrant a separate chapter.

Augusto Pinochet Ugarte

In 1973 General Augusto Pinochet Ugarte, at the request of the Chilean legislature, prevented Salvador Allende Gossens from transforming Chile into a Soviet satrapy, a fact to which USSR International Department chief, Boris Ponomarev, and his boss, Leonid Brezhnev, effectively attested at the time. But Pinochet did more than this, for, with the help of the free-market economist, Arnold C. Harberger, and others, he transformed the economic destruction bequeathed by Allende into the economic miracle of the hemisphere. The Hemispheric Left (HL), of course, has thirsted for revenge since that time and was able to initiate a vendetta against him in 1998.

Captain General Augusto Pinochet retired from a lifetime of service to his native Chile in the spring of 1998, taking his seat in the legislature as a senator-for-life. In the fall of this year he traveled to Britain for medical treatment and fell victim to a Disinformation Operation (DO) hatched by a pair of Spanish leftists and supported by the British leftists now in power in that nation. Although, with the close of 1998, the outcome of this transparent "vengeance" attempt by the International Left (IL) is unpredictable, LANS has, at least preliminarily, treated various facets of this affair in the various reports which follow.

The assignment of an order here for the various reports is not an unambiguous task: a choice must be made. LANS has chosen to begin by setting the stage with the report on Pinochet's retirement (Wkly 5.10). This will be followed by a description (Wkly 6.17) of what has been described as a "Gestapo-like" arrest of Sen. Pinochet in London. The arrest of an 82-year-old man, unprotected and immobilized by surgery, at midnight in hospital by 50 police is certainly "Gestapo-like." It appears appropriate here to follow this with the review of the Chilean best seller, *Europe vs. Pinochet: Unjust Proceeding* (Spcl 6.11), because of the general nature of the tome's treatment of the situation. This review should leave little doubt that "vengeance" is an important part of the proceeding, this leading naturally to the excellent study by Dr. Vial Larrain (Spcl.6.18).

"MISSION COMPLETED"
(WKLY 5.10, 11 MARCH 1998)

At 1010 local time on 10 March 1998 octogenarian Captain General Augusto Pinochet Ugarte turned over command of the Chilean Armed Forces to Lieutenant General Ricardo Izurieta Caffarena, closing his own 25 years as commander in chief. The change of command and the general's retirement ceremony were both held at the Military Academy.

"For 65 years," the general said in his retirement speech, "I have followed the path of duty and discipline, and, on completing my active career, my soldier's heart is shaken and murmurs from its depths: Thanks, my Country, thanks." He went on to speak of his family, of his loyal men who fell in Castro's murder attempts against him[1] and of the removal of the Marxist physician, Allende.

"The possibilities of Chilean self destruction were evident! The Armed Forces had the duty, in those extreme circumstances, to declare itself."

After these ceremonies the now retired Pinochet took his lifetime seat in the Chilean Senate, of course to be greeted by that chorus of contrived accusations with which the Hemispheric Left (HL) has greeted every attempt, successful or unsuccessful, to oppose Marxist Leninist (ML) takeovers.

Pinochet had led the effort which averted Allende's dash toward the creation of a second Castroite Cuba. But he had also, through his recruitment of Professor Arnold C. Harberger,[2] introduced Chile to the free market and produced the Latin American "economic miracle."[3]

The retiring General Pinochet could well say, "Mission completed."

SALVADOR ALLENDE GOSSENS

A great deal of doubtless highly informative analysis has appeared to enlighten us as to "why" Allende, "the fondest hope of the Kremlin," attained the Chilean presidency. There is, of course, a simple arithmetical reason for Allende's victory (Wkly 2.10). From this the reader may analyze as he chooses.

In 1964 Christian Democrat Party (PDC) candidate Frei Montalvo won the Chilean presidency with 56.09 percent of the vote against the 38.93 percent of the "Marxist physician" and also ran, Allende. Four years later the same Allende won the presidency with a smaller percentage of the vote (36.6 percent) than he had enjoyed in defeat (38.93 percent). The losing PDC candidate, Radomiro Tomic, received only half the percentage of the vote (28.1 percent) which Frei had received; the Independent Jorge Alessandri received the other half (28.1 percent). Therefore, both Allende and his PDC opponent *lost* votes, half of the 1964 PDC votes moving to the Independent.

That Allende was indeed the "fondest hope of the Kremlin" has been attested by no less a figure than Boris N. Ponomarev. Ponomarev had emerged from the Communist International (COMINTERN) when it was allegedly dissolved in 1943. In reality, it was simply moved, as Schapiro[4] has pointed out, from its Gorky Street address to its new home in the International Department (ID), Central Committee, CPSU. Ponomarev was for many years ID chief. As this dapper, moustached, if now deceased, ML pointed out in a *Kommunist* article of 1971,

> Events of major historical significance...the victory of the National Unity Bloc[5] in Chile...lead us to believe that the revolutionary process here is continuing to develop at a pace faster than in other parts of the nonsocialist world...as the Chilean comrades themselves loudly state, its victory is largely the result of the solidarity...The CPSU, as always, is giving practical support to the revolutionary struggle of the Chilean people....

Ponomarev's boss, Soviet Premier Leonid Brezhnev, did him one better. This Soviet "optimist"[6] told the 24th Party Congress:

> The victory of the Popular Unity Forces in Chile was a most important event. There, for the first time in the history of the continent, the people have secured by constitutional means the installation of a government they want and trust.

The Radical Party militant, Gabriel González Videla, was Chilean president from 1946 to 1952, a position he attained through the support of the Chilean Communist Party (PCC). In return for the favor, González was the first hemispheric chief of state, save for Cuba's Batista in 1940, to appoint communists to posts in his cabinet. The point here is that he was hardly of the anti-Left, this rendering his remarks on Allende's removal more meaningful than they might otherwise have been. Videla said that he

> does not have words to thank the armed forces for having liberated us from the Marxist claws...they have saved us and will permit us to live in democracy, inasmuch as the totalitarian apparatus which had been prepared to destroy us has itself been destroyed.[7]

As ex President Frei Montalvo told Falcoff, "...there is no doubt whatever that what was eventually envisaged [by Allende] was a government of a totalitarian type. No doubt whatever."[8] But Allende's objective of transforming Chile into a second Kremlin satrapy has been attested by higher authority than his presidential predecessor, for this Marxist physician himself told Debray,[9] after he was safely ensconced in the La Moneda Palace in 1970, two things worth remarking here.

First of all, Allende declared that the so-called "Statute of Guarantees" of democratic freedoms, which he had concluded with the PDC was but a "tactical necessity."

"The important thing," the Chilean then told the Frenchman, "was to take power."

Which he had done, and which his burgeoning ML "Militias" were beginning to assure while his "official" government began that incremental seizure of power and property as had that of the Cuban ML caudillo over a decade before. And, *inter alia*, those ML neighborhood watch committees, the Committees for the Defense of the Revolution, were springing up[10] as they had in ML Cuba and would in ML Nicaragua.

It will be recalled (pp.57ff, YRBK97)), with regard to Brazil, that the military takeover of 1964 was a counter coup to prevent Jango Goulart's ML coup,[11] not the simplistic putsch which the HL has persuaded many to accept. The case of Chile was much the same. As Ambassador Nathaniel Davis put it,[12]

> ...the generals and admirals did not rush to their task of overthrowing their president...they went to see [Allende] again and again...and asked the president to reconsider his policies and control the extremists. They squirmed, temporized, and

looked for ways out...[the transition] from planning to talk to decision and action was made slowly. It was late...when the armed forces moved collectively beyond the point of no return....

And so Allende was out by his own hand in "the smoking ruins of his own palace." But a disappointed IL was not about to leave the battlefield, and, amidst its wailings and imprecations, continued its campaign for Chile. The campaign was highlighted by a remarkable Soviet-Cuban attempt at Vallenar (Wkly 2.13) which was well described by the now apparently beleaguered Brock.[13] But neither this nor subsequent attempts to deliver Chile to the HL were successful. All of which was respected by the Chileans who, in a 1987 Gallup Poll, declared Pinochet Man of the Year.

SENATOR PINOCHET UGARTE IN ENGLAND
(WKLY 6.17, 29 OCTOBER 1998)

Immortalized by an AFP wirephoto, jubilant MLs, various of them "ex" terrorists, paraded their red banners with the hammer-and-sickle emblems through the streets of Santiago de Chile last week. The reason for their celebration? The man who had prevented them from making another Cuba or another Nicaragua out of their homeland[14] had been arrested in the United Kingdom in what had all the earmarks of another HL DO.[15] And Pinochet had added insult to injury by transforming a Chilean economy which they would have destroyed into the first and, so far, the last Latin American (LA) "economic miracle." These same MLs had tried unsuccessfully for years to murder this now 82-year-old senator for life, and perhaps his imprisonment would finally satisfy their thirst for vengeance. As the murder of Somoza in Asunción by a Sandinista hit squad had satisfied those Nicaraguans.

Pinochet's retirement as commander in chief of the Chilean Armed Forces and assumption of his place in the Chilean Senate as senator-for-life has been treated above (Wkly 5.10). Therein the reason for the HL vendetta against him has been touched upon. Throughout Pinochet's years as head of state and commander in chief the HL has carried on against him, through its scores of collaborating individuals and organizations, the only successful sort of attack it has ever mounted, the DO. It did appear last week that the method might have brought another victory to the HL.

For further information on an oft misrepresented account of Pinochet's accomplishments, LANS is particularly grateful to Editor

Carlos Ball of the Inter American Economic Press Agency (AIPE) for permission to reproduce an article by the former Independent candidate for the Chilean presidency, José Piñera.

PINOCHET: THE HISTORICAL TRUTH

JOSÉ PIÑERA
AIPE
SANTIAGO DE CHILE

The mother of all defamatory remarks that are made about ex President Pinochet is that he overturned the "democratic government" of ex President Allende. This is a monumental historical falsification.

It is true that Salvador Allende was elected in 1970 in a democratic election but with only 36.6 percent of the vote.[16] Nevertheless, it is equally true that his government lost its democratic character, violating the Constitution repeatedly.

In effect, President Allende transformed his government into a tyranny[17] when he violated his solemn oath to respect the Constitution and the Chilean laws. This was not only evident to an immense majority of Chileans in their daily lives but was also established by almost two thirds of the Chamber of Deputies in its momentous Accord of 23 August 1973 and in a parallel decision of the Supreme Court.

In this Accord there were listed the constitutional and legal violations by the Government of President Allende, and it was accorded "to present" this "serious breaking of the constitutional and legal order of the Republic to," among other authorities, "the Armed Forces." This same accord "represented to them that, by virtue of its functions, of the oath of fidelity to the Constitution and to the laws which have been sworn,...corresponds (the duty) to put an immediate end to all the situations of fact described, which infringe the Constitution and the laws."

There not existing in the Chilean Constitution a viable mechanism for removing a president who had lost his democratic character, the Chamber of Deputies, with the vote of all the representatives of the PDC "represented to" the Armed Forces that "it is up to them to put an immediate end" to this grave situation. This was, in fact, an unequivocal call to remove President Allende.

The Armed Forces, led by (the man) who was at that time Commander in Chief of the Army, General Augusto Pinochet, complied with the Accord of the Chamber of Deputies 18 days later, 11 September 1973. Therefore, the origin of the military government is as "democratic" as a revolutionary government (can be) which has no choice but to use force for the removal of a tyrant. And, as Benjamin Franklin well said, "rebellion against a tyrant is obedience to God."

When a president elected by a third of the population was removed, and especially if his government had incited the creation of armed militias, it is inevitable that a state of "civil war" is created. In some countries, conflicts of this nature produced hundreds of thousands of casualties. Thus, for example, the Spanish Civil War had produced a million dead. As did the US Civil War of more than a century ago, wherein it was not clear whether the right of secession of the states in the union existed or not and which resulted in 650,000 dead. In that war the total of the fallen exceeded the numbers in all the US wars of the Twentieth Century.

Although every human life is sacred, it is necessary to reflect on the fact that the Report of the Commission named by the government of President Aylwin[18]—antagonistic to Pinochet—concluded that in the 17-year period of the Pinochet Government around 2000 people died. To those responsible, on both sides, for those who did not fall in combat, all the rigors of the applicable laws should be applied. Indeed, it was precisely by virtue of these laws that the general and ex director of the National Intelligence Directorate is serving a sentence of seven years in prison. But to try to blame some of these incidents on ex President Pinochet is absolutely unjustified. Therefore, his arrest in London has not only overturned the principle of diplomatic immunity, but also constitutes a grave violation of his human rights.

Moreover, the successful economic transformation realized during his government, the transcendental achievement which avoided a war with Argentina and the voluntary transition to a democratic government, the historical truth about his era demands that it be recognized that President Pinochet headed a legitimate rebellion against a tyranny.

[Translated from the Spanish by the LANS Editor]

EUROPE VS. PINOCHET: UNJUST PROCEEDING (A REVIEW)
(SPCL 6.11, 15 OCTOBER 1998)

The action against Chilean Senator Augusto Pinochet Ugarte was initiated in Spain during the fall of 1998 with the rabid support of the IL. To anyone familiar with the DOs which are the lifeblood of this IL, this was clearly one more such trumped up accusation. But this DO was fated to enjoy much more success than it deserved because of the leftwing British Government. This government had been installed at least partially through the bounty of the US Clinton Government in the guise of its "political advisor," Stephanopolous, who guided the Socialist International (SI) militant, Anthony Blair, into the prime minister's office.

The "Marxist physician," Salvador Allende, mouthed the muzzle of the machine gun given to him by the terrorist boss of the HL, Fidel Castro, and pulled the trigger, writing *finis* to his planned communization of Chile. That the attempt by the IL to blame this suicide on the Chilean military is simplistic propaganda has been attested by the last person to see Allende alive, his personal physician, Dr. Patricio Guijón Klein. Also in the La Moneda Presidential Palace at the time of Allende's demise was one Joan Garcés, some times incorrectly "Juan" in English accounts. Garcés was a Spanish marxist and close collaborator of the deceased, and so the Armed Forces shipped him back to Spain.

That was 25 years ago, long enough for the Spaniard, for a while cum Chilean, Garcés, to locate a brother IL member, Baltasar Garzón, later a judge, and create a DO which they intended to use in bringing Senator Pinochet before their kangaroo court. The book under review here is perhaps the first to have discussed this DO with something more realistic than that hand-waving which has characterized much of the press in treating the Pinochet case.

Europa vs. Pinochet: INDEBIDO PROCESO. Hermógenes Pérez de Arce. Editorial El Roble Ltda. Santiago de Chile. 1998. 154 pages. References by chapter. ISBN: 956-7855-00-5. Reviewed by the LANS Editor.

The author, Hermógenes Pérez de Arce Ibieta, is a journalist and an attorney specializing in economic affairs. For some twenty years he has had a bylined weekly column in the Santiago newspaper, *El Mercurio*.

In his Preface the author defines the objective of his book as seeking "to be a defense against the unjust accusations of which he [Pinochet] has been the object." In this effort Pérez de Arce has been successful in reaching a large audience as attested by the rapid rise of his book to Chilean "best seller." In this same Preface he makes a remark which is particularly cogent in the case of the Pinochet DO:

> If the accused had been any private citizen in a moderately civilized country, a *habeas corpus* petition on his behalf would have been rapidly received and he [Pinochet] would have obtained his immediate release.

The author goes on in this Preface to list seven glaring violations of Pinochet's "human rights" (HR) which, had any IL member suffered them, would have evoked howls of anguish and a media *cause célèbre*. Here it need only be remarked that most of them will be encountered again.

Setting the stage for the book amounts to synopsizing the "Pinochet Period," 1973-1990, and the attempt by the IL to wreak "vengeance" (Spcl 6.18) through its prosecution of Pinochet. The first three chapters discuss the realities of Allende's ouster. In Chapter IV the fatuous charge of "genocide" against the Chilean Armed Forces commander is discussed, the following five chapters treating the routine allegations by the MLs relating to casualties, "disappeareds" and so on which are routine to an HL DO.

Genocide

The essential anti-subversive actions of the Military Government are the excuse, not the basis, for the charges of "genocide, terrorism and torture" against Pinochet and 37 others by Spanish Judge Baltasar Garzón. LANS has reported the attempt by the HL to bring such charges, more than a decade after the incident, against the Argentine military. The Argentines were taking back a barracks seized by ML terrorists, and the HR advocates supporting this HL accused them of violating these criminals' HR by not "aiming" precisely enough.

To an attorney such as the author, Pérez de Arce, the "genocide" accusation trumped up by the Garcés-Garzón Duo (GG Duo), was ludicrous on the face of it.[19] Article 2 of the UN Convention for the Prevention and Sanction of the Crime of Genocide was promulgated on 9 December 1948, during the Soviet tyranny of Dzugashvili (aka Stalin).[20] Be this as it may, the Convention defines genocide as those acts "perpetrated with the intention of destroying, totally or partially, a national, ethnic, racial or religious group as such." The author goes on to delineate further the details of the "elimination" as detailed in the Convention.

He then reproduces the charge against Pinochet which the GG Duo created. They allege—with no proof—that Pinochet conceived "a plan previously designed for systematically and selectively eliminating political opponents, segments or sectors of the Chilean national group with the objective of eliminating any ideological discrepancy and 'purifying' the Chilean system of life attacking those who spread socialist or communist [ML] political postures..." The travesty of truth which is this charge is best demonstrated by Pérez de Arce in his Chapter V, "The Casualties of the Confrontation," which will be further discussed below. The conclusion is that neither the total casualties nor the casualties by date indicate any program of genocide.

But in their enthusiasm the GG Duo proceeds to the sublimely ridiculous by accusing Pinochet of genocidal intentions against Chilean Jews and Mapuche Indians. As to the first the Duo claims "The purpose of this action was to achieve the installation of a new order—as Hitler sought in Germany..." Pérez de Arce describes the Chilean Jewish community as "horrified" by these charges. One of Pinochet's ex minister, Sergio Melnick, was of the Chilean Jewish community. He penned an extensive article wherein he pointed out that "Many things can be said of the government of General Pinochet, good and bad, but clearly it cannot be said that it was an anti-Semitic government. It was precisely the opposite!" (*El Mercurio,* 21 Nov 98).

Further testimony is provided by Elimat Y. Jason, president of the Chilean Committee Representing Chilean Jewish Entities. President Jason said that his organization, which represented "that union of the country's Jewish communities and institutions, expresses emphatically to you that in the period in question [during the military regime] Chilean Judaism did not see itself affected by organized anti-Semitic manifestations, was able to develop its religious, cultural and educational work without setback" (*El Mercurio* 22 Nov 98).[21]

As far as "genocide" against the Mapuche Indians is concerned, the author makes the valid point that it would be difficult to reconcile Pinochet "genocide" against these people with the gratitude and honors which they bestowed on him. The General Commission of

Mapuche Chiefs, representing the 300,000 near Cholchol in the south of Chile, that is in the heart of their lands, designated Augusto Pinochet Maximum Conductor and Guide (Ullmen F'ta Lonko). The Commission awarded him a signed parchment stating that this recognition was conferred for his "having concerned himself from the beginning of his presidential mandate that the Mapuche People recover their dignity and receive the social benefits and the propriety of their land which was historically denied to them" (*El Mercurio* 14 Nov 98).

Pérez de Arce provides other examples of the meaningless nature of the GG Duo's unfounded "genocide" charge, only a trivial one possible of repetition here. The Duo asserts as "proof" of genocide the death of four Pehuenches on 12 September 1973 at the hands of police in the Allto Bío Bío zone: "A 'genocide' of four people!"

Casualties

The National Truth and Recociliation Commission was formed in 1990 by now ex President Aylwin, its purpose the analysis of HR violations in the Chile of the Military Government (MG). Its findings were contained in the Rettig Report, so called after the name of the commission chairman who had been an official in the Allende Government. The report was put together "almost exclusively" from testimony by opponents of the MG. Therefore, the bias of this report is anti MG. The casualty figures used by Pérez de Arce are taken from Volume III of this report, these given in the two tables below.

Table I. Casualty Figures by Organization

Socialist Party (PS)	405
Left Revolutionary Movement (MIR)	384
Communist Party (PC)	353
Unitary Peoples Action Movement (MAPU)	24
Manuel Rodríguez Patriotic Front (FPMR)	19
Radical Party	15
Christian Democrats	7
Christian Left	5
National Party	4
Other Parties	15
Without known party affiliation	1,043
TOTAL	2,279

By year the casualty figures are given as follows.

Table II. Casualties by Year

1973	1261	1979	13	1985	50
1974	306	1980	15	1986	50
1975	119	1981	36	1987	34
1976	139	1982	8	1988	27
1977	25	1983	82	1989	26
1978	9	1984	74	1990	2
				TOTAL	2,279

The first and obvious conclusion demanded by these numbers is that there were not many casualties, as opposed to the *impression* for which the IL propaganda strives, with the witting or unwitting assistance of the communications media.[22] The second is that the "genocide" charge by the GG Duo can be dismissed as nonsensical. Otherwise, the first set of numbers is descriptive of the relative importance of the various terrorists groups seeking to seize the government by "force and violence."

Pérez de Arce (Chapter III) uses an interview by Politzer[23] with former PS President Carlos Altimirano in order to arrive at the number of armed terrorists involved by organization, certainly a source with ample anti-MG bias. Altimirano's testimony that the PS had 1000 to 1500 armed terrorists, the MIR 3000 to 5000 and the PC 2000 should therefore be reasonably reliable. MAPU and the Christian Left had about 1000, but they were making themselves scarce.

One final consistency in these numbers is worthy of mention, the jump in casualty figures between 1982 and 1983. Gladys Marín (b. 1942) is the haggard "ex" terrorist boss of the Chilean PC who again has her hat in the ring for next year's presidential election. She has the dubious distinction of having founded the FPMR in the early 1980s. The reader will have no difficulty in discerning from Table II that her terrorist activities were not well underway in 1982 but were in progress by 1983.

And More

A few of the highlights as discussed by Pérez de Arce have been reproduced here. But these can only indicate the value of this book and the wealth of material in its 153 short pages. A word on a DO with which "everyone" is familiar, the Letellier Case, must close this review.

In Chapter IX, "The 'Terrorism' Accusation," the author discusses, *inter alia*, the Letellier killing on 21 September 1976 for which the Pinochet Government was blamed. Therein the most telling testimony as to Pinochet's innocence was provided by the dead man's son, Juan Pablo Letellier:[24]

> ...[as] I have said time and again ... there is no evidence which has flowed from the thousands of sheets of testimony which allows one to maintain that there was participation of the Army or its Commander in Chief in the assassination of Orlando Letellier. (*El Mercurio* 4 Jun 95)

A MYTH OF REVENGE

JUAN DE DIOS VIAL LARRAÍN
FORMER PRESIDENT
CATHOLIC UNIVERSITY OF CHILE
SANTIAGO
(SPCL 6.18, 24 DECEMBER 1998)

EDITOR'S INTRODUCTION

This article appeared in Spanish in *Diario La Segunda* in Spanish. It is reproduced here in an English translation for which LANS expresses deep appreciation to the Chilean Reconciliation Movement.

* * *

Nothing will be understood about what is happening to Pinochet if nothing is known about the myth surrounding him and the how and why of it coming to pass. It should be called the myth of revenge. What happened in Chile in the seventies was a prelude to another great happening to come later—the fall of the Berlin Wall. This fall buried an ideology that had fed humanity for half a century. But when such an ideological cavity appears, where everything one believed in is buried, the wound in the soul is such that it may never close. The shadows of this pain and this absence grow ominously, and amongst other things, weave a myth.

I believe that, historically, Chile has been a country on alert. The Communist Party in Chile arose at the time of the Russian Revolution and is a contemporary of Lenin's. In the forties it had several ministers in government unlike anywhere else. The Christian political ideology preached by Maritain became government in Chile in the sixties, again unlike anywhere else. At the point in time of maximum Marxist political expansion, the ideology was preparing to emerge in human form, that is, not storming into power but grabbing it from democracy in closing its pincers on Latin America. It was precisely then in Chile where Marxism demonstrated its complete inability to govern, its complete political ineptitude and the violence that it carried in its veins. Marxism failed thunderously in Chile whilst dominating the world.

Picture the following circumstances—a prostrated nation: economically on the verge of bankruptcy; militarily threatened by its neighbors; socially on the brink of a civil war encouraged by Joan Garcés, an Allende advisor (in a delirious gesture of a young Paris intellectual who has forgotten the million dead in his own homeland)—and epitomized by Castro's symbolic presentation of a machine gun to Allende. It was under these circumstances that a large national majority backed the rising of the Armed Forces.

The task that the Armed Forces took on was extremely difficult. But there were three politically essential things of which Pinochet had an extremely clear vision. First, that he had defied and badly wounded an enormous international power: the ideology that strangled all consciences; the military powers loyal to Lenin that covered the greater part of the globe; the power that had decisively infiltrated its ideology into the global media. He understood that his fight was against Marxism.

It was then immediately clear to him that he could not get out of this swamp by established political means and that he would be required to exercise a power that the ancient Romans had institutionalized. This was not the tyranny of one man, but a power exercised with notable efficiency by the Armed Forces especially in selecting their collaborators. This efficiency was largely due to the fact that the power was not exercised for someone's benefit, but was used as a means of national salvation, and put into action by an institution which, in our context, could well be deemed glorious.

Finally, he understood that the task could not be improvised, could not be negotiated and would require a long adjustment period that would allow the consolidation of an economic regime and a political Constitution.

The battle fought was minimal, fundamentally because in its inception, the rising enjoyed total support. Its costs, always painful, were very low in comparison to analogous situations. Remember Russia and Spain, and in Latin America: Nicaragua; Guatemala; Colombia; Peru; Argentina; Uruguay, with their internal guerrillas and subsequent repression.

But there were two mistakes committed by the military government. The first was due to naiveté and the second to clumsiness. The first was to ignore the sinister reaction of the power that had been hurt and that rose beyond its frontiers. This same power is the one that is showing itself in all its spite, not only against Pinochet, but against Chile, that small and remote country that was maybe the first to dare not let that power get its own way. The country that is not even given the courtesy to be heard by the gentlemen of the law. "Human Rights" will be the grand name for revenge.

The second error was exile, in most cases unjust, which enveloped an important portion of the Chileans in an atmosphere of hate abroad and which forced him to live in a climate where he suffered from the uprooting but in which he also benefited. But these people came back to the country and have greatly contributed in a spirit of reconciliation to the continuity of the works of the Pinochet Government. It is a spirit of reconciliation, only unknown to those who live in the old way, notably those who saw Stalin as a father and Lenin as a prophet.

That the action against Pinochet is revenge is clearly demonstrated by one thing: Revenge always dresses nobly. Here it is clothed in its guise of "Human Rights." What a lovely theory is that which is now upheld even by people who hadn't believed in anything but the rule of force, the will of power or in the pure positive force of the law. Now they maintain that there are rights which are above all positive and territorial laws, and that protect that same humanity of mankind! Bravo! That is a natural right, that is justice. But is justice, is that right which is above the law, that which Garzón (a frustrated politician with a desire for stardom) is acting as an agent for? Are not justice and a man's essential rights being ridiculed when these are associated with an act of revenge, exercised by a judge of marked political orientation, acting on a petition that has been faxed by the president of the Communist Party of Chile to a government noted for its hostility to the person hounded?

Are the continents and nations where Stalin murdered millions, where Hitler murdered millions, where over a million Spaniards killed each other, where the English have murdered in Ireland, where Milosevic orders women and children killed to obtain ethnic purity and is then received in Paris, where Castro, who has violated human rights in Cuba, is decorated in Madrid; are these continents and nations the rightful judges on human rights, torture or genocide? Are these the agents of a superior justice? This ridicules justice and rights. It is a step back to revenge exercised by anyone against anyone for anyone.

Faced with myth and revenge we are possibly very weak. But we have one strength in our favor: justice. Not a charade with that name, but an effective social process which is reconciliation, penal sanctions, amnesty and mutual forgiveness amongst men of good faith.

THE PINOCHET CASE
(WKLY 6.21, 26 NOVEMBER 1998)

Those military personnel, who have done their duties in opposing the terrorists attacks against their countries, all supported by the HL — in Argentina (pp.159ff, YRBK97), Bolivia (Spcl 4.12), Brazil (pp.57ff, YRBK97; Dulles[25]), etc. –, appear never to have realized the continuity of the relentless HL war, fed by the endemic hatred of the MLs for their societies. It appears that, therefore, the military of all these nations failed to appreciate the absolute necessity for closely and continually monitoring the stream of distorted and fabricated information which issued from the Leninist adherence of these terrorists to the lie as a primary weapon. The facts of the DO Pinochet to this point are as follows.

In 1997 two leftist Spanish judges opened "investigations" of the alleged HR abuses by anti-ML regimes in Chile and Argentina. Neither judge conducted on-sight probes in either country or, as LANS Associate Editor James Whelan points out, did anything "beyond cribbing" from existing investigations in the two nations. In initiating these bizarre "legal" proceedings, both acted under the urging of Spain's Communist-led United Left coalition.

The "genocide" charges which this pair produced were the demonstrably nonsensical ones already discussed (Spcl 6.11 above). Indeed, one of the judges, Manuel Garca-Castellon, even removed himself from the process in September 1998 with the remark that "I must have very solid evidence. I do not have it." When Garca Castellon threw up his hands, the militant Baltasar Garzón enthusiastically took up the trumped-up charges by default. It is particularly important to remark here that the Spanish attorney general argued against these judges' behavior and, at the time Garzón issued his arrest "warrant" for Pinochet, he had not yet received a reply from the Criminal Division of Spain's Audiencia as to whether he had jurisdiction. Even had the charges not been the trivial contrived ones, the legality of the entire proceeding was open to serious question. Which is the point at which the simple DO nature of this action became even more evident.

At this point Pinochet made his sixth visit to England of recent years. And the notorious "HR" organization, Amnesty International (AI), tipped off Garzón that the senator had arrived there. Garzón hurriedly, and illegally, began to spring his trap with what would be the obvious collusion of the British.

The retired general was operated on 8 October. By Thursday, 15 October, a leftist European press had enthusiastically spread the word of the Spanish judge's intentions, but the Chilean's party, lulled by their belief in British law, was not particularly concerned. Even so, Chilean Ambassador Mario Artaza informed the British Foreign Ministry that Pinochet would depart for Chile on Tuesday, 20 October, the Chileans being assured that there would be no problem. Clearly aware of this, Garzon increased the rapidity of his plotting with the collusion of the British Government.

With no approval from the Audiencia the leftist Garzón hurried off his "arrest order" to Britain on Friday, 17 October. And the midnight, Gestapo-like arrest of the ailing Pinochet took place. On 28 October Britain's High Court unanimously overturned the arrest order, but this was only a momentary setback for the plotters, those in the British Government and AI now joined by others in the notorious Human Rights Watch. By 25 November, Pinochet's 83rd birthday, the case had been appealed to the Law Lords, and a three to two decision against the former chief of state handed down. The deciding vote, that of South African Lord Stanley Hoffman, was cast with no consideration of charges or "evidence," merely a statement that he supported a colleague. The last move for 1998 had effectively been made.

Collusion Between Spain and Britain

The British Government's activities against Pinochet were either the work or under the direction, of the lifelong leftist, Interior Minister Jack Straw who had been under MI5 observation during the 1960s and 1970s. These activities could assuredly be described as hand-in-glove with Garzón's court.

Pinochet's attorneys had soon discovered how defective was the warrant which the Spanish judge had hurried to Straw's ministry. The British Government found this out at about the same time, and its subsequent behavior in hurrying the document back to Garzón for "correction" is worthy of being described as "collusion." Nor is Straw to be removed from the process of appeal to the Law Lords.

No sooner had Lord Chief Justice Bingham ordered the release of Pinochet and the payment of $600,000 to him in legal costs than the Crown Prosecution Service, representing Spain, appealed to the Law Lords and won. About that time a Santiago tabloid revealed that Lord Hoffmann, the swing voter who did not bother with details, was married to a woman who had been a ranking official of AI for 25 years. The noble lord himself, it was discovered, headed the fund-raising arm of that dubious organization.

Which led to a reversal of the earlier decision and the scheduling of a January 1999 rehearing of the "case."

Collusion Among the US, Spain and the United Kingdom

The Pinochet DO is clearly a cooperative effort by certain forces in the Clinton Government of the US, the Madrid Court of Baltasar Garzón and the Blair Government of the UK, although it is apparently true that the attempts by the US have not been particularly helpful to Baltasar's non-case. The impression is given that the Clinton Government did what it could to assist but provided little if anything useful.

That there was something more than mere "good relations" between the Clinton Government, and the Spanish court is indicated by the scope and extent of the documentation which has been furnished to the latter by the former. EFE reported on 28 October 1998 that Garzón and his associate at that time, Garca-Castillon, "requested in February and July 1997 US support" in its attempted prosecution of Pinochet. The extent of the reaction by the Clinton Government spoke eloquently to its motivation. US Justice Department spokesman, James Rubin, stated that "hundreds of documents" had been turned over to Garzón in "almost a year." Perhaps even more interesting, "some of the documents ... were secret and were declassified..." Whether this report is precise, it is true in its general outlines. Which leads to a question which LANS has been unable as yet to answer.

These documents are available from the US Government only through a Freedom of Information Act (FOIA) request of the Justice Department. FOIA documents usually contain considerable blacked-out material. This blacking out can be used to eliminate material which might compromise continuing US intel operations or it can be artistically used to change the content of the material in the report. Not of course that anyone in the Clinton Government would do such a thing. But that such behavior is not beyond the realm of speculation is indicated by various considerations.

The Government of Pres. W. J. Clinton has alleged connections with the IL, both through Mr. Clinton and through certain members of his government. The allegations referring to Mr. Clinton's record during the Vietnam War, his travels to the USSR, and so on, are in insufficient detail to be of use here. As are the reports which LANS has received of certain ranking Clinton Administration figures who were connected with the Venceremos Brigades and even that ML terrorist foreign legion so active in Chile before the Allende removal, Left Revolutionary Movement (MIR). But from the LANS coverage of Mr. Clinton's sojourn in 1997 Argentina, a more specific indication of the reason for the apparent collaboration may be gleaned.

Mr. Clinton appears to "believe," or feels it beneficial to his political objectives to avow belief, that the ML position on military opposition to HL terrorist activities in the LA countries is the correct one. As described in Spcl 4.11, Mr. Clinton's trip to Argentina in October 1997 included a meeting with a cozy circle of apparently admiring reporters in one of his hotel rooms, these being Julia Cass of *The Buenos Aires Herald*, Roberto Guareschi of *Clarín*, Germán Sopeña of *La Nación* and Nelson Castro of Radio del Plata. In reply to a question by Mr. Sopeña, Mr. Clinton held forth on the reason behind the change for the better in US-Argentine relations.

"Most recently, the most important change is that Argentina withdrew from the military governments *which repressed and assassinated people* (emphasis added) toward a democracy under President Menem ...," Mr. Clinton declared, thus clearly misrepresenting the military actions in that nation and taking a position in complete support of the continuing anti-military DOs in LA. In this position he was strongly supported by Mrs. Clinton who, meeting with Rosa Roisinblit of Grandmothers of the Plaza of May (APM), accepted the "30,000 disappeareds" which the APM was claiming (pp.145ff, YRBK98)). Among the "shadows cast by the trip of Pres. Clinton" (pp.150ff, YRBK98) as reported by the LANS correspondent in Buenos Aires, this meeting with the stereotypical leftist was one of the longer ones. For purposes of this discussion, it was assuredly relevant to US support of the HL position.

Judge Garzón is "socialist," presumably a member of the Socialist International (SI) which, as has frequently been remarked here, is the lineal descendant of Heinrich Karl Marx's First International. As Ramón Díaz (*Diario las Américas* 17 Oct 98) has pointed out, it was only in 1995 that British Prime Minister Blair, also a SI stalwart, was able to have the "adhesion to marxism, contained in the Organic Charter" of the SI suppressed. Whether Mr. Blair did this for public relations or philosophical reasons may be argued, but various militants of this same SI continue to be prominent in the defense of the MLs and in the support of their DOs. This of course goes to motivation which is difficult to determine precisely. But Mr. Garzón's phraseology and material appears to come straight from the HL handbook.

The third element in the Pinochet DO Triumvirate (US-Spain-Britain) is of course the Blair Government. In addition to Blair's relations with the Spanish socialists through the SI, Mr. Clinton has remarked on several occasions that Mr. Blair is his "good friend." Clinton's allegedly former staff member, Stephanopoulos, handled—or was important to—Mr. Blair's reelection campaign, an activity which would have been unlikely if it had not met with Mr. Clinton's approval.

Daniel Ortega Saavedra

The ML tyranny in Nicaragua was initiated in 1979 when the Sandinista National Liberation Front (FSLN) occupied the power vacuum which had been created there (Chapter 4). Rule was by a Politburo (Nine Commanders, National Directorate) wherein all were equal, save that the Ortega brothers were "more equal" than the other seven (Roger Miranda and William Ratliff, *The Civil War in Nicaragua, Inside the Sandinistas*, Transaction, 1993. ISBN: 1-56000-064-

3). Daniel was more equal as *de facto* head of state, Humberto as head of the party army, the Sandinista Peoples Army (EPS). Miranda (*ibid*), who, as an aide to Humberto, should know, feels that the first presidential "election" (1984) was put off these five years to assure that the Ortega supremacy was maintained. As it was, not simply through the end of Daniel's presidential term (1990), but thereafter through his iron grip on the party.

The so-called Protocols of Transition essentially allowed the Oretegas to maintain their control of the nation by "governing from below" (1YRBK97) after the strange administration of Doña Violeta de Chamorro allegedly replaced that of Daniel Ortega. Daniel, although refusing to admit it, lost the second "democratic" election in 1996 (1YRBK97) then began a raucous and continuing campaign, replete with threats "to take up arms again" against the Alemán Government. The campaign continued through 1998, enlivened with charges from Ortega's adopted daughter, a militant Sandinista, of Daniel allegedly long-lasting and continuous sexual abuses. As seems "normal" in such circumstances, this does not appear to have had any effect on the alleged molester's iron grip on the FSLN.

ATLANTIC COAST ELECTIONS IN NICARAGUA, 1 MARCH 1998
(WKLY 5.9, 5 MARCH 1998)

ADOPTED DAUGHTERS AND SEXUAL ASSAULT

Practicing Marxist-Leninists once professed militant atheism although, with the advent of Liberation Theology (LibTheo),[26] such no longer remained a rigorous requirement. In the case of Daniel Ortega Saavedra, an ML allegedly "found God" during his 1996 presidential election campaign. In early October of that year Tomás Borge told Nicaraguan television that Daniel "now believes in God." He had become a God-fearing free marketeer in cowboy trousers and white shirt with a proclivity for throwing white flowers in the air. This transmogrification was apparently typified at the Ocotal rally of that fall by the slogan *"Después de Dios, Daniel Ortega"* (After God, Daniel Ortega) which appeared on a blanket. How real was the tranformation?

Rosario Murillo is the consort of Daniel Ortega who had several children by one Jorge Narvaez, now deceased. Ortega is alleged to have adopted these children, one of whom is known as Zoilamérica

Ortega, a young lady now 30 years old. Ms. Ortega recently published an open letter which accuses her adoptive father of sexually abusing her, apparently over a period of time. Various pundits have claimed that this could result in Daniel losing (1) his seat in the National Assembly, (2) his place on the Sandinista Directorate and (3) his chance at another presidential run in 2002. The letter follows:

Monday, 2 March 1998

Dear Friends:

I write this for those who with their company, esteem and solidarity accompany me daily, not only in my activities in the professional and political fields but in my personal life. I do it with full confidence that the things which have brought us together are going to leave us equally close.

In some form I have shared with you my reflections and my decisions concerning facts and situations of my life which, although individual, go beyond the realm of the personal, involving aspects of principles and ethical values which can impinge on multiple aspects of the national life.

The process through which I have passed has been neither short nor easy. Although I have counted on the esteem and healthy advice of my good friends, the decisions are, in the final analysis, mine alone. I have profoundly reflected on and analyzed all that I have implicitly encountered, the possible derivatives thereof, the human, political and ideological effects which I could cause. As a consequence, the implications are of a strictly individual form.

Tomorrow, Tuesday, I begin a new stage of my life, which I hope also to share with you. Perhaps the most important aspect of this relates to my recovering my name with everything which that means.

On the one hand, I am abandoning use of the name Ortega, which does not belong to me and with which, for ethical reasons, I do not identify. Since eleven years ago I was repeatedly assaulted sexually for many years, by one who, in spite of his position as father of the family, abused his power, sowed in me (then a child) fear and uncertainty and emotionally affected the development of my childhood and my adolescence. To overcome the effects of that prolonged aggression, with the embarrassment, threat, pressure and blackmail which have accompanied it, has not been easy.

On the other hand, I assert my right to be the master of my own future as I have not been of my own past. I demand my right as a citizen, as a woman and as a militant Sandinista to proceed according to the dictates of my own conscience. In my human condition, I have lived through an internal process of healing wounds, which permit me to pass from sadness, fear and impotence, toward dignity, faith and strength. I am raising my view today toward the future, definitely a future of love and promise.

[The remainder to include the signature is omitted. Translated by the Editor, LANS]

THE CHAOS CONTINUES IN NICARAGUA
(WKLY 5.20, 28 MAY 1998)

In spite of his widely-publicized peccadillos with his adopted daughter, Zoilamérica Ortega (Wkly 5.9 above), Daniel Ortega Saavedra remains the boss of the FSLN and hence the source of most of the chaos that is Nicaragua. One powerful force for continuing disorder is the fact that what is now called the Nicaraguan Army is little more than a private Sandinista army which is essentially unaccountable to the civilian government.

Although there have been two "free elections" (pp.28ff,YRBK97) in that benighted land, Pres. Alemán has been unable even to abolish the effects of the "piñata." This is the Sandinista program whereby properties, personal and commercial, were "liberated" from their owners by the Sandins and distributed to themselves and their cronies. Although since 1990 two "freely elected" National Assemblies have sought to do away with the piñata, returning the properties to their rightful owners, that effort has been only partially successful. In latter April 1998 the Nicaraguan Supreme Court ordered the National Commission on the Revision of Confiscations (CNRC) to cease the return of the "liberated" properties to their owners. Two weeks later the generally rabid Sandin chieftain, Bayardo Arce Castaño, declared that "Sandinism is proud of the piñata," and, if returned to power in 2002, will introduce a new one.

The Andrés Castro United Front (FUAC) was an armed band of some 500 ex Sandinista military who operated in northern Nicaragua during the four years before 1998. As has been routine with such outlaw bands, they signed a "demobilization" accord with the government on 4 December 1997 wherein they were promised land, technical assistance and credit in exchange for "peacefulness." At the time this was felt to be the "last" such armed band operating in the country. Then in January 1998 some 80 men, allegedly of FUAC, invaded fincas in Matagalpa Department, supposedly in order to pressure the government to live up to its promises.

Some were reported not quite demobilized by 10 May. *La Prensa* (Managua) reported that the discovery of two human heads stuck on the ends of sharpened sticks "caused profound agitation in the country." As well it might. The heads belonged to two FUAC members, Nerio José Jarquín Torres and Servando Cantillano Sevilla. It would not appear that the Nicaraguan landscape has yet assumed a "peaceful" aspect.

DANIEL ORTEGA, MAXIMUM LEADER OF SANDINISM
(SPCL 5.20, 20 JUNE 1998)

Incestuous behavior, whether within the framework of consanguinity or affinity, would hardly be of any interest here save in those cases where the political implications loom large. But here the individual accused of incestuous behavior is the ML boss of the Nicaraguan FSLN and commuting HL luminary, Daniel Ortega Saavedra, so that a certain amount of attention must be paid to this distasteful episode. For the FSLN, whether the "first" or "second" political force, has made a complete mockery of the much touted "democracy," which is supposed to have come to Nicaragua with the election of Doña Violeta Chamorro in 1990, with its continuous and almost total war against the "government" of that benighted nation. War was re-declared by Ortega after his party lost—if narrowly in the Congress—the second such elections in 1996 (pp.101ff, YRBK 98).

"We are going to have a Sandinista Front battling in the streets, I see no other alternative," Ortega declared (AFP 1 Jan 98) with the New Year. He was allegedly fomenting this to "protest" the "outrages" (*atropellos*) being perpetrated by the Alemán Government. In a letter which he sent soon after to his boss in the HL, Fidel Castro, Ortega essentially defined the "outrages" with "socialism continues to be the unique option and alternative path in order that they (the people) can attain justice, liberty and democracy as Cuba has demonstrated" (AFP 7 Jan 98). With such a bizarre mindset, it is small wonder that this ML has been able to keep his native Nicaragua in a chaotic state which has prevented it from emerging from the economic devastation of his regime.

Nor has Ortega's slowed his destructive campaign to prevent the Alemán Government from doing anything to bring Nicaragua out of the economic collapse which his, the Sandinista, government brought about. By early June 1998 the FSLN boss in the Nicaraguan National Assembly, Victor Hugo Tinoco, had established an alliance which had shut down the Assembly (AFP 4 Jun 98). Since only 36 legislators—34 from Alemán's Liberal Alliance and two minority— could be mustered in the chamber, the legislative body lacked a quorum, and the session had to be suspended.

Said Tinoco in ML-speak, acting as mouthpiece for Daniel Ortega, "we are not going to make a quorum until it is agreed to discuss a new legislative agenda of a social character which benefits the people." What amounted to a diatribe against any attempts to bring Nicaragua out of its Sandin-created economic malaise could have been written by Castro and originally was. The FSLN, indeed, the HL theory is clear enough: Create enough chaos, and a benumbed populace will eventually turn to you.

The Nicaraguan legislature was shut down for about a month (AFP 11 Jun 98), only to open with a new quorum cobbled up largely by the Sandins who appear to have remained in a rigid bloc, minority parties and "dissidents" from the Liberal Alliance. How many such "dissidents" there may be is not clear, but the most important one is clearly Eliseo Núñez, ex chief of the Liberal parliamentary bloc. LANS has described (p.30, YRBK97) how Antonio Lacayo bribed a Center Group (GC) out of the United Nicaraguan Opposition (UNO) in order to hand over the Assembly to the FSLN during the Chamorro regime. Unfortunately, there is no Toño Ybarra available to testify in the present case.

The question here is: Will he be able to maintain his iron-fisted control of the FSLN—and perhaps even the legislature — in the face of the incest charges? So far the answer is yes.

Zoilamérica Narváez (Ortega)

Zoilamérica is the daughter of Daniel Ortega's consort, Rosario Murillo, and Jorge Narváez (deceased); she and several other of Ms. Murillo's children were adopted by Ortega. On 2 March 1998 Zoilamérica released a letter which has been largely reproduced in Wkly 5.9 above. In this letter she stated, *inter alia*, "I am abandoning use of the name Ortega ...Since eleven years of age I was repeatedly assaulted sexually..." by her stepfather, Daniel Ortega.

Since this original announcement a number of interesting, and apparently related, events have taken place; the evidence indicating Ortega's guilt appears to mounting, although the testimony taken until quite recently has largely been that of the plaintiff, Zoilamérica. The FSLN boss has replied to the charges by describing them as nothing more than "a campaign of defamation and a conspiracy" against him and his family (EFE 17 Jun 98). He has, however, so far refused to testify, basing his refusal on his "immunity" as a deputy in the National Congress. Meanwhile, Ms. Narváez has taken her charges to court, where they have been considerably amplified, having failed to receive any substantial support anywhere else.

One week after releasing her letter of 2 May she made a further declaration to the review, *Confidencial*, on her charges (AFP 11 Mar 98) wherein she stated that "His (Ortega's) obligation to recognize the injustice and abuse of power in the sexual aggression committed against me since 1978"—she would later state in her deposition that "(he) first violated me in 1982" (AFP 27 May)—"at the age of 11, until 1990; and the harassment all the years of my marriage until January of 1998." She told the same periodical that she had revealed the situation to a member of the Sandin National Directorate (Politburo) who had listened to her "with much humanitarianism," the last time she had approached the Directorate being December 1997.

At that time there was a member of the Politburo, Victor Tirado López (aka El Mejicano), who called upon Ortega to withdraw from his campaign for "reelection" at the upcoming FSLN Congress (DNN[27] 20 May 98). At the same time López told DNN that he "doesn't believe he can be reelected" to the Politburo. (López was wrong.) Ortega was reelected at the FSLN Congress which took place on 24 May 1998, his "delaying tactic" *modus operandi* having proved quite successful to this point.

Henry Petrie is vice secretary of the FSLN Managua Departmental Committee; William Rodríguez is leader of the Sandinista Youth. Both came out in support of Ms. Narváez, and both were forced to leave a Sandin assembly on 4 March which was considering a "declaration of respect" for Daniel Ortega (EFE 8 Mar 98). On 9 March Sandin Deputy Xanthis Suárez, who was supporting Zoilamérica, announced that she had been receiving telephone threats that she would be "taken care of" (AFP 10 Mar 98). Xanthis has apparently not been "taken care of," but the psychologist, Douglas Guerrero, may have been. *La Prensa* (Managua) has reported that Guerrero's death could have Ms. Narváez's charges as "background" (*trasfondo*), reporting that Guerrero had offered psychological assistance to Narváez for some time. Police authorities reportedly formulated the hypothesis that the murder "is a warning to those who know (too) much about the relation that could have joined Ortega to his adoptive daughter." If it was not a warning, early April 1998 would have been a most opportune time for the "satanists" to have carved him up.

Zoilamérica would claim that various Sandins were aware of what was going on, but, not surprisingly, they have hardly come forward.

But the US "writer and photographer" (EFE 19 Apr 98), Margaret Randall, distributed an open letter in which this staunch ML resident of Nicaragua from 1980 to 1984 declared that she knew what was happening but kept silent because of her interest "in supporting the Sandinista revolution."

Some two weeks after her original denunciation, *La Prensa* reported that Zoilamérica had engaged a staff of attorneys to bring charges against Ortega in the courts for the crimes of illegitimate seduction, sexual harassment, incest and violation. Later that month she moved out of the "liberated" home which the Sandin boss had bestowed on her. The following week she and her attorneys—Nelba Blandón and Guadalupe Salinas—held a press conference asking Ortega to come out from behind his parliamentary immunity and stop "intimidating, provoking and pressuring" those who stood by her (EFE 21 Mar). Come out from behind his immunity Daniel did not.

Allegedly for these reasons, Ms. Narváez and her attorneys announced that they were going before the courts (EFE 2 Apr) and then did so (AFP 27,28 May; EFE 29 May). The result was a 40-page document recording her testimony on "kinky" sexual encounters, apparently forced upon her by Ortega. The prurient details need not be repeated here; perhaps most importantly, she names various "comrades" of the FSLN boss who were aware of the situation and who, if they do not possess Ortega's "parliamentary immunity," could be brought in to testify.[28] If Zoilamérica's testimony is not true, it certainly has the quality of a very elaborate hoax.

During all this Daniel Ortega rumbles occasionally of "vast conspiracies" of which he claims to be a victim while remaining ensconced behind his "immunity." The case was assigned to Judge Marta Lorena Quezada Saldaña of the Managua Criminal Court. Still with lips sealed, save to mouth "conspiracy," a wirephoto (AFP 17 Jun) shows Ortega handing Judge Quezada a document from the Supreme Electoral Commission (CSE) which claims that the ML has immunity. Judge Quezada subsequently declared her court to be "totally paralyzed" and therefore is forwarding the matter to the National Assembly for resolution. From the discussion above, it appears that this august body will support Ortega immunity.

In the unlikely event of this matter moving against the FSLN chief, perhaps a lengthier repetition of his recent Cuba trip (DNN 3 Jun) can be anticipated.

The Rebel Armed Forces (FAR): Another Arm of Ortega's Sandinistas

This group of rearmed Sandinistas has been called the Revolutionary Armed Forces by AFP and the Revolutionary Armed Front by EFE, neither of which is precisely correct. Professor Zelaya Blanco[29] has described FAR to LANS as made up of two Sandin groups, the Ramón Raudales Northern Front (FNRR) and the Andrés Castro United Front.

Carlos Fonseca and Ramón Raudales

Carlos Fonseca Amador (b. Matagalpa 1936) was the illegitimate and rejected son of Somoza Debayle's financial manager, Fausto Amador, and the founder of the FSLN terrorists (1961). His mortal remains do not lie beneath the "eternal flame" burning on the hill behind the Intercontinental Hotel in Managua. As the LANS Editor learned in the 1980s from individuals related to Fonseca, he lies in an unmarked grave in a Managua cemetery. One of the ways his somewhat the worse-for-wear cadaver was identified was by the entry and exit wounds from a bullet taken at El Chaparral, a wound from which he of course recovered in Cuba.

Castro had scarcely occupied the Cuban power vacuum before the "legend in his own mind," Ernesto Guevara, began sending groups of his motley MLs on *opera bouffe* "invasions" of Nicaragua. One of these, a 50-man force commanded by a former Nicaraguan National Guard lieutenant, was rounded up by the Honduran Army at El Chaparral before reaching the border. In the rounding-up Fonseca took a round through the lungs while one Ramón Raudales was killed. Whoever put together the FNRR apparently felt this epic enough to name the FNRR after him.

In Wkly 5.20 above FUAC, a relatively new Nicaraguan terrorist group, has been discussed, this done largely as an example of the chaos which FSLN rule and subsequent hi jinks have fostered on that nation. In early May the proliferation of such groups was highlighted by the pleas of Bishop Leopold Brenes (Matagalpa) to the Government of President Alemán that it "once and for all" put an end to the violence, "the campesino population is unprotected in the presence of these rearmed (personnel)." Among the groups which the bishop and others mentioned as guilty of "numerous crimes" was FAR (AFP 12 May 98).

Reminiscent of the Peruvian Sendero Luminoso terrorists, FAR, called an "armed strike" to last until 24 May (EFE 20 May 98), threatening to burn "any vehicles which did not comply." The police and military huffed and puffed and apparently did little else. Or at least the Músun Transportation Cooperative (COTRAMUSIN) did not think that they would, for it kept its vehicles in their barns. Why COTRAMUSIN may have acted wisely had been discussed by Zelaya Blanco (*Diario las Américas* 22 May 98).

"But the members of FUAC and FNRR," said Zelaya, "composed of Sandin henchmen deeply involved with the commission of all sorts of crimes...have made successive demobilizations a lucrative business, obtaining payment for each rifle and amnesty, always waiting to reinitiate their huge criminal careers in agreement with the interest of the Sandin National Directorate" of which Daniel Ortega is boss.

Antonio Ybarra Rojas was Nicaraguan Vice Minister of the Presidency from 1990 to 1992 in what Cardinal Obando y Bravo called the Chamorro-Sandin "co-government." The Minister was, of course Doña Violeta'a son-in-law, Antonio Lacayo. In the LANS files there is a copy of the Ybarra deposition which was taken in Cochabamba, Bolivia, from 18 Feb to 9 Mar 1993. Supporting testimony for this deposition was obtained by the LANS Editor in Managua not long after. While this deposition is hardly the sole source of information on Sandinista narcotrafficking activities, there is probably more detail there than elsewhere. Prof. Zelaya goes on: "In order to sabotage government efforts" by the Alemán Government "the czars of such criminal organizations, in common accord with the Sandin National Directorate, decided to reactivate its rearmed groups...."

"The appearance of the rearmed Sandins is a recurrent phenomenon." Zelaya went on. "The object is to guarantee control of the routes used by the narcotraffickers ... All of which forms part of a perverse conspiracy among Sandins and drug capos."

William Jefferson Clinton

Mr. W. J. Clinton of Arkansas was elected to the US presidency by a plurality in 1992 and entered the Presidential Palace as 65th president of the US in 1993. His unusual career, both before and after inauguration is of no interest here save as it impinges on Latin

American affairs. His remarkable progressions through various portions of LA, the curious behavior of his ambassadors and his apparently duplicitous policy toward Castroite Cuba have been discussed (pp.117ff, YRBK98).

A *New York Times* (Spanish) article greeted Mr. Clinton's arrival in Caracas, Venezuela, with "Bill Clinton will practice campaign diplomacy during a period of seven days...," a remark which the LANS coverage of his peregrinations through South America proved to be prophetic. This "campaign diplomacy" can probably be taken as another facet of what various Latin Americans have described to LANS as the "new Yankee Imperialism." In what follows, this appears to be borne out as does the fact that he has apparently won the heart, or at least the lips, of the hemisphere's top ML terrorist, Fidel Ruz Castro.

US PRESIDENT CLINTON IN CHILE
(SPCL 5.13, 22 APRIL 1998)

US President William Clinton arrived on the morning of Thursday, 16 April 1998, in Santiago, Chile, aboard Air Force One. He was accompanied by certain cabinet members to include State Secretary Albright and Mrs. Hilary Clinton. Air Force One is a Boeing 747 specially modified to transport the US president, his direct advisors and a Secret Service security guard. The over $200 million aircraft has, inter alia, 85 satellite serving telephones and 1000 m^2 of deck space containing a conference room, a kitchen, separate quarters for Mr. and Mrs. Clinton and special work areas.

The traveling aerial cavalcade appears to have been somewhat smaller than the one which accompanied Mr. Clinton last fall in his tour of South America, but it was still sizable. The C-5 Galaxy, carrying many of the accouterments which accompany him, arrived on Tuesday, 14 April. It carried six helicopters, three limousines and an array of armored vehicles which should have been enough to render his travel about the Chilean capital comfortable and secure.

El Mercurio (Santiago) reported that "One of the huge commotions which the Clinton visit has caused is the gigantic security arrangements which have descended on Chile, considered one of the most vast which can be recalled." Insofar as security is concerned, something like 120 personnel had arrived to assure this, some of them undercover personnel who had been in Chile for over a month. Officially, of course, the Chilean police were primarily responsible for Mr. Clinton's safety.

With the US president's arrival on 16 April the complex security systems, allegedly intended for all hemispheric heads of state, were put into effect. As Police Commander Manuel Castillo pointed out, security perimeters were established around the presidential (1) Palace of La Moneda where, inter alia, the summit would open, about the (2) Hyatt Hotel where the Clintons resided, (3) the Sheraton Hotel, (4) the former National Congress where the summit would close and the (5) Mapocho Station where the foreign ministers, considerably lower in the pecking order, were to arrive. Perimeter (2) was established at 0600 on 16 April, perimeter (3) not until 0700 on 18 April. Perimeters popped up here and there depending on where the host (*anfitrion*) of the 1994 CLA happened to be.

Apparently the security about Mr. Clinton was tight enough so that no one broke out machine guns (MG) and grenades as a greeting in his vicinity. However, at shortly after 0600 on 17 April a group of what appear to be some six Clinton objectors took the occasion of his arrival to attack an importer of US Chrysler, Dodge and Jeep vehicles. A grenade and a MG were used to cause damage to seven vehicles which the service manager estimated at one million pesos ($2,210.00). The ostensible reason for the "demonstration" was a protest against holding the "political"[30] prisoners who were on a "hunger strike." Although not proven, the fine Italian hand of Hemispheric Left (HL) boss Castro is probably discernible in this fiesta. Which is strange when Mr. Clinton's subsequent behavior is remarked.

Clinton Comments on the Allende Affair

In Argentina the military had no choice but that of removing the government from the hands of Perón's widow, Doña Isabel, and dispensing with the ML terrorists responsible for the continually escalating terrorism in that nation (pp.158ff, YRBK97). In Argentina in latter 1997 US Pres. Clinton told a group of reporters, *inter alia*, "Most recently, the most important change is that Argentina withdrew from the military governments which repressed and assassinated people..." (pp.143ff, YRBK98). This month the US president did much the same thing in Chile.

In Wkly 5.10 above LANS has reviewed the military takeover in Chile which prevented the fondest hope of Boris Ponomarev,[31] Salvador Allende, from converting Chile into another Cuba. On 17 April 1998 Mr. Clinton "in controversial precision emphasized" *[El Mercurio* (Santiago)] that "in the saddest moments [democracy][32] honors its soldiers for their promise to defend the people and not for putting themselves at their head." Apparently the US president feels that the Chilean military should have helped Allende to Cubanize Chile, against the wishes of the Chileans, instead of preventing it. At any rate, after stating that the "the day of the dictators has ended," he later refers to Chile as "a special star in the constellation of the Americas" because of its economic achievements. This would appear to be a curious *non sequitur* since it was the military government of Gen. Pinochet which, through the direction of Prof. Harberger, introduced that free market that has produced this "LA economic miracle."

On this occasion, however, this curious behavior on the part of Mr. Clinton was not allowed to pass unremarked. Senator Jorge Martin Busch, the former commander of the Chilean Navy pointed out that it was "improper that the president of the US had passed judgment on the internal affairs of our country." In effect, he went on to reject any such lessons in democracy from the US president. There were other criticisms of the Clinton remarks which need not be recorded.

The US First Lady's Solo Flight

On Saturday, Chilean First Lady Marta Larraechea escorted her fellow first ladies to the La Barnechea commune for the elderly, explaining the programs which her spouse's government has in mind for this ancient part of the population. The assembled ladies were then treated to an "artistic-cultural" performance which included folkloric and musical performances. After lunching at the Palacio Cousiño, she escorted the group to the Summit Exposition (*Expo Cumbre*) in the Mapocho Station where the various nations had stands displaying their arts and wares. But this happy throng lacked one rather well-known member.

For Mrs. Clinton, ignoring the pleas of those responsible for her security who would doubtless suffer the consequences of anything untoward which happened to her, was off on a solo flight to Temuco, a city some 430 statute miles southwest by south of Santiago. She went there because most of the nation's Mapuche[33] Indians are located in the region. What she did there was of symbolic significance but hardly anything more. Mrs. Clinton inaugurated the Mapuche Cultural Center at Villa Trumen discoursing on the "democratic process" and the "Indian reality" in so doing. In this symbolically cluttered day she then proceeded to the Maquehue Episcopalian Hospital to be feted by Indian dignitaries and Indian dances. From there she proceeded to a "brief encounter" with Aucán Huilcamán, the *werken* and in charge of foreign relations for the Council of All the Lands (CTT).

Meanwhile, or perhaps all the while, some 200 Mapuches from the CTT were "peacefully" marching up and down, apparently concerned about the adverse effects which the free commerce treaty would have upon them. They duly presented a document to Ms. Clinton during the next, and apparently ultimate, symbolic activity, a "round table and direct dialog" at the Temuco Centennial College. Having apparently completed her scheduled Indian activities, she boarded her aircraft and returned to Santiago for a gala evening.

BURGEONING US IMPERIALISM IN LATIN AMERICA
(WKLY 6.8, 27 AUGUST 1998)

In 1979 the Soviet-Cuban Axis reestablished the mainland base which the USSR had enjoyed in Guatemala (pp.214ff, YRBK98) until 1954, although this base was somewhat to the southeast in Nicaragua. The Nicaraguan base was considerably more active, it being the location for the formation of terrorist groups in other countries[34] and the base for logistical supply of such groups.

This Nicaraguan HL base being an obvious security concern to the US, it was appropriate for the Reagan Government to eliminate it. Unfortunately, the US bungled the job; for whatever reasons, the results were disastrous. It would appear that those selected to create the Nicaraguan Anti-Communist Resistance were of insufficient experience to accomplish the objective. For example, Edén Pastora, the Counterfeit Countra (pp.150ff; YRBK97), was actually selected to run the Southern Front. But perhaps the greatest failing by the Reagan Government was its apparent unfamiliarity, and seeming incapacity to deal, with the principal weapon in the HL armory, the DO (pp.191ff, YRBK97). Although the Bush Government put the best face possible on the Nicaraguan elections of 1990, the ML

Sandinistas have yet to be removed from power in the country which they economically devastated. Indeed, these "elections" were held under the Esquipulas II Accords (pp.261ff, YRBK98) which would bring "peace" treaties advantageous to the terrorists in El Salvador and Guatemala.

Broadly speaking, it can be asserted that the basis for US "policy" in LA shifted with the advent of the Clinton Government from concern with US security in LA to the promotion of a generally meaningless and always ethereal "Human Rights" (HR) crusade. HR is taken by the Clinton Government as basis for dictation in the internal affairs of one LA sovereign nation after another. The masters of the DO and hence the manipulation of HR to its own ends is the HL, and the Clinton Government has fallen into various traps laid for it by this HL and ended by supporting HL objectives as a consequence. But is the interest really in HR and not simply in imperial power and control in the hemisphere?

The list of *known* examples of recent US interference in the internal affairs of LA nations is long. Mexico has recently told the Clinton Government to cease and desist its interference in Chiapas—presumably the US does not wish for Mexico to reestablish its sovereignty in that Mexican state (Chap. 4). It seems likely that the US will seek to "help" solve the Nicaraguan-Costa Rica border dispute. The Great Gringo DO (Chap. 6) is simply the latest interference in the internal affairs of Colombia, the US having used fraudulent "HR" charges in interference there for some time. And, during the Bucaram Affair (Wkly 3.7ff, YRBK98), LANS correspondents reported both Ecuadoran civilian and military "scared to death" to make a move without clearing it with the US ambassador. This does not complete the list (cf. Chap.3, YRBK98), but it is sufficient for background to Peru.

The Clinton Government has attempted various activities in Peru which can be described as imperialist meddling, perhaps the most obvious the US ambassador's bizarre call for changes in the Peruvian budget. For this the Peruvian Foreign Minister called in the US ambassador and, apparently, admonished him. Mr. Fujimori was dealing with the Tupac Amaru Revolutionary Movement (MRTA) terrorists' seizure of the Japanese Embassy with a consummate skill which eventually led to complete success. According to LANS sources, the Peruvian president did not even answer a telephone call from Mr. Clinton and subsequently ignored offers of "help."

The list of Clinton Government attempts at interference in the internal affairs of sovereign Peru is long and appears to be continuing to lengthen. Among the many items on it is that of the US terrorist, Lorene Helene Berenson, who will be encountered again and who may be an important facet of *l'affaire Valle Riestra*.

JAVIER VALLE RIESTRA OF PERU

The Peruvian Government of President Alberto Fujimori has carried out the most effective, if not the only effective, campaign against the Marxist Leninist terrorists of the HL. While the presidents of Colombia to the north have devoted almost two decades to unsuccessful attempts to establish "peace" with their ML terrorists, Fujimori, in a few years after his 1990 election has broken the back of Peruvian narcoterrorism, refusing to deal with the criminals of the MRTA in the Japanese Embassy affair. While politicians like Pérez de Cuellar are enemies primarily because they want the presidential throne themselves, much of the drumbeat of attack against Fujimori has been precisely because of his success against the HL.

On 28 July 1990 Fujimori succeeded the avowed Marxist and admirer of Sendero Luminoso (SL) "principles," Alan Garcia, as Peruvian president. Garcia had been the college roommate of MRTA terrorist boss, Polay Campos, was the standard bearer of the Peoples Revolutionary Alliance (APRA), the "socialist" who had led the country almost into the Marxist abyss. In 1992, with the overwhelming approval of the Peruvian people, Fujimori abolished the courts and the congress by decree and soon had begun to establish order in Peru, reelected subsequently under a new constitution (pp.169ff, YRBK97). In accomplishing this much Alberto Fujimori of course became the target of what Johnson identified as the "great human scourge" of the Twentieth Century, the professional politician.[35] His reaction to this appears to have been generally muted and has frequently been difficult to understand. What appears to have been one reaction was his appointment of one Valle Riestra to the position of prime minister (PM). Quite recently, and following a series of Valle attacks on Fujimori, the Peruvian president fired Mr. Valle.

In somewhat more depth, the bizarre story of Valle Riestra begins with his appointment as president of the Peruvian Council of Ministers by President Fujimori in June 1998. Valle is a member of APRA, this a Social Democrat party and member of the SI, the lineal descendant of the International Working Man's Association or First International formed by Heinrich Karl Marx on 28 September 1864. He therefore ranks in that gala of luminaries which include Venezuela's Carlos Andrés Pérez and Peru's Alan Garcia. The press described him with the fanciful term, "populist," which *Webster's* defines as a party "purporting to represent the rank and file of the people," that is, a socialist.

Mr. Valle was reasonably well known as being in opposition to everything for which President Fujimori stands; indeed, if Garcia were not avoiding prosecution for what is alleged to be substantial embezzlement, it is difficult to suppose that his position would differ from that of the new PM. The HR bogey, many allegations of which have been shown to be little more than DOs, the attacks on Fujimori and the military, the calls for self-defeating leniency toward the ML terrorists, all these things and more typified the positions embraced by Mr. Valle. All these things lead to two questions:

(1) Why did President Fujimori appoint Valle?
(2) Why did Valle accept the appointment?

1.

President Fujimori stated that his decision to appoint Valle was taken "to reinforce the politic of my government which seeks to strengthen democracy and fundamental rights" (EFE 7 July 1998). The words were scarcely out of his mouth before his new PM began his anti-Fujimori drumbeat typified by "nothing is going to slow me in my task of democratizing Peru" and direct attacks such as "I say to you (Fujimori): heal the environment, achieve reconciliation with public opinion... I am in the government to tell you that, from 2000, he who defends human rights, who has no disappeareds-detaineds will..." The complete litany of the left to which Fujimori does not appear to belong.

The Peruvian president has shown no previous signs of simple mindedness so that it may be presumed that (a) he was aware of how Valle would behave and (b) saw some benefit to be derived from such behavior by his appointee. And there have been some arcane theories advanced to account for this which may or may not have any merit: This is all to create a smoke screen to obscure the real problems in Peru, or it has the object of creating a "false opposition" which is divorced from the "true" opposition—represented by Pérez de Cuellar?—and can be expected to undermine it. Perhaps there is some merit in these "answers," but they sound as likely to work against as for the Fujimori Government.

2.

It is not at all difficult to imagine an "old politician" such as Valle entering into such an arrangement, however short-lived—this one less than three months—for the notoriety which he can gather therefrom. But there is a speculative explanation of Mr. Valle's entry into this farce which would surely not be foreign to present US imperialist policies.

Could it be that Mr. Valle Riestra has been encouraged by the US to enter into this *opera bouffe* as a method of rendering LA's most effective head of state more amenable to whatever the Clinton Government's plans may be? This question has been raised in connection with the US interest in, and the Valle position on, a pardon for the US MRTA terrorist, Berenson. Not, of course, that the US could be restricted to this consideration only, although LANS has not yet obtained substantial supporting data on what the other considerations may be.

THE GREAT GRINGO DISINFORMATION OPERATION REVISITED
(WKLY 6.10, 10 SEPTEMBER 1998)

It has recently been attested again that the USSR "funded every major (Vietnam) antiwar group"[36] in the US. These erstwhile "activists" tend to aggregate around the executive and legislative branches of government, and there are those of them who have not lost the roseate illusions of their youth. These would be "putty in the hands" of those experienced Russian Military Intelligence (GRU) operatives who are almost assuredly involved in the Great Gringo Disinformation Operation (GDO).

For some time the HL and the HL Support (HLS) have of course been busily fabricating HR charges against the military which have been dutifully disseminated by various Non-Governmental Organization (NGOs), with or without malice of forethought. But it was *The Washington Post* which, doubtless unwittingly, first carried the water for the GDO in its article of 10 April 1998, "Colombian Rebels Seen Winning War." An aside.

Disinformation in *The Los Angeles Times*

In 1990 an article appeared in *The Los Angeles Times* entitled "In El Salvador, It's the Army That Seems to Be in Trouble." A subhead read in part, "the insurgents may have the upper hand." From the headline to the end of the story, the information was demonstrably fabricated, and the Editor was commissioned to demonstrate this after an individual saw the article on the desk of a "high State Department official" who appeared to be impressed. A few days in San Salvador and San Francisco Gotera were all that were required. (The information which the Editor gathered on the article's author and photographer was interesting but hardly conclusive.)

There were childishly nonsensical statements in the article, all aimed at creating a totally false impression, such as "In the capital of San Salvador...darkened tanks patrol the streets at night." The Editor then verified that El Salvador did not possess any tanks. It had armored personnel carriers, manufactured locally by welding three-quarter inch steel plate to appropriate chassis. For a good many years the Editor had been observing occasional armored personnel carriers on the Panamerican Highway although none in, say, the Colonia Escalon. As he wrote at the time, "The inferred idea of a Beirut in Central America bears no relation to reality."

In creating a totally false impression the author then wrote, "Soldiers have set up outposts throughout the city..." This was simply false as the Editor took the time to verify. The guard posts which, for many years, had been at the Estado Mayor, the Escuela Militar, I Brigade headquarters, etc., were right where they had been, but there were no "outposts."

Finally, as concerned the capital, the author quoted an unidentified real estate agent claiming that "People are leaving" because of fear of terrorist attack "and renting their house...(and) nobody wants them..." This was easily shown to be nonsensical by comparing the classified section of *La Prensa Grafica* for 2 October 1989 with that for 28 September 1990.

The LANS Editor had visited San Francisco Gotera, the headquarters of Destacamento Militar IV, a number of times over the previous five years The *Times* author stated that he and his photographer trekked there, an assertion to which The DM-4 commander, Col. Leon, attested with a smile. That author then fabricated a totally fantastic account of a military formation on the square which, *inter alia*, probably shows an unfamiliarity with the military that he shares with various of his brethren.

But most importantly, he wrote that "patrols have been halted." The Editor asked Col. Leon about this; he merely laughed and asked, "Why would they be?" Why indeed. On this same trip the Editor made a very low-level chopper flight back and forth across the northern tier of Salvadoran states in order to photograph the terrain for an organization which was building a "terrorist detector." This was a Hughes chopper, doors removed, with none of the Hughie's M-60s but with Salvadoran Army markings. Had there been any terrorists anywhere, the chopper would have offered a "fish in a rain barrel" target, but nothing happened. We spotted one two-platoon strength patrol which the pilot thought might be terrorists but which Col. Leon quickly identified as his own at our fuel stop.

This totally fabricated account, which appeared in the "news" section of *The Los Angeles Times*, doubtless had some effect on the Farabundi terrorist "victory through peace." Since, however, the US has shown little interest in investigating *why* it has lost all its wars since 1945, the extent of the influence does not appear to be known. With which we return to what may be an analogous situation in *The Washington Post*.

The GDO

In eight years the scene has shifted from El Salvador to Colombia, the "reporting" periodical from *The Los Angeles Times* to *The Washington Post*, but there is a disturbing sameness about the "report." Now it's the Colombian Army "which seems to be in trouble." But it is "in trouble" according to a Defense Intelligence Agency (DIA) report which never existed. If it did exist, the DIA spokesman lied to the LANS Editor, and the DIA commanding general lied to the Colombian Armed Forces (FAC) commanding general, General Manuel José Bonett[37] Locarno. For both the DIA spokesman and the DIA commander stated unequivocally that no such report existed. Furthermore, LANS maintains, from on the ground investigations in Colombia, that, if the report did exist, it would be nonsensical. LANS is seemingly the only organization which has covered the three "bases" for this anti-FAC allegation as they occurred.

Las Delicias—Patascoy—El Billar

The GDO, as it appeared in the spring of 1998, based its "FAC losing" allegation on these three trifling engagements, treating them as they would have treated, say, the French capture of Guderian's XIX Corps in 1940. The facts are quite different. (That the FAC has never made any tactical mistakes is not being claimed, albeit, it is not a LANS obligation to pontificate on what has happened. However, to attempt—as has repeatedly been attempted with other terrorists—to claim some sort of military superiority for the narco-terrorists of the Colombian Revolutionary Armed Forces (FARC) is simply bizarre.) The first of the three is Las Delicias.

In the summer of 1996 a less than Company-strength unit of FAC was manning a cobbled-up outpost at Las Delicias. This hamlet is in Putumayo Department, on the right bank of the Caquetá River, 31 statute miles (sm) southwest by south (SWS) of Tres Esquinas for which see Spcl 6.4, "Colombian Joint Task Force South" (Chap. 5). In "Landmark FARC Victory"[38] (pp.209ff, YRBK98) the overrun of this outpost by some 400 FARC terrorists has been described. During the next 10 months the Samper Government contributed to the propaganda victory which FARC enjoyed from this capture by acceding to FARC demands.

Another overrun occurred at Patascoy in December 1997 with another small unit (Chap. 5, "Another Colombian Terrorist Coup"), although some military heads did roll for inefficiency in this case. Patascoy was little more than a relay antenna on a mountain top guarded by a platoon. It was located on the ridge of the mountain range defining the border between Nariño and Putumayo Departments, a short distance north of the road linking the capital of the latter (Mocoa) and the capital of the former (Pasto). There were apparently serious security mistakes made, and FAC removed the brigade and division commanders from command as a consequence.

As the LANS Editor learned at Tres Esquinas (Chap. 5), the FARC terrorists made their escape from Patascoy by a "backwoods" river route which took them all the way into Ecuador, a nation which appears not to have minded their presence. And "escape" is the *mot juste*; this was no "victorious army," it was a terrorist gang.

The third such incident occurred at El Billar which is 47 sm about due east of Tres Esquinas. Once again, a small unit was overrun by a large FARC group. The personnel captured at Patascoy and El Billar are still in the hands of the terrorists: another propaganda victory was thereby handed to these outlaws.

These incidents were the basis for the GDO which appears to have been more or less initiated with *The Washington Post* article of last April. And then came the guns of early August. LANS has not treated these situations previously because of its search for reliable details which are now available on perhaps the most important incident.

Miraflores

Brigadier General Euclides Sánchez Vargas is the Inspector General of FAC. General Sánchez submitted a report on Miraflores to the FAC commander in chief, a report of which LANS has obtained a copy. It would appear that the LANS readers are capable of reading this report themselves and hardly require the Editor to tell them what it says. Therefore, an English translation of the "The Inspector General's Report" appears in Chapter 5 and is synopsized below.

Terrorist strength at Miraflores was reported by *El Espectador* as "400" and "at least 500" in two articles on the same day. The report itself has the troops which were attacked maintaining that there were 1000 of these bandits. LANS' sources in Colombia feel that the number was close to 800.

The effective strength of the infantry unit at Miraflores was 2 officers, 10 non-commissioned officers and 98 privates, that is, a company.

Guaviare Department is to the southeast of Meta Department, its capital San José de Guaviare (Spcl 6.1), on the Guaviare Rive which separates the two departments. San José is some 230 km southeast of Bogotá, Miraflores about 25 km from the Vaupes Department border on the Vaupes River.

The terrorist began the "attack" on the small military installation at 1930 on 3 August 1998, "attack" meaning they began bombarding it with whatever was at hand. At this point two platoons appear to have been on patrol, these encountering overwhelming numbers of the enemy and never returning. Weather generally prohibited any air support and, at 1720 on 4 August, the captain commanding reported that the corporal's guard remaining had been overrun.

La Uribe

La Uribe is slightly over 200 km west northwest of San José de Guaviare in Meta Department. According to EFE (Bogotá 9 August 1998), there was a detachment of 60 military and six police stationed there at 0530 on 4 August 1998 when the post was allegedly "attacked" by "several hundred" (*varios centenares*) terrorists from FARC Front XLI.[39] The attack was abandoned by the terrorists at 1930 that evening.

Apparently there was little left of the military or police post, and the casualties of both were reported as 46 dead and 16 wounded, although this was not an overrun. General George S. Patton, who had considerable combat experience, stated in no uncertain terms that, if casualties figures exceeded something like 10 percent, they were to be ignored.

Urabá

As has been pointed out (Wkly 6.6), General del Rio, commander of XVII Brigade, inflicted many defeats on FARC terrorists in the Urabá area and divested them of their influence with the banana workers. This led to DOs against him for HR violations, DOs demonstrably fabricated as will be discussed if and when the opportunity arises. The general was headquartered in the Apartadó region in Antioquia Department, the area 30 km or so east of the Choco Department border and perhaps 40 km from the border of Colombia with Panama.

Which more or less serves to define the location of Urabá, described in the press as the "jungle zone between the Antioquia and Choco Departments near the Panama frontier." It was in this region that combats, routinely described by the press as "violent" (AFP 20 August 1998), took place between 14 and 16 August.

Neither La Uribe or Urabá resulted in a terrorist victory, but the press consolidation of these two with Miraflores can be—and probably has been—read as some sort of further demonstration of the FARC superiority DO.

Notes

1. As Cuban General Intel Directorate (DIA) Capt. Enrique Garcia told a LANS colleague, he was undercover in La Paz at the time of Castro's most famous murder

attempt against Pinochet (Wkly 2.13). That the Cuban dictator was personally involved was maintained by Garcia.

2. For the work of University of Chicago Prof. Harberger, cf., Arnold C. Harberger, *Cuatro momentos de economía chilena:versión de las conferencias ofrecidas entre 1974 y 1976 en Santiago de Chile* (Fundación de Estudios Economicos BHC, Santiago, 1976) and Arnold Harberger *et al, Institucionalidad económico e integración financiera con el exterior:...* (El Instituto, Santiago, 1979).

3. As LANS Associate Editor Whelan has pointed out (p.925, *Out of the Ashes* and private communication), "Nobel laureate Milton Friedman, one of the intellectual mentors of the regime's 'Chicago boys,' was summoned to Chile in 1975 to advise on shock treatment. As a result of one or two such "lightning trips" to Chile and publicity such as that from *El Mercurio* (11 May 74), Friedman was popularly given credit for what Harberger accomplished.

4. Leonard Schapiro. "The International Department of the CPSU (Communist Party of the Soviet Union)." *International Journal*, Winter 1976-7.

5. In reality Allende's Peoples Unity Alliance (CUP).

6. Leonid I. Brezhnev, *We Are Optimists. Report of the Central Committee of the Communist Party of the Soviet Union to the Twenty-sixth Congress of the CPSU* (International Publishers, 1981. ISBN: 0-7178-0586-7).

7. As quoted by Whelan (p.557, *Ashes*).

8. P.318 of Mark Falcoff [*MODERN CHILE 1970-1989: A Critical History*, Transaction Publishers, 1991].

9. Regís Debray. *Conversations with Allende*. Random House. 1971

10. Robert Moss. *Chile's Marxist Experiment*. Newton Abbot. 1973.

11. This has been laid out in exquisite detail by John W. F. Dulles [*CASTELLO BRANCO: The Making of a Brazilian President*. Texas A&M University Press. 1978], University Professor of Latin American Studies, University of Texas.

12. Nathaniel Davis. *The Last Two Years of Salvador Allende*. Cornell University Press. 1985.

13. David Brock. "Communists Raise the Stakes in Chile." *INSIGHT*. 15 December 1986.

14. This may not be entirely true since other MLs from the International Left such as the Basque Homeland and Liberty (ETA) terrorists have long been prominent in LA.

15. Various examples of such operations have been given in 4YRBK97 and Chapter 7, this volume.

16. In 1964 PDC (Christian Democrat) candidate Frei Montalvo won the Chilean presidency with 56.09 percent, the "Marxist Physician" (Falcoff, *ibid*) trailing with 38.93 percent. In 1970 Allende received fewer votes in victory than he had in defeat, CD candidate Tomic received half the votes Frei had received while half of Frei's votes simply moved to the Independent candidate Alessandri.

17. As has been pointed out in these reports, Allende was, to the delight of the International Department (Central Committee, Communist Party of the Soviet Union) boss Boris Ponomarev, turning Chile into another Cuba (cf. Falcoff, Note 3 and Robert Moss, *ibid*). In particular, his creation of the ML militias is worthy of note.

18. This is the National Truth and Reconciliation Commission which is discussed in Spcl 6.11 immediately below.

19. Pérez de Arce does not mention the fact, but, had the Military Government really wanted to eliminate the MLs, as ML governments routinely eliminate anti-MLs, it would have dropped Garcés down a deep hole instead of shipping him back to Spain.

20. This "Convention" enunciates the "Principle of Selective Indignation." If MLs Ulianov (aka Lenin), Dzugashvili(aka Stalin), Mao Tse-tung *et al* slaughter their citizens by the tens of millions, as they did, this is not worthy of attention. But let an ML terrorist be killed by a defender of the law, and it is "genocide."
21. It is important here to recall the ML anti-Semitism which has been discussed, *inter alia*, by Louis Rapaport (*Stalin's War Against the Jews: The Doctor's Plot and the Soviet Solution*, Free Press, 1990. ISBN: 0-02925821-9).
22. LANS has produced (pp.312ff, YRBK98) an analysis of the 200,000 casualty figure claimed for Guatemala during its period of Guatemalan National Revolutionary Union (URNG) terrorist siege. What the analysis shows is that this wildly exaggerated number is just one more DO which may be traced to the terrorists themselves.
23. Patricia Politzer, *Altimirano* (Melquíades, Santiago de Chile, 1990. ISBN: 9506990204).
24. The LANS reader may recall the analogous pricking of a HL DO balloon by Pedro Joaquin Chamorro's mother who attested that Tacho Somoza Debayle had not murdered her son.
25. John W. F. Dulles, *CASTELLO BRANCO: The Making of a Brazilian President*, Texas A&M University, 1978. ISBN: 0-89096-043-7
26. Or the marxization of theology as Rev. Dr. Miguel Poradowsky calls it (4YRBK97).
27. This is the excellent news service, Del Noticiero Nicaragüense, out of Managua.
28. Among the alleged "accomplices and coverors" in a statement submitted to the court by Daniel Olivas Zúñiga was the Maryknoll LibTheo cleric, Miguel D'Escoto Brockman, foreign minister in the Ortega regime (EFE 18 Jun 98).
29. Professor Roberto Zelaya Blanco is an electrical engineer and a professor of mathematics who has experienced Sandinista "juctice" firsthand. He was seized as a political prisoner on 24 Jul 79 and condemned by a Sandin "Peoples' Tribunal" to 30 years in prison and confiscation ("liberation") of all his property. He was released on 17 Mar 89 because of pressure put on the Sandins by the international community. The Sandinista Government of Nicaragua was condemned for violation of his rights in a decision specifically delineating torture of Zelaya and awarding him indemnification. Prof. Zelaya is among the best informed on FAR.
30. A Marxist-Leninist (ML) terrorist, whether captured for murder, kidnapping, narcotrafficking or other common crimes, is *a priori*, a "political" prisoner. This ploy is often supported by press reports which simply quote the "political prisoner" claim with no further explanation. The cry of the ML is of course "Give me an MG and applaud my crimes."
31. Boris Ponomarev was the longtime head of the International Department, Central Committee, Communist Party of the Soviet Union.
32. Mr. Clinton apparently left out the word, not *El Mercurio*.
33. In the early 1970s an estimate of 360,000 Mapuches was common. Now the total indigenous population is estimated at 675,000, "most of these Mapuches."
34. The FSLN had been in power scarcely a year when Castro's man, Redbeard Piñiera, used Managua as the formation site for the Farabundi terrorist grouping (pp.146ff, YRBK97) and the Guatemalan National Revolutionary Union (URNG) terrorist grouping (pp.138ff, YRBK97).
35. P.510, Paul Johnson (*MODERN TIMES: The World from the Twenties to the Nineties*, Harper Collins, 1991. ISBN: 0-06-433427-9)
36. *THROUGH THE EYES OF THE ENEMY: Russia's highest ranking military defector reveals why Russia is more dangerous than ever* (Stanislav Lunev and Ira Winkler, Regnery, 1998. ISBN: 0-89526-390-4). Colonel Lunev is still in the Witness Protection Program.

37. General Bonett told the LANS Editor of this conversation in his July 1998 interview.
38. The "landmark" nature of the victory has to do, not with the overrun of the small unit by much greater numbers of terrorists, but with the supine Samper Government's refusal to allow FAC to go after its own which were used by FARC to hold Colombia hostage.
39. There is something strange here. Since, as LANS has pointed out on various occasions, these fronts run about company size, there must have been terrorist personnel from more than one front.

4

The Hemispheric Left

Introduction

There are four scenarios that have been advanced to explain the events of 1991 in the USSR: (1) The Marxist Leninist (ML) dictatorship of the USSR transmogrified itself into a free-enterprise democracy. (2) The Committee for State Security (KGB) weathered the "unpleasantness" of that year with an even firmer grip as absolute master of the USSR/CIS. Yevgeny Albats (*THE STATE WITHIN A STATE: The KGB and Its Hold on Russia—Past, Present and Future*, Farrar, Strauss, Giroux, 1994. ISBN: 0-374-18104-7), the Russian journalist, was perhaps the most articulate advocate of this view. (3) Any transmogrification that took place was restricted to a change of clothes for the "criminal mafia" running the USSR according to Lev Timofeyev (*RUSSIA'S SECRET RULERS: How the Government and Criminal Mafia Exercise Their Power*, Knopf, 1992. ISBN: 0-394-58639-5), there being agreement by Stanislav Lunev (*THROUGH THE EYES OF THE ENEMY: Russia's Highest-Ranking Defector Reveals Why Russia Is More Dangerous Than Ever* (with Ira Winkler), Regnery, 1998. ISBN: 0-89526-390-4) who, as a lifelong Military Intelligence (GRU) officer, maintains that the GRU, not the KGB, controls the mafias. (4) The transmogrification was a carefully-planned Disinformation Operation (DO) is the view held by Anatoliy Golitsyn (*The Perestroika Deception*, Harle, 1995. ISBN: 1-899798-00-5), a KGB defector.

If one or some combination of these theories is actually "correct," it would of course have some effect on affairs in the Western Hemisphere as did the termination of the immense annual subsidy which, for some 30 years, the USSR paid to Castroite Cuba. But there is a great deal of evidence available that the Hemispheric Left (HL), while suffering a temporary setback with the alleged transmogrification of the USSR, has since been steadily improving its position and its strength, perhaps most importantly, having replaced the immense Soviet subsidy with immense revenues from its narcotrafficking.

In 4YRBK97 the HL has been described as a loose association of amorphous Marxist and militant ML left organizations. That lineal descendant of Heinrich Karl Marx's First International, the Socialist International (SI) may be taken as an example of the former. The HL chief is Fidel Ruz Castro, his hemispheric organization made up of ML terrorist and "ex" terrorist groups, of left political parties ranging from the Mexican Democratic Revolutionary Party (PRD) of Cuauhtémoc Cárdenas to the Brazilian Workers Party (PT) of Luiz Ignacio "Lula" da Silva. Castro's principal umbrella organization for his HL is the São Paulo Forum (FSP), which has been described in considerable detail (4YRBK97 *et seq*). It was put together by Lula and Fidel in the Havana of 1989. As 1998 drew to its close the FSP had placed various of its militants in important governmental positions— Cuauhtémoc Cárdenas, for example—and one in a presidential palace.

And Castro has cleverly adopted an anti-neoliberal, i.e., anti free market, agenda as his solution to the economic woes of the hemisphere. That this ML architect of the devastated Cuban economy can lecture the world on "what should be done" economically is bizarre but only to be expected when he has no opposition in the international arena. Instead he has cleverly adopted the anti-neoliberal line to his marxism— privatization will cost you your job—being careful to avoid any mention of the origin of LA's economic woes.

The background of Castro, the consummate Professional Politician (PP) when he has no opposition, has been described in 4YRBK97 and subsequent and will not be repeated here. Suffice it to say that his 1961 declaration that he had "been a ML all his life" is one of the few accurate statements which he has ever made. That he has no intention of forsaking or softening his ML dictatorship, as certain of those outside his island appear to believe he may do, is almost continually demonstrated in the press.

A report in *Diario las Américas* (23 July 1998) by Luis Mario is accompanied by an AFP wirephoto of Castro shaking his finger at a foreign press which he had just driven out of a "parliamentary" (Peoples Power) session in Havana. According to the ML dictator the foreign press was "discrediting socialism (ML), demoralizing this revolution, combating it with lies and intrigues of all kinds..."

They were in the service of the same old ML enemy, "imperialism," and "did not share our noble ideals." The important part of course is that, before that time, at that time and thereafter, the Cuban dictator has said he has no intention of relaxing his tyranny. Nor has he any intention of relaxing the attempts of his FSP which has specifically stated its devotion to the creation of "supra national countries" in LA as a "sort of re-edition of a soviet-type union in LA" (4YRBK97 *et seq*).

In this chapter, Castro's relevant activities during this year are first considered, his HL then brought up to date and terrorist and terrorist-related activity in the hemisphere discussed by country with an important exception.

In YRBK97 and YRBK98 ML terrorism in Colombia was treated together with that in the other LA nations in the chapter allocated to the HL. Nothing has changed in Colombian terrorism save for the so-called "Pastrana Peace Process." As a consequence of this change, ML terrorist activity has warranted and received a level of attention by LANS which has removed the subject into a separate Chapter 5.

Fidel Ruz Castro

THE PAPAL VISIT TO CUBA
(WKLY 5.6, 12 FEBRUARY 1998)

Preliminaries

Fidel Castro arrived in Rome after midnight on 15 November 1996, the ostensible object of his visit being an appearance before the World Summit on Nutrition of the Food and Agricultural Organization (FAO). At that meeting he delivered his routine attack on the free market as the root of the world's woes (pp.91ff, YRBK97), a demonstrably false position if only the misery produced by his own Marxism Leninism is considered. But from its inception Castro's Roman November may have had another, even more important, objective.

For the sympathizers with the ML Cuban dictator used the occasion of his journey to Rome to prepare his apotheosis[1] which, by the time of his arrival had been transformed into a sort of "beatification" as ANSA[2] (*La Segunda* (Santiago) 14 November 1996) described it, a beatification which seems to erase from world memory the panorama of the crimes committed by, and misery produced by, Cuban communism. The tyrant's visit produced a Roman fever, more than

2000 journalists soliciting interviews (*La Epoca* (Santiago) 15 November 1996), the rich and famous courting him (*Corriere della Sera* (Rome) 19 November 1996). All of this doubtless encouraged his bizarre declaration that "the communist revolution brought benefits to the Cuban population" (*O Estado de São Paulo* 18 November 1996). An aside.

These LANS reports have never wittingly attempted to foretell the future which includes predicting the future of ML caudillo Castro. For a good many years, however, they have reported the predictions of Castro's imminent political demise by various and sundry, predictions which appear to have been based more on *wishful* than on *realistic* analysis. Since "man proposes and God disposes," he may of course depart this veil of tears at any moment, but his political demise does not appear to be immediately assured judging by the continuing successes of his HL—largely reported here—and support such as was demonstrated in Rome.

On 19 November 1996 Castro was received by His Holiness John Paul II, the ML caudillo awarded the honors reserved for heads of state (*O Estado* 19 November 1996). Amador J. Piñiero (EFE 19 November 1996) reported that it was "the general impression in the Vatican" that this visit "broke the isolation of the Castro regime." "It is an encounter which strengthened the international image of Castro" (*La Repubblica* (Rome) 20 November 1996). Small wonder that the ML caudillo should boast on his return of "the recent diplomatic successes of Cuba" and claim that his regime "has more friends than ever." Nor should his remark, "I feel proud of being a communist," encourage those seeking his political demise.

This political performance in the Rome of latter 1996 apparently led to the announcement the following year that His Holiness John Paul II would visit the headquarters of the HL early in 1998.

What effect the Vatican expected this to have may not be clear, but various Castro opponents were optimistic. It appeared, however, that Castro had no intention of ameliorating his militant ML as he demonstrated by his performances at the Young Communist League (UJC) (pp.162ff, YRBK98) and the V Congress of the Cuban Communist Party (PCC) (p.166, YRBK98). And his subordinates behaved accordingly.

Ricardo Alarcón is the head of Castro's "legislature," now euphemistically referred to as the "Cuban Parliament." The month before the papal visit this ML told *El Nuevo Dia* emphatically that this visit would bring no political changes to Cuba.

"The visit of the pope," Alarcón continued, "is going to put Cuba on the highest level in terms of informative publicity. It will show that Cuba has relations with many other countries, including the Vatican State. Then it will demonstrate that there is a normalization of relations with the Catholic Church."

It would appear that the Castroites anticipated at least these benefits from the papal visit.

Papal Itinerary in Cuba

21 January 1998, Wednesday: Pope John Paul II was scheduled to land at José Martí International in Havana at 1600, all times local. His nights would be spent at the residence of the Papal Nuncio in Havana.

22 January 1998, Thursday: Santa Clara is about 150 miles east southeast of Havana. His Holiness said mass in Santa Clara at 1015, later that day having a meeting with Castro in the Palace of the Revolution in Havana.

23 January 1998, Friday: Camagüey is about 145 miles southeast of Santa Clara. The pope said mass in Camagüey at 1035. At 1830 John Paul II visited the University of Havana in honor of Reverend Félix Varela and met with the "world of culture" (*mundo de la cultura*).

24 January 1998, Saturday: Santiago is about 165 miles southeast of Camagüey. At 1110 His Holiness said mass there and crowned the Virgin of Caridad del Cobre, patroness of Cuba. At 1900 the pope had an encounter with the "world of pain" (*mundo del dolor*) in the sanctuary of San Lázaro in Havana Province.

25 January 1998, Sunday: At 0800 the pope had an "ecumenical encounter" and an encounter with the Hebrew Community in the Nuncio offices in Havana. At 0930 he offered mass and the prayer of the "angelus" in the Plaza of the Revolution in Havana. At 1245 he had an encounter with the Cuban Conference of Catholic Bishops, in the archbishopric in Havana. At 1700 there was a liturgical celebration with the clerics, deacons, other religious, seminarians and laity in the Cathedral of Havana. At 1845 the official departure ceremony took place in José Martí International. At 1930 the papal aircraft departed for Rome.

The Pope Is Coming

It was reported from Las Villas Province the week before the pope's arrival that officials of the Cuban Ministry of Interior visited zones where opponents of the Castro regime are located. They asked permission to enter their properties under the pretext of preventing acts against the Supreme Pontiff. Those living in the vicinity of Santa Clara, where the first mass was to be celebrated, were told to inform the police of any visits to their homes between 12 and 22 January. "HR activists, opponents and independents" in the province were told that they must not leave their municipalities on the twenty-second. On the other hand, the mobilization of the youths going into military service was ordered, allegedly in order to maintain order during the coming religious ceremonies.

Castro began one of his interminable harangues on Cuban television at about 2100 on Friday, 16 January, preceding the papal arrival, finishing it at 0251 the next morning. The first two hours or so saw the caudillo warning and fulminating. His warnings were against "raising one single placard," "hoisting a single sign," "allowing oneself to prompt the least provocation." His "calling upon" his followers "to collaborate with the police" can also be taken as a warning that they do so. For the first time in 39 years he warned against any "vivas" for himself or anybody else for that matter. His fulminations were against the US.

"The president of the US, with all his nuclear arms, battleships, aircraft, rockets...does not dare to come to this island. There has been no North American president who has dared to come to this country to see what is happening and to speak to the Cubans..." This was followed by what amounted to a challenge that a US president come and discourse on Castro's pet hate, neoliberalism or the free market, a stance which the Cuban dictator apparently felt quite safe in taking.

At about 2320 he is reported to have begun talking about the visiting John Paul II, perhaps the salient feature of which was his claim of "freedom of religion" in his fiefdom which today has "the people as the unique and irrevocable witness."

Love, Hate and Ché Guevara

In speaking to reporters on his aircraft inbound for Havana Pope John Paul II is quoted as saying that "the marxist revolution is the revolution of hate, vengeance and victims," while "the revolution of Christ is that of love." These sentiments are in keeping with the position which he has routinely taken in the past. The remarks on Guevara which were attributed to him (EFE 22 January 1998), however, were quite something else again, and some have wondered whether the reporter had somehow garbled them.

The pope is quoted as saying that "it will be God who will judge his [Guevara's] merits...[but] I am certainly convinced that he wanted to serve the poor." Of course, such a remark might be considered politic at a time when Castro is carrying on his great Guevara propaganda fest (pp.192ff, YRBK98).

Guillermo Cabrera Infante is the exile from Castro's island who has recently won the Cervantes Literature Prize. In Barcelona on the same day which saw the pope inbound to Cuba, Cabrera was telling a news conference in Barcelona that the visit of Pope John Paul II "will reverberate in favor of Fidel Castro.

"If the people go [to the Havana mass]," he said, "it is because he [Castro] tells them, not because the pope tells them."

The author went on to say that Fidel Castro and John Paul II "are two fishermen in a little pond." He added that the pope is going to a Cuba from which Castro expelled 60 nuns and priests and shot Catholic political militants of the Association of Christ the King. "This," he concluded, "is a past which the pope does not want to remember."

Cabrera Infante was Cuban cultural attache in Brussels from 1962 to 1965, later defecting to the United Kingdom where he has become a British citizen. While his opinion is somewhat pessimistic, the opinions expressed, for example, by *La Prensa* (Managua) were quite the opposite.

"...[the pope] achieved more in five days than has the US in 37 years..." *La Prensa* headlines includes "Winds of Liberty Blow Through Cuba," "The Pope Eclipses Castro," "He Censures Atheism and Exhorts Religious Liberty" and the like.

The Papal Arrival in Havana

Pope John Paul II deplaned from his Alitalia (McDonnell Douglas) MD-11 to be greeted by Cuban Caudillo Castro with a speech echoing his propaganda performance of last year before the Congress of the PCC. In their own way Castro's remarks could be taken as being as insulting as were those of the Sandinistas 15 years before.

"We sincerely admire your valiant declarations on the events relating to Galileo," said the dictator, "the known errors of the Inquisition, the episodes of the Crusades, the crimes committed during the conquest of America and on the scientific discoveries which in your time were the object of so much prejudice and anathema."

Having presented history to his marxist taste, he continued, describing his Cuba and Cubans as "A people with fewer inequalities, fewer citizens without shelter, fewer children without schools, more teachers and physicians per inhabitant than any other country in the world which Your Holiness has visited." He then described what he called the thesis of the Church as a "happy idea," this "the equitable distribution of riches and solidarity among the peoples should be globalized." The latter was apparently a seizure on the papal remarks aboard his aircraft against neoliberalism, or the free market, perhaps Castro's principal *bête noire*.

In marked contrast to Castro's performance, the papal reply was couched in the language of civilized human discourse and contained a telling riposte to Castro's historical attack. He began by giving thanks to God, "Lord of history and of our destinies" for permitting him to come to "this land described by Christopher Colombus as 'the most beautiful that human eyes have seen.' On arriving in this island, where now more than 500 years ago the cross of Christ was planted—a cross zealously conserved today as a treasure in the parish temple of Barracoa—I salute you all with particular emotion and great affection."

He then stated his happiness that he could "reply to the invitation by the bishops of Cuba, now some time ago, an invitation that the president of the Republic also made to me and repeated personally in the Vatican...in November 1996..." After greeting his "brothers in the Episcopate," he goes on to describe the purpose of his "apostolic journey." "I come in the name of the Lord in order to confirm them in the faith, animate them in hope and encourage them in charity...in the history of this noble people thirsting for God and spiritual values which the Church in the five centuries of its presence has not failed to dispense..."

The papal reply continued in this vein, ending with thanks for the warm welcome and blessing the "hearts of all and particularly the poor, the sick, the outcasts and those suffering in body or spirit. Praised be Jesus Christ."

Anti-Neoliberalism

"Speak to us about the injustice of capitalism," the jeering crowd of Sandinista hecklers shouted at John Paul II during the mass he celebrated in the Managua of 1983 (Spcl 5.2, below). Which, according to some observers, is what the Pontiff did during his 1998 visit to Cuba. The details of his condemnation of capitalism (the free market)—even the phrase "savage capitalism" (*capitalismo salvaje*) is to be found among his quoted remarks—need not be reproduced or "analyzed." The position is the point because of its proximity to that of the ML caudillo, Castro, and his HL.

As some observers have suggested, in these remarks the pope may be referring to the sentiment expressed in the Biblical passage suggesting that it is as difficult for a "rich man" to enter the Kingdom of Heaven as for a laden camel to pass through the "Eye of the Needle." (The Eye of the Needle was, of course, a gate into the Holy City and not some part of a sewing instrument.) But Castro can be expected to use the papal remarks to his own ends to whatever John Paul II may be referring, the "devil quoting Scripture."

And the Cuban may be expected to use the adverse papal comments on the so-called "embargo" of Cuba which is not really an embargo at all. US President Clinton, immediately before the papal visit to Cuba, made sure that this non embargo retained its impotent status by suspending for the fourth time (*Diario las Américas* 17 January 1998) that Title III of the Helms-Burton Law. Without this title Helms-Burton is nothing more than Castro's paper tiger. In the final analysis, the visit of Pope John Paul II to Cuba left the question:

Cui Bono?

JOHN PAUL II, CASTRO AND THE SANDINISTAS
ROBERTO J. ARGUELLO[*]
(SPCL 5.2, 12 JANUARY 1998)

The battle between the Vatican and the Fidel Castro regime becomes, as the date of the Holy Father's visit approaches, continually stronger. On 10 January important communications media informa-

---

[*] Roberto J. Arguello is a prominent Nicaraguan attorney and syndicated columnist now resident in Miami, Florida. Mr. Arguello is the author of the recently published book, *La Vida Secreta de los Sandinistas* which may be obtained by sending $14.95 to him at 700 Brickell Ave., Miami, FL 33131.

tion sources "at 11 days before the visit to Cuba," reported that the papal visit was on the point of being suspended. Vatican security officers had encountered a microphone in a church residence in the interior of the country which had been put at the disposal of John Paul II for his relaxation. The Cuban espionage artefact having been encountered, the Papal Nuncio sent a strong protest note to the Cuban Ministry of Foreign Affairs to "replan" the papal visit.

Castro's "open" agenda for the visit is obvious. This will serve to demonstrate to the world that the Cuban political system is supported by the majority of the Cubans and that his regime promotes international investment in certain areas such as tourism. The "swindle" agenda of Castro is to minimize the political impact of the visit of John Paul II on the Cuban people who demand their liberty daily.

Moreover, Castro hopes that his regime will emerge from the visit having been strongly favored in two ways. First, favored with the $20 million left in Cuba by the 15,000 people who will be attracted to that island nation by the visit of John Paul II. Second, he expects to benefit from the publicity provided by the 4000 journalists who have submitted their credentials in order to cover the five days of John Paul II's visit which will begin on 21 January.

John Paul II has vast experience in negotiating and dealing with totalitarian regimes throughout the world. Certainly, all those countries, which he has visited and which have been under the influence and control of dictatorial and inhuman regimes, have eventually been converted into free countries as has been the case in Nicaragua.

The papal visit to Cuba has enormous similarities to that which John Paul II made to Nicaragua in 1983. During the decade of the 80s that nation was converted into a colony of Castroite Cuba wherein nine Sandinista leaders governed as directed from Cuba by Fidel.

Negotiations Between the Vatican and the Sandinistas

At the beginning of 1983 John Paul II decided to tour Central America and Haiti. The principal purpose of this journey was to support the Pastoral Letter of 27 February 1983 from the bishops of Nicaragua. There were strong and tense negotiations between the Sandinista Government and the Vatican on the protocols of this papal visit to the CA nation. Monseñor Andrea Cordero Lanza de Montezemolo was negotiating on behalf of the Vatican, Daniel Ortega for the Sandinistas. The Vatican demanded little, the most important such demand being that, during the mass which would be offered in the Plaza of the Republic, there would be a crucifix in place of a Sandinista mural, and that five clerics, among whom were Ernesto Cardenal, Miguel D'Escoto Brockman and Alvaro Arguello, would resign from their posts in the Sandinista Government.

John Paul II Betrayed by "Someone in the Vatican"

The famous historian, Malachi Martin, in his book *THE JESUITS*[3] says that John Paul II concluded, after his visit to Nicaragua that "someone" in the Vatican informed the Sandinistas of his agenda and plans in that nation to include informing Daniel Ortega and his associates beforehand of his speeches.

On 4 March 1983 John Paul II landed in Nicaragua. Daniel Ortega, in military uniform, instead of giving a cordial welcome to the Holy Father, profited by the occasion in order to attack the international policies of the US Government then presided over by Ronald Reagan.

250,000 Nicaraguans were present "while the entire world saw through the television" when Sandinista mobs led by Daniel and Humberto Ortega screamed vulgarities during the religious service. As was to be expected, Ortega and his companions in arms failed to keep their word since in place of the crucifix which was to have been behind the altar was a banner with the photo of the founder of the Sandinista Front, Carlos Fonseca Amador, and the legend "John Paul is here thanks to God and to the revolution."

What Can Be Expected from the Papal Visit to Cuba

Fidel Castro hopes to capitalize on the image of a statesman and on that of a stable and prosperous Cuba in which exists freedom of religion. For Castro the papal visit has the double symbolism of image and money. Castro will do everything possible in order that John Paul II has a pleasant stay in Cuba, therefore the microphone incident will be minimized by the Castro dictatorship.

For John Paul II, his visit is the beginning of the end of atheism, as a process accelerating toward a free Cuba where democracy and liberty exist.

[Translated from the Spanish by the LANS Editor]

EDITOR'S NOTE: THE NICARAGUAN PAPAL VISIT

Because John Paul II's 1983 visit to ML Nicaragua was indeed prologue to his 1998 visit to Cuba, and because Arguello's detailed treatment of the earlier visit would have been inappropriate to his subject matter, a note on the earlier papal encounter in Managua is an appropriate addition here.

On the morning of 4 March 1983 Pope John Paul II's Alitalia DC-10 touched down at Sandino International in Managua, Nicaragua. In symbolic gesture, the Pope knelt down to kiss the ground. Then in alleged greeting ML caudillo Daniel Ortega launched into a 25-minute diatribe against the US for the benefit of the assembled international media. In his reply the Pope praised the besieged Managua Archbishop Obando y Bravo and denounced the "People's Church"—Liberation Theology (LibTheo)—as "a grave deviation from the will and salvation of Jesus Christ." The Pontiff's remarks were all but drowned out by the crowd of well-orchestrated hecklers.

Only one of the top LibTheo clerics gracing Ortega's ML government, Ernesto Cardenal, was present. Of the others Foreign Minister Miguel D'Escoto was in New Delhi; OAS Ambassador Edgar Parrales and State Delegate Alvaro Arguello were at home "watching on TV" and Fernando Cardenal was "somewhere else." On encountering Ernesto Cardenal[4] the Pope wagged a finger at him and said, twice, "You must regularize your situation!" As Martin[3] says, "The reception at Sandino Airport was but a thin and reedy overture to the full symphony of humiliation that had been orchestrated for John Paul."

The main event of the papal day was the mass which John Paul II would celebrate that evening in the Plaza of the Revolution. According to official estimates, 600,000 would be present, all of whom had been "neatly sorted out and massed in prearranged blocs." Details of the sorting have been given by Belli.[5] The décor had been carefully stage managed.

One end of the Plaza boasted a massed array of "revolutionary" billboards bearing a pantheon of Sandinista "heroes." Across the Plaza a platform, on which the Pope would celebrate mass, bore a linen-draped plain table, the altar. To one side of this altar and on the platform was an official viewing stand for the Sandinista Politburo—National Directorate—members, to the other a similar stand for the Junta members. The backdrop to the altar was not the promised crucifix but banners bearings the likenesses of the patron saint of Sandinism, Carlos

Fonseca, and its titular deity, Augusto Calderón Sandino.[6]

Microphones had been strategically distributed through the preprogrammed audience, specifically so that the hecklers could compete on better than even grounds with the microphone provided John Paul II. And the "mass" which followed turned into an exercise in typical ML misbehavior. The unequal contest that followed saw the Pope vainly shout three times for "Silencio!" only to be ignored, then furiously taunt with "Miskito Power!" referring to the Atlantic Coast Indians whom the Sandinistas had harried out of the country. Among the spectrum of taunts with which his attempt to celebrate mass was disrupted were

"Power to the People!" "National Directorate, give us your orders!" "Speak to us of the poor!" "We want a united Church on the side of the poor!" "Power to the People! Christ lives in the People's Church!", that is of course LibTheo. "Power to the People!" "It is possible to be Marxist and Christian!" Speak to us about the injustice of capitalism!"[7]

The papal day in Nicaragua was concluded, fittingly from the Sandinista point of view, by a deliberate delay in the departure of the papal aircraft. As a finale to the Sandinista attack on the Roman Catholic Pontiff, the government radio then insisted that John Paul II should apologize for *his* behavior. His departure was followed by what amounted to catcalls from Borge, a Politburo member and a LibTheo Maryknoll missioner.

* * *

CASTRO'S WEALTH
(WKLY 6.1, 2 JULY 1998)

That ML is practiced, not to advance the dictatorship of the proletariat, but, rather, the power and perquisites of power of the ML bosses is unavoidable in a realistic scrutiny of these people. Indeed, it is unavoidable under almost any scrutiny.

The review, *Forbes Global*, in what can hardly be classified as a "careful scrutiny," recently credited the Cuban dictator with a fortune of $100 million from "tourism, mining and sugar," a modest sum indeed. About four years ago a ranking Cuban General Directorate of Intelligence (DGI) defector estimated to the LANS Editor that the wealth of the HL boss was over $2 billion which is probably more realistic. *Forbes*, however, cannot be faulted, for example, for having been unable to estimate Castro's immense agglomeration of wealth from his narcotrafficking activities (cf. pp.164ff, YRBK97).

CAUDILLO CASTRO AT THE CARIFORO SUMMIT
(WKLY 6.9, 3 SEPTEMBER 1998)

Although apparently a minority, some have used the recent wild gyrations in Wall Street equities to predict the worst for the economic future. These people should be heartened by the support which their position received on 24 August 1998 from that internationally known expert on economic affairs, the Cuban ML dictator, Fidel Castro.

"I predict," the architect of the Cuban economic disaster asserted, "that the people of the United States will suffer a depression worse than that of 1929" [*Listin Diario* (Dominican Republic) 25 August 1998].

Nor was this the extent of his predictions. The world, he went on to assert, will suffer a great economic crisis which will provoke a gigantic battle for human survival. The battle will include all social classes from the richest to the poorest. Since Fidel's billions place him in the former category, this "Caribbean buffoon" will not be left out. Buffoon he may be, but his recent triumphant progress through the Dominican Republic (DR) again illustrates the growing danger which he represents for the Western Hemisphere.

CARICOM

The Caribbean Community and Common Market (CARICOM)[8] was formed in 1973 by the Treaty of Chaguaramas signed in Trinidad. Its member and associate member states have been given (pp.333ff, YRBK98). The First CARICOM-US Summit was held in Barbados on 10 May 1997 (pp.129ff, YRBK98).

US President Clinton appears to have campaigned his way through this gathering in routine fashion, declaring, *inter alia*, that the American commitment was "as deep as the waters that link our shores" (*sic*). Perhaps the most interesting aspect of this largely ceremonial affair was the outright demand by many Caribbean heads of state for the admission of Castro's tight little ML dictatorship, which still supports HL terrorism, into the American "family of nations"—the Organization of American States (OAS) and so on. Mr. Clinton apparently voiced no noteworthy opposition to Castro's reinstatement. This stoked the fires of speculation on the real attitude of the Clinton Government toward Castroite Cuba.[9]

The Lomé Convention

In 1963 the European Economic Community (EEC) signed a non reciprocal trade agreement with the Associated African States and Madagascar (AASM). This was the Yaoundé Convention which was replaced on 28 February 1975 by the Lomé Convention between the EEC and the African, Caribbean, Pacific (ACP) States or, more commonly, the ACP Group. At the 1975 signing of Lomé I there were 46 African, Caribbean and Pacific countries which, according to the ACP Group Secretariat, located in Brussels, Belgium, has by now grown to the more respectable number of 71. Lomé I was followed by Lomé II in 1979, Lomé III in 1985 and Lomé IV in 1990 to endure until 2000.

This Lomé Convention is generally described as a "trade and aid agreement" between the European countries and their foreign colonies. The aid efforts are organized under the European Development Fund (EDF), and the Secretariat press releases allege that it guarantees all those politically correct (PC) platitudes which are popular among contemporary statesmen (politicians): "Sovereignty" is supposedly recognized and the development strategies and policies are claimed to be centered on people and "the respect and promotion of human, political, social and economic rights." Mr. Castro's entry into this entity would appear to "guarantee" almost anything else.

The mission of the ACP Secretariat is "to accelerate...(in the ACP Group) rates of development and to reduce the levels of poverty." And, presumably, to organize annual summits. There are various other tasks assigned to the Secretariat, mainly having to do with supporting those ACP Group councils, assemblies and other types of administrative units in the organization. These need hardly be listed. Nor need the 48 African members or the 8 Pacific members. However, the 15 Caribbean members would appear to be appropriate because they essentially correspond, not only to CARICOM but also to the Caribbean Forum.

The Caribbean Forum (CARIFORO)

The CARIFORO members are: Antigua and Barbuda, The Bahamas, Barbados, Belice, Dominica, The Dominican Republic, Grenada, Guyana, Haiti, Jamaica, St. Kitts and Nevis, Saint Lucia, Saint Vincent, Surinam and Trinidad and Tobago.

Susana Lee is or was the special correspondent in the DR for *Granma*, the Cuban mouthpiece for Castro and his Central Committee (CC). Her primary mission was, of course, the greater honor and glory of "Comandante Fidel Castro," a mission she accomplished through her interview with DR Secretary of State Max Puig who ecstacized appropriately over the imminent arrival of the ML caudillo at the CARIFORO Summit.

Dr. Puig apparently "affirmed" that Castro's presence as an observer in the ACP Group places a major emphasis on the view that the Caribbean without Cuba is not complete. Turning over her adulatory duties to the Dominican press, Ms. Lee does a workmanlike job in assigning the roots of this Summit in the November 1997 Central American (CA)–DR heads of state (pp.359ff, YRBK98) whereat the DR expressed "its desire to make common cause with the Caribbean and CA."

The Forum took place as scheduled, beginning on Thursday, 20 July 1998, and concluding on Saturday, 22 July. This routinely prescripted Forum was supposed to have been held in order to determine just what CARIFORO would recommend for the "post Lomé IV"—Lomé V has been mentioned but not as frequently—period of a bright new XXI Century. From the press coverage it appears actually to have been choreographed for the promotion of "Commander in Chief Fidel Castro, First Secretary of the CC of the PCC (Cuban Communist Party) and President of the Councils of State and Ministers" (pp.162ff, YRBK98). One cannot help but suppose that part of the choreography was the establishment of a DR consular mission in Cuba in February and the reestablishment of Cuba-DR relations on 17 April 1998. The CinC etc. duly arrived in two aircraft, an aerial cavalcade proportionally greater than that of the lavish entourage featured by US President Clinton.

No complaint could be voiced against the dictator inside the DR, but from outside, Ricardo Bofill (EFE 23 August 1998) of the Cuban

Human Rights Committee (CCDH) complained of Fidel's flight arrangements and accommodations which consisted in "renting entire hotels for his security guard" while "asking support from the UN because of danger from the drought."

Caudillo Castro in the DR

A paunchy Castro in his ML caudillo uniform arrived at Las Américas de Santo Domingo Airport (AFP wirephotos 21 August 1998) on 20 August to be greeted effusively by DR President Leonel Fernández. By Decree 313-98 President Fernández had designated a commission to accompany Castro made up of various DR dignitaries to include the foreign minister, the vice foreign minister, two presidential secretaries, the chief of customs and various other raking members of his government. But President Fernández had issued an earlier decree.

Decree 314-98 declared that the Grand Cross of Gold of the Order of Merit of Duarte, Sánchez and Mella was to be awarded to Fidel Castro. The award was presented during the evening of 22 August. A photograph of Fernández and Castro, apparently applauding themselves, shows the Cuban dictator, who has exchanged his ML caudillo uniform for a suit and tie, replete with a dinner-plate sized medal on a blue and white sash extending from right shoulder to left hip.

Mr. Fernández's comments during the award ceremony are worthy of reproduction (*Listin Diario* 23 August 1998).

According to this newspaper account, Fidel Castro led a revolution which transformed the historic destiny of Latin America, his figure forming a "living force" which has "channeled the aspirations for justice and well being of millions of human beings." [This is a truly remarkable statement, and the sycophantic hyperbole could hardly have been more exaggerated by Castroites such as the former Haitian president, Jean-Bertrand Aristide, or the now deceased Dominican, Peña Gómez.]

"That which has made possible the conversion of Dr. Fidel Castro into a symbol of the dreams of redemption of an important part of humanity," the DR president continued, "is that this portion has to see in him a distinctive sign: his character rebellious when confronted with anything which he deems unjust, unworthy or inappropriate."

It is of considerable interest that it has only taken Fernández the two years since he bested Castro's candidate for the DR presidency,

Peña Gómez, to learn all these interesting things about the Cuban. But after these comments all the other adulation is anti climactic. And Castro's comments and behavior, before and after the ceremony, evinced no obvious evidence of any remarkable transmogrification.

After Fernández had secured the decoration on the dictator, Castro assured all and sundry that the DR chief of state could anticipate "difficult times and foreign pressures" for having reestablished diplomatic relations with Cuba. He went on to claim that "both Caribbean countries, although small like David, are capable of fighting and overcoming giants." Presumably the "giants" are the US; they are certainly not Canada, Mexico or Lula da Silva's Brazil. And is the US really opposing the Cuban dictator? It should be of interest to see if the DR suffers for its recognition of Cuba or, as may be more likely, gains substantially from it.

Castro Visits Old Friends

Francisco Peña Gómez was the Castroite Dominican presidential candidate who led the field in the first round of those 1996 elections but who lost to Fernández in the second round. That he was of Castro's HL was emphasized by his appearance as the foreigner on the platform at the Sandinista National Liberation Front (FSLN) rally in the Managua of January 1995. But Castro could hardly be delivered to Peña in his armored Mercedes, the latter having departed this veil of tears last May, albeit, his widow, Pegy Cabral, was so honored. As was Juan Bosch.

Listin Diario, with a grand disregard for the historical realities, describes Bosch as having been "overthrown by a group of military who accused him of being communist." A deceased associate of the Editor, who knew the DR as the back of his hand, described Bosch with considerably more accuracy as a member of the Caribbean Comintern.

The Juan Bosch tale begins with the assassination of the Dominican caudillo, Rafael Trujillo, the latter's security chief, Arturo Espaillat[10] maintaining that "Mutt and Jeff" of the CIA did the job. The more popular story is that Trujillo's own security was responsible. No real attempt has been made to learn the truth of Trujillo's assassination, but the CIA theory appears somewhat self serving. Bosch rode into the presidency two years after the assassination and followed almost the precise course which Allende Gossens would choose save for the suicide finale.

Whether Bosch was ever a "communist"—at the time the Dominican chief of staff told the *Herald Tribune* he did not think so, he simply felt Bosch knew not what he was doing in putting communists into key positions—is irrelevant. The "Peoples Militias" were being created, arms were on their way in, and so on, the result predictable. It all began with an operation initiated in 1962 by Santiesteban Casanova of the Cuban DGI and escalating through the presidency of a Bosch who was indeed putty in the hands of the MLs.[11] Nor did Bosch's removal stop the chaos, US President Johnson's intervention essential to this result, a tale told to the Editor by the ambassador in charge of the operation.

But that Bosch was at least friendly to the Cuban dictator, then and thereafter, is easily demonstrated by the fact that he and his wife have long had one of the official residences in the "exclusive" Miramar district of Havana assigned to them as even *Listin Diario* (24 August 1998) felt it necessary to remark.

The Statement of Santo Domingo

This statement runs to 4½ typewritten pages and bears the title: THE CARIBBEAN ENCOUNTER: TOWARD THE 21st CENTURY. As with all such documents it was presumably written before the Summit by the ministry clerks.

Sprinkled with favorable references to Castroite Cuba — though hardly as favorable as were Fernández's remarks — PC references to a kaleidescope of international organizations, the document appears to be almost exclusively concerned with "reassertion" of this or that fealty, recommitment to this or that organization, etc. At the time, those interested in these details could have gone to the web site: http://www.presidencia.gov.do/boletines/220898/statstodgo.htm.

Finally, the participants expressed their delight at participating in the 500th anniversary celebration of the founding of the city of Santo Domingo de Guzmán.

JOSÉ RIVERA SENDS THE ORDER BACK
(SPCL 6.17, 17 DECEMBER 1998)

The year 1369 was of some consequence in the history of Spain for, as an allegedly direct consequence of the cruelty[12] and treachery of Pedro the Cruel, the Trastámara Dynasty, in the person of Pedro's bastard half-brother, Enrique II, was firmly established on the throne of Castile. This was finalized at the Battle of Montiel. As the good Jean Froissart (c1337-c1410) tells us,[13] by the time of the battle:

"...there were many good knights on King Enrique's side, Bertrand Du Guesclin..." who is familiar and a number of others who are not. By this time also the Black Prince (of Wales) had had a surfeit of Pedro's unreliability and withdrew from his service. In a sparkling denouement, King Enrique follows King Pedro into the quarters where he had taken refuge:

> As he (Enrique) came in he said: "Where's that Jewish son of a whore who calls himself King of Castile?" Then King Peter stepped forward, that bold and bloody man, and said: "You're the son of a whore, I'm the son of good King Alfonso."

With which Pedro threw Enrique down on a conveniently placed bed and began to dispatch him and would have done as much save the Viscount of Rocaberti "caught hold of his foot and twisted him over so that King Peter was underneath and King Henry (Enrique) was on top. The latter drew a long Castilian knife ... and drove it upwards into his brother's body."

Enrique's men hurried in and tidied up the job, albeit, Froissart found what happened next distasteful: "Those who had killed him left him lying on the ground for three days which in my opinion was a cruel thing to do." The Spanish account of the affair has Du Guesclin bringing Enrique to Pedro's room, but perhaps Froissart's account of Le Bègue doing so is the more reliable.

Whoever deserves the credit for directing Enrique to Pedro, it established the Trastámara Dynasty in Castile. From these fragile beginnings evolved what would be Castilian hegemony over the Iberian Peninsula, albeit, it would require over 100 years of cut, thrust and diplomacy, most of which must be ignored.

On 19 October 1469 Isabella, to be known as "The Catholic" and descended from John of Gaunt on both spear and distaff sides, married Ferdinand of Aragon. Five years later, on 11 December 1474, Isabella's brother, King Enrique IV of Castile died, and Isabella was proclaimed Queen of Castile. The archbishops of Toledo and Seville confirmed the principle of female succession and the sharing of the throne. On 19 January 1479 King Juan II of Aragon breathed his last, bequeathing the Kingdom of Aragon to his son, Ferdinand. The accession of Isabella in Castile (1474) and Ferdinand in Aragon (1479) effectively consolidated the Iberian Peninsula. Ferdinand and Isabella were joined in alliance by King João of Portugal (1481) and "the institution of monarchy recovered its luster, the reconquest was completed, the route to India...was opened, and the new world was discovered."[14]

The Royal Order of Isabella the Catholic

The Royal Order of Isabella the Catholic was established by the Royal Decree of King Fernando VII on 24 March 1815.[15] Beginning with modifications in 1847, the Order was modified, suppressed and reinstituted as the "republican" winds of change blew in, out and about the Iberian Peninsula. This Order was the only one not suppressed when these breezes had attained hurricane force in July 1931. When the flurries from that "scourge of the Twentieth Century," the PP, had somewhat subsided, the King of Spain was Grand Master of the Order, there being 25 Caballeros del Collar, 500 Caballeros Gran Cruz and various lesser lights who need not be enumerated here. Among the Gentlemen of the Grand Cross was José I. Rivero.

José I. Rivero

Rivero had been owner and editor of one of the foremost Latin American papers, *Diario de la Marina,* before the advent of the Cuban dictator. Generalísimo Francisco Franco bestowed the Grand Cross of the Order of Isabella the Catholic on Mr. Rivero and granted him a two-hour private audience in El Pardo Palace. Among other things, Franco explained to him: "As you see Rivero, I cannot break with Fidel Castro because Cuba still owes us a great deal of money."

Rivero explained to our friend and colleague, Ariel Remos: "Franco won the war against communism. King Juan Carlos, Aznar and Fraga Iribarne are going to lose it all with their open comradeship *(compadrazgo)* with the tyrant of the Cuban people, Fidel Castro." This sentiment was among those the journalist expressed in the letter to King Juan Carlos which accompanied the Grand Cross which he returned in a profound action which should, in turn, affect the scheduled visit of the Spanish King to the Cuban ML dictator but which has not yet interested the press or the monarch.

As Mr. Rivero said in his letter, which amounted to withdrawal from the Order of Isabella the Catholic, Spain has turned its back on the tragedy of Cuba. The visit which the King will make to Cuba "is not to embrace the suffering people but to embrace and ingratiate himself with the tyrant and fraud 'sovereign' who is oppressing them."

CASTRO STILL HEMISPHERIC DRUG LORD
(SPCL 6.17, 17 DECEMBER 1998)

LANS has been treating the narcotrafficking activities of the billionaire ML terrorist, Fidel Castro, in various reports, the first of which appeared over two years ago (pp.163ff, YRBK97). Brian Crozier (*L'Express*, 26 December 1986) demonstrated that Khrushchev recruited Castro into narcotrafficking. In what originally amounted to a "suppressed"[16] book, Joseph D. Douglass, Jr. (*RED COCAINE: The Drugging of America*, Clarion House, 1990. ISBN: 0-9626646-0-X), the debriefer of the ranking Soviet Bloc defector, Czech General Jan Sejna, details most of the evidence relating to ML narcotrafficking in LA, pointing out that "Cuba and Czechoslovakia first established drug operations in the early 1960s." What had recently been only a suspicion at LANS as to "why" the "mainstream" press knows nothing about Soviet and Cuban narcotrafficking has recently been verified. First, however, further details have been furnished to LANS by Brian Crozier, certain of which had appeared in *The Sunday Times* (London 28 January 1990).

As Mr. Crozier told the LANS Editor during December 1998, he had extensively discussed Soviet and Cuban narcotrafficking with General Sejna in 1983 and 1985. As secretary to the defence council of the Czech CP, Sejna had participated in a secret meeting in Moscow in 1960. It was at this meeting that Khrushchev launched his strategy of a drug campaign against the US, a strategy which has been more successful than the blubbery Soviet dictator could have imagined. From the first, Cuba was to play a key role, Castro establishing a hemispheric center for narcotrafficking in return for Soviet armament and training. That narcotrafficking has evolved into a key role for various ML groups from Nicaragua to Colombia and Peru is one indicator of the campaign's success.

In his valuable *Times* article Crozier discusses a second meeting which took place in Havana during the 1966 Tri Continental Conference (TCC) (pp.95ff, YRBK97), a meeting managed by Czech and Cuban intel personnel. To this meeting Gen. Sejna attested and from these beginnings Castro's position as hemispheric drug chieftain evolved until, as Crozier has told us, narcotrafficking was bringing some $10m per month into his coffers. As has been discussed (pp.165ff, YRBK97), the tale soon directly involves such as the fugitive US citizen, Vesco, and indirectly two US presidents, Nixon and Clinton. But, of perhaps greatest interest, why, in spite of continuing reports on the reality of Castroite narcotrafficking, is this subject still tabu in the US?

The immediate answer appears to be that the US Government, under whatever president, did not wish to "offend" the Soviets and apparently now has no desire to "offend" the Cuban despot. To this Gen. Sejna attested to Mr. Crozier. The astute reader may well ask why, in his book (Jan Sejna, *We Will Bury You*, Sidgwick and Jackson, 1982. ISBN: 0283991534), for example, Gen. Sejna did not mention Soviet-Cuban narcotrafficking. The Czech told Crozier the answer to this.

Since only the naïve are unaware of the Soviet program of eliminating those defectors who posed a potential threat to them, the background of this continuing program need not be laid out. Sejna posed a threat, and it would have proved nothing for him not to have entered a witness-protection program, probably the only possibility of avoiding some exotic murder device wielded by Soviet intel. And so he went into a Defense Intelligence Agency (DIA) witness-protection program. Since the general did not depart this veil of tears until last year, it appears to have been as successful as could have been hoped. But there is a caveat involved in such programs.

The potential victim must assuredly behave as his "protectors" tell him to behave or he could figuratively end "in the street" with probably fatal consequences. And both the DIA and the Central Intel Agency (CIA) told Sejna not to "embarrass" the Soviet or Cuban dictatorships with his first-hand knowledge of Soviet and Cuban narcotrafficking. Such an order is clearly not negotiable.

Castro's Narcotrafficking Continues

What has and has had all the earmarks of a US cover-up of Castro's narcotrafficking activities continues. The reasons for the cover-up may be various and speculative. Nevertheless, the pattern has been a consistent one. But, because of the I Amendment to the US Constitution, the press cannot have its freedom overtly abridged save, of course, by itself. In the matter of Castro's narcotrafficking, however, it has generally abridged its own freedom, the "informed" citizenry learning about Castro's behavior only from certain maverick members of the media. But these have existed, and the fashion in which their revelations have been countered by the US Government are of some interest.

The US allegedly has a serious effort underway to interdict drug shipments from "Colombia." A well-publicized part of this effort is the Joint Interagency Task Force with headquarters at Bone Key in Florida. As *The Washington Times* (3-9 Auguust 1998) learned, this agency had issued a rather interesting report[17] on "Colombian" narcotraffickers' operation in Cuban airspace and Cuban territorial waters, but there was no indication that the chief terrorist there had any part in it. The report declared that, during the last six months of 1997, 39 narco flights had passed through—or "near"—Cuban airspace while Cuban territorial waters were used for amphibious narco shipments. Spokesmen for the Castro dictatorship maintained that they were making "indescribable" efforts to intercept these flights.

To this claim, Congressman Bob Menéndez (D, NJ) answered, "It is ironic that Cuba can send its MiGs to disintegrate two civilian US aircraft[18] and cannot defend its airspace against narcotraffickers." Congressman Lincoln Díaz-Balart (R, FL) was a bit more specific:

"The participation of the tyranny in narcotrafficking has not diminished but has increased. And the Clinton Administration continues systematically covering up that participation in spite of the fact that the North American intel community knows the details of said participation very well." This appears to sum up what has happened under Republican Administrations and what is happening under a Democratic Administration.

THE VII CONGRESS OF THE UJC
(SPCL 6.18, 24 DECEMBER 1998)

In Chapter 7 below, LANS discusses the LA Economic System (SELA) conference in the Havana of December 1998 and the remarks of Lech Walesa on what he considers the anachronism of the ML which typifies Castro's Cuba. Were Walesa correct, the VII Encounter of the UJC would be nothing more than a bad joke, a bit of posturing which the civilized world could ignore at no risk. But, as is also discussed in that chapter, the evidence indicates that such a position may pose grave dangers. To some extent, such an attitude toward Castro and his "bandit band" in the Sierra Maestre, before

Matthews et al transmogrified him into a "Robin Hood," allowed him to occupy the Cuban power vacuum. However trivial such performances as the VII UJC may appear, these ML posturings should hardly be ignored.

This same UJC celebrated its 35th Anniversary in 1997. The "Central Act" of this Anniversary consisted primarily of an oratorical performance by Fidel Castro on 4 April 1997 in the (Heinrich) Karl Marx Theater in Havana. Every word of the Castro oratory has been of course enshrined in print by his mouthpiece, *Granma*, and was discussed in some detail (pp.162ff, YRBK98).

In December 1998, in a gathering which *Granma* has described both as a "congress" and an "encounter," 1500 representatives of "the communist militancy" met somewhere in Havana primarily to listen to Fidel but allegedly "to debate themes which most concern Cuban society and the role of the UJC in present circumstances." Castro, who "assisted *(sic)* at each one of the sessions," sounded just as he has wherever he has appeared.

The last such meeting of the UJC occurred in 1962. In "closing" this one, Castro declared, "I am not pronouncing the words of closure, I am not summing up but leaving matters open[19] because this congress should continue at least a year longer." The orders to this debating group having been given, it will, in some form, continue its sessions "a year longer."

Two others among the "1500" attendees are mentioned. José A. Echeverría of the Higher Polytechnic Institute dutifully stated that "the University is not only a place of instruction for the present but of formation for the future." The secretary of the UJC at the University of Havana, Javier Dueñas, delivered himself of various remarks, concluding with, "There are some youths who think only of their material interests. What should the base committees do?" As the reader may note elsewhere in the account of the festivities, the members of the base committees will doubtless do whatever they feel will enhance their chances of joining those UJC whose members "within 20 years will direct the ministries." But, of course, most of the talking was done by Castro.

The Cuban dictator expressed his pride at various "accomplishments" of his regime. He alleged that, in 1959, there were only four experimental stations, "today there are 222 research centers supported by 1.8 scientists for each 1,000 people, one of the most outstanding indicators in the world."

This human epitome of excellence concluded his remarks with "virtue is developed in the battle against vice."

Virtue may be inferred to be a state of UJC militancy, Vice as anything else.

The HL: Umbrella Organizations and Activities

THE VIII FORO SÃO PAULO
(WKLY 6.8, 27 AUGUST 1998)

Perhaps the most important of the HL umbrella organizations is the São Paulo Forum (FSP) (pp.97ff, YRBK97 and various other of these reports). The FSP was put together by the Brazilian leftist, Luís Ignacio (Lula) da Silva, and the Cuban caudillo, Fidel Castro, in the Havana of 1989 (*Granma* 12 January 1989). Lula is busily engaged again in what appears to be a losing race for the Brazilian presidency. The themes of the perhaps most important FSP encounter, IV in Havana, were anti-neoliberalism, anti-Yankee imperialism and the creation of "supra national countries" in Latin America (*Granma* 23, 24 July 1993) as a "sort of re-edition of a soviet-type union in Latin America." Particularly since the alleged demise of the USSR, such bombastic pronouncements have largely been ignored in the press and by governments and citizens.

Perhaps they are worthy of acceptance as nothing but bombast, but such intentions are hardly worthy of being swept under the rug and ignored. For, whatever proves to be the final outcome, the HL has made substantial advances in the last few years. Further, it is seldom acknowledged that this FSP welcomes, not only allegedly "ex" terrorist groups such as the Salvadoran Farabundo Martí National Liberation Front (FMLN)[20] but active terrorist groups such as the Colombian Revolutionary Armed Forces (FARC) and still threatening "ex" terrorist groups such as the FSLN. Nor are such groups alone in a cold world without a Cold War. For FSLN boss Daniel Ortega, who has been mumbling recently about "taking up arms again" and hence leaving the "ex" terrorist ranks, had his recent presidential campaign financed by Moamar el Khadafy.

On 19 July 1998 the FSLN celebrated the nineteenth anniversary of its "revolution." Boss Daniel Ortega was the last orator of the day, following a denunciation by the indefatigable Tomás Borge who, *inter alia*, attacked the "repugnant and cowardly conspiracies" against the FSLN Politburo. This referred of course to the charges of molestation brought against Ortega by his adopted daughter, Zoilamérica (Chapter 3 above).

The maximum "leader" then took the podium. "The enemies of the revolution," he intoned, "now come and want to take the lands from the campesinos and the houses and lots from the poor." (This is with reference to the eight years of largely fruitless attempts to correct the piñata wherein the Sandinistas "liberated" properties in Nicaragua and bestowed them on themselves and their cronies.) He fulminated on about the piñata, concluding with "that the Sandinista Front cannot permit." After more rhetoric about the non-Sandinistas wanting "...not a valiant people...(but) a cowardly and humiliated people," he promised "an armed uprising, a new revolution..." "The FSLN is disposed to take arms when necessary to defend the revolutionary conquests" (*La Tribuna* 20 July 1998). Does this include Cuadra's Sandinista army and the Sandinista police? But as to other HL advances.

The Mexican representative of the FSP and liaison with the Zapatista National Liberation Army (EZLN) terrorists, Cuauhtémoc Cárdenas, now has perhaps the second most important elective position in Mexico: governor of the Federal District. Castro's man in Caracas, Hugo Chávez, has what the Cuban dictator's mouthpiece, *Granma*, quite recently and correctly described as a "comfortable lead" (*Granma* 25 August 1998) in the Venezuelan presidential race. The so-called "peace accords" in Central America have placed both the Farabundis and Sandinistas in legislative positions of near equality with those of the parties holding the presidential palaces, and the same thing might very well emerge from the "peace process" which is underway in Colombia. Nor is this dreary listing complete, but it is indicative and brings us to the subject of this section.

The VIII FSP will be held in Mexico in October 1998. But a preliminary meeting scheduled to prepare the agenda for the upcoming FSP encounter was held in Managua, Nicaragua, in latter July and was attended by 11 of the "largest left parties in Latin America" (AFP 22 July 1998), the meeting appropriately convened in the Sandinista Auditorium. Among those present were delegates from Lula's PT, from Cárdenas' PRD, from the Broad Front (FA) of Uruguay, from the PCC, from the Salvadoran FMLN and, of course, from the Nicaraguan FSLN.

ANOTHER BANNER YEAR FOR THE HL
(WKLY 6.21, 26 NOVEMBER 1998)

Introduction

The Yeltsin Performance has been likened to a puppet show wherein the malleable, frequently inebriated and clownish Boris goes through whatever motions his handlers desire. The various "explanations" of the "change" in the USSR have been listed in the Introduction to this chapter.

The reader should feel quite free to profess one or all of these explanations, the point here being that, whatever happened, it caused the anti-ML governments of the world to lower their guard. "The Cold War is over," became the watchword even though the Peoples Republic of China (PRC) and various other ML regimes remained alive and well. In the slaughter department, for example, the PRC had outdone by tens of millions the immense slaughter perpetrated by the USSR. And Fidel Castro, the boss of the HL, continued his ML tyranny which has assuredly been the worst seen in this hemisphere. But, since "the Cold War is over," these tyrannies—and their methods —vanished from conscious thought. Which was much to their benefit, for, although their continuing campaign for hemispheric conquest slowed not at all, it was easy for those who should oppose it to ignore it. Unfortunately, this was a greater contribution to the effort than would two divisions have been.

During 1998 the HL has enjoyed a number of generally unremarked victories and moved toward additional ones. The MLs of the HL, whether under the command of Castro since 1960, or that of Boris Ponomarev[21] between 1954 and 1960, has won only two complete victories, these by the DO, hardly by "force of arms" (YRBK97). The victories, which have been won in CA and bode well to be won elsewhere, are all fruits of similar DOs. Four looming possibilities for victory have made themselves quite clear during 1988 and deserve special mention:

(1) The Esquipulas II Accords have brought "Victory Through Peace" to the MLs of various CA nations, Spcl 1.6 (pp.146ff, YRBK97) specifically demonstrating how this was accomplished in El Salvador, extensive documentation of the same sort of results to be anticipated in Guatemala (YRBK98). That the present "peace negotiations" in Colombia will probably bring victory of even greater scope to the common criminals of FARC and the National Liberation Army (ELN) appears likely.

(2) Lt. Col. Hugo Chávez Frías has been a strong favorite in the polls almost since he threw his hat into the ring for the December 1998 Venezuelan presidential elections. It is not really important why he chose to be a Castroite, but choose he did, a choice which makes him an even more interesting subject. His election would be a resounding victory for the ML dictator and HL leader, Castro.

(3) The HL and the HL Support was kept from victory in all save two LA nations by the Armed Forces of those nations. The drive to destroy these Armed Forces continues in order that the HLs still active plan for the creation of "supra national countries" as a "sort of re-edition of a soviet-type union in LA (Latin America)" (cf. *Granma* 24 July 1993 and p.99, YRBK97) may be brought to fruition without opposition. On 25 November 1998 the decision of a five-man panel of the British House of Lords turned down the appeal of Chilean Senator Pinochet Ugarte against the Spanish court's attempt, based on a long-running DO, to extradite him for trial. Although, it is possible that Pinochet will not be turned over to Spain, it appears probable that he will be, this in an immense victory for the HL, a victory which may well lead to clear fields for such HL operations in future.

(4) At the same time that the Pinochet process was proceeding through the English courts, the leader of hemispheric terrorist operations for 40 years, Fidel Castro, was travelling freely about Europe, feted and treated as something quite other than the terrorist he is. His "acceptability" continues to grow, his island paradise having just been admitted (EFE 7 November 1998) as a "full member" of LA Integration Association (ALADI) while he was embraced by the King of Spain on returning from a remarkable reception at the VIII Iberian American Summit in Oporto.

THE DEATH OF CASTRO'S TERROR CHIEF
(WKLY 5.12, 25 MARCH 1998)

Manuel (Barbaroja or Redbeard) Piñiero Losada (65) died early on 12 March allegedly of a heart attack (miocardial infarction) following a traffic accident. He was succinctly described in an AFP dispatch of 13 March 1998 as "the organizer from Havana of Cuban participation in guerrilla and insurgent movements in Latin America and Africa." Which is perhaps acceptable as far as it goes, but it omits certain facts relating to one of the most important figures in Castro's HL.

After Castro seized power in Cuba Redbeard Piñiero was chief of the Oriente Military District, a post from which he was shifted to Matanzas Province.[22] From there he was reassigned to Castro's General Staff as assistant to G-2 chief Ramiro Valdez. At that time (1959-1960) KGB Colonel Vadim Kotchergine was organizing Cuban intel.[23] Valdez then took over the Ministry of Interior (MININT) and Piñiero assumed command of G-2 as vice minister of MININT. The Soviets were then organizing the DGI of which Piñiero assumed command.

The importance of the DGI to the HL was demonstrated in October 1963 when the Colombian Army captured a letter from DGI Chief Piñiero. In this letter he threatened a reduction or cutoff of the terrorists 20,000 pesos-per-month stipend from Cuba if they did not follow Cuban instructions to the letter.[24] There has been a certain amount of confusion in the literature as to the evolution of the Piñiero domain within the DGI into what would be the "liberation war" headquarters for the HL in the CC, PCC. This was of course the Americas Department (AD) which for so many years Redbeard commanded. The "angels on pinheads" exercise which is the careful tracing of this evolution is not essential here: Barbaroja assuredly ran the AD from 1974 to 1990, but remark the last date.

During this 16-year period the most familiar AD operations were (1) the fusing of the squabbling FSLN in the spring of 1979, (2) the amalgamation of the Salvadoran terrorist groups into the FMLN in the Managua of 1980, (3) the amalgamation of the Guatemalan terrorist factions into the Guatemalan National Revolutionary Union (URNG) at the same time and in the same place and (4) the High Andes terrorist army which arose out of the III Congress of the PCC.[25]

On 5 October 1990 Piñiero's position appears to have changed. From a highly visible and obviously important officer of the HL, he disappeared into a Castro "reorganization." The objective of the reorganization was alleged to be that of "reducing paperwork and other examples of bureaucracy" (*Granma* (Havana) 5 October 1990). The result, insofar as Redbeard was concerned, was the disappearance of himself and his AD into a new Department of Ideology, Education, Science and Sports, and International Relations. This new department was headed by Carlos Aldana Escalante. Barbaroja would no longer enjoy the rank and importance which had been his. Was he another Camilo Cienfuegos who disappeared in what was apparently a fatal "accident"?

Brazil

THE MST, DEMOCRACY, JURIDICAL SECURITY AND THE ELECTIONS OF 1998. I JOSÉ CARLOS GRAÇA WAGNER[26]
ASSOCIATE EDITOR, LANS
(SPCL 5.17, 25 MAY 1998)

EDITOR'S INTRODUCTION

Brazil's Landless Peasant Movement (MST), one of the principal components of the Hemispheric Left (HL) campaign, has been discussed [pp.106ff, YRBK97; pp.168ff and 185ff,YRBK98]. That the entire Agrarian Reform (AgRef) concept in Brazil is based on fraud has been demonstrated [cf. *Reforma Agrária semeia ... MISÉRIA E DESOLAÇAO*, TFP, São Paulo, 1996], a fact which has rendered it no less useful as an HL weapon. Johnson [*Modern Times*, Harper Collins, 1991. ISBN: 0064334279] has shown that "human engineering" by the left in this century has resulted in greater slaughter than in the entire previous history of mankind. While abortion has not been as generally unpopular as other "social engineering" activities, it is perhaps the principal one of these activities at present. The LANS files contain a copy of the report on "population control" efforts referred to by Dr. Graça Wagner below. Its title page reads: NSSM (par) IMPLICATIONS OF WORLDWIDE POPULATION GROWTH FOR U.S. SECURITY AND OVERSEAS INTERESTS (PAR) December 10, 1974. It was originally classified "CONFIDENTIAL," declassified on 31 December 1980.

* * *

The Present Challenge

The national picture is becoming extremely serious as the newspaper headlines and photographs from all over the country demonstrate. The hijacking of a truck, the 13 on a Pernambuco road threatening motorists with scythes, all this demonstrates the use of force in a manner worthy of totalitarianism. João Pedro Stédile[27] is now declaring that the invasions will continue in the same way under the eventual government of Luiz Inácio (Lula) da Silva with the objective of changing the regime, its model the government of Fidel Castro. This same Lula, in *Granma*, the official organ of the Cuban Communist Party (PCC), declared that Cuba is the model for Latin America (LA). Among the modern techniques of taking power, according to the French psychologist, Roger Mucchielli (*La Subversion*, C.L.C., 1976. LCC: 77451951), is the demoralization of authority giving maximum publicity to the acts of provocation, thus intimidating the forces capable of resisting the revolutionary process. Thus, the MST invites the press to witness the hijacking of trucks, confrontations with the Military Police and the Assemblies at which these lawless acts are planned. This is the sort of "democracy" the MST wants for the country. All this was dutifully published by the journalists summoned by the MST.

The MST never was a social movement. It is and has been from its beginnings a revolutionary movement which exploits the social as well as the political. That it uses social discourse does not change the nature of its movement.

The Involvement of Outside Strategies

This analysis is an attempt to clarify the international aspects of what is happening in Brazil, this the last attempt by the international left in this century to modify its historical panorama after the "collapse" of the USSR. The analysis has, as its point of departure, the investigation made at the beginning of 1993 which developed a cognizance of the two entities whose strategic objectives, for LA, are unknown to the majority of those in positions of responsibility in the countries of the region.

One of these entities is the FSP with its "Utopia" the making of a socialist revolution in LA and Africa, a "Utopia" corresponding to that behind The Berlin Wall before its fall. The second entity is the "Inter-American Dialog (DI)," which has as its principal objective the introduction of an ironbound control of birth through the promotion of legalized abortion, sterilization and homosexual union. This is like those methods which have been taken as necessary to prevent Latin immigration to the US. In an official document of 1974 such immigration was considered as a national security problem because of the profound change which it could induce.

The São Paulo Forum

The idea of forming a new entity arose in a January 1989 meeting in Havana and was later articulated by Frei Betto in his book, *Paraíso Perdido—Nos Bastidores do Socialismo* (Geração Editorial, 1993. LCC: 94831959). The meeting was between the hierarchies of the PCC and the PT[28] to include Fidel Castro and Lula da Silva. The meeting participants had foreseen the dismantling of the USSR and sought to create conditions conducive to the construction of a union of socialist republics in LA. Such a plan was much to the liking of Fidel Castro who had always considered his *raison d'être* the leadership of LA in its confrontation with the "Giant of the North." Such a messianic view of himself explains his forty years intervention on the continent as it does his formation of the FSP.

The election of Lula to the Brazilian presidency was of primary importance to the 1989 Havana meeting. In the case of da Silva's defeat they imagined a possible victory for Leonel Brizola, a life-long militant of the HL (cf.pp.58ff, YRBK97), Fernando Collor de Mello (*ibid*) not yet even in the wings. Under these conditions they were seeking the organization of an entity which united the movements of the left, preferably of a castroite character, a movement which would include LibTheo. The LibTheo inclusion was at the behest of Frei Betto who understood its importance to the socialist revolution.

As a result of the meeting, the FSP was founded in São Paulo, Brazil, in July 1990 with 48 left organizations present, these including the guerrillas. In 1991 the II Encounter was held in Mexico under the patronage of the PRD and Cuauhtémoc Cárdenas, ex presidential candidate and prefect of the Mexican Federal District (DF). *In that meeting the Forum was defined as a deliberative entity.* In 1992 the III Encounter of the FSP was held in Nicaragua, the basic policy of the organization being defined.

The IV Encounter took place in the Havana of 1993 and was attended by 112 organizations of the continental left. Here the priorities of the Forum to the beginning of 1995 were laid out as: (a) Solidarity with Cuba through the mobilization of all possible economic support which the integrants of the Forum could obtain in their respective countries in order to overcome the effects of the cessation of Soviet subsidies. (Lula obtained from then Pres. Itamar Franco, through his Minister of Health, Jamil Haddad, the purchase of $300 million in drugs from Cuba at a critical moment for that nation. For these transactions cf. *O Globo* and *Estado de São Paulo*.) Within this priority was realized also in the Havana of latter January 1994 an International Congress of Solidarity with Cuba. There were 1200 delegates present, largely from LA. The Brazilian delegation was presided over by Senator Amir Lando, chairman of the congressional investigation of P. C. Farias, Collor's "treasurer." (b) The election of Lula in Brazil was the first step in the fundamental project of the Forum. The election of other presidential candidates by parties affiliated with the FSP was also sought in the 14 countries having elections during the subsequent 18 months. (Jorge Castañeda, an integrant of the FSP and the DI, coordinated this priority in the continental press.[29]) (c) Opposition to globalization would begin with implementation of the North American Free Trade Agreement (NAFTA), in Mexico, on 1 January 1994, the day on which there was the "uprising" in Chiapas which resulted in the "liberation" of part of the Mexican territory from the sovereignty of the central power.

On p.14 of *Folha de São Paulo* (6 May 1998) under the headline "Zapatistas Establish a Parallel Government" appeared the report of that group adopting an "organized anarchy" which it "substituted for the traditional structures which furnish education, health care and other services to the populace." This was described as reminiscent of the MST camps (which have received resources from the Federal Government), although that organization considers the government as the "enemy," as it does the latifundists, the security forces, the law, the judiciary and the impresarios. These are considered by MST as institutions and beneficiaries of "bourgeois democracy" which José Rainha Junior[30] described as "nauseating."

The Present Phase of the FSP and the MST

The V Encounter of the FSP was held in Montevideo in May 1995. Its objective was the assessment of the 14 presidential elections which had been held between August 1993 and May 1995 in which the Forum candidates had obtained the extraordinary total of 25 percent of the votes. They had not elected a single presidential candidate. At this encounter the Zapatistas were received into the Forum to which they now belong informally, and it was argued that Chiapas would be the new model for battle by the HL. The EZLN would be the advance guard, through the MST which is a FSP integrant, as are also the PT and the Workers Central (CUT) which would have to share in its strengths.

In 1996 the VI Encounter of the Forum assembled in El Salvador. The V Encounter of the FSP took place in the Porto Alegre of 1997. The meeting was complete with a logo dedicated to Che Guevara through the review, *América Libre,* the official organ of the FSP directed by Frei Betto. The performance boasted the presence of the LA and European left. At this VII Encounter the vanguard mission of the MST was reaffirmed, this in strict liaison with the Zapatistas, in the battle for the socialist revolution on the continent.

The National Congress of the MST was held in Vitória de Espírito Santo in early 1998. A theatrical drama, Lula present, was staged at which a Peoples Tribunal in the Upland Palace condemned to death Fernando Henrique Cardoso, Antonio Carlos Magalhães and Clinton. This was a sermon of hate unusual in Brazil.

The Inter-American Dialog

DI genesis may be traced to a US State Department document of 1974 (NSS-M200) which identifies immigration as a matter of national security for the US. The DI was founded in 1982. One of the founders was Fernando Henrique Cardoso who was joined by other politically active intellectuals such as Raul Alfonsín, Pérez de Cuellar, Oscar Arias, Jorge Sanguinetti, Lozada da Bolivia and impresarios of various stripes. The DI posited the major cause of the migration was poverty in LA which was the fault of the elites who, in 500 years of civilization, counted on the support of the Catholic Church and the Armed Forces. Thus, the elites and their supporters had to be considered as adverse forces. Therefore, the selection of the LA founders of the DI was oriented toward Social Democrats of agnostic and academic evolution. With the "collapse" of the USSR, the radical left ceased to be considered an adversary. Its orphaned status could be avowed through the DI, keeping in mind the need for political reinforcements.

Within this theoretical formulation, the Princeton meeting at the beginning of 1993, coordinated by Fernando Henrique Cardoso and Jorge Castañeda,[29] envisioned a political pact between the FSP and the DI. This was created through the elite of American political liberalism, of Protestant origin, well removed, nevertheless, from any religious contact, but hardly pragmatic, with heavy political, economic and academic weight in their pronouncements. Five presidential candidates, including Lula, were invited to participate by Cardoso, who also proposed them for membership in the DI, a proposal accepted by Lula. On that occasion Cardoso beckoned with his support the candidacy of Lula. With the support of the Brazilian Social Democrat Party (PSDB) Cardos's commitment to Lula was broken when, appointed Finance Minister, he realized he had the opportunity of seeking the presidency himself through his Plano Real. The support of the Liberal Front Party (PFL) in March 1994 convinced him.

The Political Pact Between the DI and the FSP

The points proposed for accord were: (a) the cessation of the armed battle with the transformation of the guerrilla organizations to political parties (such as Minister of Policy Raul Jungmann is now proposing to the MST) assuring the DI the political support and permanency on which a FSP candidate could not always rely. This aspect could reduce immigration to the US, provoked by the armed battle and repression. (b) The renunciation through denunciation of the foreign debt having as its counterpoint economic support to the elitist candidates. (c) A promise of legalized abortion, sterilization and homosexual union as a method of preventing immigration.

Lula asked, moreover, for the examination of the Haitian question where the president elect had been deposed by the military and admitted that Cuba would have to initiate a major economic opening in that maintained by the Fidel Castro regime. The IX National Encounter of PT changed the program with relation to the denunciation of the foreign debt, which would have been automatic had Lula been elected, in order to lull the creditors. It tried also to introduce into the program abortion, sterilization and homosexual union. But the resistance of the Catholic faction, linked to LibTheo, forced the temporary abandonment of these programs.

[Translated from the Portuguese by the LANS Editor]

[Editor's note: The second part of this discussion appears in Chapter 2, BRAZIL.]

Cuba

Editor's Introduction

The Eisenhower Government (EG) of the US was in power when the lifelong ML, Fidel Ruz Castro, occupied the vacuum resulting from the isolation of Batista and his flight. The EG decided to remedy this error by sponsoring an invasion of the HL terrorist boss' satrapy by his disillusioned countrymen. And then the Republican EG was replaced by the Democrat Kennedy Government (KG) which modified and carried out this invasion sponsorship. The Left was of course unanimous in "condemning," this attempt, it honing certain propaganda techniques in declaring the failure as foregone. Under the KG a report was submitted on the operation by the Inspector General, the report having a pro-KG bias which the reader should be able to recognize. Whether the EG, the KG or both was (were) ultimately responsible for what occurred at La Bahía de Cochinos may be judged as the reader finds pleasing to his prejudices, but the report is worthy of reproduction. The reader will probably find his doubts resolved in Grayston L. Lynch's *DECISION FOR DISASTER: Betrayal at the Bay of Pigs* (Brassey's, 1998. ISBN: 1-57488-148-5) which is reviewed in Spcl 7.8, *Yearbook 1999*.

* * *

IG'S REPORT ON THE BAY OF PIGS OPERATION. 1[31]
(SPCL 5.7, 2 MARCH 1998)

EDITOR'S NOTE

If anything was learned from World War (WW) I it was that timid tactical tampering (von Moltke the Younger) with a strategic plan (von Schlieffen) is unacceptable. If anything was learned from WW II it was that local air superiority over the battlefield must be maintained. In the Bay of Pigs (Bahía de Cochinos) operation[32] both of these axioms were violated by the US, assuring failure. This report attempts to deny this elemental fact as do various commentators. While the operation *might* have resulted in failure later in the campaign, there would be no "later" in this campaign to test such a theory. Whatever the name, rank or serial number of the report author, the subliminal impulse to shift responsibility from the KG to the EG is visible in the report. The resulting propaganda victory of the Cuban dictator has probably never been adequately assessed. This report was declassified as a result of a Freedom of Information Act (FOIA) request submitted by the National Security Archive. The report has been abridged, but the original language has generally been maintained. Square brackets indicate space-reducing replacement of excess wordage.

* * *
TOP SECRET
TS No. 173040

INSPECTOR GENERAL'S SURVEY OF THE
CUBAN OPERATION, October 1961
[TABLE OF CONTENTS omitted]

A. INTRODUCTION [p.1]. 1. This is the Inspector General's (IG) report on the CIA's...attempt to implement national policy by overthrowing the Fidel Castro regime...[by] a covert paramilitary operation. 2. The purpose of the report is to evaluate...[CIA] performance of this task, to describe weaknesses and failures...and to make recommendations for their avoidance... 3. The report concentrates on the organization (org), staffing and planning of the project...on the conduct of the covert paramilitary (para) phase...including...intelligence (intel) support, training and security. It does not...detail the...military phase... 4. The supporting annexes...illustrate the evolution of national policy as outlined in Sect. F...Annex A is the basic policy paper approved by Pres. Eisenhower on 17 March 1960. Annex B...[was] prepared by the project's operating chiefs for the briefing of Pres. Kennedy in February 1961. Annexes C, D and E are the planning papers successively prepared during March and April 1961...5. The report includes...roles played by CIA officials in ...conferences and...meetings at which policy decisions...were taken, but...no evaluation of...any official not employed by the CIA. 6. ...the IG and...[staff] interviewed...125...CIA employees...and...[many documents].

B. HISTORY...[p.3] 1. The history...begins in 1959 and...[here] ends with the invasion of Cuba...on 17 Apr 61 and its defeat...in the next two days. 2. Formal US...adoption of the project occurred on 17 March 1960, when...Pres. Eisenhower approved a [CIA] paper..."A Program of Covert Action Against the Castro Regime" (Annex A) and thereby authorized...this program: a. Formation of Cuban exile orgs to attract Cuban loyalties (*sic*), to direct opposition activities and to provide cover for CIA operations. b. A propaganda offensive... c. Creation inside Cuba of a clandestine intel ... apparatus...responsive to...the exile org. d. Development outside Cuba of a...para force...[to be inserted] into Cuba to organize, train and lead resistance... 3. The budget...estimated at $4,400,000...breakdown...Political action $950,000, propaganda $1,700,000, para $1,500,000, intel collection $250,000 4. This document...was...the only US...policy paper issued...[on] the project...The Cuban exile council would serve as cover for action which became publicly known. CIA personnel in contact with Cuban exiles would be documented as representatives of ... private...business...

Preparatory Action 5....preparation had preceded presentation ...In August 1959 the Chief of the CIA's Para Group (PMG) attended a meeting...[on] creation of a para capability...[for] LA...The Chiefs of the PMG prepared...staff studies for the Western Hemisphere Division (WHD) on ... covert limited warfare ... urged the creation of a ... staff. He also set up ... [an] airline ... for support...6. In September 1959 the WHD assigned an officer to plan ... CIA [contingency] action ... [for other] LA countries. There was a lack of ... operational information on potential target areas ... [there] resulted a three-volume operational study[33] 7. By December 1959 ... a plan was produced for training a small cadre of Cuban exiles ... as ... instructors ... [for] ... recruits, in a LA country, for ... infiltration into Cuba ... as leaders ... [of] anti-Castro dissidents.

Organization of Branch 8. On 18 January 1960 the WHD organized Branch 4 (WH/4) ... to run the ... operation. The initial Table of Organization (T/O) totaled 40 ... 18 at Hq, 20 at Havana Station and 2 at Santiago Base. 9. The branch ... [sought] a Panama training site. Its officers ... [checked] Miami [for various logistical and communications (commo) requirements] ... and bases for ... [operations (opns) against Cuba]. 10... Hq and ... Havana Station [studied opposition leaders to create] ... a unified political front ... [and sought] a site for ... [a] radio station.

Preliminary Progress 11... the CIA...[reported] considerable preliminary progress ... and [predicted] early performance in ...[carrying] its request for policy approval to the president in March 1960. 12. [The CIA reported that it]...was in...touch with leaders of three major...anti-Castro groups...[which] would form a unified opposition council within 30 days;...was already supporting opposition broadcasts from Miami;...[would do so from] Massachusetts...a "gray" station, probably on Swan Island, could be...ready in two months; publication of an exile edition of a confiscated Cuban newspaper...arranged;...controlled action group was distributing propaganda inside Cuba...anti-Castro lecturers...on LA tours. 13. The president...[was told] that an effective intel and action org inside Cuba...could probably be created within 60 days... preparations for development of an adequate para force would require "a minimum of six months and probably closer to eight."

Policy Discussions 14. Discussion...preceded [report] submission...In [latter] 1959 the Special Group (SG)[34]...considered...exile broadcasts to Cuba. During Jan and Feb 1960 the Director of Central Intelligence (DCI) informed the SG of CIA planning...14 March was devoted to [program] discussion...[There was concern over time for exile training, discussion of US overt action capability.] The Chairman of the Joint Chiefs (JCS)...[allegedly] said that forces...[of] 50,000 were ready...the first...could be airborne within four hours...formation of an exile junta [urged]...The CIA...[intended to request] funds to pursue the program... 15. ... [unseating] Castro had...become a major CIA activity with...highest sanction...[using] activity of...[an] expanding operating branch requiring...[continuous] attention in higher...echelons and...liaison with other agencies... 16. The activities...continued [rapidly]...but the financial approach... [was] cautious.

Financial Preparations 17. On 24 March 1960 the project was approved by DCI...[with] $900,000 for ...Fiscal...1960...two weeks later...WH/4...reported...85 percent of [this]...obligated... By 30 June an additional $1,000,000...obligated. 18. [DCI told WH/4 in Apr he would draw personnel worldwide. Between January 1960 and 16 April 1961 WH/4 grew from 40 to 588 personnel, its T/O not including air personnel of the Development Projects Division (DPD) or support personnel.] 19. ...early...[in] the project there were...[strong] efforts to organize an exile front group, to... [create] a broad...propaganda program...to being a para program and to acquire sites...for training...recruitment...and offices. 20. The..."Bender Group,"...of project political action officers, was set up to provide cover for dealing with the Cubans...a nominally unified Frente Revolucionario Democratico (FRD)...of several Cuban factions, was...[accepted] 11 May 1960.

Propaganda Activity 21. Radio broadcasts from Miami...continued... Preparations were made for...publication of *Avance*, ...Havana plant seized by Castro. Anti-Castro propaganda...was intensified...[in] LA...a boat for marine broadcasts...purchased. Swan Island station... completed and on the air by 17 May. 22. The...instruction-training program was being prepared, and $25,000...[in] sterile arms...sent to the Panama training base...activated 11 May...Useppa Island, Florida, was acquired...[for] Cuban para candidates...training radio operators. Screening of para recruits...in Miami in Apr...training in Panama began in June. 23... Miami Base... opened...25 May in...Coral Gables business district...cover...New York...[personnel] firm...

[with] Department of Defense (DOD) contract...on 15 June a commo site, with Army cover... opened at the former Richmond Naval Air Station... Safe houses...acquired in the Miami area ...use of other sites for project activities... 24. Project officers...in liaison on...[various]...Apr ...agreement with the Immigration and Naturalization Service (INS) on special entry procedure for Cubans...[in] the operation...[consultation] with Voice of America (VOA) and the US Information Agency (USIA) on propaganda operations...and with the Federal Commo Commission (FCC) on...Radio Swan and with DOD...[on] cover. The State Department (State) ...regularly consulted...

<u>Uneasy Front</u> 25. ...Cuban leaders..."front"...an uneasy one...[there was no] agreement... among themselves or with CIA...on politics or operations. 26. Power struggles...early in...the PRD. The Cuban leaders wanted...[voice in] the course of para operations...[in] May 1960 one ...prominent leader was urging an invasion...from a third country. 27. By June the American press...[had wind of] the operation, principally at Radio Swan...[poor] operational security... [indicated by] Cuban naval attache [defector who said] that it was common knowledge among exiles...that a Cuban leader [had CIA backing] and that "there were entirely too many Americans...around...waving money." 28. On 22 June the Deputy DCI briefed the National Security Couuncil (NSC)...[The briefing stated the training objective to be a 500-man force of about 25 teams, each adept at organizing and leading dissident groups, each with a radio operator. Also in preparation were an exile air force and a maritime support capability for paras.] 29. This briefing...[expressed] doubt that a purely clandestine effort...[could] cope with Castro's increasing military capability... [It stated that para success would depend on dissident forces which had not yet emerged.]

<u>Training in Panama</u>

30. ...air training program began...in Jul 60...[asked] Defense[35] for 12 AD-5s and the Navy... [for] 75...personnel. 31. ...[by] mid Jun 29...arrived in Panama for...[infiltration] training... 32. ...PRD resisting CIA attempts...to move its Hq to Mexico...[and reluctant to support] recruiting of Cuban pilots...[PRD] presented budget for $500,000 a month, excluding para costs...[granted] $131,000 if...[moved] to Mexico... [PRD agreed] to furnish 500 paras...[and moved] to Mexico. It remained there only a few weeks because of

harassment by the Mexican Govt [contrary to agreements]. It appears...PRD...[opposition to third country base was based on desire for] official channel to the US Govt.

Emphasis on Resistance

33. In Aug WH/4 [prepared briefings for Pres and JCS.] By...1 Nov...500 paras and 37 radio operators [expected to be] ready ... this group...available for...infiltration teams...[or] invasion ...briefing paper for JCS...[stated] "... successful implementation of any large-scale para opn is dependent on widespread guerrilla resistance..." 34. ...[briefing paper for Pres] identified 11 groups or individuals [with] assets in Cuba [and with whom CIA had contact]...[paper for JCS described] problems of obtaining support bases and trained man power and warned that an exile invasion force might have to be backed by a contingency force, augmented by US Special Forces ... 35. [Terms "invasion," "strike" and "assault" appear in these documents] although the strike force concept does not seem to have been given...policy sanction until the Special Group meeting...toward the end of 1960.

Plan of Operations

36. The Presidential briefing paper of August 1960 outlined the plan of opns as follows: "The initial phase of para opns envisages the development support and guidance of dissident groups in... Pinar del Rio, Escambray and Sierra Maestra. These groups will be organized for concerted guerrilla action... (¶) "The second phase...a combined sea-air assault by PRD forces on the Isle of Pines coordinated with guerrilla activity on the main island...establish a close-in staging base...(¶) "The last phase will be an air assault on the Havana area with the guerrilla forces... moving on the ground...[into] Havana..." 37. Expenditures...running beyond the original estimates...WHD estimated operating costs [for four weeks beginning 1 Jul] at $1,700,000 and for the fiscal year at...$25,000,000. On 19 Aug additional $10,000,000...obtained...half of this [$10mil ?] was the [para cost] another $2,000,000...or propaganda.

Anti-Castro Broadcasts

38. Propaganda [started early and] developed rapidly... Radio Swan had gone on the air first with anti-Trujillo, then with anti-Castro broadcasts. Radio programs were originating in Miami and (blacked out)...*Avance in Exile* [in publication by summer's end, weekly magazine planned]...some successful black opns. Most such

opns...without [FRD participation]. 39. [FRD lawyer team by August for LA propaganda tour, Radio Swan broadcasting with] worldwide reception...anti-Castro comic book...Spanish TV program... 40. [By August WH/4 found no bilingual Radio Swan announcer. One found 28 December quit by 18 January.] 41. September 1960...first maritime opn and first air drop over Cuba. [The first successful, the second a failure, para executed.]

Maritime Operations

42. Several successful maritime opns...[latter] 1960 before severe winter weather...only one boat...available...supplying and building up a resistance movement...slow...[Castro] strengthened with 30 to 40 thousand tons of Bloc arms, and Cuban internal security tightened. 43 ...strike force concept...[playing] greater role in WH/4 planning...role dominant in September 1960 with assignment of [Marine amphibious opn expert]. 44. In October Nicaragua Govt offered CIA use of air strip and docking facilities at Puerto Cabezas...250 miles closer to Cuba than Guatemala ...CIA asked Army...[for] 38 Special Forces personnel...[arrived in Guatemala 12 January 1961].

Switch in Concept

45. On 4 November 1960 WH/4...[changed course by] expanding the size of the para unit [with training] along more conventional military lines...Guatemala Base...had 475 air and ground trainees on 10 November [increased recruiting efforts in Miami]. 46. [By November] Miami Base...had recruited and dispatched to Guatemala 101 air and 370 para trainees plus six specialists (doctors, dentists and chaplains)...base had recruited 124 maritime personnel... 47. [Strike force strength 644 on 28 January 1961, 685 on 3 February, 826 on 10 March, 973 on 22 March, 1,390 on 6 April 1961.] 48. On 3 November 1960 WH/4 reported...only $2,250,000 left for [rest of Fiscal 1961] by 16 December this was almost gone... additional $28,200,000 was obtained from the Bureau of the Budget.

IG'S REPORT ON THE BAY OF PIGS OPERATION. II
(SPCL 5.10, 28 MARCH 1998)

<u>Freedom Fund Campaign</u> 49. ...financial problems... To publicize Radio Swan...the Cuban Freedom Fund Campaign was organized in November...budgeted at $900,000 for Fiscal...1961, [received] $330 in gifts... 50. <u>Bohemia Libre</u>...magazine, budgeted at $300,000...[cost]

$35,000 an issue...bad luck...in advertising... Additional funds sought...developed a circulation of 126,000... 51. ...the project moved forward [equipment, training, negotiating, public relations]...[attempts] to move arms, men and propaganda into Cuba...the FRD...[made] little progress toward unity. 52 Members [of FRD] would resign ...Each faction [wanted all the supplies]...groups inside [Cuba] reluctant to receive infiltrees sent...[by] FRD. The FRD coordinator...made unauthorized broadcasts.

Provisional Government Plans 53. ...a provisional government...first discussed with FRD leaders in December...intrigue and bickering...did nothing to advance the cause of unity. In mid-January Miami Base reported..."[problem is] to maintain...[FRD] as an operational façade until...provisional government...established." [Deadlock on how and by whom.] 54. ...dead center...resolved by an ultimatum to the FRD...agree on the...Revolutionary Council (RC) or risk...support. 55. ...FRD...[partially] responsive and useful...[example:] counterintelligence and security service... 56. By mid-March this security organization had 86 employees of whom 37 were trained case officers...[had] graduated four classes from its own training center...

Security Activities 57. ...[FRD] ran operations into Cuba...[created] card files on Cuban personalities...[reported on FRD meetings with other groups and] political maneuvering within the FRD...[helped recruit] strike force...when political leaders were sabotaging the effort. [Security and counterintel teams trained, mission: secure documents during invasion, establish martial law after] 58. ...[FRD] radio monitoring...interrogations and debriefings ...supplied...first information on...C-54...forced down in Jamaica after a mission over Cuba. 59. ...[during first quarter 1961] Army Special Forces...in Guatemala, the brigade trainee quota only half fulfilled...[call] for special recruiting teams...[in] Miami. ...[trainees in the camp] had no contact with the political front... Disturbances...[three FRD persuaded to visit the camp].

Training in the US 60. ...Nicaraguan air strip...and two new training sites were activated. Although...[no US policy on US training of Cubans] 25 tank operators were [trained at Fort Knox]. ...project acquired use of Belle Chase Ammunition Depot near New Orleans...for training [company-sized unit for diversion landing and as undersea demolition team]. 61. ...between the US national elections and the inauguration [policy-making slowdown]...piecemeal decisions...[i.e., tactical air strikes and American contract pilots]. 62. Pres. Eisenhower ...general go-ahead on 29 November [reaffirmed 3 January 1961]. [Example of slow down, denial of propaganda drop on 13 January. On 19 January a "high-level" meeting—State and Defense secretaries—reaffirmed basic concepts.]

Preparations Endorsed 63. ...[on] 22 January...project and current preparation were generally endorsed. [On 28 January the CIA and Pres. Kennedy met, the former] authorized to continue present activities [and submit plan to JCS]...By 6 February JCS [evaluated favorably with suggestions]. 64. ...[On 17 February CIA outlined three courses of action] to the president...against Castro. 65. ...paper described the growing strength of the Castro regime under (Soviet) Bloc support...[and estimated that after six months] it will become militarily infeasible to overthrow the Castro regime...[without] a sizable military force... 66. ...paper...[eliminated] small-scale guerrilla groups...advocated a surprise landing of a military force, concluding that the brigade had a good chance of overthrowing Castro...[without US commitment]... 67. ...[presidential decision postponed for two weeks...action to expand the force up to 1,000 [withheld] for the time being.

Movement of Agents 68. ...WH/4 Branch was still...[supplying] the underground... [6 successful boat opns in February, 13 in March, 2 air drops in March. 15 February personnel in Cuba: 20 counterintel, 5 intel, 2 propaganda, 4 paras. 15 March: 21, 11, 9, 6.] 69. [Invasion date strength Miami Base 160.] 70. Successive changes in the operational plan and postponements of the strike date... Detailed policy authorization...either never...clarified or only resolved at [last minute]...central decision...[on] employ strike force...in doubt to...embarkation. 71. ... In early March [State]...asked the [CIA] not to announce formation of the RC or...[do anything] until after the 5-9 March Mexico City Peace Conference...[Cuban disagreement on post-Castro platform; counterintel problems in Guatemala] ...

Sabotage Action 72. [12 March Landing Craft, Infantry (LCI) "Barbara J" in successful opn against Texaco refinery at Santiago] 73. [13-15 March project chiefs prepare revised plan to meet State objections. To president 15.] 74. [Mid March 10 more FRD executive committee members. Survey. Impatience in Guatemala.] 75. José Miro Cardona was unanimously elected Chairman of the RC. 76. [Late March Swan Island radio closing down.] Ships with strike force equipment ...arriving in Nicaragua...Guatemala camp still receiving trainees...[by] 4 April.

Overflights Suspended 77. [Cuban overflights suspended 28 March. Two reasons]: (a) ...aircraft (a/c) needed to move strike force from Guatemala to Puerto Cabezas, Nicaragua, for embarkation ...(b) ...to avoid any incident [downed a/c, etc.]...during...pre-invasion period. 78. [Papers on defection program and internal Cuban support for White House meet 29 March.] 79. On 5 April the B-26 "defection plan" was prepared [Effort to eliminate part Castro air before D-Day in "State-pleasing" way. Abort "plan": divert force to Vieques Island for demob.] 80. **On 12 April** at a meeting with the president it was decided that Mr. Berle would tell Miro Cardona there would be **no overt US support**...President...announced [on 13 April all WH/4 hq sections (sects) on 24-hour duty. RC to be briefed in stages on the military aspects. 14 April RC agreed to "isolation" for the landing phase.] 81. ...raids on three Cuban airfields...by eight B-26s on 15 Apr... destruction of half Castro's air...[estimated from] post-strike photos. (Editor's note: Note that no, repeat no mention is made that this was the only strike; all other planned strikes called off.) [Pilot landed Florida reported bombing by defectors from Castro air. Diversionary expedition trained in New Orleans failed to land on two successive nights.] 82. [Just prior to D-Day radio broadcasts, medium wave 18 hours/day, short 16. (Editor's note: In the same paragraph it is stated that these totals were increased after D-Day to 55 hours and 26 hours, respectively. Presumably this adds the hours from the various medium stations for 55 per day.) 12 million pounds of leaflets dropped on Cuba.] 83. [D-Day = 16 Apr 61] **Late on 16 April ...air strikes ...to knock out the rest of Castro's air on the following morning were called off. The message reached the field too late to halt the landing opn, as the decision to cancel the air strike was made after the landing force had been committed.** (Editor's note: This statement appears to be incorrect; see Grayston L. Lynch , *DECISION FOR DISASTER: Betrayal at the Bay of* Pigs (Brassey's, 1998. ISBN: 1-57488-148-5) to be reviewed in *Yearbook 1999*.) 84. The invasion fleet...assembled off south coast Cuba [late 16 April: 2 CIA LCIs, 1 US Navy Landing Ship, Dock (LSD) carrying 3 Landing Craft, Utility (LCU), 4 Landing Craft, Vehicles and Personnel (LCVP) all preloaded, and 7 commercial freighters. 3 of the freighters in follow-up not employed. Vessels armed with 50 cal

MGs (no spec (ns)), LCIs with 2 75mm recoilless.] 85. [Equipment in addition to personal: "Sufficient" Browning Automatic Rifles (BAR), Caliber 30, M1918-M1922, origin since intro various), MGs (ns), mortars (ns), recoilless (ns), rocket launchers (ns), flame throwers, 5 M-41 tanks, 12 trucks, fuel tractor, bulldozer, 2 water trailers and various "small" trucks and tractors.] 86. ...invasion brigade [included 5 infantry companies (cos), 1 heavy weapons co, intel-recon co, 1 tank platoon and 1 airborne infantry co (177 men not in the landing party). Total personnel 1,511.] 87. ...troops...moved by air on 3 successive nights from Guatemala to Nicaragua...where they embarked on [New Orleans pre loaded] ships. [Separate courses to rendezvous 40 miles offshore. "Unobtrusive" Navy escort. Then to point 5,000 yards from landing area.] 88 ...three follow-up ships [one to arrive D+2, other 2 at sea south of Cuba. Additional supplies in Guatemala, Nicaragua, Florida and Alabama.] ...30,000 dissidents expected to rally to the invasion force. 89. ...landing at 3 beaches about 18 mi... [apart on Zapata Peninsula] [From left flank to right:] Red Beach at...Cochinos Bay; Green Beach [right, no location]...Blue Beach [center, no location]...coastal strip [of] about 40 mi... separated from the interior by an impassable swamp [3 roads through, flanked by coast road from east]. 90. ...early...17 Apr Cuban...teams led by American contract employees, ashore to mark Red and Blue...[Small fire fights but marking successful.]...troops began moving ashore in small aluminum boats and LCUs...small militia forces...offered little opposition... 91. ...after daylight airborne infantry co...from C-46 a/c (Editor note: Number a/c not given.) to 4 of the 5 ...drop zones...[for] sealing off approach roads. 92. At dawn began the enemy air attacks which the project chiefs had aimed to prevent by the planned dawn strikes with Nicaragua-based a/c against Castro's fields. [Castro's B-26s, Sea Furies (this is the British carrier a/c Hawker Fury 2) and T33s (the trainer version of the Lockheed F-80) sunk a supply ship, beached a transport and damaged an LCI. Green Beach landing abandoned, troops ashore at Blue Beach. Shipping withdrew.] 93. ...air attacks continued...B-26s of Cuban exile force...no match for the T-33s...4 of Castro's a/c shot down by MG fire from maritime craft, assisted by friendly air... 94. ...Red Beach hit by... waves of militia...[throughout] 17 April. While ammunition lasted ... beaten off with heavy enemy casualties...several [Castro tanks] destroyed by ground or friendly air ...On... 8 April, the Red Beach

Force...retired...to Blue Beach... 95. [Friendly B-26s sank Castro vessel and attacked Cienfuegos air strip. 4 shot down, 3 back to Nicaragua, 4 to friendly bases.] 96. [Attempts at ammunition resupply by air next two nights. Resupply by sea aborted due to enemy air action.] 97. At Blue Beach enemy ground attacks [with air support] began from 3 directions...18 April. 6 friendly B-26s, 2 of them flown by Americans [destroyed "several" tanks and 20 troop carrying trucks in column from west] Air support to Blue Beach [continued on 19 April, 3 friendly a/c down]. **Jet cover from the Navy aircraft carrier Essex had been expected to protect the 19 April sorties, but a misunderstanding over timing hampered its effectiveness.** 98. ... resupply of ammunition had now become impossible....On the night of 18 April...the Cuban brigade commander refused an offer to evacuate his troops...morning of 19 April...the brigade was still able to launch a futile counterattack... 99. In the last hours...the brigade commander sent a series of...messages to the task force command ship ...: "We are out of ammo and fighting on the beach. Please send help. We cannot hold." "In water. Out of ammo. Enemy closing in. Help must arrive in next hour." "When your help will be here and with what?" "Why your help has not come?' 100. ...last message...: "Am destroying all equipment and communications. Tanks are in sight. I have nothing to fight with. Am taking to the woods. I cannot repeat cannot wait for you." 101. An evacuation convoy was headed for the beach on the afternoon of 19 April...the convoy reversed course. 102. During the next few days 2 Americans and a Cuban frogman crew... [rescued 26] from the beach and coastal islands.

[Editor's Note: Section C appears to be largely devoted to an apologia for Pres. Kennedy as innocent of any blame (par. 1,2) for having removed the air cover. The thesis is advanced that the operation might have failed anyhow (par. 3) because of all sorts of CIA mistakes (par.4-5). That this crystal-ball "evaluation" might be true is irrelevant.]

C. SUMMARY OF EVALUATION [p.34]

1.In evaluating the CIA performance it is essential to avoid grasping (*sic*)...at the explanation that the President's order canceling the D-Day air strikes was the chief cause of the failure. 2. Discussion of that one decision would merely raise (*sic*) this underlying question: If the project had been better conceived...[etc.] would that precise issue ever have had to be presented for Presidential decision at all?...3. [Opn "possibly doomed in advance," etc.] 4. ["The fundamental cause of the disaster was the CIA's failure" (sic) to do a litany of things to include organization, personnel and command.] 5. [Deficiencies in the areas of par 5 resulted in "pressures and distortions" yielded another litany of "mistakes and omissions."

In Section D, "EVALUATION OF ORGANIZATION AND COMMAND STRUCTURE," various command and staff faults are discussed, these exemplified by the inadequate rank of the project chief who did not have the powers of a task force commander. Section E, "EVALUATION OF STAFFING," finds predictable mistakes.

F. EVALUATION OF PLANNING (p.46)

3. [Plan approved (17 March 1960) by Pres. Eisenhower for slow buildup of guerrilla forces in Cuba.] 4. [13 months later amphibious landing replaced original plan.] 5. [By November 1960 SG decided that Castro's increased Soviet-supplied strength made plan obsolete.] 7. [November 1960 SG submitted plan for air infiltration (80) and amphibious landing (650-700). Draw "dissident" elements.] 8. [Pres. Eisenhower "in effect" said proceed and let new Administration make "definitive decisions."] 10-11. [Mid January 1961 request by CIA (a) use US contract pilots, (b) use US air base and (c) start air strikes dawn of D-1 turned down. Use of Puerto Cabezas approved.] 12. [Conflict between "political acceptability" and "military effectiveness."] 27. [CIA matching 1,500-man brigade against Revolutionary Army (32,000) and militia (200,000) with 30 to 40,000 tons Soviet materiel according to US Intel Board reports, "The Military Buildup in Cuba," (30 Nov 60, 9 February 1961).[32]] 31. [Four mistakes in planning: a. no plan appraisal, b. president not advised that success dubious and recommend aborting, c. plan became overt, d. no request for specific approval of plan papers.] <u>Existence of Warnings</u> (34.-36.), <u>Consequences of Cancellation</u> (37.-44.), <u>Piecemeal Policy</u> (45.-46.) 47. [Evening of 16 April the President instructed State Secretary that the D-Day strikes set for the following morning should be cancelled.] <u>A Civilian Decision</u> 48. [Earlier on evening of 16 April the project chief and his para chief warned the Deputy Director Plans (DD/P) that cancellation of the strikes would produce disaster. The DD/P, a civilian without military experience, and the Deputy Director of Central Intelligence (DDCI), an Air Force general, did not follow the advice. The president made this vital, last-

minute decision without direct contact with the military chiefs of the opn.] 49, The President may never have been clearly advised of the need for...[air superiority] in an amphibious opn...

CUBAN COMMUNISM NINTH EDITION
(SPCL 6.6, 31 AUGUST 1998)

It is almost forty years since the "lifelong" avowed ML, Fidel Castro, became the dictator of Cuba and began converting it into a human and economic charnel house from which hundreds of thousands of Cubans have fled and in which unknown numbers have been imprisoned and slaughtered. Only in the last week, however, the Dominican communications media has chronicled his progression through that nation in attending the CARICOM meeting there as if portraying the progress of some sort of abused international hero and savior (Wkly 6.9 above).

This reality, together with a spectrum of related realities, renders the almost simultaneous appearance of *CUBAN COMMUNISM* not only a welcome, but also a sorely needed antidote.

CUBAN COMMUNISM. Irving Louis Horowitz and Jaime Suchlicki (Editors). Transaction Publishers. New Brunswick (U.S.A.) and London (U.K.). 849p+xx. Two Appendices. Ninth Edition. ISBN: 0-7658-0456-5 Reviewed by the LANS Editor.

This wide-ranging yet detailed book should be in the library of any individual or institution that has an interest, not only in Cuba, but anywhere in that Latin America on which the island has had, and continues to have, such an important influence. Because this Ninth Edition is so wide-ranging, this review can only scratch the surface of its forty-eight articles produced by its fifty distinguished authors.

By dividing the work into its five parts and two appendices, however, the editors have provided a facile way of sketching its contents. Part 1 deals with the "History" of Cuba, Part 2 with its "Economy," Part 3 with its "Society," Part 4 with its "Military" and Part 5 with its "Polity." The two appendices were prepared for, and first published in, this Ninth Edition and offer a most useful addition. Appendix 1 (or Chapter 47, pp. 837- 870), "Chronology of the Cuban Revolution: 1959-1998," is a year-by-year compilation of events in Cuba and those global events which have affected Cuba. It will provide an excellent fingertip reference for all sorts of historians, latin americanist and otherwise.

Appendix 2 (or Chapter 48, pp. 871 - 886), "Current and Past Revolutionary Leaders," contains generally brief biographies of nineteen such leaders, beginning with the familiar Ricardo Alarcón, proceeding through the fleetingly familiar Camilo Cienfuegos, but skipping one important old acquaintance, now "accidentally" deceased, Manuel (Barbaroja) Piñiera Losado. The list terminates with Sergio del Valle Jiménez.

The authors largely occupy university positions, less than half of them in what may loosely be defined as independent research organization. Bringing up the rear are some four writers from the communication media, two from the *New York Times* and one from Radio Martí. As with topic details, this effectively eliminates the possibility of any remarks on these authors' biographies save for the case of the two editors who are also contributors themselves.

Irving Louis Horowitz is University Professor and Hannah Arendt Distinguished Professor of Sociology and Political Science at Rutgers University. His fellow editor, Jaime Suchlicki, is Professor of History at the Graduate School of International Studies at the University of Miami and was formerly executive director of the university's North-South Center. And as to the articles which they have edited, we can at least begin by pointing out those which have (apparently) not appeared in editions of *CUBAN COMMUNISM* previous to this Ninth Edition (CC).

The four articles which were identified as being first published in CC9 are:

(1) Jorge Salazar-Carillo, "The Cuban Economy as Seen Through Its Trading Partners."

(2) Ramón C. Barquin III, "The Castro Regime Under the Bretton Woods System."

(3) Juan M. del Aguila, "The Cuban Armed Forces: Changing Roles, Continued Loyalties."

(4) Josep M. Colomer, "After Fidel, What? Forecasting Institutional Change in Cuba."

Those articles published elsewhere at the time of the Eighth Edition (1995) will be assumed not to have appeared in CC8. Those articles published after 1995 will also be assumed not to have appeared in CC8. Therefore, the following additional papers may be presumed new:

(5) Jorge F. Pérez-López, "Cuba's Socialist Economy: The Mid-1990s," *J. Communist Studies and Transaction Politics 11*, p.125 (1995).

(6) Jaime Suchlicki, "Cuba: Without Subsidies," *Cuba Brief*, 3 (March 1997).

(7) Michael Radu, "Cuba's Transition: Institutional Lessons from Eastern Europe," *J. Inter-American Studies and World Affairs 37*, 83 (Summer 1995).

(8) Edward González, "Actors, Models and Endgames," *Cuba: Clearing Perilous Waters*, RAND, 107 (1996).

(9) Pamela S. Falk, "The U.S.-Cuba Agenda: Opportunity or Stalemate," *J. Inter-American Studies and World Affairs 39*, 153(1998).

(10) Irving Louis Horowitz, "Political Pilgrimage and the End of Ideology," Lecture, University of Miami (1996).

In their Introduction to CC9 the editors first marshal the "significant events (which) have taken place in the Cuban infrastructure" as (1) "economic reforms initiated in 1994-95 have come to a halt"; (2) "Castro clamped down harshly on dissident groups in the island"; (3) the Cuban caudillo "downed in international waters two small unarmed civilian planes"; (4) "the Clinton administration responded by supporting the passage of the Helms-Burton Act"; (5) "in October 1997 Castro held the Fifth Communist Party Congress, reaffirming his anti-Americanism and commitment to...a ML system"; (6) "Pope John Paul II visited the island criticizing both Cuban violations of human rights and the U.S. embargo"; and (7) "the U.S. government reacted...offering an olive branch to the Cuban dictator..."

The remainder of this excellent Introduction enlarges on this set of significant events, perhaps with greatest emphasis on the Fifth Party Congress. "The final party document and Castro's long speech to the Congress showed a determination to stay the (ML) course...The Party Congress...reasserted Raúl Castro's position as the undisputed heir to Fidel Castro's dynasty." Which very nearly says it all, save for certain cogent remarks on the papal visit.

"The visit...while changing very little internally on the island, seems to have energized those groups advocating a change in U.S. policy. The Castro government seems to have provided the Church in Cuba greater space...(although) the Church remains at the mercy and benevolence of the regime." The conclusion appears unescapable:

> Yet the Pope's visit and subsequent statements and pressure from the Vatican and others is forcing presidential politics in the United States to return to its policies of the pre-Helms-Burton era...concessions and constructive engagement did not work in the past. They are not likely to work in the future.

The "good things" in this book are legion. However, the one area in which a statement could be made on things which might be improved is in that of references. Since most of the writers herein wallow in references as a way of life—as of course they should—this may seem a bit harsh. However, one encounters that set of tabus which is imposed on those who devote themselves to "research" in the humanities—there are also a rather bizarre set evolving in the sciences—one rather fuzzily-described tabu being that of PC and Political Incorrectness (PIC).

PC & PIC

One of the most luminous bits of PC in today's world has to do with the alleged transmogrification of the USSR from an ML totalitarian tyranny to a free-enterprise democracy. While this reviewer is unqualified to take a position on this, there is a body of opinion[36] which considers this view pollyanna. Yevgenia Albats[37] may be included in this group, although she might not agree. In any event, the reviewer suggested this book to a friend a few years ago. The friend called the publisher's shop and was told there was no such book. Obtaining the publisher's name and telephone from the reviewer, he contacted him and had no difficulty securing a copy. Do we have KGB agents at Farrar etc.? Probably not, what we have is PC in the lower echelons.

Tacho (Anastasio) Somoza (Debayle), Nicaraguan caudillo, had his Praetorian Guard and appears to have appropriated whatever was "not nailed down" but was a paragon of "human rights" (HR) compared to Arce, Borge, Cerna, the Ortegas, Pastora and the other MLs who succeeded him. But he has, nevertheless, been the object of an impressive PC campaign. As has "his"[38] book. Cox first encountered what one might call publisher's PC in seeking a publisher, finally settling for publication by The John Birch Society's house organ, an organization the level of whose PIC is sufficient for it to have been censored from the scene. But the book is of considerable value, if only, as one of our associate editors remarked not long after its appearance, "for the Pezzullo tapes."[39]

While the lead in examples above have nothing to do with CC9, the reviewer's perhaps too superficial perusal of its references seems to indicate a routine and generally deliberate ignorance of that rich lode of material available from the hearings of the US Congress. Of particular interest are the hearings of the House Committee on Un-American Activities and the Senate Sub Committee on Internal Security (SSIS), the hearings before the latter perhaps of the greater interest of the two. As reference material, only one set of hearings by the SSIS can be briefly considered.

Perhaps most worthy of mention are the hearings entitled "Communist Threat to the US Through the Caribbean" which began in 1959 (Y4.J89/2:C73/27/pt.1; hereinafter, Threat 1) and continued through 1971 (Threat 25).

Where the description of the Bogotazo (cf. pp.109ff, YRBK97) appears in CC9 is hardly important. What is important is that it could have been improved by reference to various testimony in these hearings, perhaps in particular by the sworn testimony of US Ambassador Spruille Braden (Threat 5) and US Ambassador William D. Pawley (Threat 10). Nor is the valuable coverage of the Bogotazo limited in these hearings to this testimony: the invaluable contributions to real understanding of that COMINTERN operation from the book[40] of the Colombian security chief at the time is almost worth the trek through these hearings.

Nor is it important where the reference to the alleged murder of Camilo Cienfuegos Gorriaran appears in CC9. But it could have been improved upon by the testimony under oath of Juan Orta Cordoba (Threat 14), the director of Castro's personal office who defected in 1964. Orta heard Castro's plaintive query of his brother, "Isn't it true that this can't be, Rául?" This, of course after Camilo had been reported "found" on a local station which was to suffer for its inaccuracy.

And, finally, the hackneyed, "We didn't know Castro was a ML," reminiscent of the lament that the Chicoms were just "agrarian reformers." Robert C. Hill was US ambassador to Mexico during the period. His testimony under oath (Threat 12) contained a report which he had prepared at the request of Governor Bowles and Robert Kennedy. Only a portion of the key paragraph in this report need be reproduced here.

> Study of adequate intelligence information on Castro could have prevented the mistaken policy of sympathy for him before he took over Cuba. His Communist affiliations were well known to our Embassy in Mexico, when he was a refugee in that country in 1955. They were fully reported in Washington, yet we went ahead 3 and 4 years later and kidded ourselves that Castro was not a Communist.

Mexico

CUI BONO?
THE ACTEAL, MEXICO, MASSACRE
(WKLY 5.1, 8 JANUARY 1998)

At the beginning of Christmas Week 45 members of a support base for the terrorist EZLN were massacred during what was allegedly a Christmas celebration in the village of Acteal. This account is that of an EZLN spokesman who blamed members of a "paramilitary organization made up of Institutional Revolutionary Party (PRI) militants." Who did what?

During the funeral, which was held on Christmas Day, the arrests of those identified as belonging to the group which carried out the massacre began. Indians were massacred and other Indians were apprehended. The HL began its campaign against the "paramilitary" and the PRI the following morning, original information disseminated by EZLN spokesmen. Who did what?

Whoever did it—and there is no "evidence" yet available linking anyone but the paras to the deed—there is no question as to who won and who lost. The EZLN, a member in good standing of the HL, and the new DF governor, Cuauhtémoc Cárdenas, are substantial winners and have taken every opportunity to build on this advantage. The losers are the PRI and the paras.

The communications media has contented itself with wallowing in an orgy of horror and has apparently had neither the time nor the inclination to investigate any information save that originally furnished by the terrorists. And they may be right, the EZLN simply fortunate to have this opportunity thrust into its lap and adept indeed at taking immediate advantage of it. As of course have all the professional HR organizations. But were PRI and the paras really this moronic?

The target and the date of the massacre could not have been more ideally chosen for effect. There were allegedly 9 men, 21 women, 14 children and 1 baby killed. (It was originally reported that 15 children were killed, but this was later changed to 14 and 1 for accuracy or effect.) Although the women and some of the children have occasionally proven as deadly as the men in their service to the HL, this hardly mars the effect. The massacre occurred about noon on Monday, 22 December, thus assuring that the mass funeral with all its attendant publicity would occur on Christmas Day.

In the same vein a report by the Bartolomé de las Casas HR Center (CDHF) stated that the Attorney General of the Republic (PGR) "rescued" another 80 people "threatened" by the paras, the most interesting part of this report being that the Polhó Autonomous Council, described as a "pro Zapatista" group, "assisted" the PGR personnel. An attack by terrorist boss Guillen on the Mexican and State of Chiapas Governments is discussed in Spcl 5.1 below.

There are three obviously possible scenarios for this affair which will be discussed, following which various facts relating to the EZLN, its associates and its supporters will be reviewed.

Three Scenarios

Scenario 1. LANS distributed Spcl 5.1 below prior to the distribution of this report in order that the reader may be familiar with the scenario presented by the EZLN. Had the stereotypical ML propaganda contained in their "communiqué" been a bit less blatant, it would seem that it might have been more effective than it is. But with the gullibility or sympathy of a press, which has been carrying EZLN "testimony" as if it were news, perhaps such is not the case.

The EZLN scenario is simple: The Zedillo-PRI Government has been creating "paramilitary" organizations for several years for the express purpose of slaughtering pro-EZLN Indians. Acteal was simply an incident in this campaign.

The Mexican Government has apparently, and quite properly, been forming Self Defense Patrols (CAP) which have proven immensely effective throughout LA in protecting farmers and ranchers against the depredations of these ML terrorists. The woes of such "country people" usually receive short shrift from the press, much of which often appears to have a built-in bias in favor of the ML. A long account of this appeared in the Mexican weekly, *Proceso* [No.1105, 4 January 1998]. It should be of interest in this context, but its title, "Plan of the Army in Chiapas Since 1994: To Create Paramilitary Bands, to Displace the Populace, to Destroy the EZLN Support Bases..."—the subtitle is worse—should invoke caution in its use, and the accuracy of the material therein cannot be guaranteed.

Scenario 2. The EZLN carried out the slaughter itself as part of a substantial disinformation operation. The arrests which have been made to this point appear to render this scenario improbable.

There are contradictions which must first be introduced in order even to consider this situation. The EZLN [Spcl 5.1 below] states that there were no survivors, and yet "survivors" are allegedly the ones who "identified" the guilty parties who have thus far been arrested. The EZLN cannot "have it both ways." If there were no survivors, how were the "guilty" identified? Although the assumption is not without weaknesses, it can be assumed that there were survivors.

These would probably know some of the local CAP people; they would certainly, as EZLN or pro-EZLN, know the local Zapas. Therefore, one of them, as a near victim, could be expected to inform on his friends. Of course, if there were no survivors, only well-coached outsiders, the argument loses much of its weight.

The EZLN was apparently defending itself from possible implication in declaring that "the Zapatista arms, in their immense majority, are sticks provided by various trees of the forest..." Nonsense, replied the Minister of the Interior in a seven-page report, the [small] cache of EZLN arms found at Yalchiptyc, Chiapas, were not sticks but the sort of weapons used at Acteal [*El Universal*, 2 January 1998]. Furthermore, such arms are readily available at La Mesilla, Guatemala, from the flow originating with the disarmed terrorist groups to the south [*El Universal*, 3 January 1998].

Scenario 3. Some sort of confrontation between the EZLN and the CAP is obviously the third possibility. The argument against it is that there have been no reports of wounded CAP members. Otherwise, the innocence of the "gathering" which has been reported may or may not have any significance.

For example, the children's group Las Abejas (The Bees), which was doing something at Acteal which allegedly led to its victimization, is mentioned prominently. It, or the EZLN in its name, issued the following abstracted statement [*Proceso* No.1104 28 December 1998]:

"Making a superhuman effort to emerge from the stupor occasioned by the events of the 22nd, and participating intensely in the wake and burial of the 45 bodies of brothers, sisters and children, today, 25 December, which for the rest is a very special day, and enveloped in a special atmosphere of Christian acceptance and resignation, we were directing ourselves toward the camp of Acteal, the last resting place of the massacred, when into the road bumped a three-ton truck, property of the City of Chenalhó and occupied by the ringleaders of the paramilitary groups which perpetrated the massacre...The scene appeared extracted from a realistic 1930s US novel..."

It goes on to describe, screams, cries and fears of the paras being lynched, but all is well with these well-meaning Abejas. A perhaps more realistic example of such a "well-meaning" EZLN youth group has been given in the LANS description of the EZLN "Intercontinental Encounter for Humanity and Against Neoliberalism" (pp.100ff, YRBK97):

"A stereotypical performance closed this opening. First, the 'youth group,' '9 de Febrero' sang 'El horizonte,' another danced 'El Colas.' Then a mob of boys with cardboard hats and wooden rifles, and masked girls in colored dress, recited, then sang, the verses of 'Carabina 30-30'; 'With my thirty-thirty, I am going to march/In the ranks of the rebellion...'"

As they have been known to do.

Zapatista Chief Rafael Guillen

Rafael Sebastian Guillen Vicente [aka Subcomandante Marcos, aka El Mejicano, aka Jorge Narvaez] was groomed from birth [b.Tampico 19 May 57] to be an ML terrorist, first by his father, Rafael, then by the Jesuit-run Tampico Cultural Institute. He received a degree from Mexican National Autonomous University (UNAM) in 1980, his government profile stating that "the majority of elective course taken by...[him]...are connected with the study of ML." With thousands of young terrorists from all over the world, he arrived in Nicaragua in 1979 as a member of the "promotion of culture brigades" which was in the bailiwick of the LibTheo cleric and Sandinista Minister of Culture, Ernesto Cardenal. Cardenal's assistant, Luz Marian Acosta, has recently testified to his being the man in Chiapas.

The year 1984 divides Guillen's time in Nicaragua into two phases, the first spent in intense political activity with frequent trips abroad, particularly to Cuba and El Salvador. As Oliver Bodán, Sandinista militiaman and *Barricada* (Managua) reporter has written, Guillen's immediate superior was General Directorate of State Security (DGSE) secret police chief Lenín Cerna, his training unit Brigade 3-68. His alias was "Jorge Narvaez" among the Sandins, "El Mejicano" in the mountains of the north.

As Pedro Cifuentes reported from Cuba in the fall of 1994, the commanders of the EZLN operation received training in that island nation, Guillen being no exception. Certain additional detail has been provided on Rafael whose training neither started nor stopped at the time of the well choreographed EZLN "uprising" on 1 January 1994, the anniversary of Castro's Cuban takeover. Journalist Gustavo de Anda, for example, discovered that he took the first of his Cuban trips in October of 1981, a fact which Santiago Aroca verified through the testimony of his roommate, Eradio Morena, the Sandin mayor of San Juan de Río Coco. The mayor lived with him and "shared many of his ideas as to how to bring the revolution to Mexico." As he has done.

The ML EZLN

The "Intercontinental Encounter for Humanity and Against Neoliberalism" was hosted in Chiapas by the EZLN in the summer of 1996 and described in some detail (pp.100ff, YRBK97). This was an effort which had been organized at the hemisphere level by the FSP which, in turn, Castro and Lula da Silva had created in the Havana of 1989 (cf. pp.87ff, YRBK97)). At this left encounter Guillen described his EZLN as "formed in the mountains by a group which comes with the tradition of the LA guerrilla of the 1970s, [a] vanguard group, [of] ML ideology, which seeks the transformation of the world, trying to arrive in power in a dictatorship of the proletariat" [*La Jornada* 30 July 1996].

This ML grouping was, as has been discussed, known to exist at least two years before its anything but spontaneous "uprising" on 1

January 1994. Oppenheimer[41] has stated the following, and Roberto Arguello has confirmed it to LANS after an interview with Ortega. Immediately after the EZLN officially surfaced, Sandinista Peoples' Army (EPS) chief, Humberto Ortega, and "ex" FMLN terrorist, Joaquín Villalobos, hurried to Mexico for a closed-door meeting with Mexican President Salinas de Gortari. The pair advised Salinas to "declare" peace. He immediately did so, and the ML terrorists of the EZLN have effectively controlled a substantial portion of this Mexican state since that time.

LibTheo Clerics

The familiar LibTheo cleric and Sandinista, Ernesto Cardenal, has thus given support to Guillen in the latter's "chosen profession," making him an appropriate choice here for a description of LibTheo.

"In order to be a good Christian," Cardenal said over Chilean television, "it is primarily necessary to be a ML."

As with Cardenal, Chiapas Bishop Ruiz has been of substantial assistance to Guillen's efforts and continues to be so. That he is a LibTheo cleric has been clearly stated in various press reports and books [cf. Oppenheimer, *ibid*], but the reality of LibTheo is carefully either misstated or undefined. As LANS pointed out (pp.193ff, YRBK97), the theologian Rev. Dr. Miguel Poradowsky has demonstrated that the end result of LibTheo is the four-step Marxization of a portion of the clergy through (1) Saduceeism, (2) horizontal Christianity, (3) demythologized Christianity and (4) atheistic Christianity.[42]

Paramilitary

Recently the term has been used almost exclusively for what had been called CAPs, that is, organizations of campesinos set up to defend villages or areas against ML terrorist depredations. The word "paramilitary" appears to be used as a pejorative, and much "reporting" out of Colombia effectively now equates "paramilitary" with "terrorist." One viewpoint holds that this connotation has a definite objective, that of denigrating and disbanding all such organizations because of their successes against the terrorists as demonstrated, *inter alia*, in Peru, Colombia and Guatemala.

If the EZLN and their allies are somehow involved in the Acteal massacre, the paras would qualify as ideal goats.

Cuauhtémoc Cárdenas

Whoever carried out the massacre and for whatever specific reason may not be known, but the individuals and groups which have benefited from the massacre are obvious. The first is, of course, the EZLN which is already wringing additional concessions out of a terrified Mexican Government.

The other is the Mexican representative at Castro's FSP, the PRD, and its chief, Cuauhtémoc Cárdenas. The participation of the PRD in the FSP encounters and the "arrangement" which Cárdenas has with the EZLN have been discussed in these reports. Whatever the truth of the massacre, Cárdenas, like the EZLN, has used all avenues of approach to gain whatever political advantage the massacre may offer.

EZLN COMMUNIQUÉ ON THE ACTEAL MASSACRE
(SPCL 5.1, 5 JANUARY 1998)

EDITOR'S INTRODUCTION

The Massacre at Acteal, Mexico, is generally discussed in Wkly 5.1 above. This affair is not generally understood, a situation requiring as much information as is available. The ML terrorists of the EZLN can of course be expected to provide voluminous information. While this EZLN propaganda communiqué is *a priori* deserving of no credence, it is valuable as to technique and reveals certain information its authors had no intention of revealing. An example is provided by Pt.9, p.3, on cutting open pregnant women's abdomens and removing the fetus as a trophy. This shows nothing but the close connection between these terrorists and those of the URNG. The following has been taken from the 28 December 1997 issue of *La Jornada* (México).

* * *

COMMUNIQUÉ FROM THE CLANDESTINE INDIGENOUS REVOLUTIONARY COMMITTEE [CCRI]-HEADQUARTERS OF THE ZAPATISTA ARMY OF NATIONAL LIBERATION [HQ-EZLN]. MÉXICO

26 December 1997

To the people of Mexico:
To the peoples and governments of the world:
To the national and international press:
Brothers:

The EZLN is reporting to national and international public opinion on the progress of our investigations of the massacre in Acteal, Municipality of San Pedro de Chanlhó, Chiapas:

First—In Acteal there are living some thousands of [those] displaced from other indigenous communities of Chenalhó. They are to be found there [as] refugees in order to protect themselves from the attacks of paramilitary bands which "take by assault" the communities which are not government supporters.[43]

All the refugees were indigenous tzotziles, civilians; they professed the Catholic religion. There were Zapatistas and non Zapatistas from the independent organization, the Bees of Chenlhó.

None of the refugees had firearms.

Second—The majority of the attackers are [sic] indigenous tzotziles, [the majority] belong to diverse communities of the municipality of Chenalhó, [the majority] profess the Catholic religion and [the majority] is priista (from the PRI or the Partido Cardenista,[44] it is the same).

All the attackers had fire arms and some, even, edged weapons [*armas blancas*[45]]. The majority of the long arms were model AK-47, caliber 7.62x39. The short arms or pistols were of squad[46] model, caliber 22 long rifle.

Third—Some minutes after the massacre was initiated, the vehicles of the paramilitary were detected by indigenous EZLN support bases which were to advise the refugees in Acteal in order that they leave and they alerted the National Mediation Commission (CONAI). A group of approximately 15 people managed to leave, but the rest claimed that they could do nothing because they had done nothing bad and that [it would be] better [if] they went to pray, which they were doing when they were attacked.

Fourth—At midday [on] 22 December, when the attack had scarcely begun, Zapatista support bases heard the first explosions and communicated with CONAI in order to inform them of what was happening. CONAI replied to the comrades [*compañeros*] that they were leaving to advise the State Government. Thus it happened. At 1200 on 22 December the State Government received the report from CONAI. At 1900 the advisory was repeated. The State Government said that everything was under control.

Fifth—The paramilitary command which carried out the massacre was mobilized in vehicles [which were the] property of the PRI municipal president [mayor] of Chenalhó and private persons.

Sixth—All the members of the aggressor group wore uniforms of dark color.

Seventh—The vehicles, as well as the armament, uniforms and equipment of the aggressors was obtained with money provided by the Federal Government. Specifically, from the Secretary of Social Development.

Eighth—The paramilitary finished off the wounded whom they encountered and the pregnant women [whose] abdomens they opened with machetes.

Ninth—Ending the attack, agents of the Public Security Police of the State of Chiapas set themselves to the task of collecting the cadavers and "disappearing" them inside a cave and at the bottom of a hill.

Some conclusions from the above are:

1. A religious conflict is not being treated [since] as much the assassins as the assassinated profess the Catholic religion. (Editor's note: This is nonsense, the LibTheo militant almost unrelated to the non-LibTheo militant.)

2. An ethnic conflict is not being treated [since] the dead and [those] who killed them are indigenous tzotziles.

3. A confrontation (as the Federal and State Governments wish to present it) is not being treated. The dead were unarmed, the attackers had heavy caliber arms. There was no armed collisison. It was, plainly and simply, an execution.

4. The objective was to finish off everybody, that no accusatory witnesses remain and "to clean up the evidence." The government plan was that the action was not [that] of the public sector. The authorities first wished to deny the massacre, then minimize it, now they want to confuse public opinion on the true motive for the crime.

5. When the Government of Chiapas replied to CONAI that "everything is under control," it was not referring to avoiding a bloodbath, but to [the fact] that the government was the one which was directing the attack.

6. It diverted federal funds for the financing of various paramilitary structures. In the Jungle, North and Heights of Chiapas [this] is not unknown to federal and state authorities. Since 1994 the assignment of federal economic resources in Chiapas has been carried out using a politico-military criterion; those who are disposed to confront the Zapatista communities and the neutrals can obtain money under the condition of complying with what is called "basic preparation" and being in readiness to respond to the so-called "managers" of dealing with the projects in Ministry of Social Development (SEDESOL). It is not only [a case] of buying loyalties, it is true recruiting, a "levy" in order to make government war against the indigenous...with indigenous.

7. The attack included the military phases called "approach," "making contact," "attack" and "exploitation of the victory" [*éxito*], even of "total extermination of the adversary." It is evident that the aggressor group counted on military preparation of the so-called "special command." Its arms, equipment and uniforms are those of a militarized organization and reveal that a concerted action is being dealt with, [an action] prepared and directed by people and authorities who did not participate directly in the happenings.

8. The paramilitary obtained their armament and equipment by supply from officers of the federal army, judicial police and, principally, from the so-called "State Public Security," the Government of the State of Chiapas (in charge of the "dirty work" in this Zedillian[47]) [which] in turn obtains the armament in the black market which exists among the various police associations of the country. The police and the military divert the arms (which they collect in the confiscations) for clandestine sale, and they sell them to landowners, bodyguards, governors, municipal presidents and "important people."

An authentic "arms laundering" is being dealt with. They are "dirty" or "black" arms, so called because they were used in the commission of some crime, which are "laundered" [by] selling them to the regional or local powers.

9. The bloody ritual of opening the abdomen of the pregnant women and exhibiting its contents as a trophy,[48] forms part of the "teachings" which the Guatemalan military (of the so-called "kaibiles") imparted to their Mexican counterparts immediately after the Zapatista uprising. After 1 January 1994, the Guatemalan Army offered to its Mexican equal "advice and preparation" in

counterinsurgent battle. A select group of the Federal Army took the course "kaibil." Since then new groups are [have been] prepared in the neighboring country.

10. The victims were not selected at random. The place, date and hour of the crime were selected so that the addressees of the bloody message received it and understood it. The addressees are the rebel indigenous communities and the message is "nothing will live which is independent of the government."

11. The Mexican Government feigns to act surprised by the massacre of Acteal. Through the press and private national television, the tense situation which exists in the Heights and North of Chiapas was in the public domain. The crime of the 45 Indians was warned [of] in time.

12. From the beginning of the deterioration and crisis of the social situation in Chiapas, [a] product of the government counterinsurgency strategy, the CCRI-CG of the EZLN positioned its support bases in order that they avoid at all times, even at the price of losing its small membership, confrontation with other Indians. For us it was clear that the government intention was and is that we will change from enemies and confront us with other Indians. Therefore, each time we were attacked we did not respond in a violent manner but only resorted to CONAI (the existence of which the Federal Government fought with every decision) and the national and international press (the informative professional labor of which bothers governments so much (*sic*)).

Through both channels, as much the Federal Government as the State, they were well informed as to what was gestating in the Heights of Chiapas.

Time and again, the national public press published documented reports on the signs which may now be clearly read in the blood of Acteal.

To the professional journalists notes the State Government replied with paid insertions, with letters of denial and with ample bribery for some who call themselves journalists.

Meanwhile, the Federal Government did not continue doing that. The Minister of Interior continued the policy of the ostrich and "disappeared" following the belief that if a problem is not mentioned, this is the solution.

CONAI, while it supported government aggression of all types, continually kept the Chiapas Government and the Minister of the Interior informed on each and every one of the occurrences which, as we know now, culminated in the Acteal massacre.

13. It is undeniable that the Minister of the Interior knew in plenty of time of the series of threats which sifted over the indigenous inhabitants of the Heights.

Some periodicals of national circulation spent months covering and disseminating information which today is part of the historical antecedents of the worst crime in the last 29 years in Mexico.

On a private Mexican television channel were objectively documented the conditions of persecution and hostility in which the Chenalhó Indians live. All the interviews denounced the presence and actions of the White Guards.

There is no doubt that the Minister of the Interior read these periodicals, as well as saw the program. The proof is that he protested the "prejudiced and alarmist tone" of the information televised and vetoed its repetition.

When it is seen again it will have to be remembered that some of the Indians who were interviewed in that "prejudiced and alarmist" program are now dead, assassinated by those who, like the Minister of the Interior, complained of the grave accusations which emerged from the report.

14. In the Acteal massacre the [country's] leaders cannot be tried for negligence, precisely because they had set out to carry out the "operation." The negligence lies in the fact that they did not know how to [do it] or could not do it with discretion. They forgot that since January 1994 Indian blood weighs heavily, and the opportune informative labor of the communications media brings to light that which came to rest in a cave or at the foot of a slope.

15. The intelligence services of the EZLN detected rumors of the paramilitaries from mid November 1997. Something was being prepared. At the beginning of December an imminent paramilitary action was spoken of. We thought that that "something" was related to the visit to Chiapas by the papal nuncio. It was our communiqué wherein we warned of a possible outrage against Señor Justo Mullor. We were wrong, the victims were going to be, again, on the bottom shelf. Now we know.

16. Conforming to the evidence encountered, it is deduced that the Acteal crime was prepared in plenty of time, with full awareness,

with the direction of state government authorities and the complicity of various ministers of the Federal Government among whom are distinguished the Minister of the Interior, of Social Development and of National Defense as well as the national directors of the Institutional Revolutionary Party.

17. The politic of taking away the indigenous social base of the EZLN [having] failed, the Federal and State Governments opted for that which they considered more sensible: to annihilate that social base, they valued the price which the federal Army would have to pay very high if it participated directly in this plan. Therefore, they reverted to their party structure, leaving a "healthy distance" and making use of the organized structures of the PRI in order to do what they know best, that is, to rob and kill.

18. The present war in Chenalhó was not initiated in the 1930s. It began to be gestated in August 1995, when the Federal and State Governments accorded their present anti-Zapatista policy. Before that, more than a year and one-half after 1 January 1994, pacific coexistence among different political groups had been possible. Still some months ago the authorities of Chenalhó had accorded with the autonomous (*sic*) [people][49] mutual respect and tolerance. But the order to "hurry up" finishing with the rebels arrived...

19. The slant, which the authorities, who they say are investigating the crime, wish to give is completely false. Neither a religious conflict, nor an ideological dispute, much less an intra- or inter-community conflict is being dealt with. That history of such conflicts in Chenalhó comes from the 1930s [and] is a confidence job by those who call themselves investigators and grows out of anthropology. Not in the 1930s, but almost 30 years ago another massacre of equal magnitude shook the world. And at Tlatelolco 1968[50] the sister [outrage?] of Acteal 97 innocent blood flowed. Also then, as now, the government spoke of dialog and peace with its hands filled with death.

Brothers and Sisters:

The Acteal massacre was a slaughter and was carried out with malice of forethought, premeditation and advantage.

The motive is political, military, social and economic. It is concerned with annihilating the indigenous rebels.

The intellectual authors are high in the Federal and State Governments.

The 41 detainees are minor pieces of the complicated and bloody war machine against the Indian peoples of Mexico. And the elimination of minor pieces does not affect the functioning of the machinery, they are simply replaced.

In order to implement the replacement and not to avoid a repetition of Acteal 97, the Federal Government is sending anew thousands of soldiers to Indian lands and millions of dollars to some state authorities which have discovered that the war, but above all the dirty war, is a great job.

This is what we have put forward in our investigations.

Democracy!   Liberty!   Justice![51]

From the Mountains of Southeast Mexico. CCRI-HQEZLN. Mexico, December 1997

[Translated from the Spanish by the LANS Editor]

ACTEAL REVISITED
(SPCL 6.19, 29 DECEMBER 1998)

Weekly Report 5.1, above, and Special Report 5.1, above, were devoted to the Christmas Week massacre in Acteal, State of Chiapas, Mexico. Although there appeared to be little, if any, doubt that it was a slaughter of Indians by other Indians, the background and details of the affair were not immediately obvious. Three possible scenarios for the massacre were set forth in Wkly 5.1, the first of these being what was probably the least likely, that the Mexican Government was simply carrying out a "plan" which it had put in place in 1994. The "plan," which the MLs of the EZLN laid out in their "communiqué" of 26 December 1997 and which was reproduced as Spcl 5.1, was to "create paramilitary bands" for the express purpose of slaughtering "the EZLN support bases."

The second scenario had the EZLN carrying out the killing and then, as did their titular deity, Ulianov (aka Lenin), with the Greens, pinning it on the "class enemy" (p.188, Richard Pipes, *Russia Under the Bolshevik Regime*, Knopf, 1993. ISBN: 0-394-50242-6), in this case anti-EZLN groups such as the CAPs. Both this and the third scenario were, in the final analysis, perhaps equally unlikely, the third being a confrontation between a self-defense patrol and the EZLN terrorists. Such a confrontation appears unlikely based on the sex of the victims. Of the 45 dead, only 9 were men, 21 were women and 15 children.

It would now appear that there was no one of these scenarios which was precise. The EZLN influenced the situation leading to it, and it assuredly made what hay it could out of it, but it was only one among a number of factors which apparently produced the massacre.

Mexican Federal Government Reaction

Amidst the fabricated howls of the EZLN, its support base, national and international, and those portions of the press which never encounters an ML whom it does not like, the Mexican Federal Government moved into what appears to have been an efficient investigation of the slaughter.

The killing of the 45 Tzotzil Indians and wounding of 25 others took place on 22 December 1997. On 23 December 1997 Mexican President Zedillo Ponce de León instructed the PGR to assume jurisdiction over the Chiapas investigation if it was legally possible for him to do so. On 23 December the PGR assumed jurisdiction and ordered an Assistant Attorney General, eight agents of the MPF (Federal Prosecutor's Office), seven (presumably forensic) "experts" and 40 Federal Judicial Police (PJF) to Chiapas. On 1 April 1998 agreement A/23/98 (*Official Journal of the Federation*) established a Special Prosecutor (FE) for the crimes committed in Chenalhó Municipality, State of Chiapas.

A quite complex situation appears to have been thoroughly and rationally investigated by this staff and described in detail in the *White Paper on Chiapas* which was issued by the PGR in December 1998. The factors which militated toward the massacre were first studied, these covering virtually all aspects of human existence: demographic geography, sociology, religion and politics. However, perhaps for political reasons, the report does not really emphasize the common thread that runs through all these factors, namely, the arrival on the scene of the MLs of the EZLN, a terrorist group led by a non-Indian (Guillen) which has devoted itself to utilizing the "indigenous" theme as a catalyst in its revolutionary attack on the existing political order.

Geography Demography

The County (*Municipio*) of Chenalhó is, according to the National Institute of Statistics, Geography and Informatics (INEGI) (*Anuario*

Estadístico del Estado de Chiapas, Mexico, 1993), one of the largest counties in the Los Altos region of Chiapas, it covering a land area of 139 km² and having a population of over 30,000. It is located about 34 km north of San Cristóbal de las Casas and surrounded by the Counties of Simojovel to the north; Chalchihuitán, El Bosque and Larrainizar to the west; Chamula to the south; and Mitontic, Cancuc and Pantelhó to the east.

In 1994, of the 30,680 Chenalhó residents, 28,631 were Tzotzil speakers, 1,307 Tzetal speakers with 33 percent of the total population monolingual and 51 percent illiterate (INEGI, XVII Censo Ejidal, 1994). The population is scattered among over 100 small communities. It is perhaps best to begin with their origin, Chenalhó incorporating three indigenous towns that had lived separately from the Viceregal to the post-Revolution period: San Pedro Chenalhó is just north of the Chamula County border; Magdalenas (Aldama) is almost on the Larrainzar County line; Santa Martha is apparently outside the county. In 1990 it was estimated (Jacinto Arias, *Chenalhó*, 1990) that the county contained 27,022 people from San Pedro, 2,178 from Chamula County, 2,570 from Magdalenas and 1,160 from Santa Martha.

At present, the county seat (San Pedro Chenalhó) has a population of 12,925 while the other communities considered "most important" are: "Belisario Domínguez" Ejido[52] (a few kilometers west of San Pedro) has 1,403, Yibeljoj (a few kilometers east of Acteal in the north) 1,227 and Manuel Utrilla Egido (northwest of Belisario Domínguez) 1,065.

Insofar as the tensions arising among these different communities is concerned, only one of the examples appearing in the report can be reproduced here. Tzakukum is a few kilometers to the west of Acteal. In March 1983 the community allegedly refused to cooperate with the "traditional" authorities of Chachihuitán County in dealing with boundary problems between that county and Chenalhó. The refusal continued until the Tzakukum inhabitants were attacked on 24 March 1983, a group allegedly organized by the "traditional" authorities attacking and burning their town, killing 11 people and wounding eight.

Religion

Religious diversity, a subject which the government report treats with "kid gloves," was indicated in 1994 with 43.45 percent of the inhabitants Catholic, 19.69 percent Protestant and 24.41 percent of no discernible religion. The Catholics were split into "traditional Catholics" and "Catholics of the Diocese of San Cristóbal," the latter variety apparently hewing to the leftist line of the LibTheo Bishop of San Cristóbal, Samuel Ruiz.

The Protestants were given by Viquiera and Ruz (*Chiapas: Los rumbos de otra historia*, Mexico, 1995) as Presbyterians, (Seventh Day) Adventists and Pentecostals. Finally, the inhabitants of the oldest *teclums* (communities) have their "traditional" religions, which careful phraseology of course means polytheism or paganism. Which, in addition to demonstrating the Siglo XX PC of admitting any religion—devil worship included—as equal to any other, calls for an aside.

Michael D. Coe (*The Maya*, Thames and Hudson, 1987, 4th edition. LCCN: 83-72969) is probably as worthy of quotation on the Maya as anyone. Taking up his history of the Tzeltalan about 100 BC, by AD 400 they were pioneering settlements of the mountain valleys around San Cristóbal de las Casas, although hardly so identified at that time. Coe claims that "There many thousands of their descendants, the Tzotzil and the Tzeltal, maintain unchanged the old Maya patterns of life." Perhaps, but certainly not in toto. While any number of their modern descendants may indeed believe the earth flat on the body of a "monstruous crocodile" and facing the body of the sky serpent, few of them apparently practice that human sacrifice which constituted such an appealing portion of the Mayan eschatology.

In the real world, as compared to the PC world of late in this century, religious differences have been the root of any number of slaughters, but it is almost exclusively expulsions which are treated in the PGR's report. Perhaps more interesting than what was done is what was claimed, the one about the other. According to Hugo Esponda (*El presbiterianismo in Chiapas*, Mexico, 1986) there were about 10 Presbyterians in Chimtic (northeast of San Pedro) in 1957. Religious problems arose when their neighbors found that they "studied the Bible" in Chimtic, this apparently a serious ecclesiastical crime. The Catholics allegedly improved on this accusation by calling the Presbyterians "children of the devil" because they believed they ate human flesh. Apparently this vibrant religious hatred arose because the Presbyterians preached that the images the Catholics worshipped were in fact powerless idols. This of course is quite an old cause of dispute which, although generally based on mutual misunderstanding, is nevertheless a potent force for creating a donnybrook. As is power and privilege, government and land.

Government and Land

Leftist ideologues and leftist governments of course venerate primitive collectivist societies: the cacique with his peasants working communal lands. This has had a strange appeal to political "scientists" from (François Marie Arouet de) Voltaire to Fidel Castro. In Chenalhó the burgeoning bureaucracy—San Pedro is quoted as having 62 county agencies—was certain to replace, either peacefully or otherwise, the "happy peasant" society of the cacique. The EZLN made what little progress it made with the notion of stopping this transformation, in whatever mystical language such a notion may be couched. Of course this was nonsense, the Zapas dedicated to installing an even more rigid "happy peasant" society pending a successful conclusion of their "uprising." But to a doubtless unknown extent, this bureaucrat-cacique struggle added to the tensions which were apparently growing in the area.

A great deal of effort by the IL has gone into the use of raw government power to manipulate the private ownership of land, and this so-called AgRef continues to be one of the main thrusts of the HL. The PGR's report devotes two pages to what is really not a very good discussion of this alleged "problem," it being influenced by what appears to be a bias against private property. Such is to be expected in a nation such as Mexico whose Constitution deals with the inalienable right of private property as follows:

> Art. 27. Ownership of the lands and waters within the boundaries of the national territory is vested originally in the Nation...The Nation shall at all times have the right to impose on private property such limitations as the public interest may demand...to ensure a more equitable distribution of public wealth...measures shall be taken to divide large landed estates...

But, whatever the relationship between private property and free men may be, the question of land, whether arising naturally or artificially introduced, can be taken as yet another source of conflict among the people of Chenalhó.

Political Change

Whatever the number and extent of the frictions, such as those which have been so far discussed, a catalyst is necessary to the sort of reaction which was observed at Acteal. And such a catalyst is routinely an organized political effort. Before going further into this, however, it is necessary to reread a bit of history which could hardly have been expected to appear in the PGR's report.

No matter how "democratic" the society, all of the world's political parties seek to gain, through legitimate or illegitimate means, absolute and perpetual control over the nation in which they operate. Such a statement should precede a description of the Mexican PRI because of the bad press it has received in recent years for doing just this. The man who arranged "perpetual" power for PRI was Plutarco Elias Calles, nominated president of Mexico on 30 November 1924. By Art. 83 of the Constitution of 1917, however, no one may serve more than one term as president so he formed the PNR on 1 February 1928 in order to wield power through puppet presidents. That scourge of the Twentieth Century, the PP, need only be shown a power device once so Calles could be certain that his device would be unaffected by his departure from this veil of tears. By the time of the 1940 elections only the name had changed, from the PNR to the PRM. The PRM became the PRI after the elections of 1946, and the Mexican ship of state has sailed under these colors ever since.

The Bolshevik Revolution (1917) introduced the marxist notion of AgRef, the leftist Mexican Government of Lazaro Cárdenas was one of the first to introduce it into the Western Hemisphere.

The Cardenista Party (PC) was one of the leftist parties from which the party of Lazaro's son, Cuauhtémoc Cárdenas Solorzano, would arise. The PGR's report states that the PC began to make its Chenalhó presence felt in the late 1970s. Another forebear was the Socialist Workers Party (PST) which moved into the area about the same time. These two precursors of Cuauhtémoc's PRD are worthy of remark because of LibTheo Bishop Ruiz, whose resignation the Pope had long sought.

The Gutiérrez brothers were attacked on 9 December 1992, one of them murdered, their wives raped. Five people were arrested for the crime, and Bishop Ruiz's CDHF defended them. They were simply released for "lack of evidence." The PGR's report states that "the PST... was pushed out by the PRD" after the Zapa uprising of

January 1994, the PRD-supported candidate, Amando Avedaño, elected governor of Chiapas. "Pushed out" can be interpreted as "replaced by," the leftist party of young Cárdenas obviously offering a haven to the leftist PST militants.

As has frequently been pointed out in these reports, (1) Cárdenas' PRD is a member of Castro's FSP (pp.168ff, YRBK98), the core organization in his HL (pp.83ff, YRBK97). Further, (2) that the EZLN is a ML organization has been freely admitted by its militants, for example, at the "Intercontinental Encounter for Humanity and Against Neoliberalism" (pp.100ff, YRBK97). The EZLN's most ballyhooed militant is the non-Indian Rafael S. Guillen (aka Marcos), a red-diaper baby who was trained for his role in Cuba and in the Nicaragua of the FSLN (pp.124ff, YRBK97). The HL-PRD-EZLN relationship is completed by (3) the EZLN-Cárdenas "arrangement" which has appeared in the press, albeit, Cuauhtémoc's connection with the Zapas has never been seriously camouflaged.

The catalyst, functioning in whichever direction is assuredly present for the Acteal tragedy, was assuredly the EZLN.

BACKGROUND AND DETAILS OF THE ACTEAL MASSACRE
(SPCL 6.20, 31 DECEMBER 1998)

In Spcl 6.19 above a brief survey of those inter-group tensions which led to the Acteal massacre has been given. Although all of these tensions militated, to a greater or lesser extent, in the background, there is no question but that the catalyst for the slaughter was the EZLN. The PGR report, Section 9, arrives at five conclusions which can be drawn about the killings, only three of which will be reproduced here.

> First. ...the Acteal massacre...was undoubtedly motivated by a long-standing confrontation among socially and politically opposed groups in Chenalhó municipality (county) that had already been responsible for the murders of several members of both factions.
>
> Second. The Acteal massacre is also an indirect result of the existence of an armed group (the EZLN) that has operated in various communities in Chenalhó since 1995....
>
> Fourth. Acteal exists in an environment of disregard for the Rule of Law...ravaged both by those who advocate the non-observance of laws and disrespect for institutions in the name of a "new revolutionary legality"[53] and by those who believe that having formally joined the institutions meant they have "carte blanche" to break the law....

The other two points basically involve the virtual absence of any law enforcement authorities, particularly since the advent of the ML EZLN.

In a word, the existence of an EZLN against which most of the population had no recourse, while not *justifying* this slaughter of women and children, was assuredly the *reason* for it.

Members of the pro Zapa organization, Las Abejas, were the victims in the slaughter. In typical ML fashion the EZLN terrorists had moved into Chenalhó County and proceeded, totally illegally, to take over the county institutions. In doing so, they took over land illegally and forcefully replaced the Constitutional Chenalhó County Government with what they called, in typical ML fashion, the Autonomous County Council, a group reminiscent of Ulianov's (aka Lenin) Soviet Socialist Republics (SSR). A few of these Zapa activities will be reviewed after a brief discussion of the victims.

Las Abejas

A confrontation on 9 December 1992, involving the Las Abejas predecessor group, Pueblo Creyente (Believing People), resulted in the death of one man and the wounding of two others, The transformation of Pueblo Creyente into Las Abejas followed the next day (10 December). The PGR report describes the position of Las Abeyas as "undefined." On the other hand, the supporters of PRI and the PC declared them to be Zapas, this viewpoint appearing to be the more probable of the two.

First, Las Abejas "demonstrated" outside the jail, where the accused in the 9 December killing were being held, until the suspects were released on 7 January 1993. Although stepping with extreme caution around the subject, the PGR report does admit that "their main links are with the CDHF which belongs to the Diocese of San Cristóbal de las Casas" and is hence the bailiwick of the leftist, LibTheo Bishop Samuel Ruiz.[54] As has been pointed out (Spcl 6.19 above), the Chenalhó County Catholic population is made up of "traditional Catholics" and "Catholics of the San Cristóbal Diocese." Bishop Ruiz also presides over the CDHF and has consistently been supportive of the Zapas.

These observations would tend to support the PRI-PC view that these are Zapas. As does the report that Las Abejas "is one of the very few groups that can visit the community of Polhó"—a few kilometers south of Acteal—"with which it maintains close communications." As the group does with Las Casas.

Whichever view is correct, this appears to be why Las Abejas were chosen for slaughter.

The "Autonomous" Communities

Since the patron saint of the ML terrorists, Ulianov (aka Lenin), appeared on the scene, these revolutionaries have enjoyed levels of popularity ranging from low to miniscule. This has also been the case in Chiapas (Spcls 5.8 and 5.9, Chapter 6 below). But much of the press appears to accept and regurgitate the Zapa propaganda as if it were meaningful—in particular, cf. pp.100ff, YRBK97—which renders it so for many of its readers. The forcible occupancy of local governments by a terrorist force such as this might have some justification were the local campesino support what these MLs claim it to be. But even this excuse is invalid, and the establishment of these "autonomous" communities by the ML Zapas with weapons is simply one more terrorist act.

The EZLN allegedly erupted on the scene in January 1994, and President Salinas, at the behest of "ex" Sandinista terrorist Humberto Ortega and "ex" Farabundi terrorist Joaquín Villalobos, declared "peace" (pp.100ff, YRBK97), leaving the EZLN terrorists a free field for operation. There is hardly space here to detail their operations under this "license to steal," but one of the most interesting of them is the establishment of these so-called "autonomous communities." Such a community was directly related to the Acteal massacre.

In routinely pompous ML fashion the EZLN issued a communiqué on its so-called "military campaign," a "campaign" having no opponents but having a title, "Peace with Justice and Dignity for Indigenous Peoples" (PJD) (*sic*). What such communiqués say is not to be taken literally, but the contents are indicative. PJD stated that in 26 of these municipalities "the civil populations had appointed new authorities and had declared (33) new rebel municipalities and territories in the area." The "civil populations" were of course the Zapa terrorists with guns.

The process was not only unconstitutional and illegal—restructuring counties in the territories with settlements of indigenous peoples is to be carried out by the state legislatures—it was also against the will of the indigenous people these Cuban-trained terrorists are using as a front.

It will be recalled that the Chenalhó County authorities are located at the county seat, San Pedro Chenalhó in the southern part of the county near the Chenalhó County border. On 13 April 1996 the "Polhó Autonomous County Council" was established by the EZLN at the village of Polhó, a few kilometers south of Acteal. (In the early 1960s it was fashionable amongst the North American left to make the pilgrimage to Cuba and wallow in the ecstasy of Castro's revolution. The same sort of pilgrimages have been made by the IL for wallowing in these local marxist councils (Wkly 5.23 below).) It would appear that, with the howling accompaniment of the IL, the Mexican Government is reestablishing its sovereignty over the State of Chiapas. Araceli Burguete Cal y Mayor[55] has carried out an apparently cogent study on the division, violence and displacement of large numbers of people brought about by the aggressions between various groups as a result of these illegal "councils." The study probably gives the Zapas more influence than they have, but, here, perhaps this is as it should be.

> ...the Zapatista autonomous counties and regions...are not compact entities, but virtual boundaries that the Zapatistas themselves have drawn in accordance with their areas of influence, which include all their followers, but not all the people who live in the areas marked off. In many counties, Zapatista presence constitutes the majority and the main force, but in others that is not the case; however, in both circumstances the autonomous governments established a set of norms and rules ... that the Zapatista inhabitants accept, but that the non-Zapatistas are unwilling to obey. This is the preamble for the confrontation that reached its maximum expression in the case of Acteal.

Terrorist Acts

Terrorists commit terrorist acts. Several of these have been gathered in the PGR report, but only a brief sketch can be reproduced here, the case of the Majomut Sandbank and the attacks on certain PC supporters of the constitutional government of the county.

In 1995 the Majomut Sandbank (Rancho San José Majomut) was acquired by the Mexican AgRef Department in order to give it to the children of the Miguel Utrilla Los Chorros Ejido (MULCE) members.[56] (Majomut is between Acteal and Polhó.) On 22 January 1995 the property was turned over to 118 beneficiaries. On 13 August 1996 a group of 14 people led by Polhó Autonmomous County Mayor Javier Ruiz Hernández, toting firearms and machetes, took over the sandbank and issued a typical ML proclamation that "...everything that is the heritage of the nation belongs to everyone,[57] and everything that the Government grants in concessions will be taken over (stolen) by the people who sympathize with the EZLN..."

On 16 August 1996 Polhó Autonomous informed Chanalhó County that it would "administer" the sandbank. From this time, those campesinos venturing near the sandbank were detained with threats of death or murdered.

In Section 3.2 of his report the PGR lists various examples of beatings and murders by the Zapas of those who were not supporters of the Polhó Autonomous Council. This is a dreary litany which need not be repeated here. However, it does appear worthwhile to close this section with a quote from that section:

> The conflict over the sandbank was the start of the clashes between the "Polhó Autonomous County Council" and the MULCE which would culminate in Acteal.

The Anti Zapas Form a Self Defense Group

The PGR claims to have documented the "existence of armed civilian groups in Chenalhó, which are not linked to, organized, trained or financed by the Mexican Army or any other government agency." There are two reasons for believing this claim. (1) The terrorist claim of a government "plan" to liquidate all Zapa supporters is typical ML propaganda having no credibility. (2) The PGR report details the formation of these self defense forces (CAP), most of whom are now in prison awaiting trial. A brief review of CAP formation demonstrates the value of (2).

The PGR found that the main group behind the killings belonged to "a number of villages supportive of the Chenalhó County Council and the PT." The first meeting from which the CAP would arise took place in September 1997 near the local school in MULCE. The assembly was joined by the "influential" Antonio López Santiz and 31 others, these "rebuking" the ejido commissioner for failing to defend his people and "wage war on the Zapas." According to the PGR report, López and his associate ringleader "forced" the residents to join under threat of fines. Perhaps. At that meet López Santiz was elected president of the CAP. On 16 September López had trenches dug around MULCE, guards subsequently mounted from 1800 to 0300.

Subsequent meetings were held in October and early and late November 1997. During November 1997 various alleged attempts by the CAP to convince Las Abejas members to join their CAP were reportedly unsuccessful. From September through November 1997 conflicts increased between Zapatista and Priista-Cardenista supporters. On 29 October the press reported that "in Chenalhó County since May ...nine people allegedly opposed to the Zapatistas have been killed by them and a further 21 wounded, while ...one Zapatista has been killed and two more wounded."

In latter October the PRI-PC faction requested the presence of the Mexican Army, claiming that "the Zapatistas are training, they are levying a 'war tax' on the highways, and in several communities they do not allow those opposed to them to sow their fields." They stated further that they were going to "defend themselves against any aggression..."

In early December 1997 talks were held between the two sides at Las Limas, about half way between Chenalhó and Polhó. A second meeting was held after an adjournment, a commission weighted in favor of the Zapas was created, and, finally, the Zapas broke off further talks.

The Slaughter

At a final meeting on 21 December in Quextic, just north of Acteal, the "attack" was planned. That same day, in an interesting twist, Agustín Ruiz Pérez invited members of the Public Security forces stationed there to dine with him. Their commander Berzaín Martínez agreed to loan the CAP members their uniforms, giving 12 of them to Pérez. The PGR report states that:

> ...it can be seen that the intention of the people who had gathered was to take the lives and steal the possessions of an indeterminate number of 'Las Abejas Civil Society' members who were in the Los Narajos camp in Acteal....

They did.

As of the date of the PGR report, his office had brought 135 people before the federal judicial authorities and 10 criminal proceedings involving 97 detainees were being brought before the Chiapas First and Second District Courts. Eighty-four of those being prosecuted are civilians, 11 are former officers of the Chiapas Public Security General Coordination, one is a former Chenalhó mayor and one a former soldier. Thirty-two additional arrest warrants were waiting to be served.

TENTATIVE ATTEMPTS TO RECAPTURE MEXICAN SOVEREIGNTY
(WKLY 5.23, 18 JUNE 1998)

On 1 January 1994, the 35th anniversary of the occupation of the Cuban power vacuum by the ML dictator, Fidel Castro, the EZLN terrorists officially initiated their "uprising" in the State of Chiapas, Mexico. The Mexican Army was well on the way to dispensing with this lawlessness when Pres. Salinas de Gortari suddenly declared "peace" and left the EZLN in effective control of a substantial chunk of the national territory. As has been discussed in these reports, Salinas had called the "ex" Sandinista terrorist, Humberto Ortega, and the "ex" Farabundi terrorist, Joaquín Villalobos, who had told him to declare "peace" which he did.

Much of the Mexican press has been favorable to the EZLN terrorists, perhaps most strikingly demonstrable in the press tendency to write down as "news" whatever bizarre statements these MLs make. Here, only of direct interest is the strange antipathy of the press toward the PRI. If the pundits of the media are to be believed, this antipathy is rooted in the "lack of democracy" which characterizes PRI. The truth or falsity of this allegation shimmers into inexplicable ambiguity when compared with the treatment this same press gives to Castro's island tyranny. The new course, which the Mexican Government of Pres. Zedillo Ponce de León has recently taken, is suffering the same fate.

Pres. Zedillo took office with the "peace" surrender of Mexican territory by Pres. Salinas well emplaced, forced, therefore, to pick his way rather carefully through the booby traps which the HL, the HLS, the EZLN's political front, Cárdenas' PRD, the peripatetic HR Activists of the IL and others were laying out for him. It would appear that the time has come to take back Mexican national territory. It is difficult to assign appropriate importance to the effects of the Acteal massacre (Wkly 5.1 above) on this decision, but it had some.

Revolutionary Tourists Wanted

There are apparently some who feel left out at having never joined their leftist brethren in an HR tour of some ML utopia such as Chiapas or Cuba. Now these poor souls can "visit Chiapas for $800" on a tour which includes "Autonomous Municipalities" and an "interview with Samuel Ruiz." This golden opportunity was provided in mid

May by Global Exchange, a "travel agency" located in San Francisco, California, which was founded in 1988 by "Ted Lewis" and which specializes in "Reality Tours."

The tour in question was titled "Chiapas and Cuba: Revolutionary Cultures," although, in addition to these garden spots, the revolutionary traveler can select a tour to Haiti, the Amazon jungle or Palestine-Israel. Should you be unsatisfied with the delights of this tour, you can, at some unspecified later time, include yourself in a two-month stint as a "volunteer worker" at a "civil peace camp" in Chiapas. Such centers are under the direction and coordination of the CDHF, the bailiwick of none other than Bishop Samuel Ruiz. Since 1995 Global Exchange has relied on "Peace House" (*Casa de la Paz*), which is located in Bishop Ruiz's San Cristóbal de las Casas and which has the task of "supporting international visitors." If this sounds suspiciously like those *Venceremos Brigades* which shipped a few thousand aimless US youths to Cuba in the early 1960s to wallow in the ecstacy of Castro's "revolution," it should.

Global Exchange is located at 2017 Mission Street, #303, San Francisco, CA 94110, telephone 415/255-7296, FAX 255-7498. For more details on Revolutionary Tourism consult www.globalexchange.org.

THE PARTY (PRI), THE LIBTHEO CLERIC (RUIZ) AND THE TERRORIST (GUILLEN)

The statesman (politician) is born of an overweening desire for power and its perquisites. Therefore, when the essentially collectivist[58] Constitution of the United States of Mexico was enacted in 1917, Art. 83 left the professional politician with something of a conundrum. How were these leading statesmen going to function when "A citizen who has held the office of President of the Republic ... can in no case and for no reason again hold that office"?

But this did not daunt President Plutarco Elias Calles. Inaugurated on 30 November 1924, Calles formed the National Revolutionary Party (PNR) on 1 February 1928, in doing so developing one of the world's foremost political machines. He indeed put himself and his successors in the position of being able to maintain power and its perquisites for over eight decades. The faces remained the same; the name changed.

By the 1940 elections the PNR had become the Mexican Revolutionary Party (PMR), another change of name rendering it the PRI after the 1946 elections. Now it might be difficult to claim that PRI has run a remarkably "democratic" system, depending on your definition of "democratic." Which has been the reason given by a substantial portion of the press for its antipathy toward PRI. But, at the same time, there is little question of the antipathy in the breasts of opposition politicians envious of PRI successes. Whatever the motivation, the press tends to exult in PRI misfortunes and in the condemnations of this once all-powerful political machine.

This fact has multiplied the problems Pres. Zedillo of PRI has experienced at the hands of the press. And in the person of Cuautémoc Cárdenas, the son of leftist president and PNR chief Lázaro Cárdenas, the press has certainly found "someone to support." Cárdenas won the election for chief of state in the DF in the 6 July 1997 elections, certainly one of the most important positions in Mexico after that of the president. This is the same Cárdenas who is the Mexican representative in Castro's FSP, the man with the "arrangement" with the ML Zapatistas, the man with the vendetta against his father's party.

In short, the problems in dealing with the EZLN terrorists have been aggravated by the fad of siding with anyone in opposition to PRI. Although PRI has probably had a more anti-clerical history than otherwise, it now faces a clergy, an important portion of which has its eyes on the Marxist Kingdom of Earth rather than the Christian Kingdom of Heaven. Prominent among such LibTheos is the bishop of San Cristóbal de las Casas, Samuel Ruiz. Bishop Ruiz is consequently supportive of the ML Zapatistas and opposed to any Zedillo efforts to return the sovereignty of Chiapas to Mexico.

While the prescripted EZLN "uprising" of 1 January 1994 was playing out, certain Mexican newspapers were more amenable to the truth about clerics like Ruiz than they are now. But the future was being foretold by the counterattack launched by the Jesuit provincial in Mexico, José Morales Orozco, and one of his clerics, Carlos Bravo (EFE 6 July 1994). Morales simply labeled charges of Jesuit involvement with the Zapas "false," blamed it all on *ultra right groups*" and spoke of Jesuit mistreatment in El Salvador, now "being suffered by Guatemalan Jesuits." These clerical counterattacks, mostly by LibTheo clerics, may well be responsible for both the press and the Papal retreats which have since taken place.

As is routine in the press, the change is more obvious in what is not printed than in what is, "what is" being what the Zapas say and claim to do. What has been less frequently reported is opposition, both to clerics such as the bishop and to the EZLN.

Mary Ball Martínez (Chap 5) has discussed the widespread Indian opposition to these Zapatista MLs.[59] This was reflected, if not widely, in the press by the coverage in *EL NORTE* (Chiapas 27 February 1995) "500 Protest Against Bishop," the piece accompanied by a photograph of the burning-in-effigy of the bishop. All of which was "anti-Christian" declared the bishop. In early 1994 *Siempre!* ran a cartoon wherein the director with a star and "Samuel Ruíz" on the back of his chair and propped up by an automatic weapon, was grooming Manuel Camacho for his performance. Seated in the next chair, complete with "Sub" star and "Marcos," that worthy was grooming himself for performance. Since then, however, the situation has changed to the point that, while the details of the denunciations of Bishop Ruiz are difficult if not impossible to find, the denunciations of the denunciations fill the media.

Luis Pazos (*Diario de Juárez* 20 April 1994) declared that Ruiz's conduct during the previous 15 years had been condemned by the Vatican, publishing a portion of the letter to Ruiz by Bernardin Cardinal Gantin, Prefect of the Congregation. Dated 23 September 1993 it maintained that he should leave his diocese because he "offered an interpretation of the Gospel which made use of a Marxist analysis giving a demeaning vision of the person and work of Jesus Christ." He "maintained a pastoral approach on a fundamental doctrine not conforming in all its aspects to the teachings of the Church." He "brings into being a pastoral exclusivism which rejects the collaboration of those who—clerics, religious, laity –do not accept the suppositions of same and which imply an incompatible attitude with the catholicity unique to the Church."

Nor was Cardinal Gantin alone in expressing the Pope's wishes at that time. The next year Cardinal Juan Sandoval Iñiguez of Guadalajara called on Ruiz to resign "because of his involvement in the earlier stages" of the armed uprising and after its emergence (AFP 8 February 1995). But, as Cardinal Iñiguez went on to point out, Pope John Paul II "has not wished to act drastically because of the possible international repercussions" to a forced resignation. And Ruiz, who presides over, *inter alia*, the CDHF, has continued with his own agenda. By 1998 the Pontiff has reversed his position, or at least it would appear so from the fact that the *new* Papal delegate is supporting Bishop Ruiz.

What the bishop is supporting has been frequently discussed here. In a word, the ML EZLN which may be sketched through its chief (pp.124ff, YRBK97). Rafael S. Guillen Vicente (aka Subcmdt Marcos, aka El Mejicano, aka Jorge Narvaez) was groomed from birth (19 May 1957) to be an ML terrorist, first, by his father, then at the Jesuit-run Tampico Cultural Institute and finally in that "vast net of subversion which Castroites and Sandinistas wove in the Latin America of the 1980s." His ML terrorist training in Sandinista Nicaragua and Cuba began in 1979, continued well into the 1980s and has been described (pp.124ff, YRBK97; Wkly 5.1 above, etc.). As with the other HL successes during the last half of Century XX, Guillen's have been obtained for him by the disinformation operations of the HL and the HL Support.

Ya Basta

Guillen is alleged to be fond of the phrase *Ya Basta* (Enough Already [*The Economist* 16 May 1998]). It was therefore appropriate that an Italian "HR" group of the same name (*Gia Basta* [GB]) sent 134 of its members to Chiapas to assure that none of these ML's HRs were being violated and to cause the Zedillo Government as much grief as possible.

GB was allegedly formed three years ago by Fausto Bertinotti, the leader of the "hardline faction" of the Italian Communist Party, *Rifondazione Comunista*. LANS wonders if it might not have been two years ago following a Bertinotti visit to the international ML extravaganza hosted by the EZLN, the "Intercontinental Encounter for Humanity and Against Neoliberalism" (pp.100ff, YRBK97). Whichever the case, GB arrived in Mexico on 2 May with 10-day visas and 134[60] warm bodies among which were those of "four leftwing Italian members of Parliament." In the manner of such "revolutionary tourists," these "HR observers" headed for Chiapas, arriving at noon on 3 May in San Cristobal de las Casas. In actuality 118 of these people arrived in Chiapas. Of these 10 had visas to visit Agua Tinta and Taniperlas, but all were determined to go. This being clearly against the law, the Mexican Government had the entire group out of the country by 11 May.

This GB operation made a great deal of noise in Mexico but almost none in its "native" Italy save in *Rifondazione Comunista*. Italy's largest-circulation daily, *Corriere della Sere* devoted a brief comment to it, the second-largest, *La Reppublica*, failing to mention it.

Autonomous Municipalities

But the attempted GB invasion of the ejido Taniperlas emphasizes perhaps the most important campaign presently in progress in Mexico, that of reclaiming territorial sovereignty from the ML terrorists of the EZLN. In Taniperlas the Zapas had established one of their so-called "autonomous municipalities," done by the simple expedient of appropriating the functions of a legitimate municipality, this one called by them "Ricardo Flores Magón." With considerable care the Mexican Government had moved in the military and dismantled this outlaw "government," the first such operation. Another, "Tierra y Libertad," was dismantled later (1 May 1998).

On 4 May Chiapas Governor Roberto Albores Guillén announced the immediate dissolution of all the "autonomous" municipalities formed by "sympathizers" of the Zapas "for being unconstitutionally constructed." It would appear that the revolutionary tourism of GB did not affect this effort.

PRESIDENT ZEDILLO CONTINUES RECLAMATION OF MEXICAN SOVEREIGNTY
(SPCL 6.2, 11 JULY 1998)

The communications media continues to disseminate misinformation and disinformation relating to the EZLN terrorists, their boss the ML "red-diaper baby" Rafael S. Guillen Vicente (aka Marcos, aka El Mejicano, aka Jorge Narvaez) and their apologist, the LibTheo cleric Bishop Samuel Ruiz. For this reason, it remains almost impossible to approach the Chiapas situation without a "reality review."

That Guillen is nothing more than an ML terrorist, nurtured in what Ruiz Pavon aptly described as that "vast net of subversion which Castroites and Sandinistas wove in the Latin America of the 1980s" has been extensively enough discussed in these reports (cf. pp.124ff, YRBK97), most recently in Wkly 5.23 above. That his EZLN is simply one more ML group with roots in Castroite Cuba has been demonstrated in detail in the LANS account of the FSP-directed "Intercontinental Encounter for Humanity and Agaist Neoliberalism" (pp.100ff, YRBK97) hosted by Guillen in 1996. But the drumbeat of disinformation of course continues.

President Zedillo Ponce de León was left a badly tainted legacy by his predecessor, President Salinas, the Mexican State of Chiapas effectively in the hands of the MLs of the (HL). This had been effected by the Salinas panic and surrender to the advice of the MLs from the Nicaraguan Sandinistas (Humberto Ortega) and the Salvadoran Farabundis (Joaquín Villalobos). "Declare peace," these "ex" terrorists had told him and declare peace he did, an astonishing action comparable only to, say, turning over Cook County, Illinois, to the Capone Mob. But it was an action which the IL has continued to support.

After almost three cautious years of dealing with the Chiapas subversion, Zedillo began to take back Mexican sovereignty in the area as has been preliminarily described in Wkly 5.23 above. The specifics of this campaign began with a careful reclamation program for the so-called "autonomous municipalities" which had been established by the EZLN through the simple expedient of appropriating the functions of legitimate municipalities. With considerable care the Mexican Government had moved in the military and begun dismantling such outlaw "governments" in Taniperlas in the first operation. Then on 4 May Chiapas Governor Roberto Albores Guillén announced the immediate dissolution of all such outlaw "municipalities" for having been "unconstitutionally constructed."

As an indication of bizarre press bias, *Proceso* (Mexico 5 July 1998) had the temerity to begin an article with "In his fifth visit to Chiapas this year, President Ernesto Zedillo gave a speech in Simojovel, *Zapatista territory*..." This of course has no basis in reality, the only meaning attributable being "Zapa territory by right of Salinas surrender." In any event, the tenor of the article may be inferred from this whammo opening.

In his talk the Mexican president made the key point that no "paramilitary group" would be tolerated under any conditions. This of course makes the entire point: the EZLN is the perfect example of just such a "paramilitary group." Not that this made any impression on either the HL or the IL—the presence of European leftists in the service of the Zapas has been remarked from time to time—all of whom are allegedly opposed to para groups. As indeed they are if such groups are anti-ML in nature.

That Mr. Zedillo appears to be serious in his attempts to reclaim Mexican sovereignty in the State of Chiapas has been indicated by his tenacity in continuing the removal of Zapa outlaw "governments" and in his establishment of a substantial military headquarters in southeast Chiapas.

LANS has learned that the accelerated construction of a military headquarters had begun in Maravilla Tenejapa and was underway in early July 1998. LANS has been informed of an extensive base, remarkable in the area for its three-story buildings and all the accouterments of a modern city. Tenejapa is not on most maps, it having been little more than a wide spot in the road. It is, however, close to Margaritas which is some 22 statute miles from the border. The projected base should render it easy to deal with the Zapatista paramilitaries. Only one final point remains to be made.

In Operation Casablanca US intentions may have been of the most pristine, having no imperialist bias. In the case of Zedillo's attempts to reassert Mexican sovereignty in Chiapas, they are apparently quite something else. In June US Secretary of State Albright (AFP 18 June 1998) began to fulminate against Mexican conduct of affairs in Chiapas, a fulmination which, on this occasion, was met head-on by Mexican congressmen of both the PRI and the PAN, the latter calling the Albright pontifications "insolent." Mexico is apparently not prepared to allow the US to interfere. The leftish US congressmen who took up the Albright interference cudgels in July are hardly worthy of mention save to indicate one more group which is susceptible to the blandishments of the HL and the HLS. Through it all, however, it does appear that the Zedillo Government may cleave to its intention of repairing the Salinas surrender in Chiapas.

Nicaragua

CARTER, PEZZULLO AND THE SANDINISTAS
I. PANAMANIAN CAUDILLO TORRIJOS
(SPCL 5.19, 20 JUNE 1998)

The MLs of the HL have attained two complete victories since the ML government of Guatemala was removed in 1954 (pp.219ff, YRBK98), that of Cuba (1959) and that of Nicaragua (1979). The subject of Nicaragua has recently arisen again, partly through the jaded defense *(Diario las Américas* 24 May 1998*)* of one of the principals in the affair, Ambassador Lawrence A. Pezzulo [b.New York, 3 May 1926]. Therefore, it seems worthwhile to lay out some of the facts on this case which LANS has gathered.

James E. Carter [b.Plains, 1 October 1924] assumed the presidency of the US in 1977. He immediately began the isolation of the Nicaraguan Government of Anastasio Somoza Debayle which led to the power vacuum caused by the flight of Somoza. Since the MLs of the FSLN had the guns, they filled the vacuum left by his flight. That such would happen was well known before Mr. Carter came to power. Why did Mr. Carter follow such a course or allow such a course to be followed by his subordinates?

The reason alleged was the change which he was supposed to be making from a foreign policy based on the national interest of the US to one based on "democracy" and HR. But Carter's "high principles" proved to be very selective indeed: The US president virtually doted on the Panamanian caudillo, Omar Torrijos, who was more "undemocratic" than Tacho Somoza while he totally ignored the hemispheric HR violator *par excellence*, Cuban ML dictator Castro. Even though the behavior of *homo sapiens* is seldom sapient, the level of Carter inconsistency was something to behold. Was there discernible motivation in the behavior of the US president? Probably.

Mr. Carter was one of those men of the parlor left who apparently feel, as Heinrich Karl Marx[61] is alleged to have felt, that they can transform this veil of tears into some sort of earthly paradise. This sort of person brushes aside any inconsistencies in his own behavior and any disagreement with the bases of this behavior. When this man spurred his white horse into the White House he was already under the spell of such as US Senator Patrick J. Leahy and US Senator Claiborne Pell[62] who were and remained vociferously anti-Somoza and pro Sandinista. That the Naval Academy graduate, Carter, had any deeper motivations has not been suggested. But that he acquired somewhat similar reasons for his anti-Somoza vendetta has been.

Whether or not James E. Carter arrived in the presidency determined to turn the Panama Canal over to Panama, it was not long before he had decided on this as one of the legacies with which a grateful world would keep his memory forever alive. And in doing so found a beneficial ally in the leftist dictator of Panama, Omar

Torrijos, and his right-hand man, Manuel Noriega, both of whom were moving toward the Cuban dictator and his HL.

As Gibbon has remarked, "Like Augustus, Diocletian may be considered as the founder of a new empire."[63] In reality, with Diocletian the transformation of the Roman Empire into an Arabian Caliphate had been completed. In 305 the Emperor laid down his sceptre to take up pacing the walls of his Dalmatian castle, and, after an 18-year hiatus, Flavius Valerius Constantinus (Constantine the Great) emerged as emperor. This of course occurred after the battle with Maxentius before which a flaming cross in the sky with the legend, "By this conquer," either was[64] or was not[65] seen by Constantine. The only point of this Constantinian diversion is that certain men of the left behave as if just having experienced such a miracle, perhaps a burning shield in the sky emblazoned with "HR."

Anastasio Somoza Debayle

The communications media of the latter 1970s was alive with anti-Somoza propaganda, this ranging from demonstrably nonsensical HR allegations such as the castration of Borge to allegations of Somocista guilt in whatever might have happened most recently. A notable example of the latter occurred with the murder of Pedro Joaquín Chamorro which even Chamorro's mother later declared was no fault of Somoza. But there is no obvious reason for seeking to resuscitate Tacho, murdered in 1980 by a Sandinista hit squad; much more to the point is the nature of his enemies and those US citizens who created the vacuum that they filled. For this we turn to Jack Cox.

Although Tacho Somoza was in the West Point class the year after that of the LANS Editor, the latter can hardly claim to have known him well. Jack Cox, an acquaintance of the Editor deceased nine years ago, was something else again. Cox was a friend of Tacho's. He was a native Texan, a World War II veteran who had served as a Texas Legislator and Republican gubernatorial candidate in 1962. In Nicaragua at various critical times to include its fall to the Sandinistas, he trekked to Asunción, Paraguay, in 1980, happily arriving there before the Sandinista hit squad. He finished an intensive three-month period of interviews from which he produced what was essentially Somoza's autobiography, *NICARAGUA BETRAYED* (Western Islands, 1980, ISBN: 0-88279-235-0). Needless to remark, the book is PIC and dismissed out of hand by those who have been influenced by the DOs of the HL; nevertheless, it is valuable for anyone interested in reality. Specifically, however, there are two important points made therein which LANS has independently verified. The first of these is the abstract of Lieutenant General (LTG) Sumner's testimony before the US House Subcommittee on the Panama Canal in Chapter Seven, which will be presented in this report, the second the Pezzullo tapes which will be presented in a later one.

LTG Gordon Sumner, Jr.

General Sumner [b. Albuquerque 23 July 1924] was a field general as opposed to a political one. He began his career in Armor, served a short term in Korea in 1946, returning there in 1950. In November 1950 he was wounded and captured by Chicom forces north of Pyongyang. Escaping after two days, he returned to Japan to serve on the staff of General of the Armies Douglas MacArthur. After various duties in the ZI, he returned to artillery command in Korea in 1965, then assumed command of the 25th Divisional Artillery at Cu Chi, Vietnam, in 1968 returning to Washington in March 1968. His duties in Washington were thereafter associated largely with LA affairs. He was assigned as Chairman of the Inter-American Defense Board (IADB) in August 1975. Disgusted with what he saw the US doing in Central America (CA), he retired on 31 March 1978. His testimony before the House Subcommittee on the Panama Canal appears on pp. 122-151 of *PANAMA GUNRUNNING* (Hearings on The Involvement of the Government of Panama in the Purchase and Shipment of Arms Destined for the Use of Revolutionaries in LA, June 6, 7, and July 10, 1979. Y4.M53:96-22).

General Sumner's testimony of 7 June 1979 in these hearings is self explanatory and will be presented with minimal commentary in what follows.

> Unfortunately, the facts of Panamanian involvement in supporting leftist/communist terrorist groups in CA have been denied the American people. I saw a great deal of this when I was Chairman of the IADB. There was a blackout of this particular subject, not only in the media, but also, I felt, in the US Government.
>
> But I think of even greater importance is the strategic significance of these efforts by Gen. Omar Torrijos in de-establishing the entire CA Region. This is only one part,

obviously important, of a strategic effort by the Soviets and their surrogates, the Cubans, to deny the US access to the Caribe basin.

I have watched this over three years experience as the Chairman of the IADB; and the frustration of being unable to get this, though, to the American people, but also to the officials of the Federal Government. That is one reason why I retired from active military duty. [Sumner goes on to point out that, as Chairman of the IADB, Carter, Somoza and Torrijos were all his bosses. Editor]

My personal knowledge of Panama's involvement [in gunrunning to the Sandinistas. Editor] came from a 2-hour conversation with Gen. Omar Torrijos in November 1977. He told me then of his intention to support the Sandinistas, to support the insurrection in not only Nicaragua but also El Salvador; and during this 2-hour conversation he expressed the opinions that the Sandinistas were his good friends ... just a bunch of good old boys [Sumner's aide, a Panamanian native Major Dubrai, was the only other person present at this meeting. Editor]

... The Panama Canal negotiations were getting cranked up, and I saw at this time that this was really a bad development.

When I met with General Torrijos, I brought this up, and I expected him to give me a denial. Well, much to my surprise, he not only did not deny it, but as I say, he said he would continue the support, and defended the Sandinistas. He told me at the time, he said you people get too worried about these Communists. This is not really a problem. He said you know there is a lot going on, socialism is the way of the future, and you people are behind the power curve on this. [On returning to Washington Sumner submitted a memo on this to Joint Chiefs Chairman Gen. George Brown and talked with "responsible officials in State and Defense," memo and words disappearing from human ken. Editor]

... My decision to testify against the Panama Canal treaties before the Senate Armed Services Committee was, in part, influenced by my experience both in Managua and Panama. It was quite clear that General Torrijos was expanding his horizons to include support for revolution in CA, and I believed then, and I believe today, that he is under the influence of Communists/Marxists within Panama and Cuba, and particularly Colonel, or I believe General Noriega.

General Torrijos expressed to me great admiration for Fidel Castro at this meeting. The whole tone of the meeting was one, as far as I could determine, and I had not detected this degree earlier, that Omar Torrijos was moving very quickly to the left as he expressed it that he was getting out in front of the movement to lead it. I believe that the unseemly haste of the group of people advising President Carter at that time to consummate these treaties was just one more piece of a plan which was designed to polarize this hemisphere into left and right...

We divided up all of LA into good guys and bad guys. They are being designated as "human righteous." The fact that these "Good Guys," the guys with the white hats, are supplying arms, which you see here, they are supplying the training, money, support, a lot of this is coming out of the US taxpayers' pocket, perhaps indirectly, to murder and maim as General Noriega did in Nicaragua, without discrimination. As far as I'm concerned, that makes a mockery out of the President's human rights policy.

... We have a vital interest in this area and it is about time we realized it. I think Gen. Omar Torrijos is actively aiding and abetting leftist subversion in this area.

As a footnote to this the two thieves, Torrijos and Noriega, are believed by some to have fallen out, leading to the former's aircraft hitting a mountain. However, Noriega, in charge of the investigation, declared the crash to have been an "accident," and all was well.

CARTER, PEZZULLO AND THE SANDINISTAS
II. THE PEZZULLO TAPES
(SPCL 6.3, 20 JULY 1998)

The MLs of the HL have attained two complete victories since the ML government of Guatemala was removed in 1954, that of Cuba (1959) and that of Nicaragua (1979). The subject of Nicaragua has recently arisen again, partly through the jaded defense (*Diario las Américas* 24 May 1998) of one of the principals in the affair, Ambassador Lawrence A. Pezzullo [b. New York, 3 May 1926]. Therefore it seems worthwhile to lay out some of the facts on this case which LANS has gathered. In Part I above the testimony of General Sumner has been used to demonstrate what a singularly lopsided HR program the Government of President Carter was implementing, supporting the leftist dictator and Sandinista supporter, Omar Torrijos, while isolating the friendly anti-ML government of Anastasio Somoza and providing that vacuum which the known MLs of the FSLN would occupy by default. In this report, the details of the Carter isolation of Nicaragua are first enumerated.

THE CARTER GOVERNMENT DESTROYS
THE GOVERNMENT OF NICARAGUA

James E. Carter [b. Plains, 1 Oct 1924] assumed the presidency of the US in 1977. He immediately began the isolation of the Nicaraguan Government of Anastasio Somoza. A number of years ago LANS put together a list of some 11 actions by the Carter Government which assured that Nicaragua would be helpless before its ML enemies, the well armed Sandinistas. These may be summarized as follows:

(1) On taking office (January 1977) Mr. Carter issued an executive order halting the sale of all arms and ammunition to Nicaragua;

the necessary export licenses were cancelled. An Administration attempt to cut Nicaragua out of the military assistance bill was defeated in the US Congress.

(2) On 27 September 1977 US Deputy Secretary of State Warren Christopher ordered that military assistance to Nicaragua by Congress be held up and that $12 million in economic aid be halted.

(3) On 22 February 1978 Nicaragua was denied the right to buy arms from the US under the fiscal 1979 military aid bill.

(4) On 18 April 1978 the Administration blocked a US Embassy-approved request for 101 revolvers for bank guards opposing Sandinista holdups.

(5) On 1 November 1978 the Carter Administration blocked a $20 million standby credit loan for Nicaragua in the International Monetary Fund.

(6) The Carter Government pressured shipping companies to boycott Nicaragua under the guise of dangerous port conditions which did not exist. As a consequence the Republic was unable to export either coffee or beef in 1979, the result being almost complete economic strangulation.

(7) The US Embassy in Nicaragua pressured businessmen in their host country to transfer their dollar denominated assets from Nicaraguan to American banks. The idea was to deprive the Nicaraguan Government of dollars for possible arms purchases.

(8) On 8 February 1979 the Carter Administration cancelled two projects which had $10.5 million in aid for nutrition and rural education in Nicaragua.

(9) On 8 February 1979 the military assistance held up on 27 September 1977 was ultimately cancelled.

(10) In June 1979 an Israeli ship with a cargo of arms and ammunition, already paid for, approached the Nicaraguan coast. US Intelligence had learned of the ship's cargo, and sufficient pressure was applied to force its return, still fully loaded, to Israel.

(11) While staging bases for Sandinista terrorists in Costa Rica, Panama and Cuba were ignored, sufficient pressure was put on potential Nicaraguan allies such as Guatemala so that all defensive treaties with the Republic of Nicaragua were abrogated.

A defenseless Nicaragua was thus assured of lying prostrate for Sandinista plucking , and it was—prostrate and plucked. The OAS

Resolution of 23 June 1979 was little more than a formalization of what had already been accomplished. At a meeting in Washington, DC, on that date the US proposed the ejection of the Somoza Government, and the OAS duly disposed. In his testimony of a few days before, General Sumner, former IADB Chairman, had warned of what would happen then, and it happened.

Early on the morning of 17 July 1979 Anastasio Somoza Debayle, his Cabinet, General Staff, the departmental commanders, the Congress of Nicaragua and the Board of Directors of the Liberal Party flew into exile. That the ML Sandinistas took over and brought decades of misery to Nicaragua which have yet to really end is well enough known to require no repetition here. What is not well known is the part played in this plot by the US Ambassador to Nicaragua, Lawrence A. Pezzullo.

The Carter Government, whatever its motivation, created the power vacuum in Nicaragua which the ML Sandinistas predictably filled with disastrous results for that nation. This is a fact and a reasonably familiar one. The operation whereby this vacuum was created may be described as "clandestine" since, according to the testimony of General Sumner (Spcl 5.19 above), the IADB Chairman's attempts to warn the people of the US were carefully blocked. One of the important instruments of this clandestine operation was one Lawrence A. Pezzullo, a public school teacher (1951-1957) who was appointed vice consul in Juarez (O-8) on 15 June 1958, plodding upwards in the diplomatic service until appointed US ambassador to Nicaragua in June 1979. Here he was to play an important role in this affair.

Nicaragua Delivered to the Hemispheric Left

As Sumner has illustrated, by the summer of 1979 it was well known that the FSLN was a part of the Moscow-Havana Axis. While it appears to be true that there were considerably greater numbers of anti-Somoza Nicaraguans in the Broad Opposition Front (FAO) than Sandinistas, the latter had the guns which, in the final analysis, is what counts. Until the last moment the US Government maintained what can only be called "the fiction" that it wished to prevent a Sandinista takeover after Somoza was forced out. This was important in order that Somoza and any allies he may have had in the US and elsewhere would not "rock the boat." One of the principal instruments for this opposition was Pezzullo.

Had the US had any intention of opposing FSLN takeover, it would have had two options, (1) use its own military personnel to prevent it or (2) support the Nicaraguan National Guard in order to do so. It was to this second option that the US pledged itself during those talks which arranged the exile of President Somoza; it was Ambassador Pezzullo who acted as the go between in making this "pledge."

The Pezzullo Tapes

With apparently good reason Somoza did not trust Pezzullo and his government. Therefore, in November 1978 he began tape recording his conversations with representatives of that government, most importantly with Pezzullo. The LANS Editor had various discussions with Jack Cox, the custodian of these tapes after Somoza's murder, but has made no attempt to disturb his survivors on the subject. There were seven audio tapes which he reproduced in Chapter 18 of *NICARAGUA BETRAYED* (Western Islands, 1980, ISBN: 0-88279-235-0), Cox's "autobiography" of Somoza.

These tapes demonstrate that, through Pezzullo, the Carter Government pledged itself to option (2) above, support of the Nicaraguan National Guard, if Somoza would leave the country. This pledge is fully revealed in the following excerpts.

The first excerpts are from Tape 5, the record of a conversation of 29 June 1979 during a meeting among Somoza, his son Tacho, Pezzullo, US Congressman John Murphy (D,NY) and three other Nicaraguans.

> PEZZULLO: ...Because this structure will hold and the Guard will survive, not in the same form, but it will survive...Because they are disciplined officers who made a commitment to defend their country, and to defend and protect the interests of Nicaragua, and to preserve their order. And that's the discipline they have to draw on...
> SOMOZA: Mr. Ambassador, let me say this, because of the structure of the National Guard, I was not ready to do anything but to go...And these people, Mr. Ambassador, mainly are not fighting for Somoza, they are fighting the enemy they have fought for the last eighteen years, Communist Castroites. That's why you have not had any success in getting these people to turn on me, even in the overtures the United State has made...
> PEZZULLO: Oh but, please, please, we have never done that element. We have never sought to undercut you. I ought to know.
> SOMOZA: You have done that publicly...What I am trying to tell you, Mr. Ambassador , is that these people are quite aware of who their enemy is. That's why they are fighting like cats and dogs...But mainly, Mr. Ambassador, these men are fighting against Communism. They are not fighting for the Somoza regime. Philosophically, these people are democratic...
> TACHO: What we have to make sure is, that whatever happens in this damned country,

people within a couple of years, people can go out and vote for what they want.
PEZZULLO: That's, that's the key...
TACHO: ...That whatever happens for as long as the US makes sure that elections can take place in this country, that no half-assed, crazy son of a bitch is going to come in here and prevent the situation...
PEZZULLO: That's where we are.
TACHO: I just hope that you people can, I really hope that you people can stand the initial pressure when you start in a situation that will guarantee the ability of every little guy to be able to grow up free...

The remainder of the excerpts reproduced here appear on Tape 6, a meeting in July 1979 between Somoza and Pezzullo.

SOMOZA: There is much political fiction about myself. Due to this political fiction and because we are losing so many lives, that is why I told you the first day that I'm ready to go. But I plead with you, don't let these people suffer. When I go, goddam it, take all the sanctions away and give these people a chance...
PEZZULLO: ...I'm very much concerned about everything you've said and I'm telling a lot of people about it, and we'll try to put this into place as soon as we can and I'll be back to you to set a date.
SOMOZA: All right. What's most important...is that Nicaragua not fall into the Communists' hands. The national interests of the US will not be served well if the Communists take over the country.
PEZZULLO: Agreed, agreed.
SOMOZA: Mr. Ambassador, you should know that 90 percent of the entire officer corps of Nicaragua have gone through various United States military schools.
PEZZULLO: I know that.
SOMOZA: Well, you cannot discount that because of Somoza...
PEZZULLO: We will not. We will not. I told you that our interest is in preserving the National Guard. Even if the name changes, there will be some, we want this thing to survive as an institution.

Thus the evidence indicates a commitment by the Carter Government to prevent the takeover by the ML Sandinistas; instead the Sandinista slaughter of the National Guard was permitted after Somoza left.

On 17 July 1979 President Somoza's resignation was read to the Nicaraguan Congress which selected Dr. Francisco Urcuyo to succeed him. In the meantime Somoza had been "permitted" by Pezzullo to select Colonel Federico Mejia González to assume command of the National Guard before Tacho left Nicaragua. By this time, the Pezzullo proposals to maintain the National Guard had come to be known as the "Washington Plan."

On 18 Jul 79 President Urcuyo, General Mejia, his brother Dr. Luis Mejia and Pezzullo met in the president's office.[66] The meeting was important, but it can be succinctly summarized by Pezzullo's

statement,
"There is no Washington Plan."

What Should Somoza Have Done?

No attempt will be made to answer this question. However, among those Guard personnel whom the LANS Editor has since interviewed, there is a difference of opinion, the dissenting view perhaps adumbrated by the excellent Guard General Ivan "Loco" Allegret some two years before that black summer of 1979. Said Loco, "In the plane that Somoza leaves on, there won't be room for me."

Those who feel Tacho had no choice but that of flying away apparently feel there was reason to believe the Carter Government. But they must also believe Somoza'a remark that the Guard was out of all ammunition including small arms ammunition. One Guard ranker told the Editor, however, that on 12 July 1979 he viewed 3000 to 4000 boxed M-16s and an "immense" number of rounds of M-16 ammunition in La Loma Fortress.

Assuming the truth of this report, some believe that Somoza should have put himself at the head of an assembled guard and cut his way into Honduras. Right or wrong, such was not to be, history recording the slaughter of a scattered National Guard. Thanks to the Carter Government, the HL had won its second complete victory.

Peru

OPERATION CHAVÍN DE HUÁNTAR
(WKLY 5.4, 29 JANUARY 1998)

In 1992 Peruvian President Alberto Kenyo Fujimori Fujimori introduced and implemented the most effective, if not the only effective, anti narcoterrorist program in Latin America. That same year both terrorist organizations, Sendero Luminoso (SL) and the Tupac Amaru Revolutionary Movement (MRTA), were decapitated with the capture of their respective chiefs, Abimael Guzman and Victor Polay Campos. The latter, who had been the college roommate of the Marxist president who preceded Fujimori, Alan Garcia Pérez, "escaped" from prison in 1990. Guzman surrendered in his cell the next year. What may have been the last gasp of Peruvian narcoterrorism, the Japanese Embassy Operation (JEO) began in December 1996.

On 17 December 1996 the JEO began with the seizure of the Japanese Embassy in Lima (pp.174ff, YRBK97) in an operation with which the Fujimori Government dealt in completely successful, copybook fashion (pp.238ff, YRBK98). The result was the demise of all the terrorists involved in the JEO and the survival of all save one of the hundreds of hostages, that one indirectly as a result of a wound-induced heart attack. As has been stated in previous LANS reports, however, this could probably not have been accomplished by any contemporary Latin American politician save Fujimori—La Golconda as LANS Associate Editor Emanuiloff-Max calls him—whom the ML terrorist knows will not surrender to their blackmail.

OPERACIÓN CHAVÍN DE HUÁNTAR: Rescate en la residencia de la Embajada del Japón. General de Ejército Nicolás De Bari Hermoza Ríos. Talleres Gráficos de Fimart S.A. Lima. 1997. ISBN 9972-9077-0-0 Reviewed by the Editor, LANS.

The book is replete with colored photographs. Although this will furnish the pre-programmed HL with fodder for charges that it is a mere puff piece, this is valuable to the student of the affair. For example, the proverbially, and understandably, unapproachable intel chief, Montesinos, appears in a number of photos.

In his prologue to the book the Peruvian intel chief, Dr. Vladimiro Montesinos Torres, aptly describes the atmosphere in which the Peruvians had existed during the 15 years preceding the JEO. "A ghost roamed the Peruvian land causing terror, desolation and death; during more than ten years the Peruvian's life had no value. We could die on a street corner, inside our homes or on our lands with our farm tools in our hands. The country and the city were converted into essential aspects of the SL ghost...[they] entered the city which was, conforming to the ideology of these criminals, only 'a supplement.' That is, when on 16 July 1992, they perpetrated the outrage in Tarata Street, without any concern for the lives of so many, the strategic equilibrium concept for the fanatic terrorist idea was at it midpoint. They considered themselves with the capacity to develop the first actions of a 'guerrilla war.'"

In his Introduction and first chapter General Hermoza presents a concise and useful review of Peruvian ML terrorism from April 1980 to the opening of the JEO on 17 December 1996. A general officer on active duty can hardly be expected to discuss those statesmen (politicians) who contributed, wittingly or unwittingly, to terrorist success. It should still be emphasized (1) that the regime of General Juan Velasco Alvarado[67] swung the country's political axis toward the Soviet Union"[68] such that "if something favored Sendero's development and silent growth, it was clearly Peru's military regime in the first place."[69] And (2) that the regime of the avowed Marxist President Alan Garcia Pérez exacerbated the problem.

But it is appropriate for the general to review the behavior of the nation's political leader, President Fujimori, from his assumption of that role in July 1990. And to preface this with a simple reference to the fact that between 1980 and 1990, narcoterrorism was largely treated as a "police problem"[70] and actions against it limited "to administering the subversion." President Fujimori's attempts to deal with the terrorists were blocked by the Peruvian Congress as "militarization of the country" until his immensely popular (91 percent favorable rating on 5 April 1992) Government of National Reconstruction dissolved Congress and the Garcia Judiciary (pp.170ff, 3YRBK97).

Hermoza describes the "New Strategy" which was then introduced as "1. Reorganizing the role of the Armed Forces...2. Significantly promoting the National Intelligence System...(and) orienting its efforts toward the location and capture of the principal chiefs of the terrorism...3. Creating the institutional mechanisms for channeling the active participation...of the population through its own organizations[71] (such as the Campesino Patrols (RC) in the rural areas and the Self Defense Organizations (OAD)[72] in the urban areas)...4. Restructure the Judicial Power..."

The general describes the three SL objectives as "a) Counteraction of the Andean axis...b) Encircling the great cities, principally Lima...c) Development of an economic zone of withdrawal and subsistence..." He then goes into the success enjoyed in destroying these SL schemes, concluding with the sentiment expressed on Army Day, 9 December 1994:

> It is easy to criticize when the rivers of blood of innocent people no longer devastate your life or the lives of your children; it is easy to offend the soldiers who know the law forbids them to raise their voices in reply...After the war the usual happens...Instead of asking of the enemies, the criminals who committed the unspeakable bestialities against our brothers...what has been achieved since 1992 appears an impossible dream: to conquer the enemy who....

With the second chapter Hermoza refines his treatment to include only the terror group of principal interest here, the MRTA. His description of the Tupas history is particularly useful—19 terrorist acts in 1984 escalating to 580 in 1989—as is the account of its "cooperation agreements" with the narcotraffickers and its own with the SL "converting the Valley of Alto Huallaga into the logistics base" for them.

His next chapter (3) is first devoted to the terrorist embassy campaigns worldwide, quoting effectively from Laquer's classic[73]—"terrorism succeeded in becoming almost respectable and created an important majority in the UN." For reasons on which LANS has frequently dwelled, Hermoza points out that, in spite of the barbaric and sadistic behavior of SL, "no self-described human rights group criticized it. Nor was there heard any condemnation of the...(JEO) by the MRTA [although] there was such against the Peruvian Armed Forces and Government for rescuing the hostages." Some of the embassy seizures are quite familiar—the US Embassy in Iran (1980)—some less so—the seizure of the Dominican Embassy in Bogotá by M-19 (pp.112ff, YRBK97)—but the general success of these terrorist efforts, particularly in the realm of favorable publicity, is obvious.

The name of the rescue operation, Chevín de Huántar, was chosen by President Fujimori for two reasons. First, perhaps largely because the planning for the operation, for security reasons, took place in the caverns associated with the ancient Peruvian "Chavín de Huántar" Culture.[74] And, second and more importantly, if this culture is taken as crucial to the concept of Peru, the operation itself had "the...significance above all of being the RESCUE of the DIGNITY of Peru at a crucial moment of its battle against [a] terrorism...which...seeks national dissolution..."

The terrorist seizure of the embassy is treated by the general in Chapter 4, LANS' earlier treatment (238ff, YRBK98) generally covering this action. However, the accounts of several individuals, e.g., Foreign Minister Tudela, emphasize the success of Operation Chavin by detailing the terrorists preparations to murder their hostages if attacked. And in one interesting passage Hermoza recognizes what LANS considered perhaps the most disturbing aspect of the entire JEO, the apparent breakdown of that Peruvian intel and counterintel which had made the successful Peruvian operations possible. He could hardly be expected to reveal much about this breakdown. Nevertheless, he does indicate the concern which should have been, and apparently was, felt with: "...through negligence in established police levels (*determinados niveles policiales*), which are subjects for investigation and judgment by the Military Jurisdictional Organ, it was not considered necessary to take special security measures" for the reception at which the attack took place.

Chapter 4 also contains the details of the hostage releases through 26 January 1997. In the next chapter the conversations, whereby, through firmness and refusal to "negotiate" with these terrorists, Fujimori kept a threat against the lives of the hostages at bay. From the first Cerpa and his outlaws had been threatening to begin the murder of their hostages if their demands were not met. Because the Tupas knew Fujimori would act as he had promised, not one was murdered. Other heads of state could never have succeeded in such an attempt had they tried to do so. In this "conversations" chapter is likewise included an account of President

Fujimori's trip to Cuba, "clandestine" in that, save for the president, the presidential party—and the press—thought it was returning to Peru from the Dominican Republic until it heard "we are arriving in Havana, Cuba." The Fujimori-Castro interview is reported as open and amounting to a query of the Cuban dictator as to whether or not Cuba had offered support or would offer it. The caudillo said he would if asked. Reports (cf. EFE 21 December 1997) of Salvadoran FMLN preparation of the Tupa terrorists in Peru for attacks was not the sort of support which was under discussion.[75] LANS has described the successful operation which resulted in the elimination of the Tupa terrorists and the rescue of all 72 hostages alive (pp.238ff, 3YRBK98), one of whom succumbed to a heart attack after a bullet wound. In Chapter 6, General Hermoza recounts much the same account, although he cannot describe "in detail each of the actions for reasons of security," these details still classified "Secret." As he points out, however, the victory of 22 April 1997 was not forged in December 1996 "when planning for Chavín began" but "beginning in 1992 when the basic (intel and military) concepts were restructured."

The last two chapters recount the victory and offer a tribute to the two heroes, Colonel Juan Valer Sandoval and Captain Raúl Jiménez Chávez, who died in Operation Chavín de Huántar. A fitting tribute to the operation was rendered by General Manuel Bonnet, Commanding General of the Colombian Army.

> (Beginning today) all students of the military art and science have heard the courage and strength of Peruvian combatants...we respect their efforts, we celebrate their future triumphs and we appreciate their personal leadership.

THE PERUVIAN CIVIL SELF DEFENSE COMMITTEES
(SPCL 5.11, 10 APRIL 1998)

Peruvian terrorism now consists basically of the SL and the MRTA. These branches of the HL have been discussed in these reports (pp.169ff, YRBK97; pp.223ff, YRBK98), the JEO or Operation Chavín de Huántar receiving extensive treatment.

SL had its beginnings in 1980 (p.189ff *ibid*). Peruvian Pres. Fernando Belaunde's conclusion at that time that these were simply criminals[76] and hence a police problem would prove to have been a serious error. It was not until December 1982 that Belaunde recognized his error, a recognition apparently forced upon him by the total defeat of the police, and assigned the military to deal with the situation. For reasons which were various, among them Belaunde's distrust of his military intel sources as Alberto Bolívar O. ["Intelligence and Subversion in Peru," *Low Intensity Conflict and Law Enforcement*, Winter 1994] has emphasized, matters still did not proceed favorably for the nation in this war against ML terrorism. In 1985, Belaunde was replaced in the presidency by Alan Garcia, and matters, if anything, deteriorated.

That Garcia was a Marxist, had been a college roommate of the MRTA terrorist boss, Victor Polay Campos, and apparently expressed his admiration for SL "principles" are facets of his personality which assuredly had some influence on his inept prosecution of the Peruvian war against ML terrorism. If nothing else these characteristics had an adverse effect on the military's ability to perform. And Polay Campos did "escape" from duress vile about the time that the new president, Alberto Fujimori, took office in 1992. Pres. Fujimori has since enjoyed immense success against the ML terrorists of the HL and hence has been the target of an almost continuous disinformation operation by various elements of the HL and HLS. Contributing to this success, however, was an anti-terrorist element which has proven itself immensely important to anti-terrorist warfare wherever it has been encouraged to do so: the CAPs.

For the ML terrorist may fulminate against "bloated landlords" and other pet hates, but most of their terrorist activities end by being directed against the campesino. And when the latter is appropriately organized and armed, even poorly armed, he has been a threat to the terrorist which no armed forces have been able to match because of the sheer magnitude of the territory involved. In a recent issue of *COMANDO EN ACCION* (No.20, 1977) there is a tribute to the CAPs of the Village of Cangallo in Ayacucho Department "where what would become one of the most ominous terrorist actions of the republican story of Peru started 17 years ago." The book which will be reviewed here is a detailed study of those CAPs. These, in concert with the military, have brought most of Peru out of the shadow of the ML terrorists.

Las rondas campesinas y la derrota de Sendero Luminoso. Carlos Iván Degregori (Editor). Contributors: Carlos Iván Degregori, José Coronel, Ponciano del Pino and Orin Starn. Instituto de Estudios Peruanos (IEP). Lima. 1996. ISBN: 84-89303-55-X. 269 p. Reviewed and quotations translated from the Spanish by the LANS Editor.

C. A. Degregori is an anthropologist, principal investigator of the IEP and professor at the San Marcos National University. José Coronel is an anthropologist, Ponciano del Pino an historian, both professors at the San Cristóbal National University of Huamanga. Orin Starn is an anthropologist and professor at Duke University. The publication forms part of a program on Governability and Public Policy supported by the Ford Foundation. The book consists of five separate, referenced contributions, Chapters I and IV written by Degregori, II by Coronel, III by del Pino and V by Starn. In IV (p.189) Degregori begins with a concise early history of SL.

> When SL initiated its war in May 1980, it was a party made up largely of school teachers, professors and university students. Its presence among the regional campesinos was weak. Nevertheless, when, after the Christmas season of 1982, the Armed Forces assumed politico-military control of Ayacucho, SL had succeeded in easily displacing the Police Forces from ample rural areas of the northern provinces of the department and preparing to encircle the departmental capital. (pp.189-190)

In Chapter IV ("The Self Defense Patrols[77] and the Defeat of SL in Ayacucho") Degregori goes on to describe SL's attempts in Ayacucho Department which appeared about to succeed in the second half of 1982 when "something special happened." The Peruvian Communist Party (PCP)-SL celebrated its II National Conference and began the final stage of its "plan" of "Deploying the Guerrilla War." Whether Degregori's analysis of what happened next is precise or otherwise, his "Inattention in the midst of success incubates failure" is universally true. And the author traces the check in SL's Ayacucho successes to its *"batir el campo"*[78] campaign having enticed it into beginning "to construct its new power."

While no criticism of studies such as this one is intended, they necessarily suffer the constraints imposed by taking the ML terrorist and his avowed objectives seriously. In the observable cases, however, the objective of their operations is power and the perquisites of power for the chiefs and the apparat. This was true of Ulianov (aka Lenin) as it is true of Castro, Ortega, Handal and, assuredly, Guzman, to say nothing of those who have made "peace," walking off with the loot this had showered upon them.

When SL began replacing the *varayoq*[79] or *alcalde vara* in the small rural communities with what amounted to its commissars, it foolishly sought to destroy the complex fabric of indigenous tradition. To which it added the foolishness of AgRef with the accompanying theft of crops and slaughter of farm animals amidst the weeping of the campesinos who escaped being SL victims themselves. And the CAPs were born.

In I Degregori discusses the baneful fruits of the war in Ayacucho Department. In the third section of this chapter he deals with "The event which marked the transition between despair and vitality, it constituted by the [national] extension of the CAPs, also called *rondas campesinas*. According to the Institute for National Defense Investigations (INIDEN), in March 1994 there existed in Ayacucho and Huancavelica about 1,655 CAP containing 66,200 ronderos[80] and having 6,060 shotguns provided by the government." At this point the author provides a footnote which is of sufficient interest to reproduce.

"The numbers were provided by General Cano in an INIDEN seminar and cited by Tapia.[81]...in 1994 there existed nationally 5,786 CAPs with 400,360 ronderos and 15,390 rifles distributed by the government. These figures include a significant proportion of the rondas of Piura and Cajamarca, which arose in the 1970s in a different context...When in 1992 Legislative Decree 741, which legally recognizes the Comités de Autodefensa, was promulgated, a portion of these northern rondas opted for conversion into CAPs." He discusses the difference between these earlier CAPs and the later, the difference largely being a considerably smaller arms to personnel ratio.

It is of interest and relevant to LANS earlier reports that, although these CAPs indeed preceded the arrival of Fujimori in the presidency and the departure of Garcia, it was the Fujimori Government which nationalized and legitimized these immensely important instruments of terrorist control. It is of passing interest to remark the decrease in accuracy of Degregori's remarks with distance from his base of operations. In closing I he accurately remarks that a portion of the Colombian campesinos in arms were converted into hired assassins ... [for] narcotraffickers."[82] He is simply quoting HLS disinformation when he typifies Guatemalan counter-insurgent strategy as "genocide."[83]

In Chapter II Professor Coronel deals with "political violence and campesino response in Huanta Province" of Ayacucho Department. He treats the diverse responses of the Iquichuas of the mountains and the small, independent campesino proprietors of the valley to the violence between 1980 and 1993, the result of his field work in the area between 1992 and 1993. The central thesis of the study is that the CAPs spread in the Valley of Huanta toward the end of the decade of the 1980s as a result of the convergence between the goals of the campesinos and those of the state counter-insurgent strategy. The various authors in this work agree that, for a period of two or three years after the military replaced the SL-ousted police, the campesino had substantial problems with such strategy before this convergence took place.

The state, about the mid 1980s, abandoned its fundamentally "repressive actions" in order to attempt a rapprochement with the campesino. This rapprochement was effected at a time when SL was carrying out "military" actions in the attempt to attain "strategic equilibrium" in its "war" against the state. The scene favored the build up of the CAPs which "isolated socially and overturned politically" SL in the province. After the capture of Guzmán by the Fujimori Government in 1992 (p.171,YRBK97), the CAPs "assumed tasks of collaboration [with the Armed Forces], not only in defense but in the reconstruction of the communities."

In Coronel's Section II, he details (part 2) "1980-1982:The Sendera Expansion," (part 3) "1983-1985: The Marines Attack the Valley

Campesinos and SL the Mountain Communities," (part 4) "1986-1989: A Dream of Peace" and (part 5) "1990-1993: Spread of the Rondas and Isolation of SL." The chapter includes a number of useful tables for the student, for example, The Highland Communities Attacked by SL (Table 3) and The Highland Families Displaced, 1983-1989 (Table 4) and useful maps such as Expulsion and Reception Zones for the Displaced (Map 2).

In a Chapter III entitled, "Times of War and of Gods. Ronderos, Protestants and Senderistas in the Valley of the Apurímac River," Professor del Pino discusses just what his title implies. Insofar as Ronderos and Senderistas are concerned, an interesting description of the advance of the CAPs down the Apurímac River is displayed as Map 2.

In its journey to the Amazon, the Apurímac flows out of the high mountains of Ayacucho Department, then proceeds roughly northwest, it removed by one valley as it passes Cusco to the southwest. The river first defines the northeast border of Apurímac Department, then the northeast border of Ayacucho Department, finally splitting into the Ene River to the northwest and the Montaro River to the west. The northwest extension of the CAPs is traced along this river from its beginnings in 1983, to the northwest through 1984 and farther to include the Cusco region in 1985-1988. By 1991-1993 the CAPs had moved on to the northwest to extend well beyond the river's branching into the Ene and the Mantaro.

This author also details the spread of Pentecostal and Presbyterian churches in three regions (p.137), Table 2 itemizing the Presbyterian Churches which the SL terrorists attacked. Both the SL counterattack of 1985-1987 had certain interesting features such as the alleged "consent of some military...[the officers] offered gifts, money and feminine companionship for not acting." But the CAPs recovered even from this to a success which was not rendered any easier by the narcotrafficking problems which the author discusses. The chapter is rendered even more useful by the typical T/O which appears in it (p.153).

As Professor Starn tells the reader in his Chapter V ("Unexpected Senderos. The Rondas Campesinas of the South Central Range"), Ayacucho is the Quechua word for Corner of the Dead (Rincón de los Muertos). The city is the site of San Cristóbal University of Huamanga which nurtured the terrorist Guzmán during the 1970s and hosted a visiting Starn in 1993. According to the latter, "toward the end of 1982, Army troops carried out frequent incursions into the university to kidnap and murder alleged rebels." Such statements have "frequently" been the subject of disputation. In his essay, Prof. Starn sets out to examine "the history of the rondas campesinas. Born of the presumption that the simplistic characterizations of the ronderos, be it as brutish hobbesian ruffians or noble tolstoyan defenders of the national sovereignty..."

Notes

1. Council of Ministers Human Rights Commission (CDHCM) President Paolo Ungari "censured the Italian press for preparing an 'apotheosis' in favor of the Cuban leader" (*Clarin* (Buenos Aires) 13 November 1996).
2. The Italian News Agency—Agenzia Nazionale Stampa Associata.
3. Malachi Martin, *THE JESUITS: The Society of Jesus and the Betrayal of the Roman Catholic Church* (Simon and Schuster, 1988. ISBN: 0-671-54505-1).
4. That these LibTheo clerics share the common ML lust for other people's property has just been illustrated again by Ernesto Cardenal. *La Prensa* (Managua 15 January 1998) reported that a judge in the San Carlos District had issued an order for the imprisonment of Ernesto for failure to turn over his "liberated" property. The selfless ones of LibTheo have, of course, abrogated the Commandment referring to "not covet(ing) thy neighbors goods."
5. The Marxist convert (1977) to Christianity, Humberto Belli (*NICARAGUA: Christians Under Fire*, The Puebla Institute, Costa Rica, n.d.) also describes this all out attack on the Pope.
6. Sandino's name was not Augustus Caesar, as even Martin calls him, but, as the illegitimate son of the maid, Calderón, Augustus Calderón. Now doubtless Martin knows this, but using the "Augustus Caesar" title is nevertheless an historical inaccuracy which redounds only to the benefit of the ML Sandinistas.
7. Interestingly enough, this is just what John Paul II would speak about to the Cuban people 15 years later.
8. CARICOM replaced the Caribbean Free Trade Association (CARIFTA) which was founded in 1965.
9. The "US Cuba Gambit" (Wkly 4.15) covers many of those indicators which had arisen by its date of publication (15 October 1997). These indicators run the gamut from the Clinton dinner with Castro's good friend and unofficial ambassador, Gabriel García Márquez, and others in September 1994 to the various official and semi-official visits to Cuba thereafter. Any number of usually excellent sources maintain that none of the teeth in the Helms-Burton Act have been allowed to function since Mr. Clinton signed the bill creating it. Finally, as has been mentioned before, the LANS Editor was informed by a former DGI officer that several high ranking members of this government had been Venceremos Brigade members in the 1960s.
10. Arturo Espaillat (*Trujillo: the last Caesar*, Regnery, 1963. LCC: 63021921) graduated from West Point in 1943, two years before the LANS Editor, three years before Tacho Somoza. He outlived his boss by only two years, his demise perhaps interesting, perhaps not.
11. Having served to the Castro takeover as Embassy Press Officer in Cuba, Paul Bethel (*The Losers: The definitive account, by an eyewitness, of the Communist Conquest of Cuba and the Soviet penetration in Latin America*, Arlington, 1969. LCC: 6916944) was in the press corps in the DR at the time of the unpleasantness.

12. For those who feel that the cruelty of the Fourteenth Century has been left behind in this "enlightened" Twentieth Century, the barbarism of the USSR, the Peoples Republic of China, Nazi Germany, Castroite Cuba et al far surpasses anything that has preceded it, even the skull pyramids of Timur I Leng (1336-1405) were tactical weapons and not the "human engineering" holocausts (Paul Johnson, *MODERN TIMES*, Harper Collins, 1991. ISBN: 0-06-433427-9) of this Candidean "best-of-all-possible" centuries.
13. Pp.173-4, Jean Froissart (*Chronicles [by] Froissart*, Translated by Geoffrey Brereton, Penguin, 1968. LCC: 68143144). In 1368 he was in the party with Geoffrey Chaucer which went to Italy for the wedding of Edward III's son, Lionel of Clarence, and presumably met Petrarch who was present at the festivities.
14. P. 577, Joseph F. O'Callaghan (*A history of medieval Spain*, Cornell University Press, 1975. LCC: 74007698).
15. Those wishing more detail than can be given here should consult Alfonso de Ceballos-Escalera y Gila (Marqués de la Floresta), Almudena de Arteaga y del Alcazar and Fernando Fernández-Miranda y Lozana (*LAS REALES ÓRDENES Y CONDECORACIONES CIVILES DEL REINO DE ESPAÑA*, Montalvo, 1997).
16. Distribution of Dr. Douglass's book had been arranged before publication but mysteriously evaporated after the book came off the presses. Harle has since published an updated version, *RED COCAINE: The drugging of America and the West* (Harle, 1999. ISBN: 1899798048). Order from: bookorders@edwardharle.com.
17. A few years ago a LANS source in the DEA (Drug Enforcement Agency) reported certain examples of narco moles in that organization. The details of the operations in which they figured are unimportant, but the methods—evaporation of leads, changes of narcotrafficking plans indicating knowledge of DEA operations, etc.—which indicated penetration are of some importance.
18. Castro's FARC (Cuban Revolutionary Air Forces) used a MiG-23MF and a MiG-29 to blow two unarmed Cessna aircraft, over international waters, out of the sky (p.93, YRBK97)
19. The phrase is "haciendo las conclusiones, sino las inconclusiones."
20. During the 1992-1994 period LANS received various reports of Sandinista and Farabundi caches of arms, one, which appears to have been correct, having been photographed on a southern road out of Managua during this period by the Editor. The Government of Mexico has recently (EFE 12 August 1998) asked Salvadoran President Calderón Sol to investigate reports of Farabundi arms shipments to the EZLN. Will he investigate and will the reported results be reliable?
21. The dapper, moustached Ponomarev, now dead, was long the boss of the Americas Department of the CC (Central Committee), CPSU (Communist Party of the Soviet Union), and, as such, was of course in overall charge of terrorist operations in Latin America.
22. Cf. p.568 of *Communist Threat to the US Through the Caribbean*, Part 8A, Testimony of Lt. Aurelio Silva Hernández, Cuban National Police [Senate Subcommittee on Internal Security, 1960, Y4.J89/2:C73/27pt.8A].
23. Cf. Paul Bethel, note 11 above and Claire Sterling (*The Terror Network*, Holt, Rhinehart and Winston, 1981. ISBN: 0-03-050661-1).
24. Cf. the Bogotá press for 17 October 1963.
25. Our colleague, Ariel Remos, reported on this in March 1986 from sources he had within this Congress.
26. Doctor José Carlos Graça Wagner, now Coordinator of International Affairs for the Tancredo Nevis Institute of São Paulo, has devoted himself to public affairs since his days as a student. During this time he has participated in various political, social

27. Stédile (44) was called the "Brains of the MST" by *Jornal do Brasil* (4 February 1996).
28. Lula perhaps best described his PT in Pierre Broue [*Quand le peuple révoque le président: le Brésil de l'affaire Collor*, L'Harmattan, 1993. LCC: 93193369) by classifying its militants as "Trotskyites, Castroites, activists of the Brazilian Communist Party (PCB) ... liberation theologists ... Sandinistas" and more.
29. the LANS Editor, at about that time, sought a record of the meeting from Princeton but was told that no record was kept of this meeting directed by Castañeda. Attempts to contact Castañeda by telephone were fruitless.
30. Rainha was the ML boss of MST whose home boasted four photos of Mao and "various works of Frei Betto" (*Veja*, 17 January 1996).
31. In Spcls 5.7 and 5.8 only the two-page "Introduction," the 32-page "History of the Project" and the two-page "Summary of Evaluation" will be reproduced in condensed form.
32. In excellent account of this operation has been given by Néstor T. Carbonell [*AND THE RUSSIANS STAYED: The Sovietization of Cuba*, Morrow, 1989. ISBN: 0-688-07213-5]. The numbers given in this IG report mean nothing without considerable analysis.
33. A remark here on Marxist-Leninist (ML) control of Cuba has been removed as redundant (3YRBK97).
34. The SG included representatives of various departments and agencies and was charged by NSC5412 with approval of major covert operations.
35. It does not say "DOD." What it means must be guessed since "Navy" is apparently a branch of "Defense."
36. Cf. Note 3, p.181, YRBK97.
37. Yevgenia Albats, *THE STATE WITHIN A STATE: The KGB and Its Hold on Russia—Past, Present and Future* (Farrar, Strauss, Giroux. 1994. ISBN: 0-374-18104-7).
38. Of course the book was hardly his; it was ghosted for him by an acquaintance of the reviewer, Jack Cox, the book *NICARAGUA BETRAYED* (Western Islands, 1980. ISBN: 0-88279-235-0).
39. These are of course important to the Pezzullo Case for which cf. Spcl 5.19, this chapter below.
40. Alberto Niño H., *ANTECEDENTES Y SECRETOS DEL 9 DE ABRIL*, Libreria Siglo XX, 1949.
41. Andres Oppenheimer, *BORDERING ON CHAOS* (Little Brown, 1996. ISBN: 0-316-65095-1)
42. Miguel Poradowsky, *El Marxismo en la Teología*, Imprenta LaHosa, 1983. The LANS Editor worked closely with Dr. Poradowsky in the latter 1980s in the translation of this book into English.
43. The word is *gobiernista* by which the terrorists refer to the governing party, PRI [Institutional Revolutionary Party]. They certainly do not mean the PRD [Democratic Revolutionary Party] whose chief, the governor of the Federal District, Cárdenas, has an "arrangement" with them.
44. This small party [cf. Wkly 4.1] is named after the father of Cárdenas, a leftist president of the 1930s. The candidate it fielded in the DF elections against Cárdenas was a flying-saucer enthusiast.

45. *Armas blancas* is literally "any sharp instrument." Presumably, if "knives" were meant, or "machetes," this could have been used. Swords and spears?
46. This is generally considered the smallest tactical infantry unit, there being three or four in a platoon.
47. The word used is *zedillista* which of course means "of Pres. Zedillo."
48. If the Zapatistas were not well known as part of the HL [Hemispheric Left], this charge, reminiscent of the silly charge against the Guatemalan Army of tossing babies about on bayonets with rifles which do not take a bayonet, would be enough to identify them.
49. The phrase used here is *las autónomas*, presumably meaning "las autónomas personas" because of the gender. The word *autónoma* is an adjective unless the noun meaning "self-employed worker or person" is intended which appears a *non sequitur* here.
50. This was the alleged "massacre" of "leftist" Mexican students for which the Army was blamed and with which the HL (Hemispheric Left) of course had a field day. In actuality it was orchestrated by the KGB in a complex operation which John Barron (*KGB: The Secret Work of Soviet Secret Agents*, Bantam, 1974. ISBN: 0-553-20254-5) describes in exquisite detail in his Chapter XI, "The Plot to Destroy Mexico."
51. Democracy, Liberty and Justice appear on separate lines as does the material on the next line.
52. "Ejido" derives from the Latin "exitus," "the way out." In Spain before the conquest it was applied to common land attached to a village and used by the villagers primarily to pasture their cattle and gather firewood. In the Western Hemisphere the term was applied to the common land held by the Indian communities and used for agriculture.
53. This statement is not precisely accurate. This "revolutionary legality" is at least as old as the Bolshevik Revolution (1917).
54. Cf. pp.191 of YRBK97 (*Latin American Political Yearbook 1997*, Transaction, 1998. ISBN: 1-56000-350-2) and later reports. As discussed in Wkly 5.23, the Pope has long sought Ruiz's resignation unsuccessfully, specifically, through the letter of Bernardin Cardinal Gantin, Prefect of the Congregation, who in 1993 stated, *inter alia,* that Ruiz had "offered an interpretation of the Gospel which made use of a Marxist analysis giving a demeaning vision of the person and work of Jesus Christ." Cardinal Juan Sandoval Iñiguez asked for his resignation "because of his involvement in the earlier stages" of the armed uprising, this in 1995. The Vatican appears to have given up the effort, and more recent eyewitness accounts received by LANS are insufficiently documented for publication.
55. Araceli Burguete Cal y Major, *Remunicipalización en Chiapas*, CEMOS, No. 114, August 1998.
56. AgRef is, of course, a fraud perpetrated by the PPs for political reasons. Any logical extrapolation of this continuous division of agricultural property demonstrates that it should not be long before a "farmer" will be fortunate to feed himself, let alone any other individual. But of course, as with most "programs" of the PP, it is fraudulent so perhaps this dire consequence will not ensue.
57. Especially the ML bosses, as has been demonstrated with Dzugashvili's (aka Stalin) and the jewels (Gordon Brook-Shepherd, *The Storm Petrols*, Ballantine, 1977, ISBN: 0-345-30164-1), Arbenz and everything not nailed down (Select Committee on Communist Aggression, *Communist Aggression in Latin America*, GPO, 1954. Y4.C73/5:L34/2), Humberto Ortega and his horse-training estate (Roger Miranda and William Ratliff (*The Civil War in Nicaragua*, Transaction, 1993. ISBN: 1-56000-064-3)) and any other MLs who are investigated.

58. This adjective is based primarily on Art.27 and the premise that, without the property right, there is no individual liberty. "Art.27. Ownership of the lands and waters within the boundaries of the national territory is vested originally in the Nation ... (which) shall at all times have the right to impose on private property such limitations as the public interest nay demand..."
59. The LANS Editor has, at various times over the years, interviewed Guatemalan campesinos, finding just what Ball found (cf. Spcl 3.10, YRBK98), the Guatemalan Indians by wide margins having no use for Castro's ML terrorists.
60. *Diario Yucatán* (6 May 1998), for example, reported 135, but its strength claim appears to be in the minority.
61. Not that Mr. Carter is a Marxist. It would appear unlikely that he could make a lucid presentation on the mumbo jumbo of diamat.
62. The LANS files contain a photograph of these two worthies, taken on 14 February 1982, Leahy and Pell in a *tete a tete* with the ML, Bayardo Arce of the Sandinista Politburo, this taking place in Arce's Managua home which had of course been "liberated" from some alleged Somocista.
63. Chapter XIII of Edward Gibbon (*The decline and fall of the Roman Empire*, Modern Library, 1983. LCC: 83005460). Gaius Valerius Aurelius Diocletianus (245-313), if (like Heinrich K. Marx) a confused economist, was one of the few honest men among recorded politicians as attested by his retirement after 20 years on the throne as promised.
64. This according to Eusebius, Bishop of Caesarea (*Uber das Leben Constantius*, Vol. I of *Werke*, J. C. Heinrichs, 1902). Eusebius does not mention this in his *Ecclesiastical History* [Catholic University Press of America, 1965 (Translated by Roy J. Deffarari)] and, although claiming to have heard it from the Emperor's own lips, mentioned it not until after the latter's death.
65. Zosimus (*Historia Nova; the decline of Rome*, Trinity University Press, 1967 (Translated by James J. Buchanan and Harold T. Davis). LCC: 67026544) wherein the Pagan indeed recounts what may be called a rather ribald story of Constantine's conversion.
66. The LANS Editor has onterviewed two of the participants in this meeting, the view of General Mejia attested to him by his brother
67. The regime lasted from 1968 to 1980
68. P.122 of Simon Strong, *SHINING PATH: Terror and Revolution in Peru* (Times Books, 1992. ISBN:0-8129-2180-1).
69. Alberto Bolívar Ocampo, "Intelligence and Subversion in Peru" (*Low Intensity Conflict and Law Enforcement*, Vol.4, p.410, Winter 1994).
70. As has been pointed out in these reports, the so-called "peace" with the ML terrorists in El Salvador specifically moved, through the Chapultepec Accords, to treating subversion, foreign-based or otherwise, as a "police matter" out of the purview of the military.
71. The efforts to destroy these organizations, for example, in Guatemala and Colombia, have been frequently discussed in these reports and are to be treated further in later reports. Such efforts are basically traceable to the Henispheric Left (HL) and have been intensively channeled through various Non Governmental Organizations (NGOs).
72. *Las Rondas Campesinas y la Derrota de Sendero Luminoso* (Instituto de Estudios Peruanos (IEP), 1996. ISBN: 84-89303-55-X) will be reviewed in Spcl 5.11 below. Cf. also Francisco Reyes [*Hablan los Ronderos*, IEP, 1992] and Carlos Tapia [*Auto Defensa Armada del Campesinado*, CEDEP, 1995].
73. Walter Laqueur, *Terrorism* (Little, Brown, 1977. LCC : 77994872).

74. Cristóbal Campana D., *El arte chavín: análisis structural de formas e imágenes* (Universidad Nacional Federico Villareal, 1995. LCC: 97191367).
75. The continuing close liaison between FMLN boss Shafik Handel and HL boss Castro indicates that both would have been aware of these activities.
76. Which, in reality, they were but with a broader base than, say, the Al Capones of the world. As with the other ML terrorists of the HL, there is no crime in which they do not engage: "Give me a machine gun and an ideology and applaud my crimes."
77. These are simply called *rondas campesinas*, that is, campesino patrols, but it appears appropriate to render this as "self defense patrols."
78. Literally, "whip the countryside." Cf. Gustavo Gorriti Ellenbogen, *Sendero: historia de la guerra milenaria en el Peru* (Editorial Apoyo, Lima, 1990-, Vol.1. LCC: 91122055).
79. The indigenous mayor of one of these Andean campesino communities.
80. A member of a CDC or a *rondero campesino*.
81. Carlos Tapia, *Las fuerzas armadas y Sendero Luninoso: dos estrategias y un final* (Instituto de Estudios Peruano, 1997. LCC: 97143490).
82. The CDCs or CAPs in Colombia will be discussed in future reports.
83. The deliberate distortion of operations in Guatemala in order to produce allegations of this kind has been discussed in various reports (YRBK97, YRBK98). As have the two principal HR organizations in that nation and the mythical figure of 100,000 to 200,000 dead in the terrorist unpleasantness. The same sort of viewpoint appears to be evidenced by Prof. Starn, both these authors referencing Americas Watch reports on Guatemala.

5

The Hemispheric Left (HL) in Colombia

Introduction

In previous editions of this yearbook it has been feasible to include all hemispheric terrorism in a single chapter. During 1998, however, the concatenation of circumstances in Colombia has justified a change in this procedural arrangement. That year was witness to an increase in the amount of attention which Colombian terrorism demanded that raised the subject to a level of importance overshadowing that of any other such activity in the hemisphere. In doing so it has justified this separate chapter for its treatment. Under these conditions the extent of the LANS coverage of Colombian terrorism has increased to the point where the subject should be divided into sections for comprehension.

Section A is devoted to "The Diplomacy of the Subversion." This notation was developed by the LANS correspondent in Bogotá, Doctor Miguel Posada. The term means both (1) those Disinformation Operations (DOs) by means of which the Hemispheric Left (HL) wins all its victories and (2) that "diplomatic corps" of "Human Rights" (HR) Non Governmental Organizations (NGOs) and those Hemispheric Left (HL) or Hemispheric Left Support (HLS) activists who act as "diplomats" in spreading this disinformation.

Section B, "Minor Terrorist Coups Used in Subversive Diplomacy," is a discussion of those basically trifling engagements on which the Subversion has fabricated such elaborate DOs abroad. Particularly noteworthy here is the Great Gringo Disinformation Operation (GDO). As with most such Marxist Leninist (ML) DOs, the GDO is not particularly well conceived or well executed, it deriving its success from its reception by an ill-informed and left-biased press.

The Self Defense Patrol (CAP) is perhaps the most important auxiliary which the military has in dealing with ML terrorists. Which means that the terrorists and their auxiliaries can be expected to wage strong, and generally nonsensical, Subversive Diplomacy against them. The success of the terrorists in this battle is described, as are the CAPs themselves, in Section C, "The Self Defense Patrols."

In 1998 Andrés Pastrana Arango of the Conservative Party was elected president of Colombia. After actually obtaining the endorsement of the criminal terrorists of the Colombian Revolutionary Armed Forces (FARC) for his candidacy, he won the run-off election. His bizarre "peace process" has demanded a level of attention which LANS has supplied in Section D, "The Pastrana Peace Process." Finally, the Liberation Theology (LibTheo) terrorist cleric who had long bossed the National Liberation Army (ELN) died during the year, returning to the headquarters of HL terrorism, Cuba, to do so, as all good ML terrorists should. This event is probably most important as one more testimony to the continuing reality of cohesion in the criminal left and, as such, deserves the separate Section E, "Death of a Terrorist Cleric," which the notice has been given.

A. The Diplomacy of the Subversion

COLUMBIA: THE NEXT VICTIM?
(WKLY 6.3, 18 JULY 1998)

Colombia promises to be a repetition of the laboratory "experiment" which has been nearly completed in Central America (CA). The CA experience has largely been viewed through the myopic and clouded eyes of a US and European press which appear to confuse it. The process resulted in victories for the ML of the HL, victories which bode well for completion. While it cannot yet be said that the process will be repeated to the same conclusion in Colombia, the probability of this would appear high. El Salvador may be taken as the example of the fruits of Esquipulas II,[1] Nicaragua being one so obvious as to need no repetition, Guatemala much the same.

HL Victory in El Salvador

Amidst a barrage of disinformation, the US took unto itself the alleged task of preventing the MLs of the Farabundo Martí National

Liberation Front (FMLN) from assuming power in El Salvador. In doing so, however, it assumed ultimate control over the Government of El Salvador (GOES) with its continuing threat to cut off economic aid, military and otherwise, if its wishes were not accepted as commands. In the media-event "war" that followed, the US, succumbing to the pressure of the HLS, provided sanctuaries—in "refugee" villages and border "pockets"—from which the terrorists could operate with impunity. Both the US and the USSR, before and after its "implosion," badgered GOES to make "peace." As LANS has shown,[2] the peace of the Chapultepec Accords was the peace of surrender, and the FMLN obtained a political power which its political and "military" impotence would never have gained for it. Which leads to a somewhat more specific treatment of Colombia.

Colombian Terrorists and the Colombian Military

The ML terrorists in Colombia are, as were the Salvadoran Farabundis, common criminals who live by the entire litany of crimes which the Liberation Theology (LibTheo) "clerics" among them might once have considered "sins": Murder, narcotrafficking, kidnapping, extortion, grand theft, statutory and other rape, and so on. And the only forces which have prevented the complete takeover by such forces of many, if not all, of the LA nations have been the Armed Forces of those nations.

The LA armed forces do not need "defending" by LANS or any other group. What they "deserve" is the exposure of the HL and HLS organizations which have been tireless in fabricating DOs against them, DOs without which the terrorists of the HL would have gained no victories in Cuba and Nicaragua, no partial victories elsewhere and none of the victories which loom on today's horizon. In Europe and the US in particular, the flow of money and moral support to them is largely due to a press which, wittingly or unwittingly, regales the public with the terrorist lies about the military and thus gains the support of the honest burghers of Darmstadt and the well-meaning feather merchants of Kalamazoo for the ML criminals of Urabá. When these DOs are investigated on the ground, it is found that they are amateurishly contrived, but why do better? To an historically illiterate—and frequently uninterested—press and public they sell well and hence accomplish their purpose.

As in El Salvador, the Colombian Armed Forces (FAC) could deal with the noisy terrorists of the Colombian Revolutionary Armed Forces (FARC) and the National Liberation Army (ELN) were they given government support and the simple mission: Destroy the terrorists. [Specifically, this means that FAC must destroy their staff and command, their infrastructure and their support structure, depositing them, like Guzmán of Peru, in jail.] Such a realistic approach has been and would be rendered more difficult by the ML connections of a number of individuals in the Colombian Government—Serpa,[3] for example, was the Liberal Party presidential candidate and has been closely linked to the terrorists. These "sympathizers" tend to "protect and serve" the terrorists at the expense of the FAC.

A more realistic treatment of the DOs and the so-called "Human Rights" (HR) organizations would tend to ameliorate this difficulty within the country and it would appear that progress is being made in this direction. A brief example of the routine HR DOs will be given. First, however, it is crucial to describe a new tactic in the war against FAC. Still based on a DO, its objective is to establish the inability of the Armed Forces as a complement to their alleged brutality. This DO appears to have been initiated in *The Washington Post* (WP) of 10 April 1998 and extrapolated on the front page of *The New York Times* (NYT) of 1 June 1998. It may be recalled that, when Smith was appointed US ambassador to Cuba, he was sent to Herbert Matthews of NYT to be briefed.[4] This State Department contact with the man "who made Castro" (p.192, YRBK97) is important in itself but perhaps more important as an example of State-NYT liaison and worth the ruminations of the student. In order to consider this WP-NYT DO, a sketch of the events on which it is allegedly based is essential.

Las Delicias—Patascoy—El Billar

In the summer of 1996 a less than company-strength unit of FAC was manning a cobbled-up outpost at Las Delicias. This hamlet is in Putumayo Department, on the right bank of the Caquetá River,[5] 31 statute miles (sm) SWS of Tres Esquinas which will be encountered below. This outpost was overrun by some 400 FARC terrorists (pp.210ff, YRBK98). During the next 10 months the Samper Government contributed to the propaganda victory which FARC enjoyed from this capture by acceding to the terrorist demands.

This affair was repeated at Patascoy in December 1997 with another small unit (below), although some military heads did roll for inefficiency in this case. Patascoy was little more than a relay antenna on a mountain top guarded by a platoon. It was located on the ridge of the mountain range defining the border between Nariño and Putumayo Departments, a short distance north of the road linking the capital of the latter (Mocoa) and the capital of the former (Pasto). There were apparently serious security mistakes made, and FAC removed the brigade and division commanders from command as a consequence.

The third such incident occurred at El Billar which is 47 sm about due east of Tres Esquinas, again a small unit overrun by a large FARC group. The personnel captured at Patascoy and El Billar are still in the hands of the terrorists,[6] and, as a result, another propaganda victory was presented to the terrorists.

The Great Gringo Disinformation Operation

None of these three minor engagements were of any consequence, although FAC should—and has in the Patascoy case and perhaps in that of El Billar—deal with those responsible and assure that such propaganda bonanzas for the terrorists do not happen again. But the bonanza was blown out of proportion by the press, little if any of which has any notion of the military or of military operations. And the bonanza led to what has been called the great Gringo Disinformation Operation (GDO) (Wkly 5.18, Chapter 6 below).

This GDO began with the WP article mentioned above. In the article the existence of a Defense Intelligence Agency (DIA) report was claimed, this allegedly predicting the defeat of the Colombian Armed Forces by FARC terrorists within a few years. This is obvious nonsense[7] as anyone familiar with the situation in Colombia on the ground can attest. But even more importantly, and rendering the WP account a DO, is the fact that no such report exists.

The LANS Editor questioned the DIA spokesman some time ago and was emphatically informed that there was no such report. On 14 July 1998 the LANS Editor interviewed General Manuel José Bonett Locarno, Commanding General of Colombian Military Forces. Gen. Bonett told the Editor that the DIA commanding general had attested to him that there was no such report.

The intellectual author of the GDO can only be guessed. Perhaps the author of the WP article, one Douglas Farah, could be, but this seems unlikely. He probably picked it up from some individual or organization, perhaps one of the more violent "non violent" HR groups. And, once dispatched, such anti-military and pro-left delicacies quickly gain a life of their own as may have been the case with the NYT extrapolation. But while the "who" may thus be indeterminate, the "why" of the GDO can be confidently stated.

It constitutes an effective attack on FAC if "public opinion" can be thus swayed to believe that, not only is FAC guilty of HR violations, but the terrorists are going to beat the military in any event. Thus, the notion of making "peace" with the narcoterrorists, the Al Capones of late Siglo XX, however much of a surrender it may involve, is not only a "just" but also a "wise" course of action. This will make it easier for some foreign power, allegedly involved in "helping" Colombia, to turn it over to the terrorists instead.

The US Wants to "Help"

The requisite atmosphere had thus been emplaced with the cloud of HR DOs and, finally, the great GDO. Now "peace" must be pursued.

Oscar Arias, the "peace" prize recipient for his alleged importance to Esquipulas II, has been fulminating for years for the elimination of LA armies, the only bulwark against the HL. Within the last year he has been seeking to inject himself into the Colombian "peace process," advocating the application of "his" Esquipulas Accords to this process. Finally, however, the last piece was placed in the puzzle[8] with the AFP dispatch of 3 July 1998, "EE.UU reitera oferta de apoya a Colombia en procesa de Paz" (US Repeats Offer of Support to Colombia in the Peace Process).

The US was able to prevent Salvadoran victory in the media-event "war" in that nation with HR charges leading to protected sanctuary for the terrorist operations. In the WP article of 10 April which kicked off the great GDO, the throw-away remark, "Colombian military's dismal HR record in recent years," has already been used as a basis by the US for offering "aid" which will be tied to these same DOs on HR. Various of the DOs will be discussed in future reports, but one remark only can be included here.

In the annual report put out by the US State Department on "Human Rights" in Colombia, one demonstrable DO was reported as an

HR violation. Various Colombian authorities were able to demonstrate to State that this was one more fabricated DO. Or so it would appear, for the "violation" did not appear in the report for 1997. However, no retraction of this unfounded charge was offered by State, and those palpitating for HR charges are probably still using this as proof of Colombia's "dismal HR record in recent years."

A Touch of Reality

An aura of sanctity appears to gather about a NGO which declares itself to be concerned with "HR," and it is clearly not "politically correct" for a journalist to seek beneath this aura for the reality of the group. The fact is that many of these groups are sympathetic to, or infiltrated by, MLs, in Colombia, MLs associated with the narcoterrorists. Routinely, these NGOs fabricate DOs intended to destroy those military commanders whose records demonstrate them to pose a threat to the terrorists.

In future reports LANS will detail several interesting cases wherein these HR accusations have been fabricated by such groups, each accusation targeted at an officer whose honorable military service against the terrorists was devastating to them in its success. One of the DOs, which will be detailed, was that against General Ivan Ramírez. This really rather poorly contrived DO was used by the US as a reason for denying Gen. Ramírez a visa (EFE 21 May 1998). From such as this have arisen the allegations in the US of the "dismal HR record" of FAC.

The dismal record is, rather, that of these NGOs. Army Intelligence, in a painstaking investigation involving various NGOs which these reports will detail, was able to prove the infiltration of them by the ELN (*El Tiempo* 8 November 1997). This excellent operation was rewarded by a concerted DO maintaining that the military was "making war on the NGOs." This handed the terrorist accomplices a victory in the bizarre dismantling of the 20th Intel Brigade (AFP 20 May 1998).

THE DIPLOMACY OF THE SUBVERSION. I

MIGUEL POSADA[9] LANS CORRESPONDENT

BOGOTÁ, COLOMBIA

(SPCL 5.5, 7 FEBRUARY 1998)

As in the interior of the country the subversion aspires to replace the Democratic State, so also abroad it engages in diplomatic activity in order to achieve support for its cause, dazzling public opinion and foreign governments alike by its criminal actions and generating therewith a false image of the State and its Armed Forces (FA). In this the subversion is supported by the International Left (IL) and uses direct and open action as it uses indirect action. In the indirect action the HR NGOs play an important role, as much domestically as abroad. The Colombian State facilitates these labors by omission and commission: by omission in failing to divulge the reality of the Colombian conflict; by commission in appointing members of the subversion to the diplomatic corps.

In August 1994, for example, the government appointed the following "reinserted"[10] guerrillas to positions created the previous month: (1) Gustavo Petro of the 19th of April Movement (M-19) as First Secretary in Belgium, (2) Eduardo Chavez of M-19 as First Secretary in France, (3) Vera Grave of M-19 as First Secretary in Spain, (4) Anível Palacio Tamayo of the Peoples Liberation Army (EPL) as First Secretary in Great Britain and (5) Bernardo Gutiérrez of EPL as First Secretary in The Netherlands

These positions were therefore filled by persons who, were it not for amnesties and indulgences, would have been in jail for murder, kidnapping, extortion and various other crimes. The national or international NGOs said nothing about this. On the other hand, when the present government tried to name Col. Alfonso Plazas Vega (Ret) from the consulate in Hamburg, to a position in South Africa or in the consulate in San Francisco, the NGOs, specifically National Centrum Boor Ontwikkelingssamenwirkung (NCOS) and Samen Anders Gaan Ontwikkelen (SAGO) from Belgium, with the support of others unknown, succeeded in stopping it.

The First Secretary of the Embassy of Colombia in Belgium devoted himself to undermining the position of the ambassador in that country. It is logical to suppose that the other guerrillas mentioned devoted themselves to similar tasks.

More recently, Mr. Carlos Roberto Saenz occupied a position in the Colombian delegation to an organism of the UN in Geneva. Mr. Saenz is no less than the brother of Guillermo León Saenz, aka Alfonso Cano,[11] most recently a member of the FARC Secretariat. How important is the Diplomacy of Subversion? The present article attempts to present a brief analysis of this subject in the case of the Colombian conflict. In other recent conflicts, such as El Salvador and

Guatemala, the foreign "political war" played a critical role in the peace processes which occurred there and in the power relation between the parties involved.

1. The New World Order and the New Thematic Agenda

The end of the Cold War marked a changed attitude in the US and Europe toward the internal conflicts in other countries. Until that time countries suffering internal conflicts from the action of subversive Marxist groups could count on the support of the West. Today, this support has evaporated. A conflict like that in Colombia does not concern the West as a threat to its security.

This is a mistaken attitude because it fails to recognize the connections between terrorist groups internationally and the emulation of methods which these connections produce. Only a few months ago the Department of State (State), obliged by a recent US law, classified the groups which it considered terrorist. On said list were included FARC and ELN, but in spite of this the position of State toward the Colombian subversion has been ambiguous.

On the other hand, during the Cold War, the subversive groups could count on material support from the socialist countries. Today, there remain few socialist countries, and these are impoverished. Nevertheless, paradoxically, the subversion is receiving private and even governmental support from some developed countries. In a recent Military Intel operation in Bucaramanga, the connection of some national NGOs with the ELN and its financing by some European Union (UE) organisms was made apparent.

With the disappearance of the battle against Communism as a central foreign policy concern of the developed world which we call the West, the following concerns became important: (1) Battle Against Narcotrafficking, (2) Promotion of Democracy, (3) Human Rights, (4) Protection of the Environment, (5) Free Commerce and Protection of Foreign Investment, (6) Terrorism.

2. Objectives of the Subversive Diplomacy (SD)

Subversive "diplomacy," as opposed to official diplomacy, has clear objectives. These can be summarized as: 2.1. To give the impression that there is a conflict between a repressive state, which is defending its aristocratic interests, and an idealist subversion which is defending the oppressed classes. The state is alleged to be a brutal violator of human rights. This objective is linked to the following: 2.2. To maintain pressure on the country from abroad with the threat of commercial restrictions in order to weaken or suppress military and civilian support for the anti-subversive battle. [The attacks on the Rural Security and Vigilance Cooperatives (CONVIVIR).] 2.3. To achieve economic support in the developed countries for the subversion. 2.4. To prevent military support and the sale of armament to the FA. 2.5. To hide the criminal nature of the guerrilla activity (violations of human rights,[12] narcotrafficking, use of "quiebrapata" mines,[13] recruitment of children, etc.) To control international perception of the actions against the environment by the subversion (blowing up of pipelines and felling of jungles for the cultivation of coca and poppies). 2.6. Weakening of military intel. 2.7. To establish the attitude of the developed countries with an eye to their participation in future negotiations. To try to establish equal guilt.

3.1 Parameters of Analysis

For Colombia, not all countries have the same importance in what touches upon the internal conflict. How can relative importance be determined? Some parameters for analysis can be offered:

(1) The vulnerability of Colombia to a given country is directly related to our exports to that country.

(2) The sensitivity of a country to the conflict and the Colombian state is directly related to the level of capital investment of that country in ours.

(3) The diplomacy of the subversion functions better in those countries which have a strong left.

Using these three parameters we can analyze our relations with, and the importance of subversive "diplomacy" to, pertinent countries.

3.1.1 INVESTMENT IN COLOMBIA (IN MILLIONS $US) (source: Bank of the Republic) Total: 8,343; US 3,876; Panama 807; Spain 441; United Kingdom 357; Venezuela 315; VirginIslands 322; Switzerland 253; Netherlands 217; Canada 203; France 196; Germany 195; Japan 132.

Subsequently, there have been important Chilean investments in the electric sector. There is also a significant investment, which has appeared as of other origin, but which is actually Mexican, in the cement sector.

3.1.2. COLOMBIAN EXPORTS 1996 (MILLIONS US$) US 4,087; UE 2,408; Andean Group 1,839; Rest of the World 2,227; TOTAL 10,561.Within the UE the most important numbers are (MILLIONS $US): Germany 600; Netherlands 359; Belgium 292; France 273; United Kingdom 193; Italy 166; Spain 158.

3.2. Attitude Toward the Subjects by Groups of Countries

The attitude toward these themes, which can be called transnational themes, is different for different groups of countries. For purposes of this discussion we can group them as follows: US; UE; Latin America (LA); Japan and the Asian Capitalist Powers; Russia, China and the Third World.

Japan, the new Asiatic powers, Russia and the Third World countries do not evince must interest in the internal affairs of other countries nor in subjects other than commercial. With them, moreover, commerce is not very significant. Although Japan's imports are important for Colombia, they are not significant for that country. Our exports to those countries are negligible. For these reasons this analysis will be limited to the US, the UE and LA.

3.3. Attitude and Importance of the Countries

US. The US is our major market, and, although it has important investments in Colombia, our vulnerability toward this country is great. It does not have a Communist Party (CP), but there are elements of the left in academia and the press. Although there is some direct action by the Colombian subversion, the principal labor is done indirectly, that is, through the NGOs. Relations are tense on the subject of narcotraffic. It is the seat of the Washington Office on Latin America[14] (WOLA) and Americas Watch.

On State and on some members of Congress, the HR NGOs, inclined to support the subversion, exercise considerable influence. The section of State concerned with HR and Democracy is headed by Mr. John Shattuck, whose connection with the American Civil Liberties Union (ACLU) is a clear indication of his inclinations toward the left. The last report of this organization on HR in Colombia is based on statistics from the international and Colombian left. Based on such perceptions, support for the Colombian FM has been denied. The present ambassador, Dr. Juan Carlos Esguerra, who had been Minister of Defense and is aware of the situation, has succeeded in influencing some elements of Congress favorably.

The US media has a strong tendency toward the Left. It amplifies the "successes" of the subversion, the reports of so-called HR violations, provides a "showcase" for the voices of the subversion, etc. (An example is CNN.) This tendency has been demonstrated during the Vietnam War, the Salvadoran conflict and the recent outrages in Mexico. The subversion has direct access to the media.

Important factors: (1) Colombian diplomacy with relation to that country is not strong, it having neither adequate means nor adequate personnel. Different government functionaries "lobby" without any coordination by the chancellery or the ambassador. (2) Guerrilla activities in narcotrafficking, kidnapping, violation of children's rights and destruction of the environment could be exploited. This has not been done. (3) There exists a strongly anti-Communist Cuban exile sector. It would be feasible to seek its support. (4) There is an important Colombian colony which could exert pressure on opinion and politics were it oriented and motivated. (5) One could count on the support of those US enterprises which have investments in Colombia. There are entrepreneurial organizations which support Colombia.

Europe. GERMANY. It is the major European importer of Colombian products. It has a small investment in Colombia. This indicates great vulnerability toward this country, accentuating its great weight within the UE. *The subversion has achieved its greatest successes in Germany.* There it has attained its objectives of stopping the sale of armament to the FA and attains important financing from German sources. Colombian diplomacy has demonstrated complete ineptitude in managing the country's image there. Immediately after the Mauss case (pp.192ff, YRBK97) it was to be observed that there clearly exists an active ELN diplomacy in this country.

FRANCE. It is an intermediate case. There are neither sources of its imports from, nor investments in, Colombia, although the latter are greater than those of Germany. Having recently had colonies, its attentions are centered in these former colonies. Nevertheless, it has a strong left and some NGOs which support the subversion. Among the NGOs having connections with the subversion is France Liberté, directed by Danielle Mitterand,[15] widow of François Mitterand, the deceased socialist president, and open admirer and friend of Fidel Castro.

UNITED KINGDOM. It is not a great importer of Colombian products. Its investments are increasing. This country is living through the manipulation of the HR theme. Recently it was condemned in an absurd decision by the European Court of HR for the deaths of some terrorists of the clandestine Irish Republican Army (ERI) who were blown up while activating an explosive device. It has confronted subversive conflicts in Kenya, Malaysia, Greece. For these reasons the subversion cannot easily influence its government.

The good relations of the petroleum enterprise, British Petroleum (BP), with the FA, necessary for the secure development of its investment, suffered the attack of an English member of parliament, Richard Howitt, socialist, in the media and in the European parliament where he was supported by the "greens" and other members of the left. Members of the Colombian subversion, abusing the right of political asylum, have established NGOs there dedicated to attacking the Colombian State and BP. These are the Colombian Refugee Association (CORAS) and the Colombian HR Committee (CHRC), among whose directors are to be found Asdral Jiménez, known member of the EPL, and Freddy Pulecio, a high director of the USO, connected to the ELN and free under a court order prohibiting his leaving the country. The first NGO is directed by Virgilio Zapata. Jiménez is also a member of a third NGO called PRAXIS (Practice).

Recently, nevertheless, the subversive diplomacy has suffered some reverses in the UK. There was an important debate in the House of Lords during which Lord Waverly emphasized the true nature of the Colombian subversion. BP has taken up clarification of its action with a quiet but effective presentation before ill-informed but well meaning organizations.

For many reasons the UK is a potential ally and, given its importance in the UE, could be an important factor.

SPAIN. The DS has been very active in this country. In a recent conversation with a member of the European Parliament (PE), Señora Ana Miranda, Spanish representative, the author was able to learn the level of influence which the subversion has achieved with personalities from this country. Its commercial relations are increasing, especially its investment. Spain has suffered the same sort of terrorism from the Basque Homeland and Liberty (ETA). For these reasons, although the subversion has exerted great efforts, that country can be a support for Colombia. The recent rout of the left Spanish Socialist Workers Party (PSOE) is encouraging.

OTHER EUROPEAN COUNTRIES. Holland and Belgium are important as being the seats of a goodly number of HR NGOs. The latter country is the seat of the UE. They do not have large investments in Colombia. In proportion to their size, however, they are substantial buyers of Colombian products.

Italy, Austria and the countries of Eastern Europe are not especially interested in Colombia. Switzerland is important only as the seat of the International Red Cross (CRI) and other multilateral organisms. Norway has played important roles in the Mid East and Central America as "facilitator" of peace processes.[16] Recently its foreign ministry has displayed interest in the Colombian conflict, inviting spokesmen from different sectors to a forum dubbed "conversational," at which its functionaries were present. Three members of the CAS presented their points of view at this event. Sweden, reacting to the kidnapping of some of its citizens in Colombia, recently declared the Colombian guerrilla terrorist.

[Translated from the Spanish by the Editor, LANS]

THE DIPLOMACY OF THE SUBVERSION. II

MIGUEL POSADA

LANS CORRESPONDENT

BOGOTÁ, COLOMBIA

(SPCL 5.6, 14 FEBRUARY 1998)

Latin America. The neighboring countries are directly affected by the Colombian subversion. In the areas of influence of these countries, Colombia can hope for support in its battle against subversion. Increasing commerce with these countries makes them interdependent with Colombia. It is important to establish good coordination of efforts in order to prevent the frontiers from becoming useful to the guerrilla, the corrupt elements in those countries facilitating armament for the bandits. It is also obvious that the subversive movements existing there provide support to the Colombian subversion. Likewise, the HR NGOs in these countries, with their proclivity for the subversion, will give support to their Colombian counterparts. The strongest subversive movements in the neighboring countries are Sendero Luminoso and Tupac Amaru in Peru.

Other LA countries have been victims of armed movements. Their governments are natural allies of Colombia. The case of Mexico, which for years took in subversives of all countries, is interesting. The recent appearance of armed subversive movements in that country will oblige the Mexican Government to change its policy.

Brazil and Argentina are potential sources of useful armament in the anti-subversive battle and in these countries it is unlikely that the left will succeed in stopping its purchase by our armed forces.

Chile lived through communism. Given its recent connection with important investments in our country, it has been converted into our natural ally, especially in its impresarial sector.

Multilateral Organisms. UN ORGANISMS. The UN has two establishments for dealing with affairs relating to HR: The Human Rights Commission (CDH), which supervises the High Commission for HR (ACDH) and the HR Committee (CDH), which functions as a tribunal. The principal seat of these organisms is in Geneva, and there are some 30 NGOs certified to appear before them. There is likewise developed a subversive diplomacy through the NGOs. Many of the international NGOs accredited to the UN lend their voices to elements of the Colombian extreme left. The Office of the High Commissioner (OAC) has a special delegate for Colombia, Señora Almudena Mazarrasa, who runs an office in Bogotá, under a mandate negotiated by the Colombian Government with the Commission.

INTER-AMERICAN SYSTEM. Colombia is subjected to the Inter-American HR Pact (PIDH), a pact which establishes a Commission, an organism of a political character, integrated by ambassadors, and a Court, a tribunal which judges the activity of a country in relation to its citizens and has the power of imposing sanctions on its member countries. The commission is usually the organism which brings the cases before the Court. In the case of Colombia, through the initiative of the government, Law 288 of 1996 establishes that Colombia will pay indemnities based on the decisions of the Commission. This is highly irregular and probably unconstitutional.[17] The Commission, with its seat in Washington, has suffered from the influence of the DS, and its concepts are hardly impartial. The Court, with its seat in San José, Costa Rica, is generally impartial.

EUROPEAN UNION. The executive organ of the Union is the Commission, made up of representatives of the executive power of the member countries. A European Parliament also exists with little real power, especially in matters of Union foreign relations, but with the power of opinion. This last organism has been occupied by the subject of Colombia and is strongly influenced by the subversion.

4.0 Methods Used by the Subversion Abroad

Direct Diplomacy. The subversion maintains "direct delegations" traveling in Europe, Mexico and Costa Rica. In these countries two FARC directors, Marcos Calarcá and Juan Antonio Rojas, operate. These "delegations" are in permanent contact with parliamentarians of the left in those countries and with NGOs which they can influence. They occasionally enter the US as "conferees," but, in that country, the recent classification of the Colombian armed groups as terrorists will limit their action. Obviously there are members of the subversion who remain in Havana.

Utilization of the Columbian Diplomatic Apparatus. On many occasions the Colombian Government has appointed "ex" guerrillas, who remain faithful to their ideology, to diplomatic positions as official representatives of the country. In this way they succeed, thanks to public funds, in dedicating themselves to promoting the subversive line. On other occasions the government has sent functionaries partial to the subversion to forums and conferences on HR to "defend" the Colombian position.

Utilization of the HR NGOs. The most effective activity is that which the international NGOs carry out under the influence of their fellow countrymen partial to the subversion. The Colombian NGOs fabricate HR violation cases and distort or amplify real cases. On the other hand the guerrilla discourse minimizes its participation in kidnappings and massacres. Suffice it to say that the kidnapping of foreigners has damaged the credibility of the guerrillas with some international NGOs. On the other hand, the government has turned over certain positions having to do with the HR theme to persons sympathetic to the subversion. When the international NGOs of good faith come to these organisms in order to deal with information received from the national NGOs, what they receive is confirmation.

Utilization of Useful Idiots. In Colombia many politicians, academics, artists, etc. in order to be "politically correct," concern themselves with spreading the subversion's version. These people effectively put their prestige at the service of the subversion without being conscious of their own manipulation. The artistic and academic left circles abroad reward these positions with professional recognition.

5.0 Columbian NGOs Partial to the Subservsion

Peoples Education and Investigation Center (CINEP). Directed by the cleric,[18] Francisco de Roux, brother of the ex presidential HR councilor, Carlos Vicente de Roux (recently named magistrate of the Inter-American Court (CI)). This NGO is the source of the information for many NGOs, and foreign governments accept its information as accurate. It produces, in collaboration with Justice and Peace, the periodical *Noche y Niebla*, where there appear specific accusations against agents of the state, Paramilitary and Guerrillas. It manages a data bank on HR and has a payroll of more than a hundred "investigators." Its principal source of financing is the Social Group (GS), a financial conglomerate of the Jesuits. It was recently entrusted with an important "social" program for the Magdalena Media financed by Ecopetrol and other entities, among them the World Bank.

Inter-Congregational Commission of Justice and Peace (CIJP). Directed by the cleric, Javier Giraldo Moreno, it actively participates in the "Juridical War" (GJ) occupying itself with pushing the cases against officers of the Military Forces (FM) which are presented to the Attorney General and Prosecutor. It relies on an international network of similar NGOs. It recently combined its data bank with that of CINEP. Its is especially active in the promotion of the GJ, especially in zones of influence of the ELN

Colombian Commission of Jurists (CCJ). Earlier a section of the Andean Commission of Jurists (CAJ), it was disconnected from this NGO which is based in Peru. Gustavo Gallón and Carlos Rodríguez direct it. It participates actively in the GJ. It acts before the HR Commission of the OAS. It promoted the Isidro Caballero—María del Carmen Santana Case. In this case Colombia was condemned by the CI, then later it was proven that María del Carmen Santana was a fictitious personage.

The CINEP, CIJP and CCJ can be considered First Level and most influential abroad. Some of the many other NGOs which function in Colombia are the following: (1) LA Institute of Alternative Legal Services (ILSA) represented by Héctor Moncayo.(2) Committee in Solidarity with the Political Prisoners (CSPP) is directed by Jaime Prieto. Recently, an operation by military intel and the Attorney General, in Bucaramanga, revealed its connection with the ELN.[19] (3) Permanent Committee for the Defense of HR (PCDDH) is directed by the "conservative" ex chancellor Alfredo Vasquez Carrizosa. The representative is Héctor Pinzón. (4) Regional Committee for Defense of HR of Barrancabermeja (CREDHOS) is directed by Osiris Bayther, the Bucaramanga section by Jorge Gómez Lizarazo. The latter individual acts in the international arena with UN connections. (5) Association of Families of Detained and Disappeared (ASFADES) is directed by Jeanette Bautista, sister of the celebrated Nydia Erica Bautista, allegedly killed by military intel elements under the command of General Velandia. (6) Association for Human Promotion (CORPHU) was recently linked to the ELN in Bucaramanga and likewise to LA ESCUELA, Association for Social and Economic Rehabilitation of the People Displaced from the Northeast (REDES), COINCOPROCO and Educational Association of Investigation and Consulting of the East (CORPORIENTE).

Also active in Colombia are another dozen NGOs of lesser status such as: Peoples Training Institute, Prisoners Committee of Bucaramanga, FUNPROCEP, Colombian Peace Group, MINGA, Colombian Clerical Conference, Utopias Association, ANDAS, ANUC, Civic Committee for HR and Citizens Initiative Network Against War and for Peace.

The majority of these NGOs describe their activity as "investigation, legal services, public reports and event organization."

This is the enemy which confronts the officers and noncoms of our Military Forces in the "judicial war."

6. *International NGOs*

1. Amnesty International is based in London and operates worldwide.[20] It also criticizes some socialist regimes. 2. Americas Watch is based in the US, collects and amplifies the versions of the Colombian NGOs. 3. Washington Office on LA (WOLA). 4. Pax Christi operates in Europe, principally in Holland and Germany, echoing the reports especially if they come from Colombian NGOs directed

by clerics. Recently their position has been less biased toward the subversion.

Of lesser prestige, but active in the attack on the government and Military Forces of Colombia, the following groups may be mentioned as patronizing the books, *Terrorismo de Estado* and *Tras los Pasos Perdidos de la Guerra Sucia*: (1) National Centrum Boor Ontwikkelingssamenwerking (NCOS) has its seat in Brussels and had, until recently, Paul Van Steenvoort as its secretary. (2) SAGO has connections abroad. (3) Terre des Hommes is based in Lausanne, Switzerland, its director Bernard Boeton. (4) Commission of Churches on International Affairs. (5) International Confederation of Free Trade Unions. (6) Commissie Rechtvaarddigheid en Vrede. (7) World Organization Against Torture (OMCT) in Geneva, Eric Sottas director. (8) American Association of Jurists (AAJ) has its seat in Buenos Aires. (9) LA Federation of Associations of Families of Disappeareds (FEDEFAM). (10) French Justice and Peace Commission (CFJP) has its seat in Paris, its secretary general Antoine Sondag. National Center of Cooperation in Development (CNCD) is related to the NCOS. (11) LA Peace and Justice Service (SERPAJAL) has its seat in Guayaquil, Ecuador, its coordinator general Nelsa Curbelo. In some case replicas of these groups exist in various countries as is the case with SERPAJAL for example.

International Peace Brigades, in Switzerland and other countries has delegates working with CREHDOS, its "mission" to escort, without arms, HR activists in countries where HR are violated.

Colombia Support Network is a kind of grouping of NGOs which include individuals from WOLA, AI, Solidarity Network with Colombia, Justice and Peace and others. Based in Madison, Wisconsin, the "capital" of the radical left in the US, it is concerned with maintaining the Internet site "Gloria Cuartas" among other things.

Others. One must classify here the NGOs, established in other countries but directed by members of the Colombian subversion such as CORAS, CHRC and Praxis, mentioned earlier and established in the UK.

7. The Present Situation and Possible Courses of Action

Undoubtedly the subversion has been successful in its activity abroad. Official diplomacy has been inactive and inefficient in counteracting its activity. The Colombian embassies have had neither instructions nor written material so that they could disseminate a version different from that which the subversive apparatus is spreading, and, what is worse, these embassies are infiltrated. But, apart from governmental action, those interested in supporting a solution to this serious problem can:

Create their own NGOs. These can work independently but provide mutual support and coordinate some activities such as: (1) Investigate and produce material on the conflict appropriate to foreign target audiences. (2) Investigate and locate influential entities in the foreign countries of interest, establish contact with them and maintain a flow of material which divulges the Colombian reality. (3) Maintain contact and coordination with the MF but without subordinating yourself to them in order not to suffer the consequences of the lack of continuity and of subjection at the whim of the government of the moment. This permits action in the medium and long term. (4) Open web-sites on the Internet in order to reach the new "navigating" public. (5) Establish contacts in order to achieve publication abroad from the democratic point of view. (6) Open at some locations abroad, under the auspices of private enterprise, offices of investigation and reporting.

The guerrilla and the subversion are committing acts which militate against humanity's interest today in the environment, HR, narcotrafficking and democracy. It is vulnerable to the reporting of its acts.

[Translated from the Spanish by the Editor, LANS]

B. Minor Terrorist Coups Used in Subversive Diplomacy

ANOTHER COLOMBIAN TERRORIST COUP
(WKLY 5.2, 15 JANUARY 1998)

Prologue

The ML terrorist group, FARC, has, for many years, been the "military arm" of the Colombian Communist Party (PCC). This PCC issued a communiqué on 8 January 1998 which demanded "1st. Concrete actions to stop the criminal escalation of [the actions] of [the] paramilitary groups. 2nd. Concrete actions to stop the arrival of paramilitary in the Department of Arauca. 3rd. Investigation and punishment of the different elements of the Armed Forces connected with the operatives and massacres of the paramilitary groups, according to the denunciations of the national and international organisms of human rights, as proof that the paramilitary action does not correspond to an official strategy."

Therefore, the FARC terrorists, while continuing their depredations, are demanding government actions against the CAPs, that is, the "paramilitary." The HL, to which both FARC and PCC belong, and the HLS are stepping up their campaign against the only real enemy they have in Colombia, the CAPs, a campaign which has the support of the Colombian and US Governments.

Introduction

On 30 August 1996 FARC overran the military camp at Las Delicias in Caquetá Department, murdering[21] 27 military personnel and taking 60 army and 9 marines hostage (pp.119ff, YRBK97) whom they kept for almost a year [until 15 June 1997] in scornful defiance of a Colombian Government which had surrendered to them (pp.209ff, YRBK98). Colombian military intelligence and planning appears to have broken down before the attack, but this in no way affects this description.

After midnight on the night of 21-22 December 1997 such an overrun occurred again, this time the target a platoon outpost in Nariño Department as will be detailed. The Army appears to have acted more appropriately after the fact than it had at Las Delicias, but the Samper Government appears as if it will continue its surrender policy. Although repetitious, it is worthwhile to recall just who these terrorists are.

FARC is nothing more than an organization of criminals who justify their criminality with ML verbiage. They are murderers who engage in narcotrafficking, kidnapping, extortion and unbridled vandalism. They are supported by LibTheo [Liberation Theological] clerics, some of whom, as in the "clerics' terror group," the ELN [National Liberation Army], actually put their hand to this criminality.

NGOs

FARC and ELN are also supported, to a greater or lesser degree, by various so-called HR NGOs.[22] In an excellent article,[23] Plinio Apuleyo Mendoza analyzes the HRV [Human Rights Violations] reports which certain "perfectly unreliable" NGOs send to HRW [Human Rights Watch]. With no attempt at verification, HRW forwards these reports to, *inter alia*, the communications media and the US State Department which accepts them with "surprising blindness" as the recent behavior of State has demonstrated. One example of such NGOs must serve here.

Mendoza specifically mentions the CCJ which furnishes HRW with "constant and copious reports." "Don't they know," he asks, "that this [the CCJ] is one of the many front organizations of the communist party [PCC] whose military arm is this same FARC?"

Mount Patascoy is Overrun

Nariño Department, Colombia, borders to its west on the Pacific Ocean, to its south on Ecuador and to its east on Putumayo Department. Pasto, the capital of Nariño is some 330 statute miles southwest of Bogotá, Mount Patascoy about 15 miles as the crow flies southeast of this. This mountain rises to some 13,100 feet above sea level, and, according to legend, at least three dozen people have died trying to climb it. "Patascoy" means "place of ashes" in the Cotche language of the Quillacingas, it apparently acquiring this name as a now extinct volcano the last eruption of which in 1430 wiped out the Indian tribe which had occupied pre Colombian Pastoco.

This mountain top is on the Nariño-Caqueta border and accessible by two rugged paths, one from the interior of Nariño and the other from Caqueta, both of which must be negotiated single file. This eyrie was the site of a military communications center guarded by a platoon made up of one officer, four noncoms and 29 men. The platoon in question belonged to the Boyacá Battalion headquartered in Pasto.

An account of the terrorist attack on this post was given a few days later by one of the three who made good their escape, the platoon second in command, Hugo Fernando Naranjo. According to Naranjo, the attack began at 0205 on 21 December with the cry of "surrender, you pimps" (*ríndanse, chulos*) as the first grenade fell in the encampment and 400 terrorists of the FARC Southern Bloc began their attack. The noncom had heard rumors that the post was going to be attacked, but, since the approaches were mined and the unit had ample ammunition, they were apparently not overly concerned. But the 400 FARC terrorists far outnumbered the defenders who were "in the midst of an inferno into which rained grenades and fire from M-60 rifles" [*El Espectador* Bogotá, 24 December 1997]. This demands an aside.

There is apparently no M-60 rifle. There is of course the familiar air-cooled M-60 machine gun, but this is hardly in context. There is, however, a Serbian-made M-60 rifle grenade which is produced in both anti-tank and anti-personnel varieties and which is fired from the Serbian produced 7.62mm M70B1.[24] Note that this rifle is based on the AK-47. Therefore, this apparently should read "grenades and fire from M-70 rifles."

By 0500[25] Naranjo realized that he should withdraw with however many of his fellow soldiers he could gather. He gathered Leonardo Buitrón, Franco Cansimansi and one Bermúdez. Moments later, a rifle grenade[26] left Acevado, who was also going, so seriously wounded that he could not accompany his fellows. Visibility was restricted to two meters by weather conditions, and the four decided on a straight ahead descent of the precipitous mountain. Bermúdez slipped and fell into "an abyss surrounded by cascades." Naranjo, Buitrón and Cansimansi made good their "odyssey" and arrived somewhat the worse for wear in Pasto. This account was appropriately concluded by the words of Ana Rosa de Cansimansi whose son did not make it out. Her remarks were reminiscent of the Roman matron who told her son to come back "with your shield or on it."

Sra. de Cansimansi, campesino mother of eight, declared, "I am not mourning,[27] and I am going to command my three other sons to give military service because the guerrilla is not going to conquer us, he is not going to intimidate us."

Hostages

By 27 December Army intelligence had learned, through intercepted radio communications between Suárez Briceño (aka El Mono Jojoy) and another FARC boss that the attack had left 10 dead and 18 hostages. [It should be remarked that this 28, the 3 who escaped plus the 2 lost in the escape *almost* totals the 34 uniformed personnel.] This FARC intercept agreed with the "18 disappeared military": to which the XXIV Brigade commander referred. And "mediation" by Bishop Julio Enrique Pardo of Pasto immediately became a topic of discussion.

Toward the end of December the Nariño Department Peace Commission (CDPN), Bishop Pardo president, began agitation for another mediation "which will permit the return of the soldiers to their families." Which, in reality, will lead to one more important FARC victory. In a telephone conversation, allegedly received by Radio Carocol in Medellín, the FARC Southern Bloc gave full play, which was faithfully repeated, to their propaganda efforts. According to the terrorists, the soldiers were "in good condition" and the attack on the outpost was a complete success which had resulted in the complete destruction of the "microwave system"—presumably some sort of relay station—and the acquisition of a substantial supply of armaments.

FARC Terrorists on the Ecuadoran Border

On this occasion the Colombian military, apparently not yet ordered to surrender to the terrorists, is continuing its search for the 18 hostages as reported by Armed Forces commander General Manuel José Bonett Locarno. According to Ecuadoran General René Vargas, Retired, speaking on Teleamazonas TV on 30 December, there began intense activity by terrorist forces on the Colombia Amazon border, the general urging the Ecuadorans to reinforce their side of the border against this activity.

According to Colombian government sources the terrorists, who overran Mount Patascoy, were refugeeing in this border area. At that time at least the Colombian military was apparently on the track of these terrorists. It will be of interest to see if the military continues this operation or if a supine Colombian Government again surrenders to the "peace makers" of the NGOs and the terrorists. In the meantime, the end of the first week in January saw what was described in the press as "an unprecedented action."

It has been remarked earlier that there was a breakdown either in military intelligence or in military preparedness. The high command of the Colombian Armed Forces apparently thought so as evidenced by its action of 7 January 1998 when it relieved of their commands the III Division Commander, General Eduardo Camelo Caldas, and the commander of III Brigade, General Julio Eduardo Charry Solano,[28] these two being in the chain of command which included the Patascoy post. The division commander was replaced by General Néstor Ramírez Mejía, previously secretary of the Inter American Defense College with seat in the US, the brigade commander by General Jaime Ernesto Canal Albán, now chief of Army Intelligence.

Military Analysis of Potoscoy

An analysis of the Potoscoy affair was published in *El Espectador* [Bogotá 13 January 1998]. Here a compacted summary of the verbatim statements of the two general officers is given.

Retired General Alvaro Valencia Tovar stated: "...an axiom...states that the commander is responsible for everything that his unit does or fails to do...In the case of Mt. Patascoy, and ignoring the conclusions deduced by the Army commander from his personal inspection, direct responsibility begins at the operating level: division command. From there it descends vertically to the brigade and, in this instance, to the battalion...The division commander...[is] responsible for keeping himself informed of enemy activity through his intelligence service ...At the brigade level it is the responsibility to do the same but with major effort directed toward his battalion commands...to verify the state of defense of his bases...tactical action to avoid surprise, morale of his men, possibility of reinforcement [as required]...In the case of Patascoy, it is evident that intelligence reported an imminent risk. Brigade command issued orders to confront it. Were such orders complied with? ...What was done to verify compliance and what additional methods were necessary...On the replies to this and other questions doubtless rests the decision of the Army commander to relieve battalion, brigade and division commanders. I had a commander who would say that 'They pay me 25 percent for giving orders and 75 percent for verifying that they are carried out.'..."

Retired General Miguel Maza Márquez was director of Administrative Security Department (DAS). He begins by saying, "Intelligence is the art of leading the state in the best way...there are two different kinds of intelligence...tactical intelligence which permits perfecting... the fight against crime...and strategic intelligence is that which should be managed by DAS...Both intelligence services suffered serious reverses during the administrations of Gaviria and Samper...During the mandate of President Samper, state intelligence remained in the [office of the] head of the Ministry of Interior [the Serpa domain]. As a consequence of those improvised and erratic policies, the state remained without intelligence, replacing this by millionaire rewards...whose results were, perhaps, effective in the last century for US sheriffs...[in order to] guarantee vigorous efficacy in the solution of the various conflicts, it is necessary that efforts be redoubled...[and the problems] be the object of scientific and technical diagnostics which permit positive solutions in the short and medium term...Intelligence...must be taken on with more coherence and [in] greater depth...than has characterized it recently..."

As was the case at Las Delicias, the Colombian Armed Forces have no desire to surrender to the FARC terrorists. Judging by past performances, it is entirely possible, however, that the Colombian Government, urged on by the HL and the HLS to include various NGOs, will make some sort of virtue out of doing so.

COLOMBIA, FEBRUARY 1998
(WKLY 5.7, 19 FEBRUARY 1998)

The effects of the papal visit (Chapter 4, this volume) have been widely assessed with conclusions which bode ill for the Cuban dictator and, by inference since the existence of the entity is not widely acknowledged, for his HL. Whether such predictions bear any relation to reality remains to be seen. In the meanwhile, however, the HL appears to be doing quite well. Perhaps most remarkably, in Central America (CA) where the Esquipulas II Accords (pp.251ff, YRBK98) of 1987 have allegedly brought peace by 1997. As has been pointed out so frequently in these reports, they have brought substantial victory to the ML terrorists of Castro's HL. Or the "appearance of peace," as an old-line intel source in Guatemala has expressed it to LANS with that wry humor necessary to mere survival: the "stop-sign mentality."

The type of successes enjoyed by the HL in CA have been percolating into Colombia for some time, an interesting example of this occurring in early 1998. The first of the three-tiered Colombian elections, that for departmental governors and local officials, has been discussed (pp.49ff, YRBK 98). In Antioquia Department Alberto Builes Ortega won the governorship and was duly installed in office in early January 1998. There are two principal political parties in Colombia, the Liberal Party (PLC) and the Conservative Party (PC). It is important to point out that Builes is in the PC only as one more example of the policy these parties share in their so far totally unsuccessful dealings with Colombian narcoterrorism. For it was at his inauguration that Governor Builes announced the appointment of Manuel Conde Orellana, a Guatemalan, as his "peace" advisor. Conde came to his new post from a CA wherein he had "participated in various peace processes" (EFE 4 January 1998), i.e., Esquipulas.

Of these two principal parties, the PLC is considerably the stronger, although the PCC has occasionally won the presidential palace. And, in spite of the chaos of last fall's elections and the unpopularity of President Samper of the PLC, this party has to this point more or less maintained this superiority. Perhaps there will be no change in this power structure in the coming elections. If such is the case, the progress toward what may well be a "victory through peace" by the narcoterrorists of the FARC and the ELN can apparently be expected to continue. But the possibility that this HL victory could be avoided will be touched on below.

Another straw in the wind is the behavior of the Colombian military in the matter of the most recent FARC terrorist kidnapping of military personnel which will then be discussed together with more details of the Patascoy terrorist attack. Finally, what has all the earmarks of one more ML DO, this one in Puutumayo Department will be touched upon. Together these situations do much toward filling in the reality of Colombia 1998.

Terrorists and Presidential Candidates

The presidential elections of this spring will be covered in detail after the fact. Here, however, their relation to Colombian terrorism is more or less clear now and worthy of remark. There is, as usual, a plethora of candidates, but here only four will be considered: Serpa, Pastrana, Valdivieso and Bedoya. The first two are the official PLC and PC candidates both allegedly bent on "peace" with the terrorists, the last two on dealing realistically with the terrorists. It should be stated again that these ML narcoterrorists are not romantic figures from a Sigmund Romberg operetta, they are common criminals who deal in narcotrafficking, murder, kidnapping, extortion and whatever other criminal acts are profitable to them.

Horacio Serpa Uribe is now the official candidate of the PLC, having received this accolade as incumbent President Samper's man at the recent convention. This would not appear to mean as much as in the past, however, as will become clear with Valdivieso. It is an acknowledged fact that Mr. Serpa has "friends" in both the narcoterrorist organizations. Allegations that his youthful activities placed him within the actual narcoterrorist ranks have not been verified by LANS.

Andrés Pastrana Arango was the PC candidate who lost in the 1994 runoff against now President Samper with 49.1 percent of the vote as against the latter's 50.9 percent (pp.19ff, YRBK97). It would appear that he will obtain his party's nomination in the near future. On 9 February 1998 he told 5000 party faithful assembled in the Bogotá Sports Palace that he "will meet personally with the guerrilla (terrorist) chiefs" if he wins the presidency. This can probably be believed, and once again Colombian dealings with narcoterrorism will apparently undergo no change whichever standard bearer triumphs.

Alfonso Valdivieso Sarmiento may be one of those men for whom Diogenes is reputed to have searched. He is a member of the PLC, now a dissident one, and gained quite a favorable reputation as Attorney General of Colombia. As has been reported here, he was leading the polls early in the race, although this situation does not appear to be holding.

General Harold Bedoya, Retired, is the most recent in the long line of Colombian military personnel who have been removed from their positions by Colombian presidents. Bedoya was apparently fired because he wished to oppose Samper's surrender to FARC terrorists in their immensely successful hostage operation (pp.209ff, YRBK98). The general filed for the presidency in August of 1997. Whether he has any realistic chance of winning that post is probably not predictable, but he has been rising in the polls to occupy a quite respectable position. Although LANS has suggested the reason, in his article, "Why Bedoya's Rise" (*SEMANA* (Bogotá) 12-19 January 1998), Plinio Apuleyo Mendoza has succinctly stated this reason:

> The dialog...is an old remedy proposed a thousand times, with FARC and the ELN. Dialogs with vast peace commissions proposed by Belisario (Betancur); dialog with a National Rehabilitation Plan proposed by Virgilio Barco; dialog with humiliation and a new Constitution proposed by Gaviria; dialog in all forms and with all manner* of concessions proposed by Samper and his minister Serpa. And nothing has been achieved...but more assaults, more blood.

Military Heads Roll

It will be recalled (Wkly 5.2 above) that Mount Patascoy is on the border of Nariño and Caquetá Departments in southern Colombia, a military communications center located atop this mountain which

FARC terrorists overran on 21 December 1997. That there were serious errors made up the chain of command has become apparent since this unfortunate incident.

During the last week of September 1997 various campesinos in the vicinity of Patascoy noticed the arrival of a stranger in the area whom they reported to the military patrol in the area at the beginning of October. The patrol did not encounter him, but, when the patrol left he showed up again.[29] The Patascoy inhabitants had already reported the stranger to the headquarters of Batalla de Boyacá Battalion in Pasto, the department capital. In this Nariño capital the Army concluded that the activity had something to do with terrorist traffic in arms to make up for the immense expenditure of weaponry which had taken place during Army Operation Destroyer in Llanos de Yari. The Pasto military alerted other organizations in the region such as XXIV Brigade operating in Putumayo.

Other information being received indicated that an enormous arms traffic was developing. Then on 8 October the Army scored a triumph in locating and seizing 252,000 rounds of ammunition for Galil, R-15, AK-47 and G-3[30] weapons in the Puerto Colombia region,[31] jurisdiction of Puerto Asís, in Putumayo. The munitions were found in front of Patascoy.

In the second week of November new intel information alerted the Armed Forces to the fact that the terrorists were planning something, first, because of the return of the unknown to the Patascoy vicinity and, second, because the chief of FARC's Southern Front, Milton de Jesús Toncel (aka Usurriaga) was located with a group of his men near the Ecuadoran border not far from Mount Patascoy. Army headquarters in Bogotá soon had the information, and the inspector general, Air Force General Héctor Fabio Velasco Chávez, spent three days at the installation during the third week of November. Velasco's 10-page report contained 30 recommendations. It was distributed to various departments of Bogotá headquarters and to III Division and III Brigade in the chain of command to Patascoy.

On 14 December Intelligence Battalion 3 (Cali) sent the following radiogram: "Permit me to report that command information indicates a FARC southern bloc bandit concentration numbering approximately 200, Fronts 2, 14, 32 located 7.5 kms. Southwest Santiago municipality and 20 kms. North Mount Patascoy, coordinates 01 06

53³² north latitude and 76 59 27 east longitude. Mentioned trying to set a course next days to occupy military base Patascoy or military base Puerres...(use) extreme security measures to alert personnel under your command."

It was reported that the battalion CO, Colonel Julio Burgos was concerned and ordered a chopper. The aircraft could not operate above 4100 meters to supply food and weaponry. The attack took place about a week later. After retrieving the 10 bodies and establishing that 18 troops were kidnapped, the Army began an internal investigation. The conclusion was that the division CO, General Eduardo Camelo Caldas, the brigade CO, General Julio Eduardo Charry and the battalion CO, Colonel Alvaro Ruiz, moved to Bogotá a few days before the attack, were negligent.

It is no secret that the taking of the outpost was carried out by various fronts belonging to the Southern Bloc. One conversation intercepted by the Army was between Jorge Briceño (aka Mono Jojoy), FARC Eastern Bloc chief, and another terrorist chief. The pair had spoken of the results of the attack of 21 September.

The Army Goes After Its Own

Perhaps the worst facet of the FARC hostage operation of 1996-1997 was the refusal of the Samper Government to allow the military to go after its men. Instead, that government allowed the narcoterrorists to control its actions for nine months, capitulating to their every whim. The result was a coup for the terrorists of inestimable dimension. On this occasion, the Colombian Government apparently made no attempt to prevent the Armed Forces from attempting to rescue their personnel, although there were cries from certain HR organizations for "negotiations." Military intel continued to gather information on the situation and move toward the rescue.

These reports indicated that the 18 troops had been divided into three groups. One of these groups was sighted about 7 January in a rural portion of the municipality of Buesaco in the northern part of the department (a few miles northeast of Pasto), the second in the Caucan boot (toe of the department, the Ecuadoran border and Putumayo forming the two sides) and the third on the San Miguel River defining the Ecuadoran border (which could be in either Nariño or Putumayo).

In the meanwhile General Mario Hugo Galán announced on 30 December that he was sending more than 4000 men to the southern zone to rescue the personnel. These troops consisted of four battalions of special anti-terrorist forces of III Division supported by choppers and aircraft. "We are going to get those men back and, God willing, soon," General Galán told the press (AFP 1 January 1998). Three weeks later the Armed Forces commander, General Bonnet, was telling the press that "My mission is to seek them. We are doing that with over 3000 men and...the army hopes to have good results soon" (EFE 23 January 1998).

FARC was particularly quiet about the hostages, a silence explained by a message which the Armed Forces intercepted: "We," the terrorists said, "are aware that if this operation fails we will lose everything that we have gained with Las Delicias." Las Delicias was the operation wherein FARC took 60 hostages and kept them for nine months. "But if it is successful we will multiply what we gained on that occasion."

In some quarters it is felt that various "demilitarization" demands will be made; in others that the simple holding of these troops for a while will gain considerable advantageous publicity for the terrorists. Either one of these speculations could be realized if once again the Samper Government surrenders to the terrorists and stops the Armed Forces' rescue attempts.

Allegations Against the CAPs

The importance of the CAPs—"paramilitary" to the HL and much of the press—has been frequently emphasized in these reports. In this report the *absence* of CAPs in the Patascoy region has been seen to be at least partially responsible for the success of the terrorist assault on the military post there. Now, however, the CAPs have suddenly appeared—or have been conjured up—and have allegedly begun to murder "innocent" civilians.

The reader will be presumed familiar with Pasto, the capital of Nariño Department. Puerto Asís is across the departmental border in Putumayo, at the confluence of the Putumayo and Guamués Rivers. Patascoy is roughly on a line between these two towns. Beginning on 12 February, reports began to appear in the Bogotá press of "terror" in the region where 40 to 50 people had been killed since the first of the year. These reports were allegedly carried by what appear to be FARC sympathizers and accuse

"Paramilitary" personnel of the slaughter.

When the military commanders in the region were questioned about CAP presence in the area, their reply was that there were none, and they professed themselves confused as to what their questioners were referring. All the signs of one more ML DO surround this story.

Unfortunately, LANS has no definitive data on what is happening and can hence draw no solid conclusions. Space does not allow extensive consideration of the testimony available at this time, and, if it did, it would lead to no unassailable conclusions. These allegations will be considered again in connection with the ongoing study of the HL campaign against the CAPs. Two specific bits of information are, however, interesting.

Initial testimony from the "refugees" said that "300 heavily armed men" (*El Espectador* (Bogotá) 12 February 1998) arrived in the area. Which, with the usual accuracy of such strength reports, can be equated to the 200 men reportedly in the FARC terrorist group that attacked Patascoy. One tale bearer reported that the men carried R-15s (*El Tiempo* (Bogotá) 12 February 1998) as if this had some special significance. The large cache of FARC ammunition discussed above included R-15 rounds.

COLOMBIA: ANOTHER AMBUSH IN THE CAGUÁN
(WKLY 5.12, 25 MARCH 1998)

Various pundits and various "authoritative" overnight visitors to El Salvador in the 1980s pontificated that "there is no military solution" to the terrorist unpleasantness. The statement had no validity. However, if this statement had been changed to "there is no military solution under the restrictions forced upon the Salvadoran Armed Forces (FAES) by the US," it would have been quite accurate. The restrictions were of course the allowance of sanctuaries to the Farabundi terrorists (pp.146ff, YRBK97). The present situation in Colombia poses a more serious, but similar, problem.

That an army travels on its stomach, as the Emperor is reported to have said, would appear difficult to deny. But traveling and "protecting the environment" are no excuse for the existence of an army; warfare is. As, any number of people have said, an army fights and, in particular, wins on its *esprit de corps*. And the *esprit* of the FAC is bound to have been seriously affected by the series of "no-win wars" which have been thrust upon it by the series of "peace-seeking" presidents stretching at least back to President Betancur and his "white flag of truce" in the mid 1980s. Which is irrelevant, neither to the three notable disasters suffered by the FAC in the last year and one-half, nor to the favorable publicity showered on the ML terrorists of the FARC during the period.

The first of these was at Las Delicious (pp.209ff, YRBK98) and the second at Patascoy (Wkly 5.2 above). As with the Japanese Embassy Operation (JEO) (pp.229ff, YRBK98), there was apparently an intel breakdown in these two disasters, and certain heads have rolled as a consequence of Patascoy (Wkly 5.7 above). As they may well roll, and properly so, as a result of the third disaster which is the subject of this report. But they have also given various pundits the excuse for calling down imprecations on the heads of the military. It is quite possible that, were these critics somewhat more familiar with military realities, this successful terrorist activity might be partially blamed on a series of "peace-seeking" Colombian governments.

The Aftermath of Patascoy

Unlike the nine-month government surrender which followed the terrorist overrun of Las Delicias (pp.119ff, YRBK97), the FAC mounted an operation to recover the men it lost in the terrorist overrun of Mount Patascoy.[33] But the operation had an additional objective, that of gaining control of the Caguán.[34] This sparsely-populated region has been important to FARC narcotrafficking activities—coca-leaf growing, processing labs—from which the lion's share of the terrorist funding is derived. The unit which was apparently spearheading the operation was appropriately an anti-terrorist one, Mobil Brigade (MB) III. MB III had an advanced post of about 150 men located at El Billar.

El Billar

Florencia is the capital of Caquetá Department wherein El Billar is located. This capital is located on the eastern slope of the East Range of the Andes, some 220 sm southwest by south of Bogotá. Las Delicias, which was overrun about 1½ years ago, is located on the right bank of the Río Caquetá some 105 sm southeast by south of Florencia. The El Billar of interest here is on the right bank of the Río Caguán some 95 sm southeast of Florencia.

During the week before the 8 March congressional elections (Wkly 5.11, Chapter 1 above)—the "week of reflection" between campaign and vote—two columns of FARC terrorists converged on, and overran, this base at El Billar. These columns were originally reported as having a strength of 200 men each for a total of 400. A report the following day stated that there were "400 to 500" terrorists. The number of military personnel was generally given as about 150, although the routinely unreliable FARC claims had this number as high as 198 (AFP 13 March 1998).

The first word of the attack was received from Major John Jairo Aguilar, the commander of the El Billar outpost, after he had succeeded in withdrawing with a few survivors into the jungle and communicating with the base at Tres Esquinas.[35] That the terrorist boss of FARC Front XIV, Fabian Ramírez, accused the major of "running off in the middle of the combat and leaving his men" (*El Pais* (Cali) 17 March 1998) is probably of no probative consequence at all, but should be mentioned for the record.

The number of military casualties was variously reported by the terrorists, but, since the military reports are routinely more reliable—and more subject to verification[36]—than those of FARC, that given by FAC second-in-command General Fernando Tapias (AFP 14 March 1998) will be reported here: 62 dead, 43 hostages and 47 rescued by FAC.

This was admittedly the worst single blow suffered by FAC, but, as FAC chief General Manuel José Bonett Locarno pointed out,

> I can guarantee that Colombia at the moment is not the Titanic, and we are not going to sink or run aground.
>
> The military forces, especially the Army and Air Force, are ready to continue this offensive to wherever and for however long it may take. The soldiers are highly inspired. The troops are entering the area with high morale....

An additional 1000 men had been sent into the area on Wednesday, 4 March, to withdraw the casualties and continue the operation against the terrorists. These and other FAC units reported finding three clandestine graves with 35 terrorist cadavers in each, a routine ML attempt to cover their own casualties. The operations of FAC were continuing, and, indeed, even President Samper was supporting them.

Task Force Caguán (FTC)

The unit name is a LANS creation, — it has been announced as the Joint Task Force (FTC) — but it is appropriate to the mission which has been assigned to the newly-formed organization. The following description of the unit has been taken from Colombian press reports.

The mission of the new unit has been described in *El Tiempo* (Bogotá 12 March 1998) as "combating the 16 fronts of the most powerful bloc of FARC" which is of course the so-called Southern Bloc. Presumably, the so-called "secret" meeting of the Colombian Joint Chiefs of Staff assigned the mission of "destroying" rather than "combating" these terrorist fronts.

The FTC is to be made up of three MBs, MB III, now headquartered at Florencia, MB XII and MB XXIV, now reportedly headquartered at Santa Ana[37] in Putumayo Department. There will be Marine "detachments" within the organization, although LANS has no detail on this save that the unit(s) previously belonged to the Unified Southern Command with headquarters at Leticia.[38] The FTC "command post" will be at the Tres Esquinas Air Base. There will also be Colombian Air Force support.

The FTC commander will be Major General Rafael Hernández López who has been described as having "vast experience' in operations against terrorists and has been the Inspector General of FAC. General Hernández' Second in Command and Chief of Staff is to be Brigadier General Jaime Humberto Uscátegui who has been Chief of Army Operations

The reports on the strength of FTC are conflicting but probably interpretable. *El Tiempo* (Bogotá) headlined its article of 12 March that 5000 men were on the way to the Caguán. In the same article it stated that the FTC would have "approximately 2000 men." It may be presumed that attached and support personnel make up the difference, but this has not been specified.

COLOMBIAN JOINT TASK FORCE SOUTH
(SPCL 6.4, 25 JULY 1998)

There have been several overruns of small—company size or less—isolated military units in southeastern Colombia by overwhelming numbers of FARC terrorists. Units of generally less than 100 personnel have been attacked by terrorists in numbers upwards of 400, the military overrun after their ammunition is exhausted. LANS has covered the first three of these operations, the Las Delicias (Putumayo Department) affair in August 1996 (pp.209ff, YRBK98), the Patascoy overrun in December 1997 (Wkly 5.2 above) and El Billar (Caquetá Department) in March 1998 (Wkly 5.12 above). These incidents, for all practical purposes, provided the bases for the GDO which has been described (Wkly 6.3, Chapter 6 below) and which appears to have as its objective the attainment of a "Victory Through Peace" for the Colombian narcoterrorists.[39]

A week after El Billar the formation of FTC was announced. The LANS Editor arrived at the FTC headquarters scarcely three months later, and this report covers what he found.

Local Geography

The local geography must be capsuled again for this treatment. The East Range of the Andes drops off rapidly south of Bogotá, until, as it turns west to absorption by the Central Range near Florencia, it leaves that capital of Caquetá Department at about 800 feet above sea level. The region roughly to the east and south of this East Range is the sparsely-populated Amazon Basin, mostly jungle and ideal for the narcotrafficking operations which the FARC terrorists have conducted there for 18 years now.

Caquetá extends some 250 sm to the east southeast of Florencia, Putumayo and Amazonas Departments to its south and defined by the Caquetá River. To the north are the Departments of Meta, Guaviare and Vaupes, largely separated from Caquetá by the Ajaijú and Apaporis Rivers. The FTC headquarters is at Tres Esquinas (Three Corners) where the Orteguaza River empties into the Caquetá. El Billar—El Villar on some maps—is but a few miles east, Las Delicias but a few miles south southeast.

Commercial air is sufficient for the Bogotá—Florencia flight, but military chopper is demanded for that from Florencia to Tres Esquinas. Colombia, in both its Air Force and its Army Aviation, uses primarily one model of US and one of Russian choppers. The US is mainly the Black Hawk UH60L, the Russian the MI-17-1V prototype of their military choppers. The LANS Editor had discussed the relatively new Army Aviation Command with its commanding officer and learned that Colombia is now emulating the US in having its aviation command separate from its Air Force. For close ground support this continues to make sense. The commander commented on the different characteristics of the US and Russian choppers, each having certain advantages over the other. What he did not comment on is an equally valid reason for not putting all Colombian assets into the US basket:

A well-known US senator threatened Salvadoran President Cristiani with the immediate cutoff of all military aid if he did not immediately release the US citizen who had been caught working hand-in-glove with the Farabundi terrorists in 1989. And there is little doubt that the Farabundi "victory through peace" in 1992 was a direct consequence of the pressure the US could apply against El Salvador through its control of the purse strings. It is to be assumed that the Colombians, in obtaining equipment from, say, Russia, have this potential for US pressure in mind. Not, of course, that any of their people will say as much.

In any event, the LANS Editor made the jaunt from the Florencia airport to the strip at Tres Esquinas by Black Hawk.

Joint Task Force South

From intelligence reports LANS has detailed (pp.119ff, YRBK97) the FARC Southern Bloc force which overran Las Delicias, it consisting of over 400 terrorists from Fronts III, XIV, XV, XXXII, the Teofilo Forero Company of Front LV, Bloc Special Forces and Company Timanco. This was apparently also the terrorist aggregation that carried out the Patascoy and El Billar attacks. Incidentally, the Editor learned the terrorist escape route from Patascoy while at Tres Esquinas, it being a backwoods river route which quickly delivered them to the Ecuadoran border. This they crossed, spending eight days in that country. Although the Colombian military personnel are understandably unwilling to discuss the matter, it is obvious that, were the Colombian Government indeed interested in eliminating narcoterrorism, establishment of some sort of border control in the area would be attempted.

The FTC mission statement is worthy of verbatim reproduction:

> The Joint Task Force South with the operational command of the National Navy, the Colombian Air Force and the operational control of the anti-narcotic police and the other state security organizations in the area of interest, demarcated by the Departments of Meta, Guaviare, Caquetá and Putumayo, conduct offensive operations against the narco-subversion with the purpose of neutralizing the action of the Southern Bloc and the Secretariat of FARC stopping the cultivation, processing and export of cocaine.

Which calls for an aside.

As has been frequently discussed in these reports, the US has, for many years and under several presidents, refused to acknowledge the immense role of Fidel Castro and his HL in narcotrafficking (cf.pp.163ff, YRBK97). In what appears to be an extrapolation of this, the US is now "helping" Colombia to fight narcotrafficking — but *not* the ML narcoterrorists—and "helping" them to make "peace" with the narcoterrorists. The latter are, of course, euphemistically referred to as "guerrillas," but it is *a priori* impossible to battle the narcotraffickers without battling the narcoterrorists. It would be impossible for this fact to be unfamiliar to the US Government, this indicating one more convoluted behavior pattern which will possibly end by defeating both objectives. [Note: Relevant to this behavior was the Bogotá press conference on 13 August 1998 given by Drug Enforcement Administration (DEA) director Thomas Constantine. Constantine said, "Insofar as the relation that exists between the paramilitary and guerrilla groups of Colombia and narcotraffic, the priority of the DEA are the criminal organizations which are connected directly with drug traffic." Was Mr. Constantine long for the world of DEA? The answer proved to be "No."]

Insofar as the makeup of the FTC is concerned, it is neither advisable nor necessary to enter into extensive detail. In what is a deliberately flexible organization, there are two infantry brigades and a mobil brigade: XII Brigade, normally headquartered at Florencia, XXIV Brigade of III Division, headquartered at Cali and the Second Mobil Brigade of no particular headquarters location. There are of course police units and a naval squadron made up in mid July 1998 primarily of five of the high-performance, heavily-armed *piraña* boats (for which see photographs at the LANS website). The commanding general of the Task Force is General Hernández, although General Uscategui, the chief of staff, was in command during the Editor's visit.

Concept of the Operation

The general operational plan was set forth by the FTC itself as:
A. To block the lines of communication by river,[40] to intercept the communication agents and control land, air and river points, stopping logistical, military, consumables and precursor chemicals[41] of the narco-subversion.
B. To intensify technical intelligence and combat efforts in order to facilitate direct support for the operations of the maneuver units and the anti-narcotics police against the activities of the narco-subversion, coca cultivations, cocaine labo-

ratories and clandestine airstrips.
C. To develop sustained and extended land, water and air offensive operations in order to effect the capture and, in the case of armed resistance, to combat the nuclei of the armed narco-subversion.

Narcotics Cultivations and Production

The cultivation of narcotics-producing plants as of mid July 1998 was given to the Editor as follows (to slide-rule accuracy):

Coca (cocaine)	196,000 acres	(79,500 hectares)
Poppies (heroin)	16,300 A	(6,600 H)
Marihuana	12,300 A	(5,000 H)

The poppy acreage is in northeast César Department, eastern Antioquia, northeast Cauca, southeast Nariño and much of Huila. The marihuana cultivation need not be specified here. Of greatest interest is the coca cultivation.

Coca is produced in the Llanos, the plains area to the south and east of the East Range. Broadly speaking, the coca is produced in the Departments of Putumayo, Caquetá and Meta-Guaviare, with a relatively small cultivation in southeast Vichada. Putumayo production is centered about Puerto Asis, a river hamlet about 90 miles southwest of Tres Esquinas and some five miles up the Putumayo River from Ecuador. There is also a spillover into this department from Caquetá upriver from Tres Esquinas. An extensive boomerang-shaped coca region surrounds Tres Esquinas in Caquetá with smaller outcroppings to the north and northwest.

The Meta-Guaviare plantings are perhaps the most extensive, these taken together because there is more overlapping than in the other departments. The salvation of San José de Guaviare has been discussed in Spcl 6.1 above, of interest here because the coca area is roughly centered on this village. A U-shaped horse head pointing west gives a qualitative notion of this planting, the open mouth extending west into Meta, the trailing edges covering the entire Meta-Guaviare border and much of southern Guaviare.

The region of FTC responsibility, as viewed from a chopper, is basically jungle with occasional clearings in which can be seen the cattle of some campesino who is doubtless paying the terrorists for the "right" to run his cows. In destroying coca plantings and labs here then, both human intelligence (HUMINT) and technical intelligence (TECHINT) are required. The division between the two becomes somewhat fuzzy in the case of the aerial photography which has been used to locate plantings and/or labs in clearings, the LANS Editor having been shown a number of these.

Following such a location choppers and Gooney Birds (C-47), effectively equipped with the Gatling Machine Guns (20mm) for pre-landing preparation of the area, are used to destroy the labs, spraying to destroy the plantings. The DEA has contributed substantially toward the TECHINT required for similar operations in jungle areas where visual or photo observation is impossible.

Sale of the precursor chemicals from the US is legal. Before these chemicals leave the US, however, the DEA includes a beacon in the chemical drums which can be zeroed in on by the appropriate airborne radio equipment. Therefore, the lab at which such a drum of precursor chemical awaits use can be located in whatever jungle it is situated, the procedure from there being routine. [Note: The narcoterrorist probably knows nearly as much about this routine as does the DEA. Even so, no further details will be given here in case there is something which they have missed.]

There is another facet to the narco problem, the clandestine airstrips which are of course essential to these operations. Since these are dirt strips, explosive devices, obstacles and so one are only temporarily effective. The existence of these clandestine strips is, however, a matter of interest. As of mid July 1998 there were 13 such strips in Putumayo, 44 in Caquetá, 48 in Guaviare and 78 in Meta.

The results of these operations in mid July 1998 can be approximately summarized with: 54 labs destroyed, about 30,000 acres of coca sprayed, 11.45 tons of pure cocaine and 9.73 tons of coca base seized, 141 million pesos in cash seized.

Operations Against the Terrorists

The anti-narcotics operations are, of course, basically anti-terrorist operations. However, there have been a series of operations which have rid certain key locations of the FARC terrorists themselves. A typical such operation of several years ago has been discussed in Spcl 6.1 above wherein the ML terrorists, who, with certain paras, had been bullying the citizens of San José de Guaviare for some time, simply vanished when the military arrived. This is of course to be contrasted to the recent overruns of small military detachments by overwhelming numbers of terrorists.

The LANS Editor inquired as to what areas have been cleared of terrorist by the FTC, keeping in mind of course that there is no rational reason for again leaving small, unsupported detachments anywhere until the Southern Bloc is destroyed. A series of small villages on the Caguan River were located for him on the map.

From north to south, these are Cartgena del Chaira (90 sm southeast of Florencia), Santa Fé—a few miles north of El Billar, Peñas Coloradas, Puerto Camelias and Ramolinas del Caguan perhaps 90 sm east of Tres Esquinas.

THE INSPECTOR GENERAL'S REPORT ON MIRAFLORES. I
(SPCL 6.5, 29 AUGUST 1998)

EDITOR'S INTRODUCTION

The GDO is revisited in Wkly 6.10, Chapter 6 below. This GDO rests on two primary assumptions, the reality of various HR Violation (HRV) DOs and the ML terrorist superiority over the FAC DO. The Miraflores affair of early August is important to the latter and has not been treated in detail in these reports. When it is treated in detail the FAC DO falls of its own weight. LANS has obtained a copy of the report on Miraflores by Brigadier General Euclides Sánchez Vargas, the Inspector General of FAC. This speaks for itself. Here we only add information on (1) terrorist strength and (2) Miraflores location. (1) Terrorist strength was reported by *El Espectador* as "400" and "at least 500" in two different articles on the same day. LANS' sources feel that terrorist numbers were about 800. (2) Guaviare Department is to the southeast of Meta Department, its capital, San José de Guaviare (Spcl 6.1 above), on the Guaviare River which separates the two departments. San José is some 230 km southeast of Bogotá. One of the LANS maps, this procured "on the street" in Bogotá, shows two Miraflores, one about 10 km from the Vaupes Department border, the other about 25 km, both on the Vaupes River. The other maps show only one. There would appear to be no ambiguity, however, since the Tactical Pilotage Chart [TPC L-26C] indicates an airstrip at the most distant of the two from the border, an airstrip which will be encountered in the report.

* * *

FUERZAS MILITARES DE COLOMBIA
EJERCITO NACIONAL

Santafé de Bogotá, D.C.

No. : CEIGE-PER-893
SUBJECT : Miraflores Actions
TO : Commanding General of the Army

Through this communication I am writing to send to the Commanding General of the Army the report of the actions occurring on 3 August of the present year at the Military and Anti-Narcotics Police Base located at the Municipal Center of Miraflores (Guaviare) when the self-styled Colombian Revolutionary Armed Forces (FARC) attacked this base with the following results:

Batallón No. 19 "Joaquin Paris"

Dead	Wounded	Missing	Uninjured	Effectives
00-02-09[42]	01-02-15	01-05-69	00-01-05	02-10-98

1. **BACKGROUND**

JANUARY-98 : The mission of the Fundamental Unit (an infantry company) of the Miraflores Base is to conduct military control operations in the area and to furnish security for the National Police in their fumigation of the illicit cultivations in Guaviare.

28-FEB-98 Through official communications No. 1829 BR-7 B-3 OPE-375, the commander of the Seventh Brigade (BR-7) solicited the Commanding General of the Fourth Division (DIV-4) not to leave troops in Miraflores and to move them into support of the troops which were to be found in Caserío el Retorno because of the constant threats, extension of the lines of communication, aerial support difficulties and supplies for the Miraflores Base.

06-MAR-98 Regional Intelligence Center No.4 (CIR-4), through radiogram No. 2-0139 BR-20 BITE-4 S-2 (Intel) 252, reported to DIV-4, BR-7, BIPAR (Joaquín París Infantry Battalion)[43] and PONAL (National Police), (that) bandits of the I and VII Fronts of the FARC ONT (Narco Terrorist Organization) planned to carry out terrorist actions against the Miraflores Anti-Narcotics Base.

26-MAR-98 Through official communication No. 1741 BR-7 B3 OP-375, the BR-7 commander submitted for consideration to the commanding general of DIV-4 the critical situation in which the BIPAR company in Miraflores was to be found owing to the order of increase of the two anti-guerrilla battalions of BRIM-3 (Anti-Terrorist Mobil Brigade), because of the increased capacity acquired by the bandits and their numerical increase.

For the above reasons and because of the impossibility of supplying the troops since the aerial enterprises were threatened, the brigade commander solicited air support in order to bring in rations and to bring out personnel for rest.

03-APR-98 The commander of BIPAR, through No. 4671 BR-7 BIPAR S-2 252 to the commander of BR-7 reported the way in which the road from Port Arthur to San Vicente del Caguán was being constructed on the right bank of the Caguán River, a cocalera (coca-leaf grower) area controlled by the guerrilla and a strategic corridor for them.

22-APR-98 In the operations diary of BIPAR an entry at 1300 reports a harrassment from the urban area against the Miraflores base.

28-APR-98 In the BIPAR operations diary Capt. Gómez reports harassment from the end of the landing strip. Personnel reacted without results.

01-MAY-98 The BIPAR operations diary registered the capture of an individual on 30 April and on the date of the subject's capture a handle of FARC Front I.

21-MAY-98 The BIPAR commander, through No. 0217 BR-7 BIPAR DM72, informed the BR-7 commander of the disadvantages and limitations which BIPAR had in putting troops in Miraflores and Anzuelo, (these) because of the restrictions on the effectives, the extended distances and restrictions on air and tactical air support, (complicated by the fact that) the aviation enterprises which travel to Miraflores are not committed to bringing supplies to military personnel because of being threatened by the narco-guerrilla.

29-MAY-98 CIR-4, through bulletin No. 147, reported that Front VII was carrying out intel activities in the Miraflores urban center.

31-MAY-98 The BIPAR operations diary recorded the throwing of a hand grenade and the firing of a rifle against the voting place to which the reaction was without results.

02-JUN-98 Radiogram No. 0238 BR-7 BIPAR S-2 INT-252, from the BIPAR commander to the commander of Miraflores Base, reports FARC (is) possibly going to attack the base, alert the personnel.

10-JUN-98   CIR-4, through No. 20689 CIM CRO4 PD6 252, informs the DIV-4 and the CIM that FARC is planning to carry out actions against the BIPAR troops at the Miraflores military base and the Anti-Narcotics Police there.

18-JUN-98   In the BIPAR operations diary, there is recorded a meeting engagement without results.

20-JUN-98   The BIPAR commander, through Radiograms No. 0263 BR-7 BIPAR and No.5394 S-2 INT-252, solicited from the commander of BR-7 tactical air support for a possible guerrilla incursion at the Miraflores base.

27-JUN-98   The mayor of Miraflores resigned and elections are programmed for next Sunday (operations diary).

28-JUN-98   When the election of the mayor was in progress in Miraflores, the voting place was harassed with pistol shots, the reason there was no voting.

28-JUN-98   CIR-4, through radiogram No. 2803 CIM RIM4 PD1 252, reports to DIV-4, BR-7 and BIPAR the presence of 400 bandits around the Miraflores Municipality.

JUNE-98   Through pamphlets FARC ONT reports that they will take the Police and the troops out of the Miraflores locality.

01-JUL-98   The BIPAR commander, in radiogram No. 0290 BR-7 BIPAR S-2 INT-219, reporting to the patrols, "enemy detected(,) a ground patrol next has to be attacked."

06-JUL-98   The BIPAR commander, in radiogram No. 0298 BR-7 BIPAR S-2 INT-252, reported that the population of Miraflores is evacuating the hamlet before a possible Guerrilla incursion.

07-JUL-98   Report from Miraflores, they have evacuated 12 houses around the PONAL and BIPAR bases (operations diary).

08-JUL-98   BIPAR weekly intel summary No. 027 concluded (that) next week will be carried out a terrorist wave (with the) end of creating insecurity (among the) population of Miraflores to cope with it.

10-Jul-98   They harrassed the Miraflores base from the houses of the hamlet center, the troops carried out a search without results (operations diary).

15-JUL-98   The BR-7 commander, through No. BR-7 B-3 OP-275, solicited the DIV-4 commander for the movement of the Fundamental Unit from Miraflores to a location closer to San José de Guaviare, recommending Calamar[44] or Port Arturo for lack of aerial support, having found that it is 155 km from San José.

18-JUL-98 Some homes are burned in the urban center of Miraflores municipality, destroying a goodly number (operations diary).

22-JUL-98 By radiogram No. 0320 BR-7 BIPAR S-2 INT-252, the BIPAR commander alerts the base at Miraflores, about the FARC movement, by the Vaupez River, with the objective of attacking the base.

23-JUL-98 BIPAR Weekly Intel Summary No. 029 concludes that in the next (few) days the FARC ONT will increase terrorist attacks especially in the Miraflores Municipality.

31-JUL-98 BIPAR Weekly Intel Summary No.030 concludes that the FARC ONT continues planning an attempt against the troops cantonned in Miraflores.

02-AUG-98 According to Pvt. Marco Fidel Castro Ladino, two days before they (had) notified them that they were going to attack with cylinders of gas,[45] therefore, the captain ordered the anti-guerrilla (platoons) Aguila 1 and Aguila 2, which were to be found on the base near the hospital, left and located themselves in the tangle (vegetation), they (the terrorists) made as if to leave, and the next day (the terrs) attacked.

03-AUG-98 The BIPAR commander informed the BR-7 commander (of) developments at Miraflores Base, reporting lightly wounded and soliciting air support Plan Alpha and Plan Beta.

Capt. Rubio, commander of Miraflores Base, reported that the combat was worsening with grenades,[46] gas cylinders and machine guns, and they (the terrorists) are trying to reach the base.

The commander of Aguila Company reports to the battalion commander the loss of communication with the platoons outside the hamlet.

04-AUG-98 In the report lists of the BIPAR Communications Center there are no entries after 1800 from Aguila 6 (Capt. Rubio) until the next day.

At 0515 Capt. Rubio reports that the Base was destroyed, that now they are taken and that the Police are surrendering.

04-AUG-98 In the interview with the captured subject, who had taken photographs of the disasters which the guerrilla left in Miraflores, he reported that the guerrillas had said that they had 50 hours to take the Anti-Narcotics Base and BIPAR in Miraflores.

06-AUG-98 According to the survivors, the attack was (made) with approximately 1000 guerrillas, large quantities of gas cylinders, grenades as well as long-range munitions without it mattering how much was expended nor the human lives which were lost.

2. SUMMARY OF EVENTS

02-AUG-98 Capt. Rubio Moreno, commander of Miraflores Base, ordered the two platoons which were on the army base to carry out a perimeter search of the hamlet.

03-AUG-98 Lt. Bermeo, with the platoons which were located in the Y initiated a search of the area at 1830, detained a civilian who said that he was checking the cattle; they let him go, and farther along they saw the guerrilla; they cried who is it,[47] and Lt. Bermejo asked them (if) they were troops, and the guerrilla replied to them, they spread out and dug in as it was going to rain lead, and they began to fire; the combats continued until 0100 on 04-AUG-98.

The squad, which went with Sgt. Delgado Argote Arbey, opened up and tried to go up to the base, but encountered the guerrillas at the edge of the road in a pasture, and the sergeant shouted at them, identify yourselves; the soldiers saw that they were bandits and opened fire; the guerrillas in great numbers surrounded them; Sgt. Cáceres Cifuentes Daladier (el Enano—the Dwarf) got up and put himself in front, firing against the guerrillas, putting down more than three bandits, but he was killed together with six other soldiers, and Sgt. Delgado and some soldiers were taken.

03-AUG-98 at 1930 they began the attack with gas cylinders, grenades and bursts (of machine gun fire) at the first platoon which was encountered on the base together with the Police post and the church; this continued strongly all night; at 0730 on Tuesday, 04 August during a momentary cease fire the Captain called the soldiers in order to reorganize their disposition; the 81mm mortar remained inoperable and (the commander questioned?) how they could, with the 60mm mortar and the troops (he had), continue fighting.

The Base Platoon together with the Police, during the entire day of Wednesday continued fighting from their positions, receiving fire from mortars, gas cylinders launched catapult style, rockets and Rifle Propelled Grenades (RPGs), destroying a wall of the base where the bandits succeeded in entering.

The wounded soldiers tried to leap the trenches behind the Base, but they were being murdered.

The wounded were arriving at the Field Hospital on their own, and the guerrillas were seeking the least wounded to bring them; the medic and the nurse made certain how serious some of the soldiers (were).

The guerrillas numbered approximately 1000 bandits, belonged to FARC Fronts I, IV and XLIV (and) were uniformed as Police with a tricolor sash across the chest; they emerged from the houses around the base and from the pasture.

The civilians and the guerrillas cried that they had to finish us because the troops did not let them work (there were only coca cultivations there).

Air[48] support began to be received at 2245 on 03-AUG-98, with an AC-47 FLYING MISSIONS Alpha and Charlie, which withdrew for supplies of fuel and munitions and because of bad weather; at 0100 on 04-AUG-98[49] air support was renewed with the AC-47 and OV-10 aircraft.

Beginning at 0200 on 04-AUG-98 air support was rendered impossible by an abrupt variation in the weather in the combat zone, obliging the aircraft to return to San José del Guaviare and Villavicencio.

At 0830 air support (was) reinforced by anti-narcotics police helicopters; the bandits increased the intensity of the combat which was being carried on by isolated nuclei outside the base, radio contact with them by the captain being lost.

Beginning at 1100 on 04-AUG-98, air support was again impossible because of bad weather in the combat zone, obliging the aircraft to return to San José del Guaviare and Villavicencio. Before the imminent capture of the nuclei which were resisting outside the base they withdrew.

Twenty-four hours after the reinforcements from the Anti-Guerrilla Battalion No.7 (BCG-7) "Heroes of Arauca" with 120 men in two UH-60 choppers, one M-1 and two UH1H from the Anti-Narcotics National Police, who deplaned boldly without air support; immediately at approximately 10 km from the urban perimeter of Miraflores they (these forces) initiated support to the Miraflores Base through a maneuver to contact along converging lines.

1720, 04-Aug-98, the captain commanding the base asked support because he was wounded, and there only remained to him six soldiers and a noncommissioned officer; six police fell back toward the sector where the captain was to be found, and one of them told him that Sgt. Vanegas of the National Police had killed himself and that the rest of the police had begun to surrender; reorganizing the soldiers with the Police, they stationed themselves in one of the trenches whence they could observe that the Police were surrendering and the guerrillas were inside the Police Base, they began to fire at them, but other guerrillas who were going to advance fired toward the sector where the captain with the soldiers and the Police were to be found entrenched, defending themselves (and) inflicting casualties on the bandits inside the base; they maintained contact until, through the action of grenades of 40mm[50] and mortars (the enemy) wounded various Police and Soldiers.

During the course of the night the personnel still maintained (their) positions and in the locality isolated combats developed, without radio contact between the reinforcing units and those being supported.

Captain Rubio Moreno W., commander of Miraflores Base, declares that each search, which was carried out on the urban perimeter, was done with the Police; the captain coordinated with Lt. Donato, commander of the Anti-Narcotic Police in order that they always patrolled in a strong group made up of Police and Army.

In like manner the captain reported that during the attack he boosted the morale of the Chief and Agents who withdrew toward the sector of the Military Base, in order that they did not surrender their combat equipment, maintaining control over the situation and over the men who were fighting with him until they were overwhelmed by enemy fire.

Defense plans were rehearsed up to four times per week, (these) integrated with the police and directed by the captain.

On 05-AUG-98 the evacuation of wounded personnel was initiated with the support of a Red Cross aircraft, Air Force and Anti-Narcotics Police helicopters as well as 120 effectives of BCG-7, who immediately established contact, knocking out three armed bandits, among whom was a woman, and putting the subversives to flight.

On 06-AUG-98 BCG-7 "Heroes of Arauca" reestablished control of the area leading to the locality.

[Translated from the Spanish by the LANS Editor]

THE INSPECTOR GENERAL'S REPORT ON MIRAFLORES. II
(SPCL 6.7, 3 SEPTEMBER 1998)

EDITOR'S INTRODUCTION II

The area of responsibility of Infantry Battalion No. 19 "Joaquín Paris" (BIPAR) will be seen to include extended portions of Meta Department and Guaviare Department. In Meta, for example, there is Mapiripan which is some 60 km northeast of San José. The latter and Miraflores are at "opposite ends" of Guaviare, both the specific responsibility of BIPAR. Both departments are in the Llanos or Plains area on the eastern slope of the Andes. On the LANS maps only a single highway transits Guaviare, about due south across the state, the roads in Meta little more. A note warns that these roads are transitable only in summer.

* * *

Personnel Murdered (00-02-09)[51]

(Here the names of the dead personnel are given. Only the numbers will be given as above.)

Personnel wounded (01-02-15)
A. Personnel evacuated to the Military Hospital Bogotá (01-02-10)
B. Personnel evacuated to the dispensary (at) San José de Guaviare (00-00-05)
C. Personnel disappeared, apparently kidnapped by the ONT FARC (01-05-69)

D. War Materiel Lost

Galil 7.62mm SAR (Short Assault Rifle)[52]	08
Galil 7.62mm AR (Assault Rifle)	93
M-60 7.62mm all-purpose machine gun[53]	03
Multiple Grenade Launchers[54]	07
60mm Soltam Mortar[55]	03
81mm Soltam Mortar	01
40mm Grenades (probably for MGL)	327

Rifle grenades	22
Hand grenades	170
Belted ammunition (probably for M60)	5000
7.62mm Ammunition	33800

E. Communications Materiel Lost

(The various kinds of radios lost will not be recorded here.)

III. CONCLUSIONS

A. The officer, non-commissioned officer and private personnel assigned to the Miraflores Base fought heroically for 18 hours, with valor and nobility, battling until the reserve ammunition was largely exhausted and developing individual initiatives in seeking protection since air support was neither timely nor permanent. Among these personnel were distinguished:

PVT. SABOGAL HENRY GIOVANNY
PVT. CASTRO LADINO MARCOS
PVT. GALEANO RION ALEXANDER
PVT. CACERES CIFUENTES DALADIER (el Enano—the Dwarf)

B. The Army is not carrying out the mission entrusted (to it) by the National Constitution, it is to be found carrying out a multiplicity of tasks for which it is not prepared.
C. The commanders of the smaller, tactical operational units, with their staff officers, proved (to be) superior personnel (who, located themselves immediately to the front of the position (in order to give) direction and coordination of the required supports.
D. The commanders of BIPAR of the BR-7 and the DIV-4, through documents, reported the strategic error of maintaining a Fundamental Unit (company) isolated at Miraflores through the lengthening of the lines of communications and the difficulties of air support.
E. BIPAR has isolated units in an over extended area of responsibility which cannot depend on immediate aerial support.
F. The BIPAR Operational Plan did not (appropriately) assess the (level) of operations, before or after assuming (responsibility

for) the security of Miraflores Base.

G. The battalion did not develop counterintelligence methods in order to fool the enemy; (this is suggested) since it appears he knew the location of the unit, numerical data (on it) and support which was arranged.

H. BIPAR is not sufficient to provide security to the locations ordered by the High Command (Mapiripan, Miraflores, Retorno and San José) and, at the same time, carry out operations in an overextended area having various gangs (of terrorists).

I. CIR-4, BIPAR intel and brigade intel was very timely, providing information on the enemy to the commanders from approximately three months before (operations commenced).

J. There was no operational unity of command for the Army, Police and Air Force during the combat.

K. The Miraflores Base commander, in spite of having an integrated plan of defense, reaction and counterattack with the police of the Miraflores Anti-Narcotics Base, was not effective for lack of obstacles, early warning alarms and traps which could retard the enemy advance.

L. The troops and police which operated in Miraflores routinized (rendered routine) their activities, movements and places of rest.

M. The troops and the police underestimated the enemy, believing that they were prepared to receive an attack from a group smaller than that which they sustained.

N. The base was not provided with fortified installations and trenches in order to sustain a high trajectory attack.[56]

O. The bandits utilized the principle of mass, attacking in waves;[57] the loss of human life was not important to them, nor (was) the amount of ammunition expended.

P. The employees of the health clinic, the operator of the village power plant and some civilians supported the Public Forces by hiding them and making them appear as gravely wounded.

Q. The fumigation mission assigned to the National Police in Miraflores is almost fruitless owing to the limitations which it has faced with the great extensions of coca cultivation existing in the jurisdiction.

R. According to the information from the survivors and civilian personnel, the number of bandits was approximately 1000 men, distributed throughout the area and within the central area of Miraflores.

S. The availability of air transport was neither timely nor sufficient to support the troops in Miraflores, the support of FAC and PONAL only counted on one M.1 (chopper) and arrived late.

T. The Plan of reaction and counterattack of the Miraflores Base was not brought up to date; Capt. COMEZ PACHECO CESAR, the departing base commander, elaborated (the plan) which he turned over to the Army Inspector General; it is badly developed, does not obey the General Staff Manual, does not integrate the platoons or the police and was not revised by the S-3 (plans and operations) officer of the unit.

U. The Vaupes River, guerrilla river expressway,[58] was not covered for lack of troops to avoid displacement toward Miraflores and the withdrawal of the narco guerrillas.

V. With the attack at Miraflores (Guaviare), cocalero (coca grower) heart of the ONT FARC, the relation of these (terrorists) with narcotrafficking is obvious and (as is) the obstacle which the troops represent to development of these illicit activities.

W. Capt. Rubio Moreno William, base commander, maintained relative control of his troops and supported (them) to boost the morale of the soldiers and police who were at the military base until they were taken by the narcoguerrilla.

X. The Fundamental Unit, which was located at Miraflores, carried out in coordination with the Anti-Narcotics Police periodic inspections in the hamlet perimeter up to four times per week.

Y. The subversion has modified its way of operating, trying to move to a higher phase of revolutionary war forecast in its strategic plan for taking power, (this) designated "war of movement," in which a considerable force of insurgents is concentrated which makes it very superior at various locations simultaneously.

Z. With the above the narcoguerrilla seeks to give conclusive blows of capture to the troops disposed in a designated location, demonstrating itself to public opinion as a powerful and victorious force executing its actions without it mattering how many dead it loses during the armed actions, these (casualties) hidden from public awareness.

AA. The terrorist ascent to the national level, the response capacity at Miraflores diminished, permitting simultaneous actions at

various places in the country, the resources of the (Armed) Forces are rendered temporarily powerless to deal with the situation.
BB. The selection of the site for the location of the (Army and Anti-Narcotics) bases was not the most adequate, permitting the planning of an attack from the beginning.
CC. The narco-guerrilla employed the principle of mass effecting his attack with numerical superiority (5 to 1).

IV. RECOMMENDATIONS

A. The Army Inspector General submit to the Army Commander for consideration the recognition for heroism of Pvt. Cáceres Cifuentes Daladier (El Enano). (Q.E.P.D.) for a posthumous promotion and for the survivors who remained at Miraflores until the last moment.
B. To increase instruction in the defense of positions, reaction and counterattack.
C. Because Miraflores is to be found at a distance of 155 km approximately from San José de Guaviare, the jurisdiction of BIPAR is overextended, with the influence of the guerrilla in the area, for which reason the maintenance of an AGAT in San José de Guaviare is required.
D. To carry out offensive operations when information of an imminent seizure or guerrilla attack on fixed points, reinforcing them taking into account the necessary methods for a defense of position.
E. To revise the strategic disposition of the Army troops, and the factors of enemy, weather and terrain.
F. To revise and elaborate the different plans of logistical and aerial supply of the troops, especially for those located in isolated areas.
G. To invest in the construction, fortification and methods of defense of the base installations which merit being fixed.
H. If the presidential order is to maintain troops in Miraflores, it is necessary to construct some fortified installations impervious to mortar fire with the necessary basics for a counter-guerrilla battalion and a communications satellite.
I. To add a counter-guerrilla battalion to BIPAR with the object

       of providing security at the Anti-Narcotics Police base and for carrying out military operations.
J.   To order disciplinary and criminal investigations into what took place.
K.   To solicit the central government to promulgate a law which prohibits the transport of chemical precursors for these regions where (there is) the processing of narcotics.
L.   To provide to the Air Force methods permitting that it deal with at least two simultaneous situations in each division with missions of support, fire and troop transport.
M. To analyze the present disposition of the Army in order to render it adequate to the new circumstances, avoiding the dispersion which presently maintains the vulnerability which this entails.
N.   To recommend to the National Police to reinforce the dispositions of the isolated units with passive, active and anti aerial (mortar, artillery) security means.

[Translated from the Spanish by the LANS Editor]

C. The Self Defense Patrols

COLOMBIAN SELF DEFENSE PATROLS. I
(SPCL 6.1, 5 JULY 1998)

Until the decade of the 1990s and the alleged "implosion" of the USSR, the ML terrorist groups in LA were supported, coordinated and, generally, directed by Castro's HL out of Havana.[59] That such was the case was evident throughout the Sandinista evolution after Fonseca's death, in the formation of the Guatemalan National Revolutionary Union (URNG) and FMLN in 1980, in the coordination of such as the Montoneros in Argentina, the FARC and the ELN in Colombia and so on. Now the terrorist bosses go to Havana to die (Colombia's Pérez), or to be treated (Nicaragua's Ortega) or to confer and plot (El Salvador's Handal and a stream of others).

The situation changed somewhat with the advent of the 1990s and allegedly due to the reduced funding by the transmogrified USSR.[60] However, the terrorist groups, in particular, of Colombia and Peru have been transformed into narcoterrorist groups which are funding themselves while still allegedly operating under the aegis of Dialectical Materialism (Marxism) and Weltoktober (Leninism). With this narco bonanza, they have been well able to overcome any maladjustments in their terrorist "life style" which the USSR transmogrification might otherwise have induced.

Through it all, however, in spite of their ML mumbo jumbo, the terrorists have preyed on the (relatively) lowly campesino or countryman, happy of course to blackmail, harass and kill the farmer and rancher. While the Armed Forces of the various LA nations have done a creditable job of dealing with these terrorists, it has normally been impossible for them to maintain a global presence. Therefore, the campesinos in an area are routinely preyed upon when the army is elsewhere. The result has been that, with or without government support, the countrymen have banded together for necessary self defense.

Certain examples of government-supported self defense have been discussed in these reports. The impressive anti-terrorist successes of the Peruvian self-defense forces (*Rondas Campesinas*) have been discussed in Spcl 5.11 ("The Peruvian Civil Self Defense Committees") (Chapter 4 above). The Guatemalan CAPs broke the back of the URNG in 1982, and the bosses of that terrorist group thenceforth ran their media-event "war" from the safety and comfort of Mexico to victory. The DO against them calls for an aside.

DOs by the HL have been extensively discussed in these reports, the fact that these ML organizations have succeeded in none of their efforts save by this contrived propaganda being of immense importance. From this it is straightforward to conclude that the level of concern of the HL about a given anti-ML operation may be judged by the effort put into these DOs. The Contra Drug DO has been discussed (pp.196ff, YRBK97). It hardly stood alone among the DOs aimed at the Contras by the HL; however, the magnitude and number of these were such as to guarantee the seriousness with which this anti-ML effort was taken by the HL.[61] In like manner, the self defense forces have been an almost continuous object of such attack, important because it tells us the serious threat they are considered by the HL.

An example of the DO directed against the Guatemalan PACs (pp.217ff, YRBK97) serves as an measure of the seriousness with which they are taken. The Mexican situation remains confused (cf. Wkly 5.1, "CUI BONO? The Acteal, Mexico, Massacre," Chapter 4 above), but Mexico likewise appears to have sponsored self-defense organizations since the arrival of the Zapatista National Liberation Army (EZLN) terrorists. This, of course, has been routinely distorted by the terrorists whose allegations, however nonsensical, are solemnly written down and disseminated by the press.

In Colombia, however, the so-called "self defense patrols" have developed quite differently, the process having been considerably complicated by the MLs having introduced the term themselves. Thus, when a press account simply makes the bald statement that the oldest terrorist of them all, Tirofijo, founded FARC in 1957 as a "self defense" force, the account is technically correct but basically meaningless. The behavior of these ML "self defense" forces would soon, rather like Pompey stamping his foot, call up anti-ML "self defense" forces. This, incidentally, has led to another press *non sequitur.* Although seldom referring to the terrorists as "ultra left" (ultra izquierdista) it is common to refer to anyone opposing them as "ultra right" (ultra derechista). Therefore, those "self defense" forces which oppose the ML terrorists are commonly and meaninglessly described as Ultra Derechista.

The Evolution of Colombian ML "Self Defense" Forces

The Bogotazo and Castro's involvement therein have been extensively discussed in these reports (pp.109ff, YRBK97). The Soviet-sponsored IL was ultimately unsuccessful in this 9 April 1948 operation which these terrorists took as a call for reorganization and further plotting. On 22 October 1949 the PCC launched its slogan, "self defense of the masses." This was followed up at the 12th Plenum of the Central Committee (CC) with typical ML rhetoric: "the proletariat and the people cannot triumph" without "a strong CP, expert and disciplined, at their head" (*30 años del lucha del PCC*, Edición Paz y Socialismo, 1960).

In 1950 the PCC concentrated a large number of families in the Chaparral area of Tolima Department. A political organization was developed in which the adult men were considered PCC militants, the children inserted into the Sucre Battalion, the women in feminine committees and the youths in Communist Youth. This last organization was added to the agrarian unions and to the Juntas de Autodefensas (Self Defense Groups), the result considered as the basis of FARC. In usual ML fashion, the 13th Plenum (1950) was followed by the VII Congress (1952) and another blustering manifesto (26 June 1953) which declared, *inter alia*, that "the Colombian people...have learned to battle with arms in their hands..." (p.104, *Cuadernos de Campaña*, M. Marulanda Vélez Ed., 1974) and will not abandon their "liberating battle."

It has been stated here in the past, on what appeared to be good authority, that Tirofijo created FARC in 1957 as a "self defense force," albeit, clearly linked to the PCC. Which can be harmonized with the statement by the terrorists that FARC was "officially" formed in the Second Conference of the Southern Bloc on 25 May 1966 as a reaction to the military operations of 1964 and 1965 against the "independent republics" which the PCC had formed. It could well be that Tirofijo's organization changed its name somewhat, but this appears to render the formation date unaffected. The 1965 conference was officially the Second National Self Defense Conference.

An exhaustive study of this subject would require the details of the "Second Version" of ML Self Defense, which emerged from the XII Congress of the PCC (5 December 1975) and the "Third Version" which was the Peoples Militias of the EPL. Space here does not allow the inclusion of these two versions, however.

Anti-ML Self Defense Forces

The immense increase in Colombian subversion extended the insecurity over an extensive portion of that nation. The area was defined by the Middle and Lower Magdalena, northeast Antioquia Department, the Hi Sinú (defined by the river of the same name in Bolivar and Antioquia Departments) and various other regions. As the terrorists' organization became larger, its demands and requirements increased in proportion. Among the extortion methods used by the MLs to gather funds was (1) the *vacuna ganadera*, an extortion from ranchers proportional to the number of their cattle, (2) *impuestos de guerra* or war tax, (3) *contribuciones*[62] and, practically speaking, any other criminal activity which occurred as justification for additional theft. From this terrorist behavior spontaneously surged the self defense forces of Colombia. And these arose among the most humble. The terrorist had taken everything they had, to include their sons and daughters, save their lives. As a terrorist deserter told it:

"Some months ago now we were working with my Papa in the parcel which he had in San Vicente de Chucuri when the guerrilla arrived. There were 15 men, dressed in uniforms looking like those of the army and armed with rifles and machine guns...They go to the farms, knock down the campesinos, rape the women without caring if they be children and ...steal the cattle and the chickens...Three of the men knocked down my Papa, stretched him out on the floor, put a rifle to his head and told him: 'The boy is going with us and it is better that you don't resist.'" (*SEMANA,* 16 March 1993) The boy's life as a terrorist lasted the 17 months until his desertion. The important part of the tale is that, as was being done in various regions, FARC trained him for "self defense." He was later found to be utilizing that training, but against the terrorists, not in their service.

And over the years CAPs did arise, but the situation was hardly straightforward in Colombia. For while there were certain legitimate ones, formed, say, by cattlemen to protect them from ML terrorist depredations, there were also some very bad ones. The latter will be discussed below. The case of the Batallón Bárbula commander, Colonel Luis Bohórquez Montoya (*El Tiempo* 21 May 1989), illustrates, with a case which may well remain a conundrum, the structure of the "HR" DOs against the Colombian military which use the so-called "paramilitaries."

Colonel Bohórquez: Hero or Black Sheep?

Colonel Bohórquez was, until early May 1989, commander of Bárbula Battalion with headquarters in Puerto Boyacá. At that time he retired from the service, hounded out by charges which may have been false. His story is worth relating, albeit, it did him little good.

Some eight months earlier, in latter 1988, Gilberto Vieira, boss of the PCC[63] introduced into the Congress a document which "appeared to have originated in DAS." It was claimed in said document that Bohórquez had an "arrangement" with *sicarios* (assassins) or "paramilitaries"[64] whereby he gave them refuge after they had been out massacring innocent civilians.

Bohórquez apparently did not question that DAS was the source but maintained that the charge was based on the testimony of a fraudulent physician, one Miguel Viafra, who was actually in the M-19 terrorist group, later an assassin in Medellín. The colonel made no bones about cooperating with self defense groups unconnected with narcotraffickers and limited to 16 and 20 gauge shotguns as armament, but flatly denied ever having any connection with the "sicarios." As to the charge that he was the guest of honor at a narcotraffickers gala:

"I had more than 500 witnesses that I spent that time with my wife...in a year and a half I destroyed five [of their] laboratories valued at $15 billion pesos..." and it would hardly have been sensible of them to invite him to a 24-31 December gala.

LANS cannot demonstrate that this is true, although future reports will discuss quite similar cases wherein the military man charged with aiding and abetting the "paramilitaries" is simply the victim of a DO. However, the case is of interest here as an introduction to the sort of "Self Defense Forces" which are hired and supported by the narcotraffickers.

San José de Guaviare

San José de Guaviare is a small town on the right bank of the Guaviare River which separates Meta Department to the north from the sparsely-populated Guaviare Department to the south. Apuleyo Plinio Mendoza (*El Tiempo* 25 June 1989) described the hamlet in 1987 as "an inferno. It had no law in an era which demanded arms; the entire department from the Guaviare River to Vaupés [Department],[65] was a sea of coca cultivation, a bewildering morass of adventurers, buyers and guerrillas making up the unique authority." At a kilometer from the confluence of the Ariari and Guaviare Rivers a banner between two poles read "Welcome VII FARC Front." There was no other state than FARC.

Plinio Mendoza describes in an exquisite detail which cannot be repeated here how the strutting terrorists of FARC ran the town; how nothing save coca was cultivated; how the Union Patriotica (UP),[66] with FARC personnel at the voting booth, consistently "won" 8 of the 9 council seats. But FARC was also charging the narcotraffickers a 20 percent "tax" on the paste, 40 percent on the coca refined in the laboratories, a policy rendering matters even worse for the local citizens.

For the narcotraffickers brought in "self defense" forces, mostly from the emerald-producing region of Boyacá to clean the zone of MLs. These assassins were the "paramilitary" who have so confused the self defense situation in Colombia. Their instructions were to clean the zone of MLs, not simply by killing the UP militants but also those campesinos who arrived from the FARC-controlled zones such as that to the southeast controlled by Front I. Plinio Mendoza graphically describes the terror that ensued.

As he describes the "miraculous change" wrought by General Harold Bedoya and his VII Brigade when he arrived in the area on 21 December 1987. As has been described in connection with Task Force South and the FARC terrorist—a current DO (Wkly 6.5) has these terrorists defeating the Colombian Army—FARC took to its heels, and San José de Guaviari was, if not immediately, turned into the "miracle" which Plinio Mendoza describes.

But the point here is not the miracle *per se*, it is this type of "self defense force" peculiar to Colombia which is illustrated by the account.

COLOMBIAN SELF DEFENSE PATROLS. II

MIGUEL POSADA S.
LANS CORRESPONDENT
BOGOTÁ, COLOMBIA
(WKLY 6.5, 6 AUGUST 1998)

Students of the Colombian low intensity conflict (LIC) have seldom analyzed the tactics, sources of funds or popular support of the self-defense groups objectively. These groups, misnamed "Paramilitaries" in an effort to link them to the official Armed Forces, would not have flourished without the support of a large segment of the civilian population in their areas of operation. Originally, many were organized by the Army when it was legal for them to do so. This was no different from the practice of regular armies in other LICs, such as those involving the British, American and French armies in many parts of the world during the Cold War and that involving the Peruvian Army at present.

In the middle 1980s, lack of support from the Army, due to budgetary problems, led to establishment of links between these groups and the Drug Lords. Due to these links, the groups were banned on 19 April 1989 when the Barco Administration (1986-1990) suspended Paragraph 3, Article 33, Decree 3398 (1965) which allowed the organization of such groups. The alliance between such groups and the Drug Lords ended, however, when Pablo Escobar, head of the

Medellín Cartel, tried to involve them in his war against the government. The end of the Cartels' financial support momentarily weakened the groups. But many farmers and ranchers, tired of extortion and kidnapping by the guerrillas, stepped in to provide the funds they needed. In other cases, small farmers actually took up arms themselves.

Why do these groups receive such support, and why are they effective against the guerrillas? Successive governments have tried, unsuccessfully, to reach a negotiated solution to the conflict with the guerrillas. Mistakenly, they have followed a policy of appeasement, progressively limiting the legal powers of the Armed Forces and establishing legal processes that favor the insurgents. As a result, the Army can do little against the guerillas' unarmed support networks. The "Paramilitaries" are subject to no such limitations. They use terror, murder and banishment against these organizations, without which the guerrillas cannot function. It is an elementary tactic in war to attack the enemy's logistics, communications and intelligence. This is exactly what the self-defense groups have learned to do.

The guerrillas and their supporters, as well as many HR NGOs, claim that the Army does not fight the "Paramilitaries" and is therefore an accomplice in their actions. They claim there are links between the Army and these groups. There is, undoubtedly, less combat between the Army and the "Paramilitaries" than there is between the former and the guerrillas. This is simply due to the fact that the self-defense groups avoid fighting the Army; it is not the Army that kidnaps, murders and extorts from their employers. But combat with the Army does occur, although the Human Rights NGOs fail to report it.

The 17th Brigade, which operates in the Urabá region, and is often accused of complicity with the "Paramilitaries," is a good example. Its troops captured 28 members of these groups and killed another 13 in combat in 1996. From January to October 1997, another five had been captured and 17 killed in combat. More recently, in February 1998, this same brigade captured 23 members of the "paramilitary" forces, among whom were included two Panamanians. This is strong evidence against the allegations of Army-Paramilitary complicity.

The "Paramilitaries" will unfortunately continue to grow in numbers and territorial coverage as long as there are farmers and ranchers unwilling to submit to the guerrillas. We can only guess at the consequences of these groups' growing power over the long term. Will their leaders become warlords, demanding under threat as do the guerrillas, protection money from the people that now willingly support them?

The only realistic solution is the restoration of effective legal powers to the Army and once again permitting the operation of well-controlled legal community defense groups. The latter was the idea behind the Security Co-ops called CONVIVIR. However, the administration and the Constitutional Court bowed to pressure from the guerrillas' political supporters and from those under guerrilla influence such as the HR NGOs and the UN Commission on Human Rights. The result was continued crippling restrictions on the operation of these Security Co-ops. The CONVIVIR have been subjected to new rules and must battle against mountains of red tape. An important example of such restrictions is that the weapons they will henceforth be allowed to carry are simply inadequate to face the heavily-armed guerrillas.

To make matters worse, the administration, in yet another "peace effort," has asked Congress to pass still another set of laws which will further weaken the Army's ability and resolve to face the guerrillas. Making the legal response to the guerrillas weaker makes support for the "Paramilitaries," and their brutal response, the only immediate practical solution for the many civilians that are the guerrillas' victims.

D. The Pastrana Peace Process

THE NEW COLOMBIAN GOVERNMENT AND PEACE

MIGUEL POSADA S.
LANS CORRESPONDENT
BOGOTÁ, COLOMBIA
(WKLY 6.4, 30 JULY 1998)

EDITOR'S INTRODUCTION

In various of these LANS reports it has been demonstrated that the so-called "peace negotiations" in LA, which emerged from Esquipulas II, have in effect been victory negotiations for the ML terrorists engaged in CA media-event "wars." These were ML victories spurred on by the "STOP sign" mentality of the US and made possible by the immensely successful DOs of the HL. To these thrusts for ML peace-victory have recently been added the Colombia-specific GDO as described in Wkly 6.3 above. In the attempted transfer of this technique to Colombia the principal players, such as Oscar Arias, see themselves showered with titles, medals and awards for their "peace-making" triumphs. The ultimate *imprimatur* has recently been placed on this bizarre process by the Middle Eastern terrorist, Yasser Arafat, who, after a meeting with Colombian terrorists in Mexico, declared that his Palestine *Liberation* Organization (PLO) was prepared to *act as mediator* between the FARC terrorists and the Colombian government (EFE 21 July 1998).

* * *

In initiating its administration, the recently-elected government in Colombia will be confronted with two major problems. Each of these is difficult, but, in combination, the pair present the most complex and dangerous situation with which the country has been faced in recent decades. On the one hand, the new government must reorder the economy, and, in order to do that, it will be necessary to carry out basic changes. Among these is the reform of the appalling Constitution of 1991. The finances of the state show a serious deficit, an imbalance which has produced high interest rates, a weakness of the currency, uncertainty among investors and a high level of unemployment.

On the other hand, in the midst of this difficult economic situation, a peace negotiation has been promised with the subversive groups, the ELN and the FARC. During the election campaign the two candidates, who would face each other in the second round, offered to achieve peace. Insofar as the election campaign is concerned, it was indispensable to do it. After the elections, the president-elect, Andrés Pastrana, met with the top leaders of FARC before assuming power. In parallel with this, there was brought to a head an encounter in Germany, promoted by the German government and the Catholic Church of that country.[67] This was a meeting among directors of the ELN, elements of the extreme left and a small group of Colombian leaders. The illusion was created that peace was close. But it would be disastrous for democracy if the new government attempts to resolve the financial crisis by cutting the budget of the Colombian Armed Forces, because, in spite of the desires and good intentions of the society and the government, peace is not just around the corner.

Erroneously, the cases of peace negotiation in El Salvador and Guatemala are taken as examples for Colombia. In both cases, however, the subversion was weakened, and it was pressured by the international community to achieve a negotiated peace when it was convenient. Moreover, another question arises. Can the Salvadoran peace process be considered a success? Recent statistics reveal murder rates to be higher there than those now existing in Colombia.

At this time, do the conditions exist for a successful negotiation in Colombia? Everything indicates the contrary. In Colombia the subversion is not weakened. If, indeed, the collapse of the socialist bloc diminished the prestige of Marxism as an economic system in the view of enlightened public opinion, it is clear that Colombian subversion survived in the midst of this ideological disaster. In the mountains of Colombia they continue to make successful use of the discredited Marxist rhetoric to motivate their adherents. Within the country moreover, they have the support, for example, of the powerful unions and state enterprises. Among the latter, is the Colombian Petroleum Enterprise (ECP) which is afraid of losing its privileges and powers of intimidation with privatization.

Abroad, especially in the US and Europe, as happened in the cases of Guatemala and El Salvador, among others, a well orchestrated DO campaign was brought to a head with regard to the Colombian conflict. This campaign successfully covered up the criminal actions of the subversion and discredited the Colombian Military Forces. In this campaign a role was played by some important parts of the communications media and many organizations allegedly engaged in promoting "HR." In the economic area the subversion achieves important income from kidnapping, extortion and narcotrafficking. To these funds are added the resources of the municipalities which it controls and money which it receives from sympathizers abroad. This has allowed the subversion to gain ground even after the fall of the Berlin Wall. Why then would it treat for peace now?

It would therefore be a serious error to place any trust in an easy and rapid negotiation. In the recent past, two opportunities for advancing peace talks have failed, both of which, however, the guerrilla utilized in order to strengthen himself. He received advance concessions which weakened the state and especially the Armed Forces, and he conceded nothing in exchange. On this occasion no advance concessions should be made previous to the consolidation of peace and the demobilization of the guerrilla. Even less should any concessions be permitted which weaken the combat capability of the Military Forces. Such capability cannot be a matter for negotiation as is sought. The same error simply cannot be repeated.

We hope that the new government will be cautious, that it will resist internal and external pressures, good intentioned or otherwise, and that it will not allow itself to be lured, in spite of the fiscal difficulties, by the temptations which an uncertain peace offers.

THE COLOMBIAN PEACE PROCESS—A THREE-RING CIRCUS

MIGUEL POSADA S.
SOCIOPOLITICAL ANALYSIS CENTER
BOGOTÁ, COLOMBIA
(WKLY 6.15, 15 OCTOBER 1998)

The present painstaking search for peace brings to mind the disastrous process which was followed by the Betancur Government.[68] It also has various similarities to the vaudeville performance into which the return of the Samper Government[69] soldiers was turned. General Bedoya[70] referred to this last show as a "circus with many clowns." This time the circus has three rings and many clowns. On that first occasion anyone who did not have their picture taken with Tijofijo[71] in Casa Verda was excluded from the jet-set. On this occasion the same thing is happening. Whoever has not met with this bandit or gone to Itagüí Prison "is nobody."

We recall the result of the "Peace of Betancur,"[72] which ended in the disaster that was the taking of the Supreme Court Building by M-19. That guerrilla obtained "political peace," establishing a new party, the UP.[73] But at the same time he did his field work in order to establish his support networks in new areas which soon allowed him to re-institute the confrontation, strengthening and amplifying his field of action. The concessions which were given in advance remain in force. Meanwhile, the Army was weakened by the process both materially and in its morale. It was not easy for its members to see hundreds of guerrillas, whose capture had cost the military much sweat and blood, leaving the prisons as if nothing had happened. Later it would cost more blood to capture them again or make casualties out of them. But it was important to no one how many soldiers were killed. It is a fact that, after 40 years of war, *there is not a single monument dedicated to the soldiers who have given their lives to protect liberty and democracy.*

The Pastrana Government peace process was begun with various terrible mistakes. The president has said that he and he alone is going to manage the process. But it is accepted that a so-called "Civil Society," selected by this same subversion and made up in good part of its thinly-disguised friends, is negotiating for the entire country. Who constitutes this so-called Civil Society? The executives of unions, for example, are named as a part of this "Society" in order to represent their members before public opinion or the State, not in order for them to dialog with the subversion. As far as I know, none of them has such a mandate. Moreover, in Colombia unions represent a negligible minority of Colombians. It is also generally agreed that a senator and some of her colleagues lack the necessary discretion in seeking the screen and prominence. And I am not speaking of the "screen" in the figurative sense, I am referring to the screens of our televisions. Is the process going to be managed by the president or Piety Córdoba?

Over and above the circus ambiance, which augurs nothing good, the process began badly. We consider the famous clearance of territory. To begin with, it is a prime concession without any reciprocity: the terrorists agree to nothing in exchange. The government is going to turn over territories with obvious violation of the rights of their inhabitants who will be left without that protection which the state owes them. Or will the "protection" which the ineffable Public Defender offers them be sufficient? Will they be able to return to their homes, those who prudently put no faith in such doubtful "protection" and leave, after the guerrilla has taken charge of the region? Is the government going to provide for them while they are displaced and indemnify them for their lost possessions? If the process fails, how much more blood of our soldiers will it cost to recover these territories?

The other senselessness is the exchange of criminals for our soldiers. Yes, it would be very good to recover 245 soldiers and police.

But these are to be exchanged for 700 guerrillas—equivalent to 10 FARC fronts—who take their orders from the bandit Tirofijo. And criminals they are, although they prefer the elegant term "insurgent" to the more descriptive "narcotrafficker," "kidnapper" or "murderer." How many soldiers died capturing them and how many more will die at their hands after they return to the bush?

God grant that I am wrong and that peace will be achieved in spite of the initial errors. But God grant that that peace does not imply our submission to that ML which has brought so much poverty and sadness to Cubans and Nicaraguans, not that the present economic model be sacrificed. The economic model which is yet under construction is the only hope of attaining sustained development in the future. It is not going to be easy. It would please the subversion, were it unable to attain Marxism, to obtain the mixed system which is now failing on our continent. It is failing with its corrupt and abusive unions, its failing state enterprises, its privileged private enterprises protected from market forces, rampant bureaucracy and asphyxiating regulations.

[Translated from the Spanish by the LANS Editor]

PASTRANA'S "PEACE PROCESS"
(SPCL 6.12, 31 OCTOBER 1998)

The PC Party candidate for the Colombian presidency, Andrés Pastrana, won the runoff last summer against his Liberal opponent and assumed the presidency on 7 August 1998. Even before his inauguration, however, his presidency appears to have been largely focussed on a "peace policy" which was initiated with FARC and ELN terrorists both in the Colombian and European bush. Dr. Miguel Posada, the LANS correspondent in Bogotá, has described the process as a "three-ring circus" reminiscent of the "peace" exercise perpetrated by the Betancur and Samper Governments (Wkly 6.15 above).

Carlos Castaño, the Self Defense Forces (AUC)[74] leader in one of the outlawed anti-terrorist groups, sent a message to Chancellor Guillermo Fernández which was released on 15 September 1998. The left and the press consistently refer to Castaño and his brethren as "paramilitaries" with the object of tarring the military with the same brush as these frequently narco-involved groups.[75] Whatever

Castaño may be, however, his message contains perhaps the most accurate description of the Pastrana Peace Process with the phrase "peace at any price." In the message Castaño went on to say that "we do not share the concept of peace at any price because we consider it dangerous for the existence of the nation and its institutions."

Peace can be obtained at any time, either in war between nations or in internal war against terrorism, by simple surrender. This is of course the ultimate stage of "peace at any price." It is difficult to see that the Pastrana Government (PG) is not simply surrendering to every demand of the ML terrorists, at the same time calling for "support" from the "international community" for its "peace process." It is particularly important to specify what such "support" has meant in the past to other "peace processes," those in Nicaragua, El Salvador and Guatemala[76] being recent, if generally misunderstood, examples. In all cases of "negotiation" with ML groups it is to be remembered that: (1) According to the teachings of the patron saint of this discredited sister philosophy of nazism and fascism, Ulianov (aka Lenin), peace treaties are expendable tools and (2) terrorism or criminal behavior is a necessary adjunct to ML success. Sufficient space has been devoted in YRBK97 and YRBK98 to the HL victories through peace in Central America. The evidence indicates that ML terrorist victory in Colombia is now being prepared with the assistance of those members of the "international community" who either see some advantage for themselves in such a "peace" or who have actually been so confused by the IL that they feel the process has some meaning other than ML victory. To this point, there has been a single exception to this myopia with regard to the HL : the Fujimori Government of Peru.

Is the PG Simply Surrendering to the ML Terrorists?

The PG has once again made it fashionable to treat terrorists such as Tirofijo as if they were something other than criminals; they are, rather, living off a criminal activity which includes that litany of crime from murder to narcotrafficking which their LibTheo clerics might once have categorized as mortal sins. It has further surrendered without a whimper to every calculated insult perpetrated by these terrorists in the continuing murder of military and civilians. The ML Soviet dictator, Khrushchev, has returned to sneer again that "You spit in their face, and they call it dew." Nor is it simply a matter of continuous surrender to continuing murder.

The PG, more by silence than from any principled position, offered no opposition either when the ML terrorists announced that they would never lay down their arms before negotiations begin, or when they demanded military withdrawal from a vast area of southeastern Colombia.[77] All of this was capped off with the ridiculous demand that the 200 odd military who are in the hands of the terrorists be "exchanged" for the almost 500 terrorists who are in government prisons. Because it is probably difficult to believe that any government would surrender to a terrorist organization to this extent *before* "peace negotiations" begin, it would appear worthwhile to catalog a portion of these terrorists' continuing demonstration of contempt for the PG.

Colombian Terrorists Provocative Actions

Only the highlight can be touched upon here, but it appears appropriate to sketch a few FARC-ELN terrorist actions since Mr. Pastrana assumed the presidency on 7 August.

06 August 1998: The terrorist attack on the detachment in Miraflores has been described by the LANS translation of the Inspector General's Report (Spcl 6.5 and Spcl 6.7 above), an attack on this company-sized post by 1000 terrorists according to survivors. On 4 August it was reported that the terrorists were reported as saying they had "50 hours" to take the base, that is, it had to be taken by the eve of Pastrana's inauguration. The taunt here is blatant.

07 August 1998: Inauguration day itself was celebrated with terrorist activities in various departments. The terrorists call them "attacks"; they are simple terrorist acts such as the car bomb with 100 kg of dynamite in Medellín. The day's death toll in various parts of the country was reported the next day as 29. While incoming Pres. Pastrana, complete with neckchain, was toasting outgoing Pres. Samper (AFP wirephoto 7 August 1998), Tirofijo and Jorge Briceño (aka Mono Jojoy) were directing their 1200 terrorists in mopping up Miraflores.

08 August 1998: By this day a continuing terrorist attack in Uribe had killed 24 (EFE 9 Aug). ELN terrorists kidnap four in Antioquia (AFP 9 August).

10 August 1998: Raul Reyes, one of seven FARC chiefs, taunted the government again with "We should all know that peace is going to be achieved in the midst of war" (*El País* (Madrid)).

14-16 August 1998: Continuous attacks in the Antioquia-Choco zone.

17 August 1998: Pastrana is constrained to suspend his birthday celebration at the seaside resort of Cartagena de Indias when a number of military are murdered (AFP 17 August). At least three campesinos are kidnapped in the northeast (EFE 17 August). In a "not-to-worry" press conference Pastrana's Minister of Defense, Lloreda, says that, in spite of the violent attitude of the terrorists, the government will maintain its "will toward dialog" (AFP 19 August).

19 Aug 98: Since early August the ELN terrorists have kidnapped seven mayors in Antioquia, an action which can only de interpreted as a deliberate disregard of the "accord" this group signed on 15 July in Germany "to humanize the conflict" (AFP 19 August). On this same day the ELN terrorists continued their murders in Norte de Santander.

This is being prepared in latter October 1998. The FARC and ELN terrorism, of which a few examples are given above, has continued to the present time, but it would not appear necessary to continue this dreary recital. Instead, it will be concluded with a report by the LANS correspondent in Medellín of an unusually heinous terrorist action which the ELN recently perpetrated in Machuca.

THE ELN CAUSES A TERRIBLE TRAGEDY

LANS CORRESPONDENT
MEDELLÍN
COLOMBIA

At 00:30 on 18 October the Marxist ELN blew up an oil pipeline in Antioquia, a central department of Colombia.[78] A few hundred meters away, the inhabitants of Machuca, a small gold-mining hamlet, were startled out of their sleep by the sound of the blast. The light crude flowed into a stream that bordered the town and the highly combustible fumes invaded the narrow streets and the wooden huts. A few minutes later, all was in flames. Hundreds were burned, and, within seven days, the death toll had risen to 60 innocent civilians, more than one third of whom were children. By press time the toll had risen to 70.

In an effort to shift the blame for this tragedy, ELN leaders agreed to accept responsibility for blowing up the pipeline but to accuse the Colombian Army of setting the fire. Unfortunately for these terrorists, they had come to this agreement over the radio in a series of transmissions which were monitored and then broadcast by Army Intelligence.[79] This planned terrorist DO was patently fabricated on the face of it.

As the Armed Forces commander, General Tapias, was quick to point out, the closest Army units were hours away from the scene, the nearest base 17 km removed, and could not possibly have "slipped in" behind the terrorists and set fire to the crude. In reality, Army troops arrived at the site in helicopters at dawn with a medical team to evacuate these victims of continuing terrorist violence. LANS has learned the way in which this fire was probably started from a former Colombian oil company executive.

The source informed LANS that there is often a time lapse between an explosion such as that set by the ELN and the ignition of the resulting fumes. These are ignited by hot pieces of metal once a flammable mixture of fumes and air has been reached. The fumes can then ignite the liquid which was flowing downstream on the water. These fumes could also have been ignited by candles or other open flames—cooking is done on wood or coal fires in a poor village like Machuca. The troops' humane behavior has been corroborated by the surviving inhabitants of Machuca.

That events could not have occurred as this terrorist DO seeks to maintain is borne out by the facts of the case. But this has rendered this DO no less supportable by the HL, the crowd of HR NGOs which follow the HL lead and, perhaps most importantly, by the *idiotas útiles* (Useful Idiots). This in spite of further terrorist behavior with which the ELN followed up this outrage during the next week, setting up a road block, kidnapping a half dozen people and attacking an Attorney General's investigating unit. In the last incident these terrorists kidnapped four members of the unit, although 16 succeeded in escaping.

The setting for all this terrorist activity was an ongoing strike by government employees which had been called by the Marxist labor unions. The strike was supposed to be a protest against the government's attempt to control runaway expenses by limiting pay raises; its real objective was a test of the government's will by the powerful unions. By 20 October the government had held its ground, and the strike, which had not paralyzed the country, appeared to be running out of steam. Non-union employees, with Army protection, were successfully operating the refineries. It is apparently not known how importantly the Machuca tragedy was related to this general strike, but the question arises because of the Oil Workers Union (USO). This union has been an important player in the strike, and this USO has long been thought to have an intimate connection with the ELN. In any event, these linkages are hardly to be ignored.

Nor is the murder by an unidentified hit-man of a union official. Union officials immediately and vociferously blamed the Government, the Army and the "paramilitaries," and the obliging press coverage of the ensuing protests overshadowed Machuca. A question surely arises, however:

Are the paras really to blame, or did the ELN and the ML union leaders, sorely in need of a distraction and a new grievance against the government, produce their own "necessary" martyr? This question should be asked, but asking it inside Colombia could be hazardous to one's health.

During all this hubbub Colombia had an important visitor, Mrs. Mary Robinson, the UN High Commissioner for HR.[80] LANS learned just last week that the press had seriously misquoted Ms. Almudena Mazarrasa, Mrs. Robinson's Colombia representative, and failed to quote certain strongly-worded statements from them both. The press had the lady asking that the heavily infiltrated Civilian Courts try military personnel. In reality, Robinson made some strong statements on the Machuca atrocity that the press simply ignored. It has further been learned that Mrs. Robinson's findings in Colombia convinced her that things were not as simple as she had been led to believe by the HR NGOs: It was not a simplistic case of a Brutal Army versus Guerrilla Freedom Fighters.

Ms. Mazarrasa is a Spanish diplomat who was sent to head the office that the UN set up to monitor HR in Colombia. The MLs wanted a *Relator*, which is viewed internationally as a sanction. Two years ago, the Colombian government obtained a change in the office which now has a mandate to study violence, not just from "government agents" but also from illegal armed groups. It turns out that, unlike many of those in such HR organizations, Ms. Mazarrasa shows no ML leanings. Various ML HR NGOs, these including American Lawyers for HR and a long list of Colombian NGOs, have tried to manipulate her and failed to do so. The result was an effort to remove her last March, but the Spanish Government, which finances her operations, stood firm, and she has remained in her job.

There is a footnote to the demand for an "inquiry" on Machuca. As Gen. Tapias pointed out, the evidence of ELN guilt for the holocaust is overwhelming. The only result of such an "inquiry" would be a delay of the punishment of these ML terrorists for this outrage.

COLOMBIAN TERRORISTS CONTINUE SEEKING "PEACE"
(WKLY 6.18, 5 NOVEMBER 1998)

> "There were guerrillas everywhere.
> They came out of the underbrush, fired and hid like rats."
> — *Colombian soldier after driving the FARC terrorists out of Mitú.*

LANS had scarcely completed Spcl 6.12 above, "Pastrana's 'Peace Process,'" before what some described as the "next crop of bloody fruits of the process" was reaped. For, on Halloween 1000 FARC terrorists arrived at Mitú and destroyed that town. (See also, pp. 343ft, this chapter). Before going into more detail on this operation, a word on the geography of the situation is in order.

Vaupes Department is one of the easternmost departments of Colombia, it abutting on Brazil to its east, Guainía Department to its northeast, Guaviare Department to its north, Caquetá Department to its southwest and Amazonas Department to its south. It is basically a jungle department in the Amazon Basin with few to no land communication routes. The eastern protuberance of the department into Brazil is primarily defined by the Vaupes River. On this river and about 40 km., as the crow flies, west of the Brazilian border is the departmental capital of Mitú. Operational Navigational Chart (ONC) L-26 shows that Mitú has a 4900-foot dirt strip at an elevation of 680 feet on the right bank of the river.

Various rivers define the Guaviare-Vaupes border. Slightly over 300 km to the northwest of Mitú, in Guaviare on the Guaviare River is San José del Guaviare which has been encountered before in these reports and which will be encountered again here. Also to be encountered again here is Villavicencio which is 210 km to the northwest of San José in Meta Department.

Mitú

The police headquarters for Vaupes Department was located at the departmental capital of Mitú. There were 120 police assigned there, the unit commanded by Colonel Herlindo Mendieta. All told, there were 5 officers, 2 non-commissioned officers, 77 patrolmen, 6 agents and 30 auxiliaries.

The Terrorist Operation

For an understanding of the terrorist operation it is necessary to answer the following questions. (1) What was the objective of the operation? (2) Why did it take place when it did? (3) How many terrorists and terrorists units were involved? (4) Who commanded the operation? (5) How was the advance on Mitú made? (6) When was it made? (7) When did the "attack" begin? (8) Of what did the "attack" consist? As is frequently the case, of course, the first information coming in from an isolated site such as this one was garbled and generally unreliable. In this case it was rendered even more so by the early terr destruction of the communications towers. It does appear that the information should be reasonably reliable by this time. The objective of the attack (1) and the timing (2) will be discussed last.

Terrorist Numbers. The "attack" began on Sunday morning, 1 November. One early report had the terrorist numbers as low as 200, but this was quickly increased to 700. When the affair was over the number had grown to 1000 which will be taken as correct. The terrorist units were Fronts VII, XLIV, LI, LIII and LV, perhaps reinforced with additional personnel.

Terrorist Commander. It originally appeared that Jorge Suárez Briceño (aka Mono Jojoy) was the top boss of the operation. It will be recalled that Suárez is one of the bosses in the area (cf. Wkly 5.2 above); he was quoted early here as refusing to allow the evacuation of the wounded. Since he has been associated with the FARC Southern Bloc, it seems reasonable to suppose that he was in charge. However, according to the Red Cross chief for the department, Tormbaum, who got into Mitú on 1 November, the chief of the operation was Henry Castellanos (aka Romaña). This appears unlikely in that elsewhere Castellanos is identified as the chief of Front LIII. He may be, and he may also have been in command of the "attack." However, he had other units under him if so, this based on the fact that 1000 is much too large for one front. Therefore, in the absence of other data, it still appears that Suárez was the overall boss of the operation.

Terrorist Advance. The terrorists arrived at Mitú by the Vaupes River route. They came either downstream from inside the department or upstream from the Brazilian border area. There appears little doubt that they arrived from the south as may be assumed from the Brazilian situation which developed and which will be touched upon below. The military destroyed 17 of their launches on retaking the area, but this was probably a relatively small percentage of them.

Arrival and Attack. The terrorists arrived in Mitú around midnight on Halloween. Moving this many people in on vessels of assuredly limited capacity would have taken long enough so that "around" is precise enough. The attack has been described as beginning at dawn and beginning at 05:00.

Attack Method. The terrorists apparently surrounded the small town and hence the police garrison and used homemade mortars—as described in Spcl 6.4 above, cutoff gas cylinders—fragmentation grenades and machine guns to reduce most of the town to rubble. Amongst the rubble was the hospital, the high school, the grammar school, city hall and so on. The press takes a perverse delight in reporting the number of dead and wounded among the police and, later, the military. Of more intrinsic interest are the number of such personnel that the terrorists kidnapped and carried off with them in their retreat. However many it proves to be, it will be added to the almost 300 already in their hands which the Colombian Government has made no attempt to rescue.

Terrorist Objective and Timing. The terrorists have stated publicly that they made the attack in order to gather more hostages for their "exchange" of these for their imprisoned comrades. If this is a reason, it is probably not the principal reason. The principal reason is almost certainly one further taunt against the Colombian Government, one further demonstration to their supporters at home and abroad that this country is powerless before them. Such motivation is quite rational and has been proven out by the success of the GDO (Wkly 6.10, Chapter 6 below); it will apparently lead to the same sort of terrorist "victory through peace" that has been enjoyed by the CA terrorists. The fact that this operation was launched immediately before the PG began withdrawing and effectively surrendering to the terrorists vast areas of the southeastern portions of the nation is further substantiation for such a motivation.

The Government Reaction

The FAC occupy a most uncomfortable position: They have the responsibility for protecting the nation from these ML terrorists, but they do not have the authority to do so. LANS has described how this intolerable situation has been progressively worsening for many years. Small wonder, for example, that the number of general officers on active duty has been declining of recent years. Even in the face of the Mitú outrage the PG has huffed and puffed a bit, but the Colombian president made the incredible statement that "The Peace is not threatened."

The High Commissioner for Peace, Richard G. Ricardo, behaved in much the same way in his letter to Marulanda (aka Tirofijo), a letter dated the day the latter's terrorists were moving on Mitú. Marulanda, with his customary contempt for reality, had been accusing the military high command of trying to sabotage the "peace process." And so Ricardo wrote him what reads like a pleading letter (*El Tiempo* (Bogotá) 3 November 1998) enumerating all the terrorist demands to which the government was surrendering before "negotiations" even began. Mr. Ricardo even "warned" the world's oldest active terrorist against "the risks of off hand remarks."

The Military Does Its Job—Again

The ML terrs occupied Mitú for some 72 hours because weather and, particularly, fuel problems seriously complicated the delivery and support of ground personnel. Such deliveries originated largely from San José del Guaviare and Villavicencio. There is a 6500-foot strip, altitude 520 feet, at San José. LANS' information has the operations out of Villavicencio originating at Apiay Air Base. (On the ONC L-26 chart this base appears as Gómez Niño AB.)

On Sunday, 1 November, the FAC flew a few preliminary sorties with Black Hawks,[81] OV-10s,[82] MI-17s,[83] and a "mystery" aircraft (*avión fantasma*).[84] But fuel was the problem, and the Colombians asked the Brazilians for permission to land at their Yauarete Base for refueling. The Brazilians threw up their hands with an "impossible," and four hours later the Colombians began landing at the Brazilian strip, Querari. Happily, the Colombians were allowed to do this for humanitarian reasons—evacuating wounded and the like. Before leaving the not overly cooperative Brazilians, the question as to the origin of the river attack on Mitú might be raised again. Would the Brazilians really interdict ML terrorist operations out of their territory?

By Tuesday, 3 November, 400 effectives of Anti Terrorist MB III had been assembled some 20 kms. from Mitú. At 17:00 that day the Army Commander, General Jorge Enrique Mora, from the Joaquín París Battalion headquarters in San José, gave the order for the advance on Mitú. As is routinely the case with these terrorists when facing the military, face them they did not. Divided into nine-man squads for the night attack that followed and assisted by aircraft dropping flares from a reported 3000 feet, the troops moved into the town. By 01:00 on 4 November Mitú had been cleared of terrorists, block by block and house by house.

Would the government withdrawal now proceed as if nothing untoward had happened? Would this latest blood letting by the ML terrorists of FARC be rewarded by even more advantageous "peace" terms?

An Expert Opinion

The maximum operating radius of the OV-10 and Black Hawk is about 300 km. A Colombian expert on these terrorists was consulted by LANS; he informed us that these range considerations probably led FARC to believe that they were not vulnerable to air attack. Therefore, they operated under the assumption that the relief force would be forced to use the rivers in a slow operation. This expert feels that, relying on this scenario, the terrorists probably established observation posts and ambushes along the river. The government has now imposed a curfew on Vaupes, Guainía and Guaviare Departments, and he points out that, since the jungle affords little food, it will be interesting to see what these terrorists will do if access to the river is denied to them.

THE COLOMBIAN THREE-RING CIRCUS CONTINUES
(SPCL 6.15, 1 DECEMBER 1998)

Andrés Pastrana initiated "negotiations" with the ML terrorists after he had won the Colombian presidential race but before he has assumed the office on 7 August 1998 (Spcl 6.12 above). These negotiations have been described as a "peace process" and as a "three-ring circus," support for the former description having eroded steadily since the performance began last July. However much the citizens of Colombia may desire "peace" with the terrorists of FARC and the ELN, the behavior of these narcotrafficking kidnappers and murderers, however strong their foreign support, may be finally convincing an exhausted Colombian populace that "peace" with them is impossible.

President Pastrana has bent over backward to meet the most unreasonable demands of the terrorists, and the terrorists themselves have continued and even augmented their depredations, the FARC operation against the isolated police post at Mitú having been discussed in Wkly 6.18 above, the murderous ELN attack on the innocents of Machuca a part of Spcl. 6.12 above on which more below. It has been conjectured that these are hardly the actions of subversive groups desiring peace but those of such groups bent on showing their strength. Terrorist refusal to even enter into meaningful negotiations would appear to indicate the same thing.

Territorial Surrender Without Quid Pro Quo

Fresh from "smoking a Cuban cigar" with FARC boss Tirofijo (alias) (EFE 11 July 1998),[85] Pastrana allegedly "accepted" (AFP 12 July 1998)—with what authority it would be difficult to say—the withdrawal of Colombian military and police forces from five municipalities[86] totaling 43,000 km² in the Departments of Meta and Caquetá. The five municipalities are San Vicente,[87] Macarena,[88] Vistahermosa,[89] Uribe[90] and Mesetas.[91] About two months later (AFP 9 September 1998) the Colombian president denied having promised military withdrawal to the terrorists, albeit, this may be hair splitting as will be seen.

Although LANS does not yet have the exact boundaries of this area, twice the size of El Salvador, it appears to be about the same area which was abandoned for the terrorists in 1997 (pp.209ff,

YRBK98). La Uribe (6000 km²), Meta Department, is worthy of remark as having been the location of the FARC Secretariat until driven out by the military in 1990. Also important in the group is San Vicente, Caquetá, which Defense Minister Gilberto Echeverry says correctly is the world's major coca zone. Such of course was pointed out in the LANS descriptions of the earlier debacle.

Having publicly stated in early September that he had not "promised" before assuming office to denude the five municipalities of troops and police, Mr. Pastrana's Minister of Defense, Rodrigo Lloreda, announced on 15 October that this was precisely what was being done. That day Mr. Lloreda revealed that "the withdrawal from the five municipalities is now in progress" (AFP 16 October 1998). He went on to point out that the evacuation will be complete by 7 November when the region will be "in the hands of the local authorities."

What of the Citizens?

Realistically speaking, this means that this vast territory, inhabited by 92,000 Colombian citizens, will be in the hands of the terrorists. The LANS correspondent in Bogotá accurately described this as "a prime concession without any reciprocity" (Wkly 6.15 above). He went on to point out, "The government is going to turn over territories with obvious violation of the rights of their inhabitants who will be left without that protection which the state owes them." The behavior of these ML terrorists toward such hapless civilians is hardly described by the public relations releases which the terrorists provide the media and which the media dutifully reports as "news."

That such is no exaggeration was made quite clear by the FARC terrorists themselves on 6 November when they announced to the inhabitants of the "demilitarized zone" a catalog of "rules of conduct" (EFE 8 November 1998). In accordance with that "code," the terrorists will charge taxes on commercial operations, restrict nocturnal vehicular traffic, impose a schedule for cattle slaughter, prohibit prostitution[92] and fine gossip and street fights. Although not reported, they will doubtless join their ML brethren of other nationalities in the "liberation" of desirable properties. Earlier this year, then Pres. Samper suggested the study of surrendering the local budget to the ELN terrorists (AFP 17 January 1998). Pres. Pastrana appears to have "advanced" far beyond this concept.

As this unnecessary FARC "conquest" of the zone was being implemented, "many" of the legitimate residents there (EFE 8 November 1998) were leaving or had left the zone, clearly willing to sacrifice whatever they had to escape the terrorists. And yet, according to Pres. Pastrana, all would be well. He declared that the mayors in the area would be in charge and that unarmed police would deal with minor matters, the terrorists apparently not considering this face-saving attempt worthy of even their contempt.

And the results need not be predicted in detail, although it does seem worthy of remark that such governmental failures are hailed as "peace efforts." There is more to this situation than this, however, there is the unconstitutional behavior of the Colombian chief executive and the behavior of apparently supportive foreign governments.

Is President Pastrana's Behavior Illegal?

The case has been made in Chapter 5, YRBK98, that the Esquipulas II Accords, the basis for "peace" in Central America are unconstitutional. A portion of the introduction to these reports is perhaps worthy of recall:

> ...a scrutiny finds these accords to be unconstitutional and hence illegal and outside the law. While "peace" may be a desirable objective, obtaining it through violation of the law—the only protection of liberty and individual rights—can in no way be so characterized.

In that same press conference, Mr. Lloreda revealed the same sort of extra legal attitude on the part of Pres. Pastrana when the Defense Minister declared that the president had "awarded" the status of a "belligerent political force" to the narcoterrorists of FARC. These are the people whose immense incomes—doubled during the term of office of Pres. Samper—are obtained largely from narcotrafficking but also from kidnapping and extortion of various kinds, people whose principal method of operation is murder. Which is perhaps an appropriate point at which to remark on the inscrutable behavior of the US ambassador.

Curtis Kamman is the US ambassador in Bogotá, the successor to a curious one who appeared quite ready to accept any anti-military disinformation furnished by the so-called HR organizations. In the latter part of November Mr. Kamman captured at least the attention of EFE (20 November 1998) when he delivered himself of a statement to the effect that he was "confident" that the demilitarized zone will not be a "drug corridor." Since no one will remember his statement when the opposite occurs, perhaps this was of some therapeutic benefit for the ambassador.

In leaving the question of illegality a remark of Pastrana's in latter November is perhaps worth remarking. In essence, Mr. Pastrana pointed out that peace is not compatible with narcotrafficking (EFE 25 November 1998). A LANS contact in Florencia, who refused to be identified, commented on this with the question: "How can this 'peace' be anything but compatible with narcotrafficking when he is making it with the hemisphere's most active group of totally unreformed narcotraffickers?"

Foreign Support for the Pastrana "Peace"

Fidel Castro has been demonstrated in these reports to be the boss of a healthy HL of which FARC and ELN[93] are important adjuncts. Quite remarkably, Mr. Pastrana has invited Castro's ML Cuban dictatorship to form part of the "Friends of Colombia" group which is to "help" bring about this "peace" with the terrorists. Even more interesting, however, is Mr. Pastrana's expressed admiration for the words of advice given to him by Castro (AFP 4 November 1998).

"As one day President Castro recommended to me," Pastrana told the Venezuelans, "and I want to remember it here: for peace one must have patience, much patience." That Mr. Pastrana has never heard of the terrorist Castro's position in the hemisphere could be inferred from this statement. Since Fidel is on the side of FARC and the ELN, this is clearly a formula for terrorist victory, not "peace." This "support" cannot of course be surpassed, but that given by the VIII Iberian American Summit (IAS) is worthy of remark and not unrelated to the Cuban dictator.

The IAS has been described, for example by *El Nacional* (Caracas) as Spain's answer to the client-state collections of its European associates. This client state collection has the dubious distinction of being almost alone in having the Cuban ML dictator, Fidel Castro, among its chieftains. Last year Castro performed at VII IAS in Chile (pp.259ff, YRBK98), this year at VIII IAS in Oporto, Portugal on 18 and 19 October. If, indeed, one can tell the value a man places on himself by the length of his speeches, Castro ranks himself stratospherically. As Antonio Martínez remarked (EFE 20 October 1998), "Fidel Castro set back the closing of VIII IAS by more than three hours, hogging with his proverbial oral incontinence the signing of the Declaration of Oporto..."

Various authors have remarked that the issuance of "declarations" are the only function of the plethora of such gatherings. Mr. Pastrana asked his fellow heads of state at Oporto for "unconditional support" in his "peace process." Arriving in Oporto for the festivities on 17 October he had stated that this was to be the "Summit of Peace." At least in verbiage, it was all of that. In the Peru-Ecuador case, the catch phrase appears to have been appropriate; in the case of Colombia, it may have been a somewhat premature celebration, albeit, not of any real concern to the participants.

Through November 1998 the talk about government-terrorist talking continued, but the only subject which surfaced was that of getting those last 130 Colombian troops out of the "demilitarized zone," leaving the FARC terrorists free to solidify their control of the region, the natives to flee if they can. And, all the while, the tempo of the murderous attacks by both of the terror groups continues as if neither one has any interest in "peace," particularly a drug-free peace. As they probably do not have. While it cannot of course be said with certainty, the HL "victory through peace" which has been extensively discussed in these reports may be on the verge of fruition.

Finally, a follow-up to the LANS Medellín correspondent's report on "The ELN Causes a Terrible Tragedy" which appeared in Spcl 6.12 above.

Murder at Machuca

At 0300 on 18 October the ELN blew an oil pipeline in Antioquia Department only some few hundred meters from the village of Machuca. By press time the dead men, women and children in the village had reached 70. The ELN pleaded "innocent," as always trying to blame the military. The point of interest now is that they have since withdrawn their guilty plea, this probably indicating that their innocence claims were not supportable under the best of DOs and the deed itself—the death toll had risen to 73 by latter November—was too much even for their jaded supporters.

In the latter part of November they were reported (EFE 25 November 1998) as "indemnifying the families of the 73 dead" with $65,000 (100 million pesos), less than $1000 per killing. It is quite difficult to believe that, with their many years of pipeline blowing experience, they had no idea of the possibility of this disaster.

E. Death of a Terrorist Cleric

THE DEATH OF A TERRORIST CLERIC
(WKLY 5.20, 28 MAY 1998)

Manuel Pérez (aka Poliarco) (62) was a Spanish cleric. His claim to fame, however, was that he was a ML terrorist. He was, *a priori*, a LibTheo cleric, a living example of the "Marxization of Christianity" which, according to Rev. Dr. Poradowsky (pp.193ff,YRBK97), is what LibTheo represents. But he was considerably more. For, as a terrorist, he was guilty of all the crimes the flesh is heir to: murder, kidnapping, extortion, theft, narcotrafficking and the rest. And, if "pollution" be added to the contemporary litany of mortal sins, his spreading of millions of barrels of oil over the Colombian countryside qualifies him here also.

In 1968 Pérez and Alonso Ojeda put together the EPL.[94] Pérez moved to the ELN in the early 1980s, this fact eminently worthy of yet another aside.

"Students" of terrorism and the terrorists themselves delight in assigning philosophical labels to the different terror groups. The former enjoy doing it because it provides them a simple method of classification, allegedly "philosophical," of these groups for ease of discussion and study. The latter enjoy it because it sets them apart from the other groups with which, like the Nazis and the Communists, their "turf battle" is in progress. Except perhaps for some of the innocents who have been recruited (drafted) into the terrorist ranks, this "philosophy" argument is meaningless. The EPL has long been described as "Maoist," the ELN as "Guevarist." The meaninglessness of this was once again demonstrated when Poliarco migrated from the former to the latter following the death of another famous terrorist cleric, Camilo Torres Restrepo.

He migrated into what has been called the "clerics' terror group," the ELN having been reported (AFP, 24 October 1989) with 20 clerics in its command structure. By later 1989 Pérez was claiming (AFP, 24 October 1989) 20 years with the ELN. By April 1998 Poliarco was being reported dead, the report of course garbled by the terrorists for reasons which, though speculative, appear obvious.

First, a pair of ELN terrorists, Francisco Galán and Felipe Torres, imprisoned in Itagüí, reported that Pérez had died on 14 February 1998 of hepatitis in the mountains of northeast Colombia. The ELN "Central Command" confirmed what military intel would later demonstrate to be nonsense. His successor was allegedly Nicolás Rodríguez (aka Gabino), described as a "hard-liner," another conceit which is mistakenly taken as meaningful in some quarters.

But, as with the accounts of the terrorist's life, the account of his death was incorrect also as the II Division commander, General Mario Fernando Roa pointed out. He had died in Cuba which, as headquarters for the Hemispheric Left (HL) and, according to its own propaganda, one of the world's premier medical facilities, is demonstrably more appropriate for an ML terrorist chief.

Notes

1. The basis of the CA "peace process" is Esquipulas. LANS has pointed out (pp.268ff and pp.306ff,, YRBK98) the inconsistencies and unrealities in these accords which appear to be in violation of the Guatemalan Constitution (pp.268ff, YRBK98).
2. This was done by comparing the Farabundi intentions (pp.146ff, YRBK97), as determined from the documents on a Farabundi chief's cadaver, with the specific agreements in the Accords.
3. The cover of *SEMANA* (13-20 July 1998) was emblazoned with a picture of a smiling Pastrana, Serpa's winning opponent in the recent presidential race, posed with the oldest terrorist of them all, FARC boss Tirofijo (alias).
4. Earl E. T. Smith, *THE FOURTH FLOOR: An Account of the Castro Communist Revolution* (Random House, 1962. LCC: 638331).
5. It should be remarked that the West Range of the Andes forms the Pacific watershed while the Central and East Ranges form the Atlantic watershed. The Atlantic watershed may be conveniently divided into that which feeds the north coast of South America through the Magdalena River and that which feeds the eastern coast through the Orinoco Basin to the north and the Amazon Basin to the south. The Caquetá finds its way to the Amazon.
6. The Special Forces commander at Tres Esquinas showed the LANS Editor the route—much on river—which the terrs took from Patascoy. It is too "back woods" to explain here, but it penetrated Ecuadoran territory. While the Colombian military will not, understandably, discuss the subject, it would appear that Ecuadoran-Colombian cooperation in anti-narcoterrorism may leave something to be desired.
7. The LANS Editor spent 17 July 1998 at Tres Esquinas, accessible only by chopper from Florencia, gathering proof positive of this statement, but the important coca hamlets which Task Force South has pacified in the short three months of its existence are all that need be mentioned.
8. This is no vast conspiracy. It is clearly a continuing cooperation between those of like mind in the HL and HLS, these assisted by the always important *idiotas utiles* (useful idiots).
9. Doctor Miguel Posada S. is Director of the Sociopolitical Analysis Center in Bogotá, Colombia, and a syndicated columnist with the International Economic Press Agency.

10. These are those who have signed a "peace" treaty and allegedly become "ex" terrorists.
11. Cano has been encountered during the Las Delicias disaster (pp.209ff, YRBK98).
12. As specifically outlined in the Laws of War, the Geneva Convention and the Hague Accords.
13. "Legbreaker" mines, Salvadoran terrorists used "quita pies" or footblower mines. In both cases these are targeted on civilians.
14. Salvadoran Farabundi boss Shafik Handal sent his brother, Farid, to the US in 1980 seeking support. The Salvadoran Army published Farid's trip report in which the importance of WOLA and other HR groups to such ML subversion is emphasized.
15. She was prominent at the Zapatista encounter of 1996 (3YRBK97).
16. LANS has been informed by reliable intel sources that the US established a "slush fund" in Norway which that nation has used at State urging to promote the Central American "peace" process.
17. The apparent unconstitutionality of the Esquipulas II Accords has been discussed in these reports (pp.268ff, YRBK98).
18. Liberation Theology (LibTheo) is appropriately dubbed the "Marxization of Theology" by Rev. Dr. Poradowsky (pp.193ff, YRBK97).
19. NGO chief Alirio Uribe gained considerable publicity last fall by accusing XIII Brigade of producing a report linking various NGO personnel to the ELN. Then CO Gen. Euclides Sanchez stated that no such report had been produced, although there would have been nothing wrong with having done so.
20. LANS has given examples of AI using terrorist reports. Editor.
21. The FARC killing of military personnel is murder as surely as was its killing of political candidates last fall when it identified them as "military targets" [Spcl 4.13] if they did not withdraw from their races.
22. One of the most amusing examples of this occurred last summer. On 23 January 1989 a band of Argentinian ERP [Peoples Revolutionary Army] took over the barracks of the 3d Infantry near Buenos Aires in La Tablada. Last summer the CIDH [Inter American HR Commission] recommended an "independent" new judicial investigation in order to determine if the Army had "violated the HR" of the terrorists in taking the barracks back.
23. Plinio Apuleyo Mendoza, "¿Son santas las NGOs?," [*SEMANA*, Bogotá, No.815, 15-22 Dec 97].
24. Cf. *Jane's Infantry Weapons* (Nineteenth Edition, Edited by Ian V. Hogg, 1993-1994, ISBN: 071061067X).
25. The terrorists would later claim that their attack was a complete success in 15 minutes, whether true or false.
26. An *El Espectador* account gives "granada de mortero," but this may be incorrect unless they refer to the variety home-made from cut-off gas cylinders. If the approach terrain is as difficult as is described, it appears highly unlikely that "real" mortars were carried up.
27. The lady used the phrase "echarse atras" meaning "back down," but this appears to render her meaning.
28. Of course the division commander was probably a major general, the brigade commander a brigadier, but LANS does not have this information.
29. The immense importance of the CAPs to anti-terrorist operations is pointed up here. The reason why the HL and its sympathizers are so vehement in their opposition to the CAPs—designated "paramilitary" by them—is likewise obvious.
30. Briefly, assuming these all to be rifles, the Galil (Israel) is the 5.56mm modeled after the AK, the R-15 apparently the 5.56mm AR-15 (USA), the AK-47 the 7.62mm (various) and the G-3 the 7.62mm (Germany).

31. The word used here is *corregimiento* which is the region of authority of a *corregidor* (judge).
32. Read as 1 degree, 6 minutes, 53 seconds.
33. There is little, if any, question that, had legal self-defense forces been active in the area, this terrorist coup could have been prevented. This is not to say that it could not have been prevented as matters stood.
34. This term arises from *Région de Caguán y Caqueta* of what was once *la Comisaría de Caqueta* of 22,500 hectares (55,600 acres). This is largely to be found in Caqueta Department, now remembered to the north by San Vicente del Caguán, to the south by Cartagena del Caguán. Cf. Operational Navigational Chart (ONC) L-26.
35. Tres Esquinas is some 45 sm west of El Billar at the confluence of the Caquetá and Orteguaza Rivers.
36. News reports carry a running account of the recovery of bodies. For example, the 28 coffins in the burial ceremony in Larandia Base—a few miles south of Florencia—could be counted by anyone at all as could the 35 whose bodies were waiting to be identified (*El Tiempo* (Bogotá) 11 March 1998).
37. This may not be correct. If it is correct LANS has no record of its location, albeit, there are records of Santa Anas in Boyaca, Magdalena and Tolima Departments.
38. Leticia is in the far southeast corner of Amazonas Department, on the Amazon River at the intersection of the borders of Brazil, Colombia and Peru.
39. These FARC members are nothing more than common criminals who support their activities with every form of criminal activity, namely: murder, narcotrafficking, extortion, kidnapping and the whole gamut of criminal action. The use of the term, "guerrilla," for these people is itself a carefully crafted fraud.
40. Had this operation been in place immediately after the Patascoy affair, it is probable that the terrorist force could have been destroyed on its way to Ecuador. Miraflores is on the border of Guaviare and Vaupes Departments, some 350 kms. east northeast of Tres Esquinas.
41. These are the chemicals necessary to the transformation of the coca leaves into cocaine.
42. The first number (00) indicates the number of officers killed, the second (02) the number of non-commissioned officers and the third (09) the number of privates.
43. On the entry for 10 June this is given as Joaquín París Infantry Battalion No. 19.
44. Calamar is on Route 75 about 80 km due south of San José, 90 km as the crow flies northwest of Miraflores. Nota bene that Rte 75 is the only road across Guaviare, runs nowhere near Miraflores and is passable only in summer.
45. These are cylinders for shipment of gases from which the terrorists have cut the tops and which are then used as homemade mortars or mines. The Editor viewed a number of captured examples of these in Tres Esquinas.
46. This is given as granadas de mortero, literally, mortar grenades. These "mortar grenades" are probably the gas cylinders.
47. There are long run-on sentences throughout the report. These are repeated verbatim save for certain attempted additions of punctuation and what appear to be necessary changes in tense, the continually used present tense sometimes confusing. Editor.
48. This is given as "aerostatic" which should mean lighter-than-air, i.e., a balloon. Since a C-47 is not lighter than air, this is simply translated as "air."
49. There is a change here in the way date and time are written, 0100 04-AUG-98 being written as "0401:00AGO-98."
50. This reads "de las granadas de 40mm." These grenades are for the Multiple Grenade Launcher to be encountered in D, Spcl 6.7.

51. The word "asesinado" can mean either "assassinated" or "murdered." Since these narcoterrorists are no more than common criminals, "murdered" appears more appropriate. The first of the three numbers stands for the number of officers, the second for the number of non-commissioned officers (02), the third for the number of privates (09).
52. The rifle is manufactured by TAAS Israel Industries Ltd. The SAR differs from the AR in several particulars: Weight 3.75 kg (SAR), 3.95 kg (AR); Barrel 400mm (SAR), 535mm (AR); Length overall 915mm (SAR), 1050 mm (AR); Muzzle velocity 800 m/s (SAR), 850 m/s (AR); Rate of fire 750 rds/min (SAR), 650 rds/min (AR); Range 550m (SAR), 600m (AR).
53. The prime producer is Saco Defense, Inc. This was probably the infantry model with bipod—removed for extensive chopper installation (M60D)—either the M60 or M60E3.
54. This is given as Lanzagranadas Multiples Tipo MGL (Multiple Grenade Launcher). Presumably this fired the 40mm grenades listed below. This appears to be similar to the Italian GLF-90 but may not be.
55. This is given in the report as Soltan but apparently refers to one of the four types of 60mm mortars manufactured by Soltam Ltd. in Haifa. The 81mm mortar is also listed as Soltan.
56. "ataque con tiro curvo," literally, "an attack with curved shots." Basically "more curved than a rifle trajectory," i.e., mortars, howitzers, etc.
57. The phrase is "atacando en ordas." It is here assumed that "ondas" was intended.
58. In Spcl 6.4, "Colombian Joint Task Force South," the terrorists' river escape from Patascoy and into a disinterested Ecuador.
59. In this summer of 1998 Uruguayan President Julio María Sanguinetti expressed his shock and surprise that terrorist boss Castro was sponsoring terrorist activities in his "region" during the 1960s and 1970s. Since Sanguinetti cannot have been so encapsuled as to be unaware of this, some arcane political maneuver is apparently in process.
60. The Commonwealth of Independent States (CIS)/USSR continues to pay rent on the immense electronic espionage base at Lourdes, Cuba, and other concessions; it contracts for some rather dubious "trade" deals. Nevertheless, the more obvious subsidies and gifts appear to have dried up.
61. The intelligence organizations of the anti-ML nations have seriously underestimated the importance of these DOs, a conclusion at which one must arrive from the failure of the US Government, for example, to be aware of how Contra Drug was orchestrated.
62. In the famous disk that was found on ELN finances (*SEMANA*, 7 July 1992) there was a complete listing of "Other Extortions," these in addition to those in Arauca. The principle involved is simply that of taking everything the campesino has and find a label for the theft.
63. FARC is, and has been from the beginning, the "military arm" of the PCC. Therefore, that this may have been one more DO is an open possibility.
64. That "assassins" are "self defense forces" for narcotraffickers or other undesirables will be illustrated in the next section. The term "paramilitary" is in itself a DO which is promoted by the terrorists in an attempt to slander the military.
65. Vaupés Department is to the southeast of Guaviare Department, the former bordering on Brazil.
66. The UP was formed in 1986 by FARC as nothing more nor less than a front. It is an admittedly ML party.
67. In "The Truth About Chiapas" (Spcls 5.8 and 5.9, Chapter 6 below) Mary Ball

Martínez has described those Germans, doubtless the dupes of the HL and HLS, who have contributed substantial sums to just such organizations.
68. Belisario Betancur Cuartas was elected president of Colombia on the Conservative Party ticket in 1982, to be succeeded by Virgilio Barca of the Liberal Party in 1986.
69. Ernesto Samper Pizarro was elected Colombian president in 1994. During his term of office a large FARC (Colombian Revolutionary Armed Forces) force overran a small military outpost at Las Delicias. Samper allowed the terrorists a substantial propaganda victory by ransoming the soldiers under terrorist terms (pp.209ff, YRBK98).
70. General Harold Bedoya, commander in chief of Colombian Armed Forces, apparently unable to agree to the treatment of the terrorists by the Samper Government, retired in the summer of 1997 after the military hostages had been returned.
71. Tirofijo (Deadeye) is apparently the world's oldest ML (Marxist Leninist) terrorist, he having founded FARC in 1957.
72. On coming to power in 1982, Betancur offered the "white flag" of truce to Colombian terrorism. As Colombian journalist Guillermo Zalamea remarked in latter 1985, "the famous peace of Betancur ... has converted [the nation] into an urban and rural armed camp" (p.161, YRBK97).
73. The Unión Patriotica (UP) is a marxist party formed in 1985. For a brief treatment of the M-19 attack on the Colombian Supreme Court cf. pp.173ff (YRBK97).
74. As Dr. Posada, LANS correspondent in Bogotá has explained (Wkly 6.5), certain of the AUCs have become involved with the drug lords, others have been hired by farmers, ranchers and small business men to protect them from the ML terrs.
75. Castaño's father was a run-of-the-mill farmer who was murdered by the terrs. The Castaño brothers then dedicated their lives to the destruction of these MLs. They needed money, and they went into narcotrafficking for a while. Castaño is often accused of still being in drugs, but there is no proof of this. Some bands of Paras— there is no single para organization — in central Meta are apparently involved in the trade. Castaño has his own group and is recognized as the head of a loose confederation.
76. The HL "Victory Through Peace" in Central America is perhaps most broadly discussed in Chapter 4 of YRBK98 where the Esquipulas II Accords are analyzed. The Salvadoran Chapultepec Accords and their coincidence with Farabundi objectives are discusssed in Chapter 3 of YRBK97.
77. The Samper Government withdrew from a vast area in southeast Colombia and allowed the terrs the tremendous propaganda victory which followed in the ransoming of military personnel overrun at Las Delicias as described (pp.209ff, YRBK98). The PG is now doing the same thing, and the withdrawal of Police and Military forces from the five municipios is expected to be completed by the end of the first week in November.
78. For decades the terrs of the ELN have been creating the worst "pollution" anywhere in the world by their destruction with explosives of the Colombian pipelines, spreading millions of barrels of crude over the countryside and into the river system. That they blew the pipeline which led to the Machuca destruction they have admitted.
79. The Colombian Army and Police routinely monitor guerrilla communications which are usually radio conversations in the clear. This surveillance was carried out by the Technical Intelligence (TECHINT) Battalion of the XX Brigade. As has been recorded in these reports, XX Brigade was renamed the Military Intelligence Center.
80. Mrs. Robinson, shortly after she finished her term as President of the Irish Republic, was named UN High Commissioner for HR in later 1997.
81. The Sikorsky UH-60A Black Hawk helicopter first flew in October 1974. It was

designed to carry 11 fully armed troops plus a crew of three, but it has performed heavier duty than this more often than not.

82. The Rockwell OV-10 Bronco is a two-seat, multi-purpose counter-insurgency aircraft first flown in 1965. Various models have been developed, the initial production version the OV-10A.

83. This Russian chopper is basically an updated version of the MI-8 (NATO: Hip-H).

84. This is the name given by the Colombian press to an OV-10 or an AC-47 when operated at night. Since the OV-10 is specified in the sam report, here it apparently refers to the AC-47.

85. That the communications media routinely refers to Marulanda (aka Tirofijo) as "the legendary guerrilla"—clearly a hallmark of PC (political correctness)—speaks eloquently of the media.

86. Save for Macarena (Bartholomew), LANS has no maps of large enough scale to show the municipalities in the region. Four of the five can more or less be defined by villages which appear on the political map available in Bogotá. For the fifth we are indebted to the Bentsen Latin American Collection at the University of Texas, Austin.

87. San Vicente is in Caquetá Department about 65 km Southwest by South of Villavicencio.

88. Macarena is in Meta Department about 54 km South of Villavicencio. According to ONC (Operational Navigational Chart) L-26, there is a 3100-foot strip (La Macarena) to the North of the village.

89. Vistahermosa is in Meta Department about 30 km South of Villavicencio.

90. Uribe is in Meta Department about 32 km Southwest by South of Villavicencio.

91. Mesetas is in Meta Department North by Northwest of Vistahermosa and to the Northeast of Uribe.

92. Although the coercion of female "comrades" and statutory rape by the chiefs will doubtless continue as usual.

93. The ML terr cleric and longtime head of the ELN, Manuel Pérez, returned to his Cuban foster home to die earlier this year (Wkly 5.20).

94. An AFP dispatch of 8 April 1998 has him entering ELN in 1968, but this is simply incorrect, whatever the reason.

6

The Hemispheric Left Support

Introduction

The Hemispheric Left Support (HLS) is made of those allegedly "non-political" individuals and organizations who/which, wittingly or unwittingly, (a) furnish moral and material support to the Hemispheric Left (HL), (b) fabricate disinformation or exaggerate information in support of the Marxist Leninists (M)L of the HL and (c) either fabricate or exaggerate accounts of "human rights" violations (HRV) by Latin American governments, their police and their armies.

Liberation Theology

Liberation Theology (LibTheo) clerics are present in indeterminate numbers between the Rio Grande and Tierra del Fuego and continue to make substantial contributions to HL successes. Although operating quite openly, Political Correctness (PC) has surrounded these ML wolves in clerical sheep's clothing with an aura of invisibility which much of the press has been unable or unwilling to penetrate. LibTheo and LibTheo clerics have been discussed (pp.193ff, YRBK97), a discussion which is worthy of repetition. Here, however, only the reality of LibTheo and defining remarks by certain of its devotees must suffice.

The Reverend Doctor Miguel Poradowsky[1] defines LibTheo as the four-stage "marxization of Christianity," the phases being (1) Saduceeism, (2) horizontal Christianity, (3) demythologized Christianity and (4) atheistic Christianity. Although the work of the Reverend Doctor Malachi Martin[2] is not as focused on the theological background of LibTheo as is that of Poradowsky, it provides a great deal of valuable, perhaps more general, information on the subject.

Given the appropriate environment, these LibTheo clerics are astonishingly straightforward in their utterances. For example, on Chilean television the Nicaraguan marxist cleric Ernesto Cardinal stated that "In order to be a good Christian it is primarily necessary to be a Marxist-Leninist." Martin quotes a consequential LibTheo cleric as maintaining that "We Christian-Marxists will have to fight side-by-side in Central America (CA) with the Marxists who do not believe in God, in order to form a new socialist society..."[3] And this comment on LibTheo may be realistically concluded with:

> Throughout Latin America (LA), but especially in Nicaragua, El Salvador, Guatemala, Chile, and Peru, ... (LibTheo clerics) were laboring to spread the new Theology of Liberation, coaching high school and college students in Marxist tactics, fomenting Base Communities of *la iglesia popular*, joining guerrilla bands as fighters.[4]

Disinformation Operations (DOs)

LANS has frequently made the point that the HL has won not a single one of those "liberation wars" which its terrorists have fought in various LA nations.[5] The two ultimate HL victories were in Cuba (1959) and Nicaragua (1979). In both instances these were the direct result of DOs which led apparently "well-meaning" foreign nations, principally the US, to create a power vacuum in the country in question which was, of course, filled by the men with the guns. Although already remarked (4YRBK97), it appears worthwhile to illustrate this with Castro.

Cuba. Herbert Lionel Matthews (b. 1900), the admirer of Mussolini's Abyssinian adventure and the Kremlin's International Brigades in Spain,[6] joined the *New York Times* (NYT) in 1922. His "Robin-Hooding of Castro" formed an important part of the DO which brought Fidel Ruz Castro to his ML caudillo throne in Cuba, US ambassador to Cuba Earl E. T. Smith describing this quite succinctly with:

> Three front-page articles in the NYT in early 1957 written by the editorialist Herbert Matthews, served to inflate Castro to world stature and world recognition. Until that time, Castro had been just another bandit in the Oriente Mountains of Cuba, with a handful of followers who had terrorized the campesinos, that is the peasants throughout the countryside.[7]

Several important DOs were treated (pp.191ff, YRBK97), those in addition to LibTheo including the Contra-Drug DO and the

Harbury attack on the Guatemalan Armed Forces. Both of these were important to HL operations, but they can be given no more than passing notice here. Perhaps most importantly, these DOs demand that their investigation involves the expenditure of considerable time and effort as does their presentation.

The long-lived HL attack on the US Army School of the Americas (SOA) has been treated (pp.249ff, YRBK98) as have the probably unconstitutional Esquipulas II Accords which allegedly led to "peace" in CA. The importance of Esquipulas is immense in that investigation indicates that these "Accords" led, not to "peace," but to victory for the ML terrorists, this specifically discussed for El Salvador (Chapultepec Accords), a case wherein LANS could demonstrate that these accords gave the Farabundo Martí National Liberation Front (FMLN) terrorists precisely what they had been seeking (pp146ff, YRBK97). This demonstration was possible since the LANS Editor had been asked to translate a cache of documents found on the cadaver of a dead terrorist in 1991, the cache specifically delineating the objectives which these terrorists were seeking and which they quite apparently attained.

The Esquipulas Accords and their subsidiaries such as the Chapultepec Accords, were of substantial importance because they illuminated the modus operandi whereby the HL really seeks to attain its future victories, now most importantly, in Colombia. In this chapter only DOs on Colombia and Mexico will be specifically discussed. It is worthy of remark, however, that there is often a fuzzy line of demarcation between what is most appropriately treated as having principally to do with the HL as opposed to the HLS.

Colombia

HEMISPHERE LEFT "VICTORY THROUGH PEACE" IN COLOMBIA?
(WKLY 5.18, 14 MAY 1998)

Introduction

LANS has made the case that the Esquipulas II Accords, instead of bringing a "just peace" to CA, have brought a victory to the ML terrorists of the HL which their political and "military" impotence would never have achieved. This reality will first be reviewed. Now the "Nobel Peace laureate," Oscar Arias, appears to be making progress in foisting this same Esquipulas approach on Colombia. Important to such an attempt is the denigration and attempted destruction of the Colombian Armed Forces (FAC). Without the armed forces of the various Latin American (LA) nations the vision of "supra national countries" as "a sort of re-edition of a soviet-type union in LA" (p.99,YRBK97), so dear to the heart of Castro's cleric, Frei Betto,[8] would be much nearer to consummation. And it is to be recalled that the two outright victories enjoyed by the HL were achieved only after the destruction by disinformation-isolation of the Cuban (1958) and Nicaraguan (1979) armed forces. The same *modus operandi* is clearly in progress here, most of it, as usual, carried out for the HL, not simply by its own militants and those of the HLS, but by the *tontos utiles* (useful idiots) so dear to the heart of Ulianov (aka Lenin).

The Esquipulas II Accords: "Stop-Sign" Mentality or Conspiracy? Both. The Stop-Sign mentality is common to politicians of all nationalities. The candidate pledges to erect a stop sign at the corner of X and Y Streets if elected. He is elected, he erects and proclaims his true blue nature deserving of another term. The politician carries this mentality into the international arena – politics not "stopping at the waterline." He spoke of "peace" in his election bid, and "peace" he will achieve if it takes surrender to do so. In CA such a "peace" was attained with the Nicaraguan Sandinista National Liberation Front (FSLN), the Salvadoran Farabundo Martí National Liberation Front (FMLN) and the Guatemalan National Revolutionary Union (URNG), all creations of the HL, through the so-called Esquipulas Accords.

LANS has specifically demonstrated (pp.138ff,YRBK97), with papers taken from a Farabundi cadaver, that the "peace" accords growing out of Esquipulas in El Salvador were simple surrenders to terrorist demands. This could be done, not because of any "military" ability on the part of the terrorists, but simply because foreign pressure provided sanctuary for the latter in refugee camps and border "territorial pockets" from which they could operate with impunity until their demands were met. And of course an important support to this process was the continuing activity of the HLS with wave after wave of HRV accounts,[9] most of which were contrived. As to Esquipulas II itself.

These accords were signed by the CA heads of state in August 1987 and have been detailed (pp.261ff, YRBK98). They are apparently unconstitutional, the brief now before the Guatemalan Supreme Court having been reproduced (pp.268ff, YRBK98). The intriguing backgrounds of the signers of these accords have been detailed (pp.290ff, YRBK98). Out of these accords grew the Nicaraguan elections of 1990 (pp.28ff,YRBK97), the Chapultepec Accords of 1992 relating to "peace" in El Salvador (pp.4-5,YRBK97) and the URNG "peace" accords[10] discussed (pp.261ff, YRBK98). That the same sort of "peace" evolved in Guatemala as had evolved in El Salvador has been discussed in various accompanying reports.

This "peace process" is therefore taken as the ultimate CA "triumph" by its alleged instigator,[11] Oscar Arias. Fresh from this series of dubious triumphs, ex Pres. Arias has begun injecting himself into the Colombian terrorist problem. If the past is indeed prologue, this bodes well for Colombian terrorism and ill for that nation. And, roughly contemporary with the Arias effort, there are those incidents which have taken place and which involve the US and/or certain of its citizens. Whether as a result of planning or coincidence, these incidents form part of a DO, the target of which is the FAC.

The Washington Post Article of 10 April 1998

This article carries the byline "Douglas Farah, *Washington Post Foreign Service,*" the headline "Colombian Rebels Seen Winning War" and the subhead "US Study Finds Army Inept, Ill-Equipped." The piece runs about two columns and opens with "The US Defense Intelligence Agency (DIA) has concluded..." various things critical of a FAC which "could be defeated within five years unless" the Colombian Government does this and that. The second paragraph begins with "The report, one of the bleakest assessments..," and one must apparently conclude that this "report" is by the DIA which "has concluded..."

Assuming this, the third paragraph reads: "A summary of the report, prepared last November, was obtained yesterday by *The Washington Post*, while two sources with direct knowledge of the full text provided details not included in the summary."

The LANS Editor interviewed the spokesman for the DIA who did not wish his identity published.

> LANS Q: Has DIA issued or compiled any reports to the effect that the Colombian Government will fall to the terrorists in five years?

DIA: This organization has neither prepared nor issued such a report.
Q: Did the *Washington Post* receive a summary of such a report?
DIA: Such a report would have been classified and could only have been received illegally. We know of no such summary.

Therefore, either the basis for the article is incorrect or the DIA spokesman was lying to LANS, the latter alternative appearing to be the least likely. Since the article was thus apparently created from misinformation, the remainder of what is mostly filler loses what little importance it may have had.[12] However, on 11 April 1998 EFE picked up the story with the headline, "Informe del Pentágono avisa que la guerrilla puede derrotar al ejército" (Pentagon Report Says that the Guerrilla Can Defeat the Army), and this important piece of misinformation, perhaps disinformation, can be expected to settle into the landscape as a "truism" to the immense advantage of the HL .

Although the *Post* report appears to be phantom, such immense success has been enjoyed in numbers inflation by the HL, that a word would be in order on those claimed for the terrorists in the piece. The article alleges that the report claims that the terrorists now number 20,000. The figure is meaningless without considerable additional detail on operational personnel, support personnel and base personnel. LANS has followed the usually inflated claims which have appeared in the press on terrorist numbers, and they have been discussed on various occasions (cf. p.112ff,YRBK97). In reality, in 1992 the Colombian Revolutionary Armed Forces (FARC) apparently numbered about 6000 in 45 fronts, the National Liberation Army (ELN) 2000. These are internally consistent in that fronts in general are about company size, and 6000 men in 45 fronts is just that, 6000/45 = 130/front.

The most recent and reliable numbers in the LANS files appeared last year in a book by General Alvaro Valencia Tovar (Ret) [*Inseguridad y Violencia en Colombia*, Universidad Sergio Arboleda, 1997. ISBN: 958-9442-27-7]. Herein the consistent numbers of 7000 operational personnel in 62 fronts (113/front) are given for FARC and 3100 personnel in 33 fronts (94/front) for ELN. General Valencia is careful to make the qualification without which such numbers are meaningless: The numbers "do not include auxiliaries or members of urban and rural support networks."

There is a statement in the seventh paragraph in the *Post* article which refers to "the Colombian military's abysmal human rights record..." LANS has dealt extensively with such charges which routinely surface in press reports for which the HL or the HLS have been responsible for the fabrications. In Spcls 5.5 and 5.6 (Chapter 5) above, "The Diplomacy of the Subversion," Dr. Miguel Posada has dealt with HR operations by the various Non Governmental Organizations (NGO) HR operations which have provided such strong support to the HL. In Chapter 4 (YRBK97) and Chapter 5 (YRBK98) various such NGO groups and the DOs which have emerged from them have been discussed. The space available here allows no real repetition of this information; however, certain other information is worthy of presentation.

In a lengthy statement to the LANS Editor, General Manuel José Bonett Locarno, Commanding General of Military Forces, stated that "In public opinion polls on the credibility of public and private institutions the Military Forces appeared in the first ranks, generally surpassed (only) by the Catholic Church. However, in matters of HR, the Attorney General of the Nation...in a communication dated 19 November of last year (1997) has publicly acknowledged that the preventive measures, the educational and awareness programs within the Military Forces, like the HR policy, is having significant effects..."

Which, save for the Attorney General's remarks, is about what LANS has observed of recent years, there having been any number of DOs targeted on the military but few demonstrable cases of HRVs. The accusations improperly linking the military to the Self Defense Forces – which at times are narco involved in Colombia – or "paramilitary" are a familiar canard. On which more later.

US Congressman Dan Burton Apparently Slandered

There are various possible explanations for an article which surfaced in *El Tiempo* (Bogotá) on 1 April 1998, bylined "Andrés Cavelier Castro, *El Tiempo* correspondent Washington" and headlined "Ejército de E.U. duda de capacidad de las FF.AA" (US Army doubts the capacity of the Armed Forces). This is of course further attack, innocent or intentioned, on FAC, but the attack appears to have been nullified by a curious contention at the bottom of column two and in column three.

(A su vez...) For his part, Congressman Dan Burton reported the presence in Colombia of "Russian advisors," among them ex military and ex KGB[13] agents who would be training the guerrillas. (Par) Burton offered no further details. However, Republican assistants (asistentes republicanos del Congreso[14]) of the Congress told *El Tiempo* that this has to do with ex Russian military who pass themselves off as technical assistants but who, in reality, provide FARC with tactics for fighting the Army.

The allegation was self righteously denied by Russian ambassador Ednan Agaev as was to be expected. But what was not to be expected was that neither Burton nor his staff has ever told the news media any such thing.

The LANS Editor contacted Mr. John Williams, press secretary to Congressman Burton, and asked about the allegation that Mr. Burton and his staff had made these statements about Russian advisors. In his reply Williams showed himself to be either completely nonplussed or a remarkably seasoned actor. He denied that Congressman Burton or his staff had ever told Cavelier Castro anything at all about Russian advisors to the Colombian terrorists.

On 2 April a follow-up piece appeared in *El Tiempo* wherein the allegedly irate Russian ambassador used the distant Congressman Burton as a whipping boy.

That the entire episode is a continuation of the DO targeted on the FAC is obvious, although the precise part played by the "accusation" – or compliment – against Burton is not obvious.

EDITOR'S CONCLUSION

Under the circumstances, the allegations in the *Post* article are of little or no consequence save as an outline of the DO which is underway against the FAC. Important to this operation is the repeated allegation that the FAC is incompetent, unable "to see threats," ill trained, and so on. Such remarks are attributed to US officers of flag rank, certain of whom can be described as "political" rather than field generals. The "basis" for these remarks will be obvious to readers of these reports; they should and will be discussed further in future reports.

* * *

THE US, THE HUMAN RIGHTS ORGANIZATIONS AND COLOMBIAN TERRORISM
(SPCL 5.16, 19 MAY 1998)

EDITOR'S INTRODUCTION

In Wkly 5.18 a campaign to destroy the FAC, to the benefit of the ML terrorists, was discussed. Therein it was shown that a curious article which appeared in *The Washington Post* on 10 April 1998, which was allegedly based on a DIA report and which amounted to an attack on FAC, was based on misinformation. It was further shown that a curious and apparently totally incorrect quotation of US Congressman Dan Burton with relation to Russian advisors to Colombian terrorists appeared in the 1 and 2 April 1998 issues of *El Tiempo* (Bogotá). This was then woven in with the attack on the FAC in these articles. In Wkly 5.18 above and various earlier reports the reliance of the HL and HLS on the so-called HRV or NGO groups have been discussed. Amnesty International (AI) is perhaps the best known of these HRV groups. It was apparently not directly formed by the MLs, although it has assuredly been used by them. It has been used by them in that ML terrorist groups in Guatemala were feeding them HRV reports in 1982,[15] an HRV group formed by the Colombian Communist Party (PCC) was quite recently feeding them disinformation for regurgitation, and the LibTheo[16] clerics have assuredly used them extensively.[17] All of which hardly means that AI is wittingly in the service of the HL, but the organization has nonetheless done considerable service for it however innocent their motives. This is relevant to the following article which we have just received from our correspondent in Medellín.

* * *

STATE, THE NGOS AND THE COLOMBIAN SUBVERSION

LANS CORRESPONDENT
MEDELLÍN
COLOMBIA

Last week we witnessed a scene which a few years ago would have seemed impossible. The political supporters of the Marxist guerrillas, with the aid of the US State Department, besieged the Colombian Army.

A few weeks ago two members of the extreme left, Maria Arango and Eduardo Umaña were murdered in Colombia. Ms. Arango was a long retired communist activist; Mr. Umaña was a lawyer who had long defended accused guerrillas and actively promoted accusations against military personnel. The latter received a well organized and noisy hero's funeral, complete with a display of the ELN flag by masked guerrillas.

Mr. Vivanco, of Human Rights Watch-Americas, promptly accused Military Intelligence, specifically the 20th Brigade, of the murders, alleging he had proof of this. He did not, however, produce any such evidence. Colombian Army commanders rejected the accusations, only to be reprimanded by a spokesman for the State Department. It seems that Mr. Vivanco can act as prosecutor, judge and jury, with the full support of the State Department.

A few days latter, retired General Fernando Landazabal, a former Defense Minister, was murdered in the street. The Army did not point fingers and announced it will not do so until a proper investigation is carried out. The State Department simply found his murder "deplorable."

Next to enter the fray was AI. It demanded of the president of Colombia that he forbid any criticism of Human Rights NGOs by military personnel on active duty. The president had already forbidden any such criticism.[18] AI also demanded that this ban apply to retired officers as well, and this, under the constitution, he cannot do.[19] This was a peculiar demand, coming from an organization that supposedly upholds the right to free speech.

The next step was that General Ivan Ramirez' entry visa to the US was cancelled. This was done as a result of a terrorist accusation in support of which the MLs have yet to present any specific evidence of wrongdoing on the general's part. He is at present the Inspector General of the Army, but he has long been a thorn-in-the-side for the guerrillas. The General promoted the creation of a professional Military Intelligence service, organized as the 20th Brigade, which has since been successful in capturing dozens of guerrilla leaders. Later, as a commander of the First Division, he was successful in greatly reducing the influence of FARC, most notably, in Urabá, and in other regions in his command area. The cancellation of his US visa is a clear signal that the State Department wishes to discourage his possible promotion to Army Command. Many more visa cancellations are threatened. Can gossip and rumor, the origin of which is easy to guess, be the basis for official US policy?

The murder of the two leftist activists was extremely profitable for the Marxist left. The NGOs demanded and were given access to

Military Intelligence files. They will also benefit from the aforementioned presidential directive against criticism of human rights NGOs by military personnel and other government officials. Should not all this lead us to include the Marxists, as well as the extreme right, as possible suspects? Marxist terrorism in the past has been known to create its own martyrs.

The analysis of these events raises several questions. Was the State Department's response in support of Mr. Vivanco's unsubstantiated claim really a ransom payment for the release of four US citizens kidnapped by the guerrillas? Does the State Department really expect to be successful in the efforts to suppress illegal drug production in Colombia while at the same time helping the guerrillas (heavily involved in Drugs), by weakening or crippling Colombian Military Intelligence?

Sympathy for the Marxist insurgency was already evident in the last few State Department Reports on HR in Colombia. In these reports the Department puts its weight behind the dubious statistics and allegations produced by Colombian and foreign HR NGOs.

For example, the reports effectively condemned General Farouk Yanine, former commander of the Army, before he was even tried. The fact that the witnesses used against him were proven to be outrageous liars did not make the Department change its opinion. The last report also includes the following statement: " Although top military leaders hailed cases against guerrilla leaders, they strongly objected, and in some cases tried to obstruct, prosecution of cases against members of the armed forces and of paramilitary organizations." The first part of the statement is true. Top military leaders do hail cases against guerrilla leaders, as well they should. After all, soldiers risk their lives to capture them and turn them over to the judiciary.[20] The second part of the statement is a clever amalgamation of two disparate subjects. First, top military leaders have indeed objected to prosecution of military personnel based on false evidence. But as for the second claim, the military have never "strongly objected or tried to obstruct the prosecution of members of paramilitary organizations."[21] There is not a single case of this. These are just two examples of flagrant bias in the reports. There are many more.

It is not particularly unusual that there are supporters of the Marxist terrorists within the State Department. With the end of the cold war, Marxists and their friends are apparently no longer considered a threat by the US government. It is surprising, however, that behind the mask of the worthy cause of HR, they seem to be exerting considerable influence in the State Department. This is certainly not in the best interest of Democracy in the Hemisphere or the security of the United States.

[Translated from the Spanish by the Editor, LANS]

NGOS AND TERRORIST DISINFORMATION OPERATIONS
(WKLY 6.6, 13 AUGUST 1998)

In July 1998 the LANS Editor gathered an extensive collection of material demonstrating the connection of various NGOs, allegedly devoted to HR "causes," to terrorism in Colombia. Indeed, so extensive is the collaboration that it may not be either feasible or desirable to attempt to publish it all. However, as LANS has frequently emphasized, this cooperation has been so important to HL successes that the key portions of this documentation assuredly deserve distribution.

The HL, the HLS and their willing associates obviously have no motive for contrived HR assaults on inefficient or undedicated military personnel who have been assigned against them. And, indeed, what is found is that those officers who are attacked are the intelligent and innovative who have attained notable successes against the terrorist in quite legitimate and straightforward ways, perhaps with innovations such as some of those which will be described. He who is an efficient officer, whether a major or a major general – LANS has dealt with both – and introduces innovations in dealing with the terrorist can expect swift HR allegations to be his reward. And there is another point.

LANS files contain a number of *ORDEN DE CAPTURAS* (Arrest Orders) issued, usually for the crime of Rebellion, by a *DIRECCION REGIONAL DE FISCALIAS* of the *FISCALIA GENERAL DE LA NACION*. The National Fiscal Office will be taken as the Attorney General (AG), the Regional Office as the District Attorney (DA), this simply for convenience, and the duties are not lost in the translation. If a military unit finds a terrorist with gun in hand, he can be arrested. However, if it gathers evidence that a citizen is a terrorist, it must obtain an arrest order from the local DA. And the local DA or part of his staff may be a terrorist sympathizer who has no desire to arrest the individual in question whatever the charge. That such is hardly farfetched is demonstrated by Horacio Serpa, the Liberal Party candidate for president in the recent elections: His connections with the terrorists – all innocent "friendships," of course – have long been well known. In practice this introduces the necessity of producing overwhelming as against "reasonable" evidence of terrorist connections in order to obtain a warrant.

General Fernando Millán Pérez is just such an innovative and intelligent officer. His reward for the efficient and innovative performance of his duties as commander of V Brigade was set forth in *El Espectador* (11 August 1998):

General Millán "...was called to testify before the National HR Unit [UNDH] which is investigating him for the alleged crime of collaborating in the formation of private justice (paramilitary) groups." "Informants" are readily available, the paramilitary Vladimir, who will be encountered again, being perhaps most familiar. Their testimony is routinely repaid by reduced sentences or the like. What is most interesting in the newspaper account is "In that year (1997) and in the months of March and November..." These dates will be encountered again.

How Millán Offended the Terrorists

Barrancabermeja is the main center of oil production in the Magdalena Media area. As a consequence, the pipeline-busting "clerics' terror group," the ELN has been very active in the region. The II Division with headquarters at Bucaramanga has five brigades,[22] V Brigade responsible for the Barrancabermeja region. In April 1997 the military captured the female terrorist boss of the Yariguies Urban Resistance Front (FURY) of the ELN, one Edilma Pérez (aka la flaca Nelsy: Skinny Nelsy). She was carrying documents relating to the III Assembly of FURY, copies of which LANS has obtained in its July 1998 investigations in Colombia.

In these documents there are specific references to two "HR" NGOs as a part of the ELN, and this would prove to be only the first such to be exposed. These two were the Regional HR Committee (CREDHOS) and the Committee of Solidarity with Political[23] Prisoners (COSOP). These documents also contained testimony to the fact that COSOP was particularly useful, not having failed "the people" and having paid especial attention to the captured "comrades."[24] The document further stated that the ELN participated in, and contributed money to, CREDHOS.

The COSOP head, Yolanda Amaya, was captured in October 1997 and is awaiting trial. The president of CREDHOS is Osiris Baythen. She was in Colombia until May 1998 when, aware that her arrest could hardly be postponed much longer, she "fled" to Europe with the familiar cry that her "life was in danger." Most importantly, at that time she accused General Millán of forming a paramilitary group. The FURY document will be treated in more detail in a future report.

However, the intelligence operation was concluded in October 1997 with a raid on five NGOs, these being the Association School of Alternative and Self-Management Services (ESCOL), the Association for Human Promotion (CORPHU), the Project for Economic and Social Rehabilitation of the Displaced Population (REDES), the Association for Human Promotion (ORPHU) and the Association of Investment, Commercialization and Consumption (COINPROCO).

First, there was knowledge of CREDHOS and COSOP from which information on the others was developed. And importantly, it was discovered, as LANS has already reported from other areas, that foreign money which was contributed to these HR groups found its way to the ELN. Furthermore, ELN personnel were captured in these HR groups, among them:

(1) Javier Orlando Marín Rodríguez (ESCOP) was a member of the ELN National Directorate (Politburo) and head of the Bucaramanga Urban Front (FUB).

(2) Armando Valbueno Payares (Escuela) was responsible for FUB logistics.

(3) Yolando Amaya Herrera (COSOP) was head of the Bucaramanga Branch of COSOP and a member of the ELN.

(4) Consuelo Rincón (CORPHU) was a member of the ELN.

An arrest order was issued for Pedro José Rey Navas, the director of COSOP, but he has yet to be picked up. He is apparently (or was) in Europe.

Warrants were issued for these people largely because the evidence was simply too extensive to be ignored. In the case of several NGOs in Bogotá, however, the DA delayed for 24 hours which was enough since the birds had flown when personnel arrived to arrest them. A further complication was introduced into the operation by pressure from the government to suppress details on the operation, this pressure even going so far as to call for erasure of the information from computer storage.

The LANS correspondent in Medellín has just furnished additional information on the DO or campaign in the "Judicial War."

THE JUDICIAL WAR CONTINUES

LANS CORRESPONDENT
MEDELLÍN
COLOMBIA
(WKLY 6.6, 13 AUGUST 1998)

With the inauguration of a new administration, the command of the Colombian Armed Forces is being restructured as is customary. General Bonett, Commander in Chief, the Chief of the General Staff, and the chiefs of the Air Force and Navy will retire. This will bring many other changes down the line. This same week the Attorney General of Colombia (Fiscalia) announced that two prominent general officers, BG Fernando Millán and BG Rito Alejo del Rio, commanders of the V and XIII Brigades of the Army, will be investigated for alleged links to the so-called "paramilitaries" or illegal self defense forces. There has been a third such accusation during this eventful week.

General Ivan Ramírez is presently the Inspector General of the Army. *The Washington Post* recently accused him of having worked for the Central Intelligence Agency (CIA), this accusation following an unexplained denial of a US visa to the general. Some two weeks ago, two US congressmen accused several generals, including General Mora and General Ramírez, of HRVs.

Is the timing of all this a coincidence? This would be hard to believe. It appears to be an attempt by the political supporters of the Marxist guerrillas to prevent the promotion of the general officers that have been most effective against them. The sympathies of certain US congressmen and journalists are well known, and people with strong (and hardly secret) Marxist connections, including a niece of Aida Abella, the firebrand communist politician, staff the Human

Rights section of the Fiscalía. This is the same section that attempted to process General Yanine, using flagrantly false testimony from a convicted former guerilla and mass murderer.

General Nestor Ramírez commanded XII Brigade at the time of the "cocalero" marches, three years ago. Coca farmers were forced to march by the FARC and narcotrafickers to protest against US financed spraying of coca crops. Their aim was to control the southern departments of Caquetá, Guaviare and Putumayo. If this failed, they hoped at least to provoke a strong Army response with many marchers killed or wounded. They failed on both counts. The mobs were not allowed to occupy Florencia or any major town. The troops were remarkably well controlled in spite of extraordinary provocation. FARC even managed to pressure a local judge into ordering the Army to open the roads to the marchers. The order was overturned in higher court. The FARC effort failed. The allegations of (US Congressmen) Joe Kennedy and Torres, based on the testimony of one TV cameraman, are visibly contradicted by very extensive film footage compiled by other news organizations. But General Ramírez must be punished for his successes.

General Fernando Millán has been a thorn in the side of the Marxist guerrillas. Troops under his command captured one Francisco Galan, third in command of the ELN, and many other guerrilla leaders. Last October an intelligence operation in his jurisdiction uncovered the links between five Human Rights NGOs and the ELN. His V Brigade troops have fought well and hard and have the best record in combat of all Brigades for 1998. The solution for the Marxists is to use the powerful weapon of Judicial War against him.

The case against him was initially based on his alleged support of a supposedly illegal Convivir, a self-defense association. Once its legality was proven,[25] the charge was changed to arming this Convivir with prohibited weapons. The truth is that the Brigade did not give the Convivir its weapons, but rather confiscated those not authorized.[26]

General del Rio represents a similar threat to the FARC. When in command of XVII Brigade in the Urabá region, FARC suffered many defeats, and, most painfully, they lost their influence with the banana workers to unions controlled by the former guerrillas of the EPL. To this they responded with mass killings of EPL sympathizers.[27] The EPL sought and obtained Army protection. The response of the ML will be slander and criminal investigation by the Fiscalía against General del Rio, notwithstanding the fact that General del Rio's XVII Brigade had an impressive record of capture and combat of paramilitaries as well as guerrillas. Del Rio's main accuser is former Colonel Velazquez,[28] his onetime chief of staff, who was retired because of his excessive and improper intimacy with Apartado Mayor Gloria Cuartas.

Who in Colombia dares speak out against an investigative body that has the power to imprison anybody for months while an investigation is "in progress"? It is the MLs ultimate weapon. Even if the evidence is false, and innocence finally proved, the accused is usually morally and financially ruined by the process. Slander in the US is also a good weapon. There is no downside for the accusers. For a Colombian, legal action against a powerful US newspaper or US congressmen is prohibitively expensive.

General Mora was promoted to Army Commander. General Ivan Ramírez will retire. The fate of Generals Nestor Ramírez, Millán and del Rio is still to be determined.

We are seeing a new chapter in the "judicial war" and the great ML disinformation campaign. It serves to put the recent FARC offensive, which included all sorts of violations of the rules of war, out of the minds of nationals and foreigners. This "heroic offensive" which included firing on a Red Cross aircraft, an attack on a refugee camp, car bombs, the destruction of schools and the use of civilians as human screens, will be forgotten. The main targets of this offensive were a Police and Army antinarcotics base in Miraflores, which threatened the FARC's flourishing coca business (No comments from Kennedy and Torres).

With the new administration in Colombia committed to peace at any price, and eager to please all, MLs and HR NGOs included, this campaign will probably, at least partially, work. Will Colombia be closer to "peace"?

THE GREAT GRINGO DISINFORMATION OPERATION REVISITED
(WKLY 6.10, 10 SEPTEMBER 1998)

It has recently been attested again that the USSR "funded every major (Vietnam) antiwar group"[29] in the US. These erstwhile "activists" tend to aggregate around the executive and legislative branches of government, and there are those of them who have not lost the roseate illusions of their youth. These would be "putty in the hands" of those experienced GRU (Russian Military Intel) operatives who are almost assuredly involved in the Great Gringo Disinformation Operation (GDO).

For some time the Hemispheric Left (HL) and the HL Support (HLS) have of course been busily fabricating "Human Rights" (HR) charges against the military which have been dutifully disseminated by various NGOs (Non-Governmental Organization), with or without malice of forethought. But it was *The Washington Post* which, doubtless unwittingly, first carried the water for the GDO in its article of 10 April 1998, "Colombian Rebels Seen Winning War." An aside.

Disinformation in the Los Angeles Times

In 1990 an article appeared in *The Los Angeles Times* entitled "In El Salvador, It's the Army That Seems to Be in Trouble." A subhead read in part, "the insurgents may have the upper hand." From the headline to the end of the story, the information was demonstrably fabricated, and the Editor was commissioned to demonstrate this after an individual saw the article on the desk of a "high State Department official" who appeared to be impressed. A few days in San Salvador and San Francisco Gotera were all that were required. (The information which the Editor gathered on the article author and photographer was interesting but hardly conclusive.)

There were childishly nonsensical statements in the article, all aimed at creating a totally false impression, such as "In the capital of San Salvador...darkened tanks patrol the streets at night." The Editor then verified that El Salvador did not possess any tanks. It had armored personnel carriers, manufactured locally by welding three-quarter inch steel plate to appropriate chassis. For a good many years the Editor had been observing occasional armored personnel carriers on the Panamerican Highway although none in, say, the Colonia Escalon. As he wrote at the time, "The inferred idea of a Beirut in Central America bears no relation to reality."

In creating a totally false impression the author then wrote, "Soldiers have set up outposts throughout the city..." This was simply false as the Editor took the time to verify. The guard posts which, for many years, had been at the Estado Mayor, the Escuela Militar, I

Brigade headquarters, etc., were right where they had been, but there were no "outposts."

Finally, as concerned the capital, the author quoted an unidentified real estate agent claiming that "People are leaving" because of fear of terrorist attack "and renting their house...(and) nobody wants them..." This was easily shown to be nonsensical by comparing the classified section of *La Prensa Grafica* for 2 October 1989 with that for 28 September 1990.

The LANS Editor had visited San Francisco Gotera, the headquarters of Destacamento Militar IV, a number of times over the previous five years The *Times* author stated that he and his photographer trekked there, an assertion to which The DM-4 commander, Col. Leon, attested with a smile. That author then fabricated a totally fantastic account of a military formation on the square which, inter alia, probably shows an unfamiliarity with the military that he shares with various of his brethren.

But most importantly, he wrote that "patrols have been halted." The Editor asked Col. Leon about this; he merely laughed and asked, "Why would they be?" Why indeed. On this same trip the Editor made a very low level chopper flight back and forth across the northern tier of Salvadoran states in order to photograph the terrain for an organization which was building a "terrorist detector." This was a Hughes chopper, doors removed, with none of the Hughie's M-60s but with Salvadoran Army markings. Had there been any terrorists anywhere, the chopper would have offered a "fish in a rain barrel" target, but nothing happened. We spotted one two-platoon strength patrol which the pilot thought might be terrorists but which Col. Leon quickly identified as his own at our fuel stop.

This totally fabricated account, which appeared in the "news" section of *The Los Angeles Times*, doubtless had some effect on the Farabundi terrorist "victory through peace." Since, however, the US has shown little interest in investigating *why* it has lost all its wars since 1945, the extent of the influence does not appear to be known. With which we return to what may be an analogous situation in *The Washington Post*.

The GDO

In eight years the scene has shifted from El Salvador to Colombia, the "reporting" periodical from *The Los Angeles Times* to *The*

Washington Post, but there is a disturbing sameness about the "report." Now it's the Colombian Army "which seems to be in trouble." But it is "in trouble" according to a Defense Intel Agency (DIA) report which never existed. If it did exist, the DIA spokesman lied to the LANS Editor, and the DIA commanding general lied to the FAC commanding general, General Manuel José Bonett[30] Locarno. For both the DIA spokesman and the DIA commander stated unequivocally that no such report existed. Furthermore, LANS maintains, from on the ground investigations in Colombia, that, if the report did exist, it would be nonsensical. LANS is seemingly the only organization which has covered the three "bases" for this anti-FAC allegation as they occurred.

Las Delicias – Patascoy – El Billar

The GDO, as it appeared in the spring of 1998, based its "FAC losing" allegation on these three trifling engagements, treating them as they would have treated, say, the French capture of Guderian's XIX Corps in 1940. The facts are quite different. (That the FAC has never made any tactical mistakes is not being claimed, albeit, it is not a LANS obligation to pontificate on what has happened. However, to attempt – as has repeatedly been attempted with other terrorists – to claim some sort of military superiority for the narcoterrorists of the Colombian Revolutionary Armed Forces (FARC) is simply bizarre.) The first of the three is Las Delicias.

In the summer of 1996 a less than Company-strength unit of FAC was manning a cobbled-up outpost at Las Delicias. This hamlet is in Putumayo Department, on the right bank of the Caquetá River, 31 statute miles (sm) southwest by south (SWS) of Tres Esquinas for which see Spcl 6.4, "Colombian Joint Task Force South." Wkly 3.23, "Landmark FARC Victory,"[31] has detailed the overrun of this outpost by some 400 FARC terrorists. During the next 10 months the Samper Government contributed to the propaganda victory which FARC enjoyed from this capture by acceding to FARC demands.

Another overrun occurred at Patascoy in December 1997 with another small unit (Wkly 5.2, "Another Colombian Terrorist Coup"), although some military heads did roll for inefficiency in this case. Patascoy was little more than a relay antenna on a mountain top guarded by a platoon. It was located on the ridge of the mountain range defining the border between Nariño and Putumayo Departments, a short distance north of the road linking the capital of the latter (Mocoa) and the capital of the former (Pasto). There were apparently serious security mistakes made, and FAC removed the brigade and division commanders from command as a consequence.

As the LANS Editor learned at Tres Esquinas (Spcl 6.4), the FARC terrorists made their escape from Patascoy by a "backwoods" river route which took them all the way into an Ecuador, a nation which appears not to have minded their presence. And "escape" is the *mot juste*; this was no "victorious army," it was a terrorist gang.

The third such incident occurred at El Billar which is 47 sm about due east of Tres Esquinas. Once again, a small unit was overrun by a large FARC group. The personnel captured at Patascoy and El Billar are still in the hands of the terrorists: another propaganda victory was thereby handed to these outlaws.

These incidents were the basis for the GDO which appears to have been more or less initiated with *The Washington Post* article of last April. And then came the guns of early August. LANS has not treated these situations previously because of its search for reliable details which are now available on perhaps the most important incident.

Miraflores

General Sánchez Vargas, Inspector General of the Colombian Armed Forces (FAC), submitted a report on Miraflores of which appears here as Spcl 6.5, and Spcl 6.7 (Chapter 5 above). A brief synopsis follows.

Terrorist strength at Miraflores was reported by *El Espectador* as "400" and "at least 500" in two articles on the same day. The report itself has the troops which were attacked maintaining that there were 1000 of these bandits. LANS' sources in Colombia feel that the number was close to 800.

The effective strength of the infantry unit at Miraflores was 2 officers, 10 non-commissioned officers and 98 privates, that is, a company.

Guaviare Department is to the southeast of Meta Department, its capital San José de Guaviare (Spcl 6.1), on the Guaviare Rive which separates the two departments. San José is some 230 km southeast of Bogotá, Miraflores about 25 km from the Vaupes Department border on the Vaupes River.

The terrorist began the "attack" on the small military installation at 1930 on 3 August 1998, "attack" meaning they began bombarding it with whatever was at hand. At this point two platoons appear to have been on patrol, these encountering overwhelming numbers of the enemy and never returning. Weather generally prohibited any air support and, at 1720 on 4 August, the captain commanding reported that the corporal's guard remaining had been overrun.

La Uribe

La Uribe is slightly over 200 km west northwest of San José de Guaviare in Meta Department. According to EFE (Bogotá 9 August 1998), there was a detachment of 60 military and six police stationed there at 0530 on 4 August 1998 when the post was "attacked" by "several hundred" (*varios centenares*) terrorists from FARC Front XLI.[32] The attack was abandoned by the terrorists at 1930 that evening.

Apparently there was little left of the military or police post, and the casualties of both were reported as 46 dead and 16 wounded, although this was not an overrun. General George S. Patton, who had considerable combat experience, stated in no uncertain terms that, if casualties figures exceeded something like 10 percent, they were to be ignored.

Urabá

As has been pointed out (Wkly 6.6), General del Rio, commander of XVII Brigade, inflicted many defeats on FARC terrorists in the Urabá area and divested them of their influence with the banana workers. This led to DOs against him for HR violations, DOs demonstrably fabricated as will be discussed if and when the opportunity arises. The general was headquartered in the Apartada region in Antioquia Department, the area 30 km or so east of the Choco Department border and perhaps 40 km from the border of Colombia with Panama.

Which more or less serves to define the location of Urabá, described in the press as the "jungle zone between the Antioquia and Choco Departments near the Panama frontier." It was in this region that combats, routinely described by the press as "violent" (AFP 20 August 1998), took place between 14 and 16 August.

Neither La Uribe or Urabá resulted in a terrorist victory, but the press consolidation of these two with Miraflores can be – and probably has been – read as some sort of further demonstration of the FARC superiority DO.

Mexico

THE TRUTH ABOUT CHIAPAS. I
MARY BALL MARTÍNEZ
(SPCL 5.8, 15 MARCH 1998)

EDITOR'S INTRODUCTION

Mary Ball Martinéz is a journalist who was accredited to the Vatican from 1973 to 1988. She is a former columnist for *National Review*, *The American Spectator*, the Catholic periodical, *The Wanderer*, and various other publications. This article has been in the LANS files since January 1995, originally secured for us by our Associate Editor in São Paulo, Dr. Graça Wagner. It is being distributed now in preparation for the forthcoming article on the recently somewhat different treatment of the Chiapas situation by the Mexican Government. It originally appeared as "A VERDADE SOBRE CHIAPAS" in *Ponto de Vista* (No.3, November 1994, Rio de Janeiro.

* * *

Who financed the mini revolution in Chiapas? The CIA? Ross Perot? The US unions? British spies? Narcotraffickers? No. The answer is even more strange: the Catholics of Germany.

Michel Algrin, Professor of Law at the University of Paris, was curious about the destination of millions of francs donated by his compatriots to the Catholic Committee Against Hunger and for Progress (CCFD). He initiated a year-long investigation from which evolved Michel Algrin, *La subversion humanitaire: les bonnes oeuvres du CCFD* (J. Picollec, 1988. LCC: 8911949) which caused a scandal in France.

Disillusioned with what he had found, Algrin told the Italian review, *30 Giorni*: "I had hoped to plunge into crystal waters, but I foundered in a sewer. The CCFD reported that the money was destined for charitable works in the undeveloped world, but in reality it is used for promoting the subversives worldwide."

Algrin discovered that CCFD had sent great sums of money to Southwest Africa Peoples Organization (SWAPO), the organized guerrillas who oppose the government of Namibia, as well as to the Moçambique Liberation Front (FRELIMO), in Moçambique, to the

Peoples Liberation Movement of Angola (MPLA) and to five little groups which punish the government of Violeta Chamorro in Nicaragua.

He also found 13 other organizations similar to the CCFD, among them the Trocaire, of Ireland; Development and Peace, of Canada; Adveniat et Misere, of Germany. All these groups work together through a central headquarters known as CIDSE, in the Jesuit University of Louvain, Belgium, the annual budget for which is greater than that of UNESCO.[33]

It appears that the pious German Catholics contribute to the subversion in Mexico through Adveniat, which send funds to the Bartolomé de Las Casas Human Rights Center in Chiapas, directed through Bishop Samuel Ruíz.

The fact that the offices of CIDSE are located in the diocese of Maline-Bruxelas does not surprise me. During my 15 years as a correspondent accredited to the Vaticam I concluded that, while Rome continues administering the post-Vatican Council Church, the Jesuits of Louvain are in charge of all the questions referring to theology and ideology. Whenever a crisis occurred in some area, the correspondents were all summoned to take cognizance of how the theologians, nearly all from the above mentioned University of Louvain, had analyzed the affair. In the middle 1970s the Bishop of San Cristóbal and Bishop Romero of San Salvador, who would be assassinated a little later, were summoned to Rome to guarantee to the members of Adveniat that their donations were not being used in subversive causes.

In a trip that I made to the south of Mexico in 1983 I was received by Bishop Ruíz. Conscious of his fame as a radical, I supposed that my Vatican credentials had put the bishop on guard. It is only now, in this turbulent 1994, that I discovered the importance of 1983 for the subversive in San Cristobal. It was only in that year that the guerrilla came out of the jungle and down the mountains to unite with the professional politicians of the extreme left to form the Zapatista National Liberation Army (EZLN). The guerrilla leader who led the attack on Ocosingo explained to *Excelsior*: "We began in Tlatelolco in 1968,[34] but it was only in 1983 that the urban guerrilla united with us so that we could form the Zapatista army."

Whatever the reason may have been, Monseñor Ruíz gave evasive answers to the many questions I asked him: How many Guatemalans were camped on the frontier? Who fed them? Did the Church have anything to do with the situation? Or the United Nations? Are there guerrilla groups in the region? If there are none, who is invading the farms and killing their proprietors?

After an hour of this discouraging interview, I thanked His Excellency and left to interview Father Eugênio, but was informed that he was a prisoner under a charge of shipping contraband arms to Guatemala. I found the local seminary empty with the exception of a middle-aged man, simply dressed, who insisted that he be called only Javier. Contrary to the cautious bishop, Javier, in five minutes, clarified the two principal enigmas which intrigued the world in 1994: who invented the Zapatista Army and who financed it. Identifying himself as chief of a staff of 35 clerics who practiced Liberation Theology[35] and dedicated themselves to "awakening the conscience" of the Indians, he explained: "The Germans have been so generous! Thanks to their organization Adveniat I could spend a number of years in a German university, and now they are helping me a great deal with the refugee Guatemalans."

He showed me something that he had written; it was a pamphlet which would be printed there and then sent to Germany, translated. It consisted exclusively of descriptions of atrocities committed by Guatemalan officers and men against the campesinos. Javier did not enjoy my smile and asked me: "Why do you not believe it? I suppose that you are discovering that this is communist propaganda, no?"

Clearly yes. Here was the same line of patter of the *New York Times* correspondent, Anthony Lewis: "It is a common practice among the Guatemalan soldiers to throw babies about on their bayonets."[36] Of course it has been some decades that the regular military arms have not had bayonets, these being light assault weapons of Galil type. Javier's lies were certainly bringing in a great deal of money from the compassionate Germans and frightening the refugees out of returning to their now peaceful land.

That campaign of dirty propaganda directed against Guatemala (because it had won the war against the subversive) was very well coordinated through Bishop Samuel Ruíz, beginning at his diocese.

A polyglot woman from East (communist) Germany was in charge of talking to the national and foreign reporters about the refugees. She distributed literature similar to that of Javier and escorted the reporters on very well orchestrated visits to the refugee camps. As I had no desire to avail myself of her services, I had great difficulty in convincing the immigration functionary in Comitán that I had telephoned the Ministry of Government in Mexico City asking permission to visit the camps. The agent of the UN High Commission on Refugees (ACNUR)[37] refused to bring me to the camps, alleging that the camp inmates, at the moment, were burning their lands.

The genesis of the EZLN was, as its spokesman explained to *Excelsior*: "We were the guerrilla when we were in the mountains, without the support of the communities; our settlements gave us nothing. Later we did political work in the cities and obtained the support of the comrades and we began to receive the adherence of more campesinos to the guerrilla besides professors and workers and thus we formed the EZLN."

At that time in San Cristóbal the "comrades" of the Mexican Unified Socialist Party (PSUM) and the Mexican Workers Party (PTM) were bossed by José Alvarez Icaza, an activist of the extreme left during the Vatican Council in Rome. Alvarez was a member of the LA Training Center (CLAC) in Prague up to the collapse of international communism.

One day, having coffee in Tuxtla Gutiérrez with the regional delegate of the PMT, I asked him if his symbol was still the hammer and sickle. "Oh, no!" he replied, "don't you know we Mexicans have a horror of the hammer and sickle? Our symbol is aztec." I could not resist: "Indeed, and when you come to power?" He smiled: "The hammer and sickle, naturally." The PMT is one of the little parties which recently attached itself to the banner of the Revolutionary Democratic Party (PRD) of Cuauhtémoc Cárdenas.[38]

[Translated from the Portuguese by the LANS Editor]

THE TRUTH ABOUT CHIAPAS. II
MARY BALL MARTÍNEZ
(SPCL 5.9, 20 MARCH 1998)

"They give us nothing" was the complaint of the communist ideologues who had tried to recruit the Indians. Revolutionary leaders of the middle class, normally university students or professors, find themselves met with total indifference by the Indians with regard to their political message, and the Jesuits do not succeed in convincing the Indians of the usefulness of their efforts. Only when the method could be modified somewhat, and fear introduced through forced participation in acts of terrorism, were these marxization efforts successful.

Thus, in the first year of the Zapatista "army," Chiapas suffered a wave of terrorism. A typical case was provided by what happened in the little community of Simojovel where 40 small productive agricultural properties were invaded and devastated. The proprietors were lucky to be able to flee, leaving their livestock scattered and their crops abandoned. Meanwhile, the Pérez López family of Chalchihuitán did not fare so well. Its 10 members, varying in age from eight to 80 years, were dragged from their houses, butchered and afterwards burned on their ranch.

Margarita Michelena wrote: "Earlier, Simojovel was producing coffee, tobacco, beans, corn in abundance, and now it has practically no corn to make tortillas for the few people who remain ... meanwhile, the authorities of the diocese of San Cristóbal take the next step in their celebrated change of structures."

The participation in terrorism had given the Indians their baptism of fire, and they now must continue to fight. At the same time, during the next 11 years the constant flow of German marks will continue, complemented with funds obtained through kidnappings and confiscations; the "comandantes," who are to be found among the refugees, are in charge of practical training.

There, from the staff of 35 people headed by Javier, there are 12 parish priests from the diocese, four from the US and one from Belgium, all dedicated "cristomarxists" disposed to loan their churches for guerrilla meetings or to stockpile their provisions. If to all this is added the general atmosphere of civil and ecclesiastical tolerance in Chiapas during the last decade, it becomes clear that the emergence of an important force was inevitable. With its attack of 1 January 1994 the EZLN took its place alongside SWAPO, FRELIMO, CCDH and many other subversive organizations under the aegis of the CDSE of Brussels with its funds obtained from the parishes of many European countries.

Placed in its proper perspective, the insurrection can be seen as a local phenomenon which could have been controlled in two or three weeks if the Mexican Government had continued to act as it had begun by acting.[39] And now? The EZLN loses much of its grandeur and importance when the source of its resources are known. It should be seen as a product of the enthusiasm of a bishop who has reached old age, with a theological experience which the Post Council Church abandoned a decade ago. The mini revolution of Chiapas – in which in spite of its connection with some professional terrorists and other such politicos of the extreme left – acquires a pathetic aspect rather than a threatening one.

Samuel Ruíz, without being a Jesuit or an Indian or even a native of Chiapas, sought refuge (as did many clerics of his generation) in "cristomarxism" which the Jesuit intellectuals invented for Latin America.

In 1975 Samuel Ruiz, *La teología bíblica de la liberación* (Librería Parroquial, 1975) appeared in which he denied the fundamental principle of Christianity (Catholic or Protestant), this being that redemption is the salvation of the sinner, and substituted for this the notion that redemption is salvation from worldly suffering. In that work Ruíz describes Jesus Christ as a great revolutionary, crucified for political reasons.

This form of manipulating tradition can be diverting for some LA intellectuals, but not the common people who resent seeing their God reduced to human dimensions. For this and many other reasons, the people resisted joining the guerrillas, for which reason after 20 years and various waves of terror they have assembled only about 500 neo-zapatistas.[40]

In the green mountains of Huehuetenango, on the frontier with Chiapas, in the primitive village of San Mateo Ixtatán, I learned of the heroic resistance of a local cleric. He told me that, when a band of guerrillas arrived at the settlement and demanded that the mayor compel his inhabitants to give them food and work, the old priest refused, being tortured for that, and during four hours remained suspended through the mouth. "After that, the subversives remained in the place for two weeks, enslaving my parishioners," said the priest.

The guerrilla and poet Marío Payeras devoted the major part of his book, *Los días de la Selva*, to relating the useless attempts at regimenting the campesinos of Petén when he and 10 of his companions roamed the country for several years. Even the requests for food were received with a Maya word, *macá* (don't have). The guerrillas asked themselves many times: "Why are these people indifferent to our message?" One day, while a rancher was paying for the services of a numerous group of workers, one of the "comrades" approached him and killed him with a shot. Another began to shout in the local dialect that the revolution had been initiated and that the people were rebelling, while the students escaped before the army could encircle the suspects. A guerrilla unit had been formed.

The same thing happened in San Cristóbal. Armed only with the revolutionary mottoes of Bishop Samuel Ruíz to advance, the guerrillas attained little success with the Indians until 1983 when they introduced them to terrorism by force. The Central American Indian is not violent; on the contrary, he is pacific. Thus, the consciousness of having taken part in violence, even involuntarily, links the Indians to the guerrilla through fear of what will happen with the authorities.

If the resistance of the Indians to their message discourages the EZLN, the respect of the campesinos for the Mexican Army hurts them much more. In the little village of Chiantla in Huehuetenango, I encountered workers repairing the beautiful façade of the XVIII Century municipal palace. "They are volunteers," the mayor told me. "It is amazing to see, one day, a group of about 100 campesinos marching through the town square carrying placards which say: Long live our Army! We want our Army! And some masons among them remain working on the edifice that the subversives burned."

In March of this year, when some thousands of people in San Cristóbal marched with similar placards, and asked the government that it permit the Army to remain in its communities, their requests had no purpose save that of giving a very clear message to the neo zapatistas. For years the children and the youths recruited by the EZLN were told that the people were on their side and that if they rebelled, they would be united to them. Now the youths see that it was all lies. The cloud of white flags showed them that it was time to return to their homes.

According to Payeras, guerrilla rules require summary execution of deserters. Meanwhile, in this year of international hysteria for human rights, it would not be "politically correct" to leave cadavers scattered through the forest.

All this leaves other problems. With the radicalization of the bishops and priests of the mountains the people find themselves without pastors.

About 25 percent of the population of Chiapas has been converted to Protestantism; in Guatemala, where "evangelization" through the radio is allowed, the percentage is greater. As a Catholic, this saddens me, even when I discover the reason: it is a protest against the cristomarxism of Samuel Ruíz and his rebel priests.

With marxism and the Jesuits complicating life this side of the tomb, the people began to listen to the "missionaries" from California to hear the words of eternal life: "heaven," "hell," "redemption" and "God the Father." The question which is heard is antiquated and of Baptist style with some magical touches of the charismatics. Native questioners are rapidly replacing the North Americans.

In San Cristóbal is to be found something incredible: unemployed Catholic clerics. In a church which has lost tens of thousands of clerics since the Council, two youths are unemployed because Bishop Ruíz only concedes ministry to the priests disposed to preach marxism, while for them he must illegally locate foreigners for his parishes.

The neo Baptists frequently declare that the Church which they left "permits much." They refer to alcohol, and I only fully understood the matter later which took into account the victorious campaign of the evangelicals against the alcoholism of the male population.

What do they think now – I asked myself – of the Catholic permissivity when they see a representative of the Pope approving an amnesty for those who attacked the military installations by surprise and killed Indian youths like themselves, took hostages, dynamited bridges, burnt government buildings, destroyed archives, stole, burnt farms, sacked government departments and commercial properties?

[Translated from the Portuguese by the LANS Editor]

Notes

1. Miguel Poradowsky, *El Marxismo en la Teología* (Imprenta LaHosa, 1983). His book has been reviewed by LANS (pp.193ff, YRBK97).
2. Malachi Martin, *THE JESUITS: The Society of Jesus and the Betrayal of the Roman Catholic Church* (Simon and Schuster, 1987. ISBN: 0-671-54505-1).
3. P.19, Martin (*ibid*).
4. P.409, Martin *(ibid)*. Martin is interested in the Society of Jesus (Jesuits) *per se* and uses the name of this order specifically. LANS has here substituted the generic "LibTheo clerics," which includes those other orders whose members are similarly engaged.
5. The Venezuelan presidential victory by Chávez in December 1998, even if he ultimately establishes an ML tyranny in that nation, is not going to change this historic reality. In a manner of speaking, his entire presidential campaign can be taken as a DO.
6. Herbert L. Matthews. *THE YOKE AND THE ARROWS: A Report on Spain* (George

Braziller, 1957. LCC: 61-9963).
7. *Communist Threat to the US Through the Caribbean*, Senate Subcommittee on Internal Security [SISS], 1960, part 7, [Y4.J89/2:C73/27/pt/7]. See also Earl E. T. Smith (*The Fourth Floor: An Account of the Castro Communist Revolution*, Random House, 1962. LCC: 63-8331).
8. See also *Granma* [Havana 23-24 July 1993].
9. In the latter 1980s B. Bradford Jones compiled an account of the publishing activities of *Tutela Legal*, the public relations arm of the Archdiocese of San Salvador. By collecting the Salvadoran Armed Forces (FAES) reports on confrontations with the Farabundi terrorists and TutLeg HRV accounts published almost immediately afterward, he was able to show that TutLeg's HRV reports were created by simply changing a word or two so as to turn a simple military confrontation with the terrorists into the military slaughter of "innocent civilians." These DOs, as with most successful ones, have sunk into the landscape and are accepted without debate.
10. Presidencia de la República de Guatemala, *Los Acuerdos de Paz*, Serpúblic, 1977.
11. Arias had a college roommate in England, John Biehl, a situation reminiscent of Peruvian Pres. Alan Garcia's college roommate, Tupac Amaru Revolutionary Movement (MRTA) terrorist boss Victor Polay Campos. Biehl, left Chile with the fall of the "Marxist physician," Salvador Allende Gossens, without standing on the order of his going. He became Arias' closest "advisor," apparently actually responsible for Esquipulas II.
12. However, terrorist numbers as alleged in the article will be discussed in the next paragraph.
13. The Committee for State Security (Komitet Gosudarstvennoy Bezopastnosti) has been well described, *inter alia*, by Peter Deriabin and T. H. Bagley, *THE KGB:Masters of the Soviet Union* (Hippocrene, 1990. ISBN: 0-87052-804-1). PC apparently expects those of us amongst the Great Unwashed to believe that the KGB agents and the other denizens of the USSR have all been transmogrified into Free Enterprise Democrats (FEDs). Those with somewhat more perception may find the opinion of Yevgeny Albats, *THE STATE WITHIN A STATE: The KGB and Its Hold on Russia – Past, present, and Future* (Farrar, Strauss, Giroux, 1994. ISBN: 0-374-18104-7) worthy of perusal.
14. *Congreso* is "Congress" and not "congressman," and therefore these are not necessarily assistants to Burton.
15. Louis S. Segesvary, a State officer in Guatemala, produced a detailed report [*Guatemala: A Complex Scenario*, Center for Strategic and International Studies, Georgetown University, 1984] which demonstrated that AI had used ML terrorist "reports" as the basis for its "Special Briefing". It was observed also (p.20ff) that "there were a number of incidents that AI attributed to government forces that, in fact, should have been attributed to the guerrillas." This of course is reminiscent of Jones work with the Tutela Legal distortions favoring the Farabundi terrorists which were touched upon in Wkly 5.18.
16. As the Sandinista LibTheo cleric defined himself, "In order to be a good Christian it is primarily necessary to be a Marxist-Leninist" (p.193, YRBK97).
17. A defector from LibTheo was the Jesuit Luis Eduardo Pellecer Faena whose account claimed that much of the bad press which Guatemala and El Salvador suffered "around the world was directly due...[to the fact] that the Jesuits had a direct line to AI" ["The Priest Who Came In From the Cold," *Christianity Today*, 28 November 1981].
18. It is to be presumed that AI was already aware of the Colombian president's gag order which means this was simply a publicity-seeking ploy. Ed.

19. The presumptuousness of this organization is bizarre. Most members of the Latin American military are prevented from exercising the franchise while on active duty, a state of affairs which would not be countenanced in the US, for example. They are also muzzled while on active duty. Now this HRV organization is demanding that they be muzzled even after retirement, a very curious view of "human rights" indeed. Certain LANS informants have maintained that these NGOs have no interest in any HRVs committed against anti-MLs, military personnel or police, a claim which certainly squares with the LANS editor's experience in the John Hull Case. Ed.
20. In El Salvador the LANS Editor encountered the revolving door justice with which the courts treated the FMLN terrorists. And he was familiar with the double standard with which military and terrorists were treated.
21. LANS cannot, unfortunately, do everything at once. As soon as the forthcoming treatment of the Civil Self Defense Patrols in Peru has been completed, LANS will initiate its treatment of the same subject in Colombia. At this time, however, it can be stated that the correspondent's remarks on these CAPs and the military in Colombia are precisely correct.
22. The I, V, XIV, XV and XVIII Brigades make up II Division.
23. It is to be recalled that any terrorist picked up for any common law crime is *a priori* a "political" prisoner.
24. There are 39 pages in the holograph report, a copy of which LANS has obtained. The title of the report in rather illiterate printed capitals appears on page 1 (Editor's assigned numbers) as "3rd ASSEMBLY OF THE YARIGUIES URBAN RESISTANCE FRONT (FURY): HOTBED OF BATTLE AND REBELLIOUSNESS WITH ITS DEAD – PRISONERS AND DISPLACED CONSTRUCTING POWER ALTERNATIVE." The Agenda of the Assembly is given on p.2. The principal references to COSOP and CREDHOS are given on p.23.
25. CONVIVIR Santo Domingo, was authorized to operate in Lebrija, Santander, by the superintendency by Res.5564 of 21 March 1997.
26. Author's note: Absurdly, the ML supporters, after accusing the CONVIVIR of being legal "paramilitaries," managed to have their armament restricted to revolvers and shotguns.
27. Several members of the staff of Apartado Mayor Gloria Cuartas were indicted for the La Chinita massacre of EPL sympathizers by FARC.
28. Colonel Carlos Velasquez was at one time commander of the special Army group set up to attack the Cali Cartel. At the time he was seduced by a Cali Cartel operative. The special group, however, did produce results. After compromising pictures were published in *SEMANA*, the colonel admitted his misdeed and was forgiven. Recently, he admitted to *SEMANA* that he planned a single-handed *coup d'état* against President Samper during a presidential visit to Urabá, but was thwarted in his plan by the unexplained presence of a higher ranking officer.
29. Stanislev Lunev and Ira Winkler, *THROUGH THE EYES OF THE ENEMY: Russia's highest ranking military defector reveals why Russia is more dangerous than ever* (Regnery, 1998. ISBN: 0-89526-390-4). Colonel Lunev is still in the Witness Protection Program.
30. General Bonett told the LANS Editor of this conversation in his July 1998 interview.
31. The "landmark" nature of the victory has to do, not with the overrun of the small unit by much greater numbers of terrorists, but with the supine Samper Government's refusal to allow FAC to go after its own which were used by FARC to hold Colombia hostage.

32. There is something strange here. Since, as LANS has pointed out on various occasions, these fronts run about company size, there must have been terrorist personnel from more than one front.
33. The Jesuit involvement in Marxist Leninist terrorism is probably still best discussed by Malachi Martin, *ibid.*
34. Former Mexican President Luís Echeverría is still apologizing for the so-called Tlatelalco "massacre," apparently most recently at the Editors Club in the Hotel Marriot (*Proceso*, Mexico, 17 May 1998). He should of course be aware that he has nothing for which to apologize. That this affair was one of the KGB's most successful DOs has been demonstrated in exquisite detail by John Barron, *KGB: The Secret Work of Soviet Secret Agents* (MacMillan, 1974. ISBN: 0553202545), pp.320ff.
35. LibTheo has been frequently discussed in these reports, perhaps most extensively in the review of the book by Rev. Dr. Miguel Poradowsky, *El Marxismo en la Teología* (Imprenta LaHosa, 1983). This theologian's exhaustive treatment describes the four-step marxization of theology through (1) Saduceeism, (2) horizontal Christianity, (3) demythologized Christianity and (4) atheistic Christianity (pp.193ff, YRBK97).
36. This and related DOs have, of course, been discussed in Chapter 4, YRBK97.
37. In the early 1980s the LANS Editor had occasion to become familiar with the Miskito, Sumo and Rama Indians, fugitive from the Sandinista terrorists and encamped in Honduras. The chiefs of these Indians attested to him of the adverse behavior of the ACNUR personnel toward them. According to these Indians, the ACNUR personnel were largely supporters of the Sandinistas. This is perhaps relevant to their behavior with regard to the EZLN mentioned here.
38. That Cárdenas is the Mexican representative at Castro's São Paulo Forum (cf.p.99, YRBK97; Wkly 5.1 in Chapter 4 above, etc.) and has an "arrangement" with the EZLN has been discussed in these reports.
39. The Mexican Government had been aware of the coming Zapa "uprising" long before its official January 1994 initiation. Nevertheless, Pres. Salinas de Gortari, acting as if it was a surprise, called the "ex" Sandinista terrorist and army chief, Humberto Ortega, allegedly to ask him what to do. Ortega and the "ex" Farabundi terrorist chief, Joaquín Villalobos, flew to Mexico City and told him what to do: Declare "peace." Salinas did so. This was verified for LANS by Roberto Arguello, our colleague who interviewed Ortega on the matter (cf.pp.100ff, YRBK97 and subsequent reports).
40. The author later mentions the book by Mario Payeras, *DAYS OF THE JUNGLE: The Testimony of a Guatemalan Guerrillero, 1972-1976* (Monthly Review Press, 1983. ISBN: 0853456488) which is particularly valuable as demonstrating the fact that the fourth phase of Guatemalan ML terrorism began with the invasion of Guatemala from Mexico in 1972 by Payeras and a handful of his "comrades." By 1976 the handful had grown to only 50, more important proof that the campesino wants nothing to do with the "liberation" efforts of the HL.

7

Latin American International Organizations

General

The international organizations discussed in this chapter are largely made up of Latin American (LA) nations, although certain of these organizations, such as the Movement of Non Aligned Nations (MNNA), may contain varying numbers of representatives from other regions. Nevertheless, all of those organizations included here are importantly, if not exclusively, concerned with LA affairs.

There are of course almost any number of ways in which these organizations may be categorized. Unfortunately, there are valid objections to almost any of these categorizations so that again these have been arranged alphabetically by acronym insofar as this is possible. While this may appear to some a denigration of their relative importance, it renders their location most straightforward.

Central American Bank of Economic Integration (BCIE)

BCIE SEAT ESTABLISHMENT
(WKLY 5.8, 26 FEBRUARY 1998)

Summiteering in 1998 Central America (CA) began in Tegucigalpa, Honduras, on 19 January where the five[1] regional presidents officially established the new seat of the BCIE and stood as "witnesses of honor" at the signing of the Honduras-El Salvador border protocol. From there the presidents trekked to El Salvador where, on 4 February and in "complete secretiveness," they dealt with the CA Parliament (PARLACEN), albeit, they were, as Central America 4

(CA-4) or the Secretariat of CA Integration (SICA), to have dealt with various other matters—and perhaps did. The summiteering continued, but the presidents were replaced by their foreign ministers who appeared in San José, Costa Rica, on 10 February where they assembled with the European Union (UE) representatives in the XIV San José Meeting. The summiteers then proceeded to Panama City, Panama, for the VIII Meeting of the Grupo de Río and UE Foreign Ministers.

Several years ago the then Chairman of the Board of the BCIE, Federico Alvarez, decided to construct the impressive edifice which now graces Boulevard Suyapa in the Honduran capital of Tegucigalpa. Since the inaugural ceremonies of 19 January 1998 this building is the new home of the BCIE, boasting a $20 million [*La Prensa* (San Pedro Sula) 20 January 1998] bronze statue of the CA hero, Francisco Morazán, sculpted by the Honduran, Mario Zamora Alcántara.

Present at the christening festivities were the presidents of Costa Rica, José María Figueres; of El Salvador, Armando Calderón Sol; of Guatemala, Alvaro Arzú; of Nicaragua, Arnaldo Alemán; and of the host country, soon to be ex president, Carlos Reina, and the incoming president, Carlos Flores. These notables were joined by various banking magnates to include the president of the BCIA, José Manuel Pacas Castro; the president of the Inter American Development Bank (BID), Enrique Iglesias; and the president of the Central Bank of the Republic of China, Juan Dong Shen. Among the madding throng of other dignitaries, only Tegucigalpa Archbishop Oscar Andrés Rodríguez need be remarked.

The archbishop blessed the sparkling new installation with remarks appropriate to its expressed objective of "promoting integration and the economic and social development of the CA countries." The bishop was followed by Mr. Pacas Castro who declared, *inter alia*, that it was "a day of jubilation and happiness in the history of the BCIE and of the region because the CA heirs to the Morazanic ideal will have their own house which is the patrimony of all, thanks to the efforts of all."

Mr. Pacas went on to say that during the July 1993-December 1997 period there was a net resource transfer of $201 million. He added that the default in the bank's portfolio "is" 1.1 percent, numbers which may require further clarification. The bank has reserves for the "restructuring" of loans for $150.7 million; the net loan portfolio is $1,710.3 million, up $669.8 million from 1993. Capital and reserves are $938.5 million which is $328.7 million above that of 1993.

El Salvador-Honduras Border Protocol

The misnamed Soccer War[2] between El Salvador and Honduras began on 14 July 1969, was stopped by the Organization of American States (OAS) after 100 hours and led to border disputes which have not yet been fully resolved. These disputes in turn led, *inter alia*, to the seven *bolsones teritoriales* (territorial pockets) along the border which served as sanctuaries for the Farabundo Martí National Liberation Front (FMLN) terrorists during the Salvadoran unpleasantness which allegedly ended with the Chapultepec Accords (1992).

The common frontier between the two nations totals 374 kilometers (kms) of which only 130 kms have been agreed upon to this point. This is in spite of the Peace Treaty which the two countries signed in the Peru of 1980 and the decision rendered by the International Court of Justice in The Hague on 11 September 1992.

The remaining 244 kms will allegedly be specifically agreed upon during the year following 19 January 1998 when the Frontier Protocol was signed by El Salvador and Honduras. It was at this signing that the CA presidents acted as "witnesses of honor" (*testigos de honor*).

Diplomatic protocols are seldom simple. In keeping with this principle, the protocol in question contains seven chapters and 22 articles.

Inter-American Development Bank (BID)

THE XXXIX BID ASSEMBLY OF GOVERNORS
(WKLY 5.13, 2 APRIL 1998)

> Keynes did not add any new ideas to the body of inflationist fallacies ... He merely knew how to cloak the pleas for inflation and credit expansion in the sophisticated terminology of mathematical economics ... —von Mises[3]

Von Mises was referring to that array of international financial "instruments" including the World Bank (WB),[4] the International Monetary Fund (IMF) and BID. This whole vast structure for wealth redistribution was initiated at Bretton Woods in 1944 by two interesting characters, a Communist International (COMINTERN) agent, Harry Dexter White,[5] and a Marxist, John Maynard Keynes.[6]

"We take from the rich and give to the poor," declared Pierrot. "What poor?" asked Pierrette. "Us poor," replied Pierrot.

"... the real *piece de resistance*," say Mason and Asher in a weighty tome[7] bearing the *imprimatur* of WB President Kermit Gordon, "was an amalgamation of the Keynes and White plans into what became ... a joint statement of the experts on the IMF." In IMF Pamphlet No. 42 Chandavarkar[8] furnishes the following description: "Thus, the Fund embodies the quintessential elements of international Cooperation, namely *from* each member according to its resources (quota subscriptions and loans) and *to* each member according to its need (balance of payments)." Which is bemusing because of its similarity to Heinrich Karl Marx's "From each ... to each ..."[9]

The Inter-American Development Bank (BID)

The International Bank for Reconstruction and Development (IBRD) began operations in 1946 as an independent specialized agency of the UN. Among the various regional development banks, the oldest and once the largest was BID. This "bank" is described as "founded in 1959," it apparently coming into existence in 1960, initially capitalized at $1 billion, the US contributing $450 million. It describes itself as established "with the intention of contributing to the acceleration of LA economic and social progress." This self description continues by conjuring up the specter of former Brazilian President Juscelino Kubitschek[10] who introduced his country to the disaster that was Jango Goulart. BID claims for Kubitschek whatever the credit may be for its creation.

Beginning with 19 Western Hemisphere (WH) nations, the 1974 Declaration of Madrid extended this group to include various extra WH nations. Today the "members" include 28 WH nations, 16 European, Israel and Japan for an obvious 46-nation total. The organization of course has its seat in Washington, DC, contains two loan agencies and is geographically divided into three regions.

The subordinate loan agencies are the Inter-American Investments Corporation (CII) and the Multilateral Investments Corporation (FOMIN). CII was allegedly created to contribute to LA development by financing "small and medium private enterprises." FOMIN was allegedly created in 1992 to promote the "viability of the market economies in the region."

The first of the geographical regions into which BID operations are divided is Regional Operations Department (DRO) I which is made up of Argentina, Bolivia, Brazil, Chile, Ecuador, Paraguay and Uruguay. DRO 2 is made up of Belize, Costa Rica El Salvador, the Dominican Republic, Guatemala, Haiti, Mexico, Nicaragua and Panama. DRO 3 is made up of the Bahamas, Barbados, Colombia, Guayana, Jamaica, Peru, Suriname, Trinidad and Tobago and Venezuela.

BID has offices in each of the member countries, but its seat is, of course, in Washington, DC, the address there 1300 New York Ave., NW, Washington, DC 20577, telephone 202/623-1000.

BID Personnel

Enrique V. Iglesias has been president of BID since 1988, his third five-year term having begun on 1 April 1998. This native-born Spaniard is a naturalized citizen of Uruguay, having been foreign minister of his adopted country during the three years preceding his first accession to the BID post. He had figured importantly in such affairs as the UN Conference on New and Renewable Energy Sources in Nairobi (1981) and the Uruguayan Round of Multilateral Negotiations on the General Accord on Tariff and Trade (GATT) (1986). He has of course received a host of orders and prizes which he dutifully lists in his autobiography. As he has listed those honorary degrees and other awards which mark the successful modern man.

Iglesias' second-in-command is Nancy Birdsall, the US-born executive vice president of BID. She describes herself as having held "various policy and management positions at the WB," having been chief of the WB Environmental Division for LA Region b and accredited with establishment of the Brazil Rainforest Trust Fund. As an adviser to the Rockefeller Foundation she contributed "her expertise on the state's role in social programs"; she served, *inter alia*, on the National Academy of Sciences' Human Dimensions of Global Change Committee, and she now chairs the board of the International Center for Research on Women.

Ricardo Luís Santiago heads DRO I, this Brazilian having labored for a consulting firm between 1981 and 1990, his sojourn there apparently interspersed with positions in that nations Planning and Finance Ministries. Miguel Eduardo Martínez heads DRO II, this Argentine having received his Ph.D. from the University of Chicago, although LANS has made no effort to determine whether this was taken under Friedman or his antithesis. He was in the WB from 1974. Ciro De Falso heads DRO III, this US citizen having emerged from the Treasury Department.

The BID Mission

The expressed mission of BID is the promotion of the economic development of its member countries by "investment" in the creation or expansion of enterprises, operations and services, whether public, private or mixed. It would, according to Dell,[11] finance "not only productive projects ... but also 'social'-overhead projects ..." There would therefore appear to be no real restrictions on BID loans, and, in practice, it is difficult to find any. This is of interest for the following reasons.

BID appears to have evolved into a system wherein loans—save perhaps in the case of Chile—are largely restructured out of existence or forgiven, that is, a charitable organization which, however worthy its motivation, has little if anything to do with "banking" in what may be described as a classical sense.

From the BID Report for 1991, for example, it may be learned that the organization had approved "loans" for a total of $51.8 billion to which must be added almost $2 billion more "extended on a grant or contingency recovery basis." The money has gone for projects, the justification for which it would probably be difficult to analyze. Among those on which von Mises, for example, could be expected to cast a jaundiced eye was a 1991 loan to Bolivia of $410,000 "to improve the efficiency of state-owned enterprises."

Insofar as repayment of "loans" is concerned, there has been a great deal of "restructuring" and "forgiveness" but what appears to be relatively little repayment. In general it may be said that a substantial amount of debt has been "forgiven" by various countries, a great deal of "rollover" has taken place, and a certain amount of debt-for-equity, debt-for-aid and debt-for-nature *(sic)* swaps have occurred. The latter is perhaps worth remarking.

The Politically Correct (PC) "environmental" lobby is apparently strong enough and furnishes power enough to appeal, not only to Gorbachev, the former Soviet dictator, but to various other politicians. One way to cater to this lobby involves the debt-for-nature swap. A few examples must suffice. The first of these took place in 1987 wherein Conservation International purchased US$650,000 of Bolivian debt at *15 cents on the dollar*. In return, Bolivia agreed to set aside 3.7 million acres in three areas surrounding the so-called "Beni Biosphere" in the Amazon Basin. In 1991 the debt of the Central American Bank for Economic Integration was "purchased" at a discount unknown to LANS by New York-based Rainforest Alliance which thereby acquired land at the International Children's Rainforest. It is not known how well the conditions for these and the other "swaps" have been fulfilled by these "environmental" groups. In a non-BID swap, it will be of interest to see if Poland "cleans up its environment" in exchange for 10 percent of its debt to the Club of Paris (14 nations).

XXXIX Meeting of the BID Board of Governors

All member countries have representatives on the Board of Governors which is the "maximum authority of the bank." Generally speaking, the governors are finance ministers or presidents of central banks or occupants of similar positions. This BID Board Meeting was also the XIII CII Meeting. These meetings were held in the resort city of Cartagena de Indias on the sea. The preliminary meetings began on 12 March. The official meetings lasted from 16 March through 18 March.

These preliminary "seminars" were: 12-13 March, Seminar 1 (0900-1830), "Social Programs" and "Poverty and Citizen Participation." 14 March, Seminar 2 (0900-1830) "Promoting Citizen Coexistence (*Convivencia*): A Frame of Reference for Action." 14 March, Seminar 3 (0900-1300) "Investments in Emerging LA and Caribbean Markets: Risks and Opportunities." 15 March, Seminar 4 (0900-1300) "What Is the Employment Problem in LA and How Is It to Be Faced?"

Colombian President Samper, Panamanian President Pérez Valladares, Peruvian President Fujimori and some 4000 delegates[1,2] attended. Because Spain had hosted the last such extravaganza, the festivities were opened by Spanish Economy Minister Rodrigo Rato who duly predicted economic growth of 3.5 percent for LA during 1998, a figure slightly higher than that of BID.

Mr. Iglesias subsequently presented a rosy forecast for LA's position to withstand any problems which might arise from "Asian flu," and called down the necessity of emerging from LA's great "social debt," which he claimed to be made up of "critical poverty, exclusion and inequality." This statement may be interpreted in various ways, the first question being "What is meant by inequality?", the second "How does one *fix* it?" Mr. Iglesias of course lobbied for increases in IMF "resources," meaning that the "subscriptions" assigned to the various nations be increased (again). His remarks about redefining the functions of the State should not sit well with those who feel that LA's only chance for emerging from its slough of despond is private enterprise.

The BID president lobbied for "opening space for a private sector which operates in transparent and *supervised* markets," this so that the citizens of the resulting "harmonic" society will feel themselves (*sic*) "participants in the economic development and the consolidation of democracy." But Mr. Samper's contribution may be the most ominous.

LANS has presented (Spcls 5.5 and 5.6 in Chapter 5 above) Dr. Posada's treatment of the NGOs which have infiltrated portions of Mr. Samper's foreign service primarily in order to denigrate his country and promote the Marxist Leninist (ML) terrorists therein. Under these realities, Mr. Samper's call for "a fund for peace" in his country could contribute, not toward real "peace" but toward terrorist victory. The development of this situation should be well worth watching.

The Meaning of XXXIX BID Meeting

"There go the Sandinistas in our Mercedes Benzes," Harry Bodán Shields, the last pre-Sandinista Nicaraguan foreign minister, once remarked to the LANS Editor.

Although said with a broad smile, it was a considerably more profound remark than it might at first appear, because it honestly encapsules all that maneuvering which is politics: the quest for power and the perquisites, the Mercedes Benzes, of that power. Héctor Hernández M., writing in *El Espectador* (Bogotá) said it somewhat differently.

> Every year almost the same discourse is repeated during the assemblies...of the multilateral financial organisms. The orators change, but the content is the same: the laments for poverty and the proposals to reduce it. But everything remains the same in the third world... At the assembly will assist...more than 2,500 international bankers. Poverty and violence will be the excuse for the social encounter...BID brings 39 years of financing development... But everything remains the same.

Andean Community of Nations (CAN)

X SUMMIT OF THE ANDEAN COMMUNITY OF NATIONS (CAN)
(WKLY 5.16, 23 APRIL 1998)

The association of the nations of Bolivia, Ecuador, Colombia, Peru and Venezuela has, until recently, been referred to as the Andean Group. At about the time of the IX Summit of this group a change of name to the Andean Community of Nations (CAN) was taking place, this rendered official by the "protocol of Sucre" (April 1997). By this spring of 1998 the change appears to have been firmly established. The IX Summit took place in Sucre, Bolivia, and this, as well as the evolution of CAN has been discussed (pp.352ff, YRBK98). At this meeting were also present Paraguay President Juan Carlos Wasmosy and Panamanian President Ernesto Pérez Balladares for the signing of protocols. President Wasmosy was present as president of the Common Market of the Southern Cone (MERCOSUR), his protocol the intention of beginning negotiations between the two groups for a common market. President Pérez Balladares was present to sign a protocol to negotiate the entry of Panama into CAN.

This was in April 1997. On 20 March 1998 Venezuelan President Rafael Caldera had lunch with French President Jacques Chirac, the former telling the latter that "the conclusion of an accord is imminent." "Imminent" apparently now means "by the end of 1998." Which, according to Panamanian Vice Minister of Foreign Relations Marcel Salamín some ten days later, is also the case with Panama's entry into CAN. At the conclusion of the IX CAN Summit it was announced that the X Summit would take place in Guayaquil, Ecuador, as it did.

The "Summit" is, in actuality, a meeting of the Andes Presidential Council (CPA), the supreme "executive" body of CAN. It is to meet once per year. As is usual in such affairs, the Summit was preceded by preparatory meetings on 3 April 1998. These included the Andean Foreign Relations Ministers Council (CAMRE), the Andean Community Commission[13] and the Expanded Chancellors Council. CAMRE is a legislative body of CAN,[14] it to meet twice per year and empowered with electing the secretary general. Participating in these were the ministers of integration and foreign commerce of the five nations.

On 4 April 1998, Bolivian President Hugo Banzer, Colombian President Ernesto Samper, Ecuadoran President Fabián Alarcón, Peruvian President Alberto Fujimori and Venezuelan President Rafael Caldera opened the X CAN Summit in Guayaquil, Ecuador. On 5 April the CAN presidents closed the summit and issued the prescripted "Act of Guayaquil" (AG). About two weeks later the five would proceed to Santiago, Chile, to sign a document herein dubbed the "Declaration of Santiago" (Spcl 5.12, this chapter below), and containing much the same rhetoric, but differing in one particular, the number of nations involved.

The smiling Mr. Jeffrey Davidow, US Under Secretary of State, has captained the unsuccessful effort to subordinate all LA trading groups to the current "centerpiece" of US LA policy, the Free Trade Organization of LA (ALCA) (pp.342ff, YRBK98). In these reports MERCOSUR has been the prime target of such attempts, although CAN has shared the onslaught and evinces no overt subordination of its common-market policy to ALCA. It must be remarked, however, that its target date for "integration" corresponds to that of ALCA, 2005.

There is any amount of minutiae in AG—"create a group of experts to analyze mechanisms which facilitate the circulation of people among the five countries," etc.—but only four points will be considered here: (1) the common market among the five, (2) Bolivian outlet on the sea, (3) CAN-MERCOSUR free commerce zone (ZLC) and (4) the Peru-Ecuador border dispute.

1. By no later than 2005 the CAN presidents pledge to create a union wherein there will be free circulation of "goods and services" within the five-nation bloc. This bloc "will seek a mechanism" for a better rapprochement with the Russian Federation.[15] The CAN nations have a "particular determination" to begin negotiations of accords with Canada.

2. Bolivia has a navy but no outlet on the sea. In 1993 it appeared that it had won such an outlet, the occasion somewhat prematurely celebrated by the Peruvian and Bolivian presidents frolicking in the surf on the beach called Sea Bolivia (p.53,YRBK97). The Bolivian Navy still has no port from which to launch its ships, and this has apparently not been affected by X CAN. President Banzer spoke of this, opining that, without an agreement on this Window on the Sea, "The integration to which we aspire will never be perfected."

3. The five heads of state agreed to sign an accord on 16 April with MERCOSUR for the creation of a Free Commercial Zone (ZLC) by the two blocs. Political and commercial dialog with the UE toward the same end is to be implemented. It was agreed that negotiations with Canada for consolidation of the accords be commenced and that an accord to this effect be signed on 16 April.

4. The Ecuador-Peru border skirmish has been discussed from time to time in these reports (p.66,YRBK97). During X CAN Ecuadoran President Alarcón and Peruvian President Fujimori met and coincided "in expressing their fervent desires to concretize peace and put an end to the border differences which the two people have."

An interesting contretemps over point (2) arose not long after X CAN and when the II Summit of the Americas was getting underway in Chile. On 15 April Chilean Chancellor José Miguel Insulza announced that the request by President Banzer for a meeting with President Frei would not be granted because this request "deteriorated the political climate." On the same day the Government of Bolivia retorted to Insulza's apparently bizarre statement with, "Bolivia never solicited an encounter between Presidents Banzer and Frei."

Ecuador will turn over during June 1998 the post of CAN director to Colombia which will be in charge of organizing the next summit in May 1999.

Central American-Dominican Free Trade

CENTRAL AMERICAN-DOMINICAN TLC
(WKLY 5.16, 23 APRIL 1998)

The XIX CA Summit (CCA) was held in July 1997 in Panama as has been discussed (pp.374ff, YRBK98). What was originally billed as the XX CA Summit was held in the Dominican Republic (DR) on 5 November 1997, it being described by DR President Leonel Fernández as the Extraordinary Meeting of CA, Panama, Belice and DR heads of state. The envisioned amalgamation of CA, to include Panama but apparently not Belice, was brought closer to reality on 28 January 1998 when four Dominicans were sworn in as "permanent observers" before the PARLACEN (pp.374ff, YRBK98). Perhaps the most definitive step in the progression was taken on 16 April 1998, this of course with an eye to the immediately upcoming Summit of the Americas (Spcl 5.12 below).

On the night of 16 April the CA and Dominican heads of state signed the Free Trade Treaty (TLC) after negotiations which were reported [*El Diario de Hoy* (San Salvador) 17 April 1998] as "lasting until the eleventh hour." Finally, the provisions were allegedly agreed upon without including a "black list" of products which are not covered by the treaty. What reports seem to indicate is that there is such a "black list"; it is simply not specifically included in the treaty. The TLC allegedly establishes tariff-free trade within the bloc, but this appears to be largely in the eyes of the observer.

For example, it was reported that El Salvador did not "wish"—presumably "will not allow"—to have sugar, petroleum derivatives and ethyl alcohol enter the country. In addition to this specific example, there are various regulations established in the treaty governing "free" commerce in goods and services, governmental purchasing, rules of origin, customs procedures, safety measures, human and plant health measures, unfair commercial practices, promotion of competition, intellectual property rights and controversy solution.

Although, on posing for the cameramen on the disembarkation stair, the CA presidents and their entourages spoke glowingly of their accomplishments, the treaty may not be as close to consummation as is being claimed.

Latin American Infancy Summit (CIAL)

THE LATIN AMERICAN (LA) INFANCY SUMMIT (CIAL)[16]
(WKLY 5.15, 16 APRIL 1998)

The XXXIX BID Meeting (above) evoked an article in *El Espectador* (Bogotá) which suggested that the "poverty and violence" discussed at these assemblies served as "the excuse for the social encounter" at the seaside resort of Cartagena de Indias. March was heavy with international meetings, the first of which might perhaps be similarly described and was held in the same resort city.

The CIAL opened its deliberations in the International Convention Center at Cartagena de Indias on 1 March 1998, Colombian President Ernesto Samper welcoming the 18 first ladies and over 500 delegates with an oration bemoaning the injustices to which he claimed infancy (*infancia*) or children were subjected. The age range which may be described by "infancy" appears to be somewhat flexible.

Mr. Samper recalled that the Declaration of the Rights of the Child was proclaimed by the United Nations (UN) seven years ago and declared that "since then we have been fighting in order that the ideals therein coincide with infantile reality in the world." He then lamented the fact that "we are not achieving it." This was followed by the routine contention that more is being spent on arms than on childhood.

As is usual in such discourses, the Colombian president declared there to be no time to lose in assuring children's "rights," then told his audience of his alleged "battling in order that children are not victims of guerrilla war." The litany of reasons for "our" battle followed: "in order that they do not lose their legs to [terrorist] land mines, that they quit working in degrading places, in order that they go to school to be lovingly cared for while their mothers bring bread to the house..." and so on.

In these inaugural festivities the UN Educational, Scientific and Cultural Organization (UNESCO) "Ambassador of Good Will," Kim Phuc, figured importantly as did the Director of the UN Children's Fund (UNICEF) Office of Evaluation and Politics, Martha Santos Pais, Director General of the International Labor Organization (OIT), Victor Tockman, the First Lady of Burkina Faso, Chantal Campaore and various other national and international dignitaries such as the "First Lady" of Castro's Cuba and 19 other first ladies from the Western Hemisphere.

To the misfortunes enumerated by Mr. Samper Administrative Security Department Director Luis Enrique Montenegro Rinco added the 30,000 children involved in Colombian prostitution, giving various details such as the 270 prostitution centers in Medellín alone. As would appear appropriate, the OIT director then lectured the attendees on the "millions of youths who see their right not to work violated by socioeconomic and cultural causes."

Summit of the Americas (CLA)

II SUMMIT OF THE AMERICAS
(WKLY 5.15, 16 APRIL 1998)

Writing recently in *Diario las Américas* (Miami) US State Secretary Albright asserted that "In December 1994, with the historic Summit of the Americas in Miami, began a new era of cooperation among the democratic nations of the Western Hemisphere...The Plan of Action of Miami...produced tangible results and created a base on which can continue to be raised a better future for all the citizens of the Americas..."

This utopian "plan" has been discussed in Wkly 2.17 (*ibid*). Whether anything has yet come out of it is difficult to determine. One thing, however, is certain: it is the centerpiece of the Clinton Administration LA policy, and the US president will apparently be present in Chile on 18 and 19 April 1998.

THE II SUMMIT OF THE AMERICAS (CLA)[17]
(SPCL 5.12, 20 APRIL 1998)

"The assembly was one of the endless series of expensive inter-American exercises in ritual showmanship."— Ronald Hilton, President, California Institute of International Studies

On 19 April 1998 in Santiago, Chile, the academics Humberto Maturana and Manfred Max Neef presented the book, *The America That We Want* (La América que queremos), which is described as assembling the opinion of 32 continental "political and intellectual leaders." Included amongst these "leaders" are US Vice President Albert Gore, Guatemalan National Revolutionary Union (URNG) spokeswoman, Nobel Laureate and prevaricator *par excellence* Rigoberta Menchú,[18] ex presidents of Chile, Mexico and Peru, director of the World Health Organization (OMS) Gro Harlem, BID President Enrique Iglesias and 24 others. This is particularly relevant here because, as is the case with the II CLA, what is possible, practical or even generally desirable is apparently not important. What is important is what certain individuals or groups of individuals want or perhaps what their political leaders think they want.

Background of the II CLA

It is first important to reiterate that the CLA is the "centerpiece" of the Clinton Administration "LA policy," a fact which is apparently relevant to its aim of creating a solution to the entire gamut of human woes and conditions which prevent the existence of everyone in Utopia. I CLA has been briefly described (p.236, YRBK97); it may be reviewed using the Press Kit issued by the US State Department (State) for State Secretary Albright's trip to II CMA. One "Fact Sheet" in the Kit illustrates this with its four divisions: (1) Education: Investing in People, Defining Our Future; (2) Making Democracy Relevant, Enjoying the Fruits of Freedom; (3) Building Our Wealth Through Economic Integration and Trade; and (4) Rejecting Poverty Amid Growing Prosperity.

Space hardly permits reproduction of details, but a sketch of those topics in (1) indicates that the *modus operandi* in dealing with these problems is (a) write down whatever comes to mind relative to "Education" and (b) promise funds to "solve" all the write downs. In (1) "more funds into primary and secondary education as...for democracy, prosperity and equal opportunity"; enhance "teacher training, standards,[19] textbook availability..."; curriculum "reform for a global market"; increase "international student and teacher exchanges"; promote teaching of "democratic values" and environmentalism[20]; promote "lifelong learning including" women and displaced workers. A dollar value on spending for (1) during the next three years ($8.3 billion) concludes (1). (2) bolsters freedom and a free press; trains judges and improves justice; decentralizes government; attacks corruption, terrorism and crime; fixes disputes between states, openness in defense policies and arms transfers; enhances worker rights, eliminates child labor; ($5.9 b). (3) Free Trade Area of the Americas; fixes the financial markets; fixes environment; fixes transportation; internet and technology; ($18.9 b). (4) fixes credit, training, technology; property registration for the "poor"; reduces illness; fixes hunger and malnutrition; ($12.5 b). Should there be anything such as meteorites or other cosmic phenomena which have been left out—or any other sort of phenomena—these can be included. [And have been; see end this paper.]

The other "Fact Sheets" recount the progress which has allegedly been made toward the "goals" established at I CLA. For example. "Education and the Santiago Summit" remarks the I CLA agreement that 100 percent of the Americas' children will have access to "quality" primary schooling by 2010. "As enrollment rates nearly reach these numbers in many countries..." appears to be as close to an indication of program success as the Sheet provides, it then diverging into various "improvements" which can be anticipated. The

"Democracy and Human Rights (HR)" sheet discusses what may prove to be a seriously counter-productive program for all save the Hemispheric Left (HL), the Inter American Court (and Commission) of HR which has been encountered in these reports. In the "Climate Change and Sustainable Development" sheet the unsupportable "greenhouse gases" control is perhaps the most interesting. Apparently this transparent attack on "developed" nation technology continues to brook no challenge, not simply among the International Left (IL), but also among the "developed" themselves.

A number of treaties, protocols and so on have been signed, whether "good things" or "bad things," all PC things, but it would be difficult to determine whether anything else has occurred.

Inter Summit Activities

A number of meetings, summits and the like occurred between December of 1994 and April of 1998, these bearing some relation to the CLA. For example, the so-called Hemispheric Summit for Sustainable Development, held in Bolivia in December 1996, had advanced billing in certain quarters as the II CLA. This has been discussed in some detail (pp.235ff, YRBK97).

Immediately preceding this II CLM were the IV Entrepreneurial Forum of the Americas and the IV Meeting of Commerce Ministers, both of these held in San José, Costa Rica. These are described in Wkly 5.15, this chapter below, their predecessor meetings touched upon. It was at one of the latter that the US Government, largely in the person of the US State official, Jeffrey Davidow, unsuccessfully attempted to talk the LA nations into subordinating regional trading groups such as MERCOSUR to the US "centerpiece," ALCA. All of these, of course, were orchestrated toward the projected towering finale which would take place in April 1998 Chile.

Our statesmen (politicians) can surely be depended upon to practice that same transparency which Secretary Albright infers, if not mentions, in her various Fact Sheets (e.g., Democracy and Human Rights). Apparently, however, there are certain individuals who, in the spirit of Jefferson *et al*, do not trust their government (politicians).

"Fast Track"

Since the US is supposed to be a republic, it allegedly has no official with regal powers such as that of negotiating and ratifying treaties with foreign nations. Instead, the US Constitution states quite succinctly as follows.

ARTICLE II, Section 2. He (the President) shall have Power, *by and with the Advice and Consent of the Senate*,[21] to make Treaties, provided two thirds of the Senators present concur; ...

By the so-called "Fast Track Authority" (FTA) the US Senate surrenders its duty under the Constitution to furnish "Advice and Consent" to such treaty making, doing this by agreeing in advance to "Consent" or "not Consent" to the totality of whatever the President may negotiate and foreswearing its duty to "Advise." The justification for granting FTA is "speed" and a president thus left "unfettered" in his negotiations. Apparently those in the US Senate, who are unwilling to grant this to the present lame-duck US President, felt that such "speed"—in a negotiation process allegedly, but apparently not actually, aimed at a 2005 free-trade treaty—was hardly necessary. The US Senate may now study—and, hopefully, read—the treaty before ratifying it, perhaps avoiding, for example, environmental pitfalls such as the demonstrably unscientific "global warming" arrangements.

The Attendees

Between 0700 and 1930 on Friday, 17 April 1998, 32 Western Hemisphere heads of state arrived at the Arturo Merino Benítez Airport in Santiago, Chile, to be greeted by a Chilean minister of state, the commander of the Santiago Area Garrison, the Chief of Protocol and the ambassador from the nation of the arriving head of state. After the Honor Guard rendered the requisite ruffles and flourishes, the *arrivé* delivered his "salute" to the country, then proceeded to the Hotel Sheraton to be greeted again by the secretary general of the II CLA. The following heads of state were all, presumably, dealt with in this fashion. (Chilean President Eduardo Frei was of course present at the II CLA, but is not included in the list. President Clinton arrived four days earlier than the rest.)

Prime Minister (PM) Lester Bird (Antigua and Barbuda), Pres. Carlos Menem (Argentina), PM Hubert A. Ingraham (Bahamas), PM Owen S. Arthur (Barbados), PM Manuel Esquivel (Belice), Pres. Hugo Banzer (Bolivia), Pres. Fernando Enrique Cardoso (Brazil), PM Jean Chrétien (Canada), Pres. Ernesto Samper (Colombia), Pres. José

María Figueres[22] (Costa Rica), PM Edison James (Dominica), Pres. Fabián Alarcón (Ecuador), Pres. Armando Calderón Sol (El Salvador), PM Keith Mitchell (Grenada), Pres. Alvaro Arzú (Guatemala), Pres. Janet Jagan (Guyana), Pres. René Preval (Haiti), Pres. Carlos Roberto Flores (Honduras), PM Percival J. Patterson (Jamaica), Pres. Ernesto Zedillo (Mexico), Pres. Arnoldo Alemán (Nicaragua), Pres. Ernesto Pérez Balladares (Panama), Pres. Juan Carlos Wasmosy (Paraguay), Pres. Alberto Fujimori (Peru), Pres. Leonel Fernández Reyna (Dominican Republic), PM Denzel Douglas (St. Kitts and Nevis), PM James F. Mitchell (St. Vincent and the Grenadines), PM Kenny D. Anthony (St. Lucia), Pres. Jules Wijdenbosch (Surinam), PM Basdeo Panday (Trinidad and Tobago), Pres. Julio M. Sanguinetti (Uruguay) and Pres. Rafael Caldera (Venezuela).

II CLA SCHEDULE
SATURDAY (S), 18 APRIL, AND SUNDAY (D) 19 APRIL 1998

0845S The welcome was supposed to have been extended to the attendees at this time by the Chilean President and First Lady, this to be followed by the ceremonial inauguration of the CLA with discourses by Messers Frei and Clinton.

1200D Closure of CLA including signing of the final CLA document. This was followed by speeches and a press conference.
(Between 0845S and 1200D and after there were various culinary and cultural events which made up the lion's share of the schedule. These are not included.)

1000S First work session of chiefs of state and four representatives of each delegation.

1330S Working lunch for chiefs of state only

1545S Second work session of chiefs of state and four representatives.

0945D Third work session for chiefs of state only.

As is routine in such affairs, the final "Declaration of Santiago"— or whatever it may now be called—was pre-scripted by the ministry clerks with probably little modification arising from these "work" sessions. In abstract the chiefs of state issued the following:

Declaration of Santiago

"The democratically elected chiefs of state and of government of the countries of the Americas have assembled in Santiago with the objective of continuing the dialog and strengthening the cooperation which we initiated in Miami in December 1994.

"Hemispheric integration constitutes a necessary complement to national politics in order to surmount the unresolved problems and obtain a better development. A process of integration, in its broadest concept, will permit, on the basis of respect for cultural identities, configuring a fabric (*trama*[23]) of common values and interests which support us in these objectives.

"Globalization offers great opportunities...special attention to most vulnerable countries and groups...

"Education constitutes the decisive factor for development...

"Today we instruct our ministers of commerce to initiate negotiations for ALCA...[and] reaffirm our determination to conclude negotiations...[by] 2005.

"Volatility of capital markets confirms our decision to strengthen bank supervision in the hemisphere.

"...citizen participation at all levels [a "good" thing]...we compact to strengthen the abilities of regional and local governments[24]...and promote more active societal participation.

"We celebrate the recent establishment of [the office of] a special secretary for Liberty of Expression in the framework of the OAS.

"...combat all forms of discrimination..."

" ...problems of inequality and social exclusion have not been solved...

"With profound satisfaction, we confirm that peace...is a reality in the hemisphere. (*sic*)

"We are giving new impetus to the battle against corruption, money laundering, terrorism, arms traffic...

"We reinforce...efforts to protect the environment as the basis of sustainable development...

"We recognize...the role...of the hemispheric institutions, particularly the OAS, we are instructing our ministers...to strengthen and modernize said institutions."

The documents issued did not, of course, begin and end with this one. By and large, these correspond to the "Fact Sheets" issued by US State Secretary Albright and listed above. Their "value" is largely contained in the dollar amounts which "BID, BM and AID" allegedly will contribute to these lofty aims "during a period of three years." A partial list follows.

"Against Poverty and Discrimination $12.5 billion (b)." "Formulas for Economic Integration $18.8b." "Justice and Human Rights

$5.9b." "Education $8.3b." These numbers obviously total $45.5b but almost certainly mean as little as the $42.2b which, according to *La Epoca* (Santiago 18 April 1998), the US White House avowed would be spent *each year* on these utopian schemes.[25] This phase should probably be concluded with a remark from "Formulas for Economic Integration." [The immediate contradiction: In Albright's "Fact Sheet 1," the Education $8.3 is for the "next three years," here what must be the same is *per year*.]

In the fifth paragraph of this mini declaration is included "Application of the mechanisms of science and technology to mitigate the damage caused by El Niño and ... volcanic eruptions, hurricanes, earthquakes and floods ..." Anyone who has been involved in scientific research should be well aware that Requests for Proposals (RFP) can be issued for El Niño elimination research for the entire $18.8b, and proposals will soon have been produced for twice this amount even if no ideas exist for effecting such miraculous results.

Summit of the Peoples of America (CPA)

SUMMIT OF THE PEOPLES OF AMERICA
(SPCL 5.13, 22 APRIL 1998)

In these reports there have been discussions of the contributions by the so-called Non Governmental Organizations (NGOs) to the victories and successes of the ML terrorists of the HL. A number of these groups have been encountered which contain members of the HL, others which allow themselves to be used, wittingly or unwittingly, by that same HL. Not long ago Dr. Posada discussed "The Diplomacy of the Subversion" in Colombia (Spcls 5.5 and 5.6, Chapter 5 above), much of which is a direct result of NGO activity. This is a reality which requires a careful and continuous treatment of these groups lurking on the periphery of the II CLA.

The Summit of the Peoples of America (CPA) could apparently be called the HL Summit with considerable accuracy. On the day (16 April) Mr. Clinton arrived in Chile the CPA opened its congress to what it claimed were 1,200 delegates from NGOs in "almost all the countries of America." The "summit" was organized by the Chilean Peoples Initiative Network (RECHIP), the United Workers Central (CUT) and the Inter American Regional Labor Organization (ORIT). The stated objective of the CPA was the discussion of (1) the protection of HR, (2) the protection of the environment and (3) discrimination against the "Indian ethnicities." The discussion was intended to produce a document which was to be presented to the heads of state participating in the II CLA.

Appropriately enough,[26] the CPA presiding organization was the Praesidium which included, *inter alia*, Pedro de Jésus Alejandro, Director of the Mexican Indigenous Council (CIM), Luis Anderson, Secretary of ORIT, Manuel Baquedano, President of the Political Ecology Institute, Fabiola Letelier, President of the Peoples' Rights Defense Corporation (CODEPU) and Florentina Alegría, Director of the Bolivian Mothers Who Love (MQA). The Praesidium members were not slow in revealing their political stance.

One such member, Baquedano, asserted that his summit would constitute "a bridge beginning with which to construct a regional alliance capable of fighting to end the unequal distribution of riches." Another, Letelier, stressed what she called the necessity of "changing a society which we consider unjust, arbitrary, unequal and excluding." Ms. Letelier had considerably more to say.

Although apparently not on the Praesidium, Denise Gómez, Director of the Cuban Women's Federation was very much present, but not nearly as ML sounding as Letelier, her most remarked remark being the frequently-voiced description of the CLA as the reply to the Iberian American Summit. This hardly compares to the Letelier demand for the establishment of a permanent International Penal Court to deal with cases of "genocide and violation of international law." The idea here is quite important for it is the HL's answer to any non-HL military force which might oppose it, the NGO expertise in fabricating HL charges truly completed with such a chamber.

350 women were among the delegates, perhaps those worthy of remark being the Mapuches, Bolivian cocaleros,[27] "campesinas" from Chiapas and Cuban "directors." These ladies were vehement in rejecting "all the economic treaties because they damage the fundamental rights of the workers." As of course would Fidel Castro be.

So that North America will not feel "excluded," the remarks of Warren Allmand, President of the Canadian International Center for HR and Development (CIDHD) told the delegates and the press that it is necessary to guard "labor rights." According to Mr. Allmand, the North American Free Trade Agreement (NAFTA) has benefited only a group of entrepreneurs. "The experience with NAFTA tells us that these treaties can undermine HR, therefore, we ask that social clauses form part of them." Mr. Allmand is probably aware of how many "social clauses" already weight down these treaties.

The CPA opened at the Hotel Tupahue at 0900 on 15 April and closed at the same location and same time on 18 April. Most of the sessions were held at this location. The forums specified in the schedule were on "environment," "HR" and "Woman and Indian." To these forums were later added one on "economic integration alternatives," "campesinos," "labor union summit" and "ethics."

Of considerable intrinsic interest to the reality of this meeting was the final decision to take special interest in subjects such as "the increasing risk of military confrontation between the [ML Zapatista terrorist] Indians of Chiapas and the Mexican Army."

International Labor Day (1 May 1998) will allegedly mark the beginning of the joint activities which were agreed upon. On 23 October 1998 the first "Continental Day Against Social Exclusion" is scheduled to take place. The II CPA was scheduled for 2000.

Conference of Foreign Ministers (CMCA)

XIV SAN JOSÉ CONFERENCE OF FOREIGN MINISTERS (CMCA) (WKLY 5.8, 26 FEBRUARY 1998)

In 1985 the I San José Conference of CA foreign ministers was celebrated in San José, Costa Rica, a performance scheduled for repetition at the XIV Conference on 10 and 11 February 1998 in that city at the Convention Center of the Hotel Herradura. The ministry clerks had completed their "technical meeting" on 9 February so that the declaration to issue from this conference was already in existence. This time, however, the conference was joined by 15 representatives of the UE countries and the hierarchy of the UE's executive arm, the European Commission (CE).

The host country's foreign relations minister, Fernando Naranjo, and its ambassador to the UE, Mario Carvajal, were prominent at the affair, Costa Rican President Figueres being late in arriving from Washington for the opening of festivities. Prominent among the European visitors were the CE vice president for Spain, Manuel Marín; CE vice president for Britain, Antony Lloyd; German foreign relations minister, Werner Hoyer; Portuguese foreign relations minister, Jaime Gama; and the foreign relations ministers of Finland,

Holland and Greece. The Spanish foreign minister, Abel Matutes, did not attend, "apparently for reasons of health."

The meeting opened at 0900 on 10 February and closed, not on 11 February as scheduled, but on 10 February, allegedly because "no modifications to the preliminary draft of the final declaration arose." The more likely reason for this early termination is that the participants were in a hurry to proceed to their next stop, Panama City, and further summiteering.

The "final declaration" was the epitome of PC in which "the importance of improving the situation of the indigenous population and the children, as well as the promotion of the equality between the man and the woman" was emphasized. Predictably, it went on to mention integration processes in CA and Europe, the strengthening of "governability" and the battle against poverty, citizen insecurity and narcotrafficking. Pre conference publicity had stressed the anti-narcotrafficking theme.

The declaration acknowledged CA aspirations for a free trade treaty between the two entities, and the CE agreed to examine the question. An early leak from the embassy clerks indicated that a forum was to be organized for the second half of this year in order to treat such "economic integration." This report may not have been accurate.

Presidents of Iberian-American Democratic (*sic*) Parliaments (CPPIA)

IX CONFERENCE OF PRESIDENTS OF IBERIAN-AMERICAN DEMOCRATIC PARLIAMENTS (CPPIA)
(SPCL 5.14, 19 JUNE 1998)

This conference was held in the Montevidean Legislative Palace of the Uruguayan capital on 22 and 23 May 1998 and attended by legislators from 16 nations. The conference title was rendered a *non sequitur* by the presence of the president of Castro's ML legislature. Press conference reports once again indicated that the "final conference reports" had already been drafted when the conference opened, albeit, there were allegedly disagreements among certain of the conferees (AFP 17 May 1998) on the question of Cuba.

Jaime Trobo, president of the Uruguayan Chamber of Deputies, was quoted in the press as "reproaching" the Cuban representatives because "there is no democracy without political parties," while the provisional president of the Argentine Senate, Eduardo Menem, was telling a press conference that Cuba should be immediately reintegrated into the OAS. Interestingly enough, Argentine President Carlos Menem's brother, Eduardo, was, according to press reports, alone with Ricardo Alarcón, the ML chief of Cuba's National Assembly of the Peoples Power, in his support of Castro's tyranny.

The tortuous behavior of President Menem in recent years is again called into some question by this behavior of his brother which is difficult to accept as at odds with Carlos' wishes. At the Miami Summit of the Americas (1994) it appeared that Pres. Menem was one of the chief opponents of Castro readmission to the OAS (p.237, YRBK97). Then in the Peru-Ecuador border skirmish of 1995 (pp.68ff, YRBK97), it was discovered that Argentina had been supplying arms to Ecuador in a clandestine operation which some are still claiming (*Diario Los Andes* 19 June 1998) had to have been known to Menem.[28] In 1997 Eduardo's visit to and support of Castro (p.71, YRBK98) stands out, and as does the curious Menem behavior marked by the issuance of an Argentine stamp commemorating the terrorist Che Guevara's death (p.194, YRBK98).

In the declaration, as touted before and after the fact, there was a great deal of what some have called platitudinous praise of democracy, of rhetoric in favor of equality of states and citizens, in favor of a "radical reduction in conventional armament," against "discrimination"—which may now mean almost anything—and "nuclear arms." Such were among the allegedly utopian measures which were advocated. Most of these ring rather hollow before the platform which was provided for Cuba's ML tyranny in the person of Ricardo Alarcón.

In 1996 at the VI Iberian-American Summit (pp.232ff, YRBK97), it was Castro's foreign minister, Robaina, who defended his master's tyranny as an effective form of "democracy" with gibberish which the press faithfully recorded. His newspeak described his inability to explain "why we have only one candidate for president" while assuring that their ML system was democratic in the extreme. Castro then signed the "Declaration on Participative Democracy" with "a flourish," Chilean President Frei calling the affair "a rousing success." Castro's tyranny has remained as tyrannical as ever and still the other nations maintain a serious demeanor in the face of the continuing gibberish in May 1998 from Alarcón.

For those who follow these gatherings carefully, the X Conference will convene in Portugal in 1999, the XI Conference in Venezuela in 2000. Alarcón may be replaced as Cuban spokesman by some other ML Castroite, but the probabilities are that, as Castro continually avows, the gibberish will be the same.

Entrepreneurial Forum of the Americas (FEA)

THE IV ENTREPRENEURIAL FORUM OF THE AMERICAS (FEA)
(WKLY 5.15, 16 APRIL 1998)

For a number of years Costa Rica has been touting its central location in the hemisphere as the ideal location for that plethora of international conferences with which the region has blessed itself—or otherwise—and has done rather well by it. The next two conferences to be discussed in this report took place there in March 1998 as did a Christian Democrat meeting in April.

On 16, 17 and 18 March 1998 the IV FEA took place in San José, Costa Rica, its administrative structure appropriately located in the Costa Rican Investment and Development (CINDE) Building. This Office was headed by a Coordinator General (CG), Marco Vinizio Ruiz, his assistant, Emmanuel Haas, and a secretary having the same name as Daniel Ortega's consort, Rosa Murillo. The CG was seconded by three committees of "distinguished" impresarios and academics which advised him on local, regional and hemispheric matters. In structuring this administrative organization it was emphasized that the CG "will have to move about" the hemisphere extensively so that he would be provided "with financial means appropriate to said necessities." The CG was provided with five "modules" (committees), these "specializing in the areas of spreading news (*divulgación*), logistics, content, business conference and internet."

The mission of this forum was an essentially entrepreneurial analysis of the proposed ALCA (p.334,YRBK98), it being held immediately before the commerce ministers discussed below, both of these meetings of course in preparation for the II Summit of the Americas in April 1998. This one was allegedly held in order to provide business and industry with a vehicle for input into the formation of such a "free trade"—in reality a considerably broader based control device—organization.

In describing the event to a press conference about a week before it convened Mr. Ruiz reported that the confirmed number of continental impresario attendees was 1,112, although the total might rise to 1,500. Of these 250 were from the US, 70 from Mexico, 100 from Brazil, 16 from Chile, 83 from Argentina and 109 from CA. (The numbers which LANS received thus total 628 or about one-half the 1,112 so that presumably un-remarked nations such as Peru were represented.) In any event, the delegates duly assembled in, and presented papers to, 13 "workshops" (*talleres*), the titles of which should provide an overview of the discussions. The number of groups attending each workshop is given in parenthesis after the workshop title. These are:

(1) Access to Markets (26); (2) Rules of Origin and Customs Procedures (24); (3) Norms and Technical Barriers, Health and Plant Health Measures (21); (4) Investments (17); (5) Intellectual Property Rights (39); (6) Services (25); (7) Public Sector Buying (15); (8) Controversy Solutions (15); (9) Private Sector Participation in ALCA (22); (10) Subsidies (15); (11) Anti-Dumping and Compensatory Rights (15); (12) Politics of Competition (12) and (13) Small Economies (9).

These allegedly provide an overview of the topics discussed. For an approximate understanding of the Forum these should be coupled to a description of what organizations discussed them and what was concluded. Space hardly permits details, but, concentrating on (1), the 26 groups involved can be illustrated as follows.

These groups included such as the Argentine Industrial Union, the LA Association of Pharmaceutical Industries, the US Distilled Spirits Industry, Chambers of Commerce (CC) of the US in Argentina, Federation of CCs in the Central American Isthmus, National CC of Uruguay, Association of American CCs in LA, Motion Picture Association, American Electronics Association, Chamber of Industries (CI) of Uruguay, CI of Bolivia (similar grouping for Brazil), Industrial Councils of MERCOSUR and the Andean Community and analogous groupings.

Finally the 26 groups produced a set of recommendations on (1) Access to Markets as the other sets of groups produced recommendations on the other 12 topics. In condensed form these conclusions were (Access to Markets):

It was decided with respect to this subject:

The ratification of the subjects agreed upon at the III FEA of Belo Horizonte[29] and of those defined in the negotiation of the governments, in particular the principle of the "single undertaking,"[30] the coexistence of the sub-regional blocs with ALCA and the taking of decisions by consensus.

Next, the following points, on which the hemispheric entities involved presented their positions, were discussed.

1. The connection of the labor and environmental (l&e) subjects to the commercial.[31] The Forum participants concluded that l&e matters should be treated in specific international forums separate from the commercial.

2. The principle of the "single undertaking" and its relation to the interim accords. On the one hand there were those who maintained that the interim accords are incompatible with the principle. On the other, some felt that ALCA should not be able to restrict the possibility of putting into effect partial or sectional accords before the finalization of the negotiations. Some felt that there should exist an agreement to extend "most favored" to third countries or commercial blocs, these being more favorable than that awarded to ALCA nations.[32]

3. It was agreed that, to preserve balance and equilibrium in the negotiations, specific stages in the negotiations should not be established, declaring that this restriction does not facilitate the negotiations.

4. It was agreed that the agricultural sector and its productive network has priority of treatment with the object of liberalizing agricultural commerce in the hemisphere...(some wished to create a special group for this negotiations). There was consensus on seeking to dismantle agricultural subsidies and internal support.

5. It was agreed that non tariff barriers be identified with the object of eliminating them and agreeing not to introduce new barriers or substitutes for tariffs and establish a method of compensation before the application of shackles for tariffs...Also agreed on the necessity of agreeing on a time for elimination which permits adaptation of the countries and enterprises to the new conditions.

6. Agreed that the tax relief include all the tariffs, although different sectors could have different rates depending on their characteristics...maximum time limit on tax relief.. No consensus on moment of "stand still," some thinking it should be at the beginning, others at the end.

7. On the question of commerce from the free zone markets no consensus was achieved. Some feel that the free zones facilitate commerce and should be given treatment equal to that of the other tariff treatments...Others argue that the free zones are special and should have different treatments.

8. The Belo Horizonte Accord was reiterated with respect to the special treatment which should be awarded to lesser developed or reduced market economies. The productive sectors of these economies require a longer time to adjust to the new conditions of free commerce.

The day before this IV FEA concluded, the ALCA Economy Ministers assembled.[33]

Coexistence and Citizen Security (FCSC)

FORUM ON COEXISTENCE AND CITIZEN SECURITY (FCSC)[34]
(SPCL 5.14, 19 JUNE 1998)

On 3 June 1998 the first ladies of El Salvador (Licenciada Elizabeth de Calderón Sol), Belize, Costa Rica, Guatemala, Honduras, Nicaragua and Panama gathered in San Salvador, El Salvador, in order to sign a document which created a Regional Council for the Woman of the Rural Area (CRMR). This was described as the inauguration of the FCSC. The CRMR has the basic objective of "implementing initiatives to improve the conditions of life and development of the woman in the rural areas of the isthmus" and, presumably also in Haiti and the Dominican Republic.

Since BID President Enrique Iglesias was in town in connection with yet another forum, this one on "violence," he sat in on the FCSC, or so the press reported it. More rationally, however, he probably intends to finance whatever projects the ladies develop. Interesting enough, an AFP dispatch of 5 June 1998 reports that the initiatives which are contemplated for the campesino woman in the CA nations "were not detailed."

It was reported (*El Diario de Hoy* 4 June 1998), however, that the Salvadoran first lady spoke before "some 30 Salvadoran women field workers," bringing out the support which BID has always provided for projects "which benefit family integration and facilitate access to better conditions of life." Presumably, BID is continuing this support by providing travel expenses to San Salvador for these first ladies, although this is neither affirmed nor denied.

The first ladies did announce that they had taken their efforts outside the region in October 1997 at which time they had spoken at the Inter-American Agricultural Board. More recently they had presented a report in Bolivia on women producers of food, in the field and in the informal sector.

Grupo de Río and UE

THE VIII MEETING OF GRUPO DE RÍO AND UE FOREIGN MINISTERS
(WKLY 5.8, 26 FEBRUARY 1998)

The Grupo de Río has been discussed (pp.358ff, YRBK98), its last Summit held in Paraguay in July 1997. Panama is a member[35] of this organization and, during 1998, is filling the position of Secretariat Pro Tem in it. Which is the basis on which Panamanian President Ernesto Pérez Balladares inaugurated the XVII Meeting of Grupo de Río Foreign Ministers in Panama City on 11 February 1998. The Panama affair is probably the reason for the early exodus from San José mentioned above. But Pérez Balladares was doing something more: he was opening the concurrent VIII Meeting of the Grupo de Río and UE Foreign Ministers.

The chief executive of Panama reported that the institutionalization of the encounter between the Grupo de Río and the UE resulted from "the fact that each region recognized in the other a useful counterpart for arriving at new levels of development." Whether the surfeit of summits which characterizes the region is a "good thing" or a "bad thing" may be a matter of taste, but it would appear to be sufficiently confusing already without the additional obfuscation provided by concurrent conferences.

Since the UE representatives had already allegedly been immersed at San José in the usual litany of PC projects—battle against poverty, sustainable development, political dialog, etc.—it would have required no great effort for the summiteers to repeat their labors in Panama.

Perhaps the most interesting occurrence at VIII Meeting was the appearance of the US negotiator for the Multilateral Anti-Drug Center (CMA) (pp.82ff above), Thomas McNamara. Not that his arrival appears to have been unforeseen since, for example, the fuming Blas Julio appears to have been fulminating anew against the CMA in his "The Tip of the Iceberg" [*El Siglo* (Panama) 9 February 1998] two days before the meeting began. The details of the CMA need not be rehashed here. Suffice it to say that Mr. McNamara met "behind closed doors" with the Grupo de Río foreign ministers from 0900 until 1300 on 11 February. Later in the afternoon the US negotiator tried to enter the Contadora[36] Salon of the ATLAPA Convention Center only to be told that this was a plenary session at which only members of the Grupo de Río were allowed.

Blas Julio bases his iceberg piece on a Pentagon document to which he claims *El Siglo* "has had access." He begins by maintaining that the paper treats, not a CMA, but A Hemispheric Antinarcotic Alliance "which has been imposed by the US as part of a new strategy of world control." From this rousing opener the author builds his case with quotations from the report which appear to indicate a US intention of taking "control" in the hemisphere—of police forces through training facilities "modeled after that of Budapest," of the judiciaries through a Federal Judicial Center, of intelligence through a plan "to gain access to classified information," and of various other entities whence power flows. Space here allows no more probing description of his article or of the document itself.

Whether it is indeed the US intent, as allegedly reflected in this document, to gain "world control" or whether Blas Julio even believes what he says about such US intent is hardly the point here. From the continuing "demonstrations" against the CMA and from the existence of the article itself, it can be concluded that there is some body of opinion which does believe it and of which the student of the subject should be aware. All of which may have nothing to do with VIII Meeting, although perhaps Mr. McNamara's fruitless pounding on the Contadora Salon door indicates that it does.

GRUPO DE RÍO SUMMIT
(WKLY 6.11, 17 SEPTEMBER 1998)

The Grupo de Río arose out of Contadora which was created in 1982 by Colombia, Mexico, Panama and Venezuela specifically to oppose US policy in CA (pp.233ff, YRBK97). Its I Summit was held in Acapulco in 1989; its XI Summit was held in Paraguay on 23-24 July 1997.

Of the 12 nations which comprise this grouping, nine were represented by their presidents—Bolivia, Chile, Colombia, Ecuador, Mexico, Panama, Paraguay, Peru and Venezuela. Menem of Argentina and Cardoso of Brazil—appropriately dubbed "the giants of the southern cone" by *Excelsior* (5 September 1998)—were apparently too involved in their countries' election campaigns to attend what was largely a ritualistic performance in Panama. Uruguay's Sanguinetti was apparently likewise involved. Finally, Janet Jagan, who inherited the mantle of the guyanese presidency from her deceased Marxist husband, Cheddy, was remarkable as an observer.

The *gentil dama*, Ivette Franco Koroneos, by virtue of Panama's host position at this gathering, was president of the summit organizing committee. Under her tutelage the festivities were organized at the 24-story Miramar Hotel, which has been encountered at earlier such affairs, on Balboa Avenue overlooking the bay. The summit theme was "Education, Weapon Against Poverty." The routine objective was the issuance of another declaration, this one to be called "The Declaration of Panama."

The opening gavel was dropped on the evening of 4 September 1998 by Panamanian President "Toro" Pérez Balladares in the historic National Theater to initiate the Summit. Figuratively speaking, it dropped again the next night at the press conference offered by the GR Troika to conclude the festivities. The Troika presently consists of Mexican President Zedillo, Panamanian President Pérez and Paraguayan President Cubas, the affair only slightly enlivened by the apparent press antipathy toward Cubas.

During the Summit Bolivian President Banzer was again to be found promoting his ubiquitous, if understandable, demand for a "window on the sea," and Mexican Foreign Minister Green was again understandably, if perhaps not successfully, agitating against continuous US meddling in Mexico's internal affairs (pp.119ff above). The Declaration of Panama duly appeared.

Replete with PC platitudes, there was one "recommendation" which betrays the influence of simplistic MLs such as Castro and another reappearance of that Lorelei which is the government-controlled economy. If such government control worked, the USSR economy would still be functioning as an example to the world, the Castroite dictatorship would hardly be an economic disaster and even Venezuelan socialist President Caldera would be presiding over something other than an economic wasteland. Here the hoary Marxist myth of "capital flight" and its "government control" is revived as a "solution" to the Asian Flu, the inevitable Russian debacle and the Wall Street correction. While the figure used — $8 billion—may be correct for "capital flight" from Brazil by early September, the idea that IMF application "of methods of capital flow control"—as advocated—will do anything but exacerbate the situation is one more Marxist myth. As von Mises has pointed out:[37]

> One of the main objectives of foreign exchange control is to prevent capital flight into foreign countries…(it) only succeeds in preventing the owners of domestic investments from restricting their losses by exchanging in time…for a foreign investment…(capitalists) can never make inconvertible capital goods (fixed capital) mobile and transferable…(this) is denied with regard to circulating capital…However, the process of capital flight is in both instances the same …The investment itself is not affected; the capital concerned does not emigrate…Governments pretend that…foreign

exchange restrictions...prevent capital flight... What they really bring about is contrary to the material interest of many citizens without any benefit to any citizen or to the phantom of the Volkswirtschaft (political economy).

Common Market of the Southern Cone (MERCOSUR)

XIV SUMMIT OF THE MERCOSUR PRESIDENTS
(WKLY 6.4, 30 JULY 1998)

MERCOSUR has been discussed in some detail in various reports (pp.240ff, YRBK97; pp.338-9, YRBK98). In keeping with the proliferation of "summits," conferences and those other sessions which typify such international organizations, MERCOSUR may be increasing its efforts to receive its share of whatever media attention, resort accommodations and the like are available. Or at least the recent XIV Summit in Ushuaia, which immediately succeeded the MERCOSUR Economic Summit in Buenos Aires, might be taken as part of such an effort.

MERCOSUR has four full members—Argentina, Brazil, Paraguay and Uruguay—and two associate members—Chile and Bolivia. The economic summit found Argentine President Carlos Menem, Chilean President Eduardo Frei and Paraguayan President Juan Carlos Wasmosy agreeing to "reinforce the ties of integration and cooperation." With which all and sundry flew the 3000 miles to Ushuaia for the presidential summit.

Ushuaia is in Tierra del Fuego, virtually on the Argentina-Chile border and the sea. Actually, it is not the sea but the Beagle Canal, the breadth of which, however, should give it the appearance of being on the sea. Perhaps the spot was chosen in some sort of act of homage to the bearded Britisher. Navarino Island is of course opposite.

If the summit had any motivation other than symbolism and recreation, it was not obvious from the public remarks of the participants. Paraguay's outgoing president, Wasmosy, wanted the historic process leading to the four-nation integration remembered. The presidents of Argentina (Menem), Brazil (Cardoso) and Chile (Frei) proclaimed the health and vigor of their respective economies. As he does at every opportunity, the president of Bolivia (Banzer) lobbied for his country's "window on the sea." And the president of Uruguay (Sanguinetti) arrived from Washington, DC, posed for photographs and lapsed into (allegedly) official silence. The MERCOSUR head *pro tem* is the president of the host country. Mr. Menem turned over the baton to Mr. Cardoso, and another summit had lapsed into history. Or almost.

For Mr. Menem had invited the onetime terrorist and now (apparently) lifetime president of South Africa, Nelson Mandela, to attend the summit, apparently as an observer. And the festivities were actually closed by a speech which might have been made by Mr. Castro. In a "vibrant diatribe against misery" (AFP 25 July 1998) Mr. Mandela inveighed against "poverty, illiteracy and ignorance." While such is routine, his remark, "while we drag ourselves out of these problems we will not have much desire to speak of democracy," would appear to be rather revealing.

I MERCOSUR ANTI-DRUG ENCOUNTER
(SPCL 5.14, 19 JUNE 1998)

On 3 June 1998 the Uruguayan anti-drug czar, Alberto Scavarelli, announced a meeting of the MERCOSUR nations in Buenos Aires, Argentina, on 18 June to begin coordination of methods for combating narcotrafficking and related crimes (AFP 5 June 1998). This effort will utilize various existing organizations within the region, apparently also creating new ones.

The meeting did indeed begin on the scheduled date, Scavarelli joined in Buenos Aires by his counterparts from Argentina (Eduardo Amadeo), Paraguay (Carlos Alberto Ayala) and Brazil (Luis Matías Flach). It is proposed that the new organization deal with various aspects of the "drug problem," these being the same obvious aspects which have been proposed for treatment in the past: money laundering, chemical precursor control, narcotrafficking, community work and assistance.

While it is generally agreed that narcotrafficking in all its ramifications is a "bad thing," it is not obvious that the surfeit of meetings on the subject has proven to be a particularly "good thing."

The "Non-Aligned" Nations (MNNA)

THE XII SUMMIT OF THE "NON ALIGNED" NATIONS (MNNA)
(WKLY 6.11, 17 SEPTEMBER 1998)

Nelson Mandela

PC and its concomitant, press self censorship, has completely whitewashed the life and affiliations of South African President Nelson Mandela. In addition to being outside the LANS bailiwick, it would therefore require more space than is available to bring some sort of reality to the record. Therefore, his fulsome welcome of Cuba's ML dictator, Fidel Castro, to his country will have to serve here as the South African's introduction.

On 4 September 1998, one day after the closing of the "Non Aligned" Summit, Castro arrived in Cape Town. While members of that country's Democratic Party and Liberty Front criticized the Mandela welcome of Castro as "totally unacceptable" and worse, the South African head of state welcomed the Cuban dictator as "a great friend," entertaining him in Tuynhuys with the same sort of enthusiasm he had shown in welcoming him to Durban two days before. And, as could be said of Khadafy, he is a "great friend" of Fidel Castro. And indeed, in the AFP wirephoto of 4 September, Mandela hardly seems able to contain his enthusiasm at Castro's presence, in the photograph and in the flesh.

And Mandela is important to the discussion here because he is replacing, in the presidency of the "Non-Aligned" Nations, Colombian President Pastrana who had inherited the mantle from ex President Samper.

The "Non Aligned" Nations Movement (MNNA) DO

One of the truly masterful Disinformation Operations (DO) of the IL was the creation of the MNNA. The idea was childishly simple, but the IL could evolve it with the sure knowledge that PC would assure its acceptance at face value. The idea of "alignment" arose from the real existence of two blocs of nations, those "aligned" with the MLs of the USSR and the Chicoms, and those aligned with allegedly anti-ML nations such as the US. What more natural than the existence of a third bloc of nations aligned with neither of these two?

As Pastrana would acknowledge in his speech turning over the MNNA presidency to Mandela, the MNNA "had been arranged (*concertada*) since 24 April 1955 when the founding visionaries (*sic*) of" the MNNA arranged it. But who were these "founding visionaries"?

As LANS has pointed out in describing the strictly ML Tri Continental Conference (TCC) (pp.95ff, YRBK97), the Bandung Conference, apparently sponsored by Red China, was the first of that series of conferences which led to the TCC. It was transparently apparent that these conferences "represented only small communist or extremist groups."[38] Such was one branch of those meetings—later "summits"—which arose at Bandung. The other branch evolved into the MNNA.

At some point perhaps the latter branch should be considered in more detail. Here it is only necessary to consider a few nations and groups, representatives of which appeared at Durban for the XII Summit: Algeria, National Palestine Authority (ANP) President Yasser Arafat, South Africa, Burkina Faso, Cameroon, Cuba, India, Iran, Madagascar, Peoples Republic of China, Ruanda, Sri Lanko, Tanzania, Vietnam, Uganda, Zimbabwe, to name but a few of the 70—or 50, depending on the source—chiefs of state of the 113 "non aligned" nations. Chicom presence alone would be sufficient to make a mockery of the title. As would the cordial, photographically preserved meeting of Arafat, Castro, Mandela et al. Apparently Colombian President Pastrana's appearance on the cover of *SEMANA* in mid July with the old terrorist, Tirofijo, prepared him to hobnob with Tirofijo's superior, Fidel Castro, in Durban.

XII MNNA Summit

LANS has discussed the I Encounter of MNNA Ministers of Culture in Medellín, Colombia in September 1997, this gathering including 54 delegates from the 113 member nations. The meeting largely consisted of a speech by then Colombian and MNNA President Samper, an oration blossoming with North (America) enslaving the South and various familiar calls for PC activities such as saving the environment, fighting poverty and so on.

Apparently the PC activities called for by Samper in 1997 have not yet been attended to, for, in a voluminous dissertation running to nine printed pages, Samper's successor as president of Colombia and MNNA calls for all of the above and has space to add various words appropriate to Africa.

> ...the founding visionaries...condemned "apartheid" and colonialism. Today, thanks to the sacrifices, the tears and the blood of thousands of men and women, this Summit...constitutes a new opportunity to celebrate the elimination of "apartheid"....

This bemusing description is appropriate to the place of its delivery. However, most of the blood spilled in Africa was between the

MLs and their opponents in Angola and Mozambique or between Mandela's faction and the Zulus in South Africa. And we should not ignore those slaughters of Black African civilians by their Black African governments, these having nothing to do with "apartheid." Following it, Mr. Pastrana launches on a roseate description of all those things that MNNA is allegedly doing to make the world better for all. If his words are to be taken at face value, the only task that has been completed, however, is "proportioning the coordination of our positions...for the interests of the countries in development..." Further on, Bretton Woods arises as introductory to the manner in which this proportioning is to be carried out, that is, through various international lending agencies.

With this verbal tidal wave President Pastrana handed over the MNNA baton to President Mandela who declared that "We must renew our world." Presumably, the 50 heads of state from the 113 MNNA nations enjoyed various banquets and other festivities, undaunted by Castro's lowering prediction that "a profound general economic crisis of unforeseeable consequences" awaits them.

The Organization of American States (OAS)

THE XXVIII GENERAL ASSEMBLY OF THE OAS
(WKLY 5.22, 11 JUNE 1998)

The XXVIII General Assembly of the OAS was held in Caracas, Venezuela, from 1 June through 3 June 1998. Much of what follows will be necessary repetitions of the LANS treatment of the XXVII OAS General Assembly (pp.366ff, YRBK98).

The OAS

In 1948 the OAS emerged from the Pan American Union (pp.226ff, YRBK97) during that same Bogotazo at which Castro emerged as an international terrorist (pp.85, 111; YRBK97).

The General Assembly (AG) of the OAS is the "supreme organ" of that organization and meets annually, although it may convoke extraordinary sessions by a two-thirds vote of its member states. The AG president is elected at the first plenary session of an annual assembly, the government of the host country, here Venezuela, designating a provisional president until such election.

Articles 19 through 21 of the OAS Charter specify the activities of the Preparatory Commission in arranging the details of an AG session. The General Commission (CG) is made up of the president and vice president of the AG and the chiefs of the delegations. The CG consists of three principal, annual commissions — The First Commission [Juridical and Political Affairs], the Second [Economic and Social Affairs, and Educational, Scientific and Cultural Affairs] and the Third [Administrative and Budgetary Affairs] — and various permanent commissions and organizations, few of which demand treatment here.

The General Secretariat is the central and permanent organ of the OAS with its seat in Washington, DC, and with 700 functionaries, known as the Pan American Union until 1970. The Secretary General is elected by the AG for a term of five years; he may succeed himself once; he may not be succeeded by an individual from the same country.

The Permanent Council (PC) is composed of one representative with the rank of ambassador from each member state. The PC has the powers assigned to it by the OAS Charter and other inter American instruments as well as the functions assigned to it by the AG and the Foreign Ministers Consultative Meeting (RCMRE).

The RCMRE is held to consider problems of an urgent nature and of common interest; on being requested these meetings may be convoked by a majority vote of the PC. In case of an armed attack on the territory of a member state or within the security region established by the Inter American Treaty of Reciprocal Assistance, the RCMRE is convoked immediately. The Charter provides for a Consultative Defense Committee to advise the organs on problems of military collaboration.

The PC has established Permanent Commissions which, inter alia, deal with 1) Juridical matters through the Inter American Juridical Committee (CJI), made up of 11 jurists elected by the GA with seat in Rio de Janeiro. 2) The Managua Protocol [December 1996] established the Inter American Council for Integral Development (CIDI) which is charged with the promotion of integral and SUSTAINABLE development. 3) The Inter American Commission on Human Rights (CDIH) is charged with promotion and protection of human rights. Its seat is in San José, Costa Rica.

The specialized organisms of the OAS include, inter alia, the Pan American Health Organization (OPS) with its seat in Washington, DC, the Inter American Commission on Women (CIM) established in June 1994, the Inter American Institute of the Child (IIN) with its seat in Montevideo, Uruguay, the Inter American Indigenous Institute (III) with its seat in Mexico, DF, the Pan American Institute of Geography and History (IPGH) with its seat in Mexico, DF, and the Inter American Institute of Agricultural Cooperation (IICA) with its seat in San Jose, Costa Rica.

Member States

The Charter was adopted 30 April 1948, the Protocol of Buenos Aires establishing the present organizational structure on 27 February 1967 and the Protocol of Cartagena de Indias strengthening its hemispheric political role on 5 December 1985. Date of entry are detailed (pp.366ff, YRBK98). Here Group 1 entered in 1948, Group 2 between 1967 and 1991.

Group 1: Argentina, Bolivia, Brazil, Colombia, Costa Rica, Cuba, Chile, Ecuador, El Salvador, United States, Guatemala, Haiti, Honduras, Mexico, Nicaragua, Panama, Paraguay, Peru, Dominican Republic, Uruguay, Venezuela.

Group 2: Barbados, Trinidad and Tobago, Jamaica, Grenada, Surinam, Dominica, St. Lucia, Antigua and Barbuda, Bahamas, St. Vincent and the Grenadines, St. Kitts and Nevis, Canada, Belize and Guyana.

Permanent Observers

The OAS Permanent Observers admitted between 1972 and 1992 in Group 1 have been given in Spcl 3.8. The nations admitted between 1994 and 1998 are given in Group 2.

Group 1: Spain, Portugal, Low Countries, Italy, France, Germany, Belgium, Japan, Portugal, Egypt, Austria, Holy See, Switzerland, Greece, Saudi Arabia, Republic of Korea, Morocco, Cyprus, Pakistan, Ecuatorial Guinea, Algeria, Finland, European Community, Hungary, Tunis, Rumania, India, Poland, Angola, and Russian Federation.

Group 2: Ukraine, Lebanon, Czechoslovakia, United Kingdom, Bosnia and Herzegovina, Latvia, Ghana, Kazakstan, Sri Lanka, Sweden, Bulgaria, Yemen, Thailand, Turkey.

XXVIII GA Representatives

The OAS representatives all have the rank of ambassador; the title omitted in what follows. Those who filled this position in XXVII are preceded by an asterisk.

ANTIGUA AND BARBUDA: *Lionel Alexander Hurst; ARGENTINA: Julio César Araoz, BAHAMAS: *Arlington Griffith Butler; BARBADOS: *Courtney Blackman; BELIZE: *James Schofield Murphy; BOLIVIA: Marlene Fernández del Granado; BRAZIL: Carlos Alberto Leite Barbosa; CANADA: Peter Michael Boehm; CHILE: Carlos Portales Cifuentes; COLOMBIA: Fernando Cepeda Ulloa; COSTA RICA: *Fernando Herrero; DOMINICA: Eduard A. Alexander; DOMINICAN REPUBLIC: *Flavio Dario Espinal Jacobo; ECUADOR: *Julio Prado Vallejo; EL SALVADOR: *Mauricio Granillo; GRENADA: *Denis G. Antoine; GUATEMALA: Alfonso Quiñones Lemus; GUYANA: *M. A. Odeen Ishmael; HAITI: Guy Pierre ; HONDURAS: Laura Elena Nuñez Flores; JAMAICA: *Richard Bernal; MEXICO: Claude Heller; NICARAGUA: *Felipe Rodriguez Chavez; PANAMA: *Lawrence Chewning Farbega; PARAGUAY: *Carlos Victor Montanaro; PERU: *Beatriz M. Ramacciotti; ST. KITTS AND NEVIS: *Osbert O. Liburd; ST. LUCIA: Sonia M. Johnny; ST. VINCENT AND THE GRENADINES: *Kingsley C. A. Layne; SURINAM: Albert R. Ramdin; TRINIDAD AND TOBAGO: Michael A. Arneaud; UNITED STATES: Victor Marrero; URUGUAY: *Antonio Mercader; VENEZUELA: *Francisco Paparoni.

The XXVII AG Meeting

The inaugural session was held on Monday, 1 June 1998 at 0900 in the Teresa Carreño Theater in front of the Caracas Hilton, the festivities being opened with a speech by OAS Secretary General César Gaviria Trujillo. The speech deserves a scrutiny which must be preceded by an aside.

There is a body of opinion which maintains that the contemporary tendency is toward the eventual absorption of the sovereignties of the individual American states in a vaguely conceived hemispheric state. Whether the notion is a "good thing" or a "bad thing,"[39] it is a "thing" of which those who believe in "democracy"—and can define it — should be aware. Within Castro's HL, the notion is not "vaguely conceived" but quite specifically enunciated[40] What Mr. Gaviria lays out in his OAS inaugural address can certainly be taken as a blueprint for such a transition. Are these ideas those of Mr. Gaviria?

Probably not. As Ambassador Smith pointed out long ago,[41] the Cuban disaster which resulted in the Castro tyranny was the work, not of the upper echelons of the Eisenhower Administration, but of the foreign office clerks on the "Fourth Floor." As was apparently the case with Oscar Arias, "Esquipulas" and Biehl.[42] But whether the thoughts embodied in the speech by Gaviria are his own or those of someone else, various salient features on Gaviria, the man and statesman, are of interest: (1) His term as president of Colombia can hardly be classified as a success, particularly if the terrorist situation when he left office is considered. (2) He appears to have been the US choice for OAS secretary general in 1994.[43] (3) He informed *The Miami Herald* that he was a "friend" of HL boss, Fidel Castro, a statement which has been belied by his behavior neither before nor after the statement.

Mr. Gaviria, after a routinely flowery beginning, declares that "We are gathered here... to celebrate the dawning (*sic*) of a new OAS...we all share a common destiny...we have abandoned a sort of atavistic pessimism..." Which pearl from the speech writer's pen warrants an aside.

Mr. Gaviria's speech writer employed a fascinating, and fascinatingly descriptive, choice of words. Whatever this "pessimism" has as its object such pessimism was apparently common amongst Mr. Gaviria's "distant ancestors" but unknown to his immediate ones. This is indeed PC for the Professional Politician who can deliver himself of such meaningless mumbo jumbo as the "Declaration of Caracas" with a straight face. But to return to the Gaviria remarks.

Having exorcized "atavistic pessimism," Gaviria and his OAS are prepared to determine "how the inter-American system will confront the huge challenges brought on by globalization..." "As for the OAS, its functions have been expanded, and it must now fulfill its role as a forum for adopting inter-American legal norms, as the principal setting for political dialog, as a center...for the drafting of common or collective policies..." At the OAS Gaviria and his associates now have the "know-how to strengthen the most vulnerable democracies...protect human rights,[44] engage in de-mining efforts, carry out electoral observation missions..." The Inter-American Institute of Human Rights is to "eliminate all forms of discrimination (*sic*)...ensuring (women) their full and equal participation in all programs (p.2[45])..." The OAS is going to deal with "domestic violence...the feminization of poverty...unequal access to higher education" and assure SUSTAINABLE Development, deal with "disarmament and arms control issues" (p.3) and, indeed, virtually every aspect of human life, relationships and behavior. Nor is Fidel Castro forgotten (p.6).

In case the six pages of his speech have left any doubt, Gaviria winds up his oratory with "We hope to realize the dream of Simon Bolívar when he called together the 'Antifictionic' Congress on Panama for the purpose of 'uniting all of the new world into a single nation and a single bond that joins all of its parts together with the whole.'"

EDITOR'S COMMENTS

In both the Spanish and English versions of Gaviria's remarks, this is called the "Antifictionic Congress," although it is generally referred to as Bolivar's Congress of Panama. In the LANS files it first appears to have been discussed in the Council Meeting of Tuesday, 2 August 1825 (*Acuerdos del Consejo de Gobierno de la República de Colombia 1825-1827*, Ediciones del Consejo, 1942) recorded by Interior Secretary José Manuel Restrepo. At the meeting "the urgency of naming the plenipotentiaries from Colombia" was emphasized because "this had been compacted among all the States and Peru has already sent theirs." The Great Liberator had his Congress of Panama in 1826, and historians generally refer to it as a "fiasco" because, "despite its grandiose start...the nations which attended failed to do anything about the resolutions passed" (John A. Crow, *Epic of Latin America*, Univ. California Press, 1992. ISBN: 0-520-07868-3).

* * *

The festivities having been opened, they were inaugurated in a speech by Venzuelan President Rafael Caldera. The inaugural session having been concluded, the First Plenary Session began at 1030, it only five minutes behind schedule and thus considerably closer to its scheduled time than any of its successors. Here the president of this AG, Venezuelan Foreign Minister Miguel Angel Burelli Rivas, was elected by acclamation. The Second Plenary Session was that afternoon, the Third and Fourth on the morning and afternoon of 2 and 3 June, respectively, the Fifth and Sixth on 3 June. There were four sessions of the General Commission, these on the afternoon of 1 June, the morning and afternoon of 2 June and the morning of 3 June.

Because the general behavior was much the same as that at XXVII (1997), the LANS example from last year is simply repeated here. In 1997, the First Commission approved a report in its third session (3 June 1997) on a "Convention for the Elimination of All Forms of Discrimination by Reason of Incapacity." This report is replete with high flown language - "all human beings are born free and equal in dignity and rights ... without distinction by race, nationality, creed or sex" - and inference at the way misfortunes born of "incapacity" may be "fixed" - "the Protocol of El Salvador recognizes that all persons affected by a diminution of their physical or mental capacity has the right (*sic*) to receive special attention."[46] Nor does this "Incapacity" scratch the surface of those "evils" which the OAS apparently intends to eliminate.

What Happened in Caracas?

It appears reasonable to state that what happened was the OAS approval of the "Reaffirmation of Caracas (RC)," a pre-scripted document which is dated 2 June 1998, Caracas and begins as follows:

> The OAS member countries today reaffirm their intention of strengthening multilateralism as an expression of the unity which guides their efforts to consolidate the principles and consecrate the proposals in the Charter of the Organization.

> The "RC," approved unanimously during the Second Plenary Session of the AG of the OAS, also manifests the firm commitment to revise the institutional structure of the Inter-American System, particularly the OAS "to the end of strengthening and modernizing its capacity to respond to the challenges of the new century, adequate to the new hemispheric realities, to achieve a better complementarity among its organs and endow it with the necessary organizational efficiency."

The Declaration reaffirms...the proposition of continuing, inside the principle of free determination, a permanent and creative labor directed to the preservation and consolidation of democracy in the hemisphere and deepening a culture of peace, development and non violence.

...(the RC) dedicates special attention to the subjects of human rights, the administration of justice, economic integration, the security of the little island states and the limitation and control of arms, among other things.

...juridical instruments to protect the rights of the Indian peoples...to eliminate all types of discrimination for incapacity....

Bridgetown, Barbados, was proposed as the site of the XXXI Assembly in 2001. Guatemala will be the seat in 1999, Canada in 2000.

OAS FIFTIETH ANNIVERSARY
(SPCL 5.15, 9 MAY 1998)

On 30 April 1998 the OAS foreign ministers met in Bogotá, Colombia, in order to commemorate the fiftieth anniversary of the founding of the Organization of American States (OAS) in that same "Athens of the Andes." The meeting took place in that same Modern Gymnasium which had been host to the signing of the Charter of Bogotá on 30 April 1948. There was considerable agitation for the "readmission" of ML Cuba into the OAS, opposition by Venezuela to an allied force against the narcoterrorists and a call by Pres. Samper to "solve the problems by education not arms." But another, equally important anniversary for Colombia, was not mentioned. It too was a half century old that month and intimately involved with OAS formation.

THE BEGINNING OF COLOMBIAN TERRORISM: THE BOGOTAZO
(SPCL 1.2, 1 JUNE 1996)

At 1305 on 9 April 1948 Jorge Eleicer Gaitán, the popular Liberal Party leader, was hit by four revolver bullets as he was leaving his office in the Nieto Building (Bogota, Colombia), the shots fired by Juan Roa Sierra (26) who was literally torn to pieces by the mob but not before being gunned down by his "associates." This assassination signaled the beginning of a well-organized revolution, the Bogotazo, preparations for which had been underway for months. That it was well-organized was attested by several eyewitnesses, among them:

Inter American Workers Confederation (IAWC) President Bernardo Ibañez had an appointment at 1700 with Gaitán on the day of his death. Ibañez reported [*Inter American Labor News*, May 1948] the "crime and provocation (were) peculiar to the Russians," the careful planning reflected in the fact that "15 minutes after the attack on Gaitán all the radio broadcasting stations in Bogotá were taken over by the Communists through workers and students...Precise instructions...issued to plunder arms deposits, hardware stores..." etc. This description was generally confirmed by IAWC Vice President Juan Laro. US Ambassador to Colombia Beaulac further described[47] the organization of building burning by small groups equipped with naptha and sprayers.

The Bogotazo was a Kremlin operation, its short-range objective the disruption of the IX Inter American Conference (IAC), its long-range objective the takeover of strategic Colombia overlooking the Panama Canal and both Atlantic and Pacific Oceans.

IX IAC of 21 American republics was called for 30 March 1948 in Bogotá, US State Secretary George Marshall to attend. The IAC was to adopt a charter reaffirming the solidarity of the American states in mutual defense and resistance to international communism. Communist reaction was rapid, the Colombian Communist Party (PCC) drawing up an ambitious program to disrupt the IAC[48] (dismissed by the Kremlin), Lombardo Toledano's Marxist Latin American Labor Confederation (CTAL) loudly condemning it, a trail of agents beginning to arrive at Soviet spymaster Gumer W. Bashirov's Havana headquarters (House #6, 2d St between 1st & 3d Aves, el Reparto Sect, Miramar suburb) on 2 February 1948, the first being World Federation of Democratic Youth (WFDY) Treasurer Frances Demot with $50,000 in her suitcase.[49] On 25 February Soviet Youth Society President Basily Bogarev headed the arriving contingent including the Spanish communist Luís Fernández who was immediately sent on to Colombia. Fernández' report torpedoed the PCC plan and resulted in the dispatch of Fidel Castro and Alfredo Guevara Valdes to Colombia. What happened next is best described by Colombia National Security Chief Alberto Niño H.[50]

Rumblings from the coming storm began reaching Niño early in the year. His agents warned him that the terrorist operation would occur on "4 or 5 April"; it did not. Some in the government of Conservative President Mariano Ospina thought Gaitán behind it;

Niño did not. And "packets of various sizes" were reported moving out of a Soviet Embassy which was removing its forest of radio antennas. Red Friday (*viernes rojo*) arrived; Gaitán died, and the slaughter and havoc of the Bogotazo began. *The Daily Worker* (New York) was delighted: "Interruption of the Foreign Ministers' parley is a sock in the jaw to the big business men of the State Department" (12 April 1948).

Bogotá suffered severely, but the revolution was squelched in a matter of days by the coalition government President Ospina quickly formed with the Liberals. Using information such as that published by *El Colombiano* Medellín 3 July 1948) on four Soviet agents brought in just before the attempted coup, the Colombian Government announced on 13 April that two "Soviet agents" and 13 other foreign agents had been "caught in the act" of fomenting trouble, then broke relations with the USSR.[51] The investigation of the attempted revolution continued, detectives from the Federal Bureau of Investigation (FBI), Scotland Yard, and Military Intelligence (MI5) arriving in June.[52] A footnote on Castro's contribution:

El Pais (Caracas 27 March 1948) carried a photo of a beardless Castro and Rafael del Pino on the way to Colombia which they entered that day through Medellín, proceeding to Bogotá. According to Niño's detectives, the pair was seen with the assassin, Roa, "a few days" before the ninth. On 3 April they were picked up in the Colón Theater for throwing leaflets from the balcony, these printed in Cuba and attacking the US and Britain. The Cubans were taken to their room in the Hotel Claridge where enough material was found to warrant taking them to National Security Headquarters. Reporting back on 7 April because of passport irregularities, they were printed and mugged, all these records destroyed on 9 April with the building. On 13 April Guillermo Hoenigsberg, a Claridge guest, told detectives he had heard the Cubans boasting of their part in the coup.

During the riots US Ambassadors Pauley and Donnelly heard the following on their car radio in Bogota (Congressional testimony):

> This is Fidel Castro from Cuba. This is a communist revolution. The president has been killed, all of the military establishments are now in our hands. The Navy has capitulated to us, and the revolution has been a success.

The statements were nonsense, and Castro escaped Colombia through a mistake which Cuban Ambassador Belt long regretted.

From the Bogotazo arose *La Violencia* (LV), a 17-year bloodletting in which large numbers died. It glimmers through the murk that, in the midst of LV (1957), Pedro Antonio Marín (aka *Tiro Fijo*) founded the Colombian Revolutionary Armed Forces (FARC), the first Colombian terrorist organization. (For further discussion see pp.109ff, YRBK97.)

Commerce Ministers Meetings (RMC)

THE IV MEETING OF COMMERCE MINISTERS (RMC) (WKLY 5.15, 16 APRIL 1998)

The IV FEA concluded in San José, Costa Rica, on 18 March, the IV RMC beginning in the same city on the same day and concluding on 20 March. The number of delegates attending was given as the number which the CG of the FEA had estimated as eventually participating, 1,500. As with the earlier meeting, this was advertised as preliminary to the April 1998 II Summit of the Americas.

Jeffrey Davidow, whose smiling face adorned a number of mid-March accounts of the IV RMC, is US Under Secretary of State for Inter American Affairs. His rather testy interview with the *SUCESOS* (Punta del Este) reporter after failing to "subordinate all processes of integration"—MERCOSUR, etc.—has been discussed (pp.345ff, YRBK98). Before this ministerial meeting began he told EFE that the upcoming Summit of the Americas is going to focus "many of its efforts on education and development of human capital" in the world. Somewhat later his colleague, US Commerce Secretary William Daley of the Chicago political clan, was asserting that ALCA "is irreversible," this presumably meaning that he hopes as much.

The IV RMC then took place, this gathering duly producing The Ministerial Declaration of San Jose, albeit, the various ministry clerks had doubtless penned it some time before. The document is divided into four parts, in 20 paragraphs, and two annexes. In the Introduction (I) the ALCA negotiations are examined (¶1) and found satisfying (¶2), (¶3) then warning against "adoption of politics negatively affecting commerce." Then the importance of "the ample social and economic agenda" adopted in 1994 is reiterated as are calls "to elevate the level of life, improve labor conditions...and better protect the environment." (¶4).[53]

The reader will not be told that any paragraph is of little interest—it could be used as the basis for a future attack on him or his — but this coverage must be restricted. In Initiation of Negotiations (II), perhaps only ¶8 wherein the now conceded coexistence of ALCA and such as MERCOSUR is acknowledged. Structure and Organization of Negotiations (III) is mostly boiler plate, ¶10 establishing the Commercial Negotiations Committee (CNC) at the vice ministerial level with various officers, ¶11 establishing nine "negotiation groups." These last are precisely the IV FEA workshops (1), (4), (5), (7), (8), (10), (11) and (12) to which "agriculture" is added. These groups are co-chaired by two nations each, for example, Colombia and Bolivia co-chair (1). The seat for the meetings of these groups will be in Miami, US (1 May 98—28 Feb 01), in Panama City, Panama (1 Mar 01—28 Feb 03) and Mexico D.F. (1 Mar 03—31 Dec 04). The ALCA presidency and vice presidency will likewise rotate every six months, for example, Canada will hold the presidency first, Argentina the vice presidency, the rotation to take place at six-month intervals after the first term (5 months).

Other Subjects (IV) include an alleged reaffirmation to transparent behavior by these statesmen (¶17), a reassertion of their determination to "do something concrete by 2000" (¶18), ¶19 a bow to the Internet and ¶20 an expression of "appreciation."

Annex I deals with Objectives and General Principles, much of it already discussed. However, some readers may be interested in the fealty expressed for the World Trade Organization (OMC) in ¶c and ¶d of General Principles. Others may find certain interest in ¶e of General Objectives which urges that "our environmental politic and commercial liberalization be mutually supportive"—"sustainable development," etc.

Annex II, "Objectives for the Thematic Area of Negotiation" is largely boilerplate, under the Rules of Origin section, for example, ¶a directs the "development of an efficient and transparent system of rules of origin..."

Latin American Economic System (SELA)

XXIV SELA CONFERENCE, HAVANA
(SPCL 6.16, 5 DECEMBER 1998)

Fidel Ruz Castro

In a recent visit to Miami, Florida, ex Polish President Lech Walesa told a receptive audience of Cuban exiles that "there is some political force which wants to maintain Cuba as a museum of communism." However expert Walesa may be on Polish political matters, these remarks constitute a woeful misrepresentation of a ML tyranny which is moving toward its goal of that "collection of soviet-type states" in the Western Hemisphere.

In his public appearances, the HL boss, Fidel Ruz Castro, appears little more than a fatuous and immensely verbose font of ML inanities. Nevertheless, the Cuban dictator has shown himself to be among the most accomplished of those scourges of the Twentieth Century, the Professional Politicians (PP). From the nadir of ML influence in 1991, Castro has succeeded in rebuilding the power and influence of his HL in spite of the disaster which he and his "system" have made of his immediate fiefdom. It is true that his principal opponent, the US, has, through ineptitude or design, been of assistance rather than opposition to the process, but this hardly denies him the recognition he deserves for political acumen.

His pandering to the basest appetites of his enemies with the drug traffic has helped immensely, of course, and, here again, the behavior of those who should logically have been his opponents has contributed. His principal weapons have been (1) his adoption of the anti-neoliberal line, (2) his creation and advancement of the São Paulo Forum (FSP)—to which the Inter-American Dialog (DI) should be added as a milder but useful sister—(3) his continuing promotion of Agrarian Reform (AgRef), (4) his activity as headquarters and support staff, if no longer financier, for hemispheric terrorist activity to include the crucial financing furnished by narcotrafficking. It is to speak the obvious to say that, were it not for the PPs, none of this would have happened. It appears to be a truism, however, that the PP is typically concerned only with the immediate advantages to himself of whatever action he is taking. Under these conditions, the PP can garner advantage, for example, from adopting Castro's anti-neoliberalism (ML) and not privatizing those government "enterprises" which have brought economic disaster to his nation.

As the astute reader is well aware, Castro's rambling and meaningless tirades are important to this process. That the Cuban has an unbounded egotism is of course true. But his success demands that some more meaningful object be found for his ramblings. Of course there is one: exposure. He knows the press is prepared to parrot his ML and that the PPs care not what it is he is saying if it is potentially useful to them. And hence the tirades during which apparently intelligent individuals nod seriously. LANS has discussed his pontification at various PP international meetings, the most recent being that at the VIII Iberian-American Summit (IAS). The Castro performance there was described by Antonio Martínez (EFE 20 Oct 98) as delaying "the closing of VIII IAS more than three hours, hogging the ceremony with his proverbial oral incontinence..." In the SELA conference the Cuban performed again.

The SELA Constituent Agreement of Panama

The Constituent Agreement of Panama is the charter of SELA; it was created in the Panama Meeting of 31 July to 2 August 1975 under what it is presently PC to believe was the "benevolent" dictatorship of Omar Torrijos (pp.90ff, YRBK98). It is obviously necessary to abstract it here.

Constituent Agreement Preamble

The Preamble begins with the statement that "...it is necessary to establish an inter-regional permanent system of economic and social cooperation ... of LA, as much in the international organizations as against third countries and groups of countries." (¶) "... it is necessary that the efforts and initiatives ...to the present time to advance the coordination among the LA countries are transformed into a permanent system which for the first time includes all the states of the region ..." (¶) "... within the spirit ... of the Action Program on the establishment of a New World Economic Order..." (¶¶) "... (everything) is developed on the basis of the principles of equality, sovereignty, independence of the States, solidarity, non intervention in internal affairs ... full respect for the social and economic systems *FREELY* (emphasis added) decided by the states..."

Constituent Agreement Chapters

Chapter I consists of four articles. The boilerplate on "principles of equality (etc.)..." appears in Art.4. Art 3. "Nature and Intentions," states the "fundamental intentions of SELA:" as...(¶) "(b) to promote a permanent system of coordination and consultation for the adoption of positions and common strategies on economic and social themes, as much in international forums and organs as against third countries and groups of countries ..."

Chapter II, "Objectives" contains Art. 5 alone. There is a great deal of boilerplate having to do with whatever the clerks could think of as necessary to the creation of a best-of-all-possible worlds. Only the following will be reproduced: "The objectives are..." (¶) "1. To promote regional cooperation toward the end of achieving integral, sustainable and independent development ..." (¶) "a) To propitiate the best utilization of human, natural, technical and financial resources of the region, using the creation and development of LA multi-national enterprises. Such LA multi-nationals can be put together using *STATE, PUBLIC-SECTOR* (emphasis added), private or mixed capital ..."

Chapter III, "Members," consists of two articles. Art. 6 states that subscribing "LA States are members of SELA...," a statement which the reader may wish to mull over while perusing the list of member states.

SELA Member States

Member states are: Argentina, Bahamas, Barbados. Belize, Bolivia, Brazil, Colombia, Costa Rica, Cuba, Chile, Dominican Republic, Ecuador, El Salvador, Grenada, Guatemala, Guyana, Haiti, Honduras, Jamaica, Mexico, Nicaragua, Panama, Paraguay, Peru, Surinam, Trinidad and Tobago, Uruguay and Venezuela.

Chapter IV, "Organic Structure," establishes the organs of SELA in Art. 8 as The LA Council, The Committees of Action and The Permanent Secretariat. Art. 9 through Art. 19 deal specifically with The LA Council and will be largely paraphrased. The Council is the "supreme organ" of SELA, is made up of one representative of each member state and normally meets at the seat of the Permanent Secretariat. Each member has one vote, a "proportion" which can be modified by a "consensus" of the members. An annual meeting is held at the ministerial level, a quorum for meetings being a simple majority; the officers for each meeting are elected by the Council as are the Permanent Secretary and the Permanent Under Secretary. The Council approves "the budget and the state financing of SELA...(and) fixes the quotas of the state members." Other obvious tasks — oversee activities of the SELA organs, "approve positions and strategies of member states," call special meetings — are performed by this "supreme" organ. By Art. 17 the Council adopts its decisions by a majority of two-thirds of the members present or by a majority of all state members. By Art. 19 the Council "will adopt no decisions which affect the internal national politics of the member states."

Art. 20 through Art. 26 deal with "The Action Committees." By Art. 20 these will be constituted of state members interested in the "realization of specific program and project studies"; they will be created by Council or interested state member decision. The interested state members will be in charge of financing them. There will, of course, be annual reports. Art. 27 through Art. 31 deal with the Permanent Secretariat. The seat of the Secretariat will be Caracas, Venezuela[54] (Art. 27), the Secretariat directed, surprisingly, by a Permanent Secretary (Art. 28), it being essentially the operating organ for the decisions of the Council.

As Art. 40 states, the SELA Charter was signed on 17 October 1995.

Action Committees

The action Committees authorized by Arts. 20-26 are:

LA Technological Information Network (RITLA)
LA Organization for Fishing Development (OLDEPESCA)
LA Program of Cooperation in Regional Handicrafts (PLACAR)
LA and Caribbean Program of Commercial Information and Support to Foreign Commerce (PLACIEX)

SELA Secretariat

During the 1995—1999 period the position of Permanent Secretary was is being filled by the Argentine, Carlos Juan Moneta, that of under secretary by Luis A. Rodríguez. There are twenty members of the Secretariat.

CASTRO EMOTES AT SELA

For the first time the SELA ordinary meeting took place in Havana, Cuba, an important triumph for Castro. The Cuban dictator took every possible advantage of the triumph with his routine attacks on free economies and free trade, in this case likewise making considerable use of the Hurricane Mitch disaster.

Castro's captive "news" agency (*Prensa Latina* 3 December 1998) and the mouthpiece of his Central Committee (CC) (*Granma*) were, however, actually surpassed in their favorable coverage of the Cuban despot by the report of the "independent" wire service, *Efemerides* (EFE 3 December 1998). The second stage of the conference was initiated by the talkative Cuban caudillo with his inauguration of the High Level Panel on 2 December at 0930. The central theme of this panel was "The Dynamic of the Foreign Policy of LA and the Caribbean."

The panel included José Antonio Ocampo, Executive Secretary of the Economic Community for LA and the Caribbean (CEPAL), various financial experts and the apparent "Latin American," Barbados ex Prime Minister Sir Harold Bernard St. John. But perhaps most interesting was the US citizen, Abraham Lowenthal.

For Mr. Lowenthal is a founder of the Hemispheric Left Support (HLS) organization, DI, which has been frequently discussed in these reports. As Graça Wagner has detailed (pp.147ff, YRBK98), DI was founded in 1982, having arisen out of a US Security Memo dated 10 December 1974. The DI is basically another of those "human engineering" efforts so beloved of our Twentieth Century PPs. Blessed with raw material like Mr. Lowenthal with which to work, it is hardly surprising that the HL boss again launched into his anti-neoliberal polemic.

In the account given in the EFE dispatch of 3 December 1998, Castro compared the economic crisis "with a ship which, if it were sinking, would sink with the rich and the poor, the believers and the non believers," going on to repeat his favorite theme, "the present phenomena are the product of the globalization through which humanity is living." Having thereby dealt with the free-trade demon, which he has conjured up to waltz with the free-market demon, he goes on to inveigh against the "great giant of the north (the US)" against whom LA—and, apparently, Latin Americans like Sir Harold—must unite. EFE does not reproduce another favorite Castro theme, that of LA debt cancellation with no abatement in future lending. But the notion is there with his remarks on US "total power to count on the votes of the monetary fund and the World Bank ...and therefore not be frightened by the risks of the crisis."

Once again the Cuban dictator has launched the same mindless, if pointed and effective, ML assault against free men and free markets. His obvious (*Prensa Latina, Granma*) and his not so obvious (*Efemerides*) pressmen have reported these "economic analyses," but they have failed to report those remarks which constituted a frontal attack on that nation which has done Castro a good deal more good than harm, Mexico. Nevertheless, the attack was made (*La Jornada* 4 December 1998), and the Mexicans apparently felt it too vicious to ignore. The assault on Mexico for its participation in NAFTA was pointed and malignant, but space precludes remark on anything save "evil US influence."

In his tirade against free men and free markets, the Cuban dictator interspersed comments such as "many Mexicans can be asked who the father of the country was, and it is possible that the Mexicans do not know, but it is possible that they know who Mickey Mouse is."

Such remarks have borne fruit in Castro's long campaign against the US as was demonstrated in the fall of 1997 by Colombian President Samper. In the latter's appearance before the MNNA he showed how effective this propaganda has been (pp.362ff, YRBK98) with the following:

> [The North (America) enslaves the South] with cultural expressions which arrive electronically with all the crushing power of the medieval crusades ... because of this daily aggression our children face each new day without identity ... we are prisoners of the virtual reality of the great international networks, prisoners of their images, of their rapid assertions, which, like that detestable fast food, is also bought, used and recycled ....

But, returning to Castro's remarks against Mexico, Mexican Foreign Minister Rosario Green, a *gentil dama* in spite of the "o," reacted, demanding an explanation. The US, of course, has no Ms. Green to demand an explanation from either Mr. Samper or Mr. Castro. Apparently Castro's Alarcón will straighten out all this "misunderstanding," and the Castro campaign can continue.

Central American Economic Integration System (SICA or SIECA)

THE SIECA-AGS MEETING
(WKLY 6.11, 17 SEPTEMBER 1998)

The CA System of Economic Integration (SIECA)[55] (pp.341-2, YRBK98) was ostensibly originated for the task of creating CA economic integration. In 1997 it held its XIX Summit, a six-hour meeting taking place in El Salvador in February 1998. The meeting in latter August 1998, however, can hardly be entitled SIECA XX since it includes a broader spectrum of nations and states than those of SIECA. For it was held at Vega Alta, Puerto Rico, and included as an observer Dominican President Fernández and the state governors of the southern US. These latter belong to the Association of Southern US Governors (AGS) to include the host, Puerto Rico Governor Pedro Rosello.

From this gathering of course arose the "Declaration of Puerto Rico." This called for strengthening commercial relations and investments between CA, the Caribbean and the US, thus strengthening those "internal opportunities" which would then "discourage illegal immigration." This and various other aspects of the meeting relied heavily on claims based on the Caribbean Basin Initiative (ICC).

The ICC came into existence in 1982 when the US awarded preferential commercial treatment to the CA and Caribbean nations. As the CA nations see it with what appears to be considerable logic, the ICC fell by the wayside with the advent of NAFTA or the Free Trade Treaty (TLC) between the US, Canada and Mexico. On 28 July 1992 "The Declaration of Charlottesville (Virginia, US)" arose from an AGO-CA , meeting and can be considered an addition to the ICC. Charlottesville was intended to promote "commerce, investment and tourism."

Never at a loss for a resolution, the AGO issued another after its 4 August 1998 meeting advocating more of the same.

"The Declaration of Puerto Rico" went on to claim that the CA nations have taken "decisive and affirmative steps" to "modernize their economies" and carry out other "reforms" which allegedly indicate the wisdom of including them in governmentally arranged trade and investment.

With all due respect, the real world does not really support this roseate vision, it being seriously distorted by the HL. In Nicaragua, Ortega's ML Sandinistas have, during the eight years since "democracy" is alleged to have arrived there, kept that nation in the chaotic economic condition in which they "left" it. In El Salvador, Handal's ML Farabundis have done much the same. And that free market so detested by Fidel, without which none of these economic utopias will evolve, continues to be blocked or reversed.

THE SICA MEETING IN EL SALVADOR
(WKLY 5.8, 26 FEBRUARY 1998)

On 4 February 1998 the presidents of the nations comprising the Secretariat of CA Integration (SICA or SIECA) met for six hours in the salon of the San Salvador International Airport which is in Comalapa, some 45 kms south of the capital city. AFP (5 February 1998) identified this as a SICA meeting. It should be pointed out, however, that the meeting has also been identified (*El Diario de Hoy* (San Salvador) 3 February 1998) as a Central American 4 (CA-4) (p.334, YRBK98) meeting, apparently because it was stated therein that the four CA nations would consider the *Paso Fácil* Plan. This summit appears to have been correctly identified as the successor to XIX CA Summit (p.344ff, YRBK98).

Salvadoran President Calderón Sol had announced the coming Comalapa pilgrimage in Tegucigalpa at the BCIE festivities, the principal subject mentioned as being on the agenda the *Paso Fácil* (easy step) Plan. This allows, for example, air and surface travel among the four countries of CA-4 with identity card but without passport.

The assembled presidents, first joined by new Honduran President Carlos Flores, met in what was described by Luis Laínez as "the most complete secretiveness" (*Diario de Hoy* 5 February 1998). The results reported are therefore those given by President Calderón or some other spokesman. The general purpose of the meeting was given as the "analysis of the future of the institutions forming part of SICA." SICA, which has its seat in San Salvador and began functioning on 4 February 1993, is supposed to coordinate the efforts of some 40 institutions which have evolved since the process of CA integration was initiated in 1986.

Deputies from PARLACEN let it be known that they had presented to the chief executives a proposal for reforms in the organism to render it "more efficient." Specifically, Salvadoran PARLACEN Deputy Ricardo Acevedo Peralta told the press that the presidents "now had in their hands" the work document for restructuring the institution. President Calderón appears to have emerged from the meeting with promises to restructure *almost* as much as had already been promised at XIX CA Summit.

At XIX CA Summit (pp.374ff, YRBK98) it was stated in the "Declaration of Panama" (DP) that the number of PARLACEN deputies from each CA nation would be reduced from 20 to 10, their salaries from $5000 per month to $3000. After the Comalapa meeting Calderón told *Diario de Hoy* (5 February 1998) that the salary was currently $3000, this apparently indicating that the change had taken place. At the same time, however, he declared that there are now (still) 20 deputies per nation and that there would be a reduction to 10 or 15. Salvadoran Vice Minister of Foreign Affairs René Domínguez stated that the reforms had not been implemented because of "the multiplicity of interpretations of the DP."

Apparently the judicial bureaucracy in the CA Court of Justice (CCJ) has been reduced with the reduction of the number of judges per country to one "owing to the few cases which arrive in their court." Finally, there is the Unified General Secretariat (SGU) which the DP was to create. Calderón is quoted as stating that he and his colleagues adopted "modifications" which would create such a secretariat which will "assume the labor of 32 regional organisms." Perhaps more specific detail was given to the SGU formed by the DP, but the last seven months have apparently seen little movement toward the implementation of the SGU plans contained in the DP.

Finally, insofar as reform is concerned, a change in the BCIE structure is to be "contemplated." The presidency of the bank is no longer to rotate among the CA nations but to be bestowed on "the ideal person in the region to occupy the position" (sic).

Consistent with earlier indications, the CA presidents now agree to sign a TLC with the Dominican Republic in April 1998.

Notes

1. "CA" continues to be used to describe either a five-nation set of countries (Costa Rica, El Salvador, Guatemala, Honduras, Nicaragua) or a six-nation set which also includes Panama.
2. William H. Durham, *Scarcity and Survival in CA: Ecological Origins of the Soccer War* (Stanford University Press, 1979. ISBN: 0-8047-1154-2).
3. Chapter XXXI, of Ludwig von Mises, *HUMAN ACTION: A Treatise on Economics* (Regnery, 1966. ISBN: 0-8092-9743-4).
4. This includes the International Bank for Reconstruction and Development (IDRB) and the International Development Association (IDA).
5. According to Christopher Andrew and Oleg Gordievsky, *KGB: THE INSIDE STORY of Its Foreign Operations from Lenin to Gorbachev* (HarperCollins, 1990. ISBN: 0-06-016605-3), White entered the Chambers CPSU-GRU (Soviet Military Intelligence) spy apparat in 1935-6, soon to be complimented by GRU Colonel Boris Bykov for his activities. White's espionage activities have been further described by John Earl Haynes and Harvey Klehr, *VENONA: Decoding Soviet Espionage in America* (Yale University Press, 1999. ISBN: 0-300-07771-8)

6. While hardly a COMINTERN agent as was White, the homosexual Keynes was imbued with the Marxist world view as well documented by, say, John Costello, *Mask of Treachery* (William Morrow, 1988, ISBN: 0-688-04483-2).
7. Edward S. Mason and Robert Asher, *The World Bank at quarter century; highlights of the World Bank since Bretton Woods* (Brookings, 1973. LCC: 73178269).
8. Anand G. Chandavarkar, *The International Monetary Fund. Its Financial Organization and Activity* (IMF, 1984). Pamphlet Series No.42.
9. Heinrich Karl Marx, "Critique of the Gotha Program," Vol.ii, pp.23-4 (*Marx and Engels Selected Works*, Foreign Language Publishing House (Moscow), 1955).
10. Kubitschek won the presidency in the chaotic aftermath of the Vargas suicide and with the support of the Brazilian Communist Party (PCB).
11. Sidney S(amuel). Dell, *The Inter-American Development Bank: a study in development financing* (Praeger, 1972. LCC: 70185778).
12. If the individual delegate expense is taken as a modest $2000, travel expenses alone for this visit to the seaside amounts to $8,000,000.
13. This has been called the Commission of the Cartagena Accord (CAC) which established the predecessor of CAN, the Andean Group.
14. There is of course also the Andean Parliament.
15. It will be recalled that, although there exists a body of PIC thought to the contrary, the USSR is supposed to have transmogrified itself into a free-enterprise democracy. In the Ukrainian parliamentary elections of early April 1998 the Communist Party made gains in the 450-seat unicameral legislature which will allegedly allow it, in alliance with the Peasant Party and the Socialist Party, to block any moves by the transmogrified democrats.
16. This has also been called The Regional Infancy Summit
17. The logo for the II Summit is the arabic number "two" with a Red Star superposed.
18. Decorated by Castro with his Order of Ana Betancourt. That her life has been one long prevarication is well documented by David Stoll, *RIGOBERTA MENCHÚ and the Story of the Poor Guatemalans* (Westview, 1999. ISBN: 0-8133-3574-4).
19. Whose standards? John Dewey's or Mr. Phonics? What standards?
20. That, for example, "global warming" appears to be nothing but a power play by the International Left headed by the ex Soviet dictator Gorbachev has been discussed (pp.364ff, YRBK98), but this forms part of the "environmental" bible.
21. Emphasis added.
22. Apparently the recently-elected but not yet inaugurated Miguel Angel Rodríguez was also present.
23. As the reader is doubtless aware, *trama* also means "plot" or "conspiracy."
24. Does this mean that the American nations are to be transmogrified into local or regional governments under a One Hemisphere Government?
25. Since it is not known how serious about these schemes any of the political planners may be, it can hardly be said that any of these numbers really means anything.
26. In the Communist Party of the Soviet Union (CPSU) the Praesidium was the Central Committee successor to the all powerful Politburo for which cf. Leonard (Bertram) Schapiro [*The Communist Party of the Soviet Union*, Eyre & Spottiswoode, 1960. LCC: 60004742]. The CPSU has allegedly transmogrified itself into a free-enterprise Old Boys' Club.
27. These are of course the coca leaf growers whose raw material is used for cocaine production and whose "trade" union is an important one in Bolivia.
28. That this is no arcane "conspiracy" is attested by the fact that Fujimori's Peru has the only effective program against Castro's HL terrorists, any weakening of the Fujimori Government then in the Cuban dictator's interest.

29. The I FEA was held in Denver, Colorado, USA in June 1995, the II FEA in Cartagena, Colombia, in March 1996 and the III FEA in Belo Horizonte, Brazil, in May 1997.
30. "Nothing will be accorded until everything is accorded." This apparently has to do with the unsuccessful attempt made by the US to push its "hemispheric integration" ahead of, for example, the already well underway MERCOSUR.
31. This is of immense importance as rendering the proposed treaty considerably more far reaching than a mere device for establishing "free trade." It is, as one commentator put it, a "license to steal" for the statesmen (politicos) since "environmentalism," in keeping with its position as the new home of the International Left, offers a *modus operandi* for control of most facets of human existence. As will be seen, the impresarios were apparently aware of this.
32. Certain LA sources have told LANS that they feel the US is attempting to force "the centerpiece of the Clinton Administration LA policy"—ALCA—on them, and the May 1997 meeting of ALCA Ministers (pp.342ff, YRBK98) appears to have borne this out. It would appear that this effort continues.
33. How "lesser" is "lesser"? How "reduced" is "reduced"?
34. While the title of the forum appears thus in *El Diario de Hoy* (San Salvador 4 Jun 98), it includes the phrase "in the isthmus of CA, Haiti and the Dominican Republic" in the AFP dispatch of 5 June 1998.
35. The five CA nations are not members of the Grupo de Río, but they asked for membership at the Panama meeting.
36. Contadora was, of course, the grouping from which the Grupo de Río evolved. Is the fact that Contadora was originally cobbled up to oppose US policy in Central America of any importance or simply an amusing irony?
37. This is taken from Chapter XVIII, pp.518ff, Ludwig von Mises, *HUMAN ACTION: A Treatise on Economics* (Regnery, 1966. ISBN: 0-8092-9743-4).
38. *THE "FIRST TRICONTINENTAL CONFERENCE," ANOTHER THREAT TO THE SECURITY OF THE INTER-AMERICAN SYSTEM*, Special Consultative Committee on Security, Pan American Union, 2 April 1966.
39. For "good things" and "bad things" cf. Walter Carruthers Sellar and Robert Julian Yeatman, *1066 AND ALL THAT AND NOW ALL THIS* (E. P. Dutton, 1932). As the XX Century draws to a close there is a body of opinion equating "good things" to Political Correctness (PC) and vice versa.
40. At Castro's São Paulo Forum one encounters the idea of "supra national countries ... a sort of re-edition of a soviet-type union in Latin America" which has been quite clearly enunciated (cf.pp.98ff, YRBK97).
41. Earl E. T. Smith, *THE FOURTH FLOOR: An Account of the Castro Communist Revolution* (Random House, 1962. LCC: 638331).
42. The LANS Editor was informed by certain individuals in the Arias inner circle that, although Oscar Arias received a Nobel Peace Prize for the "Esquipulas Accords," John Biehl, his college roommate and closest advisor, was actually responsible for them.
43. Costa Rican sources informed LANS at the time that their longtime foreign minister had been in line for the job until the US exerted sufficient pressure in favor of Gaviria to assure him the job.
44. The concept of "Human Rights" is being rapidly expanded to include a spectrum of such "rights" running from equal employment to higher education.
45. The page number refers to that in the English edition of his remarks which appears at www.oas.org/agdocs/speechjunio01en.htm.
46. In the US such laws have been carried to the extreme of providing wheelchair access

to highways across which a world class runner would not venture. Other examples of such well meant but hopelessly bureaucratic regulations abound.

47. *Communist Threat to the US Through the Caribbean.* Part 2. Senate Internal Security Subcommittee. 1959. Y4.J89/2:C73/27/pt.2.
48. Reproduced in *The New York Times*, 23 April 1948.
49. Cuban journalist Salvador Diaz Verson had been photographing Bashirov's house since 1943 when he and his associates caught Castro visiting there to collect his monthly stipend as a Kremlin agent.
50. Alberto Niño H., *Antecedentes y Secretos de 9 de abril* (Librería Siglo 20, 1949). Written after his retirement.
51. *Daily Mail* (Ireland), 13 April 1948.
52. *Daily Mail* (UK), 17 June 1948.
53. This has been discussed in Wkly 2.17 (YRBK97) and provides prescriptions for most of the internal affairs of the hemispheric nations as well as for their external affairs.
54. The address is Apdo. 17035, Avenida Francisco de Miranda, Torre Europa, piso 4, Caracas 1010.
55. Until relatively recently this was more frequently written as SICA than SIECA. It now appears that SIECA has generally been adopted by the communication media.

Contributors

José Carlos Graça Wagner, a native of São Paulo, Brazil, graduated from São Paulo University Law School in the mid-1950s. He was professor of tax and economy law for fifteen years, in 1957 founding his own offices in São Paulo which now have a branch office in Brasilia and associated offices in six important Brazilian cities. A counselor to various Brazilian legal associations to include the Brazilian Bar Association, and other professional and educational organizations to include the University of São Paulo, he has authored many juridical and economic articles for prominent Brazilian newspapers and periodicals, and he is now serving as president of the Board of the Casper Libero University Foundation. His *Point and Counterpoint* publication and his widely broadcast Opinion on the Air cover various aspects of Brazilian political and social life. He is the president of the Brazilian Foundation for Economic Freedom and Social Development, and his expertise on the São Paulo Forum brought him the accolade of an unsuccessful 1994 lawsuit from da Silva's Workers Party (PT) for "election crime."

Alphonse Emanuiloff-Max is an Uruguayan political scientist, writer, journalist, and honorary consul. Dr. Alphonse Emanuiloff-Max, a native of Bulgaria, received his doctorate in political science in the 1950s in England, then moved to Uruguay and continued his career as a foreign correspondent for various publications in South America, the United States, Africa, and Australia from 1955 to present. He published an English-language weekly during the 1960s and 1970s, served on various international committees, acted as Uruguayan consul for various Latin American nations and has held posts in the Montevideo city government. He has been the director of the Uruguayan Institute for International Studies and of its publication, *Revista Uruguaya de Estudios Internacionales*, since 1982. He is now president of the POLO publishing and printing company and editor of the daily, *Ultimas Noticias*, and the Uruguayan edition of the Pan American weekly, *Tiempos del Mundo*.

Mario Rosenthal has roots in both the United States and Central America. Born in Guatemala City in 1916 of an American father and a Salvadoran mother, he grew up in San Francisco, California, attending San Matteo College during the depths of the Depression. He arrived in El Salvador for a brief visit in 1933 when the country was still recovering from the communist-organized uprising of the year before. During the 1936-1951 period he watched U.S. enterprise transform jungles into productive farms, working for seven years for the United Fruit Company, later associated with El Salvador's leading commercial enterprises while familiarizing himself with the economics and politics of the nation. The oppurtunity to enter his true vocation, journalism, arose after he became a correspondent for the Associated Press reporting from Guatemala and El Salvador. He moved to New York, published *Guatemala* (Twayne, 1961), a review of that country's history to the time of publication, and in collaboration with former President Miguel Ydigoras Fuentes of Guatemala, published the latter's *My War with Communism* (Prentice-Hall, 1962). The book detailed Fidel Castro's support of the leftist movement in Guatemala, a movement which still exists under the same leadership. He was editorial page editor of the most important Spanish-language daily in the United States, *El Diario-La Presna* of New York. He retired to El Salvador in 1979 as the twelve years of the Maerxist-Leninist insurrection was catching fire. He was editor and publisher of the bilingual *El Salvador News-Gazette* until it was sold. Today he continues bravely to express his opinions in his weekly column for *Diario de Hoy*, El Salvador's leading newspaper.

James R. Whelan. LANS is delighted to announce that James R. Whelan has joined our staff of associate editors. He has had a distinguished career in journalism which began with his work for UPI (1952-1968), first in several domestic bureaus, later as a foreign correspondent, country than division manager in LA (Latin America) (1958-1968), returning to report on the region from Washington in 1970 and 1971. Among numerous awards, he received the Overseas Press Club of America's Citation of Excellence in 1971 for the best article on LA, any medium. The author of six books on LA, his *Out of the Ashes: Life, Death and Transfiguration of Democracy in Chile*, 1833-1988 (Regnery, 1988) is the definitive work on that subject in English. *El Mercurio* (Santiago) aptly described this as "without question, the most complete history of our country published in this century, with the sole exception of the works of Francisco Encina and Gonzalo Vial Correo." His academic efforts include Nieman Fellow at Harvard University, adjunct professor at the University of Maryland, a lifetime appointment as associate professor at Finis Terrae University, Santiago, and visiting professor at the Institute of Political Science, University of Chile, (1993-1995). He was managing editor of the *Miami News* (1972-1974), vice president and editor of the *Sacramento Union* (1980-1982) and founding editor, publisher and chief executive officer of the *Washington Times* (1982-1984), *inter alia*. He is a regular contributor to *El Mercurio* and *La Segundo* (Santiago) and a frequent contributor to scores of other newspapers and magazines throughout the hemisphere. He now resides in Saltillo, Coahuila State, Mexico.

Robert G. Breene Jr., received a bachelor's degree in military science and engineering from the United States Military Academy (West Point) in 1945, and a doctor of philosophy degree in theoretical physics from Ohio State University in 1953. His career during the succeeding years was succinctly described by *Soldier of Fortune* in 1987:

> **Renaissance Writer:** Robert G. Breene, Jr. has never had had to worry much about boredom. In the last forty years he has been a fighter pilot, a test pilot for the Air Force [Flight Test Division, 1947-50], an engineering consultant in the Near East, Far East, and South America [Transportation Consultants, Inc.], a professor of physics, and a newspaper correspondent in Central America for the *Union Leader*. And in his spare time he owned and operated a 600-head cattle ranch in Nevada.
>
> Dr. Breene has also found time to write about his work along the way. In addition to many scientific papers and books, he has authored articles on Nicaragua, El Salvador, Cuba, and Guatemala, and two soon-to-be-published works on military history..."

During the latter 1980s and early 1990s, Breene has carried out investigations in Latin America for various organizations and publications.

Name Index

[Editor's Note: The 32 heads of state attending the II Summit of the Americas are listed on pages 443-4 of this volume. References to them in this listing do not appear in this Index. The OAS (Organization of American States) representatives at the XXVIII General Assembly of that organization are listed on page 465 of this volume. References to them do not appear in this Index.]

Abella, Aida, Col, 407
Acevedo Peralta, Ricardo, ES, 481
Acosta, Amylkar, Col, 36, 249
Acosta, Luz Marian, Nica, 249
Agaev, Ednan, Russ, 4, 400
Aguilar, J. J., Col, 346
Auguinsky, Marcelo, Arg, 72
Alarcón, Fabián, Ecuad, 194, 436
Alarcón, Ricardo, Cuba, 241, 437, 450-1, 479
Albats, Yevgeny, Russ, 191, 243
Albores Guillén, Roberto, Mex, 79, 275-6
Albright, Madeleine, US, 121, 194, 277, 440-1
Aldana Escalante, Carlos, Cuba, 220
Alegría, Florentina, Bol, 447
Alejandro, Pedro de Jésus, Mex, 447
Alemán Velasco, Miguel, Mex, 78
Alemán, Arnaldo, Nica, 12, 168, 172, 428
Alessandri, Jorge, Chile, 147
Alfaro Ucero, Luís, Ven, 67, 70
Alfonsín, Raul, Arg,, 92, 96, 225
Algrin, Michel, Franc, 415
Allegret, Ivan "Loco", Nica, 287
Allende Gossens, Salvador, Chile, 145-50, 152, 155, 158, 163, 176, 208
Allmand, Warren, Can, 447-8
Altimorano, Carlos, Chile, 156
Alvarez Icaza, José, Mex, 418
Alvarez, Carlos, Arg, 96
Alvarez, Federico, Hond, 428
Amador, Carlos Alberto, Parg, 459
Amador, Fausto, Nica, 117
Amaya Herrera, Yolanda, Col, 406

Anda, Gustavo de, Mex, 249
Arafat, Yasser, PLO, 365, 461243, 307
Arana, Mariana, Urug, 33
Arango, Baby, Panam, 16
Arango, Maria, Col, 401
Arce Castaño, Bayardo, Nica, 167, 243113, 162
Argaña, L. M., Parg, 30
Argote Arbey, Delgado, Col, 348
Arguello, Roberto J., Nica, 199, 202, 250
Arias, Arnulfo, Panam, 14
Arias Calderón, Ricardo, Panam, 13, 130
Arias Sanchez, Oscar, CR, 134, 308, 395-6, 466
Arias, Ricardo, Panam, 130
Aristide, Jean Bertrand, Haiti, 121, 207
Arosemena Valdes, Rubén, Panam, 15
Artaza, Mario, Chile, 161
Arteaga, Rosalía, Ecuad, 45-7
Arzú Irigoyen, Alvaro, Guat, 10, 428
Auginsky, Marcelo, Arg, 104
Avedaño, Amando, Mex, 264
Aylwin, Patricio, Chile, 151, 155
Aznar, José María, Spain, 211

Balaguer, Joaquin, DR, 76
Ball Martínez, Mary, 181, 184, 244, 415, 418
Ball, Carlos, US, 136, 138, 273
Balza, Martin, Arg, 104-5, 109
Banzer Suárez, Hugo, Bol, 16, 109-10, 436-7, 457-8
Baquedano, Manuel, 447

Barco, Virgilio, Col, 330, 362
Barr, Bob, US, 130
Bartlett Díaz, Manuel, Mex, 84
Bashirov, Gumer W., Russ, 470
Bautista, Jeanette, Col, 320
Bautista, Nydia Erica, Col, 320
Bayther, Osiris, Col, 320, 406
Beaulac, US, 470
Bedoya, Harold, Col, 35, 38, 41, 43, 329-30, 367
Belaunde, Fernando, Col, 292
Bell, Gustavo, Col, 41
Belli, Humberto, Nica, 202
Belt, Guillermo, Cuba, 471
Benza, Nicolás, Arg, 107-8
Berenson, Lorene Helene, US, 181
Bermeo, Lt., Col, 348
Bermúdez, Col, 325
Bernard Lasnaud, Jean, Franc, 103
Benardin, Cardinal Gantin, Mex, 273
Bertinotti, Fausto, Ital, 274
Betancourt Pulecio, Ingrid, Col, 37
Betancourt, Rómulo, Ven, 55, 61-2, 66
Betancur, Belisario, Col, 330, 333, 367
Betto, Frei, Braz, 20, 222-4, 396
Biehl, John, Chile, 466
Bingham, Lord, UK, 162
Birdsall, Nancy, US, 431
Blades, Rubén, Panam, 12, 16
Blair, Anthony, UK, 152, 162, 164
Bodán Shields, Harry, Nica, 434
Bodán, Oliver, Nica, 249
Boeton, Bernard, Swiss, 321
Bofill, Ricardo, Cuba, 138, 206
Bogarev, Basily, Russ, 470
Bohórquez Montoya, Luis, Col, 360
Bolívar O., Alberto, Peru, 292
Bolívar, Simón, 58, 310
Bonett Locarno, Manuel José, Col, 183, 292, 307, 326, 333, 336, 399, 407, 412
Borge, Tomás, Nica, 71, 203, 216, 243, 279
Borja, Rodrigo, Ecuad, 45-7
Bosch, Juan, DR, 208-9
Bowles, Chester, US, 245
Braden, Spruille, US, 25, 244
Bravo, Carlos, Mex, 272
Brenes, Leopold, Nica, 172
Brezhnev, Leonid, Russ, 145, 147
Briceño Suárez, Jorge (aka Mono Jojoy), Col, 325, 332, 371, 376-7

Brizola, Leonel, Braz, 19, 223
Brown, George, US, 281
Bucaram Ortiz, Abdala, Ecuad, 44-6, 50, 52
Bucaram Ortiz, Adolfo, Ecuad, 49-50
Bucaram Ortiz, Averoes, Ecuad, 48
Bucaram, Elsa, Ecuad, 52
Bucaram Ortiz, Jorge, Ecuad, 48
Builes Ortega, Alberto, Col, 328-9
Buitrón, Leonardo, Col, 325
Bunke Bider, Haydee Tamara, Germ, 110
Burelli Rivas, Miguel Angel, Ven, 468
Burgos, Julio, Col, 332
Burguete Cal y Mayor, Araceli, Mex, 468
Burton, Dan, US, 399-401
Bush, George, US, 129, 133, 177

Caballero, Isidro, Col, 319
Cabral, Peggy, DR, 208
Cabrera Infante, Guillermo, Cuba, 197
Caceres Cifuentes, Daladier, Col, 352
Calarcá, Marcos, Col, 318
Caldas, Eduardo Camelo, Col, 326, 332
Caldera Rodríguez, Rafael, Ven, 55-6, 59, 62-3, 66, 68-9, 136-7, 435-6, 457, 467
Calderón Fournier, R. A., CR, 7
Calderón Hinojosa, Felipe, Mex, 124-5
Calderón Sandino, Augusto, Nica, 203
Calderón Sol, Armando, ES, 9, 428, 481-2
Calderón Sol, Elizabeth de, 454
Camelion, Oscar, Arg, 99, 104-6, 108-9
Camelo Caldas, Eduardo, Col, 332
Campaore, Chantal, BurkF, 439
Canal Albán, Jaime Ernesto, Col, 327
Cansimansi, Ana Rosa de, Col, 325
Cansimansi, Franco, Col, 325
Cantillano Sevilla, Servando, Nica, 167
Carazo Odio, Rodrigo, CR, 7
Carbajal, Mario, CR, 448
Cardenal, Ernesto, Nica, 201-2, 249, 274
Cardenal, Fernando, Nica, 202, 250
Cárdenas del Avellano, Enrique, Mex, 82
Cárdenas Gutiérrez, Gustavo, Mex, 81, 83

Name Index

Cardenas Solorzano, Cuautémoc, Mex, 71-3, 192, 217, 223, 245, 251, 263-4, 270, 272
Cárdenas, Lázaro, Mex, 263, 272
Cardona, José Miro, Cuba, 235
Cardoso, Fernando Henrique, Braz, 17, 19, 22, 27-8, 112, 114-5, 225, 458-9
Carles, Ruben, Panam, 13
Carmen Santana, Maria del (dummy), Col, 319
Carmona, A. A., Peru, 53
Carrasco A., Diódoro, Mex, 77
Carter, J. E., US, 126, 131-3, 278, 281-2, 286-7
Casanova, Santiesteban, DR, 209
Cass, Julia, Arg, 163
Castañeda, Jorge, Mex, 224-5
Castaño, Carlos, Col, 369-70
Castellanos, Henry (aka Romaño), Col, 377
Castillo, Manuel, Chile, 175
Castro Ladino, Marco Fidel, Col, 347, 352
(Ruz) Castro, Fidel, Cuba, passim.
Castro, Nelson, Arg, 168
Castro, Raúl, Cuba, 242, 244
Cavallo, Domingo, Arg, 99, 105, 109
Cavazos Lerma, Manuel, Mex, 82
Cavelier Castro, Andrés, Col, 81, 83, 99, 400
Cerna, Lenín, Nica, 243, 249
Chamorro, Pedro Joaquin, Nica 279
Chamorro, Violeta Barrios de, Nica, 165, 168, 192, 416
Chandavarkar, Anand G., Ind, 430
Charry Solano, Julio Eduardo, Col, 326, 332
Chávez Frías, Hugo, Ven, 54-9, 62-3, 65-70, 136-8, 217, 219
Chavez, Eduardo, Col, 310
Chavez, Federico, Parg, 30
Chávez, Hugo de los Reyes, Ven, 65
Chelminski, Vladimir, Ven, 57
Chirac, Jacques, Franc, 435
Chirinos Calero, Patricio, Mex, 77
Christopher, Warren, US, 283
Cienfuegos Gorriaran, Camilo, Cuba, 220, 241, 244
Cifuentes Daladier, Cáceres, Col, 348, 355
Cifuentes, Pedro, Cuba, 249
Cipriano Garcia, Panam, 128

Clinton, Hillary Rodham de, US, 164, 174, 196-7
Clinton, William J., US, 14, 122, 129-30, 162-4, 173-6, 178, 181, 199, 204-5, 213, 440, 446
Coe, Michael D., US, 261
Collor de Mello, Fernando, Braz, 16-7, 24, 223
Columbus, Christopher, Ital, 198
Conde Orellana, Manuel, Guat, 329
Constantine, Thomas, US, 339
Constantinus, Flavius Valerius, Rome, 279
Corach, Carlos, Arg, 97
Córdoba, Piety, Col, 368
Cox, Jack, US, 244, 279, 285
Cristiani, Alfredo, ES, 9, 339
Crozier, Brian, UK, 212-3
Cuadra, Joaquín, Nica, 217
Cuartas, Gloria, Col, 409
Cubas Grau, Raul, Parg, 29-30, 457
Cueto, Maria Teresa, Arg, 98
Curbelo, Nelsa, Ecuad, 321

Daley, William, US, 472
Davidow, Jeffrey, US, 436, 442, 472
Davis, Nathaniel, US, 148
de Bonafini, Hebe, Arg, 95
Degregori, C. A., Peru, 293-4
de la Rúa, Fernando, Arg, 95-6
de Menem, Zulema, Arg, 94
Demot, Frances, Franc, 470
Debray, Regis, Franc, 148
D'Escoto Brockman, Nica, 201-2
del Rio, Rito Alejo, Col, 186
Devia Silva, Luis Edgar (aka Raúl Reyes), Col, 372
Dias, Marcio, Braz, 28
Diaz-Balart, Lincoln, US, 214
Diaz Herrera, Roberto, Panam, 13,
Díaz, Ramón, Cuba, 164
Diocletianus, Gaius Aurelius Valerius, Rome, 279
Diogenes (The Cynic), Greece, 330
Di Tella, Guido, Arg, 99-100, 105
Domínguez, René, ES, 482
Donato, Lt., Col, 350
Dong Shen, Juan, China, 428
Donnelly, US, 471
Douglass, Joseph D. Jr., US, 212
Duch, Juan, ES, 9

Dueñas, Javier, Cuba, 215
Du Guesclin, Bertrand, Franc, 210
Duhalde, Eduardo, Arg, 93, 95
Dulles, J. W. F, US, 160
Duque, C. A., Panam, 16
Durán Ballén, Sixto, Ecuad, 48-9, 51
Dzugashvili, Iosif, (aka Stalin), Russ, 153

Echeverría, José A., Cuba, 215
Echeverry, Gilberto, Col, 381
Eguiluz, Ruben, Arg, 105
Ehlers, Freddy, Ecuad, 46-7
Eisenhower, Dwight D., US, 226, 228, 235, 238, 466
Elias Calles, Plutarco, Mex, 263, 271
Endara, Guillermo, Panam, 130
Enrique II, Castile, 210
Enrique IV, Castile, 210
Escobar, Pablo, Col, 362
Escorcia, Sandra, Panam, 13, 15
Esguerra, Juan Carlos, Col, 314
Espaillat, Arturo, DR, 208
Estrada, Horacio, Arg, 107, 109
Eugênio, Mex, 417
Evans, G. Russell, US, 134
Eymael, José M., Braz, 21

Falso, Ciro de, US, 432
Farah, Douglas, US, 308, 397
Farias, P. C., Braz, 24, 228
Ferdinand of Aragon, 210-1
Fermín, Claudio, Ven, 54
Fernández de Cevallos, Diego, Mex, 71
Fernández Medina, Orlando, Ven, 64
Fernández Meijide, Graciela, Arg, 95-6
Fernández, Eduardo, Ven, 54
Fernández, Guillermo, Col, 369
Fernández, Leonel, DR, 71, 207-9, 437, 480
Fernández, Luis, Spain, 470
Ferreira, José, Arg, 105
Figueres Ferrer, José (Pepe), CR, 2, 57
Figueres Olsen, José María, CR, 2, 428
Filizzoli, Juan Carlos, Parg, 29
Fischel Volio, Astrid, CR, 7
Flavius Valerius Constantinus, Rome, 279
Flores Pérez, F., ES, 9-10
Flores Facusse, Carlos R., Hond, 11, 428, 481

Flores, Jorge, Panam, 13
Fonseca Amador, Carlos, Nica, 172, 201, 203, 356
Ford, Guillermo, Panam, 15
Fraga Iribarne, Spain, 211
Franco Bahamunde, Francisco, Spain, 211
Franco Koroneos, Ivette, Panam, 456
Franco, Itamar, Braz, 17, 223
Franke, Roberto, Arg, 108
Franklin, Benjamin, US, 151
Frei Montalvo, Eduardo, Chile, 147-8
Frei Ruiz-Tagle, Eduardo, Chile, 437, 450, 458
Friedman, Milton, US, 432
Fujimori Fujimori, Albert Kenyo, Peru, 178-80, 287-92, 295, 370, 433, 436, 438
Froissart, Jean, Franc, 210

Gaitán, Jorge Eleicer, Col, 469-70
Galán, Francisco, Col, 386, 408
Galán, Mario Hugo, Col, 333
Galeano Rion, Alexander, Col, 352
Galileo Galilei, Ital, 198
Gallón, Gustavo, Col, 319
Gama, Jaime, Port, 448
Gantin, Bernardin, Cardinal, Italy, 273
Garca-Castellon, Manuel, Spain, 160-2
Garcés, Joan, Spain, 152-3, 158
Garcia Hurtado, Jorge, Col, 41
Garcia Pérez, Alan, Peru, 20, 179-80, 287, 289, 290
Gárcia Preval, René, Haiti, 121
Garcia, Cipriano, Panam, 128
Garzón, Baltasar, Spain, 152-3, 159, 161-4
Gaviria Trujillo, Cesar, Col, 41-2, 327, 330, 465-7
Genghis Khan, Mong, 123
Gibbon, Edward, UK, 279
Giovanni, Sabogal Henry, Col, 352
Goethals, George W., US, 100
Golitsyn, Anatoliy, Russ, 191
Gomes, Ciro, Braz, 21
Gómez Lizarazo, Jorge, Col, 320
Gómez, Capt., Col, 345
Gómez, Denise, Col, 447
González Espinosa, Alvaro, CR, 4
González de la Vega, Edberto, Arg, 108
González Espinosa, Alvaro, CR, 5

Name Index 495

González González, Felipe, Mex, 78
González Videla, Gabriel, Chile, 144, 148
González, Jacinto, Mex, 128
Gorbachev, Mikhail, Russ,
Gordon, Kermit, US, 430
Gore, Albert, US, 440
Goulart, João (Jango), Braz, 19, 148, 430
Graça Wagner, José Carlos, Braz, 70, 110, 220-1, 415, 478
Gramsci, Antonio, Ital, 1
Granados Roldán, Otto, Mex, 77
Grave, Vera, Col, 310
Green, Rosario, Mex, 122, 124-5, 479
Guareschi, Roberto, Arg, 163
Guderian, Heinz, Germ, 412
Guerrero Mier, Angel, Mex, 76
Guerrero, Douglas, ES, 170
Guevara Valdes, Alfredo, Cuba, 470
Guevara, Ernesto, Arg, 110, 196-7, 224, 450
Guijón Klein, Patricio, Chile, 152
Guillen Vicente, Rafael Sebastian, Mex, 82, 248-50, 264, 274-5
Guillén, Paloma, Mex, 82-3
Gunera de Melgar, Nora, Hond, 11
Gurría, José Angel, Mex, 124
Guzmán Reynoso, Abimael, Peru, 287, 294, 306

Haas, Emmanuel, CR, 451
Haddad, Jamil, Braz, 223
Handal, Shafik, ES, 294, 356, 480
Harberger, Arnold C., US, 145-6, 176
Harbury, Jennifer, US, 395
Harlem, Gro, 440
Hayes, Rutherford B., US, 31-2
Hermoza Ríos, Nicolás De Bari, Peru, 288-91
Hernández Correa, Joaquín, Mex, 81, 83
Hernández López, Rafael, Col, 337
Hernández M., Héctor, Col, 434
Hill, Robert C., US, 245
Hilton, Ronald, US, 440
Hitler, Adolf, Germ, 111, 154, 160
Hoenigsberg, Guillermo, Col, 491
Hoffmann, Lord Stanley, S.Afr., 161-2
Horowitz, Irving Louis, US, 240-2
Howitt, Richard, UK, 315
Hoyer, Werner, Germ, 448

Hughes, William, US, 130
Hurtado Miller, J. C., Peru, 53
Hurtado, Jaime, Ecuad, 57

Ibañez, Bernardo, 470
Iglesias, Enrique, Spain. 428, 431, 433-4, 440, 454
Insulza, José Miguel, Chile, 437
Isabella, Spain, 210-1
Itamaraty, Braz, 57
Izaguirre, Maritza, Ven, 137
Izurieta Caffarena, Ricardo, Chile, 146

Jackson, Jesse, US, 14
Jagan, Cheddy, Guy, 456
Jagan, Janet, Guy, 456
Jairo Aguilar, John, Col, 336
Jarquín Torres, Nerio José, Nica, 167
Jason, Elimat Y., Chile, 154
Jefferson, Thomas, US, 442
Jiménez Chavez, Raúl, 291
Jiménez, Asdral, Col, 315
João of Portugal, 211
John Paul II, Poland, 194-7, 199-203, 242
Johnson, Lyndon Baines, US, 209
Johnson, Paul, UK, 221
Johnston, Olin, US, 55
Juan Carlos, King, Spain, 211
Julio, Blas, Panam, 129, 455
Jungmann, Raul, Braz, 114, 226

Kamman, Curtis, US, 382
Kassar, Monzer Al, Arg, 104, 106
Kelly, Raymond, US, 123
Kennedy, John F., US, 226, 228, 235, 238
Kennedy, Joseph, US, 407, 409
Kennedy, Robert, US, 245
Keynes, John Maynard, UK, 429
Khadafy, Moamar el, Libya, 216, 460
Khrushchev, Nikita, Russ, 212, 320
Kim Phuc, 439
Kotchergine, Vadim, Russ, 219
Kouri, Alexander, Peru, 54
Kubitschek, Juscelino, Braz, 430

Lacayo Oyanguren, Antonio, Nica, 117
Laínez, Luis, Hond, 481

Laino, Domingo, Parg, 25, 29-31
Lakas, D. E., Panam, 134
Landazabal, Fernando, Col, 402
Lando, Amir, Braz, 223
Lanza de Montezemolo, Andrea Cordero, Ital, 201
Laro, Juan, 470
Larraechea de Frei, Marta, Chile, 176
Laya, Alfredo, Ven, 65
Leahy, Patrick J., US, 278
Lee, Susana, Cuba, 278
Leon, Colonel, ES, 182-3, 411
Letelier, Fabiola, Chile, 447
Letellier, Juan Pablo, Chile, 157
Letellier, Orlando, Chile, 157
Lewis, Anthony, US, 417
Lewis, Ted, US, 80, 271
Li Ka-Shing, China, 135
Lleras de la Fuente, Carlos, Col, 38
Lloreda, Ridrigo, Col, 372, 381-2
Lloyd, Antony, UK, 448
Lodezma, Antonio, Ven, 54
Lombardo Toledano, Vicente, Mex, 470
López Obrador, Andrés M., Mex, 80
López Santiz, Antonio, Mex, 263
López, Cecilia, Col, 42
Lott, Trent, US, 122
Lowenthal, Abraham, US, 478
Lunev, Stanislav, Russ, 191
Lusinchi, Jaime, Ven, 64
Lynch, Graystom L., US, 227

MacArthur, Douglas, US, 280
Maciel, Marco, Braz, 21
Madrazo Cuellar, Felipe, Mex, 124
Magalhães, Antonio Carlos, Braz, 114, 225
Mahuad, Jamil, Ecuad, 45-6, 50, 115
Malavassi Calvo, Federico, CR, 6
Maluf, Paulo, Braz, 19-20
Mandela, Nelson, S.Afr, 459-62
Marín Rodríguez, Javier Orlando, Col, 406
Marín, Gladys, Chile, 186
Marín, Manuel, Spain, 448
Marín, Pedro Antonio (aka Tirofijo), Col, 358-9, 378, 380, 461
Mario, Luis, Cuba, 192
Marquevich, Arg, 97-8
Marshall, George C., US, 470
Martin Busch, Jorge, Chile, 176

Martin, Malachi, US, 201-2, 393
Martínez, Antonio, Cuba, 383, 475
Martínez, Barzaín, Mex, 269
Martínez, Miguel Eduardo, Arg, 431
Martínez, Patricio, Mex, 75
Marulanda Vélez, Manuel – see Marín, Pedro A.
Marún, Jorge, Ecuad, 50
Marx, Heinrich Karl, Germ, 19, 21, 89, 164, 180, 192, 215, 278, 430
Matías Flach, Luis, Braz, 459
Matthews, Herbert Lionel, US, 215, 306, 394
Maturana, Humberto, 440
Matutes, Abel, Spain, 449
Mauss, Werner, Germ, 314
Max, Alphonse Emanuillof, Urug, 24, 288
Maza Márquez, Miguel, Col, 327
Mazarrasa, Almudena, Col, 317, 374-5
McCaffrey, Barry, US, 122
McNamara, Thomas, US, 129, 455-6
Medrano, Antonio, Mex, 80
Mejia González, Federico, Nica, 286
Mejia González, Luis, Nica, 286
Mejia, Luis, Ecuad, 52
Mejia, María Emma, Col, 41
Melnick, Sergio, Chile, 154
Menchú, Rigoberta, Guat, 440
Mendieta, Herlindo, Col, 376
Mendoza, Plinio Apuleyo, Col, 323-4, 330
Menem, Carlos Saul, Arg, 16, 92-7. 99, 101, 103-4, 106
Menem, Eduardo, Arg, 450
Menem, Zulema de, Arg,, 94
Menéndez, Bob, US, 214
Merquevich, Roberto, Arg, 96
Michelena, Margarita, Mex, 419
Millán Pérez, Fernando, Col, 405-8
Milosevic, Slobadan, Serbia, 160
Miranda, Ana, Spain, 315
Mises, Ludwig von, Aus, 429, 457
Mitterand, Danielle, Franc, 315
Mitterand, François, Franc, 315
Mockus, Antanus, Col, 37,41
Moellor, Heinz, Ecuad, 50
Moltke the Younger, Helmuth Karl Bernhart, Count von, Germ, 227
Molina, Rita, Arg, 96
Moncayo, Héctor, Col, 320
Moncayo, Paco, Ecuad, 47, 50

Moneta, Carlos Juan, Arg, 477
Monreal Avila, Ricardo, Mex, 76
Montenegro Rinco, Luis Enrique, Col, 439
Montesinos Torres, Vladimiro, Peru, 288
Moorer, T. H., US, 135
Mora Valverde, Manuel, CR, 55
Mora, Jorge Enrique, Col, 379, 409
Morales Flores, Melquiades, Mex, 74
Morales Orozco, José, Mex, 272
Morazán, Francisco, 284
Morena, Eradio, Nica, 249
Moreno Ocampo, Luis, Arg, 96-7
Moreno William, Rubio, Col, 348, 350, 354
Moreno, Javier Giraldo, Col, 319
Moscosa de Gruber, Mireya, Panam, 12-5
Mucchielli, Roger, Arg, 221
Muñoz Céspedes, Walter, CR, 5
Murat, José, Mex, 78
Murillo, Rosa, CR, 451
Murillo, Rosaria, Nica, 165, 169
Murphy, John, US, 285
Mussolini, Benito, Ital, 1, 394

Naranjo, Hugo Fernando, CR, 324-5, 448
Narváez, Jorge, Nica, 165, 169
Narváez, Zoilamérica, Nica, 156, 166-7, 169-71, 217
Navarro Wolff, A. J., Col, 29,
Nebot, Jaime, Ecuad, 49-50
Neef, Manfred Max, 440
Negroponte, John, US, 129
Niño H., Alberto, Col, 470
Nixon, Richard M., US, 133, 213
Noboa Ponton, Alvaro, Ecuad, 45-6, 50
Noriega, Manuel, Panam, 129, 279, 282
Núñez, Eliseo, Nica, 169

Obando y Bravo, Cardinal, Nica, 173, 202
Ocampo, José Antonio, 478
Octavianus, Gaius Julius Caesar Augustus, Rome, 279
Odio Benito, Elizabeth, CR, 7
Ojeda, Alonso, Col, 385
Orta Cordoba, Juan, Cuba, 244
Ortega Diaz, Pedro, Ven, 57

Ortega Saavedra, Daniel, Nica, 11, 55, 132, 164-5, 167-71, 173, 201-2. 216-7, 243, 250, 274, 356, 480
Ortega Saavedra, Humberto, Nica, 89, 166, 201, 243, 250, 266, 269, 276, 356
Ortega, Ramón (Palito), Arg, 93
Ortega, Zoilamérica, — see, Narváez, Zoilamérica
Ospina, Mariano, Col, 479-1
Ossorio Arana, Arturo, Arg, 100
Oviedo, Lino S., Parg, 24-5, 27-30

Pacas Castro, José Manuel, Hond, 428
Pacheco Cesdar, Comez, Col, 354
Palacio Tamayo, Anivál, Col, 310
Palleros, Diego, Arg, 102, 105, 107, 109
Pardo, Julio Enrique, Col, 325
Parrales, Edgar, 202
Pastora Gómez, Edén, Nica, 177, 243
Pastrana Arango, Andrés, Col, 35-8, 41, 43-4, , 193, 304, 329-30, 365, 370-2, 375, 380-4, 460, 462
Patton, George S. Jr., US, 186, 414
Paulik, Juan, Arg, 107-8
Pawley, William D., US, 244, 471
Payeras, Mario, Guat, 420
Pazos, Luis, Mex, 78, 273
Pedro the Cruel, Spain, 210
Pell, Claiborne, US, 278
Peña Gómez, Francisco, DR, 70-1, 207-8
Pérez Balladares, Ernesto, Panam, 12-5, 125-6, 129-30, 433-4, 455, 457
Pérez de Arce, Hermógenes, Chile, 152-6
Pérez de Cuellar, Javier, Peru, 178, 181, 225
Pérez Jiménez, Marcos, Ven, 54
Pérez López, Mex, 419
Pérez, Carlos Andrés, Ven, 20, 54-6, 59, 61-3, 66-9, 138, 180, 356
Pérez, Edilma (aka Skinny Nelsa), Col, 405
Pérez, Manuel (aka Poliarco), Col, 385
Perón, Isabel de, Arg, 175
Perón, Juan Domingo, Arg, 25, 92-3
Perot, Ross, US 415
Petkoff, Teodoro, Ven, 57, 62, 66, 68-9, 137
Petrie, Henry, Nica, 170

Petro, Gustavo, Col, 310
Pezzullo, Laurence, US, 244, 278, 282, 284, 286
Piñera, José, Chile, 150
Piñiera Losado, Manuel, Cuba, 219-20, 241
Piñiero, Amador J., 194
Pino, Rafael del, Cuba, 471
Pinochet Ugarte, Augusto, Chile, 145-7, 149, 151-5, 157-62, 164, 219
Pinzón, Héctor, Col, 320
Plazas Vega, Alfonso, Col, 310
Polay Campos, Victor, Peru, 179, 287, 292
Ponomarev, Boris, Russ, 145, 147, 176, 218
Poradowsky, Miguel, Poland, 250, 385, 393
Portillo, Alfonso, Guat, 10
Posada S., Miguel, Col., 41, 303, 309, 316, 362, 364, 367, 369, 399, 434, 446
Prieto, Jaime, Col, 320
Puig, Max, DR, 206
Pulecio, Freddy, Cil, 315

Quezada Saldaña, Marta Lorena, Nica, 171

Rainha Junior, José, Braz, 224
Ramírez Mejía, Néstor, Col, 327, 408-9
Ramírez, Fabian, Col, 336
Ramírez, Ivan, Col, 309, 402, 407
Randall, Margaret, US, 170
Rato, Rodrigo, Spain, 433
Raudales, Ramón, Nica, 172
Reagan, Ronald Wilson, US, 177, 201
Reina, Carlos, Hond, 428
Remos, Ariel, US, 69, 211
Restrepo José Manuel, Col, 467
Rey Navas, Pedro José, Col, 406
Reyes, Jorge, Ecuad, 47
Reyes, Raul, Col, 372
Ricardo, Richard G., Col, 378
Rincón, Consuelo, Col, 406
Rio, Rito Alejo del, Col, 186, 407-9, 414
Rivero, José I., Cuba, 209, 211
Roa Sierra, Juan, Col, 469
Roa, Mario Fernando, Col, 386
Robaina, Roberto, Cuba, 450
Robinson, Mary, Irel, 374
Rodríguez Echeverría, M. A., CR, 2, 7
Rodríguez, Andrés, Parg, 30

Rodríguez, Carlos, Col, 319
Rodríguez, Francisco A., Panam, 129, 477
Rodríguez, Luis A., Arg, 477
Rodríguez, Nicolas (aka Gabino), Col, 386
Rodríguez, Oscar Andrés, Hond, 428
Rodríguez, William, Nica, 170
Roisinblit, Rosa, Arg, 164
Rojas, Juan Antonio, Col, 318
Roldos, León, Ecuad, 49, 51
Romberg, Sigmund, US, 329
Rosello, Pedro, PR, 480
Roux, Carlos Vicente de, Col, 319
Roux, Francisco de, Col, 319
Rubin, Robert, US, 123, 163
Rubio, Noemi Sanín de, Col, 37, 41, 43
Rueda Serboussek, María I., Col, 39
Ruiz Hernández, Javier, Mex, 267
Ruiz Pavon, Horacio, Nica, 275
Ruiz Pérez, Agustin, Mex, 269
Ruiz, Alvaro, Col, 332
Ruiz, Marco Vinizio, CR, 451-2
Ruiz, Samuel, Mex, 250, 261, 263-4, 271-2, 274-5, 416-7, 420-2

Sabino, Carlos, Ven, 89
Sabogal Henry, Giovanni, Col, 352
Saenz, Carlos Roberto, Col, 310
Saenz, Guillermo León (aka Alfonso Cano), Col, 310
Sáez Conde, Irene Lailin, Ven, 54, 57, 63, 66-7, 70
Salamín, Marcel, Panam, 435
Salas Feo, Enrique F., Ven, 62, 65
Salas Römer, Henrique, Ven, 54, 62, 65, 67, 70
Salinas de Gortari, Carlos, Mex, 250, 266, 270, 276
Salinas de Gortari, Raúl, Mex, 125
Samper Pizarro, Ernesto, Col, 36, 42, 327, 330, 367, 382, 412, 433-4, 436, 438-9, 461, 467, 479
Sánchez Vargas, Euclides, Col, 185, 393, 413
Sandoval Iñiguez, Cardinal Juan, Mex, 273
Sanguinetti, Julio María, Urug, 33, 225, 453
Sanín de Rubio, Noemi, Col, 37-8, 41, 43-4

Name Index 499

Sanjur, Conrado, Panam, 130
Santana, María del Carmen, Col, 319
Santiago, Ricardo Luís, Braz, 431
Santiesteban Casanova, Cuba, 209
Santos Zelaya, José, Nica, 11
Sarbanes, Paul S.,US, 134
Sarlengo, Luis, Arg, 101-2, 106-8
Sasson van Elsloo, Roberto, Arg, 101-2
Scavarelli, Alberto, Urug, 459
Schlieffen, Count von, Germ, 227
Sejna, Jan, Czech, 212-3
Serpa Uribe, Horacio, Col, 35-6, 41-4, 306, 329-30, 405
Shattuck, John, US, 318
Silva, Luiz Ignacio (Lula) da, Braz, 17, 20, 111-2, 192, 208, 216-7, 222-3, 225, 249
Smith, Earl E. T., US, 306, 394, 466
Somoza Debayle, Anastasio, Nica, 126, 132, 149, 172, 243, 278, 281-2, 284, 286-7
Sopeña, Germán, Arg, 163
Soto, Cecilia de, Mex, 71
Sottas, Eric, Switz, 321
St. John, Harold Bernard, Barb, 478
Stedile, João Pedro, Braz, 111, 221
Steenvoort, Paul, Holl, 321
Stephanopolous, George, US, 152, 164
Stone, Oliver, US, 14
Stornelli, Carlos, Arg, 109
Straw, Jack, UK, 162
Stroessner, Alfredo, Parg, 30,
Suárez, Xanthis, Nica, 170
Suchlicki, Jaime, US, 240-2
Sucre, Alejandro, Ven, 138
Sucre, Antonio José de, 68
Sumner, Gordon Jr., US, 280, 284

Tapias, Fernando, Col, 336, 372, 375
Thomas, Sherman, CR, 5
Timofeyev, Lev, Russ, 191
Tínoco Rubí, Victor, Mex, 84
Tinoco, Victor Hugo, Nica, 168
Tirado López, Victor, Nica, 170
Tirofijo – see Marín, Pedro Antonio
Toma, Miguel Angel, Arg, 97
Tomic, Radomiro, Chile, 147
Toncel, Milton de Jesús, Col, 331
Torres Restrepo, Camilo, Col, 385
Torres, Felipe, Col, 386
Torres, US, 408-9

Torrijos, Omar, Panam, 126, 132, 134, 278-82, 475
Tovar, Rafael, Ven, 65
Trobo, Jaime, Urug, 449
Trujillo Molina, Rafael L., DR, 208
Tudela, Francisco, Peru, 290

Ulianov (aka Lenin), Vladimir, Russ, 158, 258, 265-6, 294, 370, 396
Umaña, Eduardo, Col, 401
Urcuyo, Francisco, Nica, 286
Urso, Jorge, Arg, 100-1, 104, 108
Uscátegui, Jaime Humberto, Col, 337

Valbueno Payares, Armando, Col, 406
Valdez, Ramiro, Cuba, 219
Valdivieso Sarmiento, Alfonso, Col, 35, 37-8, 329-30
Valencia Tovar, Alvaro, Col, 327, 398
Valer Sandoval, Juan, Peru, 291
Vallarino, Alberto, Panam, 15
Vallarino, J. J., Panam, 15
Valle Riestra, Javier, Peru, 179-81
Varela, Félix, Cuba, 195
Vargas, René, Ecuad, 326
Vasquez Carrizosa, Alfredo, Col, 320
Velandia, General Col, 320
Velasco Alvarado, Juan, Peru, 54, 68, 289
Velasco Chávez, Hector Fabio, Col, 321
Velazquez, Col, 409
Vesco, Robert, US, 213
Viafra, Miguel, Col, 360
Vial Larraín, Juan de Dios, Chile, 146, 157
Videla, Jorge, Arg, 96-8
Vieira, Gilberto, Col, 360
Villalobos, Joaquin, ES, 250, 266, 269-70, 276
Viqueira, Horacio, Arg, 109
Vivanco, 402-3
Vives Pérez, José, Col, 39
Vladimir, Col, 405
Volonte, Alberto, Urug, 33
Voltaire, François Marie Arouet de, Franc, 262

Walesa, Lech, Poland, 214, 474
Wasmosy, Juan Carlos, Parg, 24-5, 27, 30, 435, 458
Waverly, Lord, UK, 315

Whelan, James, US, 160
White, Harry Dexter, US, 430
Williams, John, US, 400
Wolff, Carlos, Col, 42

Yabrán, Alfredo, Arg, 97
Yanine, Farouk, Col, 408
Yarrington Ruvalcaba, Tomás, Mex, 74, 81-3
Ybarra Rojas, Antonio, Nica, 173

Yeltsin, Boris, Russ, 10, 94, 218
Yoma, Emil, Arg, 104
Yoma, Jorge, Arg,, 94

Zamora Alcántara, Mario, Hond, 428
Zamora, Rubén, ES, 9-10
Zapata, Virgilio, Col, 315
Zedillo Ponce de León, Ernesto, Mex, 71, 122, 124-5, 259, 270
Zelaya Blanco, Roberto, Nica, 173

Subject Index

AA (Agricultural Action), Ven, 69
AAJ (American Association of Jurists), 321
AAN (Andean News Agency), 99
AASM (Associated African States and Madagascar), 205
Abejas, Las (The Bees), 248, 252, 265-6, 268-9
AC (Forward Chiclayo), Peru, 53
ACDH (High Commission for HR), 317
ACLU (American Civil Liberties Union), 313
ACNUR (UN High Commission on Refugees), 418
ACP (African, Caribbean, Pacific States), 205
Acteal Massacre, Mex, 245, 247-8, 250, 255-8, 263
Act of Guayaquil, 289
AD (Americas Department), 200, 220
AD (Democratic Action), Ven, 54-5, 59-62, 64, 66, 70
AD (Democratic Alliance), Panam, 12
AD-5, — see Pigs Opn
ADM-19 (Democratic Alliance 19 April Movement), 36-7
ADO (Democratic Opposition Alliance), Panam, 15
ADT (Tumbusina Democratic Alliance), Peru, 53
Adveniat et Misere, Germ, 416
AgRef (Agrarian Reform), 19, 221, 262-3, 267, 221, 474
AI (Amnesty International), 80-1, 161, 213-4, 265-6, 320-1
AID (US Agency for International Development), 445
AIPE (Inter-American Economic Press Agency), 41, 54, 136, 150
Air Force 1, US, 174
AK-47, 325, 331

AL (Liberal Alliance), Nica, 11-2, 168-9
ALADI (LA Integration Association), 219
ALAP (Panam Alternative Legal Assistance), 128
ALCA (Free Trade Organization of LA), 436, 442, 448, 451, 453-4, 472-3
ALIANZA, Arg, 16, 92, 95
ALIANZA, Parg, 32-3
Allende Govt of Chile, 180
Alto Parana Dept, Parg, 32
Amambay Dept, Parg, 33
América Libre, 224
Americas Watch, 313, 320
ANP (National Palestine Authority), 461
ANR (National Republican Association), Parg, 30, 32-3
ANSA (Italian News Agency), 193
Antifictionic Congress, 467
Anti-neoliberalism, 8
AP (Patriotic Accord), 16
APERTURA, Ven, 63
Apiay Air Base, Col, 278
APM (Grandmothers of the Plaza of May), Arg, 164
APRA (Peoples Revolutionary Alliance), Peru, 50, 179
Apurímac River, Peru, 296
ARDI (Left Revolutionary Group), Ven, 62
ARENA (National Republican Alliance), ES, 9-10
ARMIF (Regional Assoc for Forced Migration), 128
Army Operation Destroyer, Col, 331
Artillery Transport Gp 4, Arg, 101
ASFADES (Association of Families of Detained and Disappeared), Col, 320
ASI (Indigenous Social Alliance), Col, 40

Asian Flu, 457
ATF (Arequipa Tradition and Future), Peru, 58
Atlantic Fleet, US, 135
Atlantico Department, Col, 38-9
AUC (Self Defense Forces), Col, 369
Autonomous Communities, Mex, 266-7
Autonomous County Council, Mex, 267
Ayacucho, Peru, 293-6

B-26 "defection plan", 157
Babies and Bayonets DO, Guat, 417
Bandung Conference, 460-1
BAR (Browning Automatic Rifles), US, 237
Bárbula Battalion, Col, 360
Barco Administration (1986-1990), Col, 362
Bartolomé de Las Casas Human Rights Center, Mex, 416
Batalla de Boyacá Battalion, Col, 331
Bay of Pigs, Cuba – see Pigs Opn
BCG-7 (Anti-Guerrilla Battalion No.7), 349-50
BCIE (Central American Bank of Economic Integration), 427-8
Belo Horizonte Accord, 453
Beni Biosphere, 433
Berlin Wall, 157, 366
Betancur Government, 367
BID (Inter American Development Bank), 328-34, 438, 440, 445, 454
Billar, El, Overrun, Col, 306-7, 335-6, 338-9, 412-3
Biodiversity, CR, 4
BIPAR (Joaquín París Infantry Bn), Col, 344-7, 352-3, 355, 379
Black Hawk U60L, US, 338, 379
Bloc Special Forces, Col, 339
BM (Banco Mundial) – see WB (World Bank)
Bogotá Sports Palace, Col, 330
Bogotazo, Col, 244, 369-72
Bolivian (landlocked) Navy, 436
Bolshevik Revolution (1917), Russ, 263
BP (British Petroleum), 315
Brazilian Constitution, 1993, 17ff
Brazilian Federal District, 17-8, 23
Brazilian House of Representatives, 21-3
Brazilian Senate, 21-3

Bretton Woods, 429-30
Brigade 3-68, Nica, 249
Brigade 5, Col, 407
Brigade 12, Col, 408
Brigade 13, Col, 407
Brigade 20, Col, 402
BRIM-3 (Anti-Terrorist Mobil Brigade), Col, 345
British House of Lords, 161-2, 315
Broad Front, Ecuad, 50
Buenos Aires Province, Arg, 92-3

C-47 (Gooney Birds), 342
CAJ (Andes Comm Jurists), Peru, 319
C-5 Galaxy, 174
CA-4 (Central America 4), 427-8
Cambio 94, Panam, 13
CAMRE (Andean Foreign Relations Ministers Council), 435
CAN (Andean Community of Nations), 435-7
CAP (Self Defense Patrol), 127, 246-7, 250, 258, 268-9, 293, 304, 323, 333-4,
Capone Mob, US, 276
Caribbean Group, 102
Caribbean Legion, 3
CARICOM (Caribbean Community and Common Market), 204-5, 240
CARIFORO (Caribbean Forum), 206
CARIFTA (Caribbean Free Trade Association), 297, n.8
Carter Center, US, 12
Carter Government, 282-4, 286-7
Carter-Torrijos Treaty, 126, 132
Casa Verda, Col, 367
CC (Christian Road Party), Nica, 11
CCA (CA Summit), 437
CCDH (Cuban Human Rights Committee), 207, 419
CCFD (Catholic Committee Against Hunger and for Progress), Franc, 415-6
CCJ (CA Court of Justice), 482
CCJ (Col Commission of Jurists), 319, 324
CD (Democratic Convergence), CR, 9
CDH (Human Rights Commission), UN, 317
CDHCM (Council of Ministers Human Rights Commission), Ital, 297, n.1

Subject Index 503

CDHF (Bartolomé de las Casas HR Center), Mex, 246, 263, 265, 273
CDIH (Inter American Commission on Human Rights), OAS, 463
CDPN (Nariño Department Peace Commission), Col, 326
CE (European Commission), 448
Central Dept, Parg, 32-3
CEO (Colombian Electoral Organization), 39
CEPAL (Economic Commission for LA and the Caribbean), 478
Cervantes Literature Prize, 197
CFJP (French Justice and Peace Commission), 321
CFP (Concentration of Popular Forces), Ecuad, 49, 52
Chaco, Parg, 31-2
Chamber of Deputies, Chile, 31, 150-1
Chamber of Deputies, Col, 38-40
Chamber of Deputies, Mex, 72-4
Chamber of Deputies, Mex, by State, 75-85
Chamber of Deputies, Parg, 30-3
Chamber of Deputies, Ven, 64
Chapultepec Accords, 305, 395, 397, 429
Chevín de Huántar, Peru – see JEO
CHICOMS, 132, 135-6
Chilean Armed Forces, 148-9, 155-6
Chilean Committee Representing Chilean Jewish Entities, 154
Chilean Constitution, 150
Chilean Reconciliation Movement, 157
China Resources Enterprise, 135
CHRC (Colombian HR Committee), 315
Christian Democrats, Chile, 155
Christian Left, Chile, 155
CI (Inter-American Court), 319
CIA (Central Intel Agency), US, 213, 223, 229, 231, 233, 239, 407
CIAL (Latin American Infancy Summit), 438-9
CIDHD (Canadian International Center for HR and Development), 447
CIDI (Inter American Council for Integral Development), OAS, 463
CIDSE (NGO Hq), Belg, 416, 419
CII (Inter-American Investments Corporation), 430
CIJP (Inter-Congregational Commiss of Justice and Peace), Col, 319

CIM (Inter American Commission on Women), OAS, 464
CIM (Mexican Indigenous Council), 447
Cimpum Callao, Peru, 53
CINDE (CR Investment and Development), 451
CINEP (Peoples Education and Investigation Center), Col, 319
CIR-4 (Regional Intelligence Center No.4), Col, 345-6
Circunscripción, Col, 35
CITEFA (AF Scientific and Tech Research Inst), Arg, 102
Civil Society in Pastrana Peace Process, Col, 368
CJI (Inter American Juridical Committee), OAS, 463
CLA (Summit of the Americas), 175, 440-4
CLAC (LA Training Center), Czech, 418
Clandestine airstrips, Col, 340-1
CMA (Multilateral Anti Drug Center), 13-4, 126, 129-31
CMCA (Conference of Foreign Ministers), 448-9
CNCD (National Center of Cooperation in Development), Col, 321
CNN (Cable News Network), US, 314
CNRC (National Commission on the Revision of Confiscations), Nica, 167
Coastal Alliance, Nica, 12
CODEPU (Peoples' Rights Defense Corporation), 447
COENA (ARENA National Executive Committee), ES, 9-10
COINCOPROCO (Association of Investment, Commercialization and Consumption), Col, 320, 406
Colombia Support Network, 321
Colombian Chamber of Deputies, 38-40
Colombian Force, 43
Colombian Independent Conservative Movement, 40
Colombian representatives by department, 40
Colombian Senate Elections, 36-8
Colombian three-phase elections, 35
Colón Theater, Col, 471
Colonia Escalon, 182

Colorado Party, Parg, 24, 27-30
Colorado Party, Urug, 53
CoMaCaTe (Clandestine Officers Group), Ven, 56, 68
COMINTERN (Communist International), 147, 244, 430
Commissie Rechtvaarddigheid en Vrede, 321
Commission of Churches on International Affairs, 321
CONAI (National Mediation Commission), Mex, 252-3, 255
Concepción Dept, Parg, 33
Constituent Agreement of Panama, 475-6
Constituent Assembly, Ecuad, 45
Constituent Assembly, Ven, 58
Constitution, Col, 330, 352 365
Constitutional Province, Peru, 52-4
Contadora, 456
Continental Day Against Social Exclusion, 448
Contra-Drug DO, 357, 394
CONVERGENCIA, Ven, 63
CONVIVIR (Rural Security and Vigilance Cooperatives), 312, 364, 408
COPEI (Independent Political Electoral Organization Committee – Christian Socialist), Ven, 59, 62, 64, 70
CORAS (Colombian Refugee Association), 315
Cordillera Dept, Parg, 32-3
CORPHU (Association for Human Promotion), Col, 320
CORPORIENTE (Educational Association of Investigation and Consulting of the East), Col, 320
COSOP (Committee of Solidarity with Political Prisoners), Col, 405-6
Cotche language, Col, 324
COTRAMUSIN (Musún Transportation Corp), Nica, 173
Counterfeit Contra (Edén Pastora), Nica, 177
CPA (Andes Presidential Council), 435
CPA (Summit of the Peoples of America), 446-8
CPPIA (Iberian-American Democratic (sic) Parliaments), 449
CREDHOS (Regional Committee for Defense of HR of Barrancabermeja), Col, 320-1, 405-6

CRI (International Red Cross), 316
Cristomarxism, 377
CRMR (Regional Council for the Woman of the Rural Area), 454
CRS (Socialist Renovation Current), Col, 37
Crusades, 198
CSE (Supreme Electoral Commission), Nica, 171
CSE (Supreme Electoral Commission), Ven, 57, 65
CSPP (Committee in Solidarity with the Political Prisoners), Col, 320
CTAL (LA Labor Federation), 470
Cuban Women's Federationh, 447
CUT (United Workers Central), 446
CUT (Workers Central), Braz, 112-3, 224
CZ (Panama Canal Zone), 138

Daforel (firm), Urug, 107-8
DAS (Administrative Security Department), Col, 327
DC-8 (McDonnell Douglas, intro 1958, 4-pod jet engines), US, 106-7
DCI (Director of Central Intelligence), US, 230
DEA (Drug Enforcement Administration), US, 340, 342
Debrol (firm), Urug, 102, 107, 109
Declaration of Caracas, 466
Declaration of Charlottesville, 480
Declaration of Madrid, 430
Declaration of Oporto, 384
Declaration of Panama, 457, 481
Declaration of Santiago, 444-6
Declaration of the Rights of the Child, 439
DeConcini Amendment, 133-4
Del Carmen Santana Case, 319
Delicias, Las, Overrun, Col, 306, 335, 337, 412
Democratic Party, SAfr, 460
Department of Ideology, Education, Science and Sports, and International Relations, Cuba, 220
Departments of Peru, 37-8
Deputies, Ecuador, 51-2
Deputies, Mex, 72-85
Destacamento Militar IV, Nica, 411
Development and Peace, Canad, 416

Subject Index 505

DF (Federal District), Mex, 50-1, 223, 272
DGI (General Directorate of Intelligence), Cuba, 203, 209, 220
DGSE (General Directorate of State Security), Nica, 249
DI (Inter-American Dialog), 110, 183, 222, 224, 474
DIA (Defense Intelligence Agency), US, 183, 213, 307, 397, 400, 412
Dialectical Materialism (Marxism), 1-2, 191-2, 356-7
Diplomacy of the Subversion, Col, 303, 309-21
DM IV – see Destacamento Militar IV
DNC (Democrat National Committee), US, 135
DO (Disinformation Operation), 303, 305-9, 400, 414, 460
DOD (Department of Defense), US, 231
DPP (Peoples Democracy Party), Ecuad, 46, 49-51
DRO (Regional Operations Department - BID), 431
Drug Campaign Against US, 212-4

ECP (Colombian Petroleum Enterprise), 366
EDF (European Development Fund), 205
EEC (European Economic Community), 205
Eisenhower Government, US, 226
Ejido, Mex, 260
EL Party, Ven, 61
ELN (National Liberation Army), Col, 34, 127, 218, 304, 306, 311, 314, 323, 328, 356, 365, 369, 372, 374, 381, 398, 405, 408
EPL (Peoples Liberation Army), Col, 310, 315, 408
EPS (Sandinista Peoples Army), Nica, 165
ERI (Irish Republican Army), 315
ESCOL (Association School of Alternative and Self-Management Services), Col, 406 268
ESCUELA, LA, Col, 320, 406
Esquipulas II Accords, 121, 218, 304, 328, 364, 381
ETA (Basque Homeland and Liberty), Spain, 316

Eye of the Needle, 199
Ezeiza International Airport, Arg, 100, 107
EZLN (Zapatista National Liberation Army), Mex, 79, 81, 83, 245-52, 255-6, 258, 262, 264-6, 270, 272-5, 358, 416, 418-9, 421

FA (Broad Front), Peru, 53
FA (Broad Front), Urug, 217
FAC (Colombian Armed Forces), 183, 185, 309, 335, 354, 396, 399-400, 412
FAES (Salvadoran Armed Forces), 116, 334
FAL (Fusil Automatico Liviano) 5.56mm rifle, also produced in 7.62mm FN-FAL, Arg, 106-7
FAO (Broad Opposition Front), Nica, 284
FAO (Food and Agricultural Organization), 193
FAR (Revolutionary Armed Front), Nica, 172
FARC (Colombian Revolutionary Armed Forces), 34, 44, 127, 184, 186, 216, 219, 304, 306-7, 310-1, 318, 322-6, 328-9, 331-3, 335-7, 339, 342, 344-7, 356, 358-61, 365, 376, 398, 408-9, 412, 414
FARC Sanctuary, Col, 380-3, 402, 472
Fascists, 1
FBI (Federal Bureau of Investigation), US, 471
FCC (Federal Commo Commission), US, 231
FCSC (Coexistence and Citizen Security), 454
FD (Democratic Front), CR, 4
FEA (Forum of the Americas), 451
FEDEFAM (LA Federation of Associations of Families of Disappeareds), Col, 321
Federal District, Braz, 18, 23
Federal District, Ven, 45
Federal House of Representatives, Braz, 23
Federal Senate, Braz, 23
Federal Territories, Braz, 17-8
Fifth Communist Party Congress, Cuba, 194

FIJOF (Independent Front for Fixed Works), Peru, 53
Fine Airlines, US, 99, 101
FIN small political party, Ven, 61
FIP (Independent Peoples Front), Peru, 63
FIRJP (Peru Together Independent Regional Front), Peru, 53
First International, 164
Fiscalía, Col, 409, 410
FL (Lorteana Force), Peru, 53
FM (Military Manufacturing), Arg, 99, 101, 103
FMLN (Farabundo Martí National Liberation Front), ES, 9, 216-7, 220, 304-5, 356, 395-6, 429
FMPR (Manuel Ponte Rodríguez Front), Ven, (sometimes FPMR), 51, 63, 155-6
FNRR (Ramón Raudales Northern Front), Nica, 172-3
FOIA (Freedom of Information Act), US, 163, 229
FOMIN (Multilateral Investments Corporation), 430-1
FP (progressive Force), Col, 40
FPD (Pro Democracy Front), Panam, 15
FPMR (Manuel Rodríguez Patriotic Front), Chile, 155-6
FRA (Alfarista Radical Front), Ecuad, 49-51
France Liberté, 315
FRD (Democratic Revolutionary Front), Cuba, 230
FRELIMO (Moçambique Liberation Front), 415, 419
French National Assembly, 1'
Frente Amplio, Ecuad, 50
FREPASO (National Solidarity Front), Arg, 96
FRG (Guatemalan Republican Front), 10
"Friends of Colombia," 383
FSLN (Sandinista National Liberation Front), Nica, 11, 164, 168, 170-2, 208, 216, 220, 250, 264, 284, 396
FSP (São Paulo Forum), 17, 20, 57, 70, 110, 192-3, 216-7, 222-4, 226, 264, 272, 474
FTA (Fast Track Authority), US, 443
FTC (Task Force Caguán), Col, 336-8, 340, 343

FUAC (Andrés Castro United Front), Nica, 167, 172-3
FUB (Bucaramanga Urban Front), Col, 406
FUNPROCEP, Col, 320
FURY (Yariguies Urban Resistance Front), Cxol, 405-6
FVI (Independent Local Front), Peru, 53

G3 7.62mm Heckler and Koch, since 1959, Germ, various mod, 331
GAD (High Level Group Against Drugs), 122
Galil 7.62mm AR, Col, 351
Galil 7.62mm SAR, Col, 351
Gatling Machine Gun (20mm), 342
GATT (General Accord on Tariff and Trade), 431
GB (*Gia Basta*), 274-5
GDO (Great Gringo Disinformation Operation), US, 178, 181, 184, 303, 307-8, 338, 343, 410-2
Gecko SA8 Surface to Air missile, Arg, 106
General Assembly, OAS, 462ff
General Secretariat, OAS, 463
Genocide Accusations, Chile, 153
GJ (Juridical War), Col, 319
Global Exchange, US, 271
GOES (Government of El Salvador), 305
Government of National Reconstruction, Peru, 289
Governors, Mex, 72, 74ff
Granma (periodical), Cuba, 206, 215-7, 219
Greens, USSR, 258
GRU (Russian Military Intelligence), 191, 510
Grupo de Río, 284, 302-3
GS (Social Group), Jesuit, Col, 319
Guairá, Parg, 33
Guaraní Language, 27
Guatemalan Supreme Court, 397
Gubernatorial election, Mex, by state, 73ff
"Guevarist," 385

Harbury DO, 394-5
Hayton Trade, Urug, 102, 107, 109

Subject Index 507

Helms-Burton, US, 199
High Commissioner for Peace, Col, 378
High Court, Britain, 161
Higher Polytechnic Institute, Cuba, 215
Himyarite-Axum or Homerite-Axum struggles, after circa AD300, 55
HLS (Hemispheric Left Support), 303, 393
Hotel Claridge, Col, 471
House Committee on Un-American Activities, US, 244
Howard AF Base, Panam, 131
HR (Human Rights), 159, 306, 308-10, 317-21, 393
HRW (Human Rights Watch), 324, 402
Hughes Model 500, US, 411
HUMINT (Human Intelligence), 342
Hutchison Whampoa, Ltd, PRC, 135

IADB (Inter American Defense Board), 280-1, 284
IAS, (Iberian American Summit), 383, 475
IAWC (Inter American Workers Confederation), 470
IBOPE (Brazilian Institute of Public Opinion and Statistics), 112
IBRD (International Bank for Reconstruction and Development), 430
ICC (Caribbean Basin Initiative), 480
ID (Democratic Left), Ecuad, 49-51
IL (International Left), 145, 310, 358, 370
IL-B (Independent List B), Chile, 23
ILSA (LA Institute of Alternative Legal Services), 320
IMF (International Monetary Fund), 137, 429-30, 434, 478
Impresarial Forum of the Americas, 451-2
INEGI (National Institute of Statistics, Geography and Information), Mex, 259
INIDEN (Institute for National Defense Investigation), Peru, 294
Inquisition, 198
INS (Immigration and Naturalization Service), US, 231
Intel Brigade XX, Col, 309
Intelligence Battalion 3 (Cali), 220
Inter American Court (and Commission) of HR, 442

Inter American Defense College, US, 327
Inter-American Institute of Human Rights, 467
Intercontinental Encounter for Humanity and Against Neoliberalism, 274, 248-9
International Brigades, 344
International Children's Rainforest, 433
International Confederation of Free Trade Unions, 321
International Department, CC, CPSU, 147
International Peace Brigades, 321
International Working Man's Association, 180
Investment in Columbia, 312
IPC (Independents for the Community), Ven, 69
IRENE (New Hope Integration Registration), Ven, 61, 63, 69
Isolation of Nicaragua, 282-3
Itagüí Prison, Col, 367
Itaipú Dam, Parg, 26
Italian Communist Party, 274
Itapua Dept, Parg, 32

JA (Self Defense Groups), Col, 358
JCS (Joint Chiefs of Staff), US, 230, 232, 235
JEO (Japanese Embassy Operation), Peru, 287, 288ff, 290, 335
Joaquín París Battalion, Col, 379
John Birch Society, 244
Joint Interagency Task Force, US, 214
Joint Task Force South, Col, 184, 327-8
José Martí International, Cuba, 195
Juárez Cartel, 123
Judicial War, 269, 270

KG (Kennedy Government), US, 226
Kaibiles, Guat, 254
KGB (Committee for State Security), USSR, 191, 219, 243, 399-400
Khrushchev drug strategy, USSR, 212

LCI (Landing Craft, Infantry), US, 235
Libertarian Movement, CR, 6-7

Liberty Front, SAfr, 460
LibTheo (Liberation Theology), 165, 223, 249-50, 253, 265, 272, 275, 304-5, 325, 370, 385, 394, 401, 417
LIC (low intensity conflict), Col, 362
Life Option, Colombian coalition, 43
Lippo Group, 135
Loma Fortress, La, Nica, 237
Lomé Convention, 205
LSD (Landing Ship, Dock), US, 236
LV (La Violencia), Col, 472

M-16 (5.56mm Colt M16A2, from AR-15, 1967), US, 287
M-19 (19th of April Movement), Col, 37, 310, 360, 367
M-60 (7.62mm Machine Gun, General Purpose), US, 414
M-70 B1 (7.62mm Assault Rifle), Serbia, 325
MAD (Democratic Alternative Movement), Col, 40
Majamut Sandbank, Mex, 267
Managua Protocol, OAS, 463
"Maoist," 305
MAPU (Unitary Peoples Action Movement), Chile, 155-6
Mapuche Cultural Center, Chile, 177
Mapuche Indians, Chile, 154-5
Marx Seminary, Braz, 19
MAS (Movement Toward Socialism), Ven, 57, 62, 64, 69, 136-7
Mauss Case, Col, 314
Mayoral elections, Oaxaca, Mex, 81
Mayors, Tamaulipas, Mex, 83
MB (Mobile Brigade) III, Col, 335
MB XII, Col, 337
MB XXIV, Col, 337
MBR200 (Bolívar Revolutionary Movement 200), Ven, 56, 62, 68-9
MCPC (Peoples Civil Convergence Movement), Col, 40
MDAP (Peru Decentralized Now Movement), 53
MD-11 (McDonnell Douglas, 3 turbofan, from DC-10), US, 197
Medellín Cartel, Col, 383
MERCOSUR (Common Market of the Southern Cone), 1, 25-7, 29, 58, 435-6, 442, 452, 458-9, 472-3

Mexican Army, campesino respect for, 421
MI-17-1V (Russian chopper), 338
MI5 (Military Intelligenmce), UK, 162
MI6J (6 June Independent Movement), Peru, 52-3
MIC (Cealamaqui Independent Movement), Peru, 53
Military Intelligence, Attack On, Col, 403
MININT (Ministry of Interior), Cuba, 219-20
MIP 2000 (2000 Pucalipa Independent Movement), Peru, 53
MIR (Left Revolutionary Movement), Chile, 155, 163
MIR (Revolutionary Left Movement), Bol, 16
Miraflores Palace, Ven, 66
Miraflores, IG Report, Col, 344-56
Miskito, Sumo and Rama Indians, Nica, 11
MISP (We Are Peru Independent Movement), 53-4
MITU (Independent Tacna United Movement), Peru, 53
Mitú Overrun, Col, 376-9
MIVV (Independent Neighbors Movement), Peru, 53-4
MNNA ("Non Aligned" NationsMovement), 427, 459-62, 479
MOA (Bolivian Mothers Who Love), 447
MOIR (Independent Revolutionary Workers Party) Col, 37
MOL (Liberal Oxygen (Oxígeno) Movement), 37
MOLIRENA (Liberal Republican National Movement), Panam, 15
Moneda Palace, La, Chile, 148
MORENA (National Renovation Movement), Panam, 17
Morazán Bolsón, ES, 116
Mothers of the Plaza of May, Arg, 95, 98
MPD (Peoples Democratic Movement), Ecuad, 51
MPE (Papa Egoro Movement), Panam, 12, 16
MPF (Federal Prosecutor's Office), Mex, 259

Subject Index

MPLA (Peoples Liberation Movement of Angola), 416
MPP (Peoples Participation Movement), Panam, 15
MRC (Civilista Renovation Movement), Panam, 15
MRTA (Tupac Amaru Revolutionary Movement), Peru, 178-9, 287, 290, 292, 317
MSI (Independent Solidarity Movement), Ven, 69
MSN (National Salvation Movement), Col, 40
MST (Landless Peasant Movement), Braz, 19, 110, 112-3, 115, 220-2, 224-5
MTB (Manfra, Tordella and Brockers Banking), US, 108
MULCE (Miguel Utrilla Los Chorros Ejido), 258, 267
Municipal electisons, Mex, by State, 72ff
Mussoliniani, 1
MVR (Fifth Republic Movement), Ven, 57, 64, 69

NAFTA (North American Free Trade Agreement), 224, 447, 480
Narcotics Cultivations and Production, Col, 341
National Assembly of the Peoples Power, Cuba, 449
National Assembly, Ecuad, 51-2
National Assembly, Nica, 113
National Directorate (Politburo), Nica, 135
National Front, Col, 42
National Intelligence Directorate, Chile, 151
National Party, Chile, 155
National Party, Urug, 53
National Senate, Brazilian, 18, 21-2
National Union, Ecuad, 48
National Unity Bloc — see CUP
NAZI (National Socialist German Workers Party), 1-2, 113
NCOS (NCBOS) (National Centrum Boor Ontwikkelingssamenwirking), 310, 321
Neembecú Dept, Parg, 32-3
Neoliberalism, 89ff

New and Renewable Energy Sources, 431
New Country – Socialist - Pachakutik Alliance, Ecuad, 82
New World Economic Order, 475
NFD (New Democratic Force), Col, 40
NGO (Non Governmental Organization), 181, 303, 309-11, 315-22, 328, 399, 402-8, 410, 434, 446-7
NGOs, Lesser, Col: FUNPROCEP, etc., 320-1
NH (National House), Braz, 23ff
NI (New Left), Peru, 53
Nicaraguan Anti-Communist Resistance, 177
Nicaraguan National Guard, 285
Nicaraguan Supreme Court, 167
Nine Commanders (Sandinista Directorate, etc.), Nica, 166
Noche y Niebla (NGO periodical), 319
NP (New Country), Ecuad, 49, 52
NSC (National Security Couuncil), US, 231

OAC (Office of the High Commissioner -HR), UN, 317
OAD (Self Defense Organizations), Peru, 289
OAS (Organization of American States), 12, 116, 122, 283-4, 429, 450, 462-9
OIT (International Labor Organization), 439
OMC (World Trade Organization), 473
OMCT (World Organization Against Torture), Col, 321
OMS (World Health Organization), 440
ONC (Operational Navigational Chart), 375
Operation Casablanca, US, 123, 277
Operation Gaviota, 106
Operations and Maintenance Study, Panama Canal, 134
OPS (Pan American Health Organization), OAS, 464
Order of Isabella the Catholic, Spain, 211
Order of Merit of Duarte, Sánchez and Mella, DR, 207
Oriente Military District, Cuba, 219
Operation Chavin de Juantar – see JEO

ORIT (Inter American Regional Labor Organization), 446
ORPHU (Association for Human Promotion), 406
ORVE (Venezuelan Revolutionary Party), 55, 62
OTO Melara 105mm, Arg, 101-2
OV-10 (Rockwell Bronco), 379

PA (Arnulfista Party), Panam, 13
Pachakutik, Ecuad, 51-2
PALA (Alajuela Labor Action Party), CR, 8
PAN (National Action Party), Mex, 71, 73, 75-7, 79-82, 84, 122, 124
Pan American Union, 462
Panama Canal, 100, 126, 133, 138, 278, 280-1
Panama Ports Company, S.A, 135
Papal Visit to Central America, 200-3
Papal Visit to Cuba, 201-3
Paraguayan departments (17), 32
Parana Plateau, Parg, 32
Paraná River, Parg, 32
PARM (Authentic Mexican Revolution Party), 82-3
PARLACEN (CA Parliament), 427, 437, 481-2
Pastrana Peace Process, Col, 193, 304, 308, 369-72, 375, 380, 384
Patascoy Overrun, Col, 306-7, 324, 327, 330, 335, 338-9, 412-3
Pax Christi, Col, 320
PC (Cardenist Party), Mex, 83, 252, 268-9
PC (Communist Party), Chile, 155-6, 160
PC (Conservative Party), Col, 328
PC (Peoples Convergence), Col, 40
PCB (Communist Party), Braz, 20
PCC (Chilean Communist Party), 148
PCC (Colombian Communist Party), 322-4, 358-9
PCC (Colombian Conservative Party), 34-6, 38, 40-1, 44, 304, 328-9
PCC (Cuban Communist Party), 206, 220, 222
PCDDH (Permanent Committee for the Defense of HR), Col, 320
PCdoB (Communist Party of Brazil), 19-20

PCE (Ecuadoran Conservative Party), 48, 51
PCN (National Reconciliation Party), CR, 9
PCP Communist Party of Peru), 294
PCV (Venezuelan Communist Party), 62-3, 69
PD (Democratic Party), CR, 3, 5, 8
PDC (Christian Democrat Party), Chile, 23-4, 147, 150
PDC (Christian Democrat Party), CR, 7
PDC (Christian Democrat Party), Parg, 33
PDS (Party of the South), Chile, 24
PDT (Democratic Workers Party), Braz, 19, 22-3
PDVSA (Petroleum Monopoly), Ven, 137
Peace House, Mex, 291
PEN (National Encounter Party), Parg, 32-3
Peoples Militias, DR, 209, 359
Peru-Ecuador border skirmish, 103, 105, 450
Pezzullo Tapes, 244, 282, 285-7
PFD (Democratic Force Party), CR, 3-4, 8
PFL (Liberal Front Party), Braz, 19, 22, 113
PFL (Liberal Front Party), Braz, 23, 114, 225
PIB (Gross Domestic Product), 137
PIDH (Inter-American HR Pact), 317
Pigs Opn (Bay of Pigs), US, genl, 227-40
Pigs Opn, AD-5 (Douglas Skyraider, modif kit for 12 pass), 231
Pigs Opn, *Avance*, 232
Pigs Opn, B-26 (Douglas A-26 Invader 1942, B-26 1948) 235-7
Pigs Opn, BAR (Browning Auto Rifle), 237
Pigs Opn, Beach Blue, 237-8
Pigs Opn, Beach Green, 237
Pigs Opn, Beach Red, 237
Pigs Opn, C-54, 234
Pigs Opn LCI (Landing Craft, Infantry), 235, 237
Pigs Opn, LCVP (Landing Craft, Vehicles Personnel), 236
Pigs Opn, LSD (Landing Ship, Dock), 236

Subject Index 511

Pigs Opn, LSU (Landing Ship, Utility), 236
Pigs Opn, recoilless rifles, 2.75mm, 237
Pigs Opn, RC (Revolutionary Council), 235-6
Pigs Opn, Sea Furies (hawker Fury 2), 237
Pigs Opn, Soviet Bloc Arms, 233, 235
Pigs Opn, T33 (trainer version F-80), 237
Pigs Opn, Tanks, M-41, 237
PIM (Multi-Ethnic Indigenous Party), Nica, 12
PIN (National Integration Party), CR, 3, 5, 8
Pinochet, Ullman F'ta Loriko, Chile, 155
PINU (Innovation and Unity Party), Hond, 11
PJ (Justicialista (Peronista) Party), Arg, 16, 72
PL (Liberal Party), Braz, 20
PLA (Authentic Liberal Party), Panam, 15
Plan of Action of Miami, US, 440
Plano Real, Braz, 225
Plaza of the Revolution, Nica, 202
PLC (Colombian Liberal Party), 34-6, 38, 40-1, 44, 304, 306, 328-9
PLC (Constitutional Liberal Party), Nica, 12
PLH (Honduran Liberal Party), 10-1
PLN (National Liberation Party-Social Democrat), CR, 2-4, 8
PLN (National Liberation Party), ES, 9-10
PLO (Palestine Liberation Organization), 365
PLRA (Authentic Radical Liberal Party), Parg, 32-3
PMDB (Brazilian Democratic Party Movement), 19, 22-3
PML (Libertarian Movement Party), CR, 3, 6, 8
PMN (National Mobilization Party), Braz, 21
PMR (Mexican Revolutionary Party), 272
PNC (National Christian Party), Col, 40
PNH (Honduran National Party), 10-1
PNR (National Revolutionary Party), Mex, 263, 271-2

Polhó Autonomous Council, Mex, 246
Politburo, Sandinista, Nica, 164, 170, 173, 202, 217
Polo Patriotica, Ven, 64-5
PONAL (National Police), Col, 344, 354
Popular Union Party (PUP), CR, 7
PP (Polo Patriótico), Ven, 64-5, 67
PP (Professional Politicians), Scourge of Siglo XX, 466 and *passim*
PP (Progressive Party), Braz, 19, 22
PPB (Brazilian Progressive Party), 20, 22-3
PPD (Party for Democracy), Chile, 24
PPR (Reformed Progressive Party), Braz, 20, 22
PPS (Peoples Socialist Party), Braz, 19-21, 23
PPT (Country for Everyone), Ven, 58, 63, 69
PRAXIS (Practice), Col, 315
PRC (Civilist Renovation Party), Panam, 13
PRC (Costa Rican Renovation Party), 3, 7
PRC (Peoples Republic of China), 132, 218
PRD (Democratic Renovation Party), CR, 7
PRD (Democratic Revolutionary Party),Panam, 12-3
PRD (Dominican Revolutionary Party), 56
PRD (Revolutionary Democratic Party), Mex, 71, 73, 75, 77, 80-2, 84, 251, 264, 270, 413
PRE (Ecuadoran Roldosista Party), 49-50
Precursor Chemicals, 342
PRF (Febrerista Revolutionary Party), Parg, 33
PRI (Institutional Revolutionary Party), Mex, 71, 73, 75-7, 80-2, 84, 122, 124-5, 245-6, 252, 263, 269-70, 272
PRM (Mexican Revolutionary Party), 263
PRN (National Republican Party), CR, 5
PRODEFENSA, Arg, 101, 103
Progressive Encounter, Urug, 33
PRONA (National Order Reconstruction Party), Braz, 21
Protocol of Buenos Aires, OAS, 464

Protocol of Cartagena de Indias, 464
Protocol of El Salvador, OAS, 468
Protocol of Managua, OAS, 463
Protocol of Sucre, CAN, 435
Protocols of Transition (FSLN to Doña Violeta), Nica, 165
Provincial delegates, Ecuad, 51-2
PRP (Progressive Republican Party), Braz, 20
PRSD (Social Democrat Radical Party), Chile, 24
PRVZL (Project Venezuela), 62, 64, 70
PS (Socialist Party), Chile, 155
PSB (Brazilian Socialist Party), 20, 23
PSC (Social Christian Party), Braz, 21
PSC (Social Christian Party), Ecuad, 49-51
PSC (Chilean Socialist Party), 23
PSD (Social Democrat Party), Braz, 19-21
PSDB (Brazilian Social Democrat Party), 19-23, 113-4, 225
PSDC (Christian Social Democratic Party), Braz, 21
PSE (Ecuadoran Socialist Party), 49, 52
PSN (National Solidarity Party), Braz, 21
PSOE (Spanish Socialist Workers Party), 316
PST (Socialist Workers Party), Arg, 98
PST (Socialist Weorkers Party), Mex, 263
PSTU (Unified Socialist Workers Party), Braz, 21
PSUM (Mexican Unified Socialist Party), 418
PT (Workers Party), Braz, 20-3, 113, 222, 224, 226
PT (Workers Party), Mex, 71, 73, 75-6, 83,
PTB (Brazilian Labor Party), 20, 22-3
PTN (National Workers Party), Braz, 21
PUSC (Social Christian Unity Party), CR, 2-4, 7-8
PV (Green Party), Braz, 21
PVEM (Mexican Green Ecology Party), 73, 76, 83

Quiebrapata Mines (leg breaker), Col, 312
Quotient, Colombian election, 39

(A)R-15 5.56mm rifle (M-16 precursor), US, 331, 334
RAAN (Autonomous North Atlantic Region), Nica 11-2
RAAS (Autonomous South Atlantic Region), Nica, 11-2
Radical Party, Chile, 155
Radio America, 100,
Radio Caracol in Medllín, 326
Rainforest Alliance, 433
RCMRE (Foreign Ministers Consultative Meeting), OAS, 463
RD (Reconstruction and Development), Peru, 58
Reaffirmation of Caracas, OAS, 468
Reagan Government, US, 177
Real Plan, Braz, 111
RECHIP (Chilean Peoples Initiative Network), 446
REDES (Association for Social and Economic Rehabilitation of the People Displaced from the Northeast), Col, 320, 406
Reichstag, 1
RENACE (minor party), Ven, 61
Renewable Energy Sources (UN Conference), 431
Renovating Workers Party, Braz, 20
Residue, Colombian election, 39
Restor Metals, Arg, 99
Rettig Report, Chile, 105
RFP (Request for Proposal), 446
Rivera Sends the Order Back, 209-12
RMC (Commerce Ministers Meetings), 472-3
RN (National Renovation), Chile, 23-4
Rodman Pacific Naval Station, Panam, 131
Roman November of Fidel Castro, 193
RP (Proportional Representation), Mex, 79
RPG (Rifle Propelled Grenades), 348
Russian Advisors, Col Terrs, 399-400

SAGO (Samen Anders Gaan Ontwikkelen), 310, 321
Samper Government, Col, 204, 215, 221
San Cristóbal National University, Peru, 293
San José de Guaviare, Col, 341-2, 346, 349, 355, 361-2

Subject Index   513

San Marcos National University, Peru, 293
San Pedro de Chanlhó, Municipality of, Mex, 252
Sandino International Airport, Nica, 202
SAPB (South American Propaganda Bureau), 20
School of the Americas DO, US, 395
Scotland Yard, UK, 471
Scourge of the Twentieth Century, 211, 263, 478
Second Conference of the Southern Bloc, Col, 359
Second Mobil Brigade, Col, 340
Second National Self Defense Conference, Col, 359
SEDESOL (Ministry of Social Development), Mex, 254
SELA (LA Economic System), 214, 473, 475-7
Senate, DR, 71
Senate, Ven, 63-4
Senators-for-life, Chile, 24
SERPAJAL (LA Peace and Justice Service), 321
SGU (Unified General Secretariat), CA, 402
SH (We Save Huaraz), Peru, 53
Sherman, Fort, Panam, 131
SI (Socialist International), 164
SICA (Central American Economic Integration System), 428, 479-81
SIECA – see SICA
SISS (Senate Sub Committee on Internal Security), US, 244
SL (Sendero Luminoso), Peru, 179, 287, 292, 294, 317
SLA (State Legislative Assembly)., Braz, 18
Social Christian Party, Col, 44
Social Workers Party, Braz, 20
Soltam 60mm Mortar, 361
Soltam 81mm Mortar, 361
Somoza, murder of, Nica, 149
Soviet Youth Society, USSR, 470
SP (We Are Peru), 53
Spanish Civil War, 151
SSIS (Senate Subcommittee on Internal Security), US, 244
States General of 1789, 1
States, Braz, 18
States, Mex, 72

Stop-Sign mentality, 265, 396
Stroñato, 32
Sucre Battalion, 358
Summit of the Americas, 438-46
Supra national countries, 193, 394
SWAPO (Southwest Africa Peoples Organization), 415, 419

Tampico Cultural Institute, Mex, 248, 274
TCC (Tri Continental Conference), 142, 306
TECHINT (technical intelligence), 342
Teofilo Forero Company, 225
Terre des Hommes, Switz, 321
Terrorismo de Estado (ML DO), 321
Tlatelolco 1968, Mex, 257
Town councils, Mex, 74ff
TPC (Tactical Pilotage Chart), 343
Tras los Pasos Perdidos de la Guerra Sucia (ML DO), 213
Trastámara Dynasty, Spain, 210
Tres Esquinas, Col, 306-7, 336-9, 341, 413
Triangular Arms Smuggling, Arg, 101, 104
Trocaire, Irel, 416
TSE (Supreme Electoral Commission), Ecuad, 48
TSJE (Supreme Electoral Tribunal), Parg, 31
Tyrians and Trojans, 93
Tzeltalan, Mex, 261
Tzetal, Mex, 260
Tzotzil, Mex, 260

UCCP (Progressive Center Center Union), Chile, 24
UCR (Radical Civic Union), Arg, 95-6
UDI (Independent Democratic Union), Chile, 23-4
UE (European Union), 311, 318, 428
UH60L Black Hawk (Sikorsky Chopper), US, 338-9, 349
UJC (Young Communist League), Cuba, 194, 214-5
UNAM (Mexican National Autonomous University), 248
UNDH (National HR Unit), Col, 405
UNESCO (UN Educational, Scientific and Cultural Organization), 416, 439

UNICEF (UN Children's Fund), 439
Union for Life, Col, 43
United Left coalition, Spain, 160
Unity Coalition, CR, 7
UP (Patriotic Union), Col, 37, 361, 367
Uribe, La, Col, 414
URNG (Guatemalan National Revolutionary Union), 220, 356, 396, 440
US Civil War, 151
US Cuba Gambit, 297, n.9
US v. Roach, 133
Useful Idiots, 319
USIA (US Information Agency), 231
USO (Oil Workers Union), Col, 374

V Brigade, Col, 405, 407
Vallenar, attack on, Chile, 147
Valley of Huanta, Peru, 149
Venceremos Brigades, Cuba, 163
Venezuelan Central Bank, 137, 139
Vietnam War, 160
VII Brigade, Col, 362
Virgin of Caridad del Cobre, Cuba, 195
VMA (Venezuelan Military Academy), 68

VOA (Voice of America), US, 231

WB (World Bank), 429-30, 432, 448, 478
WB Environmental Division, 431
Weltoktober (Leninism), 357
WFDC (World Federation of Democratic Youth), USSR, 311
WHD (Western Hemisphere Division), US, 229
White Paper on Chiapas, Mex, 259
Wilson v. Shaw, Panama, 133
WOLA (Washington Office on LA), US, 313, 320-1
World Bank, 319

XII Brigade, Col, 340
XIX Corps, Wehrmacht, 134
XXIV Brigade, Col, 325, 331, 340
Yátama Party, Nica, 12
Yauarete Base, Braz, 379
Yaundé Convention, 205
YI (Yanqui Imperialism), US, 174, 277
ZI (Zone of the Interior), US, 200
ZLC (Free Commerce Zone), 436-7